Availability

This text is available
in both digital and print formats.
Pearson offers its titles in
eText format through MyLabs,
CourseSmart®, Kindle®, Nook®,
and more. And going digital
saves students money —
up to 60%.
To learn more about
our programs, pricing options, and
customization, visit

WWW.pearsonhighered.com.

Seventh Edition

Thinking through Communication

An Introduction to the Study of Human Communication

Sarah Trenholm

Ithaca College

PEARSON

Boston   Columbus   Indianapolis   New York   San Francisco   Upper Saddle River
Amsterdam   Cape Town   Dubai   London   Madrid   Milan   Munich   Paris   Montreal   Toronto
Delhi   Mexico City   Sao Paulo   Sydney   Hong Kong   Seoul   Singapore   Taipei   Tokyo

Publisher, Communication: Karon Bowers
Editorial Assistant: Megan Hermida
Senior Marketing Manager: Blair Zoe Tuckman
Senior Digital Media Editor: Paul DeLuca
Digital Media Editor: Lisa Dotson
Digital Project Lead: Sean Silver
Managing Editor: Linda Mihatov Behrens
Project Manager: Anne Ricigliano
Project Coordination, Text Design, and Electronic Page Makeup:
  Cenveo® Publisher Services
Senior Operations Supervisor: Mary Fischer
Operations Specialist: Mary Ann Gloriande
Cover Creative Director: Jayne Conte
Cover Image: Shutterstock: ADA_photo
Text Permissions Specialist: Craig A. Jones
Text Permissions Researcher: Anna Waluk/EPS
Photo Research: Stefanie Ramsey/Bill Smith Group
Printer/Binder: Courier Kendallville
Cover Printer: Courier Kendallville

Credits and acknowledgments borrowed from other sources and reproduced, with permission, in this textbook appear on the appropriate page within text.

10   9   8   7   6   5   4   3

MySearchLab with eText
Standalone Access card:
ISBN-13: 978-0-205-95561-9
ISBN-10: 0-205-95561-4

Student Print Version:
ISBN-10: 0205902359

Instructor's Review Copy:
ISBN 13: 978-0-205-91482-1
ISBN 10: 0-205-91482-9

www.pearsonhighered.com

Contents

PART III   COMMUNICATION CONTEXTS

6   Interpersonal Communication   129

Preface

TO THE INSTRUCTOR

This text introduces students to basic concepts in speech communication. In writing the text and the instructional materials, I have provided as much flexibility as possible. The text contains core material for the student to read and study. The instructional supplements contain additional materials that allow you to tailor the course to your interests and to students' particular needs.

Whereas the text itself provides a general overview, the material in the supplements allows you to fill in details in your own way. Included are standard teaching aids such as chapter outlines and test questions. In addition, I have added suggestions for supplementary lectures, handouts, discussion questions, observation guides, exercises, and assignments. I hope that these materials will allow you to take the course in the direction you want.

Additions to the Seventh Edition

Whether you take a theory or a skills approach to teaching, this text will give your students a better understanding of communication as a field of study and will help them think about communication in systematic ways. It provides a conceptual foundation for discussing communication and its effects.

Key additions to this new edition include:

- The pace of technology is breathtaking. Just when we've become used to Web 2.0, Web 3.0 comes along. What was formerly accomplished only through face-to-face interaction is now filtered through electronic devices. And what was once cutting edge is suddenly old hat. In revising this text, we gave special attention to updating discussions of mediated communication as they occur in the chapters on interpersonal, group, organizational, and public communication.

- In addition to integrated discussions of mediated communication throughout the context chapters, we have also revamped our discussion of traditional and new media in Chapter 11, considering current research on ways social network sites are providing social capital by supporting and changing offline relationships, and examining studies on the cognitive effects of computer-mediated communication.

- Although communication has always had a dark side, most textbooks pay little attention to this fact. In addition to communicating in ways that enrich their lives, people can, and often do, use communication to exploit and manipulate one another. In this edition you will find sections on a range of dark-side topics, including Facebook stalking, cyberbullying, cell phone entrapment, cyber vigilantism, and negative relational maintenance strategies, as well as the use of social robots as caregivers and companions. We hope this material will provide a jumping-off point for discussions of ways to make communication more fair and less dysfunctional.

- Nowadays we live in what Marshall McLuhan called the global village. Understanding how cultures differ and how these differences affect our ability to interact is more important now than it has ever been. We reorganized and expanded the chapter on intercultural communication to include a fuller discussion of the dimensions of difference that can, but need not, divide us.

- Language is a fundamental tool in a field that originally focused on spoken symbolic interaction. As society changes, so do language practices. To emphasize that point we included a new section on neologisms in the chapter on verbal communication. Language also has political ramifications, a fact recognized by those who seek to reclaim and redefine words they consider oppressive. We considered these efforts in our revisions.

- One of the features that makes this text unique is its overview of representative studies illustrating basic research methods in communication. This edition provides five new studies: a rhetorical analysis of President Obama's "A More Perfect Union" speech, an ethnography of the use of humor by restaurant chefs, a survey on how couples separated by war cope with long-distance relationships, an experiment on impression formation on social network sites, and disaster narratives as cultural performance. These studies were chosen because they are well designed, illustrate the range of topics studied by communication researchers, are so clearly written that undergraduates without a previous course in research methods can read and understand them, and are inherently interesting.

Despite these extensive changes, the general structure and organization of the text remain the same. You should therefore have no trouble integrating these new topics into your present classroom practices. To help in that regard, new test questions, PowerPoint slides, topics for discussion, and chapter outlines are provided. You may also note that in past editions the list of key terms at the end of each chapter was overly long (and perhaps a bit intimidating to students). In this edition, the key terms have been streamlined, although a more complete glossary of communication-related terms is provided in the Instructor's Manual.

TO THE STUDENT

This book asks you to think about a process that you can do without thinking. It asks you to look at behaviors that most of us overlook. In short, it asks you to rediscover communication. When we get too close to things, we often take them for granted. People, places, and everyday processes become invisible so that we no longer see their complexity or appreciate their uniqueness. We simply accept them without giving them much thought. Although there are some advantages to taking things as they come, there are also disadvantages. If we were to see the world fresh every day, we would pay a price in time and mental effort. We are often much more efficient when we don't think too much. Yet, we give up something in exchange for efficiency: when we act without thinking, we lose control of our behavior.

This book was written to make you more aware of the invisible process called communication. The first step in mastering communication lies in becoming more conscious of it—in taking time to think it through. It is important that we think communication through because we think through communication. How we see the world and how we act in it are determined by communication practices. When we communicate, we do more than reflect beliefs about the world: we create them.

This book is an introduction to the study of human communication. It is designed to give you the basic concepts you need in order to understand how communication works and to introduce you to some of the most important contexts in which communication occurs. It is also designed to make you more critical of your own communication behavior as both a message sender and a message receiver.

Plan of the Text

The formal study of communication stretches back thousands of years. Like students of today, students in ancient Greece signed up for courses in communication. The first chapter of this book examines the history of communication study. The second chapter provides basic definitions and models of communication. It offers a number of answers to the question "What is communication?" and demonstrates that the way we approach communication determines what we see in it.

Chapters 3, 4, and 5 look at basic encoding and decoding processes. They discuss how we interpret and construct messages. In Chapter 3 we look at listening, the complex process whereby receivers interpret and evaluate messages. In Chapter 4, we turn our attention to the basic material of which most messages are constructed: spoken language. Of course, meaning is not conveyed only through words. Time and space, movement, and appearance also convey meaning. In Chapter 5, we look at the hidden nonverbal messages that sometimes enhance, but often undermine, spoken communication.

Communication comes to us in many forms—from face-to-face conversation to mediated programming. In Chapters 6 through 13, we look at the contexts in which communication occurs. In Chapter 6 we discuss interpersonal communication, the informal, one-to-one interaction that is the most common form of communication. In Chapter 7, we move on to group communication, considering the constraints that communicating in groups places on interaction. Chapter 8 focuses on communication in complex organizations, while Chapters 9 and 10 look at face-to-face public address. Chapter 11 summarizes the impact of mediated messages on our everyday lives, with particular attention to the social and cognitive effects of new media, and Chapter 12 addresses communication between cultures, a topic of increasing importance in today's global village.

Finally, Chapter 13 gives us a glimpse into the way communication scholars make discoveries about communication. Because communication is such an essential part of our lives, the study of communication does not stop when a book ends or a course concludes. Chapter 13 discusses ways we can continue to think through communication throughout our lives.

Instructor and Student Resources

Sarah Trenholm prepares the Instructor's Manual and Test Bank (ISBN 020595717X) and PowerPoint Presentation Package (ISBN 0205897487) that accompany *Thinking through Communication*. The Instructor's Manual portion of the IM/TB includes the following resources for each chapter: Chapter Outline, Chapter Review Questions with Solutions, Glossary of Key Terms, Questions for In-Class Discussion, Critical Thinking Questions, Student Handouts, and Exercises and Assignments. The Test Bank contains approximately 750 multiple-choice, true/false, and essay questions, all of which are organized by chapter. These supplements are available at www.pearsonhighered.com/irc (instructor login required). MyTest online test generating software (ISBN 0205914837) is available at www.pearsonmytest.com (instructor login required).

For a complete listing of the instructor and student resources available with this text, please visit the *Thinking through Communication* e-Catalog page at **www.pearsonhighered.com/communication**.

ACKNOWLEDGMENTS

Special thanks go out to all those who have reviewed this and previous editions and offered useful insights and critiques. Although I have not always been able to follow all their suggestions, I have always learned from them. Reviewers include: Isolde K. Anderson, Hope College; Ann J. Atkinson, Keene State College; Bethann Bark, Suffolk Community College; Ferald Bryan, Northern Illinois University; Jerry Buley, Arizona State University; Mary Carpenter, New York University; Melissa Donley, University of Northern Colorado; Dennis Doyle, Central College; Tresha Dutton, Whatcom Community College; Leonard Edmonds, Arizona State University; Lucinda Eubanks, Ohio University-Chillicothe; Larry Galizio, Portland Community College; Katherine Hawkins, Wichita State University; Emily Holler, Kennesaw State University; Virginia Kidd, California State University; Thomas J. Knutson, California State University, Sacramento; Mark Lipton, New York University; Rita Miller, Keene State University; Steven Y. Miura, University of Hawaii, Hilo; Teresa Nance, Villanova University; Elizabeth Reeves O'Connor, Rochester Institute of Technology; Helen Sterk, Marquette University; John D. Stone, James Madison University; Jo Young Switzer, Indiana University/Purdue University, Fort Wayne; April Trees, University of Colorado, Boulder; Kyle Tusing, University of Arizona; Robin Vagenas, University of Delaware; Alice Veksler, University of Connecticut; John T. Warren, Bowling Green State University; Archie Wortham, Palo Alto Community College; and Julie Yingling, Humboldt State University.

The Communication Tradition

It is in the constant interplay between communication and experience that our world is shaped.

After reading this chapter, you should be able to:

- Identify the four periods of rhetorical study.
- Describe the way in which scholars viewed communication in the classical period.
- Describe the five canons of rhetoric.
- Explain the major characteristics of communication study during the medieval period and the Renaissance.
- Outline rhetorical study during the modern period.
- Distinguish between humanistic and scientific approaches to communication study.

Language philosopher Harley Shands once said that "people, in cultures, speaking to each other in the local tongue and following the rules and regulations of the group, are playing a great game, the central game of the human condition."[1] This book is about that game. It's about how the game is played and how playing it affects us and the world we live in. It's about the rewards that come from playing the game well, and it's also about the costs of losing. It's about a game that affects us deeply, both on a cultural and on an individual level.

No society has existed, or ever could exist, without a well-ordered system of communication, and no individual could survive for long without knowing how that system operates. Without the ability to communicate, we could not form relationships with others, nor could we understand the world around us, for it is in the constant interplay between communication and experience that our world is shaped.

In the following pages, we look at how communication affects us as individuals and how it affects us as a culture. We look at the verbal and nonverbal skills that make communication possible and at the many contexts in which it occurs. In short, we'll examine the knowledge and skills necessary to operate successfully in an age that has often been labeled the "age of communication."

A BRIEF HISTORY OF COMMUNICATION STUDY

Before we begin our study of contemporary communication, it is useful to look at the development of the field—the history of communication study. Communication has been studied seriously for many centuries. In fact, many of the communication principles we believe today were taught in ancient Greece over twenty-five hundred years ago. In the remainder of this chapter, we'll see how the formal study of communication began in fifth-century Sicily and developed in ancient Athens; we'll trace it through the medieval period and the Renaissance, discover how it evolved in the modern period; and look at some recent trends (see Table 1.1 for a summary). This brief tour should help you to appreciate the importance of the subject you are about to study and should give you a sense of how it has changed over the years.

Many of the communication principles we believe today were taught in ancient Greece over twenty-five hundred years ago.

Studying Rhetoric in Ancient Greece

If by some mysterious twist of fate you were to wake up tomorrow and find yourself in ancient Greece, you could still pursue your education, although it's unlikely that you would be able to put together the same class schedule you have today. Many of the courses and majors you now take for granted wouldn't exist. However, if you were interested in studying communication, if you wanted to learn public speaking, oral interpretation, argumentation and debate, or communication theory, you would have no problem, for in Athens, about three hundred years before the birth of Christ, communication was as popular

Table 1.1 A Short History of Rhetoric and Communication Theory

Cave paintings attest to the universal human need to record and communicate experience. Written records in all ancient civilizations (Egypt, Babylon, India, China) show that communication has long been an object of study.

Classical Period (500 B.C.–400 C.E.)

With the rise of Greek democracy, public communication became an important tool for problem solving. Rhetoric, the study of "the available means of persuasion," was a respected discipline taught by the great philosophers. The first known communication model, the canons of rhetoric, divided rhetoric into five parts: invention, arrangement, style, memory, and delivery. Classical rhetoric emphasized credibility, ways to ground arguments, and audience analysis. Major figures included Plato, Socrates, Aristotle, Cicero, and Quintilian.

Medieval Period and the Renaissance (400–1600)

In response to the rise of monolithic Christianity, rhetoric became secondary to theology. Major rhetorical acts were letter writing and preaching. Parts of the classical paradigm were kept alive, but the focus was prescriptive, not theoretical. Rhetoricians emphasized methods of embellishing and amplifying rhetorical style. Major figures included Augustine, Cassiodorus, John of Salisbury, and Erasmus.

Modern Period (1600–1900)

Once again, public rhetoric was a major force in determining public policy. The written word became an important medium as books and newspapers became more available. Rhetoric followed four paths: classical rhetoric revived the work of the ancients. Psychological/epistemological rhetoric investigated receivers' psychological responses to persuasive messages. Belletristic rhetoric saw written and spoken communication as art and developed theories of rhetorical criticism. Elocutionists focused on developing elaborate rules for delivery. Major figures were Francis Bacon, René Descartes, John Locke, Fénelon, Lord Kames, George Campbell, Joseph Priestley, and Thomas De Quincey.

Contemporary Period (1900–present)

Modern departments of communication were formed. Communication study took two paths: rhetoricians used humanistic methods to analyze rhetorical effects of public discourse. Communication theorists used scientific methods to analyze communication behavior as a social science. Communication study expanded to include interpersonal and group, as well as public, communication. The rise of electronic media signaled additional changes in communication study.

a subject as it is today. It would be quite easy for you to find a school, for there were many famous teachers willing to take on new students. You would simply have to keep in mind that in those days, the study of communication was called **rhetoric** and teachers of communication were known as **rhetoricians**.

If you were looking for a place to study rhetoric in Athens around 335 B.C., your best bet would be a school called the Lyceum. The Lyceum was founded by **Aristotle**, whose writings on rhetoric are considered by many to be the single greatest source of rhetorical theory. Born in 384 B.C., Aristotle was a student of the other great Greek philosopher, **Plato**, and attended Plato's Academy. Before starting the Lyceum, Aristotle served as tutor to the young son of Philip of Macedon, the child who grew up to be Alexander the Great.

Those of you who are male would have no difficulty attending the Lyceum, for the school was open to any young man who showed an interest in education. Those of you who are female would, unfortunately, have a problem. Although historical records show that two women managed to attend Plato's school, it was not Athenian custom for women to receive higher education. Indeed, Axiothea, one of the women who attended the Academy, resorted to the strategy of disguising herself as a man.[2]

If you were to attend Aristotle's public lectures (whether or not in disguise), you would have to rise early. Accompanied by your *paidagogos*—the attendant hired by your parents to make sure you didn't cut classes—you would make your way through the busy *agora*, or central marketplace, to the great wall surrounding the city. Outside the wall, you would enter the wooded sanctuary of Apollo the Wolf Slayer, site of the Lyceum. As you passed the huge gymnasium, you might see young men practicing throwing the discus or wrestling. If it were during one of the many periods in which Athens was at war, you could observe troops, clad in bronze breastplates and shields, taking part in military drills on the open parade ground. In Athens, as in other Greek city-states, physical activity was important to education, and teachers of philosophy and rhetoric shared space in the public gyms with teachers of physical culture and the military arts. As you neared the school library (one of the first of its kind), you would undoubtedly meet friends, and together you would look for seats in front of the colonnaded portico from which Aristotle customarily spoke.

Aristotle held his public lectures in the mornings, covering philosophy, science, and logic.[3] In the afternoons, he walked along the shaded walkways known as *peripatos*, stopping from time to time to sit in one of the roomy recesses and talk with his students about ethics, politics, and rhetoric. Because much of his private instruction took place as he strolled the peripatos, his school became known as the *Peripatetic School*.

If you were to study with Aristotle, your focus would be on persuasive rhetoric. Aristotle considered the science of rhetoric to be that of "observing in any given case the available means of persuasion."[4] He lectured about the ways in which successful arguments can be built, and he described methods of arriving at truthful conclusions.

© Bettmann/CORBIS

The need for communication is basic. It allows us to form connections and build community by sharing stories.

He also talked a great deal about proof. Aristotle believed that a speaker could sway an audience in three ways: through personal character, or **ethos**; through the ability to arouse emotions, or **pathos**; and through the wording and logic of the message, or **logos**. In discussing ethos, Aristotle became one of the first communication specialists to point out the importance of source credibility. If you were fortunate enough to study with him, you would leave school knowing the most frequently encountered types of speaking situations, rules for effective reasoning, the part that human emotions play in persuasion, the necessity for audience analysis, ways of improving style and delivery, and the place of rhetoric in maintaining and discovering truth.

The Classical Period: Enchanting the Mind by Arguments

Although he was arguably the greatest of the early Western rhetoricians, Aristotle was not the first. That honor is shared by two Sicilian Greeks, **Corax** and **Tisias**, who lived a century before Aristotle. The story of Corax and Tisias illustrates clearly that the study of communication is always prompted by practical problems.[5]

In 466 B.C., Sicily experienced political upheaval; the populace overthrew the existing tyrant and established a democratic constitution. People who had been exiled under the previous regime came back to Sicily and demanded the return of their land and property. This, of course, led to intricate legal problems. Corax recognized that many of the litigants were ill equipped to argue their own cases persuasively. This prompted Tisias to study ways in which speakers could effectively order their ideas. From these early attempts to address practical problems, the rhetorical tradition emerged.

In the next one hundred years, the study of rhetoric expanded rapidly as the great orators and philosophers of ancient Greece added insights and theories about the art of public speaking. Indeed, the rhetoric taught by the Greek philosophers is directly linked to the rhetoric taught in modern communication courses. Much of the advice a modern teacher of public communication gives a student (advice on building audience rapport, organizing ideas, arguing to hostile audiences, and delivering a speech) was given by Greek and Roman teachers over two thousand years ago.

The **classical period** lasted for about nine hundred years, from the fifth century B.C. to the fourth century A.D. It flowered under Athenian democracy, lasted through the years of the Roman Empire, and closed with the advent of Christianity. Communication study was important in ancient Greece for at least three reasons. First, Greece was a society that revered the spoken word. Although many Athenians could read and write, the stone, wood, or wax tablets they used were unwieldy. There was no light reading, no books, or magazines. Oral expression, in the form of storytelling, poetry reading, dramatic performance, or conversation, was the major source of entertainment, and ornamental speech was greatly admired.

> **The rhetoric taught by the Greek philosophers is directly linked to the rhetoric taught in modern communication courses.**

Second, the Greeks put a great deal of emphasis on persuasion and argumentation. Because Athens was a democracy, would-be politicians achieved office through their ability to speak thoughtfully and persuasively. Important political issues were defined and resolved through public debate, and individual politicians gained public notice as a result of their skills in argumentation.

Finally, for many years there was a ban on professional lawyers. Like their Sicilian counterparts, Greek citizens who wished to bring suit in a court of law had to have the forensic skills to argue their cases successfully.

In response to this practical need, a group of itinerant teachers called **Sophists** began to ply their trade. The Sophists were professional speech teachers who advertised their services by posting notices in public places where they could find an audience. Soon the gymnasia became important locations for learning: the Sophists knew they could find a large and receptive audience in the Athenian version of today's health clubs.

The major concern of the Sophists was teaching the "tricks" of persuasive speaking for use in the law courts or assemblies. Often, the Sophists supplemented their income by acting as professional speechwriters and political consultants. Philosophers such as Plato and Aristotle, who believed that the goal of communication was to discover the truth, not merely to win arguments, held the Sophists in great contempt. The Sophists seemed undaunted, however, and bragged about their skill in defeating strong arguments with weak ones.

The Greek and Roman philosophers Plato, Aristotle, Cicero, and Quintilian were more theoretical (and more ethical) than were the Sophists. **Cicero** (106–43 B.C.), a prominent Roman politician, was considered to be Rome's finest orator. He met his death when he joined the forces opposing Mark Antony after the assassination of Julius Caesar. During his lifetime, he delivered many famous speeches and wrote extensively on communication theory. By the time his works were published, the study of rhetoric had stabilized into five major topic areas, the famous **canons of rhetoric**. Cicero did much to elaborate on this early model of communication.

The canons divided communication into five parts: invention, style, arrangement, memory, and delivery (see Table 1.2). The first, **invention**, was the process of deciding on the subject matter of one's speech and of discovering information and arguments that would lead to sound conclusions. Classical rhetoricians shared Aristotle's belief that through communication, one could decide which of several possible "truths" was the most correct. In their writing and teaching, they argued that speakers should have a wide knowledge of current affairs as well as the ability to think clearly. Theories of invention emphasized ways to argue in different contexts.

Style was the second canon. It described the process of selecting the proper words to convey a message. Classical rhetoricians emphasized correct use of language and cataloged major figures of speech. Cicero believed there were three styles of speaking that corresponded to ethos, logos, and pathos, Aristotle's three modes of speech. The *plain style* built ethos by convincing the audience of the speaker's good character, good sense, and trustworthiness; it was logical, clear, and restrained. The *middle style* emphasized logos by impressing the audience with the soundness of the speaker's position; it consisted of intricate argumentation and careful philosophical distinctions. Finally, the *vigorous style* was based on pathos; it "pulled out all the stops" and was eloquent and emotional. Cicero, like other classical rhetoricians, mistrusted emotional appeals and warned speakers not to use the vigorous style without elements of the other two styles.[6]

Aristotle

Table 1.2 The Five Canons of Rhetoric

Invention

The speaker must begin by discovering what can be said about a given topic and by finding arguments that will allow others to understand it. Classical theory emphasized methods for analyzing audience, subject, and occasion of speech to find material that would move people to belief and action. Through logical thinking and clear topical analysis, the speaker could find grounds for effective arguments. Major speech occasions were three: forensic, deliberative, and epideictic (ceremonial). Modes of proof were three: ethos, pathos, and logos.

Style

The speaker must select and arrange the wording of the message carefully. Style was thought to differ in relationship to speech purpose: it could instruct, please, or persuade. Classical writers believed language should be clear, lively, and appropriate for the audience. Using figurative language was thought to be a way of increasing audience response.

Arrangement

The speaker must arrange ideas for maximum impact. Classical theory divided a speech into several parts that correspond roughly with today's introduction, body, and conclusion. Theorists agreed that the audience must be put into the proper frame of mind for receiving the message, the subject must be set forth clearly, a case must be built, and the speech must end with a summary and conclusion. Writers recognized that order of elements depends on the nature of the audience (whether hostile or friendly) and on the seriousness of the occasion.

Memory

The speaker must find a way to keep the message firmly in mind. Classical writers suggested several mnemonic devices to help orators memorize speeches. Theorists also discussed factors that make speech material memorable, including novelty.

Delivery

The speaker must present the speech in a natural, varied, and appropriate way. Voice should convey interest and emotion, and gestures should match the major ideas in the speech.

The next canon, **arrangement**, described ways to order ideas effectively. Speakers were taught that a speech must open with an introduction, follow with a statement of purpose, lead into presentation of arguments, and end with a conclusion. Classical rhetoricians also emphasized the necessity of organizing material according to audience needs and goals.

In an oral society, **memory**, the ability to hold content, style, and arrangement in one's mind, was exceedingly important. The science of mnemonics was developed during this time to help speakers keep track of complex arguments. One of the most popular mnemonic systems called for the speaker to visualize a villa with the main ideas of the speech situated in each room. During the speech, the speaker could then mentally proceed through the rooms, making each argument in the correct order. The method was developed by a rhetor named Simonides who, after reciting a poem at a banquet, was called away from the banquet hall. This circumstance was fortunate, because no sooner did he leave than the hall collapsed, killing many of the guests. When asked to help identify the dead, Simonides realized that he could remember quite easily where each person had been sitting. The incident brought home to him the power of visual memory and set him to wondering whether visualization might be used to recall other kinds of information.

The final canon was **delivery**. Delivery was considered necessary for success because if the speaker did not use a pleasing voice and graceful gestures, the effect of the speech would be undermined. Although they considered delivery less important than the other canons, the Greeks and Romans understood the importance of nonverbal communication in speech presentation. Cicero, for example, illustrated the need for nonverbal expression when he warned speakers that they would never be able to make an audience feel indignation, terror, or compassion until these emotions were "visibly stamped or rather branded on the advocate himself."[7]

> For classical rhetoricians, communication was the "queen of disciplines."

For classical rhetoricians, communication was the "queen of disciplines." Because it was through communication that a society determined policies in its own best interest, rhetoric carried heavy ethical weight. In fact, **Quintilian** (35–95 C.E.), the last of the great classical theorists, defined rhetoric as the study of "the good man speaking well." While the focus of communication study during this time was on legal and political discourse, classical theorists also expressed a concern for all forms of communication. As Plato says in the *Phaedrus*,

> *Is not rhetoric, taken generally, a universal art of enchanting the mind by arguments; which is practised not only in courts and public assemblies, but in private houses also, having to do with all matters, great as well as small, good and bad alike?*[8]

Medieval and Renaissance Communication: Truth Armed against Falsehood

With the fall of the Roman Empire and the rise of Christianity, rhetorical study declined. During the next two important historical periods, the **medieval period** (which lasted from 400 to 1400) and the **Renaissance** (1400 to 1600), little insight was added to classical thought. Only at the very beginning of the medieval period, when Augustine wrote, and at the very end of the Renaissance, with the work of Francis Bacon, do we find much original work. During the twelve hundred years following the classical period, most rhetorical works were fragmented versions of earlier thought or handbooks on rhetorical style.

The medieval period and the Renaissance were characterized by the rise to power of Christian clergy and the decline of "pagan" theories of rhetoric. With the advent of monolithic Christianity, the goal of communication was no longer to discover possible truth through debate but to instruct the faithful in certain truth, the revealed "will of God." Classic ideas of rhetoric, therefore, fell into disrepute, and "rhetoric ceased to be a vital, developing discipline."[9]

© Bettmann/CORBIS

Communication is ubiquitous. In any modern city in any country in the world, messages are everywhere. Communication scholars study the impact of these messages.

There was, nevertheless, a practical need for training in communication. The two most important communication activities were letter writing and preaching. The first was of great importance because in a world of independently held feudal kingdoms, it was necessary to communicate over large distances. In the so-called Dark Ages, most people were illiterate, and even kings, queens, and priests were forced to hire professional "dictators" who composed and wrote the political decrees, legal mandates, and religious dispensations that connected feudal society.

Preaching was also of great importance, because it was the duty of the Christian clergy to teach the word of God. **Augustine** (354–430), a major Christian theorist, argued that it would be foolish for truth "to take its stand unarmed against falsehood." If evil speakers were to sway an audience by their eloquence and false arguments, and the good were to "tell the truth in such a way that it is tedious to listen to, hard to understand, and, in fine, not easy to believe in," then wicked and worthless causes would triumph.[10]

The preacher's goal was to interpret the word of God. He (rarely she) had to study the scriptures and pass their meaning on. As a communication theorist, Augustine tried to understand this process. He believed that people communicate through signs. A sign, he said, is something that "causes something else to come into the mind as a consequence of itself."[11] *Natural signs* (for example, smoke, which causes one to think of fire) are created by God. *Conventional signs* (for example, the spoken or written word) are arbitrarily created by humans, and their interpretation is more difficult. For Augustine, communication was a process of "drawing forth and conveying into another's mind what the giver of the sign has in his own mind."[12] This view of communication as a process whereby a sender transmits symbols to a receiver who interprets and acts on them is close to the view of many modern theorists.[13]

Augustine

After Augustine, there was little original theorizing about communication. Rhetoric became secondary to theology, its subject matter was dispersed throughout the liberal arts, and what remained was prescriptive rather than theoretical. Most rhetorical works were compilations of form letters or manuals on preaching style. Although the study of rhetoric never died out, it became fragmented; the vigor and originality that had characterized it during the classical period were gone.

The Modern Period: A Rational Science of Rhetoric

The three centuries from 1600 to 1900 are known as the **modern period**. During this time, new attitudes toward knowledge revitalized the study of rhetoric. James Golden and his colleagues express it this way: "Prior to 1660, the world was viewed as a place of sin, peopled with men who were wicked. God and the devil haunted man. But from 1660 onward religion was less influential."[14] The world became more secular, and a new emphasis on men's and women's ability to determine the truth rationally and independently took hold. The rise of the scientific method meant that ideas and arguments should be *empirically* grounded (that is, based on observation). The rise of nationalism and democratic forms of government gave new importance to the practice of rhetoric. Once again, people believed that political and moral problems could be solved through the exercise of free speech.

In his analysis of modern rhetoric, Douglas Ehninger identifies four directions of rhetorical study during the modern period.[15] Those who took the *classical approach* set out to recover the insights of the great classical rhetoricians, adapting them to modern times. Others took a *psychological/epistemological approach*. They investigated the relationship of communication and thought, trying to understand in a "scientific" way how people could influence one another through speech. The *belletristic approach* focused on writing and speaking as art forms, developing critical standards for judging drama, poetry, and oratory. Finally, those who took an *elocutionary approach* designed elaborate systems of instruction to improve speakers' verbal and nonverbal presentation.

Those adopting a psychological/epistemological approach were particularly eager to find a scientific basis for the study of human communication. They wanted to understand how human action could be influenced by speech, and they wanted to describe the thought processes of receivers listening to persuasive messages. This inquiry led them to a consideration of human nature and human thought. **Francis Bacon** (1561–1626) started things off with an analysis of perceptual bias that seems remarkably modern even today. Writing at the very beginning of the modern period, Bacon identified four "idols" or distortions that get in the way of clear thinking.[16] The "Idols of the Tribe" referred to fallacies in thinking due to human nature. Bacon believed that most of us are, by nature, careless thinkers often ruled by emotion. Thus, our understanding is like a false mirror that can distort reality.

The "Idols of the Cave" are the individual prejudices we bring with us because of our own backgrounds and personalities. Each of us lives in a cave or den that "refracts and discolours the light of nature." The "Idols of the Market Place" are social in nature and center on imprecise use of language. "Words," according to Bacon, "plainly force and overrule the understanding, and throw all into confusion, and lead men away into numberless empty controversies and idle fancies." Finally, the "Idols of the Theatre" are fallacies that occur when we accept fashionable ideas uncritically. Bacon felt that received systems of thought represent "worlds of their own creation after an unreal and scenic fashion."[17] According to Bacon, we should be on guard against these prejudices and distortions in our own thought and speech and in those of others. The only true protection is to be as scientific as possible, grounding knowledge in empirical observation and rational thought, and expressing thought in clear, unadorned language.

> Those adopting a psychological/epistemological approach were particularly eager to find a scientific basis for the study of human communication.

Other modern thinkers such as **René Descartes** (1596–1650) and **John Locke** (1632–1704) also mistrusted normal uses of rhetoric and argued that truth could be obtained only through discourse that was solidly grounded in an understanding of human rationality. The ideas of these early modern thinkers were picked up by **George Campbell** (1719–1796) and combined with the teachings of the classical rhetoricians. One of Campbell's most modern ideas concerned the relationship between speaker and audience. He believed that receivers were active participants in the persuasion process and that the effective communicator studied the inner workings, or "faculties," of the human mind. Contemporary theorists still emphasize the importance of understanding the experiences and motivations of individual receivers.

The rhetoricians who took a belletristic view were interested less in the psychology of communication than in problems of style and eloquence. Nevertheless, like the classical and psychological theorists, they believed that speakers should be widely read and well educated; should use clear, lively, and concise language; should follow a motivational or psychologically based order of arguments; and should speak with a natural, extemporaneous style, matching gestures and voice to the feeling expressed in their texts.

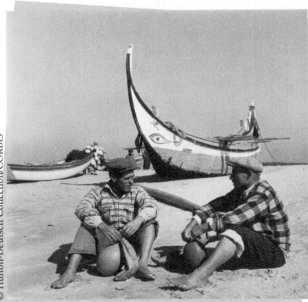

© Hulton-Deutsch Collection/CORBIS

Communication takes many forms, from the most sophisticated messages to the simplest of conversations. In every case it affects the quality of our lives.

The elocutionists focused their study of communication on the canon of delivery. Although their initial task was to describe the gestures and vocal characteristics that are naturally associated with different emotional states, their zeal for systematizing soon led to sets of artificial rules for delivery. They developed elaborate charts detailing the appropriate ways to show major emotions such as pride, shame, horror, and admiration (see Figure 1.1). By using the "self-help" books they published, speakers could mechanically map out the nonverbal behaviors that would make their delivery most effective. Unfortunately, this approach led to a florid style that was anything but natural and spontaneous and that gave a bad name to the study of oral communication for many years.

Figure 1.1 An Elocutionary Approach to the Use of Gesture

The Geometric Properties of Easy and Graceful Movement

Diagrams Showing the Speaker How to Express Appropriate Emotion

Aversion is expressed by two gestures; first the hand . . . is retracted toward the face . . . then suddenly the eyes are withdrawn, the head is averted, the feet retire, and the arms are projected out extended against the object, the hands vertical.

Veneration crosses both hands on the breast, casts down the eyes slowly, and bows the head.

Horror is seldom capable of retreating, but remains petrified, in one attitude, with the eyes riveted on its object, and the arm held forward to guard the person . . .

From *A Manual of Elocution: Embracing Voice and Gesture, Designed for Schools, Academies and Colleges as Well as for Private Learners* by M. Caldwell, 1845, Philadelphia: Sorin and Ball, pp. 248, 310, 808.

COMMUNICATION TODAY: CONTEMPORARY DEPARTMENTS OF RHETORIC AND COMMUNICATION THEORY

Throughout the history of communication study, new technologies have continually affected our ideas of what communication is. During the modern period, the new technology was printing. As written communication became increasingly important, rhetoricians turned their attention from the study of the spoken word to the study of literary works. Therefore, when American universities and colleges organized themselves into departments, rhetoric was assigned to English departments. In the early years of the twentieth century, however, teachers of public speaking and rhetoric formed their own professional organization and developed their own departments of speech communication. Today, these departments are among the most popular on campuses everywhere, but in the early days, this was not the case. At that time, serious students of communication focused on literary communication, whereas public speaking was associated with the simplistic systems of the elocutionists. Many people considered speech too simple to be studied seriously.[18]

Communication: Humanity or Social Science?

In contemporary departments, two approaches to the study of communication are evident. Many scholars continue in the rhetorical tradition. They use the historical and critical methods of the humanities in their studies of the ways in which symbolic activity shapes public response to political and ethical issues. For these scholars, rhetoric remains a humanistic discipline. Yet although their approach grows out of a long and rich tradition, the problems they address are often very contemporary.

A second school of thought takes a more scientific approach to the study of communication. At the turn of the twentieth century, many disciplines were influenced by the **scientific method**, a belief in controlled laboratory experimentation and careful, objective measurement. Scientists believed that one could understand a phenomenon only by reducing it to its most basic elements or variables, manipulating these variables in a controlled situation, and observing the results.

Scholars in the emerging disciplines of psychology, sociology, and anthropology sought ways of applying the methods of the "hard" scientists to the study of human behavior. Because many students of communication were convinced that human communication should join the social sciences, in the 1920s communication researchers began to look at communication from this new perspective. Rather than relying on introspection, communication scientists decided to observe and measure communication behaviors either in natural, real-world settings or in laboratories. Their first step was to isolate a phenomenon of interest. After looking at relevant theory and finding out what had previously been discovered, they would then pose a research question and determine the kinds of observations and measurements that might allow them to answer their questions or test their hypotheses. For example, a researcher might be interested in the phenomenon that we call *source credibility* (the extent to which a communicator is considered believable and competent). The researcher might also be interested in how gender affects credibility. He or she might then formulate a research question linking these two variables. For example, the researcher might ask, "Are women considered more credible when they address stereotypically 'female issues,' such as education or health care, than when they speak on stereotypically 'male issues,' such as crime or the economy?" The researcher could then set up a situation in which audience members would listen to a series of speeches by female speakers on different issues and then rate their credibility. As a result of the findings of this study, the researcher could do further work to determine the strategies and approaches that would help or hurt female candidates.[19] The researcher could also determine the extent to which stereotypes affect audience expectations.

In fact, early communication scientists did study phenomena such as credibility in order to understand more about audience psychology and attitude change. They also studied the effects of speech organization, use of evidence, the effects of rational and emotional appeals, and "audience variables such as sex, dogmatism, ego involvement in the subject of the message, and so forth."[20] Today, the areas of interest studied by communication scientists have expanded to include investigations of interpersonal and group interaction as well as investigations of persuasive messages.

Although their methods may differ, rhetoricians and communication scientists address similar questions.

Chapter 13 discusses in more detail how communication scientists proceed as well as how those who take a more humanistic, rhetorical approach engage in research.

Whether you believe that communication should be studied by using humanistic or scientific methods, you will find support in contemporary communication departments, where courses in both rhetoric and communication theory are taught. Although their methods may differ, rhetoricians and communication scientists address similar questions. Both want to understand how communicators affect each other as they interact.

What Do Rhetoricians and Communication Scientists Do?

One of the most attractive aspects of studying communication is that it prepares us for so many different professions. People with degrees in rhetoric and communication theory apply their interests in many communication-related professions. They may become speechwriters, political consultants or politicians, legal consultants or lawyers, advertising executives, public relations experts, counselors, organizational training and development specialists, professional negotiators, personnel managers, specialists in information storage and retrieval, radio or television performers, media consultants, and the like. Communication specialists are needed in corporate settings as spokespersons and company representatives. They are also needed in professions that provide information and counseling to the public, such as health-care professions. In fact, opportunities for individuals trained in communication are plentiful throughout the economy. Whether you plan to major in communication or to take some courses simply to explore, what you learn will be useful to you throughout your working life. Knowing how to communicate clearly and effectively will benefit you no matter what career you choose.

Of course, business and professional contexts are not the only settings in which the study of communication is important. Many communication specialists decide to teach or do academic research. Those who do so have large numbers of subjects to investigate and, as we shall see later, a variety of ways to study those subjects. In the past, rhetoricians have studied the rhetoric of films, television, social movements, political speeches, political newscasting, cartoons, popular music, psychotherapy, painting, architecture, and even science.[21] Communication scientists have studied how communication affects the development and maintenance of one's self-image, how message variables affect the way we process and understand information, the factors that lead to attitude change, how interpersonal relationships form and dissolve, how small groups make effective and ineffective decisions, how complex organizations use communication to function effectively, how the media affect audience responses, and the like.[22]

As we've seen, communication has been an important area of study for thousands of years. Now, more than ever, a firm grounding in communication is a personal and professional necessity, for we live in an age in which the ability to process and evaluate communication has become a necessary skill. As you progress through this text, you will gain a greater understanding of how communication works and, in the process, you will begin to develop more control over the way you communicate.

SUMMARY

The study of communication is not a modern invention. We can trace many of today's ideas about communication to earlier periods, in particular ancient Greece and Rome. Although the first Western rhetoricians to be recognized as such were the Sicilian Greeks Corax and Tisias, the study of rhetoric became fully developed only after the Athenian philosophers, particularly Plato and Aristotle, turned their attention to the art of communication. Early rhetorical systems provided practical training for individuals who needed to express their thoughts clearly and eloquently in political and legal contexts.

Aristotle and Plato wrote during the classical period (500 B.C.–A.D. 400). As a result of their

work and that of others such as Cicero and Quintilian, by the end of this period a full-fledged communication model had developed. This model, called the canons of rhetoric, divided the process of public communication into five parts: invention, style, arrangement, memory, and delivery. Much of the information we now study in public speaking classes originated in these canons.

During the medieval period (400–1400) and the Renaissance (1400–1600), the focus of rhetoric shifted, owing in part to the political power of the Christian clergy. Particularly important forms of communication were letter writing and preaching. The medieval philosopher Augustine viewed communication as a symbolic process, a view we shall examine in detail in the chapter on spoken language, Chapter 4.

In the modern period (1600–1900), the study of rhetoric followed one of four paths. The classical approach revived ancient Greek and Roman models. The belletristic approach focused on communication as art. The elocutionist approach consisted of elaborate, artificial systems of presentation. And the psychological/epistemological approach investigated the relationship between communication and thought, placing special emphasis on the receiver as an active participant in the creation of meaning.

By the twentieth century, a new method of inquiry, the scientific method, became popular. Some communication scholars began to use experiments and objective measurement to investigate audience response and attitude change. During the same period, a more humanistic, philosophical approach was also used. Contemporary departments of communication acknowledge the importance of both communication science and the rhetorical tradition. Communication study has a rich history. Although methodologies and concerns have changed over the centuries, the fundamental importance of understanding communication remains the same.

KEY TERMS

Listed below are the key terms used in this chapter, along with the number of the page where each is explained.

rhetoric (3)	Sophists (5)	medieval period (7)
rhetoricians (3)	Cicero (5)	Renaissance (7)
Aristotle (3)	canons of rhetoric (5)	Augustine (8)
Plato (3)	invention (5)	modern period (9)
ethos (4)	style (6)	Francis Bacon (9)
pathos (4)	arrangement (7)	René Descartes (10)
logos (4)	memory (7)	John Locke (10)
Corax (4)	delivery (7)	George Campbell (10)
Tisias (4)	Quintilian (7)	scientific method (12)
classical period (4)		

SUGGESTED READING

Bizzell, Patricia, & Herzberg, Bruce. (2001). *The rhetorical tradition: Readings from classical times to the present* (2nd ed.). Boston: Bedford/St. Martin's.

> Presents readings from the original works of the great rhetoricians; its introductions to each period present excellent summaries of the history of rhetorical thought.

Herrick, James A. (2012). *The history and theory of rhetoric: An introduction* (5th ed.). New York: Prentice Hall.

> Provides a lively and readable discussion of the history of rhetoric from ancient Greece to current times, using contemporary examples that show the relevance of rhetoric today.

Definitions, Models, and Perspectives

C ommunication is a complex process that can be viewed in many ways.

After reading this chapter, you should be able to:

- Explain why definitions are important and why there can be more than one definition of communication.
- Identify how definitions vary in terms of breadth, intentionality, sender/ receiver orientation, and importance of symbols.
- Explain the three functions of models as well as their drawbacks.
- Distinguish between the psychological, social constructionist, and pragmatic perspectives.
- Explain for any given model which perspective it belongs to.
- Criticize each perspective by describing its weaknesses.
- Understand the cultural studies perspective.
- Identify the elements of communication in Hymes's SPEAKING model.

A s we saw in Chapter 1, communication has had a long history. For thousands of years, scholars have debated the nature of communication, and students have worked to improve their communication skills. Unfortunately, this doesn't mean that it's easy to define communication. As we shall see, communication is a complex process that can be viewed in many ways. In this chapter, we consider issues that arise when scholars try to describe the essence of communication. We examine what it means to create definitions and build models of this complex process, and we explore some of the underlying philosophical perspectives that guide our understanding of communication.

We'll look at three fundamentally different approaches to communication, and as we do so, we'll consider where each locates communication and what each has to say about the characteristics of good communicators. We'll also look at a fourth, evolving, perspective.

DEFINING COMMUNICATION

A definition is a useful and logical place to start our exploration of communication. The term **definition** comes from a Latin word meaning "to determine, bring to an end, or settle." Definitions clarify concepts by indicating their boundaries. They focus attention on what is important about whatever it is we are defining. A good definition of communication tells us which behaviors count as communication and which do not. It also describes the essential characteristics of communication.

Unfortunately, no single definition of communication does this to everyone's satisfaction. In fact, in the early 1970s, Frank Dance identified 126 published definitions.[1] In the last twenty years, communication scholars have been busily adding to that list, so now there are a good many more. Why has the concept of communication produced so many definitions? To understand the reasons for this diversity, we have to look first at what it means to create a definition and then at the specific issues that arise when people try to define communication.

Definitions: Discovery or Construction?

One way to think about the world is to assume that it is made up of phenomena that exist independently of human knowledge. By carefully observing objects and actions, we can discover their essential features and express them in the form of an objective definition. According to this view, a good definition accurately records and describes something that already exists. Understanding the world and expressing that understanding in a definition are objective processes of *discovery*; theoretically, a single correct definition exists for everything we wish to understand.

> **Even the most mundane of objects can have a number of equally valid definitions.**

A second, and quite different, way to think about the world is to assume that most of the things we try to define are human constructions. As we experience the world, each of us tries to make sense of it by creating mental representations of it. Because we each have different needs and experiences, our individual understandings will often vary. According to this view, a definition is a subjective *construction* rather than an objective discovery. If we adopt this approach, then the test of a good definition is not its absolute truth but rather its practical use. Different definitions focus our attention on different aspects of a given phenomenon. A definition is useful if it helps us understand those aspects more fully.

The second approach explains how even the most mundane of objects can have a number of equally valid definitions. Even an everyday object such as a telephone can be defined in many ways. If we were to ask an American teenager, a telemarketer, and a telecommunications engineer to tell us what a telephone is, we might get quite different definitions. The teenager might define the telephone in terms of its social functions, seeing it as a way of maintaining relationships. The telemarketer might view the telephone as a way to reach customers. The engineer might concentrate on the phone's design. Each would visualize and explain the instrument in a different way, and each would be right. All three definitions are useful, because they clarify important aspects of the telephone. Clearly, when it comes to social phenomena such as communication, multiple definitions become even more likely.

Deciding What Communication Is

Table 2.1 lists a number of definitions of communication that differ on several dimensions: breadth, intentionality, role of senders and receivers, and the importance of symbols. Before you read further, consider these definitions and choose the one you like the best. If none appeals to you, try your hand at creating your own definition.

How Broad Is Communication?

One of the first questions to ask is how broad or narrow we want communication to be; this is the issue of **breadth**. What kinds of behaviors do you call communication? No doubt you include people talking to one another; that's easy. But what do you make of a situation in which one person draws conclusions about another person without the second person's knowledge? Do you call that communication? And how do you class the bond between a pet and its owner, or the signals that animals send to one another? What about someone "communing" with nature; is he or she communicating? Is it possible for people to communicate with computers or for computers to communicate with one another?

If we wish the concept of communication to include all of the activities mentioned above, we need a very broad definition. Definitions 1 and 2 in Table 2.1 are the broadest and most inclusive. Definition 1 ("Communication is a process of acting on information") includes all of the examples given above, whereas definition 2 ("Communication is the discriminatory response of an organism to a stimulus") excludes machine communication but includes behaviors of living organisms.

Whereas some people prefer a broad definition, others want one that focuses more directly on human behavior. Arguing that there are essential differences between humans, animals, and machines, these people define communication as a

Table 2.1 Definitions of Communication

Definition 1	Communication is a process of acting on information.
Definition 2	"Communication is the discriminatory response of an organism to a stimulus."[a]
Definition 3	"Communication . . . is an 'effort after meaning,' a creative act initiated by man in which he seeks to discriminate and organize cues so as to orient himself in his environment and satisfy his changing needs."[b]
Definition 4	"Speech communication is a human process through which we make sense out of the world and share that sense with others."[c]
Definition 5	"In the main, communication has as its central interest those behavioral situations in which a source transmits a message to a receiver(s) with conscious intent to affect the latter's behaviors."[d]
Definition 6	Communication is a process whereby people assign meanings to stimuli in order to make sense of the world.
Definition 7	Communication is "the transmission of information, ideas, emotions, skills, etc., by the use of symbols—words, pictures, figures, graphs, etc."[e]
Definition 8	Spoken symbolic interaction is the process by which people use words and other symbols to create meaning and to affect one another.
Definition 9	*Nonverbal interaction* is the unspoken, often unintentional behavior that accompanies verbal communication and helps us fully interpret its meaning.

[a]Stevens, S. S. (1950). A definition of communication. *The Journal of the Acoustical Society of America*, 22, 689–690.

[b]Barnlund, Dean. (1968). *Interpersonal communication: Survey and studies*. Boston: Houghton Mifflin, 6.

[c]Masterson, John T., Beebe, Steven A., & Watson, Norman H. (1983). *Speech communication: Theory and practice*. New York: Holt, Rinehart & Winston, 5.

[d]Miller, Gerald A. (1966). On defining communication: Another stab. *Journal of Communication, 16*, 88–98, 92.

[e]Berelson, Bernard, & Steiner, Gary. (1964). *Human behavior*. New York: Harcourt, Brace, & World, 254.

uniquely human process. People who hold this view prefer definition 3 ("Communication . . . is an 'effort after meaning,' a creative act initiated by man in which he seeks to discriminate and organize cues so as to orient himself in his environment and satisfy his changing needs") or definition 4 ("Speech communication is a human process through which we make sense out of the world and share that sense with others"). These definitions set different boundaries for communication.

Is Communication Intentional?

Another question about communication is whether or not it involves **intentionality**. Let's consider an example of unobtrusive observation. Assume that Brennan comes across Brianne, who is unaware that she is being watched. Brianne does something revealing; perhaps she frowns and looks annoyed. As a result, Brennan draws a conclusion about her mood. Is this communication? According to definition 5 in Table 2.1 ("In the main, communication has as its central interest those behavioral situations in which a source transmits a message to a receiver(s) *with conscious intent to affect the latter's behaviors*"), it is not communication, for Brianne did not mean to send a message.

But not everyone would agree. Some people think that it's impossible to know whether a message is intentional. They argue that what is important about the interaction between Brennan and Brianne is not what Brianne intends but how Brennan interprets her behavior. People who take this view prefer that the definition of communication include unintentional as well as intentional behaviors. Definition 6 ("Communication is a process whereby people assign meanings to stimuli in order to make sense of the world") does just that.

Is Communication Sender- or Receiver-Based?

If we accept the situation involving Brennan and Brianne as an instance of communication, we are faced with yet another question. Which of them is communicating? Some people would argue that it is Brianne who is communicating, because it is her behavior that is the source of information. Others would contend that it is Brennan who is communicating, since it is he who assigns meaning. Those people who locate communication in Brianne's behavior take a **sender-based** view of communication, whereas those who see Brennan as the communicator take a **receiver-based** stance. Definition 5 in Table 2.1 ("Communication has as its central interest . . . situations in which a source transmits a message . . . *with conscious intent*") is sender oriented, as is definition 7 ("Communication is the 'transmission of information, ideas, emotions, skills, etc., by the use of symbols—words, pictures, figures, graphs, etc.'"). Definition 4 ("Speech communication is a human process through which we make sense out of the world and share that sense with others") includes both sender and receiver, and the rest of the definitions appear to be receiver oriented.

Is All Communication Symbolic?

A final question concerns the extent to which a definition of communication emphasizes symbolic behavior. As we shall see in more detail in ensuing chapters, humans have two code systems at their disposal. We can express ourselves symbolically through words, numbers, and graphic designs. We can also convey meaning nonverbally through facial expressions, body movements, and physical appearance. Many people believe that it is the ability to use **symbols** (arbitrary and conventionalized representations) that makes humans unique and that we should focus our study of communication on the way humans use symbols to convey meaning. For these people, nonverbal behaviors are a secondary concern. Definition 7 ("Communication is the 'transmission of [meaning] by the use of symbols'") clearly limits communication to symbolic behavior, whereas the other definitions seem to include both symbolic and nonsymbolic behavior.

Multiple Definitions: Communication as a Family of Concepts

As you move from one definition to another, the boundaries of communication shift, and you focus your attention in a slightly different direction. In choosing one definition over another, consider how that definition expands or contracts the domain of communication. A broad definition is useful when you want to emphasize commonalities between human and nonhuman information processing. A narrow definition is useful when you want to focus on a particular kind of communication, say, human communication or symbolic communication. There is no right or wrong way to make your choice, nor is it necessary to choose a single definition. Indeed, Frank Dance has suggested that instead of talking about communication as a single concept, it may be more useful to talk about several kinds of communication, for example, animal communication, nonverbal communication, spoken symbolic interaction, and so on. Dance asks us to think of communication as a family of interrelated concepts, each of which has its own utility.[2]

If communication is a family of concepts rather than a single concept, then the two family members that have traditionally received the most attention are spoken symbolic interaction and nonverbal interaction. Our discipline originally focused on **spoken symbolic interaction**, the way people use symbols (primarily words) to create common meaning and to share that meaning with one another. In keeping with this tradition, most of the chapters in this book are devoted to understanding verbal communication. Nevertheless, people are often affected by unintentional behaviors that accompany the spoken word. Therefore, we will also direct attention to **nonverbal interaction**, the unspoken, often unintentional behavior that accompanies verbal communication and helps us fully interpret its meaning. And, in addition to face-to-face communication, we will look at mediated communication as well.

For many years now it has been common to divide communication into subfields, with *interpersonal communication* focusing on how individuals use one-to-one interaction to build relationships, *small group communication* examining how small collections of people can work together to discuss and solve problems, and *public communication* investigating how public speakers sway audiences. *Intercultural communication* has explored how people from different cultures, with different values and understandings, can come to understand and accept one another; *organizational communication* has considered how communication plays out in business and industrial settings; and *mass communication* has investigated how messages are broadcast to large mass audiences through newspapers, radio, TV, and the like.

Until quite recently the primary focus in these fields has been on face-to-face interaction, with mass communication being the sole area devoted to mediated communication. However, the burgeoning of digital media has expanded our view of the importance of mediated messages and reminded us that broadcasting is not the only form of mediated communication. We now recognize that instant messaging, email, social networking, and texting are changing the ways we create and maintain interpersonal relationships; that individuals can work together in virtual as well as co-present groups; and that public speeches can stream live on Webcasts. In allowing us to create as well as consume mediated messages, Web 2.0 has also shown us that, in addition to one-to-one, few-to-few, and one-to-many communication, many-to-many communication is a potent form of human interaction.[3]

HOW MODELS HELP US UNDERSTAND COMMUNICATION

In addition to defining communication, scholars build models of it. A **model** is an abstract representation of a process, a description of its structure or function. Models are useful because they help us understand how a process works. As Cassandra Book and her colleagues point out, models can help us to organize our thinking, generate research questions, and make predictions.[4] And just as there are many definitions of communication, so there are many models. Models are representations; they cannot capture a process in its entirety. Instead, each model describes certain aspects of the total process.

Modeling a social process helps us to think carefully about the form and function of that process. To create a model, we divide the whole process into its basic parts and consider how these parts are connected. Models stimulate creativity; by building models, we may find out interesting things that we might previously have overlooked.

In this section, we'll continue our examination of communication by looking at several models. We'll describe each model carefully, consider its assumptions, and discover its strengths and weaknesses. We'll also look at how each model characterizes good communication.

> **Models stimulate creativity; by building models, we may find out interesting things that we might previously have overlooked.**

The Forms and Functions of Models

Almost any object or process can be modeled, and models can take many forms. Before we consider ways of modeling communication, consider how you might model another kind of entity: a city. A model of a city could be any of the following: a street map, an organization chart of city government, a computer simulation of traffic flow, a scale model of a city's architecture, a sociological description of changing neighborhoods, even a board game. Each is an abstraction, a simplified version of the city. Each focuses on only a small part of the process. Yet each helps us to answer the questions "What is a city?" and "How does it work?"

Models aid us by describing and explaining a process, by yielding testable predictions about how the process works, or by showing us ways to control the process. Some models fulfill an **explanatory function** by dividing a process into constituent parts and showing us how the parts are connected. A city's organizational chart does this by explaining how city government works, and the sociological description allows us to see the economic and social factors that caused the city to become what it is today.

We construct prototypes and models so that we can understand how objects and processes work.

Other models fulfill a **predictive function**. Traffic simulations and population growth projections function in this way. They allow us to answer "if . . . then" questions. If we add another traffic light, then will we eliminate gridlock? If the population keeps growing at the current rate, then what will housing conditions be in the year 2025? Models help us answer questions about the future.

Finally, models fulfill a **control function**. A street map not only describes the layout of a city but also allows you to find your way from one place to another and helps you figure out where you went wrong if you get lost. Models guide our behavior. They show us how to control a process.

The Drawbacks of Models

Models are useful, but they can also have drawbacks. In building and using models, we must be cautious. First, we must realize that *models are necessarily incomplete* because they are simplified versions of very complex processes. When a model builder chooses to include one detail, he or she invariably chooses to ignore hundreds more. Models can be misleading if they oversimplify a process.

Second, we must keep in mind that *there are many ways to model a single process.* Most of us like certainty. We've grown up believing that every problem has one right answer. Unfortunately, when we study complex processes, we can never be 100 percent certain we understand them. There are many "right answers," all equally valuable but each distinct. Although this may be confusing at first, try thinking of it positively. Looking for single answers limits you intellectually; accepting multiple answers opens you to new possibilities.

Finally, we musn't forget that *models make assumptions about processes.* It's always important to look "below the surface" of any model to detect the hidden assumptions it makes. Communication models, being abstract, make many assumptions. In the next section, we'll look at two of the most important types of assumptions a model makes. We'll examine where each model locates communication; for example, does a given model imply that communication occurs in the minds of human interactants, in social norms and rules, or in patterns of moves and counter-moves? We'll also examine what value judgments the model makes; we'll try to discover what good communication is from the standpoint of each model. As we shall see, the answers to these questions are often hidden below a model's surface.

Models are simplified versions of very complex processes.

IT ALL DEPENDS ON YOUR POINT OF VIEW: FOUR PERSPECTIVES

Many interesting communication models exist. In this section, we'll look at four, each of which takes a different theoretical perspective. In the next section, we'll look at a fifth model that will provide us with a practical way to observe communication behavior.

A **perspective** is a coherent set of assumptions about the way a process operates.[5] The first three models we will look at are built on different sets of assumptions. The first model takes what is known as a **psychological perspective**. It focuses on what happens "inside the heads" of communicators as they transmit and receive messages. The second model takes a **social constructionist perspective**.[6] It sees communication as a process whereby people, using the tools provided by their culture, create collective representations of reality. It emphasizes the relationship between communication and culture. The third model takes what is called a **pragmatic perspective**.[7] According to this view, communication consists of a system of interlocking, interdependent "moves," which become patterned over time. This perspective focuses on the games people play when they communicate. As we look at each of these models, you'll begin to understand how these perspectives differ in their emphasis on individual psychology, cultural constructs, or actual behaviors.

Communication as Message Transmission

We'll begin with the most familiar approach to communication. Most models and definitions of communication are based on the psychological perspective. They locate communication in the human mind and see the individual as both the source of and the destination for messages. Figure 2.1 illustrates an example of a psychological model.

Elements of a Psychological Model

The model in Figure 2.1 depicts communication as *a psychological process whereby two (or more) individuals exchange meanings through the transmission and reception of communication stimuli.* According to this model, an individual is a *sender/receiver*

Figure 2.1 A Psychological Model of Communication

In a psychological model, messages are filtered through an individual's store of beliefs, attitudes, values, and emotions.

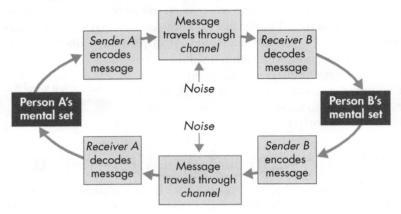

who encodes and decodes meanings. Adam has an idea he wishes to communicate to Betty. Adam *encodes* this idea by translating it into a message that he believes Betty can understand. The encoded message travels along a *channel*, its medium of transmission, until it reaches its destination. On receiving the message, Betty *decodes* it and decides how she will reply. In sending the reply, she gives Adam *feedback* about his message. Adam uses this information to decide whether or not his communication was successful.

During encoding and decoding, Adam and Betty filter messages through their *mental sets*. A mental set consists of a person's beliefs, values, attitudes, feelings, and so on. Because each message is composed and interpreted in light of an individual's past experience, each encoded or decoded message has its own unique meaning. Of course, partners' mental sets can sometimes lead to misunderstandings. The meanings that Adam and Betty assign to a message may vary in important ways. If this occurs, they may miscommunicate. Communication can also go awry if *noise* enters the channel. Noise is any distraction that interferes with or changes a message during transmission. Communication is most successful when individuals are "of the same mind"—when the meanings they assign to messages are similar or identical.

> **Communication is most successful when individuals are "of the same mind"—when the meanings they assign to messages are similar or identical.**

Let's look at how this process works in a familiar setting, the college lecture. Professor Smith wants to inform his students about the history of rhetoric. Alone in his study, he gazes at his plaster-of-paris bust of Aristotle and thinks about how he will encode his understanding and enthusiasm in words. To encode successfully, he must guess about what's going on in the students' minds.

Although it's hard for him to imagine that anyone could be bored by the history of rhetoric, he knows that students need to hear a "human element" in his lecture. He therefore decides to include examples and anecdotes to spice up his message.

Smith delivers his lecture in a large, drafty lecture room. The microphone he uses unfortunately emits shrill whines and whistles at inopportune times. That he also forgets to talk into the mike only compounds the noise problem. Other sources of distraction are his appearance and nonverbal behavior. When Smith enters the room, his mismatched polyester suit and hand-painted tie are fairly presentable, but as he gets more and more excited, his clothes take on a life of their own. His shirt untucks itself, his jacket collects chalk dust, and his tie juts out at a very strange angle. In terms of our model, Smith's clothes are too noisy for the classroom.

Despite his lack of attention to material matters and his tendency toward dry speeches, Smith knows his rhetoric, and highly motivated students have no trouble decoding the lecture. Less-prepared students have more difficulty, however. Smith's words go "over their heads." As the lecture progresses, the students' smiles and nods, their frowns of puzzlement, and their whispered comments to one another act as feedback for Smith to consider.

Smith's communication is partially successful and partially unsuccessful. He reaches the students who can follow his classical references but bypasses the willing but unprepared students who can't decode his messages. And he completely loses the seniors in the back row who are taking the course pass/fail and have set their sights on a D minus. Like most of us, some of the time Smith succeeds, and some of the time he fails.

Improving Faulty Communication

According to the psychological model, communication is unsuccessful whenever the meanings intended by the source differ from the meanings interpreted by the receiver. This occurs when the mental sets of source and receiver are so far apart that there is no shared experience, when the source uses a code that is unfamiliar to the receiver, when the channel is overloaded or impeded by noise, when there is little or no opportunity for feedback, or when receivers are distracted by competing internal stimuli.

Each of these problems can be solved. The psychological model points out ways to improve communication. It suggests that senders can learn to see things from their receivers' points of view. Senders can try to encode messages in clear, lively, and appropriate ways. They can use multiple channels to ensure that their message gets across, and they can try to create noise-free environments. They can also build in opportunities for feedback and learn to read receivers' nonverbal messages.

> According to the psychological model, communication is unsuccessful whenever the meanings intended by the source differ from the meanings interpreted by the receiver.

Receivers too can do things to improve communication. They can prepare themselves for a difficult message by studying the subject ahead of time. They can try to understand "where the speaker is coming from" and anticipate arguments. They can improve their listening skills, and they can ask questions and check their understanding. All of these methods of improving communication are implicit in the model in Figure 2.1.

Criticizing the Psychological Perspective

Although the psychological model is by far the most popular view of communication, it poses some problems, which arise from the assumptions the psychological perspective makes about human behavior. What are some of the assumptions?

First, the psychological model locates communication in the psychological processes of individuals, ignoring almost totally the social context in which communication occurs, as well as the shared roles and rules that govern message construction. This model makes individuals appear more independent than they actually are.

Second, in incorporating the ideas of channel and noise, the psychological model is mechanistic. It treats messages as though they are physical objects that can be sent from one place to another. Noise is treated not as a message but as a separate entity that "attacks" messages. The model also assumes that it is possible not to communicate, that communication can break down. All of these are mechanical ideas that may distort the way communication actually works.

Finally, the psychological model implies that successful communication involves a "meeting of the minds." The model suggests that communication succeeds to the extent that the sender transfers what is in his or her mind to the mind of the receiver, thereby implying that good communication is more likely to occur between people who have the same ideas than between those who have different ideas. This raises some important questions: Is it possible to transfer content from one mind to another? Is accuracy the only value we should place on communication? Is it always a good idea to seek out people who are similar rather than different? Some critics believe that the psychological model diminishes the importance of creativity and makes receivers appear to be empty receptacles waiting to be filled with other people's ideas.

Asking Questions from the Psychological Perspective

Models can be used not only to identify potential communication problems and to suggest ways of overcoming them but also to generate research questions. The psychological perspective is usually associated with what is called a **laws approach** to research. Communication scientists who take this approach describe cause-and-effect laws that connect communication variables. A researcher looking for lawful relationships between parts of the communication process might ask the following questions: Are multiple channels more effective than single channels for transmitting complex messages? Does attitude similarity enhance or inhibit communication accuracy? Because the psychological model is linear, it lends itself to these kinds of questions and to related research methods. Chapter 13 takes up this topic in more detail.

Communication as World Building

The social constructionist perspective takes a very different view of communication. In this view, communication becomes a means of world building. Figure 2.2 illustrates an example of a social constructionist model. According to this model, communication is not something that goes on between individuals; instead, communication is something that surrounds people and holds their world together. Through communication, social groups create collective ideas of themselves, of one another, and of the world they inhabit.

> **Communication is something that surrounds people and holds their world together. Through communication, social groups create collective ideas of themselves, of one another, and of the world they inhabit.**

Elements of a Social Constructionist Model

According to the social constructionist model, communication is *a process whereby people in groups, using the tools provided by their culture, create collective representations of reality*. The model specifies four of these cultural tools: languages, or *symbolic codes*; the ways we've been taught to process information, or *cognitive customs*; the beliefs, attitudes, and values that make up our *cultural traditions*; and the *sets of roles and rules* that guide our actions. These tools shape the ways we experience and talk about our world.

> **Most of what we know and believe about the world comes to us through communication rather than through direct experience.**

Figure 2.2 A Social Constructionist Model of Communication

In a social constructionist model, people exist within, and perceive themselves and others through, the communicative practices of their cultures.

Communication can be viewed as an act of construction. Often what we build as we talk is more lasting than we realize.

The social constructionist perspective maintains that we never experience the world directly. Rather, we take those parts of it that our culture makes significant, process them in culturally recognized ways, connect them to other "facts" that we know, and respond to them in ways our culture considers significant. According to this perspective, we construct our world through communication.

This perspective points out that most of what we know and believe about the world comes to us through communication rather than through direct experience. If everyone around us talks about the world in a certain way, we are likely to think of the world in that way and fail to question whether we are seeing things accurately. Thus, when we later encounter people who communicate in different ways, we will have problems during interaction.

Let's take an example. John has been with his company for thirty years and has five more years to go until retirement. When he first started working, there were very few women in managerial positions, but now he finds himself working with many women managers. John thinks of himself as fair-minded and easygoing. He has nothing against the fact that "girls" are now moving up in the company, but he does find it hard to understand why they get so upset over "nothing." When he calls his female secretary "Honey" (which he's done for twenty years), he doesn't understand the prickly reaction of his new colleague, Judy. After all, he's just trying to be nice. It's the way he always talks to women.

Judy is fresh out of business school and eager to make her way in the professional world. She is appalled by John's behavior. When she hears the way he talks to his secretary, she feels embarrassed and demeaned herself. Furthermore, when John treats Judy like an idiot by explaining everything to her as though she were a child, her blood boils. Judy has come of age in a time when discussions of feminism and sexism are common. She's sensitive to issues John doesn't even notice.

John's attempts to communicate with Judy fail because the two colleagues don't share collective representations of reality. When John was growing up, no one talked about sexism and sexual harassment, so for him these concepts have limited meaning. His views of male/female roles used to work, but now they are outmoded. As a result, he says things that are quite inappropriate in a modern office. In a very real way, John and Judy live in two completely different worlds.

Improving Our Social Constructions

The social constructionist model doesn't give us as many specific guidelines for improving communication as the psychological model did, but it does suggest a few concerns we should think about if we want to be effective communicators. Primarily, it emphasizes that we should take responsibility for the things we talk about and the way we talk about them. Our constructions of reality, according to the model, often distort our communication. Thus, we may accept cultural myths and stereotypes without thinking. Given the fact that symbols have the power to control us, it is useful to develop the critical ability to "see through" cultural constructions and to avoid creating them through our own talk. The ability to decipher our biases is a useful skill.

And whereas the psychological model suggests that individuals create communication, the social constructionist model suggests the opposite, that communication creates individuals. To be successful communicators, it maintains, we must be willing to follow cultural rules and norms. We must take our parts in the social drama our culture has laid out for us. We must also carefully consider whether those roles enhance our identities or inhibit them. If a role is outmoded or unfair to others, we must be willing to abandon it and find a new and more appropriate way of communicating.

Criticizing the Social Constructionist Perspective

For many of you, this model may seem to depart radically from commonsense ideas about communication. To say that we live in a symbolic, rather than a physical, world seems to contradict our most basic notions about the nature of reality. For if we can never gain access to reality but can only experience constructions of it, then how can we tell the difference between truth and illusion? The social constructionist model raises important philosophical questions as it emphasizes a relationship that has been recognized since ancient times: the relationship between rhetoric and truth.

Another troublesome aspect of the social constructionist position is that it defines good communication as socially appropriate communication. Scholars who take this perspective often talk of humans as social performers. To communicate successfully, one acts out a social role over which he or she has little control. For many, this view implies that the good communicator is a social automaton rather than a sincere and spontaneous self. Many people criticize the social constructionist perspective because it places too much emphasis on the social self and not enough on the individual self. They feel that in emphasizing the social and cultural nature of humans, the aspects that make humans unique and individual are forgotten.

Asking Questions from the Social Constructionist Perspective

When social constructionists do research, they pay particular attention to the implicit rules that guide social action. Researchers who are social constructionists often take what is known as a **rules approach** to understanding communication. Rules researchers believe that human behavior is not so much caused as chosen: to accomplish their goals, people choose certain lines of action and follow certain rules laid down by their cultures. We can understand communication behavior by understanding the rules people follow as they act. A rules researcher might ask questions such as these: How do individuals within a given culture use symbols to make sense of the world? Do men and women follow different rules to accomplish their goals? What are the major forms of communication in a given culture, and how are they valued?

Communication as Patterned Interaction

The third model takes yet another view of communication. Instead of focusing on individual selves or on social roles and rules, this perspective centers on systems of behavior. It suggests that the way people act when they are together is of primary importance, and it urges us to look carefully at patterns that emerge as people play the communication game.[8]

Elements of a Pragmatic Model

According to the pragmatic view, communication consists of *a system of interlocking, interdependent behaviors that become patterned over time.* Scholars who take a pragmatic approach argue that communicating is much like playing a game. When people decide to communicate, they become *partners* in a game that requires them to make individual "moves," or *acts.* Over time, these acts become patterned, the simplest pattern being a two-act sequence called an *interact.* One of the reasons certain acts are repeated is that they result in *payoffs* for the participants. Over the course of the game, players become *interdependent* because their payoffs depend on their partners' actions. This analogy between communication and a game is illustrated in Figure 2.3. The analogy between chess and communication holds in a number of ways. First, the game itself, not what goes on around it, is the central concern. Although it is possible to find books on chess that analyze the personality of individual players, most books focus on the structure of the game itself. Who white and black represent is not nearly as important as how they respond to one another. To understand chess, you need to understand the present state of the board and the series of moves that produced it. To understand communication, pragmatists argue, you need to do much the same thing: understand the moves people use as they work out their relationship to one another.

> To understand communication, pragmatists argue, you need to understand the moves people use as they work out their relationship to one another.

Note that in Figure 2.3, the moves are listed sequentially. At every turn, you can see what A did and how B responded. Chess books always list moves in this way, using the exact sequence in which they occurred in the game. It would make no sense to list all the moves of the game randomly. The game consists of ordered, interlocking moves and makes sense only when we follow the sequence. In the same way, an individual act or isolated behavior makes sense only in context, that is, when we see it in relationship to previous acts. According to the pragmatic viewpoint, the smallest significant unit of communication is the interact, which consists of two sequential acts. If you merely hear me cry, you know very little

Figure 2.3 A Pragmatic Model of Communication

In a pragmatic model, communication is seen as a game of sequential, interlocking moves between interdependent partners. Each player responds to the partner's moves in light of his or her own strategy and in anticipation of future action. Some moves are specific to this game, and others are common gambits or strategies. All moves make sense only in the context of the game. Outcomes, or payoffs, are a result of patterned "play" between partners.

move	A's moves	B's moves
21	. . . . . .	B offends A
22	A ignores B	B repeats offense
23	A challenges B	B ignores A
24	A reissues challenge	B offers apology
25	A accepts apology	B thanks A
26	A changes subject	. . . . . .

about what is happening. To understand what my crying means, you need to know, at the very least, what happened immediately before I cried. I may have become sad or angry, or I may have laughed so hard I began to cry. My crying may be a sincere expression of sorrow, or it may have been a move designed to make you feel sorry for me. The more you know about what happened before I cried, the more you understand the communication game I'm playing.

One of the factors that makes the game analogy appropriate is the interdependence of game players. Each player is affected by what another player does. Players need each other if they are to play. The same is true of communication: a person can't be a sender without someone to be a receiver, and it's impossible for a receiver to receive a message without a sender to send it. The dyad, not the individual, is important. Individuals don't play the communication game; partners (or opponents) do.

In a game, every action is important. Every move I make affects you, and every move you make affects me. Even if I refuse to move, I am still playing: I am resigning from or forfeiting the game. This is even more significant in communication, in which any response counts as a move. According to the pragmatic perspective, *we cannot not communicate.* If a friend promises to write to you and doesn't, his or her silence speaks louder than words. You realize that your friend doesn't want to continue the relationship. It is impossible not to communicate, just as it is impossible not to behave.

Finally, communication resembles a game in that both result in interdependent outcomes, or payoffs. In chess, the payoff is the thrill of victory or the agony of defeat. Communication also has payoffs. Sometimes, they are competitive; for example, someone "wins points" by putting down someone else. But more often than not, the payoffs are cooperative. Each person gets something out of playing. In fact, one way to view relationships is as cooperative improvised games. As people get to know one another, they learn to avoid unproductive moves, and they begin to work out patterns of interaction that satisfy both of them. This is what we mean when we say that two people are "working out the rules" of their relationship. They are learning to play the relationship game with style and grace.

Improving Unhealthy Patterns

According to the pragmatic approach, the best way to understand and improve communication is to describe the forms or patterns that the communication takes. If these patterns are destructive, then the players should be encouraged to find more productive ways of playing the communication game. Let's say that George and Martha are having problems communicating and decide to go to a communication counselor for help. The counselor taking a pragmatic approach will try to uncover the communication patterns that are the root of George and Martha's problems.

In the beginning, George may explain the problem by blaming Martha. "Her need for attention is so great," he may say, "that I'm forced to spend all my time catering to her. This makes me so mad that I have to get out of the house. She can't seem to understand that I need my privacy. She's demanding and irrational." Of course, Martha has her own version of events, which may go something like this: "He's so withdrawn, I can't stand it. He never pays any attention to me. I have to beg to get a moment of his time, and when he does give it, he gets angry. George is cold and unreasonable." Without help, George and Martha will each continue to blame the other. Martha may blame George's mother for making him the way he is. George may decide that Martha has a personality flaw.

Some scholars see communication as a complex game, where each move determines the next.

© Bettmann/CORBIS

The pragmatic therapist isn't interested in exploring background issues. Instead, the therapist tries to identify the behavior pattern that is causing the problem. In this case, George's and Martha's responses to one another are ineffective and are exacerbating the problem. The therapist will help George and Martha to work out a more effective set of moves that will make them both happy.

Perhaps the most important thing the pragmatic theorist tells us is that to understand communication, we should focus on interaction rather than on personality. When you get into an interpersonal conflict (and it's in the interpersonal and small-group arena that the pragmatic model seems to fit best), how often do you examine the pattern of events that led up to the conflict? Chances are, you don't do so very often; instead, you look for a personality explanation. When you and your roommate have problems communicating, you probably don't ask yourself, "What do I do that causes her to respond the way she does?" Instead, you try to figure out what's wrong with her. This is not the most productive solution to the problem.

Criticizing the Pragmatic Perspective

The principal problem with the pragmatic viewpoint is that it holds that both personality and culture are irrelevant. Pragmatists steadfastly refuse to ask why people act as they do. They dismiss factors such as intentions, desires, and needs. They are interested only in how sets of interacts pattern themselves. They also have little to say about the cultural context surrounding interaction. Look again at Figure 2.3, and notice that only what happens on the board is important. What happens outside the world of the game is never considered. Who the players are, where the game is played, and what other players are doing are all irrelevant questions.

Asking Questions from the Pragmatic Perspective

Communication researchers who subscribe to the pragmatic perspective do not take a laws or a rules approach. The approach most compatible with the pragmatic perspective is the **systems approach**. Systems researchers are concerned with describing interdependent patterns of behavior rather than individual behavior. A systems researcher looks at the structure, function, and evolution of a communication system, asking how communicators within the system organize their behavior, how patterns of behavior affect the way the system works, and how communication changes over time. A systems researcher might ask the following questions: How do the members of a dyad become interdependent over time? What effect do different patterns of dominance have on long-term relationships? Do small-group discussions go through standard phases?

Communication as Power Relations

A final approach to communication, the **cultural studies perspective**, now influences many communication scholars, in particular those who take a rhetorical approach to the study of communication. Unlike the perspectives we have already examined, this approach is overtly political because scholars in the field of cultural studies see a close relationship between acts of communication (called *discursive acts* or *texts*) and power.

The Cultural Studies Perspective

According to scholars who take this approach, cultures are constituted through a particular set of discursive acts. Any given culture is, in fact, a web of interconnected acts of communication, all of which carry meaning, much of which lies below the surface. These texts play off of one another, as collective beliefs and experiences move from one medium to another.[9] Because they are linked to social forces such as capitalism, patriarchy, racism, colonialism, and so on, texts exert power over the people who consume them.[10] A particularly powerful kind of discursive act can be found in popular culture: on television, in films, and in other popular art forms. Although these acts of communication may seem innocent of any political content, cultural critics believe that they serve political interests because they reproduce the structures of domination and subordination that exist within a culture and because they are often used by receivers to understand the conditions of their lives.[11] Thus, for example, crime dramas, popular films, or news broadcasts may encourage racism

Any given culture is, in fact, a web of interconnected acts of communication, much of which lies below the surface.

and homophobia, while romance novels, prom magazines, or beauty pageants may contain messages that encourage the subordination of women. Sometimes the consumers of these messages are not aware of their political content and accept them without thought.

The job of the cultural critics is to uncover and make visible the connections between social forces, particularly forces of oppression, and the messages or texts that reinforce these forces. A cultural studies critic focusing on race, for example, would ask questions like the following: How is race symbolically created? How are whole racial groups relatively empowered or disempowered by exposure to the message comprising the cultures in which we live? How are people recruited to participate in their own oppression and devaluation?[12] Cultural studies pays especially close attention to popular electronic media because media messages are so pervasive in contemporary society. But cultural criticism is not only limited to television and film. All aspects of popular culture are open to examination. In addition to crime dramas, situation comedies, and popular films, cultural critics have studied "texts" as diverse as congressional testimony, news stories, rock lyrics, shopping centers, jokes, scientific papers, public memorials, the AIDS epidemic, and magazines like *Hustler*.[13]

© Jamie Pham Photography/Alamy

Media images represent cultural values. Venues like Comic-Con allow individuals to act out media-generated fantasies.

Although power is always at stake, according to the critical studies perspective, public discourse is not the intentional production of a single individual or even of a homogeneous group of individuals. Instead, it is the product of "multiple voices, in contest over power."[14] Receivers do not always "read" a text in ways that support power structures. It is often possible to do oppositional readings, that is, to resist the political message that may be contained within a given text. Every text offers its readers a *subject position,* a role or stance to take when responding to the text. Although those who are most oppressed often accept this role by assuming that things are and should be the way they are depicted, they do not need to do so. Part of the political agenda of cultural studies is to help people recognize sources of oppression when they occur in public discourse.

Criticizing Cultural Studies

Cultural studies is by no means a unified field. Originating in the 1960s and 1970s, the cultural studies perspective is still being defined, and debates within the ranks about theory and method can often be fierce.[15] Whether you agree or disagree with the specific political stance taken by cultural studies, the perspective raises many interesting questions and draws our attention to the fact that communication has powerful effects, that texts are not always what they seem on the surface, and that it is wise to think carefully about what a given act of public communication is actually saying or doing.

WHAT TO LOOK FOR WHEN YOU LOOK AT COMMUNICATION

Before we move on, we have one more model to consider. This model, developed by Dell Hymes, is a kind of field guide for describing communication.[16] Communication teachers often ask students to develop sensitivity to different speech communities. Students may be asked to describe "locker room talk" or "children's playground talk." Or they may be asked to compare the rules governing female speech with those governing male speech. These assignments put the student in essentially the same situation as anthropologists who try to explain a strange culture; the student must do what is called an **ethnography of communication**. Hymes presents a systematic way to undertake this kind of observation. Figure 2.4 presents Hymes's model.

Hymes begins by giving a general overview of the contexts in which communication occurs. When people share common ways of thinking about communication and common styles of talk, they have formed a *speech community*. These communities may be large (as when we describe "women's speech") or small (as when we examine the way athletes on a particular team engage in locker room talk). The first step in doing an ethnography is identifying a speech community. Let's say you are studying the communication patterns of members of nontraditional religions.

> When people share common ways of thinking about communication and common styles of talk, they have formed a speech community.

You settle on the Unification Church, a Christian sect that came to the United States in the 1960s, declined in popularity, and is now working to regain converts who left the church. You are particularly interested in understanding how its members, popularly known as Moonies, managed to convert so many original members. You believe

Figure 2.4 **What to Look for When Observing Communication**

Situations	Setting and scene of interaction
Participants	Who speaks, who is addressed
Ends	Goals and outcomes of interaction
Act Sequences	Content, means of expression
Keys	Tone or spirit of interaction
Instrumentalities	Channels, or media of interaction
Norms	Rules regulating interaction
Genres	Type of communication enacted

Adapted from *Foundations in Sociolinguistics: An Ethnographic Approach* by Dell Hymes, 1974, Philadelphia: University of Pennsylvania Press.

that whenever a member joins the Moonies, he or she becomes socialized into the speech practices of the community. The Moonies, then, are your speech community.

Next, you need to catalog *speech situations* within the community. A speech situation is a clearly marked occasion that calls for a specific type of speech. By reading accounts of recruitment policies, talking to original members, and observing current church members carefully, you begin to get a sense of what these situations are in this community. You find that recruitment, weekend retreats, study sessions, and flower sales were four of the original speech situations that called for distinct forms of communication.

Each of these situations consists of a series of *speech events*, or identifiable sequences of speech. You discover that in the early days, the Moonies built cohesion during weekend retreats by playing simple, competitive games. Recruits were warmly accepted by their teams. As play progressed, group cheering and chanting often led to an almost ecstatic state. Another weekend workshop activity was called "love bombing." A "love bomber," or church member, followed each recruit everywhere and lavished attention on him or her. Chanting and love bombing were two different speech events that took place in this retreat setting.

Speech events can often be broken down into *speech acts*, or individual, purposeful acts of communication. During love bombing, Moonies may have engaged in one or more of the following speech acts: showing concern, expressing regard, helping a recruit, and so on.

A complete description of all the speech acts and events included in major speech situations of the Unification Church gives us a good idea of the way members used communication to persuade and influence prospective members. By examining the way communication works in this context, we can also develop a better understanding of persuasive communication in general.

Hymes lists a series of specific items that an ethnographer of communication observes (see Figure 2.4). Conveniently, the first letters of these items spell the word *speaking*. Hymes believes that it is important to describe the *specific situation*, or the environment in which communication takes place (including the time, place, and physical circumstances), as well as the psychological weight a given situation carries. He also believes it is important to describe the *participants* who take part in a given form of speech, as well as their goals, or *ends*. In describing act sequences, the ethnographer carefully records communication content and form, noting not only what is said or done but also how it is expressed.

Key is the tone or spirit (for example, joking, aggressive, or ecstatic) in which a given activity is undertaken. *Instrumentalities* are the channels of transmission used (for example, verbal or nonverbal, written or spoken). In looking at *norms*, the observer indicates the values and beliefs attached to a given form of communication, as well as the rules that regulate its use. Finally, a *genre* is a specialized type of encoded message. Examples of genre include prayers, orations, curses, and so on. Hymes believes the conventions governing each genre should be carefully described to gain a true understanding of communication in a given speech community. Observing communication behavior often seems to be an overwhelming task. By breaking communication down into smaller units, Hymes helps make that task more manageable.

Communication can be understood and modeled in a variety of ways, five of which we've looked at so far (the four models discussed in this chapter and the canons of rhetoric discussed in Chapter 1). Although the methods are quite different, each helps to explain a small part of a very complex process.

SUMMARY

Through the years, rhetoricians and communication scientists have not always agreed about what communication is. This chapter looks at a variety of definitions, models, and perspectives that offer insights into communication.

Definitions help to explain and limit concepts. The process of defining can be thought of as either an objective act of discovery or a creative act of construction. According to the second view, the test of a good definition is not its absolute truth but rather its usefulness, and several definitions of a concept may be valid.

One way definitions of communication vary is in breadth. Narrow definitions limit the domain of communication, whereas broad definitions expand it. Another way in which definitions differ is in the importance they place on intentionality. Further, definitions may be either sender- or receiver-based. Finally, some people believe that all communication is symbolic. We don't have to choose just one definition. Instead, we can think of communication as a family of related concepts. Historically, students of communication have studied interpersonal, small group, public, intercultural, organizational, and mass communication. More recently they have turned their attention to the ways digital media are expanding our understanding of more traditional face-to-face forms of communication.

Whereas definitions express the essence of a concept, models focus on its structure or function. A good model explains a phenome-non, allows us to predict the future, and gives us control over future events. Even good mod-els are always incomplete; there is no perfect model. Models are based on assumptions. The set of assumptions that we hold about a given concept is called a perspective. This chapter discusses three perspectives (psychological, so-cial constructionist, and pragmatic) and offers a model for each perspective.

The psychological perspective views commu-nication as a process of message transmission. A typical psychological model uses concepts such as sender/receiver, encoding and decoding, mes-sage, channel, feedback, and noise. It locates communication in the mental sets of individual communicators. Although the psychological perspective is the most widely used in our field, it has drawbacks: it ignores social context, it is mechanistic, and it places more value on accu-racy than on creativity. Researchers who follow this perspective often use a laws approach.

According to the social constructionist per-spective, communication is the collective cre-ation of meaning. It is not something that goes on between people but, rather, something that surrounds them and holds their world together. Social constructionist models stress concepts such as symbolic codes, cognitive customs, cultural traditions, roles, and rules. Critics of this view argue that its emphasis on truth as a construction can lead to relativism and that its emphasis on cultural appropriateness leaves out individual action. Researchers who follow

this perspective often use a rules approach to research.

The pragmatic perspective views commu-nication as a system of interlocking behaviors that become patterned over time. Pragmatists use concepts such as acts, interacts, outcomes or payoffs, and patterned moves. Critics regard the pragmatic perspective as a form of naive behavioralism and argue that it treats commu-nication as context-free. Pragmatic researchers often use a systems approach to research.

The cultural studies perspective is the most overtly political of the perspectives discussed in this chapter, in that it associates communica-tion and power. According to this perspective, cultures are made up of discursive practices that are embodied in texts. Because many texts uphold a culture's power structures, they need to be examined carefully. By placing receivers in certain subject positions, many texts that look innocent on the surface may oppress re-ceivers. The job of the critic is to offer receivers ways to resist the hegemonic messages con-tained in popular public discourse.

The chapter closes with a final model that focuses on what to look for as we observe com-munication behavior. Rather than describing how communication works, this model directs our attention to factors such as situations, par-ticipants, ends, act sequences, keys, instru-mentalities, norms, and genres. It also situates communication within speech communities and gives special emphasis to the identification of speech acts.

KEY TERMS

Listed below are the key terms used in this chapter, along with the number of the page where each is explained.

definition (16)
breadth (17)
intentionality (19)
sender-based
    communication (19)
receiver-based
    communication (19)
symbols (20)
spoken symbolic
    interaction (20)

nonverbal interaction (20)
model (21)
explanatory function (22)
predictive function (22)
control function (22)
perspective (23)
psychological
    perspective (23)

social constructionist
    perspective (23)
pragmatic perspective (23)
laws approach (26)
rules approach (29)
systems approach (33)
cultural studies
    perspective (33)
ethnography of
    communication (35)

SUGGESTED READING

Anderson, Rob, & Ross, Veronica. (2002). *Questions of communication: A practical introduction to theory*. Boston: St. Martin's Press.

> An involving, personalized look at theory building in communication and a lively and interesting introduction to theories and models of communication.

During, Simon. (2005). *Cultural studies*. New York: T&F/Routledge.

> An introduction to cultural critique, consisting of short essays on core topics in the field, including time, space, identity, sexuality, and gender.

Littlejohn, Stephen W., & Foss, Karen (2010). *Theories of human communication*. Long Grove, Illinois: Waveland Press.

> A comprehensive overview of theories and approaches to human communication. Although it can be a bit challenging if you are not familiar with the field, this book is the place to go if you want a detailed exploration of theory and perspective.

Decoding Messages: Listening and Perception

L istening is the forgotten part of communication, yet being able to listen well is one of the most essential communication-related skills.

A lthough people may disagree on how to define communication, everyone agrees that we use communication to make sense of the world—in other words, that we think through communication. In the next two chapters, we'll investigate communication from the sender's point of view. In this chapter, however, we'll look at how receivers listen to and process messages. You may be surprised to learn how subjective and fallible perception and listening are. Different people exposed to a single message can come away with very different understandings.

A group of scientists attending a professional conference were waiting for a meeting to begin when a door opened and two men, one wearing a clown's costume and the other wearing a black jacket, red tie, and white trousers, rushed in. The two men yelled at each other and scuffled briefly. Suddenly, a shot rang out, whereupon both men rushed out of the room. The chairperson immediately asked everyone in the room to write a complete description of what had happened. The scientists did not know that the incident had been staged to test the accuracy of their perceptions.

How accurate were their perceptions? Of the forty scientists who responded, none gave a complete description of the incident. Twelve reports missed at least 50 percent of what had happened, and only six reports did not misstate facts or add inaccurate details. The eyewitnesses could not even identify the color of the second man's suit; it was variously described as red, brown, striped, blue, and coffee-colored. In relating this story, William D. Brooks comments on the limitations inherent in perception:

> *The experiment demonstrated dramatically the fallibility of vision and hearing as avenues of information. Similar demonstrations have been made in numerous college speech and psychology classes*

since the original incident was carried out. Man does not perceive all he sees, nor does he necessarily perceive accurately what falls on the eye's screen; and yet his intrapersonal communication is limited to and based on the information he has via the process of perception from all the senses.[1]

Although perception and listening are always risky, accurate communication is possible. By understanding how perception and information processing work, you can improve both your receiving and sending skills. In the following pages, we will look at ways to listen and to process information more accurately as well as ways to design messages that are easy for others to understand.

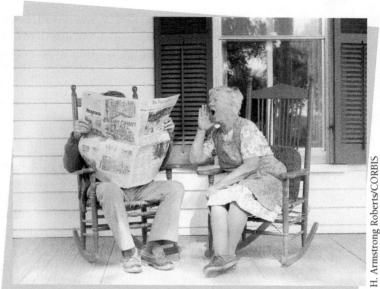

In interpersonal interactions failure to listen can lead to frustration and futile attempts to amplify messages.

H. Armstrong Roberts/CORBIS

WHAT IS LISTENING?

According to the International Listening Association, **listening** is "the process of receiving, constructing meaning from, and responding to spoken and/or nonverbal messages."[2] When we listen, we engage in a complex multi-step process that includes (1) attending to the sensory stimuli that make up a message, (2) making those stimuli meaningful by using our own experiences to interpret them, (3) critically evaluating our interpretations, (4) responding to the message, and (5) storing the message for future use. When we listen, we are not passive receivers but active creators of meaning.

Most people think listening and hearing are the same thing. But listening and hearing are quite different. **Hearing** is a physiological process that occurs when sound waves are translated into electrical impulses and then processed by the central nervous system. Listening, on the other hand, is a social cognitive process. When we listen, we assign meaning, and in assigning meaning we are influenced by our habits, expectations, and desires. And whereas hearing focuses primarily on sound, listening includes all forms of sensory data. We hear with our ears, but we listen with all our senses. When we listen to a conversation, for example, we process not only what is said but also how it is said. To understand the message fully, we need to be aware of the nonverbal cues that accompany and modify the meanings of words. When we

> Whereas hearing focuses primarily on sound, listening includes all forms of sensory data. We hear with our ears, but we listen with all our senses.

interact through electronic media, we must also listen. We now live in a world where we spend a great deal of time reading and responding to text-based electronic messages. All of the principles that apply to the accurate reception of spoken messages apply to electronic messages as well. The process of interpreting and evaluating text messages is a new but vital form of listening.

Why Listening Sometimes Fails

Despite the fact that we spend more time listening than engaging in any other form of communication, most of us have very poor listening skills. How often have you missed the point of a lecture because your attention wandered or you found that your understanding of an assignment was different from your professor's? Have you ever been caught unprepared because you forgot an appointment? Have you failed to pick up on nonverbal cues that signaled a partner's feelings? These kinds of problems are all too common, and they are all tied to poor listening.

Listening takes skill and mental effort. Unfortunately, we are not trained to develop that skill. Years ago, Ralph Nichols and Leonard Stevens conducted a revealing study. They asked teachers at various grade levels to interrupt their lectures and ask students, "What was I talking about before I called time out?" In Grade 1, 90 percent of the students were able to answer the teacher's question. By junior high, only 43.7 percent were listening, and the percentage fell to 28 percent by high school.[3] This and similar studies show that actual listening performance worsens over time. A serious gap exists between what we *can* do and what we actually *do* as listeners.

The gap between ability and actual performance may be partly due to cultural values. As Americans, we value activity and independence. We tend to believe that expressing our own ideas is more valuable than attending to others' messages. And because of the low value our culture places on listening, most of us have learned to be poor listeners. Parents and teachers make sure we develop skills in reading, writing, and speaking. Listening, however, is usually something we learn on our own, and the models that we learn from are not very good. Florence Wolff and her colleagues tell us that our parents often train us to be "nonlisteners." When parents tell a child, "Don't pay any attention to that" or "I don't want to hear that in this family," they model nonlistening. By not paying attention or by interrupting each other in midsentence, parents tell us that it is not important to hear others out.[4] In school,

> Because of the low value our culture places on listening, most of us have learned to be poor listeners.

the situation is almost as bad. Teachers, themselves untrained in listening, make up for students' listening deficiencies by patiently repeating themselves. By failing to demand high levels of listening performance, they too may be reinforcing nonlistening.

Why Listening Is Important

If listening is so difficult, why take the time and trouble to improve it? The answer is that learning to listen more effectively has benefits. First, becoming a better listener enhances job performance. A study of listening in the workplace, for example, found that more than 60 percent of business errors are related to poor listening.[5] In another study, 80 percent of the executives questioned rated listening as the most vital skill for accomplishing workplace tasks.[6] As listening expert Judi Brownell tells us, listening has been shown to play a vital role in a variety of organizational settings including health care, the military, sales, and marketing.[7]

Listening is also essential in creating and maintaining relationships. One of the major characteristics that attracts us to others in the first place is their willingness to listen. When people refuse to listen, they send a message that they don't care about us, that we don't exist for them. If we want to develop good relationships, we need to listen carefully not only to what our partners say but also to what they leave unsaid. If we can't listen in an open, accepting way, it is impossible for us to comfort and support our partners. Listening is important in both our professional and personal lives.

THE LISTENING PROCESS

Listening is a complex process. In this section, we will break that process down into parts and try to understand how each part contributes to the whole. We will begin by looking at attention, the first requirement for effective listening. We will then discuss how we interpret, or construct meaning from, the stimuli we attend to. Because listening involves evaluating messages, we will also examine some ways to become more critical receivers. Next we will consider how important it is to respond appropriately to the messages we receive from others. We will end with a discussion of how we retain and retrieve messages. As we look at each part of the listening process, we will also consider ways to improve listening performance. (Table 3.1 summarizes this aspect of our discussion.)

Attention

Because we live in a world that continually bombards us with stimuli, we have to be selective about what we pay attention to. We therefore screen out most of the sensory data that surround us, focusing only on a small subset of the information we could take in. **Attention** is the process of selectively focusing on certain events in the environment. Stop reading for a minute and focus on your surroundings. You may suddenly become aware of the hum of an air conditioner or the voices of passersby on the street. You may realize that the temperature is a bit too cool or that your chair is a bit too hard. You may also become aware of odors you have blocked out—the smell of food or the faint scent of perfume. While you were reading, all of these stimuli disappeared. When you made a conscious attempt to attend to them, they jumped into focus.

> We screen out most of the sensory data that surround us, focusing only on a small subset of the information we could take in.

Voluntary and Involuntary Attention

Scholars who study information processing often distinguish between two kinds of attention: voluntary and involuntary.[8] *Voluntary attention* occurs when we willfully focus on a stimulus; it is attention guided by personal plans and goals. When we listen to a debate to find out a candidate's position or examine a map to make sure we are going in the right direction, we are engaged in voluntary attention. *Involuntary attention*, by contrast, occurs when the intrinsic properties of a stimulus make that stimulus stand out; this kind of attention lies outside our control. When we jump because a siren starts to blare or when we suddenly stare because someone in an outlandish outfit walks by, we are engaging in involuntary attention.

Improving Attention

Because attention occurs in short bursts and because external stimuli are constantly vying for involuntary attention, it is very easy to get distracted. An effective listener is someone who can focus attention on what is important while screening out irrelevant details. One way to improve attention is to *begin by acknowledging how easy it is to be diverted by extraneous details*. A speaker's clothes or mannerisms, unusual environmental details, competing sounds or movements, or our own concerns and feelings can divert voluntary attention. Other sources of distractions are self-consciousness (focusing so much on how you are coming across that you miss what the other person is saying) and competitive turn taking (planning and plotting what you will say next rather than attending to the other person). Luckily, it is possible to refocus attention.

Because voluntary attention is guided by goals and plans, it is especially important to *have a clear purpose in mind on entering a listening situation*. In other

---

Table 3.1 Ways to Improve Listening Performance

To Improve Attention

- Avoid distractions.
- Be aware of your purpose for listening.
- Notice contextual cues.
- Keep a positive attitude; don't assume that you'll be bored.

To Improve Interpretation

- Recognize the complexity of perception.
- Prepare ahead of time by knowing about the topic.
- Use extra time to summarize and rehearse.
- When appropriate, use perception checks.

To Improve Evaluation

- Test information for adequacy and accuracy.
- Separate inference and evaluation from description.
- Acknowledge your biases and delay final evaluation.

To Improve Responding

- Realize you cannot not communicate.
- See things from the sender's perspective.
- Respond to what is *not* said as well as what is.

To Improve Storage and Retrieval

- Decide what information needs to be stored.
- Rehearse and review material.
- Use mnemonic devices or special memory aids.

words, know what you want to accomplish by listening, and remind yourself of your purpose whenever you find your attention straying. If you are listening to a lecture, your purpose may be to understand and remember the speaker's main points as well as supporting examples. In an interpersonal situation, your goal may be to understand what is bothering a friend. In either case, your goal can direct your attention.

Although a good listener needs to focus primarily on the content of messages while avoiding trivial details, this does not mean that all attention should be directed to what is said. Often, context is an important part of a message, and *how* something is said is a key element in determining *what* has been said. This is particularly important in interpersonal interactions. A friend may say she isn't upset, but if she is wringing her hands and looking away, chances are that something is wrong, something you should be aware of. As an effective listener, then, you should *notice relevant contextual and nonverbal cues.*

Finally, you can improve attention if you open yourself to others' messages. *Don't dismiss a message ahead of time because you assume that it will be boring or ignore what someone says because you dislike the person.* If you enter a listening situation expecting the worst, nonlistening becomes inevitable.

Strange or surprising stimuli stand out, capturing involuntary attention.

Alain Dejean/Sygma/CORBIS

Interpretation

Of course, listening is more than attending. It also involves assigning meaning. When we focus on a portion of the sensory world, we immediately label and categorize what we have perceived. We do so by giving incoming stimuli stability, structure, and meaning.[9] You can see how this process works by considering what you do when you

> **Often, context is an important part of a message, and *how* something is said is a key element in determining *what* has been said.**

watch television. When you turn on the TV, what you actually sense are a series of flickering lights and a jumble of undifferentiated sounds. You quickly **structure** these sounds and shadows into images and words. As the show progresses, you also impose **stability** on what you see. When the camera moves in for a close-up on one character, you are not disoriented. You understand that you are viewing a single character from a new perspective. When the camera pans across the room, you know that the character still exists even though he or she is no longer in view. Finally, you give the scene **meaning**. You begin to identify the characters, and, if you have seen the show before, you can guess what will happen next. All of this happens so quickly that you may not realize that complicated social knowledge is involved. Yet without this knowledge to guide you, you could not organize your sensations in any meaningful way.

Using Cognitive Schemata

Psychologists agree that we use shared social understandings, past experiences, and our knowledge about the world to help us interpret what we see or hear. To do so, we draw on mental guidelines, or what psychologists call **schemata** (singular: schema), to help us identify and organize incoming information. Schemata are internal representations of objects and sequences of actions. When we encounter a perceptual object, we store its image in short-term memory while we search for a schema to make sense of it. Perhaps you have a favorite TV comedy, one you always watch. If so, you have a schema for that show. You know the characters and typical plots, and it is easy for you to follow the story and identify who is who. Those who have never seen the show, on the other hand, must work out their own understandings, although a general situation-comedy schema can help them make sense of the format. Viewers from a culture without this kind of TV show, however, lack the interpretive schemata needed to understand the conventions we take for granted. Schemata make processing rapid and effortless, although, as we shall see, they can sometimes distort perception.

> We use shared social understandings, past experiences, and our knowledge about the world to help us interpret what we see or hear.

We have schemata for physical objects, types of people (including ourselves), personal traits, relationships, and sequences of actions. For our purposes, the three most important types of schemata are person prototypes, personal constructs, and scripts.[10] (See Table 3.2 for an overview of these schemata.)

Person Prototypes

We often use schemata to form impressions of other people and to interpret their messages. **Person prototypes** are idealized representations of a certain kind of person. For example, you may have a prototypical image of a professor, a used car salesman, a scientist, or a quiz show host. These images allow you to identify whether a person belongs to one of these categories. The information contained in prototypes consists of traits, patterns of behavior, and role relations that fit our idea of a certain type of person. If a person appears to have a sufficient number of these traits, and if he or she exhibits no incompatible traits, then that person is easily recognized and understood.[11]

In helping us to identify and categorize people, person prototypes make our lives easier. But they also can color the way we interpret and evaluate messages by affecting expectations. If, for example, we class Kristin as "a typical airhead," then we are unlikely to take what she says seriously, regardless of the quality of her message. On the other hand, if we decide that Sam is "an expert in the field," then we're likely to accept whatever he says, even when a moment's reflection would tell us that he's not making any sense. In both cases, we allow a prototype to affect our ability to listen.

Personal Constructs

In our daily interactions, we often use another kind of schema, called a personal construct.[12] **Personal constructs** are characteristics that we notice on a daily basis about others. Whereas prototypes are global categorizations, constructs are specific descriptors.

Some personal constructs are suggested to us by events. We use them because they have recently been "primed." For example, if we have just come back from a religious service, constructs such as "forgiving" and "kind" may be uppermost in our minds, and we may interpret others' behavior in terms of generosity and concern for others. If, on the other hand, we have been reading about the latest political scandal, constructs such as "manipulative" may occur to us.

In addition to constructs that we use temporarily because they are suggested to us by events, we also have habitual ways of judging others. Constructs that are important to us and that we frequently use, regardless of circumstances, are called **chronically accessible constructs**, and these constructs are likely to color and bias our interpretation of others and their messages. Psychologist John Bargh tells us that there are wide personal differences in construct accessibility and that this accessibility does not often overlap between individuals. Thus, two people may "pick up very different information about a third person, and interpret the same information in very different ways."[13] For example, Sheldon (who is suspicious of others) may use

---

Table 3.2 Cognitive Schemata

Person Prototypes

Person prototypes are idealized representations of a certain kind of person. They are used to identify and classify people. If you can form a mental image of any of the following, you are using a person prototype: cowboy, beauty queen, stand-up comic, feminist, politician, type-A personality. Although prototypes give us a quick take on someone, they ignore individual details and can lead to stereotyped responses.

Personal Constructs

Personal constructs are the characteristics that we habitually notice in others. They are the specific descriptors we use to answer the question "What is he or she like?" Part of the mental apparatus of the observer, they appear to be characteristics of the observed. Like other schemata, they can make perception easier and more efficient, but they can also be inaccurate and unfair.

Scripts

Scripts are representations of sequences of action. They tell us what to do next in a given situation. When communication is scripted, we can rattle off a routine without thinking about it. Well-learned scripts free us from making conscious decisions about our actions and give us the confidence that comes from knowing what to say or do next. However, they can lull us into mindlessness and repetitive routines.

We do our best to interpret what we see, but things are not always what they seem.

© INTERFOTO/Alamy

constructs such as *manipulative, insincere,* and *ingratiating* to interpret Judi's offer of help, while Marla may see the same behavior as *friendly* and *sincere*. Each of us sees what is important to us and may miss what others see. Clearly over-reliance on chronic constructs can lead to problems in interpreting messages.

Because they operate outside of our control and potentially outside of our awareness altogether, we cannot adjust for them through some intentional and controlled process. We cannot say, for example, "Oh, maybe Carol didn't mean it that way," and decide that we can still be friends with her, because as with the color of the sky, we do not question the validity of automatically produced perceptions.[14]

To examine your own personal constructs, consider a number of people you know, and write down adjectives to describe them. Looking at your completed list, you'll see the kinds of judgments you habitually make about others. Are the constructs you listed based on physical or psychological characteristics? Are they fair or unfair? What do they tell you about how you evaluate people and their behaviors and motivations?

When individuals use only simple, undifferentiated constructs, we say that they lack cognitive complexity. **Cognitive complexity** occurs when an individual has a large, rich, and varied set of personal constructs.[15] The cognitively complex person is willing to combine seemingly contradictory characteristics in creative ways, realizing that people are not all good or all bad. The person who lacks cognitive complexity tends to use one or two simple constructs, ignoring contradictory information. Cognitive complexity is a mark of maturity and is necessary for good communication. Incidentally, cognitive complexity is itself a personal construct, one that communication scholars use to explain perceptual behavior.

> **The cognitively complex person is willing to combine seemingly contradictory characteristics in creative ways.**

Scripts

So far, we have focused on how we use schemata to process information about other people. We also have schemata that allow us to interpret sequences of behavior. These are called **scripts**.[16] A script tells us what comes next in a sequence of actions. When we experience a situation repeatedly, we abstract its essential features and identify the order in which things happen. We have scripts for all kinds of simple actions: eating in a restaurant, working out at a gym, walking to class. Scripts allow us to behave effortlessly, without having to think much about what to do next. When we find ourselves in highly scripted situations, we feel confident. When we encounter unusual or novel situations for which we have no script, we feel uncomfortable and unsure of ourselves and have trouble figuring out what is going on.

We have scripts for a variety of communicative events: simple greetings, public speeches, interviews, and so on. When speakers follow these scripts, we have no trouble understanding what is going on. Part of being an effective listener is being familiar with common scripts. For example, if we know that in a public speech, the introduction will present the main idea, the body of the speech will provide supporting evidence, and the conclusion will include a summary, then it will be relatively easy to follow the speech and interpret its message correctly.

Despite the fact that scripts can help us to interpret messages, there are times when they can impede rather than enhance interpretation. If we rely too heavily on a script, we may see or hear what we expect rather than what actually occurs. All schemata have embedded within them **schematic default options**, details that are supplied when actual information is missing. Assume that you witness a car crash. Later, when a lawyer asks you whether or not glass from broken headlights was on the ground, you may answer, "Sure," even if the headlights were not actually broken. Your schema for a car accident contains this detail, one that exists in your mind rather than in the actual situation.[17]

The use of schematic default options often occurs in simple greetings. For example, when we greet a friend with a "How are you?" we assume that the answer will be, "Fine." If the other person says, "I'm terrible," we may not even notice and may respond

> If we rely too heavily on a script, we may see or hear what we expect rather than what actually occurs.

with a cheery, "That's good. See you later." The story that opened this chapter shows another example of how schemata can distort perception. The scientists described what they thought they had seen rather than what they actually saw, filling in details in ways that made sense to them but did not correspond to reality. And evidence shows that after a period of time, the problem only gets worse; as time progresses, people have more and more trouble distinguishing inferred from observed information.[18]

Becoming More Mindful

As our discussion of schemata has shown, we often process information automatically, without much conscious thought. We frequently act like "lazy organisms" or "cognitive misers," saving our conscious attention for important situations and spending much of our time in what is called **mindless** or **automatic processing**.[19] We process mindlessly when we rely on old routines and mental habits to give us information about the world. Of course, mindless processing has its advantages: it can free us to attend to "the new, the unusual, the potentially dangerous, the most informative, and the most important events going on around us at any time."[20] On the other hand, mindlessness has serious disadvantages when we rely on incomplete or inappropriate schemata.

The opposite of mindless processing is **mindful processing**. According to psychologist Ellen Langer, when we are mindful, we are in a state of "alert and lively awareness."[21] When we act mindfully, we actively think about the world, creating new understandings rather than relying on old ones. Effective listeners know when to rely on familiar scripts, but they also know how and when to switch from mindless to mindful processing.

> Effective listeners know when to rely on familiar scripts, but they also know how and when to switch from mindless to mindful processing.

Improving Interpretation

As this section has shown, the process of interpretation depends heavily on subjective factors. Listening to a message is not simply a case of recording what we hear; rather, it is a complex process involving shared social knowledge, personal expectations, and individual schemata. The first step in improving interpretation, therefore, is to *recognize how complex perception is and how easy it is to get things wrong.*

When listening for complex information, you may need to *prepare ahead of time. The more you know about a topic, the easier it will be to process information about it.* If you can identify a speaker's purpose and the way he or she has structured a presentation and you know something about the subject, it will be a great deal easier for you to interpret the presentation correctly. Consider the following example:

> *The procedure is quite simple. First you arrange items into different groups. Of course one pile might be sufficient depending on how much there is to do. If you have to go somewhere else due to lack of facilities, that is the next step; otherwise you are pretty well set. It is important not to overdo things. That is, it is better to do too few things at once than too many. . . . After the procedure is completed one arranges the material into different groups again. They then can be put into their appropriate places. Eventually they will be used once more and the whole cycle will then have to be repeated. However, that is part of life.[22]*

At first, the passage seems so incomprehensible that you may be tempted to give up and stop processing. But it instantly becomes interpretable once you discover that it is about washing clothes and once you relate what you know about clothes washing to what the speaker has said. As a listener, you should constantly ask yourself, "What's going on here?" And you should *relate what the speaker says to what you already know.* Luckily, there is a gap between speaking and processing speed that allows you time to do just that.

One of the interesting facts about listening is that we can listen much faster than we can speak. The normal rate of speaking is approximately 150 words per minute, but studies have shown that we can process messages at rates of 300 words per minute or even higher. This means that as we listen we have plenty of time to think.

When processing complex information, we should *use the time differential between speaking and processing to focus on message content and structure.* In public speaking situations, you can fill time by identifying main ideas, recalling supporting details, and looking for transitions that will identify the structure of the speech. In interpersonal contexts, you can focus on identifying a partner's feelings and checking his or her nonverbal communication. In either case, the time differential can be used to paraphrase content and relate it to prior knowledge.

In formal, public situations, communication may be primarily one way. In such a situation, there is little opportunity for you to check your interpretation of the speaker's message during the speech itself. But in less formal settings, it is often possible to *ask for clarification by using what is called a perception check.* A **perception check** is a response that allows you to state your interpretation and ask your partner whether or not that interpretation is correct. When your professor gives you an assignment, you can check your perception by saying, "So, you want us to hand in our papers by ten o'clock on this Friday, is that right?" This allows the professor to agree or to explain, "No, not this Friday. It's due next Friday." You can also comment on contextual cues when you do a perception check. Say, for example, a friend says to you, "I don't want to go. You go without me." A perception check might consist of the following: "I know you say you don't want to go, but you seem a bit disappointed. Would you rather we both went at another time?" In this case, not only does perception checking clarify the message, but it allows you to avoid potential hurt feelings and misunderstandings.

Evaluation

Living as we do, in an age of information, we are bombarded with messages. It would be absurd to accept everything we hear or to believe everything we see. Some of the messages we receive are accurate and useful, and some are not. Part of being a good listener is evaluating message quality—knowing what to reject, what to believe, and what to question. That means listening critically. Being critical, however, does not mean being negative or rejecting everything we hear out of hand; instead, it means thinking carefully about the messages we receive. It means being aware of a speaker's purpose, evaluating the quality of the information that is being presented, and recognizing logical inconsistencies.

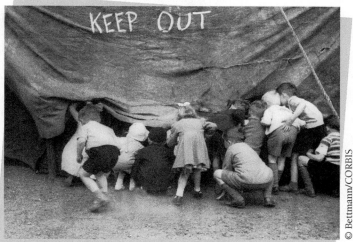

Censoring or restricting stimuli often makes them more interesting and appealing.

© Bettmann/CORBIS

Identifying Communicative Purpose

The first step in evaluating a message lies in determining its purpose. In some cases, the purpose is clear. When candidate Smith says, "Vote for me," we know that we are listening to a persuasive message. But in other cases, the speaker's intent may not be so obvious. An apparently objective lecture may actually have a hidden persuasive intent. And when the interaction is interpersonal, its purpose may be even more difficult to determine. For example, a stranger at a bus stop who remarks, "It's a beautiful day," is probably not working for the Weather Channel. The comment may be a way of passing the time, of striking up an acquaintance, of flirting, or even of softening you up so that the person can borrow the bus fare. And when someone says to you, "I'm only telling you this for your own good," it's probably wise to be suspicious; the speaker may have a hidden agenda that is unclear to you and not even very clear to the speaker. Knowing what a speaker is trying to do puts us in a much better position to evaluate the message.

Judging Information

Critical listeners are also adept at judging the quality of the information contained in a message. Although we know that we should be suspicious of new information, especially if it appears to be too good to be true, we also have a tendency to believe what we want to believe. If a message supports current beliefs, attitudes, and values, we tend to find it compelling. If it enhances our sense of self-worth, we may accept it without question. Yet it is in exactly these situations that we should be wary. By demanding good evidence and by considering the trustworthiness and expertness of message sources, we increase our ability to think critically about messages.

> If a message supports current beliefs, attitudes, and values, we tend to find it compelling. If it enhances our sense of self-worth, we may accept it without question. Yet it is in exactly these situations that we should be wary.

As we saw in Chapter 1 and will explore more fully in Chapter 9, source credibility is an important factor in judging the quality of information. Communicators who are both expert and trustworthy are much more believable than sources that are not. Whether you are communicating in a dyad or a group or are part of an audience, you should remember the old adage "Consider the source."

Identifying Loaded Language

Finally, effective evaluation means identifying logical inconsistencies and emotionally charged language. Critical listeners understand that appeals to emotion are often tied to questionable conclusions. In Chapter 9, we will consider logical fallacies in more detail, as we look at ways public speakers bypass reason in an attempt to sway audiences. At this point, it is probably enough to note that critical listeners carefully judge the language choices of speakers. Many years ago, Richard Weaver suggested that we react especially strongly to what he called **god and devil terms**.[23] *God terms* are terms that are so positive that they go unchallenged; *devil* *terms* express negative values and repel the listener. For most Americans, *patriotism* and *democracy* are unquestionably good, while *terrorism* is unquestionably evil. Words like these may inspire us to action, but they can also short-circuit rational debate because of their powerful connotations. Of course, using loaded language for persuasive ends is not new. As social psychologists Anthony Pratkanis and Elliot Aronson explain, our forefathers used loaded language to stir up patriotic feelings. Early American patriots, they tell us, "were able to increase revolutionary fervor by terming a minor skirmish with the British the *Boston massacre*."[24] To get current versions of the use of loaded language, all you need do is turn on your TV and tune in to one of the many political commentary shows, look at blogs with a political agenda, or listen to talk radio.

Evaluating Information on the Web

We noted earlier that nowadays we spend a great deal of time processing electronic messages. When you want to look up a "fact," where do you go? Chances are, you turn to the World Wide Web for the information you need. Why not? After all, the Web is a rich source of information. Unfortunately, it is a rich source of misinformation as well. Because anyone can post anything on the Web and because sources are often anonymous, evaluating information gleaned from Web pages is particularly challenging.

Librarian John Henderson offers some simple guidelines for using the Web as an information source. First, he tells us, make sure that the Web is the appropriate place to find the information you are seeking. Not everything, he reminds us, is on the Web. "An hour on the Web may not answer a question that you could find within two minutes of picking up a reference book."[25] If you decide to go to the Web, be suspicious: when in doubt, doubt. Look for ambiguity, loaded language, poor reasoning, and bias. Check several sources to verify that the fact you've just found isn't pure fiction. And always consider the source. You might assume that anyone posting information about a serious topic has credentials, but this isn't always the case. Susan Barnes reports one case in which a 15-year-old California high school student presented himself online as a legal "expert," despite the fact that almost all of his legal knowledge was gleaned from watching Court TV. In fact, he was such a popular contributor to the Website in question that even after he confessed, members still sought out his advice.[26]

As we suggested earlier, identifying the purpose of a message is an important aspect of listening. Henderson reminds us that we should try to determine why a given Website was created. "Since money talks, try to notice who is paying for the site, either through advertising or sponsorship. Both can affect content and objectivity."[27] Ask yourself whether the main purpose is to inform or to persuade. Looking at details can also help you to determine the accuracy of a Website's facts. Misspelling, poor grammar, lack of organization, distracting graphics, and links that do not work suggest carelessness and a lack of professionalism that may carry over into content.

Finally, Henderson reminds us that not all pages found on the Web are Web pages. Some Web content is created by individuals with an idiosyncratic view or by advertisers with persuasive intent, but books, periodicals, and government research reports are now accessible on the Web as well. These online sources are no more or less reliable than the same information found in print and must be evaluated like any other source. See Table 3.3 for a summary of things to keep in mind as you evaluate information from the Internet.

Improving Evaluation

As we've already seen, to be good listeners, we need to be critical consumers of information and to *question the adequacy and accuracy of the messages we receive.* One of the stumbling blocks to doing this is misunderstanding the difference between a description, an inference, and an evaluation.[28]

A **description** of fact is an actual observation of a state of affairs, made with a minimum of distortion. "John is making direct eye contact with me" is a description. An **inference**, by contrast, is a personal interpretation of the meaning behind the behavior being described. "John is aggressive" is a possible inference, as is "John is interested in what I have to say" or even "John finds me attractive." An **evaluation** goes even further, adding a positive or negative judgment. "John has a rotten attitude" and "I like the way John listens" and even "How dare John react to me in that way?" are all evaluations. It is easy to lose sight of the fact that a given behavior can be interpreted in multiple ways. Consider the following: "Elissa stamped her foot, screamed, and threw the book across the room"; "Elissa is angry"; "I hate it when Elissa acts like a child." These three statements are doing very different things. The

---

Table 3.3 A Guide to Evaluating What You See on the Web

- **Make Sure You Are in the Right Place.**

  Ask yourself: *Is this site the right place to get the information I need?*

- **When in Doubt, Doubt.**

  Ask yourself: *Do I have good reason to believe the information on the site is accurate? Can I confirm this information from another source?*

- **Consider the Source.**

  Ask yourself: *Who is responsible for the site? Do the authors have any authority or expertise?*

- **Know What Is Happening.**

  Ask yourself: *What is the main purpose of the site? Is it to inform, to persuade, to entertain, or to sell something?*

- **Look at Details.**

  Ask yourself: *Did the authors spend time making the site clear and professional, or is it full of careless errors? Are graphics helpful or distracting?*

- **Distinguish Web Pages from Pages Found on the Web.**

  Ask yourself: *Was the page designed for the Web, or was it originally something else? If it was something else, what was it?*

Adapted from *ICYouSee: T Is for Thinking,* by John R. Henderson, Ithaca College Library, www.ithaca.edu/library/training/think.html. Used by permission of the author.

second is an inference, but it is only one possible explanation for Elissa's behavior. What other possibilities might there be? And how might your evaluation of her change as a result? As effective listeners we need to *separate descriptions of fact from inferences and evaluations.*

Refusing to accept inferences without considering the facts they're based on is one way to improve listening. But we can't do this if we respond emotionally. It is human nature to jump to conclusions—to accept blindly what we want to hear and to reject without thinking what we don't want to hear. And the more ego involved we are with an issue—that is, the more we have a personal stake in the outcome—the more likely we are to lose our objectivity by not listening or by distorting the message. If you're like most people, some things that people say drive you crazy. Can you identify some of these statements? How do you respond when one of these hot button issues is raised? Most likely, you either shut down or begin to argue back before you have actually heard the speaker out. You will be a better listener if you *become aware of your biases and delay final evaluation until you have had time to think about the message.* If your interpretations of messages are biased, your responses will be biased as well.

> It is human nature to jump to conclusions—to accept blindly what we want to hear and to reject without thinking what we don't want to hear.

Responding

Picture this. You pour your heart out to a friend. As you talk, your friend stares at you blankly. When you're finished, your friend looks at you with a neutral expression, gets up, shrugs, and walks out of the room. How would you feel? Chances are that you would be hurt and confused. When we communicate, we expect a reaction. In social situations, the role of the listener involves more than simply understanding and storing information. Listeners have an obligation to respond either verbally or nonverbally. Responding in a way that lets a speaker know you are listening is called **active listening**.

Active listening takes many forms. It can consist of overt verbal responses, or it can simply be a nod, a smile, or a frown. In any form, active listening shows the speaker that you are paying attention. It also allows senders to gauge the success of their messages and receivers to check the accuracy of their perceptions. Although it can be awkward—even painful—to give or get negative feedback, even negative feedback is better than silence and a frozen expression.

Styles of Listening

Not only is it important to give feedback during listening, it is crucial to do so in the right way. Just as there are styles of speaking, there are also styles of listening, ways in which listeners indicate understanding and interest. Sometimes these styles are individual; some people are more nonverbally expressive than others. And sometimes these styles are cultural. European Americans, for example, usually expect listeners to listen silently, fixing their eyes on the speaker until he or she signals that talk is concluded. In this cultural group, such behavior shows respect. In the African American rhetorical tradition, however, a different pattern occurs. "Speaker and listener urge one another on with call and response, with messages and expressions of delight, amplification, encouragement, and echoes of words just said."[29] Eye behavior also differs; in the African American group, the speaker gazes and listeners look away. Likewise, individuals in other cultural groups listen in their own distinctive ways. Given how much we all rely on cues to tell us that our conversational partners are listening, it is important to keep in mind that listening style varies both individually and culturally and to become familiar with different listening styles.

Empathic Listening

Active listening is perhaps most important in close dyadic relationships when individuals want to show their concern for one another. In these relationships, active listening is a way to offer support and counsel. One of the most important ways to show empathy is to use **paraphrasing**. When we paraphrase, we repeat the sender's message in our own words.

Assume for a moment that a friend says to you, "I'm so far behind in my classes, I'll never catch up. I might as well drop out." How would you respond? Some people might offer immediate advice, telling their friend to work more efficiently. Others might try to reassure their friend that the problem is not serious and that everything will turn out all right. These responses are based on the same assumption: that the listener understands the speaker's problem. But problems are not always easy to understand, and people don't always clearly articulate what is bothering them. If your friend's problem goes deeper than the issue of time management, the only way to find out is to encourage more discussion, and the best way to do this is to paraphrase.

Paraphrasing enables you to check your understanding of what someone else is saying. In the example above, you might paraphrase by saying, "So you're very discouraged about your classes and ready to give up." This allows your friend to think more about the problem; it invites elaboration. Because it is a tentative statement, it encourages your friend to tell you what's really wrong. As a result, not only will you understand your friend better, but your friend will have a better understanding of the problem as well. Only when you both understand the problem can you go about solving it.

Of course, using paraphrasing should be more than just a technique. If you are simply applying a formula in a mechanical way, your response will sound as though you are playing psychologist. But if your motivation is honest, then paraphrasing will come naturally, and you will find that in your role as listener, you have given useful help.

Clearly, listening is an active process that takes attention and energy. Like other goal-directed behaviors, it can be improved with practice. Because listening is the forgotten part of communication, we seldom spend much time or effort on it. Yet being able to listen well is one of the most essential communication-related skills.

Improving Responding

The best way to improve responding is to realize that you cannot not communicate. In other words, you are always responding in some way to the people around you, whether you are saying anything or not. No matter what you do, you are sending a message. Let's say you slip into your 9:00 A.M. communication class after catching only a few hours of sleep the night before. You sit in the back and hope that by the time class is over, you will be fully alert. You are much too tired to answer questions or do much more than stare. Luckily, all you have to do is listen; there is no need for you to communicate. But you *are* communicating, even though you may be unaware of the message you are sending. Whether or not you are processing what is going on in class, your lack of responsiveness is sending the message that you aren't listening and that you aren't interested. Without knowing it, you create a negative impression. Or let's say that someone sends you a text message just to say hi, but you don't bother to reply. Don't assume that in ignoring the message, you are not communicating. Your lack of response is a message in itself, one that can have unintended but very negative results.

The point here is not that you should answer every question in class or respond to every text message or email within minutes; it is simply that you should be aware of how your responses are likely to be read and *see things from the perspective of the sender*. This means focusing on your partner instead of yourself and imaginatively feeling what he or she is feeling.

Responding may also mean reading between the lines. For example, Carlos, age nine years, suddenly says that he hates school and doesn't want to go back. To respond effectively, you need to figure out what is actually going on. Responding by saying, "Nonsense, you love school," won't help if a bad experience has made him think the other kids don't like him or if he is having trouble with math. What he needs is sympathy and reassurance and a way out of his dilemma. As a good listener, you need to *respond to what is not said as well as what is said*.

Storage and Retrieval

No matter how effectively you attend, interpret, evaluate, and respond, if you cannot remember a message, then listening fails. Telling your professor after a test that you knew the information last night won't be enough to get you a passing grade. Explaining to your significant other that you knew her birthday was today but just forgot isn't much of an excuse. Effective listeners must do two essential things: store messages in memory and then retrieve them at the appropriate time.

Factors Affecting Memory

A number of factors can interfere with storage and retrieval. First of all, most of us are highly suggestible. The sad fact is that memory is fallible. Information that is painful or unpleasant can be pushed aside, while things that never happened can be remembered as though they were true. There have been several dramatic instances of **false memory**. Anthony Pratkanis and Elliot Aronson report a fascinating case in which a previously law-abiding deputy sheriff confessed to abusing his daughters and leading a satanic cult.[30] Why did he confess to and supply false details about a crime that experts now agree never happened? The answer lies in the social pressures he endured as the case unfolded. During interrogation, he was told that it was common to repress memories of crimes of this type. In addition, everyone in his environment—members of his church, his family, and other members of the sheriff's department—behaved as though the allegations were true, and confession was held out as the only way to atone for his transgression. But perhaps the most important factor leading to his false confession was that he had to choose between believing that his daughters were lying and believing that he had committed a horrible crime. Psychologically, he responded to this untenable situation by creating a false memory.

Of course false memories are usually not this extreme; many average, well-balanced people have very vivid childhood memories of things that could never have happened. In fact, psychologist Elizabeth Loftus has demonstrated that it is quite easy for parents or family members to implant childhood memories simply by talking about events as though they were true.[31] The fact is, many of us remember doing things it turns out we never did. And many of us choose to forget information that challenges our assumptions or desires.

> **Many average, well-balanced people have very vivid childhood memories of things that could never have happened.**

In addition to psychological defense mechanisms and social pressures, the situation in which listening occurs can also affect memory. Stress is one of the biggest impediments to memory. When we are rushed, when we are in unfamiliar surroundings, when a situation is interpersonally unpleasant, or when we have simply worked ourselves up into a state of anxiety, we are unlikely to remember events accurately.[32]

Another factor that can affect storage and retrieval is information interference. This occurs when information from multiple sources merges and details from one situation become attached to another. If, as a child, you spent many summers at the lake, your memories may run together. A picnic that occurred when you were six years old may include a storm that actually happened two years later. And you may remember how your dog jumped into the water, even though that didn't happen until you were twelve. The tendency of one memory set to interfere with another can also influence how well you do on tests. An effect called **retroactive inhibition** occurs when new learning interferes with early stored material. To avoid this problem, before a test, you should study only the subject you will be tested on, get a good night's sleep, review, and take the test. Any extraneous information that you acquire between studying and taking the test can cause interference.

Improving Storage and Retrieval

As we have seen, memory is fallible. Yet it is possible to improve storage and retrieval, especially when you are listening intently and your purpose is to retain knowledge. Sometimes, especially in a college setting, you may feel overwhelmed by the sheer amount of information you are expected to remember. Just keep in mind that you seldom have to remember everything you hear exactly as you heard it. In most cases, it is better to store main ideas rather than specific phrasing. In fact, if during listening you concentrate too specifically on wording or descriptive details and not enough on ideas, you'll miss the meaning of the message. The first principle in improving retention, then, is to *decide what needs to be stored.*

> **If during listening you concentrate too specifically on wording or descriptive details and not enough on ideas, you'll miss the meaning of the message.**

Once you decide that something should be remembered, you must actively work to retain it. One way is to *mentally rehearse and review ideas that need to be stored.* Another is to take notes to ensure that you have a permanent record of a spoken message. Of course, special problems can arise during note taking. The first is that as we struggle to write something down we may tune out the rest of the message. If you have to take notes, jot down main ideas along with brief examples. Be sure you understand the idea before you start writing. In addition, notes are of little use if they are not reviewed. The information ultimately has to go into memory, and writing it in a book does not guarantee that you will remember it later. Experts on note taking suggest that you go over your notes as soon as possible after taking them, filling in details.

In special cases, you may wish to use mnemonic devices or special memory aids. When simple repetition fails to fix things in memory, other devices can be used. If you are visually oriented, you may find it easier to memorize something (say, a list) by visualizing its parts or items placed in a familiar setting—a technique that we discussed in Chapter 1. Another way to remember items is to link them visually to one another. For example, if you have to shop for a light bulb, suntan lotion, a quart of orange juice, and pencils, you could visualize a cartoon of a light bulb wearing sunglasses, lounging in the sun writing a postcard with the pencil and drinking a cool glass of orange juice. This unusual image is likely to stay with you as you pick up each item at the store. Acronyms, or made-up words, each letter of which stands for an idea you want to remember, are also useful, as are rhymes, such as "*i* before *e*, except after *c*." Whatever aid you choose, you must spend time and effort to ensure that what you have attended to and interpreted will come back to you when you need it.

DESIGNING MESSAGES THAT ARE EASY TO LISTEN TO

Not all speakers capture attention, and not all messages are easy to understand and remember. There are things the sender of a message can do to ensure that audience members do not tune out or get confused. In this section, we look at ways in which speakers can capture attention, increase comprehension, enhance message acceptance, and increase retention. Table 3.4 summarizes this discussion.

Capturing Attention

Earlier, we noted that there are two kinds of attention: voluntary and involuntary. A skilled communicator must consider both when designing messages. Voluntary attention can be increased by relating message content to receivers needs. An unemployed person, for example, will be receptive to a speech on how to get a good job. To someone with a job, the same speech is less interesting, and the speaker will have to show the receiver that the information will be useful in the future or can lead to job advancement now. In either case, *voluntary attention can be increased by giving receivers a reason to listen.*

Involuntary attention works differently. *To increase involuntary attention, one must create vivid and compelling message elements that cannot be ignored.* Marvin Zuckerman explains that involuntary attention is part of our biological makeup:

> One of our hominid ancestors in a relatively relaxed state on a plain in Africa might have little engagement of attention by the environment, but the sound of something moving in the brush, the sight of something moving in the distance, or a new smell wafting about must have had the instant capacity to engage attention and arouse the brain. Novel stimuli do have this intrinsic capacity to stop ongoing activity and to engage the attention mechanism.[33]

What kinds of stimuli have the potential to arouse involuntary attention? Stimuli that are intense, novel, complex, surprising, and incongruous.[34] Vivid colors, loud sounds, and sharp contrasts instantly capture attention. In addition, evidence suggests that we prefer visual over other sensory modalities—that a picture really is worth a thousand words. In terms of verbal material, therefore, vivid, concrete, easily visualized information draws attention more easily than does drier, more abstract information.[35] People also pay special attention to information that is surprising or that violates well-established schemata.[36]

What kinds of stimuli arouse involuntary attention? Stimuli that are intense, novel, complex, surprising, and incongruous.

Of course, vivid stimuli are not always desirable. If listeners are anxious, intense stimuli may make them feel uncomfortable. And competing stimuli in the speaking environment can distract attention. When

Table 3.4 Design Elements That Make Listening Easier

Elements That Capture Attention
- Increase voluntary attention by giving receivers a reason to listen.
- Increase involuntary attention by including vivid and compelling message elements.

Elements That Guide Interpretation
- Relate new information to old.
- Adapt content to audience's learning level.
- Use a clear-cut organizational pattern.
- Ask for feedback.

Elements That Ensure Acceptance
- Show the audience that new information is supported by prior beliefs.
- Offer an incentive for acceptance.
- Encourage favorable cognitive responses by involving receivers.

Elements That Enhance Storage and Retrieval
- Use repetition within the message.
- Personalize the message.
- Tie information to appropriate triggers.

deciding where to deliver a message, it is important for communicators to choose environments that are interesting enough to keep receivers alert but not so interesting that receivers miss the intended message.

Guiding Interpretation

Message elements can be vivid and compelling, but if the message is unintelligible, it will not be effective. Therefore, senders must design messages that are easy to understand. Message comprehension can be increased in a number of ways. The first is to *relate new information to old*. Our discussion of schemata showed that when we encounter new information, we search for schemata that will make sense of it. A skillful message sender helps the receiver to do this by using analogy, comparison, and contrast—methods that help receivers to interpret a new experience in terms of prior meaning structures.

Listeners have different levels of experience to draw on and process information at different levels. A fundamental principle of good communication is that *effective senders adapt to the learning level of their listeners, using familiar, concrete, and clear language and appropriate and unambiguous images*. This does not mean that speakers should talk down to listeners, but it does mean they must make a reasonable assessment of receivers' intellectual ability, degree of expertness, and past experience with the topic.

When complex information is presented, it is often necessary to link ideas and to construct interconnected arguments. *Use of a clear-cut organizational pattern that guides a receiver through a message enhances comprehension*. Whether people are reading an article, listening to a story, or hearing a joke, they expect message details to be delivered in a logical order. Organization is as important in a comedy routine as it is in a persuasive speech. All good communication must exhibit coherence.

Message comprehension can also be increased when the sender provides opportunities for feedback. One friend asks another, "Do you understand what I mean? Have you ever felt like that?" A person on duty in an information booth gives directions and then encourages the receiver to repeat them. A teacher quizzes students to find out whether or not they understand. In each case, the communicator is prepared to offer more information if the original message is unclear.

Ensuring Acceptance

Because receivers may understand what is said but may still block out or dismiss a message, effective senders do their best to ensure that message content is evaluated positively. *One way to increase acceptance is to show receivers that new information agrees with other elements in their belief system*. Most of us find it difficult to accept information that contradicts cherished beliefs or values. If you were to hear something shockingly negative about a close and respected friend, you probably wouldn't believe it—at least not initially. If you were to take a course with a professor who contradicts everything you have been taught, you would not know what to think. Accepting radically new information often means abandoning or reorganizing old beliefs, a difficult process. Senders can make the process easier by indicating how new information is supported by old beliefs or, when cognitive realignment is necessary, by helping receivers to reorganize belief structures.

Acceptable messages offer receivers an incentive. It is important that receivers see value in a message proposal. Receivers should understand why the information conveyed is useful and why following the speaker's recommendations might be rewarding. After all, message processing takes time and effort, and receivers won't want to expend that time and effort on irrelevant or erroneous messages.

Persuasion theorists called **cognitive response theorists** point out that people accept messages not on the basis of what a speaker says but on the basis of their own responses to the speaker's message.[37] During listening, receivers hold a kind of internal conversation with themselves. They agree or disagree, supplying supporting examples or counterarguments. These cognitive responses are what ultimately convince them to accept or reject a message. The cognitive response principle suggests that *senders who wish to increase acceptance should encourage favorable cognitive responses.* This can be achieved by getting receivers actively involved in message processing. Teachers, for example, may use experiments or exercises because what people discover for themselves is often more powerfully convincing than what they are told. Therapists may use role-playing for the same reason. And public speakers may ask audience members rhetorical questions to make them think about a topic.

Enhancing Storage and Retrieval

As we have seen, memory is not always perfect. How can senders help receivers to remember message content? First, *senders can encourage message retention by using repetition within the message.* During a message, they can also ask questions that encourage receivers to repeat what they have heard. They can provide follow-up activities that reinforce information rehearsal. They can also personalize their messages, making sure that information is relevant to receivers' experiences. *Information related to self-perception appears to be stored and retrieved more readily than is less relevant information.*

Message retrieval is often "triggered" or set off by some external stimulus. For example, we pass a restaurant and suddenly remember that we were supposed to meet a friend for lunch. Or we see an acquaintance going to the gym and suddenly recall that we vowed to exercise more often. In both cases, something in the environment jogged our memory. *Senders can increase information retrieval if they tie their message to an appropriate trigger.* Assume, for example, that a father wants his child to refuse rides from strangers. To ensure that the child retrieves the message at the appropriate time, the parent may set up a role-play. He may take the child outside, have a partner pretend to lure the youngster into a car, and make sure the child says no and runs away. In this way, the child knows when and under what circumstances to retrieve the desired response.

Clearly, listening is a complex process that takes attention and energy. It can be enhanced when senders design clear and interesting messages. And like other goal-directed behaviors, it can be improved with practice. Because listening is the forgotten part of communication, we seldom spend much time or effort on it. Yet being able to listen well is one of the most essential communication-related skills.

SUMMARY

Listening is a complex, multi-step process during which we attend to, interpret, evaluate, respond to, and store messages. Listening is not the same as hearing. When we hear, we translate sound waves into electrical signals to be processed by the brain. When we listen, we engage in a social cognitive process that focuses not just on sound but on other sensory data as well. Unfortunately, Americans are quite poor listeners, a situation that can negatively affect career and personal success.

Listening begins with attention, a process of selectively focusing on some stimuli while filtering out others. Attention can be voluntary or involuntary. In addition to being aware of distractions, we improve attention by listening with a clear purpose, by focusing on relevant contextual cues, and by maintaining a positive attitude.

As we listen, we give incoming stimuli structure, stability, and meaning. In doing so, we rely on cognitive schemata—mental models of the world that help us to process information. Person prototypes label and categorize people, personal constructs describe individual differences, and scripts describe action sequences. People who have rich construct systems and accurate schemata are more cognitively complex and therefore better able to interpret messages than are individuals who are limited to small sets of chronically accessible constructs. People who act mindfully are also better listeners than those who act mindlessly. In addition to recognizing the fallibility of perception, listeners can improve interpretation by being well informed, relating new information to old, using the speech–listening time differential effectively, and, when appropriate, employing perception checks.

Not all messages are believable. Effective listening involves evaluating information. By identifying a sender's purposes and credibility, demanding good evidence, and being sensitive to loaded language, listeners improve evaluation. Special problems exist in evaluating mediated messages. Some ways to be more critical of Web-based information include being suspicious of information that cannot be confirmed, understanding purpose and origins of a site, and being cautious about sites that are poorly or carelessly designed.

Responding is an often overlooked part of listening. Listeners are obligated to listen actively, that is, to react in ways that let speakers know they are listening. Active listening is an important part of empathic listening—listening designed to offer support or comfort to others. One effective way to show empathy is to use paraphrasing, a practice that allows listeners to check understanding, that invites elaboration, and that signals concern. Listeners improve responding by monitoring their nonverbal behaviors, seeing things from the perspective of the sender, and being aware of what is not said as well as of what is said.

The final factor that affects listening is message storage and retrieval. Memories are constructed and fallible and are affected by information interference, stress, anxiety, and social pressure. Storage can be improved when listeners consciously decide what needs to be stored, mentally rehearse and review important ideas, and use mnemonic devices or special memory aids.

Although a large part of the responsibility for effective listening lies with receivers, senders also have a part to play. Senders can help receivers by designing messages that are easy to listen to. By giving receivers a reason to listen, employing vivid and compelling message elements, and setting up proper environments, senders make attending easier. The probability that receivers will understand and interpret messages correctly is increased when speakers relate new information to old, adapt to the learning level of their listeners, use clear-cut organizational patterns, and provide opportunities for feedback. Sometimes receivers are resistant to messages. One way to increase acceptance is to show receivers that new information agrees with existing elements in their belief systems. Another is to offer incentives. Senders also increase the likelihood that receivers will agree with them by encouraging favorable cognitive responses. Finally, techniques like repetition and personalization make messages more memorable, as does associating a message with an appropriate trigger.

Listening is the forgotten part of communication, yet being able to listen well is an essential skill that can improve with practice.

KEY TERMS

Listed below are the key terms used in this chapter, along with the number of the page where each is explained.

listening (41)	chronically accessible	god and devil terms (52)
hearing (41)	constructs (47)	description (54)
attention (43)	cognitive complexity (48)	inference (54)
structure (45)	scripts (48)	evaluation (54)
stability (45)	schematic default	active listening (55)
meaning (46)	options (49)	paraphrasing (56)
schemata (46)	mindless/automatic	false memory (56)
person prototypes (46)	processing (49)	retroactive inhibition (58)
personal constructs (47)	mindful processing (50)	cognitive response
	perception check (51)	theorists (62)

SUGGESTED READING

Brownell, Judi. (2012). *Listening: Attitudes, principles, and skills* (5th ed.). New York: Prentice Hall.

A thorough discussion of listening as a complex, interrelated process, including a discussion of emotional intelligence and listening. In addition to providing a solid foundation, this book has many good activities and exercises.

Blake, Randolph, & Sekuler, Robert. (2006). *Perception*. New York: McGraw-Hill.

Provides a detailed examination of perception as a physical, social, and cognitive process and includes chapters on visual perception as well as speech perception and hearing. For the student who is interested in the science of perception.

Encoding Messages: Spoken Language

Language gives us the power to affect and persuade others. But language also exerts power over us.

After reading this chapter, you should be able to:

- Identify four important characteristics of language.
- Explain what a symbol is.
- Explain the Sapir-Whorf hypothesis and give examples of ways language affects thought.
- Identify and describe the four subsystems of language.
- Explain the four levels of context described in CMM theory.
- Describe how public and private discourses differ from one another.
- Name the functions of conversational closings.
- Identify differences between men's and women's communication.
- Explain how ambiguity, abstraction, and metaphor use affects our interactions.

"It was a bright cold day in April, and the clocks were striking thirteen." These words usher us into the bleak world of *1984*, George Orwell's chilling anti-utopia. Written in 1949, the novel describes a future world where freedom of thought has vanished—a world where Big Brother is always watching.

In *1984*, the government controls the masses through a special kind of language: "Newspeak." In Newspeak, any idea that diverges from party principles is literally unthinkable. Words such as *honor, justice, morality, internationalism, democracy, science,* and *religion* no longer exist, and words such as *free* have been stripped of connotations deemed troublesome by the government. The architects of Newspeak have reduced the number of words in the language because "the smaller the area of choice, the smaller the temptation to take thought."[1]

Orwell's novel illustrates a truth we often overlook: we think through language. This is as true of the everyday English we speak as it is of Newspeak. Language gives us the power to affect and persuade others. But language also exerts power over us. In this chapter, we look at what we do with language and what language does to us.

We'll begin by defining language and discussing its structure. We'll then move on to consider how we use language during interaction. We'll look at some pragmatic rules that govern language use, and we'll see how language is tied to group identity. Finally, we'll discuss how everyday language choices can sometimes result in unintended effects.

WHAT IS LANGUAGE?

Newspeak is frightening because it is dehumanizing. It is language "designed not to extend but to *diminish* the range of human thought, to make only 'correct' thought possible and all other modes of thought impossible."[2] Like other thinkers before him, Orwell understood the connection between language, thought, and humanity, a connection that can be found in the stories, myths, and religions of many cultures. Linguist Victoria Fromkin tells us that language is often experienced as the source of human life and power:

> *To some people of Africa, a newborn child is a kuntu, a "thing," not yet a muntu, a "person." Only by the act of learning does the child become a human being. According to this tradition, we all become "human" because we all come to know at least one language.*[3]

There are many kinds of languages. The most common are those built around the spoken word. Spoken languages are called "natural languages," emphasizing the close link between language and its expression in speech. Not all languages, however, depend on speech. Some "artificial" languages, such as computer languages, employ electrical signals, and sign languages use gestures. In this chapter, we'll focus on understanding spoken languages. In the next, we'll widen our discussion by looking at nonlinguistic codes.

In its most general sense, **language** can be defined as a rule-governed symbol system that allows its users to generate meaning and, in the process, to define reality. As we shall see, spoken language has four important characteristics: it is made up of symbols, it is a kind of knowledge, it is rule governed and productive, and it affects the way we experience the world.

Language Is Symbolic

To communicate, people must find a way to express the ideas that originate in their minds. A **sign** is the vehicle for this expression. It consists of two parts: the private idea located solely in the mind of a communicator (known as the *signified*); and the form in which the idea is expressed (or the *signifier*). In natural languages, the signifier is a sequence of spoken sounds. In artificial languages, the signifier may consist of electrical pulses, gestures, plastic shapes, marks on a page, or any of the other ingenious ways humans use to express meanings. In each case, the sign connects content and form. The French linguist Ferdinand de Saussure compared the sign to a sheet of paper, the front of which is the signifier and the back of which is the signified. Creating a word is like cutting a shape out of the paper, a shape that is both conceptual and representational.[4]

The sign relationship can be natural, or it can be produced by humans. An example of a natural sign is the smoke that indicates fire. In this case, the relationship between signifier (smoke) and signified (fire) does not depend on human intervention. In other cases, humans create signs. For example, English speakers use the sound sequence "dog" to represent a domesticated canine. The word *dog* is a special kind of sign called a symbol. A **symbol** differs from other signs in that it is arbitrary and conventional. The symbol *dog* is an *arbitrary symbol* because there is no natural connection between the idea of dog and the signifier *dog*. There is nothing particularly doglike about the word *dog*. In fact, in northern China, the signifier *gou* is used to represent the same idea. The symbol *dog* is a *conventional symbol* because its meaning depends on social agreement. Speakers of English have agreed to use the word *dog* in certain ways that speakers of other languages have not. In our language, the sound sequence "dog" has meaning; in Chinese it does not.

Of course, words are not the only vehicles to carry meaning. Cultures can assign meaning to shapes (a hexagonal sign at the end of a street means stop) and to colors. For most Americans, red means love, sex, anger, or heat; white stands for innocence and purity; and black is associated with mourning. That this color symbolism does not hold true in other cultures shows

Every culture develops its own set of symbols. Clear to members of the culture, they are impenetrable to outsiders.

how arbitrary and conventional color symbols are. Guo-Ming Chen and William Starosta explain, "for instance, to the Chinese, Japanese, and Koreans, red represents a color of longevity, splendor, and wealth; the color black is very much welcome in the Caribbean and Africa; green is a holy color to Moslems but means adultery to the Chinese; and yellow is a noble color for the Chinese and Indians."[5]

The fact that symbols call up similar thoughts in the minds of communicators even though no natural relationship between sign and idea exists has fascinated scholars for thousands of years. Aristotle recognized that symbols were ways of making inner thoughts discernible through sound, and (as you may recall from Chapter 1) Augustine thought and wrote about the nature of symbols. The Port-Royal grammarians of the seventeenth century also recognized this connection, describing language as

> the marvellous invention of composing out of 25 or 30 sounds that infinite variety of words, which tho' they have no natural resemblance to the operations of the mind, are yet the means of unfolding all its secrets, and of disclosing unto those, who cannot see into our hearts, the variety of our thoughts, and our sentiments upon all manner of subjects.[6]

Language Is a Kind of Knowledge

Language is mental rather than physical. Language is a body of knowledge stored within our brains. As such, it can never be examined directly but must be inferred from speech. Speech is the external, physical side of language, and language is the internal, mental side of speech. When we are born, we have not yet acquired the knowledge we call language. As we grow, we listen to the speech of those around us and figure out the rules that make up language. Every infant has the potential to learn the sounds, words, and sentence structures of any language. Had you been born into a language community other than the one in which you were raised, you would have mastered its language quite easily.

Language Is Rule Governed and Productive

One of the most amazing things about linguistic knowledge is that it lets us understand sentences we have never heard before. It is unlikely that you have ever before read this sentence: "The large, gray pachyderm wearing the pink tutu ate cherry vanilla ice cream and dreamed of Africa." Yet you know what the sentence means. Your ability to understand and create unusual sentences like this one is called **linguistic productivity**, and it shows that language learning is more than a matter of trial and error. When we learn language, we don't learn a set of specific word combinations; instead, we learn rules that allow us to generate meanings. Of course, most of us can't consciously explain the rules we follow as we speak and listen, but we can use them to make ourselves understood. These rules are complex and interrelated. They tell us how to make the sounds of our language, how to combine those sounds into words, how to order those words into sentences, and how to use sentences in interaction.

> One of the most amazing things about linguistic knowledge is that it lets us understand sentences we have never heard before.

Language Affects the Way We See the World

Human language is closely related to thought. Although some thought is purely visual, most is filtered through language. You can see this connection if you watch very young children think: they invariably talk or whisper at the same time. As we grow, overt verbalization gives way to silent, inner speech, but we still do a lot of our thinking through language.

Not only do we think in language, but we also store many memories in words. This phenomenon was demonstrated in a classic experiment performed in the 1930s. Leonard Carmichael and his colleagues asked people to view a set of twelve ambiguous figures (see Figure 4.1). Those taking part in the study were told to reproduce the figures as accurately as possible. As each figure was flashed before the subjects, it was labeled. A figure consisting of two circles connected by a short line, for example, was alternately labeled "eyeglasses" or "dumbbell." Results showed that subjects distorted the ambiguous figure to better fit the verbal label. Those who were shown the "eyeglasses" drew a picture in which the line connecting the circles was rounded to look like the bridge of a pair of glasses. Those shown the "dumbbell" thickened the center piece, making it look like a training weight. Evidently, people stored the verbal labels and then produced matching images, rather than storing the images themselves. As linguist Dan Slobin points out, verbal memory is thus a two-edged sword: it enables us to store and retrieve information, but in the process, it can distort perception.[7]

Figure 4.1 Figures Carmichael Used to Illustrate the Effect of Language on Memory

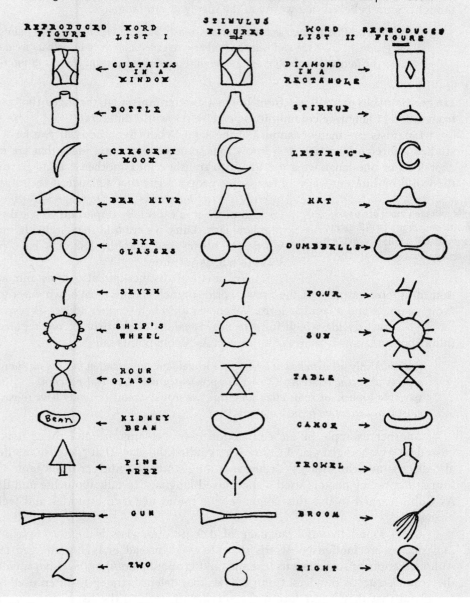

Figures in the middle column are the stimuli Carmichael presented to subjects.
Figures in both outer columns show how verbal labels distorted subjects' recall.

From "An Experimental Study of the Effect of Language on the Reproduction of Visually Perceived Forms" by L. Carmichael, H. P. Hogan, and A. A. Walter, February 1932, *Journal of Experimental Psychology, 15,* pp. 73–86.

If we think and remember linguistically, then it stands to reason that the nature of our language affects the nature of our thought. The **Sapir-Whorf hypothesis** expresses this idea. Named after the linguist Benjamin Lee Whorf and his teacher Edward Sapir, the hypothesis consists of two corollaries: linguistic determinism and linguistic relativity. **Linguistic determinism** is the theory that language determines thought. Sapir believed that we are at the mercy of our language:

> the "real world" is to a large extent unconsciously built up on the language habits of the group. . . . We see and hear and otherwise experience very largely as we do because the language habits of our community predispose certain choices of interpretation.[8]

Linguistic relativity follows from linguistic determinism. It theorizes that people from different language communities perceive the world differently.

Linguists cite many examples of the Sapir-Whorf hypothesis. If you have ever studied a foreign language, you know that some concepts and ideas that are easily expressed in one language are difficult to translate into another. Languages divide the world in different ways. In fact, some people argue that a glance at the most frequently occurring words in a language will give you an idea of what is especially important to speakers of that language. Thus, we are told that Arabic has many words for horses and that the Eskimos have many ways to talk about snow.

> Some concepts and ideas that are easily expressed in one language are difficult to translate into another. Languages divide the world in different ways.

Grammatical distinctions also draw our attention to different aspects of the social world. French speakers have two ways to say "you": a polite and a familiar form. Whenever a French speaker addresses someone, he or she must decide which form to use. Speakers of English are not required to think about relationships in the same way. As Slobin points out,

> If we suddenly all switched to French, we would find our attention focused on many aspects of social relations which were previously not of central concern. . . . In speaking French, or some other language, we would almost certainly have to pay more daily attention to such matters.[9]

Another example of the connection between language and thought is discussed by psychologist Carol Cohn, who studied the ways that "defense intellectuals" discuss nuclear strategy. In her year-long study at a nuclear think tank, Cohn found that policy makers used a specialized language to talk about life and death. As Cohn learned to use this language, she found her own attitudes and feelings changing.

Cohn found that the language of defense strategists is highly euphemistic. *Euphemisms* are inoffensive words that are used instead of highly charged terms. Although euphemisms allow us to avoid talking about painful or offensive situations, they can also act as blinders. Cohn tells us that defense strategists often used terms "so bland that they never forced the speaker or enabled the listener to touch the realities of nuclear holocaust that lay behind the words."[10] For example, a nuclear expert "sanitizes" bombs that are one thousand times more powerful than the one that destroyed Hiroshima by calling them "clean bombs." When civilian deaths are called "collateral damage," they become easier to dismiss. And when delivery of ordnance equipment results in "friendly casualties," the fact that American troops are being killed by American bombs goes almost unnoticed.[11]

Technostrategic language is a specialized jargon known only to members of the in-group. Cohn reports that gaining access to this jargon gave her a feeling of power. Knowing the jargon also made talking about defense strategy fun, in part because the language used many short, snappy words. Referring to a missile guidance system as a "shoot and scoot" made it easy to forget the darker and more serious side of nuclear scenarios.

The better Cohn got at speaking the language, the more difficult it became to express her own ideas and values. As she accepted a new way of talking, she also came to accept a new way of thinking:

> As I learned to speak, my perspective changed. . . . Speaking the language, I could no longer really hear it. And once inside its protective walls, I began to find it difficult to get out. . . . I had not only learned to speak a language: I had started to think in it. Its questions became my questions, its concepts shaped my responses to new ideas. Its definitions of the parameters of reality became mine.[12]

Language, then, has powerful effects on the ways that we think about and experience the world. Although we are not completely prisoners of language, it is easy to overlook the extent to which our language habits affect our views of the world.

Language Takes Many Forms

Languages can take a variety of forms. People who share a common language do not necessarily speak in the same manner. If you've ever conversed with an Australian or a New Zealander, for example, you know that the English language can vary in pronunciation and vocabulary. If you've attended a professional convention, you've seen jargon in action. One of the things that makes language so interesting is the way it changes to meet the needs and express the values of its users. Table 4.1 shows some of the forms languages can take.

Language Changes over Time

Language is fluid. Over time grammar and the rules for social usage change. Pronunciations shift. Old words fall away and new ones are coined. Although grammar and pronunciation change very slowly, words enter and leave language fairly quickly. In this section, we'll look at two examples of the ways word meanings change. We'll begin by considering the way new words enter a language. Then we'll look at some of the ways groups reframe the meanings of existing words.

Neologisms

Let's begin by considering neologisms. The term **neologism** has two different but related meanings. In psychiatry it refers to the made-up words a patient uses that make no sense to anyone else. Using these words can be a symptom of a psychiatric illness like schizophrenia or the result of a stroke or brain injury. Obviously the use of neologisms of this type impedes communication because communication depends on shared meaning. There is another meaning to neologism, however. The term can also refer to a new word that is in the process of entering the language but

Table 4.1 Forms of Language

Dialects

When a subgroup speaks a language using a different vocabulary, grammar, or pronunciation from others who speak that language, they are using a *dialect*. Problems occur when one dialect is defined as standard and given greater status than other dialects. "Because language will naturally show variations, showing respect and open-mindedness is more important than arguing which dialect should be . . . standard. Today's preferred dialect may be tomorrow's relic."

Pidgins

There are no native speakers of pidgins. A *pidgin* is a simple language deliberately invented so that people new to an area (often colonizers) can communicate with those who live in that area. During wartime, soldiers may use pidgins to speak to locals. The grammar and vocabulary of pidgins are often very simple. "Long time no see" is an expression originating in the pidgin used by Chinese immigrants when they first arrived in America.

Creoles

A language that occurs when a pidgin becomes permanent is called a *creole*. Haitian Creole, based on French and African languages, can be traced to a slave-trade pidgin. Gullah, spoken on the coast of South Carolina, is another example. Creoles are often devalued because of the frequently marginalized social status of their speakers.

Lingua Francas

When people from different language communities choose one language to use for trade and commerce, the chosen language is called a *lingua franca*. Swahili is used in this manner in Africa, and English has now become the lingua franca of international business.

Jargon

The special or technical words used by members of professions are called *jargon*. Legal, medical, and computer jargon are examples.

Argot

Argot refers to words whose meanings have been changed so that outsiders cannot understand them. They are often used by nondominant groups for protection and concealment. Prostitutes and prisoners, for example, use such words to refer to their activities.

Taboo

Words that are unacceptable in polite society are *taboo*. In the United States, frank discussions of bodily functions are usually considered taboo. In Chinese, the word that means "four" may be avoided because it sounds the same as the word for "death."

Neologisms

New words that are in the process of entering the language are called *neologisms*. They help us adapt to changing conditions for which there are no adequate words.

Adapted from Guo-Ming Chen and William J. Starosta, *Foundations of Intercultural Communication*. Lanham, MD: University Press of America, 2005. Reprinted by permission of Rowman & Littlefield Publishing Group.

which has not yet been widely accepted. Neologisms of this type allow language to reflect the inevitable changes that occur in the world. They enhance communication, because they allow us to express new realities for which there may not be an existing word.

Many new words stem from changes in technology, but they can also reflect social and political change, come from literature or the media, or be related to new products and services. The terms *Internet, computer mouse, hard and/or soft copy, snail mail,* and *wireless hookup* began as technical neologisms, but are by now indispensable parts of the language. The terms *red state* and *blue state* are recent additions to the language, and *truthiness* is a good example of a media-coined word that may become widely used or that may fade over time. There are a number of sites on the Internet that list recent neologisms. One particularly interesting one consists of a collection begun in 2003 by students in a linguistics class at Rice University. Included are terms like *adultolescence* (moving back in with parents after graduation), *bofro* (boyfriend), *chillax* (to calm down, chill and relax), *E-linquent* (someone who makes trouble online), and *earworm* (a song that repeats over and over inside one's head). Some of the neologisms students collected have become widely used in the intervening years while others have faded. Nevertheless, like all lists of words, they are windows into the worlds of people who heard or used them at the time. They are also indications that language is a living system that continues to change.[13]

Reappropriating Negative Labels

The addition of new words is not the only way language changes. Sometimes, old words take on new meanings. In this section we will look at how members of groups may intentionally try to change the meaning of existing words and labels. We'll start with a conscious attempt to take a politically negative term and turn it into a positive one; we'll then go on to consider examples of ways stigmatized groups have tried to redefine negative labels through a process known as **reappropriation**.

Obamacare started out as a pejorative term used by U.S. Republicans to express their disgust with what they felt was President Obama's disastrous health-care law. For a while, if you heard the word, you could bet that it was not being used by an Obama supporter. Then, in March 2012, as the United States Supreme Court was about to hear arguments on the law's constitutionality, democratic political strategist David Axelrod decided not only to accept but to embrace the term. He sent out an email that said: "I like Obamacare. I'm proud of it—and you should be too. Here's why: Because it works. So if you're with me, say it: 'I like Obamacare. . . .'" What was going on? In the words of political commentator Frank James, the Democrats "clearly were trying to bleed the word of its sting through the time-honored practice of co-opting a word."[14] They were reappropriating the word's meaning. *Obamacare* is not the first word that has been reappropriated by a political party. *Reaganomics,* for example, started out as a negative characterization of Republican Ronald Reagan's economic policies but was later embraced by Reagan himself.

Reappropriation has also been used in a more serious way; stigmatized groups have used it to turn hurtful terms into symbols of pride. When gay and lesbian individuals, for example, embrace the term *queer*, they are attempting to change its negative associations and show pride in their social identity. According to Adam Galinsky and his colleagues, the use of reappropriation by stigmatized groups depends on two assumptions: "First, names are powerful, and, second, the meanings of names are subject to change and can be negotiated and renegotiated."[15]

A classic classroom exercise by teacher Jane Elliott illustrates the fact that names are powerful and that negative connotations can rapidly become attached to them. You may already be familiar with what she did. In order to explore the concept of prejudice, Elliott divided her class by eye color, giving advantages to the blue-eyed children. By the next day a fight broke out at recess when one student called another "brown eyes." When the brown-eyed child was asked what the term meant, he responded that it meant "I'm stupid." Being stigmatized also affected the children's abilities. When the brown-eyed children wore a collar identifying their eye color, they took an average of 5.5 minutes to complete a word task; when the collar was removed, they completed the task in 2.5 minutes.[16] When asked why they had done so badly, the children said it was because they were thinking about their collars; when the collars were removed, they could concentrate on the task. Elliott's experiment was, of course, a demonstration of what goes on outside the classroom every day as individuals attempt to increase their own social status by labeling others with demeaning words.

One of the tactics that members of stigmatized groups can employ is to rename their group. The changes from "colored" to "negro" to "black" and then to "African-American" were attempts to reject negative racial labels. Another tactic individuals can use is to accept the negative name, but change its connotations—that is, to reclaim or reappropriate it. Thus, some African-Americans will use "the N word" among themselves in a positive way, just as some gay and lesbian individuals embrace the word *queer*. Galinsky and his colleagues argue that this tactic not only works to build in-group pride and cohesion, it confronts out-group users. This fact was ironically illustrated in an episode of *The Simpsons*, when Homer, in hearing a gay person use the word *queer*, yells, "You can't use the word *queer* . . . that is *our* word for you."[17]

Although reappropriation is frequently used as a form of political activism, it is still controversial. Some members of stigmatized groups feel uneasy about referring to themselves with negative labels. Others argue that reappropriation is not always effective, that taking possession of a negative word does not automatically change attitudes of outsiders. The fact that African-Americans feel free to use the "N-word" among themselves does not mean that the meaning has changed within the wider population. If people who identify as gay and lesbian use the term *queer* in a positive way, that may not mean that others use it that way. And even if Democrats carry banners that say, "I love Obamacare," Republicans may still think of the policy as catastrophic. Reappropriation is an interesting, controversial, and somewhat risky communication move.

THE SUBSYSTEMS OF LANGUAGE

No matter what form it takes, language is a carefully structured system of meaning. In this section, we'll look briefly at how language is put together, and we'll examine what it means to master the sounds, the words, the sentences, and the social context of language. Table 4.2 summarizes our discussion.

The Sounds of Language

When you first experience a foreign language, all you hear is a string of unintelligible sounds. As you learn the language, however, you learn how to pronounce these sounds and how to combine them with one another. When you have accomplished this, you have mastered the first subsystem of language: the sound system. We humans have a rich and varied repertoire of sounds that we combine in countless ways to make up the lexicon of our language. Because we

---

Table 4.2   The Subsystems of Language

Phonology: Study of the Sound System of a Language

- Phonology is the study of ways in which speech sounds form systems and patterns in human language.
- Its smallest unit is the phoneme.
- Phonological knowledge allows us to pronounce familiar words correctly, to know how unfamiliar words should sound, to know which sound variations are important in a language and which are not, to recognize foreign accents, and to make up new words that sound right.

Semantics: Study of the Meaning System of a Language

- Semantics is the study of linguistic signs (symbols), including word formation and the internal structure of words.
- Its smallest unit is the morpheme.
- Morphological knowledge allows us to divide a stream of sound into meaningful words, to store and recall both the forms and meanings of words, to understand a word's morphemic components, to recognize how the addition or subtraction of a morpheme can change meaning, and to inflect unfamiliar words (e.g., to make plurals, to change tenses, etc.).

Syntactics: Study of the Structure of Phrases and Sentences

- Syntactics is the study of the rules that govern the combination of words into permissible strings.
- Its smallest unit is the sentence or utterance.
- Syntactic knowledge allows us to distinguish grammatical from ungrammatical combinations of words, to combine words in the correct order and to understand how changes in order change meaning, to produce sentences we have never heard before, and to recognize ambiguous sentences and decode their ambiguity.

Pragmatics: Study of the Social Context of Language

- Pragmatics is the study of ways in which people use language forms to achieve goals in social contexts.
- Its basic unit is discourse.
- Pragmatic knowledge allows us to interpret another's communicative intent, to understand how context affects linguistic choices, to make language choices that communicate our intentions effectively, and to take into account information about the social world and our partner's knowledge of it.

can articulate distinct sounds, we can build a sophisticated system for expressing meaning. The ability to articulate sounds is a vitally important part of being able to communicate.

The study of the significant sound patterns of language is called **phonology**. Of all the possible sounds we humans can make, only a small portion enter our language. In any language, some sounds are important and others are not. In English, for example, only one kind of "b" sound is significant. Different English speakers pronounce that "b" differently, but these variations can be overlooked. In Hindi, however, there are two kinds of "b" sounds: one is aspirated (accompanied by a short puff of air), and the other is unaspirated. Hindi speakers hear an aspirated and an unaspirated "b" as very different sounds, whereas we hear no difference at all. English, of course, contains some sounds not found in other languages. French speakers, for example, often pronounce the English words *this* and *that* as "zis" and "zat." Their language does not have a sound comparable to our "th."

The significant sound distinctions in a given language are called its **phonemes**. In English, "b" and "th" are phonemes; they are used to construct words, and no English speaker will confuse "bat" and "that." All English speakers have learned how to pronounce the English phonemes and know their basic characteristics. They also know how to use pitch, intonation, and word stress in acceptable ways. All of these skills are part of their knowledge of the sound system of language.

The Words of Language

In every spoken language, sounds are combined into meaningful sequences called words. The study of the structure of the units of meaning in a language is called **semantics**. We all carry a kind of mental dictionary that equates word meanings with sound structures. When you memorize the words that make up your language, when you can hear a sound sequence and assign it meaning, you are acting on your knowledge of this subsystem of language.

So far, we have been talking about words as though they were the basic unit of meaning. Actually, the smallest unit of meaning in language is the **morpheme**. Some morphemes, called *free morphemes*, are equivalent to words. The words *boy* and *girl* are free morphemes. Other morphemes, called *bound morphemes*, must always be attached to other morphemes. The morpheme *ish*, meaning "having the quality of," is never found alone but must be combined with a noun, as in *boyish*. The plural

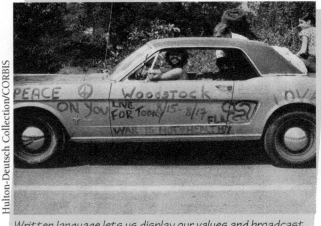

Hulton-Deutsch Collection/CORBIS

Written language lets us display our values and broadcast our messages at a distance.

morpheme *s* when added to *girl* creates *girls*, a new word with a new meaning. *Antidisestablishmentarianism* is one word made up of six bound morphemes attached to the free morpheme *establish* (anti-dis-*establish*-ment-ari-an-ism). A list of all the words of a language is known as a *lexicon*.

To know language is to know the rules of word formation. Young children often make errors because their morphological rules are not quite right. They learn that *s* indicates a plural form and *ed* indicates a past form, so they form words such as *dogs* and *barked*. But they may also construct words such as *sheeps* and *runned*. These errors show that children have inferred basic morphological rules but have not yet learned exceptions and irregularities.

The Sentences of Language

If a foreign student memorized an English dictionary, he or she would not know English, for he or she would not know how to construct sentences. To speak English, one must know the grammatical rules that govern English sentence construction. The study of the sentence structure of a language is known as **syntactics**.

Syntactic knowledge enables us to sequence words appropriately and to determine meaning based on word order. An English speaker who wants to indicate that Elliot surprised Mary on Tuesday would not say, "It was that on Tuesday Elliot Mary surprised." This way of ordering words defies the rules of English sentence structure. Neither would the speaker say, "It was on Tuesday that Mary surprised Elliot," for that would confuse Elliot's and Mary's actions. Clearly, word order and sentence structure are important elements of communication.

What do we know about syntactic knowledge? Grammarians believe that to use language, we must have a basic sense of how the different parts of a sentence (subject, verb, object, and the like) are related. To prove that we do have this knowledge, grammarians often point to ambiguous sentences; for example, "He decided on the train." This string of words can have two meanings. One meaning is "He made a decision while riding on the train." Here, "on the train" is a phrase that modifies the verb *decided*. On the other hand, the sentence could mean "He decided to take the train [rather than some other form of transportation]." Here, *train* is the object of the verb *decided on*. This sentence has two meanings not because the words are ambiguous but because the sentence has two different grammatical structures. If we couldn't understand this, we couldn't recognize the ambiguity.

Grammarians believe that syntactic knowledge contains information about the basic structures of sentences; the grammatical functions of words (for example, whether a word is a noun or a verb and where it fits in a sentence); rules for generating new sentences; and rules for transforming base sentences into different forms. Attempts to describe the syntactic knowledge necessary for even the simplest conversation are extraordinarily complex, and grammarians are still working on mapping syntactic structures. Luckily, we don't have to know complicated grammatical theories to use language. We can use syntactic knowledge automatically and unconsciously to generate new sentences and to recognize the sentences we hear.

The Social Context of Language

Knowing how to form grammatical sentences is a necessary, but not a sufficient, condition for good communication. To be really effective, speakers have to say the right thing at the right time in the right way. The fourth subsystem of language, the study of how we use language in social contexts, is known as **pragmatics**.

Speech Acts

People seldom make sentences just to show off grammatical competence. We talk to accomplish goals. Pragmatic knowledge allows us to understand the intentions of others and to make our own intentions clear. The goal a speaker intends to accomplish through speech is called a **speech act**. Successful communication involves understanding the relationship between words and sentences and the speech acts they represent. To do this, we have to go beyond grammatical knowledge and draw on social knowledge.

Earlier, we saw that a single utterance can have two syntactic structures. A single utterance can also have more than one pragmatic structure. Let's look at an example that has at least two interpretations and identify the speech act in each case. Consider the words "Do you have a watch?" The most likely interpretation of this sentence, if it is uttered by a stranger in the street, is that the speaker wants to know the time. Your knowledge of social behavior tells you that in our culture, people often phrase a request for the time in this roundabout way. If you believe that the speech act being performed is a request for the time, then the appropriate response is "Yes, it's 12:05."

Of course, the speaker may have other speech acts in mind. If he or she is carrying a clipboard and seems to be interviewing every passerby, the question might be part of a marketing survey. Then the proper response is yes or no or, perhaps, "I'm not interested in being in a survey." If the speaker is your teacher and you have just walked into class ten minutes late, the speech act is probably a criticism rather than a request for information, and the expected response is an excuse or an apology. Finally, if the speaker is a six-year-old who has been asking you a series of silly questions, the question may be part of a game, and you may decide to respond by asking silly questions of your own. To understand what is really meant by a speech act, you have to make inferences about the speaker's intentions.

Communication and Context

To make correct pragmatic choices, speakers must be sensitive to context, for context offers us, as listeners, the social information we need to understand speech acts. Context tells us who our communicative partners are and gives us clues about their assumptions and their expectations of us.

Table 4.3 shows some of the contextual information that we use to make pragmatic interpretations. This material is drawn from a larger theory of communication called the Coordinated Management of Meaning theory, or CMM.[18] **CMM theory** provides a framework for understanding how individuals use context to assign pragmatic meaning. CMM theorists believe that to communicate successfully, we must take into account four levels of context: episode, relationship, life script, and cultural pattern.

> To make correct pragmatic choices, speakers must be sensitive to context, for context offers us, as listeners, the social information we need to understand speech acts.

An *episode* simply means the situation we find ourselves in during a given interaction. *Relationship* refers to the role obligations that we feel toward one another. *Life script* is our professional or personal identity, and *cultural pattern* consists of the cultural norms we share with others. Communicators who understand these factors interpret the messages they receive correctly and communicate clearly. Communicators who can't read these contextual cues are at a disadvantage.

Language must always match context. Thus, if a speaker's professional identity is that of an aggressive defense attorney (life script) engaged in cross-examining (episode) a hostile witness (relationship) in a U.S. court of law (cultural pattern), he or she must communicate accordingly. When the speaker leaves the courtroom to have dinner with his or her spouse, however, the speaker's language style must change. A spouse can't be treated like a witness if a marriage is to survive. What is admirable in the courtroom may be unforgivable in the dining room.

Table 4.3   Levels of Context: The CMM Hierarchy

Speech Act

An act done by the speaker to the hearer. Speech acts identify the speaker's intention.
Examples: to persuade, to flatter, to inform, to comfort, to gather information

Episode

A sequence of communicative behaviors that exist as a unit with a beginning, a middle, and an end. Episodes identify the purpose of an interaction.
Examples: a friendly chat, playing a game, solving a problem

Relationship

All of the episodes that can reasonably be expected to occur between self and other, given reciprocal roles. Relationship identifies who communicators are to one another.
Examples: friends, lovers, strangers, business associates

Life Script

A person's ideas about the kind of communication that matches his or her personal identity. Life script is the individual's sense of self.
Examples: aggressive executive, creative artist, loving parent, gifted orator, sensitive friend

Cultural Pattern

General agreements shared by members of a particular cultural group about how to act in and respond to the world. Cultural patterns legitimize all lower contextual levels.
Examples: identity based on class, national, religious, or ethnic membership

Pragmatic knowledge is essential for good communication. In linguist Robin Lakoff's words,

> *Pragmatics connect words to their speakers and the context in which they are speaking: what they hope to achieve by talking, the relation between the form they choose and the effect they want it to have (and the effect it does have), the assumptions speakers make about what their hearers already know or need to know.*[19]

Pragmatic knowledge also includes knowledge about the type of discourse employed in any situation.

PRAGMATIC STYLES AND STRUCTURES

As we move from one situation to another, we use what linguists refer to as different discourse styles. Just as the basic unit of syntax is the sentence, so the basic unit of pragmatics is discourse. **Discourse** is a unit of language larger than a single sentence; it consists of connected sentences that form an identifiable structure to fulfill a communicative function. In a typical day, you may read a newspaper article, study a college textbook, listen to a professor's lecture, take part in a group discussion, write a personal essay, give a public speech, or hold a casual conversation. All these activities are forms of discourse, and each has its own structure and rules. As we shall see in Part III of this text, different communication contexts call for different kinds of discourse. One aspect of being a good communicator is understanding and following the rules that govern common forms of discourse.

Forms of Discourse: Classifying Kinds of Talk

In this section, we'll compare two forms of discourse, one relatively private and the other slightly more public. These two forms of discourse, conversation and classroom interaction, are so familiar that we engage in them effortlessly. Yet when we go from one to the other—when we move from friendly talk with friends to interaction with classmates and teachers—our pragmatic rules change quite dramatically.

Understanding Conversation

The most common mode of spoken communication is the **conversation**. Through conversations, we create and maintain relationships, explore and develop personal identities, and accomplish daily tasks. Because this form of discourse is essential for social survival, conversation has been one of the most studied of all the discourse modes.

Through conversations, we create and maintain relationships, explore and develop personal identities, and accomplish daily tasks.

Conversation analyst Margaret McLaughlin defines a conversation as "a relatively informal social interaction in which the roles of speaker and hearer are exchanged in a nonautomatic fashion under the collaborative management of all parties."[20] As the most private and most personal mode of communication, conversation differs from other forms of discourse.[21] It is the most reciprocal and egalitarian of all discourse forms because participation is equally distributed. Generally speaking, conversation allows partners a degree of freedom not present in any other kind of communication. In most cases, informal language forms are chosen and personal information is shared. Conversations are also spontaneous, or locally managed; that is, participants make up a conversation as they go along, taking their cues from one another. Thus, conversations are characterized by hesitations, restatements, repairs, and fillers, devices that signal the absence of strategy.

Some forms of discourse are publicly accessible; they are open to a large audience and are "on the record." Conversations, on the other hand, are private; in many cases, it is a violation of trust to repeat what is said. Outsiders may have difficulty making sense of conversations because participants use implicit, private codes and personal "shorthands" that reinforce the participants' unique bonds. This is important because the overall orientation of conversation is often relational. Although people may accomplish tasks through conversation, they often use conversation to get to know one another. More formal kinds of talk seldom focus on purely relational matters.

Describing Classroom Interaction

Classroom discourse is quite different in both style and substance from conversation. Whether or not we admit it, the defining characteristic of classroom discourse is a nonegalitarian distribution of power. In almost all cases, a teacher has more power than a student does. The teacher chooses the text, makes the assignments, and gives the grades. As a result, interaction is nonreciprocal. In a typical lecture-discussion class, teachers talk more than students do, and teachers set the topics for discussion. Although both students and teachers ask questions, the functions of these questions differ. Presumably, students ask questions to acquire information, whereas teachers already know the answers to the questions they ask.

Conversation is the most private and personal form of communication. Through conversation we create and maintain relationships.

© Old Visuals/Alamy

Degree of language formality varies, but generally, the syntax and vocabulary used in the classroom are formal, and topics are relatively impersonal. Certainly, classroom discourse contains more jargon than do private forms of talk. Teachers' talk is also scripted. If being too prepared in a conversation makes a speaker seem manipulative, being unprepared in the classroom destroys a teacher's credibility. Most teachers preplan their lectures, and some use the same jokes and examples from one year to the next. One of the most difficult tasks in good teaching is finding a way to make standard material fresh.

Classroom material is publicly accessible and generally explicit, and clarity is required. Finally, although teachers and students do build personal relationships, the business of the classroom is instruction, and most classes stay task oriented.

Dimensions of Discourse

The dimensions we have used to describe conversations and classroom discourse are summarized in Table 4.4. These dimensions define some of the important differences between private and public forms of talk and demonstrate how language use changes in different situations. Every time you adjust the way you talk to a different social context, you show your tacit understanding of these dimensions. We will return to these differences in more detail in Chapters 6 through 9, in which we'll discuss the nature and goals of interpersonal, group, public, and private communication.

Interactive Discourse: Coherence and Structure

In addition to knowing general forms of discourse, communicators must coordinate communication. This knowledge is of particular concern in interactive discourse, in which communicators must be particularly sensitive to coherence and structure.

Coordinating Conversational Moves

In his discussion of the cooperative principle and conversational maxims, H. P. Grice has described the most basic and simple of the conventions that guide talk.[22] The **cooperative principle** asserts that for talk to work, communicators must be willing to cooperate with one another by speaking in socially approved ways. To cooperate, they must follow four **conversational maxims**, or rules. First, they must make sure their contributions contain enough, but not too much, information. This is the *quantity maxim*. Second, speakers must be truthful. If they say something patently absurd, they violate the *quality maxim*. Speakers must also be sure their contributions are direct and pertinent; otherwise, they fail to follow the *relevancy maxim*. Finally, speakers should follow the *manner maxim*; they should be direct and clear. When communicators don't follow these rules, conversation becomes impossible. No one can carry on a conversa-

---

Table 4.4 **Dimensions of Public and Private Discourse**

Private Discourse	Discourse Dimension	Public Discourse
reciprocal	interaction pattern	nonreciprocal
egalitarian	power distribution	nonegalitarian
personal/informal	language choice	impersonal/formal
spontaneous	amount of forethought	scripted
privately owned	information accessibility	publicly accessible
implicit	meanings	explicit
relational	orientation	task oriented

tion with someone who has no regard for truth or relevance, whose style is unclear, and who has no concept of an appropriate amount of talk.

For talk to work, communicators must be willing to cooperate with one another by speaking in socially approved ways.

This does not mean that maxims are never violated, however. Sometimes we violate a maxim intentionally to send an indirect message. If, for example, Harry asks Sally a personal question and she responds, "Nice weather," her violation of the relevancy maxim probably means that she finds Harry's question too personal. If he's sensitive to pragmatic rules, he understands her indirect meaning and has the good grace to change the subject. In this example, interpreting Sally's meaning is complex, for her meaning is not just in her words but also in the fact that she purposefully violates a conversational maxim. What lesson can we draw from Grice's analysis? It suggests that *to make sense, communicators must act cooperatively; when they fail to do so by violating conversational conventions, meaning is affected.*

An important factor is that conversation is sequential. For conversation to work, each move must follow the previous move and must fit into the overall conversation. This means that *communicators must keep track of what is going on as they talk and must build off others' contributions without losing sight of their conversational goals.* This is by no means easy, and conversation analysts have spent a great deal of time and effort debating and describing the rules that make such coordination possible. Communicators must do something more as well. *Communicators must know when it is time to make a conversational move.* In conversation, knowing whose turn it is can be tricky. In formal classroom discourse, the convention of raising your hand helps to regulate turn taking. In informal conversations, communicators must rely on subtle linguistic and nonverbal cues that indicate whether one speaker wants to continue or is relinquishing a turn. Although conversational turns commonly overlap a bit, true interruptions are social blunders that are often read as attempts to dominate.

Given the complexity of conversation, it isn't surprising that people occasionally lose track of what is going on and misunderstand one another.

Given the complexity of conversation, it isn't surprising that people occasionally lose track of what is going on and misunderstand one another. A final skill that communicators need is conversational repair. *Conversational partners must be able to head off problems before they occur or, if these attempts fail, to repair misunderstandings.* By using disclaimers and licenses, communicators can ask their partners for special understanding. "I'm not sure if I have this right, but I heard . . ." or "Now, hear me out before you object . . ." keep the conversation from breaking down. If these efforts fail, communicators must be able to explain misunderstandings and repair the conversation.

Conversational Closings

Each form of communication, from the nightly newscast to the everyday conversation, has its own internal structure. A speech, for example, can be divided into a beginning, a middle, and an end, each of which does something different. In this section, we'll illustrate the importance of structure by taking a brief look at conversational endings. We'll see that even in this relatively spontaneous form of interaction, people have definite expectations for what should occur—expectations the competent communicator must meet.

Endings play an important role in conversation. They signal that interaction is about to wind down, establish a sense of closure, reassure participants that the interaction has been successful, and establish conditions for future interaction. Often, they also contain specific directions for future behavior on the part of both speaker and listener.

Because walking away abruptly the instant talk ceases is unconscionably rude, the end of a conversation is signaled in advance. A statement about upcoming commitments ("I suppose I should get back to work soon") or a comment on the interaction ("I'm so glad we could get together") lets others know the conversation is drawing to an end and establishes closure. A good conversational ending also contains a statement of concern and goodwill ("It was great to see you") as well as a brief summary of the conversation ("Now, don't worry; things will work out"). Finally, it's a good idea to mention future contact ("I'll call you"). As Robin Lakoff points out, "Farewells stress the speaker's unwillingness to depart, offering it as a necessity imposed by cruel circumstances rather than the speaker's desire. We say, 'Gotta go!' not, 'Wanna go!'"[23]

Endings are equally important in other forms of discourse. In courtroom communication, for example, the summation is a lawyer's last chance to impress the jury; it is here that he or she will summarize arguments and make the strongest appeals. Conclusions are also vital in public speeches, because a weak ending can undermine the entire effect of a speech.

Yet endings are only one part of discourse structure. To be truly competent communicators, we must understand the entire structure of a given kind of discourse. (Beginnings, for example, are another important part of messages.) Although some forms of discourse are structured and formulaic and others are open and spontaneous, all must be well organized to be effective.

Guidelines for Understanding Discourse

To communicate successfully, we must master many types of discourse. We must know the purpose, rules, and stylistic properties of each type, and we must be aware of hidden assumptions and unintended effects. To become more aware of the way a specific form of discourse works, we should ask ourselves the four sets of questions listed below.[24]

1. **What is the purpose of this discourse?**

   What do I and my partners hope to achieve? Do we agree about the purpose of this interaction? What would mark the success of this discourse, and what would mark its failure?

2. **What rules regulate this discourse?**

   What speech acts are expected of each participant? What speech acts should participants avoid?

3. **What are the normal style and structure of this discourse?**

    What specialized language choices are called for? How does one begin and end interaction? How might meanings here differ from those elsewhere?

4. **What are the effects of engaging in this form of discourse?**

    What values and assumptions are presupposed in this discourse? Do I agree with these beliefs? Can this discourse be used to manipulate or dominate? How?

LANGUAGE AND SOCIAL IDENTITY

Although modes of discourse dictate certain language choices, they do not completely control communication. Not every teacher or public speaker or lawyer communicates in the same way. In this section, we will look at how group memberships affect language use, beginning with one of our most important group identities: gender.

Gender and Language

Men may not be from Mars, nor women from Venus (as a popular book proclaims), but it sometimes feels as though we might as well be from different planets. Let's look at a few examples.

> **Men may not be from Mars, nor women from Venus (as a popular book proclaims), but it sometimes feels as though we might as well be from different planets.**

On the way to visit friends in another part of the city, Juan and Rick and their friend Denise get lost. Denise suggests that they stop and ask the way, but both Juan and Rick refuse. They are uncomfortable asking for help and believe that there's no guarantee that a stranger will give accurate information anyway. They would prefer to drive around until they find the way. This doesn't make sense to Denise, who isn't at all embarrassed about asking for information and believes that anyone who doesn't know where he or she is should admit it.

Maria can't wait until Tom gets home from work so that they can talk about the day. As Tom enters the house, Maria begins a barrage of questions. What did he do? How was his presentation? Where did he and his colleagues go for lunch, and what did everyone order? She is interested in every detail, and his evasive answers hurt her. Tom, on the other hand, feels overwhelmed by Maria's "third degree" about things he barely noticed.

Not only do we teach children to act in gender-appropriate ways, we teach them to speak like "ladies" and "gentlemen." These lessons go largely unchallenged, yet they affect us in important ways.

David Turnley/CORBIS

Michael's friends ask whether it's okay to come over to watch the game on Friday. Michael says, "Sure." When he tells his girlfriend, Alyssa, she's upset—not because the friends are coming but because Michael didn't consult her first. Had the situation been reversed, she would have asked. In fact, "I have to check with Mike" would have been a way for her to let others know that she's part of a couple. For Michael, however, asking Alyssa implies he needs to get permission. As a result of these differences, Michael thinks Alyssa is unreasonable, and she sees him as insensitive.

As a linguist, Deborah Tannen believes that these misunderstandings occur because men and women grow up with different expectations about how to use language.[25] Women are encouraged to focus on intimacy and connection, whereas men are taught to display autonomy and individual achievement. These orientations affect the ways men and women think they are supposed to communicate and determine their topics of conversation, their conversational styles, and their interpretations of one another's meaning.

The Development of Gender Differences

We are the victims of gender expectations from the moment we're born. The first question most people ask after a child is born is "Is it a boy or a girl?" And once this question has been answered, perceptions and expectations change markedly. Psychologists John and Sandra Condry asked people to interpret why a newborn was crying. Those who were told that the baby was a boy were likely to interpret his first act of communication as anger. Those who were informed that the baby was a girl assumed she was afraid.[26]

As boys and girls grow up, they learn the expectations associated with their gender. Play is a case in point. Games traditionally associated with boys stress freedom and competition, whereas girls' games focus on matters of inclusion and exclusion. Boys are encouraged to interact in large, hierarchically structured groups, playing rule-bound games with winners and losers. Boasting, mocking insults, and teasing often accompany boys' play. Girls, on the other hand, often play in smaller groups within which everyone gets a turn. Girls try to avoid the appearance of conflict by proposing rather than ordering. Instead of saying, "You stand over there," girls are more likely to say, "Let's get in a circle, okay?" or "What if you stand at that corner?" This is not to say that girls do not find ways to exclude one another, but they do it in ways that allow them to display "appropriate" gender identities.[27] Later in life, men continue to bond through shared physical activity and women through talk.[28]

As boys and girls grow older, they develop characteristic conversational styles. One example is the way each gender responds to **trouble talk**. A number of studies show that boys often respond to other boys' reports of a problem by dismissing or downplaying it or by giving straightforward advice on how to solve it. Girls, on the other hand, are likely to respond with trouble talk of their own.

This characteristic holds true in storytelling as well. Males often tell stories about contests in which they acted as either protagonist or antagonist and in which they ultimately succeeded. Females often tell stories about times when they or others violated social rules and consequently looked bad. Females exorcise their social failures by talking about them. Males, on the other hand, prefer to ignore failures and to focus on achievement. Tannen comments, "If men see life in terms of a contest, a struggle against nature and other men, for women life is a struggle against the danger of being cut off from their community."[29]

In adulthood, these patterns persist, and a verbal division of labor takes place. Women specialize in relationally oriented talk, whereas men specialize in task-oriented talk. Tannen uses the terms **rapport talk** and **report talk** to get at these differences. Rapport talk focuses on relational meaning; it is most appropriate for interpersonal topics and feels most natural in intimate contexts. Report talk focuses on content; as a style, it is appropriate in public situations when decision making or opinion exchange is expected.

Throughout their lives, men and women learn, to varying degrees, how to use language to display stereotypical gender identities. Men know that being competitive is a way of being masculine. Women recognize that stressing connection is part of being feminine. This can explain why many men would rather drive around for hours than ask directions (and reveal their lack of control). It can explain why many women want to know every detail of a man's day the minute he walks through the door (to build intimacy through shared talk). And it can also explain why a simple statement such as "I have to check with X" can be interpreted in entirely different ways.

Of course, men and women do not act stereotypically all of the time, nor do all men and women feel comfortable fitting into expected gender identities. Just as we grow up knowing how to display gender identities through language, we also make choices about whether or not to act in expected ways. Feminist scholars frequently make a distinction between "women's language" (the way women are supposed to talk) and the "language of women" (the way women actually communicate). The same can be said for men's language. One of the tasks faced by researchers who want to understand gender and language is finding out how stereotypical expectations interact with actual behaviors.

> Just as we grow up knowing how to display gender identities through language, we also make choices about whether or not to act in expected ways.

Research on Gender and Communication

Over twenty-five years ago, Cheris Kramer, Barrie Thorne, and Nancy Henley took on the task of investigating the relationship between gender and language. They posed the following questions: "Do women and men use language in different ways? In what ways does language—in structure, content, and daily usage—reflect and help constitute sexual inequality? How can sexist language be changed?"[30]

In the ensuing years, a great many answers have been given to these questions. Scholars have described and documented sexist language, and experimental researchers have found evidence that the use of this language has a negative impact on both men and women. For example, there is evidence that women's recall for facts is better when those facts are presented using inclusive, nonsexist language than when they are presented in noninclusive terms.[31] And it has also been demonstrated that when women are referred to as "girls" they are judged as being less responsible than when referred to as "women."[32] As a result of these and other findings, it is now common practice to avoid the use of language that denigrates, disrespects, or makes women invisible.

The answer to the question of whether there are differences between the ways men and women use language is more problematic. On one hand, our own experiences as well as many hundreds of studies attest to the fact that men's and women's language differs. So, in one sense, the answer to the question "Do men and women communicate differently?" is a resounding "Yes." On the other, as Ann Weatherall points out, there is no agreement on the exact nature of these differences nor is there any consensus about their theoretical explanation.[33] Table 4.5 describes some of the many findings in this area.

Problems in Interpreting Gender Differences

But how significant are these differences, and what do they mean? In recent years, feminist scholars have urged caution in interpreting research on gender differences. As Deborah Cameron points out, many of our most familiar generalizations exhibit what Shan Wareing has called the **hall of mirrors effect**: "in the course of being cited, discussed, and popularized over time, originally modest claims have been progressively represented as more and more absolute, while hypotheses have been given the status of facts."[34]

Psychologist Elizabeth Aries agrees, pointing out that although there are many statistically significant differences between male and female communication styles, they are generally quite small. She reminds us that "men do not form a homogeneous group, nor do women. There is considerable variability in the interaction styles of members of the same sex because of differences in personality, age, race, class, ethnicity, or sexual orientation."[35] In many studies of communication differences, gender accounts for only a small proportion of subjects' behaviors. It is therefore useful to keep in mind that we are much more similar than we are different.

Aries also cautions us to remember that context makes a difference when it comes to gendered communication. For example, it would not be accurate or fair to conclude that overall men are more likely than women to take on leadership roles. In point of fact, research shows that men are most likely to emerge as leaders in short encounters with strangers or when the task draws on skills that are typically associated with men. In longer encounters, when women have been given equal status and power, there are fewer gender differences in leadership behavior.[36]

More problems arise when we try to evaluate communication differences. For example, for many years, women were criticized for using what was known as the **female register**. By using *tag questions* (fragments such as "right?" or "okay?" at the end of sentences), *qualifiers* (words such as "maybe" or "perhaps"), and *disclaimers* (phrases such as "now don't get me wrong, but" or "don't get mad until you hear me out"), women were criticized for being passive and powerless. They were advised to become more assertive and direct to become credible; in other words, to be more like men. More recently, women's speech has been reevaluated. Now, use of tag questions and the like is interpreted as attempts to build mutual support and solidarity. And men's speech, now viewed against a female model, is often seen as deficient in

---

Table 4.5 Conclusions Drawn from Research on Gender Differences in Communication

Quantity of Talk: *Who Talks the Most?*

- In task-oriented cross-gender groups, men talk more than do women.
- In friendly same-gender dyads, women prefer to spend time talking; men prefer to share activities such as sports or hobbies.

Topics of Talk: *What Do Men and Women Talk About?*

- Women talk more about private matters (family, relational problems, other women, men, clothing) than do men.
- Men talk more about public matters (sports, money, and news) than do women.
- Women and men both talk about work and sexual relationships.

Vocabulary: *Do Women and Men Use Different Words?*

- Women are reported to use more detailed color terms (*mauve, teal*) than do men.
- Women more often use weaker expletives ("Oh dear," "Oh my"), whereas men more often use stronger expletives, including obscenities.
- Women use certain evaluative adjectives (*adorable, cute, fabulous*) that men do not use.

Grammatical Constructions: *Do Men's and Women's Syntax Differ?*

- Women use more qualifiers (*somewhat, kind of, I guess*) than do men.

- Women use more disclaimers ("I'm no expert, but . . . ," "Don't get mad, but . . .") than do men.
- Women use more tag questions ("Right?" "You know?") than do men.
- Women are more likely to use polite forms than are men.

Turn Taking: *Who Controls Interaction Flow?*

- In cross-gender dyads, men interrupt women more than women interrupt men.
- Women ask more questions, and men make more statements during interaction.
- Men often respond to women using delayed minimal responses ("Oh" or "right," said after a brief pause) that discourage interaction; women's minimal responses ("Hmmm, I see") occur within turns and seem to encourage talk.

Topic Control: *Who Chooses the Topics of Talk?*

- Men successfully initiate topics more often than do women.

Humor: *Do Women or Men Tell More Jokes?*

- Boys and men offer more jokes and witticisms than do girls or women.
- Girls and women laugh more than do boys or men.

Self-Disclosure: *Are Men or Women More Open?*

- Women tend both to disclose more and to receive more disclosures from others than do men.

Note: Current research supports these conclusions; however, not every study concurs, and some contradictory findings exist.

Adapted from research reviewed by Laurie P. Arliss in *Gender Communication,* 1991, Englewood Cliffs, NJ: Prentice-Hall.

intimacy, connectedness, and expressiveness. But turnabout is not necessarily fair play. As Aries states, "We now misrepresent and devalue men just as women were misrepresented using masculine models, and we continue to define men and women in position to one another and to polarize differences."[37]

One way to avoid making the mistake of viewing male/female differences as essential is to consider the **performative aspects of language**. Although it may look as though we differ in essential ways, many of these differences can be explained as social performances rather than as innate characteristics. Candace West and Don Zimmerman tell us, "A person's gender is not simply an aspect of what one is, but, more fundamentally, it is something that one *does*, and does recurrently, in interaction with others."[38] Many current language scholars argue that we do not use language the way we do because of our gender, we create gender identity through language. Deborah Tannen explains, "Ways of talking and behaving that are associated with gender are a matter not of identity but of display. In other words, the behavior is not a reflection of the individual's nature (identity) but rather of some performance that the individual is accomplishing (display)."[39] An interesting example of this idea can be found in the fact that some of the most eager readers of books on gender differences and communication are transgendered individuals "looking for guidance on how to mount an 'authentic' performance of their chosen gender identity."[40] But it is not only transsexuals or drag queens who perform gender. Most of us know how to "talk like ladies" or "act like men" in order to fit in and display an appropriate gender identity. Aries reminds us that:

> **Many current language scholars argue that we do not use language the way we do because of our gender, we create gender identity through language.**

> *Men and women behave in different ways because of their different placement within the social hierarchy, the different statuses and roles they fulfill, the different skills and abilities they acquire in these roles, their desire to display behavior to confirm their gender identities, and the consequences they face for violating expectations for gender-related behavior.*[41]

Adapting to Gender Differences

None of the scholars we have quoted denies the fact that men and women do communicate in different ways; they simply believe that these differences are more complex than was originally thought. It would be as wrong to deny true differences as it would be to accept false ones. In fact, understanding that men's and women's approaches to communicative situations often vary can be useful. Knowing, for example, that the behaviors that annoy or perplex us about another person may be based not on personality defects but on the need to perform gender roles can make us more accepting of one another.

Today's language scholars call on us to be both more cautious and more tolerant, and to be willing to experiment with traditional communicative behaviors. If habitual styles of communicating are not serving us well, we should find new forms of communication that suit us better. We should also learn to accept people who do not fit traditional gender roles, valuing them for their ability to imagine new ways of being as they find ways to escape the stereotyped expectations that control most of us.

Language and Cultural Difference

If men and women within a single language community confuse one another, you can imagine how difficult it can be when people from different countries try to communicate. Even when they have learned the vocabulary and grammar of each other's language, they may still experience problems, for languages differ in many other ways. We will discuss cultural differences in language use in more detail in Chapter 12. For now, let's look at one example: use of intermediaries to avoid directness. Not all cultures value directness. In many cultures third parties are used in situations that might cause the primary parties to lose face. In traditional Kenyan societies, for example, during marriage brokering, friends or clan elders may work out the details so that the family of the groom-to-be does not have to enter the negotiations. Similarly married couples often avoid bringing up problems. If a wife has a complaint against her husband, she will often tell her best friend and former maid of honor, who will tell *her* husband, the couple's best man, who will then talk to the husband. In this way the husband and wife themselves do not have to argue or embarrass one another.[42]

Of course Kenyans can communicate directly just as Americans can be indirect. In fact, when you were in fifth or sixth grade and wanted to let someone know you "liked" him or her, you may have acted indirectly, asking your friends to send messages to the object of your affection. Now, however, it's much more likely that you will express your feelings openly because American adults value directness.

Recognizing that different cultures have different preferences for language use is important. In our example of Kenyan culture, sojourners or aid workers who want to communicate competently in Kenya will have a much better chance if they understand how and when to be direct and how and when to use and respond to third-party communication.

LANGUAGE CHOICES AND PRAGMATIC EFFECTS

One of the themes of this chapter is that language gives us power. Our linguistic choices count: they make a difference in our lives and in those of others. If we use language wisely, we can control communication; if we do not, communication can have unintended effects. In this section, we look at some of the effects of using four kinds of language. We'll discuss ambiguity, immediacy, abstraction, and figurative language.

Ambiguity: When Not Making Sense Makes Sense

As we have seen, U.S. culture values directness and clarity. You've probably been told that language should be concrete, simple, direct, and straightforward. You've been warned that ambiguity diminishes communication. Often, this is true. In many situations, clarity is the measure of the success of a message. Legal documents or technical

Clarity is not always advantageous, even in a low-context culture like ours, and ambiguity can sometimes help, rather than hinder, communication.

instructions, for example, must be precise. But clarity is not always advantageous, even in a low-context culture like ours, and ambiguity can sometimes help, rather than hinder, communication.

Eric Eisenberg, an expert in organizational communication, discusses positive effects of using **ambiguous language**, language that can be interpreted in more than one way.[43] First, ambiguous language can give an organization the flexibility to adapt to future contingencies. When a university issues the statement "The University shall be responsive to its surroundings," the university is being deliberately ambiguous. It is assuring members of the surrounding community of its intention to act in good faith while leaving itself room to develop policy. On an interpersonal level, ambiguity allows members of organizations to perceive themselves as similar rather than different. Because similarity is a basic factor in attraction, ambiguity can increase group solidarity. We often employ strategic ambiguity unconsciously. For example, the first stages of group formation involve a great deal of ambiguity. Here, ambiguity allows members to avoid disagreements until the group is cohesive enough to deal with stress.

Eisenberg points out that people with high credibility often benefit most from ambiguity. If one's credibility is already high, clarity is more likely to decrease than to increase it. Strategic ambiguity also allows one to deny a stand if it should become unpopular. "That's not what I meant at all" gives a person a way to back down gracefully.

Janet Beavin Bavelas and her colleagues suggest that **equivocal communication**, another term used to describe ambiguous communication, is most often used when a communicator feels trapped between two unpleasant alternatives. When speaking the truth and lying are both problematic, people often equivocate. Ask yourself which response you would choose in each of the following situations:[44]

A fellow student has just given a class presentation. It was very badly done. After class he asks you, "How did I do?" Which response is best?

a. You did very well. I really liked it.
b. You were terrible; bad job.
c. Not well, but don't feel bad about it.
d. You were braver than I would be!

You have received a gift from someone you really like a lot, but the gift is awful. How would you respond?

a. The gift is perfect; I really love it.
b. I don't like the gift and am going to exchange it.
c. I like you, but I don't like the gift.
d. I appreciate your thoughtfulness.

You are torn between loyalties to two people you know and like equally well. Ann worked for you at one time. Bob is thinking of hiring Ann. Unfortunately,

Ann is nice but incompetent. You must write a letter of reference. What would you say?

a. Ann was an excellent employee; I recommend her.
b. Don't hire Ann; she was not a good employee.
c. Ann is a nice person but not a good employee.
d. It's been years since I employed Ann, so I can't answer specifically.

In each case, d is the equivocal response. If you are like most people, you were probably tempted to use ambiguity in at least one of these cases, for it is a way of responding to an uncomfortable situation without lying or hurting someone's feelings. Communication specialists differ in their evaluation of this form of communication. Some decry it as deceptive and misleading and tell us we should always be honest. Others, like Bavelas, defend it:

> *Equivocation is not the deliberately deceitful "dirty old man" of communication. It is subtle, often commendable, and entirely understandable, if only the observer will expand his or her analysis to include the communicative situation. . . . In our experience, real living messages do not fit prescriptive and judgmental models; they are more subtle, more skillful, and more interesting.*[45]

Immediacy: Up Close and Personal

Language can be inclusive or exclusive. It can place the listener at a distance or forge a close and personal bond.[46] **Immediate language** is personalized language, and it can be very effective in persuasive situations. Consider the following excerpt from a televised speech:

> *This historic room and the presidency belong to you. It is your right and responsibility every four years to give temporary custody of this office and of the institution of the presidency. You so honored me, and I am grateful—grateful and proud of what together we have accomplished.*

The speaker was President Ronald Reagan, and the occasion was the 1984 announcement of his decision to run for a second term.[47] This speech illustrates an effective use of immediacy. Reagan involves us directly and personally. We feel we are a part of his presidency, although what exactly "we" did together is not specified. Critics might say that this use of immediacy is misleading, yet it is certainly effective.

Empirical studies show that the use of verbal immediacy in public situations has positive effects, increasing ratings of a speaker's competence, character, similarity to audience members, and degree of relaxation, especially when the speaker agrees with audience members.[48] Immediacy is also effective in interpersonal contexts. If, however, it is blatantly used to create a bond where none exists, it can backfire. A low-status speaker might offend someone of higher status by being too familiar. Sometimes, norms for considerateness preclude being too immediate. As communicators, we must find a balance between familiarity and polite deference.[49]

Abstraction: Creating General Categories

I remember my grandmother's house in complete detail. If I close my eyes, I can picture the garden in back and the broad veranda where I played as a child. When I speak of this place, I use the word *house*. Yet no single thing called "house" exists, only particular houses, such as the ones you and I grew up in. A house has no particular color, shape, or size. It is simply a structure used for human habitation. "House" is an **abstraction**, a synthesis of what many houses have in common. All words are abstractions, although some are more general than others. To call my grandmother's house a "dwelling unit" or an "abode" is to abstract it even further, and to abstract something is to make it less real.

Of course, abstraction is necessary. Abstract concepts allow us to talk about the future, to make predictions, and to think logically and mathematically. In Robin Lakoff's terms, abstraction is "the basis of science, crucial to human understanding and the growth of our intellect and to our power as a species over the physical universe. It has made us what we are."[50]

Abstract language can also be false and dangerous. It is the basis of stereotyping. When my grandmother's house becomes merely a "house," it loses its individuality; it is reduced to a series of general qualities. Similarly, when my neighbor becomes a "New Yorker" or a "teacher" or an "American," she loses her uniqueness. Your idea of what she is like is shaped by these abstractions. Finally, when some people become "we" and others "they," the way is paved for misunderstanding and abuse.

Figurative Language: Metaphors We Live By

We usually think of metaphors as devices that poets use, not as a feature of everyday talk. Metaphors, however, are a figurative form of language that is found in every kind of discourse, and their presence affects us in interesting and important ways. A **metaphor** is a linguistic usage that allows us to understand and experience one thing in terms of another. Metaphors guide our thoughts and actions.

George Lakoff and Mark Johnson illustrate the pervasiveness of metaphors by looking at the common ways we talk about argument.[51] What underlying comparison is common to the following statements?

He attacked every weak point in my argument.
His criticisms were right on target.
I demolished his argument.
He shot down all my arguments.

The metaphor is that argument is a war—a common way of viewing argument in our culture. Lakoff and Johnson ask us to imagine instead another kind of culture,

[where] argument is viewed as a dance, the participants are seen as performers, and the goal is to perform in a balanced and aesthetically pleasing way. In such a culture, people would view arguments differently, carry them out differently, and talk about them differently.[52]

Metaphors allow us to grasp abstract or difficult concepts in terms of more understandable ideas. In doing so, however, they highlight some aspects of the concept and downplay others. Let's look at some common metaphors used to describe love. Love can be thought of as a physical force ("There's electricity between us," "When we're together, sparks fly"); as mystic power ("She's bewitching," "The magic is gone"); as madness ("I'm crazy about him"); or as war ("She conquered my heart," "He's besieged by women"). Each of these metaphors calls our attention to a different kind of experience and legitimizes a different kind of behavior. If love is a physical force or mystic power, it is beyond our control; there's nothing we can do but let it wash over us. If love is madness, then irrational behavior is defensible. What if, however, we were to think of love in a new way, as a collaborative work of art? Following from this metaphor, love would be something to be worked on, something that takes shape over time, and something that is beautiful and precious. Our reactions to and experience of love would be significantly different.

Lakoff and Johnson believe that the metaphors we live by have a political dimension. Metaphors are often imposed on us by people in power: politicians, religious leaders, economists, and advertisers control us by creating metaphorical values. Once we come to believe in a given metaphor, say, "Bigger is better" or "More is good," then it becomes difficult to see the world in any other way. Accumulation is valorized, and behaviors such as conservation are devalued. When, in *1984*, the architects of Newspeak force the masses to believe that war is peace, freedom is slavery, and ignorance is strength, they create ideological metaphors. Although metaphors can illuminate the way we see the world, they can also blind us. Metaphors, like other language choices, can shape our actions and experiences. They can give us power, or they can control us. For a discussion of how metaphors work in complex organizations, see Chapters 8.

Improving Language Choices

Language is a powerful tool. It allows us to abstract and store experiences and to share them with others. It allows us to make contact with and to influence, regulate, persuade, and dominate one another. It makes us the humans we are. Yet, despite the great power it gives us, language also exerts power over us. Our thoughts and perceptions are filtered through language and can be distorted by it. In the words of Aldous Huxley, "Possessing language, we are . . . capable of intellectual achievements beyond the scope of any animal, but at the same time capable of systematic silliness and stupidity such as no dumb beast could ever dream of."[53] It is important, then, that we use language with care and sensitivity, realizing that it can lead us astray as often as it can lead us to the truth.

> **Language is a powerful tool. It allows us to influence, regulate, persuade, and dominate one another. It makes us the humans we are.**

Throughout this chapter, we've explored the social nature of language. We've seen that words are social agreements, agreements to express ideas in similar ways. We get into trouble if we start believing that words are complete and accurate reflections of reality. We should *always remember that talking about something doesn't necessarily mean it is real.* Language has a peculiar tendency to reify concepts, to make us believe that they are tangible and real rather than fallible human constructions. Two old sayings remind us not to confuse reality with talk: "The map is not the territory" and "The word is not the thing."

Another important principle to keep in mind is that meanings are in people, not in words. Although we share a language with others, we each shade its words and phrases with our own experiences. Meanings are by no means objective, and, as our discussion of speech acts points out, we often mean more than we say and say less than we mean. *Uncovering meaning involves making inferences about the communicative intentions of others.* Only a madman would take as literal everything others say. A sane and competent communicator recognizes that language involves a great deal of social inference. One should always be careful to *take context into account both when interpreting others' messages and when creating one's own.*

When we encode messages through spoken language, we have to make choices. *There is no single right way to use language; language choices must depend on our purposes, our audience, and the conventions of the discourse form we use.* We use a specific kind of language to sell a used car, host a TV talk show, tell a joke, deliver a public speech, or talk to a stranger at a party. Each form of communication has its own linguistic conventions. Although most of the time language that is direct, clear, concrete, and straightforward is preferred, there are also appropriate times for ambiguity, abstraction, and figurative language. Making language choices is no simple matter. It requires sensitivity to others, a clear sense of one's own communicative intent, a great deal of social knowledge, and an overall understanding of the communication process.

SUMMARY

Although we use many encoding systems, the one most natural to us is spoken language. Spoken language has four important characteristics: it is symbolic, it is a kind of knowledge, it is rule governed and productive, and it affects the way we experience the world. The first step in understanding language is to grasp the concepts of symbol and sign. A sign is any mode of expression that connects an idea (the signified) to a form (the signifier). When the signifier is an arbitrary and conventional creation of the human imagination, it is a special kind of sign known as a symbol.

Language learning is not a matter of rote repetition. When we learn language, we learn implicit rules that allow us to generate and understand novel utterances. These rules are complex and interrelated, allowing us to make the sounds in our language and to combine these sounds into words and sentences. Ultimately, language practices affect the way we see the world, as the Sapir-Whorf hypothesis shows. Language takes many forms and is constantly changing.

Language can be divided into several subsystems. The first is the sound system. Each language recognizes certain sounds as significant and ignores others. The significant sound distinctions in a given language are called phonemes. Phonemes are combined into units of meaning called morphemes. Morphemes are roughly equivalent to words, although a single word may consist of several morphemes. In practice, human utterances are made up of strings of words. The rules that govern the way words can be combined make up the syntax of language. Although knowing how to form words and make sentences is important for communication, an understanding of pragmatic rules, or rules governing language use, is also important.

When we talk, we do so for specific reasons. The goal we want to accomplish when we talk is called a speech act. According to CMM theory, speech acts are affected by four levels of context: episode, relationship, life script, and cultural pattern. The kind of communication appropriate to a given social context is called discourse. Each form of discourse has its own style and structure. Perhaps the most common form of discourse is everyday conversation. To be successful at conversation, individuals must work together cooperatively. Their talk must follow the conversational maxims of quantity, quality, relevancy, and manner. Communicators must keep track of the conversation as it unfolds, making sure their contributions fit into what has been said previously. They must also coordinate turn taking and be able to repair problems when they occur.

All forms of discourse, whether formal or spontaneous, have a certain shape or structure. One example of structure is the conversational closing. Closings must be carried out in specific ways. They must be signaled in advance and must include an explanation of why the conversation is ending. Often, they include

statements of concern as well as summaries of what has happened. A communicator who does not understand discourse conventions such as the conversational closing will be at a social disadvantage.

People from different social groups use language differently, and this difference is often a source of social identity. Men and women, for example, grow up learning to use language to display gender identities. Studies suggest that men learn to prefer task-oriented, or report, talk, whereas women are encouraged to use relational, or rapport, talk. Although current researchers do not deny that there are differences in the ways men and women communicate, they believe that many of the generalizations we have come to accept should be treated with caution. They recognize that men and women do not form homogeneous groups, that context affects whether or not gender communication will be displayed, and that the meanings often associated with gender differences are problematic. They also urge us to think of gender as a performance rather than as an essential characteristic of humans.

Gender, of course, is not the only group membership that affects language use. National culture affects language, for example, by specifying how open and direct speakers should be. Cultural differences are taken up in more detail in Chapter 12.

Although social memberships affect language usage, we do make language choices, and the way in which we make these choices affects communicative success. This chapter closes with a discussion of the advantages and disadvantages of choosing between ambiguity and clarity, immediacy and distance, abstraction and concreteness, and figurative and non-figurative language.

KEY TERMS

Listed below are the key terms used in this chapter, along with the number of the page where each is explained.

language (66)	semantics (76)	rapport/report talk (87)
sign (66)	morpheme (76)	hall of mirrors effect (88)
symbol (66)	syntactics (77)	female register (88)
linguistic productivity (68)	pragmatics (78)	performative aspects
Sapir-Whorf hypothesis (70)	speech act (78)	of language (90)
linguistic determinism (70)	CMM theory (79)	ambiguous language (92)
linguistic relativity (70)	discourse (80)	equivocal communication (92)
neologism (72)	conversation (80)	immediate language (93)
reappropriation (73)	cooperative principle (82)	abstraction (94)
phonology (76)	conversational maxims (82)	metaphor (94)
phonemes (76)	trouble talk (86)	

SUGGESTED READING

Napoli, Donna Jo. (2010). *Language matters: A guide to everyday questions about language.* New York: Oxford University Press.

> In this intelligent and highly readable book, Napoli answers questions like "Do animals have language?" "Can computers learn language?" "Why is it hard to learn a second language?" and "What do we lose when a language disappears?"

Ravitch, Diane. (2004). *The language police: How pressure groups restrict what children learn.* New York: Vintage.

> Describes some of the ridiculous lengths people go to to guard against politically incorrect language, raising important questions about the political implications of language.

Tannen, Deborah. (2006). *You're wearing that?: Understanding mothers and daughters in conversation.* New York: Random House.

> An examination of the meta-messages that lurk underneath the words mothers and daughters use to work out their relationships.

Encoding Messages: Nonverbal Communication

Even when we are silent, invisible messages crowd around us: colors excite us, sounds calm us, the smell or look or feel of another human attracts or repels us.

After reading this chapter, you should be able to:

- Name the four characteristics that distinguish nonverbal from verbal communication.
- Identify the six basic nonverbal codes.
- Explain the kinds of meaning that are best conveyed nonverbally.
- List some of the ways nonverbal and verbal messages interact.
- Distinguish emblems, illustrators, regulators, affect displays, and adaptors.
- Describe how facial expression, eye behavior, and vocal behavior are used to communicate.
- Describe some of the ways in which time and space communicate.
- Describe how physical appearance and object language affect interaction.
- List some ways in which communicators can improve their nonverbal skills.

In 2011 a small French movie called *The Artist* was released worldwide. Surprisingly it began to win one award after another, culminating in a Golden Globe, a New York Film Critics award for best picture, and an Oscar for best actor. What made its critical success so surprising was that this film wasn't a brilliantly colored, dialogue-driven, surround-sound blockbuster, and its stars weren't Hollywood A-listers. *The Artist* was a black-and-white, silent film with a largely unknown cast of French actors. Aided by only a few dialogue cards and a script consisting of two spoken words, the story was easy to follow and surprisingly touching. A brilliant smile, a shy glance, a self-deprecating shrug, or an offhand gesture were enough to establish complex relationships between characters and to draw an international audience to the story. When asked how it was to act in a silent film, Jean Dujardin, who played the main character, answered, "It was much more instinctive than other movies, less thought out . . . and your body started to tell the story."[1]

We shouldn't be so surprised by the success of *The Artist*. After all, we live not only in a world of words but also in a world of silent messages. Every day, we accompany our talk with the languages of gesture and posture, space and time. Even when we are silent, invisible messages crowd around us: colors excite us, sounds calm us, the smell or look or feel of another human attracts or repels us. To communicate fully, we must learn to speak these unspoken languages.

This chapter is about **nonverbal communication**, the study of communication systems that do not involve words. As we will see, many human behaviors convey messages—messages that can be understood as clearly as words. Picture, for example, the following scene, familiar from countless movies and TV shows. Two men, standing several yards apart, face one another in a dusty, deserted street at high noon. One man, clean-shaven, dressed in a light-colored Western-style hat with a tin star on his vest, stands straight and tall, his face betraying no emotion, his eyes steady and intent. The other, all in black, a sneer on his face and a glint of hatred in his eye, stands opposite, his body tensed, his hands near the holsters he wears at his side. Though not a word has been spoken, we know that we are on the main street of a small town in the Old West, about to witness a gunfight. We also know something about the character and motivation of the two men. By reading their posture and gestures, their facial expressions and the symbols in their dress, we know which is the "good guy" and which is the "bad guy." All this has been coded nonverbally in a familiar language of sight and sound.

In this chapter, we examine the unspoken language that allows us to find meaning not only in this scene but also in the more typical scenes that we encounter every day. We begin by defining nonverbal communication, looking at its nature and purpose. We then examine each of the codes that make up the nonverbal system: body movement and gesture; facial display and eye contact; vocal characteristics; time, space, and touch; and physical appearance and the use of artifacts. Once we have considered each code in turn, we will list some skills that can increase nonverbal effectiveness.

WHAT IS NONVERBAL COMMUNICATION?

One of the problems of defining nonverbal communication is deciding what counts as a nonverbal message and what does not. Because all human behavior has the potential to create meaning, is all behavior communication? This question is more than academic; it has real-life implications. Consider an example. As Lorene sits waiting for her boyfriend, Jack, she swings her foot back and forth and repeatedly taps her keys on the edge of a chair. Is Lorene's behavior nonverbal communication? If we also know that Lorene is completely alone and is totally unaware of her behavior, most of us would answer no. Lorene is behaving, but she is not communicating. But what if the situation is slightly different? What if Lorene is angry with Jack and wants him to observe her anger? What if her impatient behaviors are meant to let Jack know that he should be more punctual in the future? Is Lorene's behavior nonverbal communication in this case? Most of us would answer yes. Lorene is communicating, because she is intentionally creating a message for Jack's consumption.

So far, it has been easy to see the difference between behavior and communication in our examples. Unfortunately, however, it's not always this simple. Assume now that Lorene is simply bored. She is not trying to send a message to Jack; she is totally unaware of her behavior. An observer, however, watches her and thinks, "That young woman looks tense and troubled. I wonder what's wrong." The observer received a message that Lorene did not intend to send, one that she would very likely deny sending if asked. This kind of unintended message is harder to classify. Some would argue that Lorene's behavior is not communication, because Lorene is not aware of her observer. Others would argue that Lorene is nevertheless sending a message, and therefore she is communicating.

Because unintended messages occur frequently and have powerful effects (and because it is often difficult to determine whether or not a message is intended), we will take the second view, including as nonverbal communication any instance in which a stimulus other than words creates meaning in either a sender's or a receiver's mind. According to this view, the first scenario cannot be called nonverbal communication because no meaning was created. Both the second and third scenarios, however, can be called nonverbal communication.

How Can We Know What Nonverbals Mean?

If some nonverbal communication is unintentional, how can we be certain that our interpretations are accurate? Unfortunately, we can't ever be completely sure, but we can take steps to increase our chances of making correct interpretations. Consider the following scene: Kelly shudders, crosses her arms, and moves away from Cliff. Should Cliff take this to mean that he has offended Kelly? Perhaps. But what if Kelly is just cold? Cliff can't be sure unless he gets additional information. He can increase his probability of being correct in three ways. First, he can *check the context*. If a breeze is blowing through an open window and Kelly is covered with goose bumps, Cliff shouldn't lose sleep over her behavior; she is probably physically cold rather than irritated with him. A second way for Cliff to increase his accuracy is to *compare current behavior to baseline behavior*. If Kelly usually stands quite far from people, if her body posture is generally closed, and if she habitually crosses her arms, Cliff may conclude that she is simply the kind of person who needs a lot of personal space. If Kelly is normally quite open, however, she is more likely responding to something Cliff has done. Cliff can use one final method to check his understanding. He can *ask for verbal feedback*. He can ask Kelly what her behavior means. Like Cliff, we should be aware that every nonverbal act has several different interpretations, and we should be careful not to settle on one too soon.

Characteristics of Nonverbal Communication

Nonverbal communication has a number of characteristics that distinguish it from other communication systems. We'll look at four.

Nonverbal Communication May Be Unintentional

This characteristic has important implications for our behavior as both senders and receivers. As receivers, we should not assume that every nonverbal act is an intentional message. We should always check for alternative interpretations, and we should realize that reading nonverbals is a risky business. As senders, we should be aware that unintended nonverbal messages can easily undermine and contradict what we really want to convey. We should try our best to make our verbal and non-verbal messages congruent and clear.

Nonverbal Communication Consists of Multiple Codes

The nonverbal system is made up of a number of separate codes. To be success-ful communicators, we must become aware of how each of these codes works. We must also learn to coordinate codes. When nonverbal codes work together to send the same message, their impact is intensified. When they work at cross-purposes, confusion results. In an interview, for example, a confident smile can be undermined by nervous foot tapping, and a firm handshake can be offset by a too-rigid stance. The competent communicator is able to use the full range of nonverbal codes in ways that enhance messages. Later in this chapter, we will look in detail at how these codes work. For now, Table 5.1 presents an overview.

> When nonverbal codes work together to send the same message, their impact is intensified. When they work at cross-purposes, confusion results.

Nonverbal Communication Is Immediate, Continuous, and Natural

Because nonverbals are physical extensions of our bodies, they are immediate. We can weigh our words, carefully compose our verbal messages, and wait for the right time and place before we speak. But we can't delay most nonverbal messages. They occur whenever we are face-to-face with one another. In this regard, we cannot not communicate.

Nonverbal messages are also more continuous than verbal messages. Nonverbal displays flow into one another without the discrete beginnings and endings that characterize words. If we try to isolate and separate nonverbal gestures, they lose meaning. Whether a raised arm is a greeting or a sign of impending attack can only be decided by its context.

> If we try to isolate and separate nonverbal gestures, they lose meaning. Whether a raised arm is a greeting or a sign of impending attack can only be decided by its context.

Table 5.1 Some Basic Nonverbal Codes

Body Movement and Gesture (Kinesics)	Time (Chronemics)
• Emblems	• Psychological time orientation
• Illustrators	• Biological time orientation
• Regulators	• Cultural time orientation
• Affect displays	
• Adaptors	**Space (Proxemics)**
	• Territoriality
Facial Expression and Eye Behavior	• Spatial arrangement
• Cultural display rules	• Personal space
• Professional display rules	• Touch (haptics)
• Personal display rules	
	Physical Appearance and Object Language
Vocal Characteristics (Paralanguage)	• Body type
• Vocal qualities	• Dress
• Vocalizations	• Object language
• Vocal segregates	

Finally, nonverbal messages are more natural and less arbitrary than their verbal counterparts. In most, form and meaning are connected. When we gesture to someone to come nearer, the gesture traces the path we want the person to take. When we show our concern by hugging someone, the hug is part of the natural act of comforting.

Nonverbal Communication Is Both Universal and Cultural

Although not completely free of cultural convention, many nonverbals are understandable the world over. Paul Ekman and Wallace Friesen have shown, for example, that happiness, anger, disgust, fear, surprise, and sadness are conveyed in much the same way in many different cultures. Some hand gestures, such as pointing, also transcend culture. At a very basic level, therefore, we can communicate nonverbally with people whose verbal language we do not know.[2]

Not all nonverbal behaviors, however, have universal meaning. Even emotional displays are modified by cultural rules. Although a smile conveys happiness in most cultures, in some cultures it conveys other emotions, such as embarrassment or submission. In addition, the rules for how often and when to smile vary in different cultures. And when it comes to other kinds of nonverbal meanings, such as the use of time and space, quite dramatic cultural differences occur. The implication is clear: do not assume that everyone shares your own nonverbal rules.

What Meanings Are Best Conveyed Nonverbally?

Verbal and nonverbal codes do not operate in quite the same way. What may be expressed easily in one may often be quite difficult to express in the other. We therefore tend to rely on each of these codes in slightly different situations. As we shall see, nonverbal codes are especially useful for giving us information about personal and relational topics we would be embarrassed to talk about. They allow us to express certain emotional themes that are hard to describe verbally. Nonverbal codes also allow us to refine and expand upon verbal meanings. When something can't be put into words, we turn to nonverbal channels.

> Nonverbal codes are especially useful for giving us information about personal and relational topics we would be embarrassed to talk about.

Making Initial Judgments

Nonverbal cues are often used to size up other people. It is important, sometimes even vital, to know the characteristics, attitudes, and intentions of others. In the early stages of an acquaintance, we seldom volunteer much verbal information about ourselves, nor do we feel comfortable asking others personal questions. This does not mean that we ignore personal information; it simply means that we turn to nonverbal channels. In addition to information about gender, race, and cultural identity, we can pick up cues about personality, attitude, and individual style. Nonverbal behaviors tell us whether others are friendly or hostile, shy or confident, gullible or worldly wise. They help us to determine the credibility and approachability of those around us.

Relational Information

Once we have sized up others and have decided to interact with them, nonverbal cues convey relational information, helping us keep track of how an interaction is going and what others think of us. According to Albert Mehrabian, three kinds of relational messages are exchanged nonverbally during every interaction: liking, status, and responsiveness.[3]

Liking is indicated through facial expression, eye contact, proximity, and the like. If a conversational partner smiles frequently and makes eye contact, we can be relatively sure that he or she likes us. If the partner avoids touch, however, and stands at some distance, there's a good chance that he or she does not like us very well. **Status** is often conveyed through posture and gesture, through touch and proximity, and by the objects we display. Of two individuals, the one who controls the most space, initiates the most touch, and seems the most relaxed is probably the one of higher status. A person's display of expensive or rare objects is also a good indication of high status.

Responsiveness, the degree to which we are psychologically involved in an interaction, is shown by such cues as rate and volume of speech, amount of gesture, and variability of facial display. Someone who responds to us in a monotone, staring straight ahead with a dull, expressionless look, is indicating low involvement and low responsiveness. All of these messages tell us how we are faring in an interaction and give us cues about how to communicate. Although we can ask people whether they like us, whether their status is higher than ours, and how involved they are in an interaction, this approach is rather awkward. Luckily, asking is usually unnecessary. Nonverbal communication gives us a clear picture of where we stand.

Emotional Expression

Another area in which nonverbal is more effective than verbal communication is emotional expression. When a child is frightened or unhappy, a comforting hug is worth more than a verbal explanation of why it doesn't help to cry. When we care about someone, we want to reach out and touch him or her. Talk is not an entirely adequate substitute for human contact, despite what telephone company slogans would have us believe. When people have something emotionally important to say, they need the full range of nonverbal channels. Of course, when they want to break off a relationship but also want to avoid an emotional scene, they may take the coward's way out and use a purely verbal channel, sending a "Dear John" or "Dear Joan" letter rather than announcing the breakup face-to-face.

Nonverbal Codes and Verbal Messages

Finally, nonverbal cues expand on and clarify verbal messages. Nonverbal experts such as Paul Ekman and Mark Knapp have cataloged some of the ways nonverbal messages are used in conjunction with verbal messages.[4] Table 5.2 summarizes the six ways in which nonverbal messages modify verbal messages.

Sometimes we use nonverbal cues to *repeat* what we say verbally. If I'm giving you directions, I may say, "To get to my office, go down the stairs," and, to make sure you understand where I want you to go, I may point toward the stairs. This kind of redundancy helps to ensure that verbal messages are accurately received. Nonverbal cues are also used to *contradict* verbal messages. Jason may turn to his wife, Isabel, and say, "I don't know why I ever married you. For two cents I'd get a divorce." His smile and friendly tone, however, contradict the harshness of his words and let her know he is just joking. Sarcastic comments are another example of contradiction. The words may be friendly, but the tone of voice gives the real message.

Joking and sarcasm are culturally recognized patterns; most people understand what their meaning really is. But other forms of contradiction are not easily deciphered—for example, when a close friend says to you, "I'm fine," but grimaces with pain, or when someone says, "I love you," in a cold, distant way. Communications like these send two opposing messages at the same time. They are potentially harmful to relationships and should be avoided.

Sometimes nonverbal messages can *substitute* for verbal ones. At the end of a difficult and boring meeting, two people can just sigh and roll their eyes. They don't need to put their frustration into words. We also use substitution when verbal channels are unavailable. While scuba diving or during the filming of a TV show, we can't yell out a message, so we resort to sign language.

Nonverbal messages can also *complement*, that is, modify or elaborate on, a verbal message. When Don says to his roommate, "I had a terrible day today," the slope

Table 5.2 Some Ways Nonverbal and Verbal Messages Interact

Repeating	The nonverbal message repeats the verbal message; resulting redundancy can increase accuracy. *Example:* "I'll give you three minutes," said while holding up three fingers.
Contradicting	The nonverbal message undermines the verbal message, often causing confusion and uncertainty. *Example:* "I'm glad to see you," said with a sneer.
Substituting	A nonverbal message is used instead of a verbal message. *Example:* In answer to "How was your day?" the communicator just sighs and shakes his or her head.
Complementing	The nonverbal message modifies the verbal message, letting the receiver know how to take it. *Example:* "I love your gift," said with a huge smile.
Accenting	Nonverbal cues emphasize part of the verbal message. *Example:* "And the most important thing is . . . ," said with vocal emphasis on the most important words.
Regulating	The nonverbal message manages and controls verbal behavior. *Example:* Looking at one's watch to let the speaker know it is time to go.

Liking is indicated nonverbally, through posture, touch, and facial display.

of his shoulders and the weariness in his voice indicate just how bad the day really was. These behaviors add to Don's message, telling us the extent of his feeling. Without the proper accompanying nonverbals, people do not believe others' verbal messages. If a winning contestant on a game show reacts by saying, "I'm glad I won," but fails to scream and clap and jump up and down, the audience doesn't believe that the message is sincere or that the contestant deserved to win.

Sometimes, nonverbal behaviors *accent* the important parts of a verbal message. A teacher may emphasize the main points in a lecture by nonverbally stressing certain words. A parent may make eye contact with a child to make sure the child hears an important bit of advice. The eye contact says, "Now listen carefully. I expect you to remember this and to follow through."

Finally, nonverbal cues *regulate*, or control, social interaction. When we converse, we must carefully coordinate our contributions, finding a way to take the field when it is our turn to speak and a way to relinquish it when we are finished. Because we must do this instantly, without awkward pauses or interruptions that disrupt the flow of speech, we turn to nonverbal channels. Through changes in speech tempo, eye contact, head nodding, and the like, we manage conversations. To claim our turn to talk, we raise our index finger or lean slightly forward, taking a breath as though we are about to speak and nodding our heads to hurry up the other speaker. If the other speaker responds with decreased eye contact and begins to talk faster and louder, we know that our bid to talk has been turned down.[5] Knowing the meaning of and abiding by these nonverbals are aspects of the important interpersonal skill called **interaction management**. People who are skilled in interaction management are considered highly competent communicators.[6]

THE NONVERBAL CODES

So far, our discussion of nonverbal communication has been general. Now we'll look at the specific channels that make up the nonverbal system. We'll start with body movement and gesture, move on to facial expression and eye behavior, and then consider the way vocal quality is related to verbal expression. We'll also discuss the messages conveyed by time, space, and touch, and we'll end by looking at the effects of personal appearance and object language.

© Bettmann/CORBIS

The Kinesic Code I: Body Movement and Gesture

Our bodies are an important source of nonverbal meaning. Whether we lean in toward someone or move away, whether our stance is wide and strong or narrow and weak, whether we talk with our hands or remain completely still—we tell others a lot about us. Even the way we walk can give off signals. When prison inmates arrested for assault were asked to look at tapes of people walking along a city street, they had little trouble agreeing on which were "muggable" and which were not. People classed as "easy rip-offs" moved awkwardly, taking either very long or very short strides, and their arm movements followed their leg movements rather than alternating with them. They appeared to walk around in a daze. Their walk signaled to potential muggers that they would put up little resistance.[7]

The study of body movement (including movement of the face and eyes) is called **kinesics**. People who study kinesics often classify body movement into five categories: emblems, illustrators, regulators, affect displays, and adaptors.[8]

Emblems

Emblems are kinesic behaviors whose direct verbal translations are known to all of the members of a social group. Emblems are like silent words. If you are at a noisy party and want to send a message to a friend across the room, you can use nonverbal emblems. You can "say" to your friend, "Shame on you" (by rubbing your right index finger across your left), "All right! Excellent!" (by turning your clenched fist inward at about head height, then drawing it rapidly down and back), "What time is it?" (by pointing at your wrist), or "I'm leaving now" (by pointing to yourself and then to the door). In fact, you can have a fairly lengthy (if not intellectually stimulating) conversation using emblems. In the United States, we have emblems that allow us to tell others what to do ("Wait a minute"; "I can't hear you"; "Come over here"; "Sit down next to me"; "Calm down"), that convey our physical state ("I'm hot"; "I'm cold"; "I'm sleepy"; "I don't know"; "I'm confused"), that act as replies ("Yes"; "No"; "Maybe"; "I promise"), that evaluate others ("He's crazy"; "That stinks"; "He [or she] has a great figure"), and that serve as insults, including obscenities.[9]

> Whether we lean in toward someone or move away, whether our stance is wide and strong or narrow and weak, whether we talk with our hands or remain completely still—we tell others a lot about us.

One of the defining characteristics of emblems is that they are culturally defined. We must be very careful when using them with members of different cultural groups. The sign that we in the United States recognize as the A-OK sign (thumb and index finger touching in a circle, the rest of the fingers outstretched) can in other countries stand for money, can indicate that something is worthless, or can obscenely signify female genitalia. Judee Burgoon comments on the way emblems vary in different cultures:

> For example, the head throw for "no" displayed by Greeks, Southern Italians, Bulgarians, and Turks could be mistaken for "yes" in cultures where nodding signifies affirmation. The Bulgarian turn of the head for "yes" is likely to appear to be

shaking the head, a sign of negation in many cultures. Beckoning gestures are also a source of misunderstandings. The palm-down fluttering fingers beckoning gesture observed in Asian and Latin American cultures may be interpreted as "go away" by North Americans. In sum, although emblematic differences allow us to identify cultural group membership, they can also create cross-cultural misunderstandings and unfavorable attributions.[10]

Illustrators

Sometimes, the best way to describe an object is to use gestures that indicate its size or shape or movement. If someone doesn't know what a scalloped edge looks like or isn't familiar with the term *zigzag*, you can use hand movements to illustrate what you mean. Gestures like these accompany speech and add to the meaning of utterances; they are called **illustrators**. Illustrators need not describe physical objects; they can also be used to indicate the structure of utterances. A public speaker may gesture each time a new point is raised. The gesture illustrates the central structure of the argument. People differ in the number of gestures they use. Some people are so used to talking with their hands that if their hands were tied behind their backs, they would find it almost impossible to speak.

Regulators

Regulators are nonverbal behaviors that act as "traffic signals" during interaction. They consist of the head nods and eye and hand movements that allow us to maintain, request, or deny others a turn to talk. As their name implies, they fulfill a nonverbal regulating function. Regulators usually occur so rapidly and automatically that we are not consciously aware we are using them. At a subconscious level, however, we are certainly aware of them, for without them conversations grind to a halt.

Regulators are seldom noticed—unless they are used inappropriately. Then negative attributions are likely. This can be a problem in communicating with people from other cultures, for the rules governing regulators can differ. In comparison to the Japanese, Americans tend to dominate conversations. Whoever has something to say has the floor and tends to keep it for as long as he or she has something to say. The Japanese, on the other hand, distribute the talk more equally, making sure that everyone has equal talking time.

Affect Displays

Body movements that convey emotional states are called **affect displays**. When we want to know what someone is feeling, our first instinct is to look at that person's face. The rest of the body, however, is equally expressive. In fact, experts on deception tell us that to determine whether someone is lying, we should not necessarily look at the face but at the body. When people lie, they generally experience heightened emotional arousal. If this arousal is not suppressed, it will act as a *leakage cue*, letting the observer sense guilt, anxiety, and excitement. Facial cues are least likely to leak this information, because liars pay close attention to and control their facial expressions. Body movements are less controlled and are therefore a better source of information. The voice is also a good source of leakage cues.[11]

In addition to leakage, liars may also give themselves away through their use of *strategic cues*.[12] Strategic cues are behaviors that liars use to disassociate themselves from their messages and to reduce their responsibility for what they've said. Liars sometimes seem uncertain or vague, less immediate, and more reticent than non-liars as they try to "back away" nonverbally from their lies. These cues, shown by body movement and spatial behavior, may be detected if one knows where to look. Unfortunately, the average receiver is not very good at detecting deception, perhaps because liars control those very types of behaviors that most of us associate with lying: facial and eye behaviors. If you want to detect deception, attend instead to a sender's body and vocal channels, and compare any suspicious behavior to the sender's baseline behavior.

Of course, not all emotional displays are attempted deceptions. Most affect displays are honest depictions of internal states and are easily detected. In attempting to read emotions, remember to look at the behaviors of the other person's whole body, including those behaviors that fall into our next category, adaptors.

Adaptors

Have you ever noticed how often people engage in odd, repetitive, nervous mannerisms? The next time you're in public, say, in a classroom, watch your fellow students tap their pens, kick their feet, twirl their hair, play with their jewelry, groom themselves, and so on. As often as these behaviors happen in public, they are even more frequent in private. Called **adaptors**, they are behaviors that people use to adapt to stresses and to satisfy personal needs. Some (such as scratching) are behaviors that satisfy immediate needs, whereas others (such as pen tapping) may be residual displays of behaviors that were once functional. Fist clenching or foot kicking, for example, may be residual hitting or running motions. Rocking back and forth may be a way of re-creating early childhood experiences. And playing with jewelry may be the next best thing to carrying around a security blanket. Regardless of where they originate, most adaptors are used to manage stress.

People are often completely unaware that they are using adaptors, and for this reason, adaptors are a good source of information about emotions. When people touch their own bodies (for example, by rubbing their necks or playing with their hair), they are using *self-adaptors*. When they touch objects (for example, by playing with cigarettes or shredding Styrofoam cups), they are using *object adaptors*. By observing these behaviors, you may uncover hidden information about people's emotional states.

The Kinesic Code II: Facial Expression and Eye Behavior

The face is the arena most people turn to for information about others. We believe that "the eyes are mirrors of the soul" and that people's character can be "written all over their faces." We like people with open, friendly faces, and we avoid "two-faced" people with shifty eyes or thin, mean lips. And when we want to look particularly honest or friendly, we smile and widen our eyes. All these behaviors indicate our faith in the face and eyes as sources of nonverbal communication.

Facial Displays

Where do **facial displays** come from? Experts believe that they are partly innate and partly learned. That is, the form that emotional expressions take is "prewired" into the human brain, but the way these expressions are exhibited is governed by culture-specific rules. Evidence for the basic innateness of facial expression comes from several sources. Studies show, for example, that blind and sighted children have very similar facial expressions, and cross-cultural studies show that basic expressions are shared across many different cultures.[13] These studies suggest that the reason we smile when happy and cry when sad is that smiling and crying are part of our biological inheritance.

© Kevin R. Morris/CORBIS

When we consciously make a face, we're well aware of what we're doing. At other times, we may not realize how much of what we feel is displayed for everyone to see.

When and where and how much we smile or cry, however, depend on learning and imitation. Within each culture, certain expressions are encouraged and reinforced, whereas others are discouraged.[14] People in every culture learn to modify their facial displays, *intensifying* certain emotions and *deintensifying* others. For example, most Americans feel that it is impolite to show disappointment over a gift or to gloat at our own good fortune. We may therefore pretend to like a birthday present more than we actually do, or we may downplay pleasure at our own success if a friend has failed. We also learn to *neutralize* other emotions, swallowing our disappointment by pretending not to care. Finally, we may *mask* one emotion with another. When the first runner-up hears she is not being crowned Miss America, not only does she not show her disappointment and jealousy, she looks positively joyful as she rushes up to hug the winner. Becoming a good communicator includes learning how to modify facial displays. The rules that govern these modifications occur at three levels: the cultural, the professional, and the personal.

By following what are called **cultural display rules**, people in some cultures learn to be "stone-faced" and stoic, whereas those in other cultures learn to be highly expressive. In American culture, for example, men follow a cultural display rule that tells them not to show fear in public. Women, on the other hand, are free to show fear but must keep anger in check. Women are also expected to express pleasant emotions and smile more frequently than men. In Japan, smiling is equally important, although the display rules governing smiling differ. There the smile is not only a way to express happiness, but also a way to reduce embarrassment and promote harmony. Guo-Ming Chen and William Starosta tell us that Japanese hosts are expected to smile at guests, even at funerals. An athlete who loses a competition or a student who receives a failing grade must also cover his or her concern with a smile.[15]

In addition to modifying facial displays to meet cultural expectations, people learn to follow display rules at work. Service personnel, such as flight attendants, are taught to inhibit any irritation they feel and to smile no matter what. Nurses learn to be cheerful, calm, and caring, whereas lawyers learn when to put on a "poker face" and when to show justified outrage. Rules for facial expression based on career considerations are called **professional display rules**.

Finally, people also follow **personal display rules**. These rules are learned through individual experience and are often, but not always, shared with family members. Researchers have made a number of attempts to identify personal styles in emotional expression. Ross Buck argues that people are either externalizers or internalizers.[16] *Externalizers* are good at portraying emotion, whereas *internalizers* are less adept at showing emotions.

Eye Behavior

For centuries, the eyes have been associated with mystic power. The Greek philosopher Empedocles explained vision as a flow of fiery corpuscles that pass from the eye to an object of vision and back again. This image of the glance as a fiery stream persisted; it can also be found in Renaissance love poetry, in which eyes were thought to "shoot arrows, daggers or swords [and] project fiery beams which burn the soul and kindle love's flame."[17] In addition to possessing the ability to engender love, the eyes have also been associated with suffering and death, perhaps because of our instinctive fear of the predatory gaze. Whatever the reason, primitive people in all ages have guarded themselves from the evil eye, a hostile glance reputed to kill instantly. Gerald Grumet reports that a certain mental disorder reverses the evil-eye superstition: the afflicted person avoids others in fear that his or her glance will injure them.[18]

> For centuries, the eyes have been associated with mystic power. The Greek philosopher Empedocles explained vision as a flow of fiery corpuscles that pass from the eye to an object of vision and back again.

Although modern Americans do not believe in primitive superstitions, we do recognize that eye behavior serves a number of important functions. Grumet tells us that dominant animals place themselves where they can watch their subordinates and where they themselves can be watched. Similarly, human leaders tend to situate themselves where they will command the center of visual attention, such as at the head of a table or the front of a conference room. Thus, *eye behavior serves to maintain social position.*

Eye behavior is also a good indication of both positive and negative emotions. We stare at sights we find agreeable and avert our eyes when a sight disgusts or horrifies us. Studies also show that when our interest and attention are high, our pupil size enlarges. Furthermore, research shows that people with enlarged pupils are judged more physically attractive than those with constricted pupils, a fact known as early as Cleopatra's time, when women used eyedrops made of belladonna to darken and enlarge their eyes.[19]

The eyes also signal our willingness to relate to one another. Mutual gaze is the first step in most relationships, for it signals both parties' awareness of one another.[20] During conversation, eyes act as nonverbal regulators, displaying typical patterns for listening and speaking. Listeners gaze more than do speakers, perhaps to pick up turn-taking cues. Speakers look away while formulating their thoughts, perhaps to cut down on visual stimuli that might interfere with concentration. As any student who does not want to be called on in class knows, avoiding eye contact closes communication channels, whereas inadvertently looking up virtually guarantees being called on.

> As any student who does not want to be called on in class knows, avoiding eye contact closes communication channels, whereas inadvertently looking up virtually guarantees being called on.

Finally, like other nonverbal cues, *eye behavior is associated with specific character traits.* People who make eye contact are judged as friendlier and more natural and sincere than those who avoid direct gaze. People who shift their gaze, on the other hand, are judged as cold, defensive, evasive, submissive, or inattentive.[21]

Paralinguistics: Vocal Behavior

A lot of the meaning in everyday talk lies not in our words but in how we say those words. If we were to read transcripts of conversations, we would have to mentally supply what is left out: the speakers' intonations, tones of voice, volume, pitch, timing, and the like. Characteristics that define how something is said, rather than what is said, are part of **paralinguistics**, the study of the sounds that accompany words. The importance of paralanguage was clearly demonstrated in 1974, when former president Richard Nixon, under investigation by the House Judiciary Committee, refused to supply audiotapes of his conversations and instead sent transcripts. Committee members, who needed to determine the truth value and meaning of the tapes, argued that the transcripts were incomplete, because vocal qualities and characterizers were missing.[22] The committee recognized how important vocal modifications are.

> Although the judgments we make based on vocal qualities are not necessarily accurate, we think they are. People generally agree about the connotations of different kinds of voices.

Paralanguage includes **vocal qualities** (characteristics of the voice, such as pitch, tone, and intonation patterns), **vocalizations** (special sounds that convey meaning, such as groans, cries, moans, giggles, and yawns), and **vocal segregates** (pauses and fillers, such as "um" and "uh"). All of these kinds of sounds affect the meaning of our spoken communications. They can be eloquent testimonies to emotional states, but they can also be cues used to make stereotypic judgments of personality characteristics.

It is a matter of interest that although the judgments we make based on vocal qualities are not necessarily accurate, we think they are. People generally agree about the connotations of different kinds of voices. A light, breathy voice connotes seductiveness and a lack of intelligence. A nasal voice may lead others to perceive the speaker as dull, lazy, and whiny. And the big, full, orotund voice associated with preachers and politicians can signify authority and pomposity.[23]

Judgments of social status are also associated with the way we speak. Most cultures define certain accents and ways of speaking as "prestige speech." People whose grammar, word choice, or accent deviates from these standards are likely to be judged less credible and less intelligent than people who meet paralinguistic norms. On the other hand, speaking a regional or subcultural dialect may lead to higher ratings of benevolence and attractiveness. That is, the person who speaks in perfect, pear-shaped tones may appear distant and snobby, whereas someone whose language patterns are more regional may seem like a "regular guy." Certainly, to people within a social group, accent similarity can enhance group solidarity.[24]

An often overlooked aspect of paralanguage is silence. Just as sound creates meaning, so too does the absence of sound. One use of silence is to create interpersonal distance. By not talking to someone, we can send the message "I refuse to admit your presence." The Amish use a form of silence called "shunning" to punish those who have violated important social norms.

A sudden silence can also indicate that a specific remark or behavior is inappropriate. If after telling an off-color joke at a dinner party you are greeted with stunned silence, you have likely committed a major social faux pas.

Of course, silence is not always negative. If filled by other nonverbal cues (a tender gaze, a touch), silence can signal intimacy and comfort. Silence can also be a mark of respect or reverence. We often fall silent on entering places of worship, both to show our respect and to concentrate on inner, spiritual concerns. We also become silent when someone of high status appears, indicating that his or her words are more important than our own.[25]

But although there are times when we value silence, in general, Americans like to talk. This is not true in other cultures. According to Keith Basso, who has studied Western Apache culture, silence in this culture is generally valued over talk. For example, strangers who jump into a conversation too quickly are treated with suspicion. Their desire to speak seems to indicate a kind of greed or selfishness that imposes on listeners. The Apache suspicion of those who speak too much extends to a dislike of detailed descriptions. As Basso explains:

> *A person who speaks too much—someone who describes too busily, who supplies too many details, who repeats and qualifies too many times—presumes without warrant on the right of hearers to build freely and creatively on the speaker's own depiction. . . . In other words, persons who speak too much insult the imaginative capabilities of other people, "blocking their thinking" . . . and "holding down their minds."[26]*

Chronemics and Proxemics: Time, Territory, and Space

So far, we have looked at ways we use our bodies to communicate. In this section, we will look at how the dimensions of space and time can serve as nonverbal messages.

The importance we attach to time and how we manage it are important nonverbal signals.

© Conde Nast Archive/CORBIS

We will begin by looking at **chronemics**, the study of time as it affects human behavior. We will then move on to a discussion of **proxemics**, the study of how we use space and what space means to us.

Time Orientations

Are you the kind of person who enjoys dwelling in the past? Do you retell old stories, pore over scrapbooks, and spend your time remembering past events? Or do you like making plans and imagining what the future will hold? Do you place high or low value on being punctual? Do your friends always end up waiting for you, or are you the one who is always early? The answers to these questions can tell you something about your **psychological time orientation**, the way you habitually think about and experience time.

Alexander Gonzalez and Philip Zimbardo devised a scale called the Stanford Time Perspective Inventory to measure individual differences in time orientation. Using a variation of this scale, they surveyed more than eleven thousand readers of *Psychology Today* and found seven different time perspectives: two related to the present, four focused on the future, and one concerned with the effects of time pressures.[27] Interestingly, past orientations were so infrequent that they were eliminated from analysis. The overwhelming emphasis on the future makes sense, given the values our culture attaches to progress. As we shall see, members of other cultures have a much different sense of time.

Gonzalez and Zimbardo found two kinds of people with present orientations. People who focus on the present are either impulsive sensation seekers who like to spend their time playing and going to parties or people who believe that it doesn't make sense to plan, because events will occur unalterably no matter what one does.

Four time orientations focused on the future. Some future-oriented people believe in hard work, recognizing the importance of meeting obligations and completing projects no matter how difficult or uninteresting. Others are more positive about the future and spend their time imagining the success they will achieve when their goals are met. Still others view the future in practical, down-to-earth ways; they value behaviors that make the future secure, such as saving money and buying insurance. Finally, a fourth group obsesses over controlling the details of day-to-day events. These people are the list makers and daily planners who map out their lives in specific detail.

The final orientation is slightly different from the others. Labeled the time-sensitivity orientation, it describes people who feel anxious and pressured by time obligations and who are somewhat compulsive about both their own and others' punctuality.

Gonzalez and Zimbardo believe that time orientation may be related to the kinds of employment we seek. Thus, semiskilled or unskilled occupations may be attractive to and appropriate for people with present orientations, whereas managerial and professional occupations call for future-oriented individuals. The authors also suggest that we can all benefit from developing more flexibility in our relationship to time. Although punctuality is important for success, we should not let it become an obsession. Think about your own time perspective. When does your orientation work for you, and when does it get you into trouble? Are your relationships with others hurt or helped by the way you think of time?

In addition to being influenced by our psychological orientation to time, we are also controlled by our **biological time orientation**. Humans, like other animals, seem to have built-in biological clocks that govern our daily rhythms. Metabolic processes, as well as neurochemical activities in the brain, are tied to biological rhythms. When these processes are upset by changes in clock time (for example, by flying into a different time zone or by changing work shifts), we may feel irritated, tired, and even physically sick until we find a way to reset our internal clocks. Some people are extremely sensitive to seasonal changes in the amount of available light. In the short, dark days of winter, they can fall into a depression called seasonal affective disorder, which can sometimes be treated by using artificial light. We are beginning to find out that our mental alertness, as well as our emotional stability, is affected by biological time.

A third way time affects us is through our **cultural time orientation**. People from different cultures think differently about the value and uses of time. Judee Burgoon tells us that the Sioux have no words for "late" or "waiting," that the Pueblo people start ceremonies whenever "the time is right," and that the traditional Navajo are extremely present oriented.[28] Gonzalez and Zimbardo point out that clashes between different cultural time orientations account for cross-cultural misunderstandings between North Americans and people from Latin American and Mediterranean countries:

> From their strong present and past perspectives, they see us as obsessed with working, efficiency, rationality, delaying gratification and planning for what will be. To us, they are inefficient, lazy, imprudent, backward and immature in their obsession with making the most of the moment.[29]

The silent language of time is an extremely important part of nonverbal communication.

Territory and the Use of Space

Managing territory and distance is another important aspect of nonverbal behavior. Like birds and mammals, humans need to maintain uniform distances from one another and to occupy and defend territories. Proxemics commonly consists of three areas: territory, spatial arrangement, and personal space.

The need to create boundaries, to control areas of space and make them ours, is called **territoriality**. Territoriality is a basic human need. We need to have a place to call our own, a place where we are safe from attack and, even more important, where we are free to do what we want without being observed and judged. People often feel most truly themselves when they are in familiar territory.

People occupy several kinds of territories. Stanford Lyman and Marvin Scott describe four: public, home, interaction, and body territories.[30] **Public territories** are territories that we share with others. City parks and shopping malls, for example, are open to everyone in the community, although what people are allowed to do there is often restricted. To avoid the potential disorder that can occur when strangers interact, public territories are usually patrolled by police, and anyone who is thought to be threatening community standards may be asked to leave. When we occupy public territories, we are expected to follow the rules. At most beaches, for example, we are free to play Frisbee but not to sunbathe nude.

Home territories are areas owned and controlled by individuals. In these spaces, we have much greater freedom to do whatever we want. A child's clubhouse with its sign warning "Keep Out, This Means You!" is a home territory, as is his or her parents' bedroom. The need to control space is so great that people may even try to make home territories out of public territories. We may, for example, consider a favorite table in a local restaurant "our" table and be irritated or outraged when it is occupied by someone else. In cities, gangs may lay claim to certain streets, marking nearby buildings with graffiti to indicate "their" turf. You may even consider your seat in your communication classroom as an extension of your home territory.

Whereas public and home territories may be bounded by physical barriers, such as walls, gates, or fences, **interaction territories** are socially marked. Groupings of people at a party or lovers in private conversation occupy interactional territories. Like other territories, these arenas may be made off limits to outsiders. By the way they position their bodies, make or avoid eye contact, or focus their attention, those who are inside the interaction separate themselves from those who are outside and indicate how permeable their invisible boundaries may be.

Body territories are the most private of all our territories. Our rights to touch and view one another's bodies are strongly restricted. From the time we are children, we are shown which parts of our own (and others') bodies can and cannot be

> Body territories are the most private of all our territories. Our rights to touch and view one another's bodies are strongly restricted.

touched. We are told how much clothing to wear, and we are expected to decorate our bodies in acceptable ways. In some cultures, practices such as tattooing or nose piercing are encouraged; in others, they are thought to be disgusting.

Lyman and Scott believe that our territories may be encroached in three ways: through contamination, violation, or invasion. In *contamination*, a territory is polluted or made unacceptable. After contamination, the territory must be cleansed before it can be used again. In caste societies, the presence of a low-caste person is thought to pollute sacred spaces. Vandalism can encroach on home territories, and dirty jokes can contaminate an interaction. Soiling one's clothes or spattering someone else with mud are examples of body contamination.

A second form of encroachment is *violation*, any unwarranted entry into or use of a space. Homeless people sleeping in a park, an outsider stumbling into a private conversation, a dog digging in a neighbor's flower bed, or a stranger brushing against someone in a crowded subway are examples of violations.

Invasion is perhaps the most serious form of encroachment. It occurs whenever people who are not entitled to use a space enter and take control of that space. When a motorcycle gang takes over a public park, when a visiting relative won't leave after two weeks, or when an insensitive boor dominates a conversation, public, home, and interaction territories are invaded. Rape and assault, of course, are invasions of body territories; most cultures consider these acts to be so serious that they are punishable by imprisonment or even death.

Territories are important to us. We build barriers against the approach of others, and we are often willing to defend these barriers to the death. Some barriers are easy to identify. Barbed-wire fences and border guards let us know when we are crossing national boundaries. Picket fences or hedges tell us where one yard ends and another begins. But other barriers are not as easy to identify. We do not always know when we are not wanted or when our behavior has violated a social norm. The ability to recognize the nonverbal signs that indicate we are encroaching on another's territory is an important communication skill.

Spatial Arrangement

The ways we arrange home and public territories affect our lives. Architects and interior designers know how important **spatial arrangement** can be. The way walls and furniture are arranged within structures affects the amount, flow, and kind of interaction in them. Seating choice in classrooms, for example, often predicts which students are likely to talk and which are not. In a seminar-style classroom, students who sit directly next to the teacher are less likely to be called on than are those who sit farther down the seminar table. In a regular classroom, most participation comes from the so-called **action zone**, a roughly triangular area beginning with the seats immediately in front of the teacher and diminishing as it approaches the back of the room.[31]

> The way walls and furniture are arranged within structures affects the amount, flow, and kind of interaction in them.

Furniture arrangement in offices also delivers a number of messages. To observe this phenomenon yourself, visit several of your professors' offices, and note factors such as the overall amount of space and the presence or absence of barriers between instructor and student, as well as the relative amount of space "owned" by each. Ask yourself how these arrangements affect your comfort level and how they define the role of student. Figure 5.1 shows several examples of seating arrangements and furniture placement and summarizes their effects on communication in the United States.

Figure 5.1 **Effects of Furniture Placement on Communication**
Seating Arrangements at Rectangular Tables

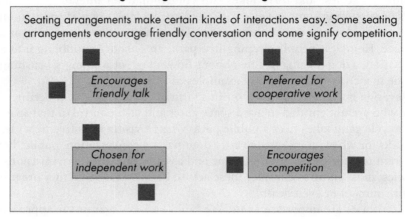

Seating arrangements make certain kinds of interactions easy. Some seating arrangements encourage friendly conversation and some signify competition.

Encourages friendly talk

Preferred for cooperative work

Chosen for independent work

Encourages competition

Office Arrangements

Office arrangements give messages of dominance and power. In which arrangement is the student treated most like an equal?

Window

Window

Door   **A**

Door   **B**

In arrangement A, chair placement allows cooperative action across the corner of the desk and space seems equally shared. In arrangement B, the desk acts as a barrier and the student's territory is cramped.

U.S. workers in general prefer private offices or cubicles, but not every culture divides up work space similarly. Bruce Feilor, who lived and worked in Japan, describes a very different arrangement. In Feilor's office, a large open space, desks were arranged in groups of nine. Within each group, four desks were lined up next to and directly facing another four desks opposite, while a desk for the section chief was placed at one end, perpendicular to the two rows. With all of the desks touching, the work surface was like a giant table top. As Feilor explains, "every conversation and every minor memo became the business of the whole group."[32]

Such an office arrangement promotes group interaction, but it does not, as it might first appear to an American, promote equality. In Japan, group membership and hierarchy are valued at the same time, and status markers are often subtly revealed. Feilor goes on to explain:

> *Younger people sat at the bottom of each line, seniors higher along, and the section chief alone at the end. As a worker advanced along this route, he was allowed to keep more paper on his desk, more cushions on his chair, and perhaps even a pair of slippers underneath. In this office, one desk stood out. It was placed in the center of the room, separate and unequal from the rest. . . . Above the desk a lone sign dangled from a fluorescent light. It read simply, shocho: Director.[33]*

Personal Space

Each one of us varies in how close we prefer to be to other people. This preference, called **personal space**, acts as a kind of portable territory that we carry with us wherever we go. If others come too close, we move away until we feel comfortable. Similarly, if people stand too far away, we move in to establish more intimacy. People with the same personal space norms have little trouble interacting. Those who vary greatly, however, find it difficult to coordinate their needs. They can be observed engaging in a complex dance; as one moves closer, the other counters by backing away.

> People who like one another usually stand closer together than do strangers; in fact, closeness is often used as a measure of attraction.

Factors that affect personal closeness include liking, status, gender, and the way we define the interaction. People who like one another usually stand closer together than do strangers; in fact, closeness is often used as a measure of attraction. The amount of personal space one controls can also indicate status, with people of higher rank being given more personal space than those with low rank. In our culture, gender too makes a difference in the way we use personal space: males generally take up more space than do females. Of course, our personal space also depends on the nature of our interaction. We expect to be at a greater distance from a teacher delivering a lecture than from a friend talking to us. Edward T. Hall investigated American cultural norms for personal space and found four kinds of interaction zones. These are described in Table 5.3.

When one's personal space needs are violated, one experiences *crowding*. Crowding has been shown to lead to heightened arousal and anxiety, decreased cognitive functioning, and increased verbal and physical aggression. To relieve discomfort, crowded individuals often avoid eye contact or verbal interaction, use body blocking to decrease their sense of contact, or use objects to build barriers between themselves and others. People whose occupations cause them to violate the personal space of others (such as servers, hairdressers, or massagers) are often given the status of **nonpersons** and are thus absolved of responsibility for the violation.

Touch

The extreme of personal closeness is touch. To touch and be touched is a basic need. People who are deprived of touch may develop physical, mental, and social disorders. In fact, studies have linked touch deprivation to depression, alienation, and violence.[34] Touch is an important form of nonverbal communication, and its study is sometimes called **haptics**.

All cultures regulate how and how often their members touch. Judee Burgoon and Thomas Saine feel that, compared to other societies, our culture is "restrictive, punitive, and ritualized" in regard to touch.[35] Affectionate contact between people outside the family is discouraged, and strict norms regulate touch within the family. Mothers, for example, are encouraged to touch male children, but fathers are not. Fathers also face strict taboos about touching post-adolescent female children. In general, touch declines from early infancy on, with senior citizens suffering the most deprivation and isolation.[36] Strong antitouch norms also affect heterosexual male–male touch. As Loretta Malandro and Larry Barker tell us, "Physical contact by a man with another man remains so potentially dangerous and unspeakable for many American males that other than a constrained handshake, no one but the dentist and doctor are permitted to touch the skin surface."[37]

> People deprived of touch may develop physical, mental, and social disorders. In fact, studies have linked touch deprivation to depression, alienation, and violence.

Touch conveys a number of messages. First, the type of touch (a pat on the back versus a lingering caress) indicates how we feel about others and defines a given relationship as playful, loving, friendly, sexual, or even aggressive. In most cultures, negative feelings such as derision are shown by touch avoidance. Touch also communicates status, the person who initiates touch being of higher status. It is a social error, for example, for a management trainee to casually pat his or her manager on the shoulder. Touch initiation is generally considered a dominant behavior; in fact, we often use touch to control or direct the action of others. For this reason, touch initiation is governed by the rules that control other forms of dominance.

Touch also satisfies our own emotional needs. When we feel stressed or lonely, we may curl up our bodies and hug our knees, wring our hands, or stroke our hair.

Table 5.3 Interaction Zones for Most Americans

Intimate Distance	Extends from contact to about eighteen inches. It is reserved for intimate interaction and very private conversations.
Personal Distance	Extends from eighteen inches to about four feet. It is used for casual, friendly interactions.
Social Distance	Extends from four to twelve feet. It is used for impersonal business relationships.
Public Distance	Extends from twelve feet to the limits of visibility or hearing. It is used for public performances, lectures, and the like.

For a more extensive discussion, see Edward T. Hall (1966). *The Hidden Dimensions*. New York: Doubleday.

The use of these kinds of self-adaptors shows a need for body contact. When we feel the need for touch, we may also gain comfort from touching animals. Some nursing homes have introduced house pets or encourage visiting pets. Being able to stroke a cat or dog and feel its warmth helps residents to overcome isolation and loneliness.

Physical Appearance and Object Language

Professional designers—whether they design clothing, graphics, or interiors—are trained in the selection and arrangement of elements to create an overall effect. In a certain way, we are all designers. When we go out to face the world each morning, we take with us a material self that is created by the way we look and dress and by the objects we display. Whether or not we realize it, our design efforts matter. Personal appearance affects the way others act toward us, as well as how we feel about ourselves. As Mark Knapp has pointed out,

> *Physical attractiveness may be influential in determining whether you are sought out; it may have a bearing on whether you are able to persuade or manipulate others; it is often an important factor in the selection of dates and marriage partners; . . . it may be a major factor contributing to how others judge your personality, your sexuality, your popularity, your success, and often your happiness.*[38]

Body Type

People have strong reactions to body shape and appearance. All cultures favor certain body types, subjecting to ridicule people who don't fit the ideal. Cultures also form stereotypes about the characteristics that are thought to go along with various body types. Whether there is any truth to these stereotypes is less important than that we believe and act on them.

Researchers who study body types classify people according to how closely they approximate three extremes. The *endomorph* is short, round, and fat; the *mesomorph* is of average height and is muscular and athletic; the *ectomorph* is tall, thin, and frail. A person's somatype is a composite score, using a seven-point scale, of each of these extremes. The **somatype** of an extremely fat person, for example, is a 7/1/1; that of a trained athlete, a 1/7/1; and that of a very tall, skinny person, a 1/1/7. Mark Knapp reports that the late comedian Jackie Gleason scored roughly a 6/4/1, that former heavyweight boxing champion Muhammad Ali rated a 2/7/1 at the peak of his career, and that Abraham Lincoln is considered to have been a 1/5/6.

Certain personality characteristics are generally associated with each of the three body types that make up the somatype. Descriptors such as placid, contented, affable, generous, and affectionate are used to characterize endomorphs. Mesomorphs are seen as energetic, enthusiastic, competitive, reckless, and optimistic. Ectomorphs seem more self-conscious, precise, shy, awkward, serious, and sensitive.[39]

One's height and body type can put one at an advantage or a disadvantage when it comes to love and career. In America, height is an advantage, especially for men. A number of studies show that—all else being equal—tall men are hired more frequently than are short men.[40] Tall men are also more successful in romance. Few women seek out a man who is "short, dark, and handsome."

Generally, North American cultural norms value men who are muscular and women who are slender, even though most Americans are overweight. Obesity is especially disliked, and fat people are often ridiculed and avoided. To escape being perceived as endomorphic, Americans will go to great lengths in exercise and diet. Victims of anorexia nervosa are quite literally willing to starve themselves to death to achieve what they consider a desirable body type.

Dress

According to Desmond Morris, clothing, or dress, serves three major functions. First, it provides *comfort-protection*, shielding us from extremes of heat and cold. Second, it preserves our *modesty* by covering areas of the body that are considered taboo. Most important, it serves as a *cultural display*, telling others about our place in a variety of culturally defined hierarchies. In earlier times, laws dictated the clothing appropriate for each profession and social class. People who dressed above their station in life could be arrested. Rank could be read in the shape of a coat or the color of a ribbon. In modern, more democratic times, we are freer to dress as we wish. Yet we are still constrained by unwritten laws, and we may still read information about socioeconomic class in others' clothing choices.

Whether or not clothes should be taken seriously, they are. Most businesses and schools have written or unwritten dress codes, and violations of dress norms are still a potent outlet for social rebellion.

Like other nonverbal signs, clothes are often read as a sign of character and are especially important in creating first impressions. The courtroom is one place where the messages of clothes are carefully scrutinized.

Trial consultants dress defendants to look as innocent as possible. Witnesses and lawyers are also careful about their clothing choices. If you were going to appear in court, say, as a character witness on behalf of a friend, how would you dress? Take a moment to imagine what you would wear. Then compare your choices to the following descriptions of clothing that, according to Lawrence Smith and Loretta Malandro, increase perceptions of credibility and likeability in a courtroom setting.[41]

To increase their credibility, men are advised to wear classic, conservative two-piece suits made of wools and wool blends. Trendy styles, unusual fabrics, and large patterns are to be avoided. Acceptable suit colors are gray and navy, but the only acceptable color for the shirt is white. Jewelry should be limited to one conservative ring, a

© Lucien Aigner/CORBIS

Appearance and adornment are often considered to be indicators of taste and status as any fashion-victim knows.

watch, and a tie bar or tiepin. Conservative tortoiseshell eyeglasses can enhance the image. Hair should be short and conservatively styled.

Advice for women is similar. A traditional two-piece suit consisting of matching jacket and skirt in a solid color should be worn with a cotton or silk (not polyester) blouse with a simple collar. The skirt length should range from just below the knee to two inches below the knee. Shoes should have closed toes and heels approximately two and one-half inches high. Acceptable suit colors include gray, white, off-white, beige, and navy, with a white or light blue blouse. Jewelry should be limited to five points, for example, nondangling earrings, a simple ring, a single strand of pearls, a watch, and a pin on the jacket. As with men, eyeglasses increase women's credibility. Makeup should be moderate.

Men and women who wish to emphasize their approachability and likeability may modify their dress by wearing jackets that contrast with the rest of the suit. Men are advised to wear tans, beiges, or browns; women may wear colors in the brown, gray, and blue families, as well as pinks and roses. Eyeglasses should be removed occasionally to increase the perception of approachability.

Although it seems patently obvious that dressing conservatively will not make one any more intelligent or more expert, violating dress norms can have serious effects. Whether or not clothes should be taken seriously, they are. Most businesses and schools have written or unwritten dress codes, and violations of dress norms are still a potent outlet for social rebellion.

Object Language

The objects or artifacts we own and display can also be an important mode of communication. **Object language** can be defined as "all intentional and nonintentional displays of material things, such as implements, machines, art objects, architectural structures, [as well as] the human body, and whatever clothes or covers it."[42] As we have already discussed body and dress, we will concentrate on material possessions, giving special attention to environmental design.

In the 1890s, philosopher William James talked about three aspects of the self: the social self, the spiritual self, and the material self. James believed that a person's possessions are a fair measure of his or her sense of self. As Franklin Becker notes, James defined a man's material self as:

> *the sum total of all that he can call his, not only his body and his psychic processes, but his clothes and his house, his wife and children, his ancestors and his friends, his reputation and works, his lambs and horses, his yacht and bank account. All things give him the same emotions. If they wax and prosper, he feels "triumphant"; if they dwindle and die away, he feels cast down—not necessarily in the same degree for each thing but in much the same way for all.*[43]

Even today our possessions act as public symbols of our values, status, and financial success, informing others of our identity and reinforcing our own sense of self.[44]

Our possessions act as public symbols of our values, status, and financial success, informing others of our identity and reinforcing our own sense of self.

Figure 5.2 Linear Perspective and Meaning

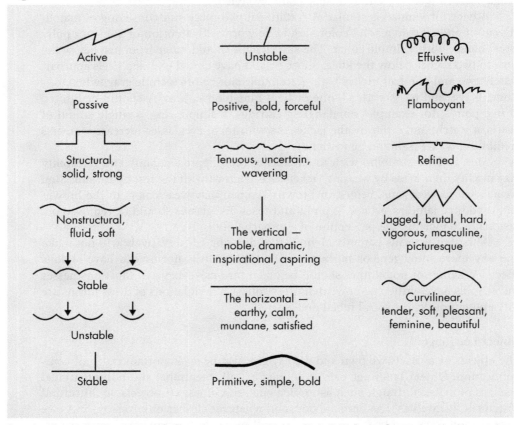

From *Landscape Architecture* by J. O. Simonds, copyright 1961, New York: F. W. Dodge Corporation. Used by permission of McGraw-Hill Book Company.

Nowhere is our status so clearly displayed as in the buildings we construct. From the outside, the look of a building tells people what to wear, how to act, who is allowed in, and what services they can expect. Once inside, interior design elements give off additional messages. Burgoon and Saine list a number of factors that affect communication in **built environments**. In addition to furniture arrangement (which we have already discussed), Burgoon and Saine cite size, shape, and texture of materials, linear perspective, lighting, color, temperature, noise, and sensory stimulation as important communicative factors.[45]

In terms of *size*, massive spaces create a sense of awe, whereas smaller spaces are cozier and more comfortable. Of course, if spaces are too small, we can feel cornered. The size of furnishings within spaces also sends messages. Large furniture (for example, a massive desk with a high-back swivel chair) often indicates power. The boss's and the secretary's desks are usually not the same size. The *materials* used to decorate a room can affect mood and comfort level. Rough surfaces give an effect different from smooth ones; softness invites us to relax, whereas hardness makes us more tense. A hard-edged modern office with highly polished metal furniture creates an atmosphere very different from a more traditional, wood-paneled room with leather-upholstered furniture.

Linear perspective refers to the ways in which lines created by walls or furnishings relate to one another. Figure 5.2 illustrates the meanings that can be created by different linear perspectives.

Lighting can vary our perception of the size of a room, as well as make us want to linger or to escape. A restaurant that wants to encourage leisurely dining usually uses muted lighting, whereas a restaurant designed for high volume and quick turnover uses harsher, brighter light. *Color* also affects moods; cool colors (such as blues and greens) are relaxing, whereas warm colors (reds, oranges, and yellows) are more stimulating. Colors also carry symbolic value. Most men would think twice before painting their dens pink, because pink is considered a feminine color.

Temperature and *noise* can either increase or decrease tension and irritability, as can the overall level of *sensory stimulation*. Environments must strike a balance between satisfying the needs for novelty and excitement and the need for consistency and stability.

INCREASING NONVERBAL SKILLS

This chapter has emphasized the importance of being aware of and making effective use of the unspoken languages available to us. In this last section, we'll look at a few ways to improve nonverbal skills.

The first lesson we should learn is to *be cautious in interpreting nonverbal messages*. Most of us share the folk belief that it is possible to read another person like a book if we are sensitive to that person's nonverbal behavior. Most of us have our own theories about what to look for to judge another's character, and we use these theories as a kind of early warning device to avoid unpleasant interactions. That we never stop to test these stereotypes seldom bothers us. Yet many of our most cherished nonverbal stereotypes are false. It's important to remember that nonverbal behaviors can have many different meanings. When Anne crosses her arms over her chest, she may be inadvertently indicating a need to protect herself from contact, or she may simply find that posture comfortable. When Larry's eyes shift during a conversation, he may be lying, he may be nervous, or he may have been distracted by some extraneous stimulus.

It is not a good idea to read deep meaning into every gesture, yet it is important to *give proper attention to nonverbal cues*. Just as some people seem too sensitive to nonverbal cues, others seem completely insensitive. People will sometimes tell us nonverbally what they will not tell us with words, and we should not ignore those silent messages. Jim, for example, never seemed to notice other people's leave-taking cues. As a consequence, his employees didn't know how to get out of a conversation with him. The usual nonverbal cues—glancing toward the door, looking at one's watch, making small movements of escape—were always ignored, while more overt methods (such as saying, "Jim, stop talking. I'm leaving now") seemed too rude. The problem was so bad that people who were scheduled to have a meeting with Jim would often ask a friend to phone Jim a half hour into the meeting. When Jim would stop to pick up the phone, the employee would sneak out the door. Although this fact-based example may be extreme, it nevertheless illustrates that some people aren't very sensitive to nonverbals. If you're the kind of person who needs to have things spelled out, if you're often the last person to figure out what everyone else seems to know, then you may not be paying enough attention to nonverbal communication.

> People will sometimes tell us nonverbally what they will not tell us with words, and we should not ignore those silent messages.

In addition to becoming more aware of others' messages, you should also *become aware of the messages you may be inadvertently sending*. As we've seen, people jump to conclusions about nonverbal behavior. And if they form judgments about other people in this way, you can bet that they also form judgments about you. Remember that what you do is as important as—and sometimes more important than—what you say. We're used to considering our words but much less used to monitoring our nonverbals. Think about the ways in which you habitually use all of the nonverbal codes. Some of these ways will be obvious to you, but others will not. Most people check out their clothes in a mirror, but fewer are aware of vocal habits, and still fewer stop to think about their use of space and time. If you're not sure what messages you're sending, ask someone you trust to give you feedback.

It's also wise to *remember that nonverbals you consider to be perfectly innocent can be invasive and even threatening to others*. When we stare at people, enter their personal space, use objects that belong to them, or make them wait for us, we may be offending them in ways we scarcely realize. That these things don't bother us doesn't mean that they don't bother others. And the potential for inadvertently committing offense is compounded whenever cultural differences exist. Take the time to find out the nonverbal meanings of others, and try to respect those meanings.

The silent messages that make up the nonverbal codes are subtle and are easily misinterpreted. Yet they are powerful modes of communication, and complete communicators are as aware of their own nonverbal messages as they are of their spoken words. If we overlook nonverbal communication, we overlook a world of meaning.

SUMMARY

Although language is an important source of human messages, words are not our only means of communication. Messages can be encoded nonverbally. In this chapter, we have looked at the nature and purpose of nonverbal communication and at the codes that make up the nonverbal system. Nonverbal communication occurs whenever a stimulus other than words creates meaning. This broad definition includes virtually all meaningful human behavior, whether intentional or not. Because behavior can convey a variety of meanings, we should be careful in interpreting nonverbal communication to remain aware of context, to compare current to baseline behavior, and to ask for verbal feedback to clear up misunderstandings.

Nonverbal communication is unique. It is often unintentional; it consists of multiple codes; it is immediate, continuous, and natural; and it may carry universal meaning. Nonverbal communication is particularly useful when direct verbal communication is socially inappropriate or difficult (e.g., when making initial judgments; when conveying relational messages of liking, status, and responsiveness; or when expressing emotion). Nonverbal communication can also expand upon, clarify, or even contradict verbal messages.

Body movement and gesture make up the first of the nonverbal codes. We use a variety of kinesic cues, including emblems, illustrators, regulators, affect displays, and adaptors. All are potential sources of nonverbal meaning. Facial displays are another important nonverbal code. People in every culture learn to modify and to manage facial expressions by following cultural, professional, or personal display rules, and each of us develops our own display style. The eyes are a particularly important part of the face. They can signal positive and negative emotions and attraction, and they are often used as cues to character. The voice is a third nonverbal code. Paralanguage includes

not only the quality of the voice but also the sounds we make and the pauses and fillers we add to our talk. Even silence can communicate.

The dimensions of time and space are rich sources of meaning. Chronemics includes the study of psychological time orientation (how we think about and experience the past, present, and future), biological time orientation (how biological clocks govern our lives), and cultural time orientation (social rules for managing time). Proxemics is the study of space. One important aspect of proxemics is territoriality. We humans need to own and control a variety of territories (public, home, interaction, and body). When these spaces are threatened, we feel compelled to defend them. This is especially true of personal space; every society has implicit rules regulating personal closeness and touch, to convey both emotional and power messages.

A final nonverbal code consists of physical appearance and object language. The way we look and dress and the objects we display affect not only the way others see us but also the way we see ourselves. For many, self-concept is tied to appearance and possessions.

With all of its complexity, the nonverbal system is a powerful source of information as well as a powerful source of misunderstanding. It is important to become more aware of our own and others' silent messages.

KEY TERMS

Listed below are the key terms used in this chapter, along with the number of the page where each is explained.

nonverbal communication (99)	kinesics (107)	professional display rules (111)
liking (104)	illustrators (108)	personal display rules (111)
status (104)	regulators (108)	paralinguistics (112)
responsiveness (104)	affect displays (108)	vocal qualities (112)
interaction management (106)	adaptors (109)	vocalizations (112)
	facial displays (110)	vocal segregates (112)
	cultural display rules (110)	

SUGGESTED READING

Ekman, Paul. (2007). *Emotions revealed: Recognizing faces and feelings to improve communication and emotional life* (2nd ed.). New York: Holt/Owl Books.

> An examination of the ways in which people express and control emotional displays; written by one of the foremost researchers in nonverbal communication.

Guerrero, Laura K., & Hecht, Michael. (2007). *The nonverbal communication reader*. Long Grove, IL: Waveland, Press.

> A collection of readings on a wide range of topics including body image, the role of perfume in perception, the power of silence, and nonverbal social norms in virtual environments.

Knapp, Mark L., & Hall, Judith A. (2009). *Nonverbal communication in human interaction* (7th ed.). Belmont, CA: Wadsworth Publishing.

> A comprehensive and popular review of research and theory on nonverbal communication.

Manusov, Valerie, & Patterson, Miles L. (2006). *The Sage handbook of nonverbal communication*. Thousand Oaks, CA: Sage.

> A comprehensive overview of the field presented in a series of chapters written by nonverbal scholars.

Interpersonal Communication

O ur survival as social beings depends in large part on our interpersonal communication skills.

It is easy to underemphasize the importance of everyday communication. Whereas public speakers often deal with issues of national importance and members of decision-making groups often design important new products, members of interpersonal dyads tend to spend their time in what seem to be less significant pursuits: gossiping, joking, or simply passing the time. Viewed in this light, interpersonal communication hardly seems to be a topic worthy of serious study.

The goal of this chapter is to show you that interpersonal communication is far from insignificant. It is, in fact, the most frequently used and, arguably, the most important form of communication humans undertake. It's possible to make it through life without ever giving a public speech or joining any decision-making group. None of us, however, can avoid interpersonal communication. In fact, our survival as social beings depends in large part on our interpersonal communication skills.

In this chapter, we look at how the everyday exchanges that make up interpersonal communication shape our lives. After defining interpersonal communication, we look at some of the problems that can affect interpersonal interactions; examine the stages in building interpersonal relationships; and review some basic skills that can enhance communication in everyday life.

WHAT IS INTERPERSONAL COMMUNICATION?

In a sense, all communication is interpersonal, because all communication occurs between people. The term **interpersonal communication**, however, was originally coined to refer to two-person, face-to-face interaction. It is often used interchangeably with the term **dyadic communication**. Since the advent of the Internet and other forms of digital communication, we have come to realize that interpersonal communication frequently occurs in mediated forms as

After reading this chapter, you should be able to:

- Explain the relationship between interpersonal communication and psychological-level rules.
- List some of the reasons people build dyads.
- Describe the three dialectics that must be balanced in interpersonal relationships.
- Understand how threats to face and disconfirmations affect relationships.
- Explain what can happen when individuals experience rigid role relationships, paradoxes, and spirals.
- Identify the stages in Knapp's relational developmental model and relate them to the social penetration model.
- List some of the cues that affect interpersonal attraction.
- Name ways people can use self-disclosure effectively and identify ways of responding to others' disclosures.
- Name five conflict styles and describe when each should be used.
- Explain some of the ways people can give each other feedback effectively.
- Discuss how new technologies affect interpersonal communication.
- Consider the ethical implications of interpersonal communication.

> **Compared to other forms of communication, dyadic communication has several unique characteristics. It is direct, personal, immediate, spontaneous, and informal.**

well. Whenever we tell a joke to a friend, ask a professor a question, succumb to a sales pitch, text our plans to a family member, IM a classmate, or express our love to a romantic partner, we are engaging in interpersonal communication. Compared to other forms of communication, dyadic communication has several unique characteristics. It is direct, personal, immediate, spontaneous, and informal.

Characteristics of Dyadic Communication

The first characteristic that distinguishes the dyadic context from other communication contexts is its *directness*. We can hide in the back of a classroom or make ourselves unobtrusive in a committee meeting, but when we communicate, either face-to-face or electronically, with one other person, we cannot let others speak for us. Because we are in such direct contact, dyadic communication is also very *personal*. Public speakers cannot adapt to every audience member's specific needs. Dyadic communicators, on the other hand, can get to know one another more intimately. They can adapt their contributions to their partner's intellect and interests.

Dyadic interaction is more *immediate* than other forms of communication because the quality of feedback is potentially high. As a member of a face-to-face dyad, we can instantly sense when our partner is losing interest, can note when we are speaking too rapidly or too slowly, and can correct ourselves on the spot if our partner looks confused or puzzled. When our interpersonal communication is asynchronous, as in a text, we expect to receive feedback in a timely manner and are often annoyed when our text is not returned immediately. In other communication contexts, feedback is less immediate.

Compared to other kinds of communication, dyadic communication is the most *spontaneous*. Members of dyads rarely, if ever, outline and rehearse what they will say to each other; public speakers almost always do. Finally, whereas communication in other contexts is often characterized by formal role relations that signal a communicative division of labor, in dyads the roles of speaker and listener are usually *informal*.

Are All Dyads Interpersonal?

For many scholars, the defining characteristic of interpersonal communication is that it occurs between two people. This view suggests that all dyads are equally interpersonal. But are they? Is the communication between a clerk and a customer in a busy store interpersonal in the same way as the communication between a parent and a child or between two best friends? Does the quality of communication stay the same as partners get to know one another? A number of scholars say "No." They believe that dyadic communication and interpersonal communication are not the same thing. According to those who take a **developmental approach** to interpersonal communication, something special must occur to turn ordinary, impersonal, dyadic interaction into interpersonal communication. When the rules governing the relationship, the amount of data communicators have about one another, and the communicators' level of knowledge change, dyadic communication becomes interpersonal.

Gerald Miller and Mark Steinberg argue that communication is governed by rules that tell us how to communicate with one another.[1] **Cultural-level rules** are general and apply to all of the members of a particular culture. We use cultural-level rules with people we do not know well. When we greet strangers, for example, we follow rules that tell us to use polite, fairly formal forms of

Relationships can be troublesome, but they give us support when life gets risky.

Courtesy of the author

address. We usually nod, shake hands, and say something such as, "Hello, how are you?" Our choice of topics is limited. With strangers, we talk about the weather, sports, or current events, not about personal concerns and fears.

When we interact with people who belong to specific groups within our culture, we use **sociological-level rules**, rules that are tied to group membership. When college students greet each other, informal modes of address, such as "What's up?" are preferred. Topics concern classes, upcoming social activities, and campus events. Each of the many groups we belong to employs a slightly different set of communication rules.

Finally, when we interact with people we know quite well, we abandon the sociological rules and move to the use of **psychological-level rules**. We make up the rules ourselves. Part of the joy of being in a close relationship is the knowledge that we are free to break everyday rules. Friends, for example, may greet each other with hugs, screams of delight, or mock blows. They may even insult one another. They use behaviors that would never do with strangers, because in the course of their relationship they have made these behaviors their own. With our close friends, we can talk about very personal and emotional matters, topics we would hesitate to mention to people we don't know well.

> **Part of the joy of being in a close relationship is the knowledge that we are free to break everyday rules.**

As we get to know one another, our sources of information also deepen. When we interact at the cultural level, we have very little data to go on. As we become more familiar, however, we can understand our partners better because we know about their attitudes and values. We begin to recognize when they are happy or upset or hiding their feelings. We pick up on cues that would not be obvious to outsiders. As a result, our level of knowledge deepens. Now, not only can we describe our partners'

© John Henley/CORBIS

Dyads provide us with comfort and support. With friends we don't have to worry about putting on a front; we can relax and be ourselves.

behaviors, but we can predict and explain them as well.

Miller and Steinberg argue that interpersonal communication is a type of dyadic communication in which partners negotiate rules, are willing to exchange information openly, and have extensive personal knowledge of one another.[2] Interpersonal communication occurs over time, as partners put effort and energy into building a personal relationship. For Miller and Steinberg, dyads start off as impersonal; only a few undergo the changes that make them interpersonal.

Why Do We Build Dyads?

In the movie *Annie Hall*, the narrator, Alvie Singer, tells a joke about a man whose uncle had convinced himself he was a chicken. When asked why the family didn't send his uncle to a psychiatrist, the man replies, "We would have, but we needed the eggs." Singer goes on to explain that that's how he feels about relationships. No matter how "totally irrational and crazy and absurd" they are; we keep going through them "because most of us need the eggs."[3] Singer understands that relationships can be difficult, but he also understands that they serve us well. Among the many other things they do, dyads give us security in an often insecure world, tell us who we are, and allow us to maintain our self-esteem.

We choose our friends in part because they tell us it is okay to be the person we want to be.

One reason we form dyads is that *without interpersonal relationships, we would fail to thrive*. Recent studies have found a surprising connection between interpersonal relationships and physical and mental health. Dyads, it turns out, "have major effects on immune, cardiovascular, and neurotransmitter systems."[4] Children raised in isolation or in threatening environments, for example, are likely to develop stress-related illnesses and suffer depression in later life.

We also form dyads because *interpersonal relationships help us develop stable self-concepts*. Our sense of self is a product of the approval and disapproval of those with whom we come in contact. To use Charles Horton Cooley's metaphor, the appraisals of others act as a kind of mirror, reflecting back to us our **looking-glass self**.[5] The other people in our lives show us ways to live and teach us who to be. They validate our perceptions of ourselves and our social worlds. We choose our friends in part because they tell us it is okay to be the person we want to be. In this sense, "friendship is the purest illustration of picking one's propaganda."[6]

Finally, *interpersonal relationships offer us comfort and support.* In an often insecure world, knowing that we have someone to turn to when things get bad provides a feeling of security. To cope with everyday life, we need to make connections with others.

MANAGING INTERPERSONAL COMMUNICATION

Although close relationships bring enormous benefits, they also involve costs. In joining a relationship, individuals take on duties and responsibilities that can leave them feeling stressed. In this section, we look at some of the inevitable tensions of relational life. We begin by reviewing three dialectical forces that must be balanced if relationships are to be successful. We then discuss the need to acknowledge and protect identity needs. Finally, we look at some of the dysfunctional patterns that can beset dyads. As we shall see, all of these problems arise through, and are resolved by, interpersonal communication.

Balancing Interpersonal Tensions

A number of authors, including Leslie Baxter and William Rawlins, have written about the tensions that beset individuals as they try to balance the demands of a relationship and their own personal needs.[7] Individuals must face three sets of tensions as they decide how much of themselves to invest in relationships. These are called the expressive–protective, the autonomy–togetherness, and the novelty–predictability dialectics.

The **expressive–protective dialectic** involves finding a balance between the need to share personal information and the need to maintain privacy. When we become close to someone, we have a natural desire to share our thoughts and feelings with that person. Close relationships are built on shared information, and we usually expect a high level of self-disclosure (the voluntary revealing of information that would normally be unobtainable) in interpersonal relationships.

On the other hand, we can feel very uncomfortable when others ask for information that is too personal. Just as we have a need to be open, we have a need to keep some of our thoughts and feelings to ourselves. The problem of how much information to reveal and how much to keep private must be negotiated by every couple. Managing self-disclosure is a basic interpersonal skill, one we will return to later in the chapter when we discuss ways of increasing relational competence.

> Just as we have a need to be open, we have a need to keep some of our thoughts and feelings to ourselves.

A second dialectic is the **autonomy–togetherness dialectic**. Here, friends and couples decide how interdependent they want to be. This problem is often experienced by first-semester college roommates. Some people come to school expecting to spend all their time with their roommates. Others feel overwhelmed by too much closeness. Of course, roommates are not the only people to feel this tension. Dating and married couples must also decide on the proper level of autonomy and togetherness. William Wilmot points out that

> some of the "craziness" and unpredictability in close, intimate relations comes from the oscillations between autonomy and interdependence. As we get farther away, we miss the other, and when we feel at "one" with the other, we sense a loss of the self.[8]

The only way to resolve this tension is to realize that others' needs may differ from our own and to talk about our feelings openly as soon as they become a problem.

Finally, partners must resolve the **novelty–predictability dialectic**. On the one hand, as individuals interact, they fall into patterns of behavior. After a time, these behaviors become predictable, and the couple spends much of their time repeating old routines. Obviously, a certain amount of predictability is necessary for coordinated activity. A long-term relationship couldn't sustain itself at the level of uncertainty found in a developing relationship.

On the other hand, when behavior gets too patterned, partners can feel bored, and everyday interaction can become flat and stale. After all, relationships do not occur in a vacuum; they occur in a constantly changing world. Relationships that aren't open to change may become obsolete. Therefore, every couple must spend some time adapting to changing conditions and finding new ways to interact. The novelty–predictability dialectic is a matter of finding ways to balance the familiar and the new.

It's important to remember that over time, relationships change. Small children are dependent on their parents, but during adolescence, older children strive to become more autonomous. Both child and parent must adapt to the changing shape of their relationship and must make adjustments according to the "cultural" rules they follow. Likewise, competent communicators must be willing and able to negotiate new relational understandings as time goes by.

Respecting Identity and Protecting Face

Communication is inherently risky. There is always the chance that others may not like us or may not see us as we want to be seen. Several communication scholars have directed their attention to describing what happens when we experience rejection. In this section we will examine the relationship between communication and identity first by looking at the concept of face, and then by describing ways we may inadvertently cause others to feel disconfirmed.

Approval and Autonomy: Balancing Face Needs

One way to think about the effects of communication on identity is to consider the significance of face. **Face** is the "conception of self that each person displays in particular interactions with others."[9] It is the person we try to be when we are with other people. Because having one's sense of self questioned or rejected is painful and disheartening, communicators must make efforts to honor and support each other's face needs. Penelope Brown and Stephen Levinson argue that we have two face-related needs.[10] We need to be respected and accepted by others and we need to feel we are free to control our own lives. The first of these face needs is called *positive face*; it is threatened whenever people criticize or disagree with us. The second face need is called *negative face*; it is threatened whenever others impose on our autonomy. Assume, for example, that you disagree with a friend and want to convince her she is wrong. This act can threaten her positive face (after all, you are disapproving of her current views) as well as her negative face (you are attempting to control and change her behavior). In order to communicate effectively, you need to recognize that your behavior is potentially face threatening and find a polite way to balance your need to persuade and your duty to support your friend's face. Instead of saying, "Your views are absurd; you can't really do that," you might instead say, "You know I respect you, but in this case I can't agree. I know you'll make up your own mind, but I hope you'll consider my position." The latter choice diminishes threats to face and keeps the relationship on an even keel. Politeness, then, is more than a social nicety. It is a way of acknowledging others' identities and saving face.

Giving advice, asking favors, enforcing obligations, and refusing requests are common communication activities that have the potential to threaten participants' social selves. So too are attempts to initiate, intensify, or terminate relationships. All necessitate careful attention to the face needs of both self and others.[11]

Disconfirmation

One way to respect face is to avoid **disconfirmations**, rejecting messages that leave recipients with a diminished sense of self-respect. Evelyn Sieburg argues that whenever we communicate we present ourselves to others. Their responses can either confirm our sense of self or can make us feel diminished and rejected. She identifies seven ways in which we can (sometimes unknowingly) disconfirm one another.[12] These are shown in Table 6.1. The first occurs when one partner ignores the other. A parent who is too busy reading the paper to listen to a child's story is giving an *impervious response*. The message is, "You are not worth noticing." A second way people disconfirm one another is by giving an *interrupting response*. An interruption is a move that sends the message, "You are not worth listening to." Occasionally, we encounter people who burst into conversations and immediately change the subject to something that has absolutely no bearing on what was said before. This is an example of an *irrelevant response*. A variation on this pattern is the *tangential response*, wherein an individual briefly acknowledges the topic but then goes on to discuss his or her own interests. Both responses send the message, "My concerns are more important than yours are."

Impersonal responses are also disconfirming. The person who uses stilted, formal, distant language is signaling, "I feel uncomfortable being close to you." Another response that indicates a desire to escape from interaction is the *incoherent response*. When someone seems embarrassed and tongue-tied, he or she says, in effect, "I feel uncomfortable with you." A final way to disconfirm a partner is by sending *incongruous responses*, messages wherein the verbal and nonverbal cues don't match. These double messages imply, "I don't want to deal with you directly and openly."

Most people are disconfirming from time to time. Out of carelessness or irritation, we may use one of the responses just described. An occasional lapse is not necessarily problematic. However, if disconfirmations become habitual, they can destroy others' self-esteem and can severely damage relationships.

Avoiding Dysfunctional Patterns

In the process of working out the general shape of their relationship, individuals create specific patterns of interaction. Unfortunately, these patterns often go unnoticed. When relationships run into trouble, partners rarely analyze their behavior patterns.

Table 6.1 Some Examples of Disconfirming Messages

Listed below are some examples of disconfirming conversations and the implicit messages they carry. Can you identify the kind of disconfirmation illustrated?

Conversation 1
　A: "Hi!"
　B: (Continues reading, ignoring A)

Implicit message: You don't count.

Conversation 2
　A: So I said. . . .
　B: "Gotta go. Bye!"

Implicit message: You are unimportant to me.

Conversation 3
　A: "He really hurt me."
　B: "Do you like my coat?"

Implicit message: You aren't important to me.

Conversation 4
　A: "He really hurt me."
　B: "Too bad. You know I got dumped last year . . ."

Implicit message: My concerns are more important than yours.

Conversation 5
　A: "I don't understand."
　B: "The dependent variables are isomorphic . . ."

Implicit message: I don't care enough to make myself clear.

Conversation 6
　A: "Do you love me?"
　B: "Well, gosh, er, I mean, well . . ."

Implicit message: I'm uncomfortable and don't want to have this conversation.

Conversation 7
　A: "Do you love me?"
　B: Sure. (Said in a bored, offhand way)

Answers: 1: impervious; 2: interrupting; 3: irrelevant; 4: tangential; 5: impersonal; 6: incoherent; 7: incongruous

Instead, they each place the blame on the other's character or personality. This is unfortunate because although patterns can be changed, people usually can't.

Dysfunctional patterns—especially our own—are often difficult to describe. We are so used to them that they become invisible to us. Yet with a little effort and a willingness to be objective, we can begin to identify and correct problematic behaviors. In the next section, we look at some common dysfunctional communication patterns. In particular, we look at what happens when partners fall into rigid role relationships, become the victims of paradoxes, and get swept away by spirals.

Rigid Role Relations

Over time, one of the major relational themes that partners address is *dominance*. Partners must distribute power within the relationship. Each must decide whether he or she feels more comfortable playing a dominant part, or **one-up role**, or a more submissive part, or **one-down role**. Although some couples share power equally, relationships often fall into one of two patterns: complementary or symmetrical.

In a **complementary pattern**, one partner takes the one-up position and the other takes the one-down. Parents and their children generally have a complementary relationship. The parent controls the child, making most of the decisions and exerting most of the influence. For the most part, the child complies, although occasional temper tantrums show the child's dissatisfaction with the one-down role.

This division of relational labor has an advantage: decisions can be made rapidly and easily. Problems occur, however, when complementarity becomes too rigid. When the submissive partner begins to resent always giving in or when the dominant partner begins to tire of being in charge, dissatisfaction can result.

The second common pattern is the **symmetrical pattern**. In *competitive symmetry*, both members fight for the one-up position. Although there are times (for example, when two athletes train together) when competition can encourage both members to do their best, in typical relationships this pattern can be stressful and frustrating and can take its toll on the patience of the partners. In *submissive symmetry*, both parties struggle to relinquish control. If you and a friend have ever spent all night deciding where to eat ("I don't care, you decide." "No, anything's okay with me; you decide"), you have experienced the problems associated with submissive symmetry. This is an especially interesting pattern, because it is paradoxical. Although both partners ostensibly avoid control, each does his or her best to control the other by forcing the other to make the decision.

Complementary or symmetrical patterns can occasionally be satisfying, but they can also take over a relationship and limit partners' options. Partners can feel trapped by a pattern they hardly realize they have created. Learning how to share the one-up and one-down positions gives a couple the flexibility they need to adapt to changing circumstances.

Paradoxes

Couples sometimes fall into the habit of sending one another contradictory messages. These kinds of double messages are called **paradoxes**. For example, we may make statements such as "I know you'll do well, but don't worry if you fail" or "I don't mind if you go camping this weekend; it doesn't matter if I'm lonely and miserable." These kinds of responses are confusing and annoying, and they place the receiver in an awkward position.

Another, and a potentially more serious, form of paradox is the **double bind**. A double bind is a particularly strong and enduring paradoxical communication wherein the receiver is simultaneously given two opposing messages but is prohibited from resolving them. When a parent says to a child, "Come give me a hug," but recoils in disgust when the child approaches, the parent is delivering a double message. The child has no way to do the right thing. Over a long period of time, double binds can damage a partner's sense of rationality and self-esteem.

Spirals

The final dysfunctional pattern we will look at is the **spiral**. In a spiral, one partner's behavior intensifies that of the other. William Wilmot gives an amusing example of how spirals can escalate:

> My son Jason at age three saw a sleek, shiny cat. With the reckless abandon of a child his age, he rushed at the cat to pet it. The wise cat, seeing potential death, moved out of Jason's reach. Not to be outdone, Jason tried harder. The cat moved farther away. Jason started running after the cat. The cat, no dummy, ran too. In a short ten seconds from the initial lunge at the cat, Jason and the cat were running at full tilt.[13]

Internet fights that sweep through a high school progressively involving more and more students are another example. Spirals can also happen to couples. In some spirals, called *progressive spirals*, the partners' behaviors lead to increasing levels of involvement and satisfaction. Claudine shows trust in Michele, who decides to earn that trust by working hard. Michele's hard work earns her more trust, and so on; over time, Claudine and Michele's relationship becomes stronger. Unfortunately, not all spirals are positive. When misunderstanding leads to more misunderstanding, eventually damaging a relationship, partners have established what is called a *regressive spiral*. Leslie begins to suspect Toby of being unfaithful. Toby becomes defensive and denies being in the wrong, but the denials only increase Leslie's suspicions. Finally, figuring, "If I'm going to be blamed, I might as well get something out of it," Toby actually is unfaithful. The relationship has spiraled out of control, and, in the process, Leslie and Toby have created an **interpersonal self-fulfilling prophecy**. Leslie's original prophecy (that Toby could not be trusted) has become true.

What can be done to stop spirals? In many cases, the partners need only sit down with one another and analyze the situation to determine what triggered the spiral and how it got out of control. In other cases, if the spiral has gone too far, the partners may need to turn to an objective third party who can help them describe their behaviors

> The key to dealing with spirals is the same as that for dealing with any relational problem: partners must focus on patterns rather than on personalities.

objectively and without defensiveness. The key to dealing with spirals is the same as that for dealing with any relational problem: partners must focus on patterns rather than on personalities.

RELATIONAL DEVELOPMENT: STAGES IN INTIMATE DYADS

Relationships are in a constant state of flux. Over time, couples redefine themselves, moving toward and away from deeper involvement. In an attempt to understand more about the ways in which relationships change, several theorists have looked for global patterns of relational development. Although these theorists recognize that each couple's relational journey is slightly different, they have nonetheless attempted to chart the paths that couples take into and out of intimacy.[14] In this section, we examine two aspects of this journey. We begin with one of the most widely known of the relational stage models, Mark Knapp's relational development model. We then consider some of the factors that lead couples to become attracted to one another in the first place, reviewing Steve Duck's filtering theory of attraction.

Paths to and from Intimacy

Mark Knapp provides us with a ten-step model of the way relationships grow and dissolve. These steps are summarized in Figure 6.1.

The Journey Toward Intimacy

The first of the **relational development stages** occurs during a couple's initial encounter as communicators and is known as the *initiating stage*. In this stage, partners work to create a favorable initial impression; observe cues about personality, attitudes, and willingness to engage in further interactions; and look for ways to open communication channels. Communication tends to be cautious, and topics are relatively shallow as individuals use tried-and-true opening lines and conventional formulas to initiate conversation.

If all goes well and initial evaluations are positive, a couple moves on to the *experimenting stage*. Here, partners search for common ground on which to begin to build their relationship. Communication at this stage consists primarily of small talk. Although the talk may be small, it is not unimportant, for it uncovers topics for further conversation, gives individuals information that reduces their uncertainty about one another, and allows them to reveal their personalities. Communication at stage two is generally relaxed, uncritical, noncommittal, and somewhat ambiguous.

> Experimenting-stage communication uncovers topics for further conversation, gives individuals information that reduces their uncertainty about one another, and allows them to reveal their personalities.

Most relationships stop somewhere in stage two, but others move on to the *intensifying stage*. Here, individuals make initial moves toward greater involvement. Self-disclosure increases, and the use of nicknames and terms of endearment becomes more common. Inclusive pronouns such as *we* and *us* begin to be used,

Figure 6.1 **Knapp's Relational Development Model**

Stages in Coming Together

Initiating
Experimenting
Intensifying
Integrating
Bonding

Stages in Coming Apart

Differentiating
Circumscribing
Stagnating
Avoiding
Terminating

Stages are described in *Interpersonal Communication and Human Relationships,* 2nd ed. by Mark L. Knapp and Anita L. Vangelisti, 1992, Boston: Allyn and Bacon, pp. 35–45.

as do tentative expressions of commitment and private symbols for shared experiences. Finally, as partners become more familiar with each other's verbal and nonverbal styles, they start to use verbal shortcuts and may even complete each other's thoughts. In this stage, satisfaction and excitement are high.

In the *integrating stage*, the individuals become a couple both in their own and in others' eyes. Attitudes and interests are shared, and social circles merge. As body rhythms synchronize, partners may even begin to talk and move in similar ways. Shared experiences and artifacts become personalized, and a couple can be overheard talking about "our" restaurant or "our" song. Finally, partners may exchange **intimacy trophies**. By wearing the other's athletic jacket or by displaying the other's picture, partners signal to the rest of the world their official status as a couple. This perception of unity is often reinforced by friends or acquaintances who now think of the partners as halves of a whole, and who may show their approval or disapproval of the relationship.

For the couple, the loss of individual identity that comes with integrating may be welcome or upsetting. Knapp emphasizes the fact that *as we participate in the integration process, we are intensifying and minimizing various aspects of our total person. As a result, we may not be fully conscious of the idea but when we commit ourselves to integrating with another, we also agree to become another individual.*[15]

With commitment often comes insecurity. An individual may wonder whether his or her partner is truly involved in the relationship and may (either consciously or subconsciously) use **secret tests** to measure the other's commitment. Leslie Baxter and William Wilmot discuss four of these secret tests: indirect suggestions, separation tests, endurance tests, and triangle tests.[16]

The secret test of *indirect suggestion* includes flirting and joking about the seriousness of the relationship. They let partners observe each other's response. If, for example, a comment on living together is greeted with laughter, this shows that the relationship is not intensifying. If the comment is taken

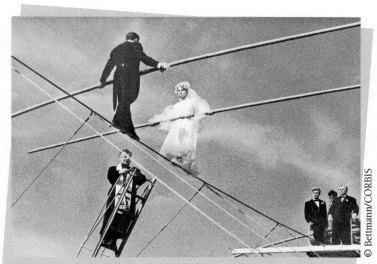

Maintaining relationships requires balance and coordination.

© Bettmann/CORBIS

seriously, however, this response indicates that commitment is high. *Separation tests* let individuals see how their partners feel about being apart. It's not a good sign if one's partner doesn't even notice a week-long absence. Daily phone calls, on the other hand, indicate strong commitment. *Endurance tests* involve making demands on the time or energy of one's partner; they show individuals just how far a partner is willing to go to maintain the relationship. Finally, individuals use *triangle tests* to see whether or not their partners are prone to jealousy. Although secret tests are frequently used, they are not necessarily good for a relationship, and they can easily backfire.

> **Throughout the entire journey toward intimacy, partners expand the boundaries of their relationship.**

Once all tests are passed and both parties are sure of their feelings, they move on to the *bonding stage.* Bonding consists of a public ritual to legitimize the relationship. Romantic couples may bond through marriage or commitment ceremonies. Friends may bond by exchanging friendship rings. Even groups can bond, as when social clubs initiate new members. In any case, bonding rituals officially legitimize the relationship and, in subtle and not-so-subtle ways, change participants' attitudes toward and feelings about one another.

Figure 6.2 **Social Penetration: Relational Depth and Breadth**

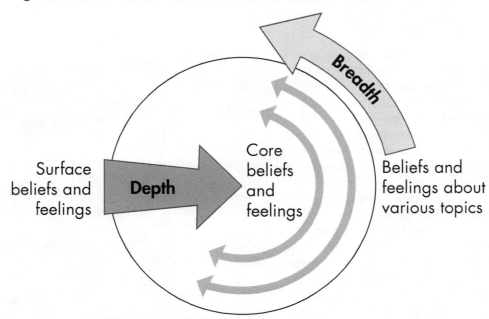

The original social penetration model was developed in *Social Penetration: The Development of Interpersonal Relationships,* by Irwin Altman and Dalmas A. Taylor, 1973, New York: Holt, Rinehart and Winston.

Throughout the entire journey toward intimacy, partners expand the boundaries of their relationship. According to Irwin Altman and Dalmas Taylor, relationships grow in breadth and depth as time progresses.[17] Figure 6.2 illustrates this idea. To expand **relational breadth**, individuals progressively share more aspects of themselves and communicate about more topics. To increase **relational depth**, they let their partners get closer to their core identities. For Altman and Taylor, the process of relational development is a matter of social penetration.

If the relationship lasts, partners continue to share intimate ideas and emotions. If the relationship cannot stand up to internal or external stresses, however, it gradually weakens; patterns of communication narrow and become more shallow, and the relationship starts to break apart. Figure 6.1 illustrates the **relational dissolution stages**.

The Retreat from Intimacy

In the retreat from intimacy, a couple emphasizes differences rather than similarities. In the first or *differentiating stage*, a couple begins to notice and comment on previously overlooked disparities. Instead of using the pronouns *we* and *us*, they begin to talk about "you" and "me." Arguments may be prefaced by comments such as "I don't understand how you could possibly like her" or "I can't believe you agree with him." Overt argument and conflict are hallmarks of this stage. One reason for differentiation is that bonding may have taken place too rapidly, before the partners were able to negotiate a satisfactory relational culture.

Short periods of differentiation occur in all relationships. By reaffirming relational goals and focusing on similarities, partners may reverse their movement away from intimacy. Sometimes, however, differentiation leads to the second stage of relational breakdown, the *circumscribing stage*. In this stage, members carefully restrict their communication. Certain topics are placed off limits because they are too painful. "Let's just skip it" or "I'd rather not discuss that" indicate that communication has become a minefield of potentially explosive topics. As a result, very little information is exchanged, and expressions of commitment decrease.

In a failing relationship, the next stage is the *stagnating stage*. This stage is characterized by silence and inactivity. Communication is infrequent, and when it occurs, it is stylized, rigid, and awkward. Talk may be overly formal and polite, with negative emotions being conveyed nonverbally. One might think that this uncomfortable stage cannot last long. Unfortunately, a couple may stagnate for months or even years.

In the *avoiding stage*, partners separate either physically or emotionally. In a dating situation, one partner may suddenly stop answering the phone or disappear for weeks at a time. In a marriage, one spouse may spend more time at the office or visit relatives for the summer. If physical separation is impossible, couples may isolate themselves psychologically, behaving as though the other does not exist.

The final stage in relational disengagement is the *terminating stage*. If both parties are aware that their relationship is dissolving, termination may come as a relief. In other cases, it may be a heart-wrenching surprise. Either way, termination is the time when individuals come to terms with the fact that the relationship is over. Knapp believes that communication during this stage fulfills the three basic functions of other forms of leave-taking. It announces the upcoming separation, summarizes what has occurred during interaction, and determines the future of the relationship.

Variations In Relational Development

Keep in mind that Knapp's model is a general overview, not a specific prediction. It describes what often happens in relationships, not what inevitably happens. If you and a partner find yourselves in the differentiating stage, for example, you should not pack your bags and decide there is no hope for the relationship. Couples can turn relationships around by going back to and replaying earlier stages. If they care enough, they can repair troubled relationships by exploring alternative forms of relating; taking on more functional roles; eliminating unhealthy interaction patterns; or searching for new ways to make the relationship rewarding.

In real life, couples do not always go through the stages together. One partner may think the relationship is at the casual, experimenting stage, whereas the other may believe the partners are ready to bond. Or one partner may be so busy that he or she doesn't notice that the other partner is circumscribing. Furthermore, not all couples take the same length of time to complete the steps, even when partners are in sync. Some couples take a long time before risking commitment. Others rush through the early stages. This latter course is dangerous; if one of the early stages is skipped or rushed, later stages may be unstable, like a building constructed with a faulty foundation. For relationships to last, couples must work out agreements and develop healthy interaction patterns, processes that take time.

Interpersonal Attraction: Filtering Theory

We have seen how relationships change over time. But what causes people to enter relationships in the first place? Steve Duck feels that attraction is really a process of elimination. According to his **filtering theory**, we use a series of filters to judge how close to others we want to become.[18] At each filter, some potential partners are eliminated and some move on. Figure 6.3 shows how this process works.

What are the filters we use to regulate attraction? Duck identifies four filters: sociological or incidental, preinteraction, interaction, and cognitive cues. *Sociological or incidental cues* are the demographic or environmental factors that determine

Figure 6.3 **Duck's Attraction Filter**

Potential Partners

Sociological or Incidental Cues
proximity, frequency of interaction, etc.

Preinteraction Cues
physical beauty, artifacts, nonverbal behavior, etc.

Interaction Cues
social rewards, conversational management, etc.

Cognitive Cues
attitude similarity, need complementarity, shared values, etc.

Friends and Romantic Partners

Adapted from "Interpersonal Communication in Developing Acquaintance" by Steven Duck, 1973, in *Exploration in Interpersonal Communication,* Gerald R. Miller, ed. Beverly Hills, CA: Sage, pp. 127–148.

probability of contact. They include factors such as where we work and live, how frequently we travel, and so on. Obviously, we cannot form relationships with people we have never met, and maintaining contact with someone thousands of miles away is extremely difficult. *Physical proximity* seems to be a key factor here. Numerous studies show that marriages and close friendships are most likely to occur between people who live close to one another. *By carefully choosing where to live, work, and play, people can increase the nature and frequency of their interpersonal bonds.*

Preinteraction cues are also important filters. People use nonverbal impressions to determine whether they wish to interact with others. We use body type, physical beauty, dress, and related artifacts to give us some idea of what others are like. Whether or not they should, surface details often determine whether future interaction will occur. At least some of the time, the old expression "You never get a second chance to make a first impression" is true. Therefore, *it is important to become more aware of the ways silent nonverbal messages affect impression formation.*

Interaction cues occur once we have made initial contact. Some interactions are smooth and comfortable, whereas others are awkward and difficult. When topics flow easily, turn taking is smooth and effortless, eye contact and facial expression indicate friendliness and approval, and attraction is high. *The ability to manage conversations and to make interaction rewarding is an important factor in increasing attractiveness.*

Cognitive cues constitute the last, and most important, filter. Studies show that the strongest factors in creating solid, long-lasting relationships are psychological. In the long run, the extent to which values are shared and attitudes and beliefs are similar is a more important determinant of friendship than is physical appearance. How do we get to know another person at this level? By communicating openly about our beliefs, attitudes, and values. This is why *it is important to disclose one's own beliefs and values and to elicit disclosure from others.* It is also important to be open to the possibilities in others. If we let initial filters keep us from getting to know people, we may be missing out on potentially rewarding relationships.

INCREASING RELATIONAL SKILLS

As we've seen, relationships wax and wane. How long a relationship lasts, and how successful it is, depends in large part on the partners' skills as communicators. Over the last twenty years, communication scholars have directed a great deal of attention to identifying the ways people keep their relationships in good working order. In this section, we address this research and look at some of the skills necessary for successful relational maintenance.

Relational Maintenance

Relational maintenance strategies are the behaviors people use to keep their relationships at a desired level. When asked how they routinely go about maintaining relationships, people report a range of strategies. Although most people report using positive behaviors such as expressing affection, comforting one another, avoiding hurtful topics, and so on, others report using antisocial methods like inciting jealousy or guilt.[19] Obviously not all of these strategies are widespread or successful. The five most often identified by scholars are: *positivity* (being positive and cheerful), *openness* (being willing to disclose personal information), *assurance* (offering reassurance), *networks* (spending time with one another's family and friends), and *task sharing* (sharing the workload).[20] *Conflict management* (handling conflict effectively) and *advice* (offering advice and support) are also frequently cited.[21] Table 6.2 lists these strategies and gives some examples of the kinds of communication they entail.

These seven behaviors are not only common but also successful. The more these behaviors occur in relationships, the more people report positive outcomes such as increased liking, commitment, satisfaction, and trust. These strategies have been found to be important in marital and romantic,[22] friendship,[23] parent–child,[24] and even friends-with-benefits relationships.[25] Secure people use them more often than do anxious or avoidant people,[26] and chronically lonely people use very few of them.[27] There is a great deal of evidence, then, that these are important communication behaviors to master if you want your interpersonal relationships to thrive.

Interestingly, not all relational maintenance behaviors are positive. There is a "dark side" to the behaviors some people use to maintain relationships. Some couples use arguments, ultimatums, and extreme tests to manage relationships,

---

Table 6.2 Positive Relational Maintenance Behaviors

Positivity

Relational partners are cheerful and optimistic, build each other's self-esteem, are patient and forgiving, and refrain from criticizing one another.

Openness

Relational partners have periodic talks about the relationship, are able to disclose their own feelings and needs, and encourage their partners to be open.

Assurance

Relational partners indicate their commitment to one another, demonstrate that they are faithful, and talk in ways that show they believe the relationship has a future.

Networks

Relational partners like to spend time with each other's families and with mutual friends and include them in their activities.

Task Sharing

Relational partners take joint responsibility for the relationship and help equally with tasks that need to be done.

Conflict Management

Relational partners know how to work out disagreements, listen to their partners' needs, and apologize when conflict occurs.

Advice Sharing/Offering

Relational partners share opinions, offer support, and use feedback effectively.

whereas others employ insolence and avoidance. In a 2008 study, Dainton and Gross identified jealousy induction, avoidance, spying, infidelity, destructive conflict, and allowing control (i.e., focusing on the partner instead of attending to other people and other responsibilities) as common negative behaviors used to keep their relationships going.[28] Table 6.3 explains these behaviors.

Although negative behaviors such as these can be dysfunctional in the long run, they are commonly used. Alan Goodboy and his colleagues suggest that using negative relational maintenance behaviors is one way partners can see to their individual needs while remaining in a relationship.[29] For example, making one's partner jealous or avoiding him or her may be ways of making oneself look more attractive to that partner while controlling the relationship and testing its strength. Despite the fact that negative behaviors are frequently employed, they do not lead to quality relationships and are often employed by dissatisfied partners.[30] Individuals with negative images of themselves or others are much more likely to use them than people with a secure sense of self. Goodboy sums up his research on negative relational maintenance behaviors in the following way:

> Ideally, given a choice of relational alternatives, adults should try to foster a committed relationship with secure partners who are generally satisfied and comfortable in their relationships and who are unlikely to use negative relational maintenance behaviors.[31]

Choosing the right way to maintain a relationship is not an easy task. Keeping a relationship on track takes a good deal of interpersonal sensitivity. In the remainder of this section, we look at some of the specific skills that allow us to preserve interpersonal connections. In particular, we focus on self-disclosure, conflict management, and ways to offer helpful feedback and advice.

Table 6.3 Negative Relational Maintenance Behaviors

Jealousy Induction
Intentionally making a partner jealous

Avoidance
Avoiding a partner or topic by giving him or her the "silent treatment"

Spying
Secretly trying to find out information about one's partner

Infidelity
Having a romantic liaison outside one's primary relationship

Destructive Conflict
Controlling one's partner through arguments and fights

Allowing control
Focusing on the partner instead of other responsibilities; letting one's partner make one's decisions

Toward More Effective Self-Disclosure

One of the most important interpersonal skills is the ability to self-disclose effectively. **Self-disclosure** occurs when we reveal information to others that they are unlikely to discover on their own: when we voluntarily open up to them. The ability to disclose in appropriate ways has many benefits. Being open about traumatic events, for example, typically diminishes anxiety and stress and can increase physical and mental health.[32] In fact, there is evidence that talking or writing about disturbing events can actually increase immune system functioning and prevent physical ailments. In addition, the support that comes from disclosing to a close and trusted friend can be comforting, and a frank discussion can help one put a problem into perspective. Disclosure can also strengthen relationships by signaling trust and commitment. Studies have shown that the partners of people who conceal information and refuse to be open often feel excluded and find such relationships unsatisfactory.[33] Disclosure, then, seems to draw people together and strengthen their bonds.

Yet not all statements about the self are true self-disclosures. "I have to be honest and share this with you. No one around here can stand you," is not a disclosure, it's an attack. This kind of "open" communication is not something that will strengthen a relationship and is not what communication experts mean when they discuss self-disclosure.

Rules for Disclosing

True disclosures can be healthy for a relationship, but only if certain guidelines are followed. The first is that *self-disclosure is not appropriate in all relationships.* In deciding whether or not to reveal personal information, try to match the level of your disclosure to the level of your relationship. We usually don't tell our personal experiences to strangers (except, perhaps, for bartenders, therapists, and people sitting next to us on long-distance airline flights). We do tell our personal experiences to close friends and romantic partners. One of the reasons for not disclosing to everyone is that disclosure is a risk. People are not always sympathetic and understanding. Disclosures can come back to haunt us, for not everyone can be trusted to keep a confidence.

Another reason for not disclosing indiscriminately is that disclosures put a burden on others by creating intimacy. The chance acquaintance who confides that he or she is in terrible trouble is asking for more than polite attention. He or she is asking for involvement. A close friend may be happy to provide the necessary counsel and comfort; a stranger usually is not. Therefore, it is important to *consider the effect your disclosures will have on others.*

Even when you know that your partner will be open to disclosure, you should nonetheless be cautious about when and where to hold the discussion. It is important to *choose the right time and place for your disclosures.* Running up to your best friend in the hall and revealing a major problem ("Guess what? I think I'm pregnant. Got to run.") right before a major test is insensitive and foolish. Disclosures should not be bolts from the blue. They should take place in an environment and at a time that allows recipients to react appropriately.

Disclosures should also be related to what is happening in the "here and now." They should be connected to what is currently going on in the relationship. Any disconnected topic—particularly an unrelated disclosure—disrupts a conversation. If Elena and her roommate are discussing what to do next weekend

Disclosures should also be related to what is happening in the "here and now." They should be connected to what is currently going on in the relationship.

and Elena suddenly says, "Dad lost his job when I was ten. We were so poor that I didn't get a birthday present for years," the disclosure is inappropriate. Elena doesn't seem to have a reason to bring up such a sensitive issue. The same disclosure might make perfect sense in another context. For example, if the roommate has just given Elena a small gift and Elena bursts into tears, the disclosure allows the roommate to understand Elena's behavior.

In general, *disclosure should be gradual.* It is a good idea to start out with fairly safe disclosures and then move on to more personal topics. As we have seen, relationships take time to develop and to deepen. We don't dive headfirst into them; we test the waters first. The same is true for disclosures.

Finally, *disclosures should be reciprocal.* In general, we expect a disclosure by one party to be met with a disclosure by the other. If one person in a relationship does all the disclosing, the imbalance may signal opposing attitudes toward openness. Participants should encourage their partners to disclose without making them feel uncomfortable. They should also learn to modify their own disclosures until an appropriate atmosphere has been established.

Responding to Disclosures

If disclosing is tricky, so too is responding to others' disclosures. It takes sensitivity to respond in useful ways. Imagine this: you run into your best friend from high school, who turns to you and says, "I'm really depressed. I have a good job and I make an adequate salary, but I'm not happy. . . . I didn't do too well in school before, but maybe I will quit work and go back to school. I don't know what I should do." What do you say? Your response probably falls into one of five **disclosure response categories** identified by David Johnson. You may give advice, analyze your friend's problem, offer reassurance and support, ask questions, or help your friend clarify his thinking by paraphrasing his statement.[34] Each of these ways of responding bears a closer look.

Most people respond to disclosures by offering advice. They think about the problem, make a judgment about what ought to be done, and offer a simple (and sometimes simplistic) solution. If your response is to tell your friend what to do, you are using an *advising and evaluating response.* People don't always want you to offer them a plan of action. Note that in this example, your friend didn't say, "Tell me what to do," but instead said, "I don't know what I should do." The advice you give may be more appropriate for you than it is for your friend. In most cases, you won't have enough information about a problem to offer advice right away. You may eventually help your friend come up with his own plan, but it's probably best to use one of the other responses first.

If your response is to analyze the causes of his dilemma, then you are using an *analyzing and interpreting response*. Telling your friend that depression is often internalized anger and suggesting that he may feel angry with himself because he dropped out of school is an example. Such a response may be insightful (if you know your friend very well), but it may be way off base (e.g., if your interpretation is based on something you heard on a daytime talk show). In either case, it is likely to cause defensiveness. As Johnson points out, "people will usually respond better when you help them think about themselves and their feelings than if you try to figure out what causes them to do the things they do."[35]

Many of you may respond to your friend's disclosure by telling him not to worry, assuring him that it will all work out. By offering sympathy, you have chosen a *reassuring and supporting response*. If your friend is so distraught that he needs to be calmed down, this kind of response may be okay. It runs the danger, however, of cutting short the discussion and of making your friend feel he has no right to be unhappy.

If your immediate reaction is to gather more information, then you choose a *questioning and probing response*. This response can be useful, especially if your friend can benefit from considering the problem more fully. Obviously, different questions define the problem in different ways. And questions can also be evaluative. "How in the world did you get yourself in such a mess?" may sound like a question, but it is really an evaluation.

Often it is a good idea to turn questions into reflective statements for the other person to respond to. Phrased as a question, "Why aren't you happy?" seems judgmental (as well as very difficult to answer). But phrased as a statement, "You're feeling very unhappy now," the response loses its judgmental tone, and the listener can more easily clarify his feelings. If your response to your friend's dilemma is something on the order of "In other words, you're depressed and puzzled because your job isn't fulfilling. Yet you're not sure going back to school will work out either," then you choose a *paraphrasing and understanding response*.

Many communication scholars believe that paraphrasing is the best of the alternatives, at least as a first step. It allows you to check your understanding of what is troubling your friend, it allows your friend to hear and think about what he has just said, and it shows that you are listening to him.[36] Its major disadvantage is that it may seem awkward until you get used to it.

Make sure that when you paraphrase, you do not parrot back exactly what was said. Instead, offer your own understanding of what your friend was trying to say. And be careful not to get carried away in your paraphrasing. "So, what I hear you saying is that you're so depressed you don't want to live, because you're a failure at everything" puts the problem into your own words; unfortunately, it also completely misinterprets what was said. When paraphrasing, try to get at the gist of the problem without diminishing or enlarging it. This may take some practice, but the practice will pay off.

> When paraphrasing, try to get at the gist of the problem without diminishing or enlarging it. This may take some practice, but the practice will pay off.

Managing Interpersonal Conflict

Relationships don't always run smoothly. It's natural for people in relationships to experience bouts of conflict from time to time. If conflict is managed successfully, it need not lead to termination; indeed, it can strengthen a relationship.

Conflict occurs whenever two people have incompatible goals. If one roommate, for example, wants to watch TV and the other wants to sleep, they'll feel that they are in conflict. Whether they resolve this conflict or whether it escalates will depend on their attitudes toward conflict and their **conflict styles**.[37]

We each have preferred ways of dealing with conflict. Some people opt for *withdrawing*. The minute they sense conflict, they walk away or change the subject. If the issue is unimportant and there is no need to build a strong relationship with the other party or if engaging in conflict would lead to dangerous escalation, the decision to withdraw may be appropriate, but most of the time, withdrawing just postpones a problem and makes it worse.

Some people use a tactic called *forcing* to get their way. When they sense conflict, they put aside the other's needs and go all out to win. If an issue is personally very important and you are not deeply invested in a relationship you may want to use this technique; for example, when buying a used car from someone you don't know, it is okay to push hard for the price and terms you want. However, forcing is an inappropriate tactic with a loved one because too much domination can destroy equality in a relationship.

Unaddressed conflict can undermine relationships and lead to relational dissolution.

© Hulton-Deutsch Collection/CORBIS

Some people try *accommodating* in conflict situations. When they sense conflicts, they give in immediately. It's all right to accommodate on unimportant issues to please someone you care for, but when important issues are at stake, it's not a good idea to give in. In long-term relationships, accommodation can often lead to unstated resentment.

What about *compromising*? Compromise usually means that each party gives up part of what he or she wants. Although this can be effective, remember that even in the best of compromise situations, both parties are somewhat unsatisfied. There is actually a better alternative than compromise: *problem solving*. Problem solving means negotiating until you come up with a new, creative solution that satisfies both parties. This is better than reaching a middle ground that satisfies no one.

If problem solving is the best alternative, why don't we use it more often? One reason is that we tend to specialize in one of the five strategies. People who withdraw or accommodate are often fearful of conflict and aren't used to arguing for what they believe in, whereas aggressive people often see problem solving or compromise as weakness. As David W. Johnson points out:

> It's important to remember that the use of certain strategies may increase the probability that other strategies will appear. When individuals cannot withdraw any more, when they feel backed into a corner and have to deal with the conflict, they are likely to strike out and try to force the other person into letting them have their way. When a person attempts to smooth, and the other person responds with forcing and anger, withdrawal may follow. That, in turn, may be followed by forcing if the other person continues to be angry and competitive.[38]

It takes time and skill to think of creative solutions, which is another reason why we don't use problem solving as often as we should. Most people seize a single position and argue for it exclusively, rather than addressing the conflict in terms of mutual interests. A **position** is a concrete solution to a problem; an **interest** is the overall goal we want to achieve. Take the example of Mandy, who wants some time alone because she is tired. She decides that the only way she can get the break she needs is to go on vacation by herself. However, when Mandy suddenly announces this decision to her partner, Diane, who has made plans to spend the vacation with her, Diane feels angry and confused. Worsening the situation is the fact that Mandy states her position (a separate vacation) and doesn't let Diane know the thinking behind it. If Mandy would discuss her thinking with Diane rather than insisting on her decision without explanation, it's possible they could resolve the problem.

Problem solving means sitting down together, directly expressing interests, defining problems clearly, and finding positions that best serve everyone's interests. This process often involves the ability to see things from the other person's point of view and a commitment to seeking options that benefit everyone.[39] It also involves a willingness to be open and direct.

Directness is learned. In general, directness is a cultural value in today's United States. Most of us believe that we should confront rather than avoid problems. After all, our needs cannot be met if no one knows what they are. The process of avoiding and postponing conflict is known as **gunnysacking**; when we gunnysack, we store up all our grievances and carry them around until the burden gets too heavy and we explode in anger. To prevent this, the best time to confront conflict is when the issue is immediate, small, and manageable.

Direct confrontation may work well for people in our culture, but it is certainly not the norm everywhere. In some cultures, direct expression of feelings is looked on with disapproval. In such cultures, smoothing and indirect statements are favored. In China, for example, indirect communication is preferred. Often, conflicts are solved by unofficial intermediaries, friends, or acquaintances of the parties to a conflict, who take it on themselves to intervene. In this way, group harmony is not disturbed. According to Guo-Ming Chen and William Starosta, "the intermediary approach to interpersonal conflict tends to be as functional in East Asia as is the assertive approach in North America."[40]

According to Richard Reeves-Ellington, "For Americans, self-disclosure is a strategy to make various types of relationships work; for Chinese, it is a gift shared only with the most intimate relatives and friends."[41] It's clear, then, that there's no one correct way to deal with conflict. When we handle conflict, we should take into account the cultural backgrounds and individual styles of the participants.

Making Feedback Effective

During conflict, as well as during other forms of interaction, it's important to give and receive feedback. **Feedback** is information that helps individuals to control and adjust their behavior. It tells people how they are doing and what they may need to change to be more effective. Competent communicators are open to feedback about their own behavior and know how to give useful feedback to others. In many cases, feedback presents no problem. "That was great!" is easy to say and is usually well received. Giving feedback about more sensitive issues, however, is not quite so simple. Let's consider five ways to make sure your feedback is effective.[42]

> Competent communicators are open to feedback about their own behavior and know how to give useful feedback to others.

The first rule is to *own your own message*. When we have to give others unwelcome feedback, we often avoid blame by refusing to acknowledge that the message is ours. We may use phrases such as "everyone's angry" or "we're all beginning to worry," when what we really mean is "I'm angry" or "I'm worried." Attributing the feedback to others is basically dishonest and confusing. Your partner is left with the idea that some unspecified others are upset, but he or she has no idea what you think. If you want to give feedback, own up to it.

Also, *avoid apologizing for your feelings*. To avoid hurting someone else, you may place all the blame on yourself. If you aren't at fault, don't act as though you were. A statement such as "I guess it's my fault that you borrowed my shirt and ruined it. Maybe I just didn't make it clear that I wanted it back in one piece" is not good feedback. This statement gives the impression that you don't really care about the shirt and that you don't expect any repayment, when in fact you do (and have every right to). The receiver of a message such as this can't be blamed if he or she doesn't understand the depth of your concern.

It is important to *make your messages specific and behavioral*. The object of good feedback is to give useful information. Saying something such as "Oh, I don't know, it's just your attitude" is not useful. "I was hurt when you didn't call me last week. It made me feel as though I don't count" is better because it relates to behavior. Your partner now knows what he or she did and what your feelings were. This kind of direct statement paves the way for a discussion of what each of you expects from the other and allows you to set norms for future behavior. People often hurt others simply because they are unaware that their behavior is a problem. In many cases, they would have been happy to change if only they had known. Specific behavioral information gives them this knowledge.

Verbal and nonverbal behaviors should support one another. People often have trouble expressing their emotions nonverbally. This is particularly true of anger. In an attempt to remain calm, an individual may smile and say (in a perfectly pleasant voice), "You know, I'm very angry right now." This double message is confusing and potentially double binding. In effective feedback, the verbal and nonverbal channels are congruent.

Finally, it is important to keep your partner from feeling defensive. This means that you should *avoid evaluating and interpreting your partner unless he or she specifically asks you to do so.* As we have seen, there are times when your partner may want to know your interpretation. In most cases, however, unsolicited judgments cause defensiveness. How helpful would it be if someone were to turn to you and say, "I think you should hear this for your own good. You are the craziest, most narcissistic, most sociopathic personality I've ever met"? Attacks like this are never helpful and can only hurt relationships.

NEW MEDIA, NEW RELATIONSHIPS

Traditionally, interpersonal communication has involved dyads communicating face-to-face (FtF). What happens when technologies emerge that allow people separated in time and space to form relationships? How does computer-mediated communication (CMC) affect interpersonal communication? In this section we'll look at some of the ways new media technologies impact relationships. After describing the characteristics of electronically mediated relationships, we'll consider how individuals create online identities and how CMC allows us to maintain long-distance relationships. We'll then turn our attention to the "dark side" of computer-mediated communication by discussing cyberstalking and cyberbullying.

Online Relationships

Although most of the people with whom we communicate online are people we already know offline, people do meet and form relationships over the Internet. Online dating services offer the possibility of new kinds of romantic attachments. Chat rooms and discussion groups provide places to share information with new acquaintances. And social networking services make it possible to collect hundreds of Internet "friends." Other media such as cell phones, text message systems, email, and instant messaging (IM) are an integral part of everyday interactions. Nowadays, few, if any, relationships are conducted solely offline.

Communication scholars used to believe that it was impossible for individuals to form deep and lasting relationships online. There is evidence, however, that online interpersonal relationships develop quickly and are often more intimate than FtF relationships.[43] Joseph Walther's **hyperpersonal theory** explains why this is the case: (1) online senders often carefully emphasize those aspects of self that make them attractive to others, thus increasing their appeal; (2) they edit their messages before sending them, creating high-quality conversations; (3) in the absence of cues to the contrary, there is a tendency for receivers to overemphasize similarities and form idealized views of their partners; and (4) the lack of emphasis on physical presence removes inhibitions to free and genuine communication.[44] Although in the initial stages of online relationships individuals are less open, they quickly adapt to the characteristics of the medium and exhibit increased self-disclosure.[45] The upshot is that relationships formed in cyberspace can be meaningful and the factors that lead to satisfaction in computer-mediated communication are similar to those emphasized in offline relationships, including trust, honesty, and commitment.[46]

Identity in a Socially Networked World

For most college-age students, sites like Facebook, YouTube, and Twitter are an indispensable part of daily life. As we shall see in more detail in Chapter 11, these sites have extended our ability to keep in touch with close friends and expanded our network of casual acquaintances. They have allowed us to be more knowledgeable, more creative, and more involved. They have also presented us with social challenges that our parents and even our older siblings never had to cope with. One such challenge is deciding what to reveal about ourselves when what we divulge can be seen, read, and judged by hundreds if not thousands of people.

Social networking sites create pressures on users to create and publish an idealized image of self. For many young teens creating a Facebook profile can be an agonizing task because they know they will be judged by the official photo they post, their lists of likes and dislikes, the groups they say they belong to, and the people they decide to friend.[47]

So powerful is the need to make a good impression, some teens have even admitted to using "shrinking" software to make themselves look thinner in their photos.[48] Although users think of their online profiles as "resumes, or strategic tools intended for marketing their 'best' selves, rather than providing completely candid self-representations,"[49] they also know that they cannot lie too overtly. If they make themselves look too thin or too glamorous, if they claim to like music their friends know they never listen to, if they brag about nonexistent talents or accomplishments, they will be called on it. What makes online impression management even more difficult is that individuals can be judged by what their friends post about them.[50] The number and recency of comments posted on one's wall as well as "tagged" photos on other people's sites give off information as well, as does the sheer number of friends an individual has accumulated. Too few friends suggest that a person is unpopular, too many that he or she is indiscriminate.[51] It would appear that in cyberspace, as well as in the "real world," we are judged by the people we know and we can know too many people for our own good.

Relational Maintenance in Cyberspace

Nowadays we have a large number of choices when it comes to communicating with family, friends, and romantic partners. In addition to FtF conversations, we use telephone, email, instant messaging, and social networking sites to keep existing relationships from eroding. CMC is especially useful for college students because it is a readily available, cheap, and convenient channel of communication. Although CMC frequently is used to check in with geographically close friends, it is particularly important in maintaining long-distance relationships. Indeed, today's students can easily stay in contact with absent friends and extended family, "resulting in their having greater numbers of social ties than their parents."[52]

For many reasons such as going away to college, military deployment, immigration, and work-related travel, people find themselves separated from friends, family, and romantic partners. For these people, mediated channels provide a means for self-disclosure and other relational maintenance behaviors. Hua Wang and Peter Andersen report that telephone, email, and IM are the primary communication channels used in long-distance friendships, followed by FtF interactions, letters, and other types of CMC. They argue that "the more intimate the relationships become, the more communication channels people adopt, and the more frequently they use these tools to keep the relationship going."[53]

Although there is evidence that the more channels people use to keep in contact with one another the better able they are to keep their relationships in tune, using IM or email is not a magic solution to relational maintenance. If, for example, one's long-distance relationships are based on "distorted pleasant memories, then the reality of a friend changing over time may lead to faster deterioration of an otherwise dormant relationship."[54] And if one's mediated messages are not reciprocal and fair, one partner may feel "under-benefitted" and dissatisfied. The key in using mediated communication is to negotiate which channels to use and to agree about how often and when to communicate. We have more options than ever before, but we must use them wisely.

The Dark Side of New Technologies

All forms of communication, whether face-to-face or mediated, have a dark side. People can be inadvertently hurtful or intentionally cruel. They can deliberately try to make their partners feel jealous and inadequate, they can be demanding and controlling, and they can obsessively pursue relationships with people who want nothing to do with them. In this section we will focus on intrusive online behavior, looking at how the Internet, and social network sites in particular, have made it easy for some people to make others' lives miserable. Although only a small percentage of individuals go to the extremes of stalking and bullying those around them, a significant percentage have experienced some form of online harassment.

Cyberstalking

Managing romantic relationships is seldom easy, and the difficulties aren't made any easier when they are played out in front of an audience on social network sites. Breakups can be particularly stressful, with some leading to inappropriate behaviors. Intimate partners have been known to send each other intimidating messages, to reveal information they promised to keep private, to take their fights online, and to monitor each others' activities obsessively. As Army Lundon and colleagues point out, "as we open ourselves to more forms of communication, we increase the likelihood that new technologies become a means of intrusion and surveillance."[55]

One increasingly frequent form of intrusion has become known as *Facebook stalking*. Examples of Facebook stalking include obsessively checking "friends'" wall posts, status updates, and photos, as well as leaving messages demanding intimacy. When this behavior is such that it would cause a reasonable person fear, it rises to the level of *cyberstalking*. A few exes have even gone so far as to create false Facebook profiles of their partners, spread untrue rumors, post embarrassing photos, and leave spiteful messages on the pages of ex-partners. What is even more disturbing is that individuals who stalk online may take their pursuit offline by bombarding targets with unwanted messages, leaving unwanted gifts, or even following and monitoring the behaviors of the object of their obsession.

Cyberbullying

Cyberstalking is one form of *cyberbullying*, the intentional use of technology to create harm to another, which can have serious, even tragic results. In addition to effects on school achievement, it can lead to drug and alcohol use, illness and feelings of loneliness, depression, and hopelessness. In several highly publicized cases, cyberbullying has even led victims to commit suicide.[56] In one of the earliest of these cases, thirteen-year-old Ryan Halligan killed himself after a classmate pretended to want a romantic relationship, and then forwarded his IM responses to her friends. When he approached her in person, she told him he was nothing but a loser and that she wanted nothing to do with him. Three years later, another thirteen-year-old, Megan Meier, took her own life when a former friend's mother used MySpace to create a fictitious profile of a sixteen-year-old named "Josh Evans," making Megan believe that "Josh" had a crush on her. When Megan received a message that "the world would be a better place without her in it," she hanged herself in her closet. More recently, a college student named Tyler Clementi was victimized by his roommate, who posted a video of Tyler in a sexual encounter with another man and then alerted other students by Twitter. Tyler too killed himself as a result.

Other less tragic, but nonetheless disturbing, examples abound. For example, a high school student named Hail Ketchum was victimized by an online video in which three other students falsely describe raping and attempting to murder her in the back of a pickup truck. The video was viewed by more than six hundred students. Unlike the others, Hail did not harm herself; instead she sued the school system for not doing anything to the boys who had posted the video. Finally, as a practical joke, a forty-year-old woman posted photos and personal information about a seventeen-year-old girl on Craigslist. As a result the young girl received phone calls, emails, and text messages from men looking for a sexual encounter. Certainly bullying occurs offline as well as online. However, because children have unsupervised access to the Internet, and because rumors can spread with incredible speed, cyberbullying is particularly pervasive and inescapable. For many young people today, cyberbullying can be a nightmare.[57]

Jealousy and Dependence

Several scholars interested in the dark side of mediated communication have noted that being in constant connection via social network sites and cell phones can lead to jealousy and dependence as well as more positive effects. Sonja Utz and Camiel Beukeboom, for example, found that people often become jealous if they find out that their partners are interacting with other people on Facebook. This is particularly true for low-self-esteem individuals with a high need for popularity. The authors believe this is in part due to the public nature of information on Facebook and the particularly face-threatening experience of knowing that others can see when your partner is in contact with a former relational partner.[58]

Another negative interpersonal effect of new media use is *overdependence*. Now that cell phones are ubiquitous, individuals report that being continuously available to others is both an advantage and a disadvantage. Jeffrey Hall and Nancy Baym report that being in perpetual contact may lead to enhanced anxiety as users find themselves pulled between a need for dependence and a desire to be independent.[59] This tension is increased as expectations escalate, putting pressure on friends to text and call continuously throughout the day. When a response is not immediate, friends often interpret this as a deliberate slight and feel rejection and dismay. Thus, one of the side effects of cell connection can be a feeling of entrapment as users try to decide how often they need to call and respond to each other. As in all forms of interpersonal interaction, unrealistic expectations can lead to relational conflict.

Human-Machine Interaction: Companion Robots

Until recently robots could be found only in the fictional worlds created by filmmakers and science fiction writers. The earliest robots to go into actual production were engineered for industrial uses, to build automobiles and the like. Artificially intelligent machines, machines that could assist humans and act as their companions, were far in the future. But that future is getting nearer. Today scientists are creating robots that can engage in social interaction and can, in at least a limited sense, act as babysitters and as caregivers for the elderly.[60] Paro, a robot that looks like a baby seal, responds to human touch by moving its head and legs and repeating behaviors it is rewarded for. It was developed to keep elderly dementia patients from being lonely. Its originators claim that it reduces stress and stimulates interaction between patients and caregivers. A Hello Kitty robot has been developed to act as a babysitter. According to the Hello Kitty Website, this robot replica of the cartoon kitten can chat with and play guessing games with a child and is "a perfect companion for times when your child needs a little extra comfort and friendship."[61] It is also equipped with a voice recognition system and can call children by their names. Some babysitting robots are equipped with cameras and can track movements, sounding an alarm when a child leaves a designated area.

In her book, *Alone Together*, Sherry Turkle, director of the MIT Initiative on Technology and Self, discusses the impact of robot companions on young children and on the elderly. She reports that when toy robots are given to children, the children think the robots have emotions and that the robots care about them. When the children are asked whether or not they would like a robot babysitter and whether or not it would be a good idea to have robots take care of old people, some liked the idea, others were uncertain, and one child asked, "Don't they have people for that?"[62]

The use of robots as companions to especially vulnerable populations like children and the elderly certainly raises ethical questions. Will the ease and convenience of handing over child- and elder-care tasks to a machine encourage people to shirk their responsibilities to one another? Perhaps not, but the following comment from one user of the Hello Kitty robot gives one pause.

> Robo Kitty puts Max to sleep, watches TV with him, watches him in the bath, listens to him read. It's amazing, like a best friend, or as Max says "Kitty Mommy!" Now when I'm working from home I don't have to worry about Max asking a bunch of questions or wanting to play or having to read to him. He hardly even talks to me at all! He no longer asks to go to the park or the zoo—being a parent has NEVER been so easy! Thank you Robo Kittty.[63]

Although Max's parent's life is a lot easier, what about Max's development? We know that attachments made in early childhood are related to relational health in later life. What kinds of attachments can one make to a machine? Even the best robot cannot empathize with us. Does empathy matter? What do you think? If a robot could take care of your child or grandparent, would you use one?

BECOMING A MORE RESPONSIBLE COMMUNICATOR

The childhood taunt "Sticks and stones can break my bones, but words can never hurt me" suggests that talk is unimportant—that words don't count. But of course, they do. Careless talk can wound others, sometimes irreparably. It's important, therefore, to reflect on our responsibilities as communicators.

There are no hard-and-fast rules that can tell you what is right or wrong in any given situation, yet there are some questions you can ask yourself to determine whether a given act of communication is ethical or not. Melinda Kramer offers two simple tests for ethical decision making.[64] The first, which she labels the **public scrutiny test**, consists of three questions:

1. Am I personally proud of this action?
2. Am I comfortable with this decision?
3. Would I feel uncomfortable or embarrassed if this decision were known to my colleagues, friends, spouse, or children?

The second, which she calls the **four-way test**, comprises the following four questions:

1. Is it the *truth*?
2. Is it *fair* to all concerned?
3. Will it build *goodwill* and *better friendships*?
4. Will it be *beneficial* to all concerned?

These tests are not exhaustive, but remembering to ask these questions may serve to focus your attention on the consequences of communicative behavior.

Here and at the end of the next four chapters, you'll find brief sections on some of the ethical issues involved in different communication contexts. As you read the following guidelines for becoming more interpersonally responsible, think about other criteria you would add to the list. The guidelines are as follows:

- Interpersonal communication has consequences. Everyday talk may seem inconsequential, but as we've seen throughout this chapter, our notions of who we are and what we are worth evolve through interactions with others. Careless comments over a period of time can have serious repercussions. Because people make themselves vulnerable whenever they communicate, communication that belittles, attacks, or otherwise takes advantage of this vulnerability is irresponsible.

- Communicating responsibly does not mean that we have to agree with or even like everyone with whom we interact. It does mean that we should show others respect and be willing to listen with an open mind to their points of view. Too often, we dismiss other people's ideas because we assume that we have nothing to learn from them. In doing so, we limit ourselves. In an ideal world, communicators would not only listen to one another, but would actively seek out each other's opinions.

- Respectful communication also involves honesty. If we truly disagree with a proposal or if we believe that what someone is doing is self-destructive or wrong, we have an obligation to offer honest and helpful feedback, even if that feedback may not be welcomed. Of course, in expressing our opinion, we should take into account our own motives as well as the needs of our partners. Selfish or manipulative comments can sometimes masquerade as honest feedback. It's important to be rhetorically sensitive while communicating honestly.

- Whenever people form long-lasting relationships, they reveal themselves to others. Sometimes, in order to be accepted, we may be tempted to present ourselves dishonestly. Although there's nothing wrong with accentuating the positive, lying about who we are in order to create a false impression is a violation of a basic interpersonal contract. Any serious, long-lasting relationship must be built on trust.

- As we build relationships, we create relational cultures. And in these cultures, we take on roles vis-à-vis one another. For example, one person may dominate while the other submits. Some division of interpersonal labor is fine, as long as the roles are mutually negotiated and mutually satisfying. But sometimes, people force others into roles that are rigid and limiting. In general, we should use communication to create roles that allow participants maximum freedom and equality.

SUMMARY

In this chapter, we begin our consideration of communication contexts with a discussion of interpersonal communication. The most frequently encountered of all communication contexts, interpersonal communication refers to two-person, face-to-face interaction. Communication of this type is direct, personal, immediate, spontaneous, and informal. If we take a developmental view, interpersonal communication is also governed by psychological-level rules. In long-term dyads, we understand our partner at a very personal level and develop unique ways of interacting.

Managing communication is never easy. In every context, we must balance conflicting demands that pull us in different directions. In interpersonal relationships, we must balance the goals of expressiveness and protectiveness, autonomy and togetherness, and novelty and predictability.

We must also respect one another's positive and negative face needs and avoid disconfirmations. Finally, we should avoid dysfunctional patterns such as rigid role relations, paradoxical messages, and spirals. Each of these patterns limits the freedom of participants and sends ambiguous and destructive messages. One key to avoiding these potential problems is to focus as much as possible on patterns rather than on personalities.

Relationships are always changing. As individuals get to know and trust one another, they go through a series of stages: initiating, experimenting, intensifying, and integrating. As they pass through these stages, a couple often uses secret tests to gather information about each other's level of commitment. Once tests have been passed, the couple may decide to engage in bonding, a public legitimation of their relationship. Unfortunately, relationships don't always work out. When relationships dissolve, they pass through the stages of differentiating, circumscribing, stagnating, and avoiding until they reach termination. During each of these stages, including the last, partners do important relational work that calls for different sets of relational skills. The extent to which a couple passes through the stages of forming a relationship is often determined by their level of attraction. Interpersonal theorists have likened attraction to a sequential filtering process whereby potential relational partners are judged and eliminated.

Relationships are built and maintained through communication. By using positive relational maintenance strategies such as positivity, openness, assurance, networks, task sharing, conflict management, and advice, we can keep relationships healthy. It is best to avoid negative maintenance behaviors such as jealousy induction, avoidance, spying, infidelity, destructive conflict, and allowing control. An essential relational skill is self-disclosure, the ability to offer our partners access to personal information. In responding to others' disclosures we should recognize when it is appropriate to advise, interpret, support, question, or paraphrase.

Relationships don't always go smoothly, so effective communicators must learn to manage conflict. Most people handle conflict in one of five ways: by withdrawing, forcing, accommodating, compromising, or problem solving. The last is usually most effective, although each approach has its place. In managing conflict, it's important to focus on interests rather than positions. Americans in general handle conflict openly to avoid gunnysacking. Members of other cultures use more indirect methods. In everyday interaction, as well as during conflict, communicators need to give feedback in clear, nonevaluative ways.

It is becoming much more common for people to develop and maintain relationships online. According to hyperpersonal theory, online interpersonal relationships develop quickly and can often be more intimate than face-to-face relationships. One reason is that we can control what we reveal to others online. Studies of impressions management in social networking sites have shown that people judge others on a variety of cues, some of which we ourselves provide and others over which we have little control. Not only are we judged by the messages and photos we post, we are judged by what others say about us and by those we choose to befriend online. Mediated channels are used not only to initiate relationships, but also to maintain current bonds. Studies show that most people use multiple channels to keep in contact with one another. However, CMC is not a cure-all. If it is not used wisely it can lead to feelings of inequity and dissatisfaction. Like FtF communication, mediated communication can have a dark side including cyberstalking and cyberbullying, overdependence and feelings of entrapment. One of the newest uses of technology is the development of intelligent sociable robots to be used as caregivers for children and elderly people.

It is easy to lose sight of the fact that our communication decisions have an impact on those around us. Yet they do, and this means we should act responsibly when we communicate. One way is to use either the public scrutiny test or the four-way test of ethical decision making to determine whether an act of communication is ethical.

KEY TERMS

Listed below are the key terms used in this chapter, along with the number of the page where each is explained.

interpersonal communication (129)	disconfirmation (135)	relational dissolution stages (142)
dyadic communication (129)	one-up role (137)	filtering theory (144)
developmental approach (130)	one-down role (137)	relational maintenance strategies (145)
cultural-level rules (131)	complementary pattern (137)	self-disclosure (148)
sociological-level rules (131)	symmetrical pattern (137)	disclosure response categories (149)
psychological-level rules (131)	paradoxes (137)	conflict (151)
looking-glass self (133)	double bind (138)	conflict styles (151)
expressive–protective dialectic (133)	spiral (138)	position (152)
autonomy–togetherness dialectic (133)	interpersonal self-fulfilling prophecy (138)	interest (152)
novelty–predictability dialectic (134)	relational development stages (139)	gunnysacking (152)
face (134)	intimacy trophies (140)	feedback (153)
	secret tests (141)	hyperpersonal theory (154)
	relational breadth (142)	public scrutiny test (159)
	relational depth (142)	four-way test (159)

SUGGESTED READING

DeVito, Joseph A. (2010). *Interpersonal messages: Communication and relationship skills* (2nd ed.). Boston: Allyn & Bacon.

> An interactive text that emphasizes interpersonal skills.

Guerrero, Laura, Andersen, Peter A., & Afifi, Walid. (2010). *Close encounters: Communication in relationships* (3rd ed.). Thousand Oaks, CA: Sage Publications.

> Discusses how close relationships begin, escalate, maintain themselves, and end.

Spitzberg, Brian H., & Cupach, William R. (Eds.). (2007). *The dark side of interpersonal communication.* Mahwah, NJ: Lawrence Erlbaum.

> Discusses destructive elements such as secrets, complaints and criticisms, bullying, infidelity, and the like.

Trenholm, Sarah, & Jensen, Arthur. (2012). *Interpersonal communication* (7th ed.). New York: Oxford University Press.

> A comprehensive introduction to the study of interpersonal communication.

7

Group Communication

Groups tell us what to think and feel and how to act. We are who we are because of the groups we have been a part of.

After reading this chapter, you should be able to:

- Identify the characteristics of "groupness."

- Distinguish tasks best done by groups from those best done by individuals.

- Explain group socialization processes.

- Identify task, maintenance, and negative group roles.

- Recognize the danger signs of groupthink.

- Understand how group identity affects in-group and out-group relations.

- Explain the normal phases of group development.

- List four approaches to leadership. Describe behaviors that keep individuals from leadership positions.

- Describe methods and findings of hidden profile research.

- Recognize behaviors that lead to defensive and supportive climates.

- Understand how the standard agenda, brainstorming, and nominal group technique can be used to enhance problem solving.

- Describe special formats for public discussion.

- Discuss ways new technologies affect group communication.

- Describe ethical responsibilities involved in group discussion.

Groups affect us throughout our lives. We are born into family groups, play and learn in friendship and school groups, and spend much of our adult life in work groups. Most Americans think of the individual as the basic social unit, but others believe that the group is even more basic, that individuals are merely products of group interaction.[1] In fact, R. E. Pittinger and his colleagues argue that it is

> *not really useful to think of individuals as the units out of which groups and societies are constructed; it is more fruitful to think of an individual as the limiting case of a group when, for the moment, there is no one else around.*[2]

In many ways, Pittinger is correct, for we are shaped by the groups we've belonged to, and, even after we leave them, they continue to live on in us. Much as we may hate to admit it, groups tell us what to think and feel and how to act. For good or ill, we are who we are because of the groups we have been a part of.

WHAT IS A GROUP?

Not every aggregate is a group. Groups, like dyads, develop over time. A **group** is a special kind of entity. It is a collection of individuals who, as a result of interacting with one another over time, become interdependent, developing shared patterns of behavior and a collective identity.

Characteristics of Groups

One way to see how "groupness" develops is by considering the development of a team. The athletes who show up for tryouts at the beginning of a season are not yet a group. At this point they are merely a collection of individuals. As they begin to train together, however, they gradually take on the characteristics of a true group.

A collection of people develops into a group through interaction. It is through *interaction* that an aggregate of individual athletes becomes a functioning team. If the team is relatively small, communication is direct and participation is equal. If it is larger, specialized roles such as trainer, captain, and assistant coach develop and messages are conveyed through specialized networks. Whichever is the case, without communication the team could not exist.

As a result of communication, *the behaviors of group members become interdependent; in a true group, any action by one affects all. Interdependence* is an important characteristic of groups, for it means that separate individuals have become a functioning whole. In athletics, it is not the individual but the team that wins or loses. If team members act independently, pursuing individual goals rather than team goals, the team never gels and may eventually disintegrate.

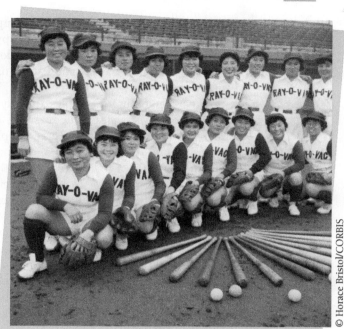

When a collection of individuals becomes interdependent, begins to share a sense of identity, and learns how to work together for a common purpose, they have become a group.

© Horace Bristol/CORBIS

In the process of becoming interdependent, *members develop and share stable and predictable norms, values, and role structures.* Each group develops a unique culture that sets it apart from other groups, a culture that tells group members how to behave, what to value, and who to be. Once these *shared behavioral standards* develop, *members experience a sense of identity and psychological closeness.* They take pride in their shared membership, and being part of the team becomes a primary identity for them. The stronger and more cohesive their sense of membership, the stronger is their *collective identity* and the more they become a true team. When all these characteristics develop—interaction, interdependence, shared behavioral standards, and a sense of membership—"groupness" has been achieved. Without these characteristics, individuals remain separate and isolated. Table 7.1 summarizes the characteristics of groups.

Group Size: How Big Is a Small Group?

In discussing the characteristics of groups, we have so far avoided one topic: group size. Exactly how big is a small group? The answer to this question is not as straightforward as it seems. Although most people agree that the lower limit of a small group is three, they disagree on a small group's upper limits. We say that a group begins at three because something special happens to communication when a third person enters a relationship, something that does not occur in a dyad.

Former newscaster Jane Pauley once remarked, "Somehow three children are many more than two."[3] Pauley is right. For a number of reasons, **triads**, or groups of three, are much more complex than dyads, and three-person communication is different from two-person. One reason is that the number of communication channels increases dramatically with three people. In a dyad, partners don't need to choose whom to talk to; there is only one channel, A to B. In a triad, there are suddenly six channels: A to B, A to C, B to C, A to B and C, B to A and C, and C to A and B. And as the number of people in a group increases, the number of channels rises dramatically. In a seven-person group, for example, the number of potential relationships is 966. Members in large groups must work harder to include one another and to ensure equal participation. Often, groups solve this problem by developing formal roles, such as leader, follower, or harmonizer, and by using specialized networks.

Groups also tend to break down into smaller units. If you have ever lived with two other people, you may have experienced the tendency of a triad to break down into a primary dyad plus one outsider.[4] Three-person groups have to work hard to maintain cohesion. If more people join a group, the tendency to divide into subunits increases markedly.

As groups increase in size, they become more unwieldy. At some point, they become too large for the members to interact directly with one another. At the point when members no longer recognize and relate to one another as equal individuals, the small group ceases to exist, becoming a large group or an organization. Under extraordinary circumstances, a small group may include as many as twenty people,

Table 7.1 Characteristics of Groups

Interaction	Groups are constructed through communication. As members interact with one another regularly, interaction networks develop, and repeated use of these communication channels links group members.
Interdependence	Member behaviors become interconnected. In a true group, each member affects every other member. People who are interdependent share common goals and a common fate.
Shared Behavioral Standards	Groups develop unique ways of doing things. Each member takes on a role within the group, and the group as a whole abides by shared norms. Members implicitly know and follow the kinds of behaviors that are appropriate within the group. In this way, the group develops a group structure.
Collective Identity	In true groups, members perceive themselves as part of a whole. They feel a sense of closeness to other members. In addition to having an "I" identity, they develop a "we" identity based on group membership.

but most of the time the upper limit is much smaller, around ten or twelve. In reviewing a study of jury deliberations, Ernest Bormann tells us that in twelve-person groups, five to seven people often hold the discussion while the others listen silently.[5] Bormann also found that groups of more than ten or eleven tend to break into smaller cliques.

> **At the point when members no longer recognize and relate to one another as equal individuals, the small group ceases to exist, becoming a large group or an organization.**

What is the ideal size for a group? Dan Rothwell tells us, "the appropriate size for a group is the smallest size capable of performing the task effectively."[6] Other experts are more specific. They feel that the optimum size for a problem-solving group is from five to seven people. A group of this size has enough members to ensure a large pool of ideas and information yet not so many members as to inhibit equal participation.

Why Communicate in Groups?

If groups are unwieldy and unstable and if one needs special skills to communicate in groups, why bother? Why not work by oneself? Because there are advantages to working in groups. Whereas some tasks are best done by individuals, other tasks benefit from the input of several people. In general, the more complex the task and the more difficult its implementation, the more it needs the multiple inputs that occur in group interaction.

The first advantage of working in a small group is that *groups provide more input than do individuals*. Often, complex problems need knowledge that goes beyond that of a single individual. Having five or six heads rather than one means that more ideas can be generated and explored. Researchers who have studied small groups often speak of an effect known as **group synergy**. Put simply, group synergy is the idea that groups are often more effective than the best individuals within them. Something extraordinary happens to people when they work with others: their output surpasses what it would have been if they had worked alone. People working in groups can pool information, share perspectives, and use one another's ideas as springboards. They can also motivate and energize one another to keep searching for a solution.

A second advantage of working with others is that *cohesive groups provide support and commitment*. Sometimes, tasks are too large for a single individual, either because they require a great deal of planning or because special effort is needed to implement them. Sometimes, problems are too serious to face alone. By sharing the workload and by offering encouragement and support, groups can take on difficult and complex tasks that individuals would hesitate to undertake by themselves.

A final advantage of groups is that *groups can meet members' interpersonal needs*. We often work with others because we like being with people and because we feel that they can help us to meet individual needs. One way to think of need satisfaction in groups is to consider the three basic **interpersonal needs** described by psychologist William Schutz: the needs for inclusion, control, and affection.[7]

The *inclusion need* is the need to establish identity by associating with others. As we saw in the previous chapter, other people give us a sense of self. Groups are especially important for enhancing identity. They tell us who we are, and, even more, they tell us that it is okay to be who we are. People with especially high needs for self-definition can find a stable sense of self in working with others.

In addition, groups satisfy control needs. The *control need* is the need to prove one's worth and competence by making effective decisions. By providing opportunities for leadership, groups can validate members' feelings of self-worth. Groups can also provide guidance and control for people who feel overwhelmed by responsibility.

Finally, groups can satisfy affection needs. The *affection need* is the need to develop close, caring relationships with others. By establishing friendships and by getting to know one another intimately, group members can satisfy their need to receive affection, as well as their need to show affection to others.

When Are Groups More Effective Than Individuals?

Although there is evidence that mature, cooperative groups often make better decisions than do individuals working alone, groups are not always superior to individuals. Group synergy occurs only under certain conditions: when the task is appropriate and when the group structure is such that each member is encouraged to do his or her best.

What kinds of tasks are most appropriate for groups? In general, the most appropriate tasks are those that are complex, need a wide range of insights and information for their completion, and depend on group commitment to be put into practice. When tasks are relatively simple and straightforward, time is limited, and implementing decisions is easy, then a single talented individual can be as effective as a group. Table 7.2 lists some of the factors that determine whether group or individual decision making is more effective.

The manner in which group members work together also makes a big difference in whether a group will be more productive than an individual. When members support one another, are accountable for the work they do, and feel committed to group goals, group synergy occurs. However, sometimes groups do not work effectively. Group synergy is

© Christian Simonpietri/Sygma/Corbis

Groups allow us to pool our talents and create an end product that is more than the sum of its parts.

unlikely in at least two situations: when social loafing occurs and when members take a free ride by letting others do their work.

Social loafing occurs when members get "lost in the crowd" and don't fulfill their work potential. This effect often arises during **additive tasks**, in which the productivity of the group is determined by adding up the efforts of each member—for example, when the entire group has to produce as many products as possible in a given time. In theory, the output from additive tasks should be directly proportional to the number of group members. This is not always the case, however. Although a ten-member group will produce a lot more than an individual will, it often will not produce ten times as much because of social loafing. Some researchers believe that social loafing can be reduced if groups build cohesion among members, set clear performance goals, and identify individual contributions.[8]

Another effect, called **free-riding**, also decreases group productivity. This effect occurs in **disjunctive tasks**, tasks in which if one person does a job, no one else has to. For example, if one person does all the research for a project, the work is done, and no one else has to contribute. In this kind of situation, it's easy for members to sit back and let others do the work for them; we call this "taking a free ride." The effects of free-riding are especially destructive because they tend to escalate; when working members perceive that others are getting a free ride, they in turn reduce their efforts. It is important, therefore, to make sure that group members feel their contributions are valued and that everyone is encouraged to participate equally. Table 7.3 indicates some of the factors that can decrease social loafing and free-riding to make groups more productive.

Table 7.2 Individual versus Group Decision Making

Tasks Are Best Left to Individuals When	*Tasks Are Best Done by Groups When*
1. the decision is simple and its rationale is apparent to all members;	1. the decision is complex and needs an innovative, creative solution;
2. a single individual clearly has the expertise to make the decision, and that individual is trusted by the group;	2. the resources of the entire group are needed;
3. time pressures are great and it is difficult to get group members together;	3. there is adequate time for group members to meet;
4. implementing a decision does not necessitate the committed action of all group members;	4. full commitment of all group members is needed to get the job done;
5. little risk is involved;	5. a good solution is risky;
6. there is substantial agreement within the group.	6. the possibility for disagreement or misunderstanding exists unless members talk about the problem.

MANAGING GROUP COMMUNICATION

To get the most from groups, members need to understand how to manage group interaction. They must be aware of potential problems that can beset inexperienced groups. In this section, we turn our attention to some of these problems and look for ways to overcome them. We'll begin by discussing two group dialectics: the need for group members to balance individual and group needs and the need to resolve the tension between task and maintenance goals. We'll then examine how poor communication can result in poor decision making, how groups can avoid the serious problem called groupthink, and how identifying with one group can damage relationships with another.

Balancing Group and Individual Needs

In discussing interpersonal communication, we saw that couples are often beset by contradictory needs—the needs for individuality and interdependence, openness and privacy, and novelty and familiarity. Couples must work out these relational dialectics if they are to create a stable and satisfying relational culture. As we shall see, groups experience similar pressures. And unless a group balances its opposing needs, group communication can fail. The first dialectic is between the needs of the group as a whole and the needs of the individual members.

Group Socialization Processes

Richard Moreland and John Levine, two social psychologists who study group behavior, see **group socialization** as a kind of contest between the individual and the group.[9] Throughout the life of their relationship, individuals try to influence the group to meet their needs, whereas the group as a whole seeks to influence individuals to do what is best for it.

Members have their own reasons for being part of a group. They join groups, at least in part, to receive individual rewards. Throughout their membership, they repeatedly

Table 7.3 Factors Related to Group Productivity

Factors That Increase Group Productivity	Factors That Decrease Group Productivity
Members have a variety of different skills and knowledge.	The group is too large to use all members' resources adequately.
Everyone is committed to group goals.	Members feel their individual efforts don't make a difference.
There is individual accountability.	There is a perception that others are taking a free ride.
All members have an opportunity to contribute.	Members lack commitment to the group.
Members have critical skills.	There is too great a desire for unanimity.
There is an atmosphere of positive interdependence.	Members have hidden agendas or conflicting goals.

measure the extent to which they are receiving these rewards. Moreland and Levine call this process *evaluation*. As a result of evaluation, the level of member satisfaction, or *commitment*, either stays the same, rises, or falls. In the first case, members determine that no change is necessary, and they simply maintain their relationship with the group. In the latter two cases, members decide that some kind of change, or *role transition*, is necessary, and they become either more or less engaged in the life of the group.

The evaluation process begins when a *prospective member* scouts out and evaluates prospective groups, committing himself or herself to the one that he or she evaluates most positively. If the group agrees to accept the person, he or she experiences the role transition from prospective member to *new member*. Often, this transition is marked by an official ceremony and is followed by some kind of orientation. Over time, new members experience additional transitions. If commitment rises, they become *full members*. If commitment falls, they become either *marginal members* or *ex-members*. (Figure 7.1 shows the major role transitions that members go through as they enter, find acceptance in, diverge from, and, finally, exit group life.)

> **If a group has high status, if it can get things done, and if its social atmosphere is positive, members will feel group commitment.**

Figure 7.1 Role Transitions during Group Socialization Processes

Processes

Prospective member

During *investigation* prospective members evaluate rewards available in group, while the group decides on the acceptability of the prospective member. If entry requirements are met, prospective member experiences role transition to new member.
  Entry occurs.

New member

During *socialization* new members seek to make the group accommodate to their needs, while the group seeks to assimilate the new member. If both agree, the new member experiences role transition to full member.
  Acceptance occurs.

Full member

During *maintenance* full members seek out satisfactory roles within the group while the group attempts to negotiate member's role identity. If agreement is reached, full member remains in the group. If not, full member experiences role transition to marginal member.
  Divergence occurs.

Marginal member

During *resocialization* marginal members try to make the group accommodate To their needs, while the group seeks to assimilate the marginal member. If agreement is reached, the marginal member becomes a full member. If not, the marginal member experiences role transition to ex-member.
  Exit occurs.

Ex-member

During *remembrance*, both ex-members and the group decide on the meaning of their association.

*For further discussion, see **Advances in Experimental Social Psychology,** 15th ed., edited by Leonard Berkowitz, "Socialization in Small Groups: Temporal Changes in Individual-Group Relations" by Richard Moreland and John Levine, pp. 137–193.*

What factors cause a rise in commitment and therefore a deeper involvement in the life of the group? If a group has high status, if it can get things done, and if its social atmosphere is positive, members will feel group commitment. In addition, members become committed to groups that allow them to act in desired ways. One member may turn to a group to demonstrate leadership ability. Another member may seek friendship or security. Only if the group gives members what they want will members continue the relationship.

At the same time that members try to influence the group, the group tries to influence members. Just as prospective members shop around for the best group available, so groups try to recruit the best members, admitting only those who meet entry criteria. Think for a minute of yourself as the prospective member and the school you are now attending as the group. In deciding to admit you and to reject others, the school was attempting to maintain its standards and identity. When you decided to attend, you became a new member. In the administration's eyes, first-year students are on a kind of probation and aren't given full status until they prove themselves.

If you are at or beyond the sophomore level, you have achieved the status of a full member of your school. Of course, at any time, if your grades fall or if your conduct violates school standards, you may become a marginal member, and the school will make special efforts to resocialize you. If these efforts fail and you completely refuse to meet the school's requirements, the administration may ask you to leave.

From summer orientation to graduation, ceremonies mark your progress. Along the way, the school tries to make you into its idea of the model student, and you either go along or resist. This process happens not only in large organizations such as colleges but also in everyday small groups. Fraternities or sororities, work or friendship groups, and even families attempt to socialize members. In each case, member and group must reach agreement on what they are to receive from one another. Both must have realistic expectations, and both must be willing to meet some of the others' needs while maintaining their own standards.

Adapting to Group Pressures

How can members adapt most easily to group socialization and find a balance between individual and group needs? One way is to *recognize that full membership comes only with time*. At different stages in one's relationship with a group, different behaviors are expected. Rookies can't make the same demands on a team that veteran players can. A first lieutenant doesn't have the same status as a general. And the brand-new, just-out-of-school management trainee doesn't sit down at the head of the table and tell the third-line manager what to do.

Before a new member can be accepted, he or she must earn the right. Using an economic metaphor, Edwin Hollander created the concept of idiosyncrasy credit to explain how groups regulate the behavior of inexperienced members.[10] An **idiosyncrasy credit** is a kind of symbolic currency earned through conformity. By meeting group expectations, members build up a "credit balance" that can later be traded in for innovative behavior. Group members who try to take over leadership too soon or who deviate from group consensus before they have earned enough credit are usually rejected by more established members. Hollander's research reinforces the idea that new members should proceed slowly, gradually increasing their participation once they have earned the group's trust.

> Group members who try to take over leadership too soon or who deviate from group consensus before they have earned enough credit are usually rejected by more established members.

Another way to make a successful transition into a group is to *recognize the written and unwritten norms that govern each level of membership.* These norms may be explicit rules, written down and available to all, or they may be implicit norms that can only be picked up through imitation. Whether or not members decide to follow all of the group's norms, they should be aware of what the norms are. This awareness takes careful and sensitive observation on the part of the member and clear messages on the part of the group.

Adapting to group life is usually easier with support from others. This support can come from more experienced members or from other new members. A full member who knows the ropes and who is willing to initiate a new member into the group culture is called a *mentor.* Mentors can help to smooth role transitions for new members by instructing them how to fit in. Support is also essential for members who decide to resist group norms. By banding together with other newcomers, new members can sometimes successfully challenge old ways of doing things. Whereas a lone member usually cannot exert enough pressure to change a group, several new members sometimes can.

Successful role transition is a matter of negotiation and balance. Perhaps the most important thing to keep in mind is that *members have a right to expect the group to meet some of their needs, just as the group has a right to expect members to contribute to its goals.* Only by recognizing the legitimacy of both parties' goals can groups and individuals successfully work together.

Taking on Task and Maintenance Roles

Another dialectic is important in group life: the tension between task and maintenance goals. Most groups exist for a reason. Often, they form to solve a problem or to reach a decision. This dimension of group behavior is called its **task dimension**, and the output of this dimension is called *productivity.* We expect groups to produce results.

At the same time, groups must also fulfill social functions. Groups must devote some of their efforts to creating a positive group climate. This dimension of a group's behavior is called its **maintenance or social dimension**, and its output is called *group cohesiveness.* Although productivity and cohesiveness are sometimes in conflict, they are closely related. Successful groups must achieve both. A group that works so hard on its task that it neglects members' feelings eventually dissolves. Cohesiveness

> A group that works so hard on its task that it neglects members' feelings eventually dissolves. Cohesiveness is the glue that holds a group together.

Groups allow people with unique and similar interests to create bonds and broadcast their identity.

Science and Society/SuperStock

is the glue that holds a group together. Similarly, a group that avoids work to focus entirely on maintenance ends up losing members, for no one wants to be part of an unproductive group. One of the keys to managing group communication is to behave in ways that advance both productivity and cohesion.

All of us find some behaviors easier than others. Often, we specialize in either task or maintenance behaviors. The key to being an effective group member, however, lies in being able to take on both kinds of behaviors, depending on the needs of the group. Behaviors that help the group to accomplish its task are called *task roles*. They include acting as information giver, information seeker, evaluator-critic, and so on. Behaviors that enhance the social climate of the group are called *maintenance roles*. Roles such as encourager, standard setter, or harmonizer are examples. Finally, personal goals that do not help the group reach either of its basic goals are called *negative roles*. Negative roles are generally dysfunctional and indicate that a member is having trouble balancing group and individual needs. Table 7.4 lists some of the roles necessary for group productivity and cohesiveness, and Table 7.5 outlines negative, dysfunctional roles.

How can one person increase group effectiveness? First, it is important to *become as flexible as possible in both task and maintenance roles*. The best group member is the one who can recognize and provide whatever the group needs at a particular time. Such a member must watch the group process carefully, realizing that what the group needs is not necessarily what the member likes to do best. Highly task-oriented members often lose patience with the group when it gets off track; they fail to understand that occasional jokes, friendly chitchat, and well-timed breaks are not a waste of time but are ways to build group cohesion. Instead of giving a steady barrage of opinions, the task-oriented group member should learn to stop and make sure other members are comfortable.

Similarly, the maintenance-oriented member should learn how to enhance task development. A harmonizer, for example, should realize that the line between relieving tension and being a clown is thin. Although maintenance is a good thing, there are times when the group must get down to work. One way to increase your own flexibility is to look at Tables 7.4 and 7.5 and determine the roles you play most frequently. Then practice playing different roles until you feel comfortable with a large repertoire.

In addition, it is important to *avoid disruptive individual roles*. We all bring our own hidden agendas to the groups we belong to. A **hidden agenda** is a personal goal that lies below the surface and that can get in the way of group performance. Sometimes, hidden agendas are compatible with group goals (for example, when a

---

Table 7.4 Task and Maintenance Roles

Task Roles

Role	Description
Initiator–Contributor	Suggests new ideas to group or offers new way of regarding group problem
Information Seeker	Asks for clarification of suggestions and for information and facts pertinent to problem
Opinion Seeker	Asks for clarification of values associated with group problem or with decision suggestions
Information Giver	Offers facts or generalizations or relates experiences relevant to group problem
Opinion Giver	States beliefs or opinions pertinent to group problem or to decision suggestions
Elaborator	Thinks of examples, offers rationales, or works out details of previous suggestions
Coordinator	Pulls together ideas and suggestions and coordinates work of various subgroups
Orienter	Summarizes what has occurred or asks questions about the path the group will take
Evaluator–Critic	Develops standards for group functioning and compares group performance to standards
Energizer	Prods group to action and stimulates greater levels of group activity
Procedural Technician	Expedites group movement by taking on routine tasks
Recorder	Writes down suggestions, records decisions, and takes minutes

Maintenance Roles

Role	Description
Encourager	Accepts and praises others' contributions
Harmonizer	Relieves tension and mediates disagreements
Compromiser	Seeks to find solution for conflict that involves own ideas
Gatekeeper–Expediter	Keeps communication channels open and facilitates others' participation
Standard Setter	Expresses maintenance standards or applies standards to group process
Group Observer	Observes group process and offers feedback about maintenance procedures
Follower	Accepts ideas of group and serves as audience

Based on "Functional Roles of Group Members," by Kenneth Benne and Paul Sheats, 1948, *Journal of Social Issues, 4*, pp. 41–49.

group member channels a need for recognition into effective task leadership), and sometimes they are incompatible (as when a team member grandstands or hogs the ball instead of passing it off). Members should examine their own agendas and guard against dysfunctional behavior. At the same time, the group should be aware of members' needs and try to satisfy them. If this is impossible, the group should discuss members' dysfunctional behaviors with those members, pointing out the effects of the behaviors on the group as a whole.

Combating Groupthink

We have seen that it is important for task groups to feel cohesive and confident. Sometimes, however, a group gets too confident and begins to make poor decisions. We call this state **groupthink**, and it can have very serious repercussions. A number of communication scholars have argued that the 1986 explosion of the space shuttle *Challenger* was a classic example of groupthink. They contend that poor decision making on the part of Thiokol engineers and NASA officials led these experts to underestimate risks, overestimate the likelihood of success, and ignore warnings and their own misgivings.[11] In this case, a failure of group communication may have led to death and disaster.

    What exactly is groupthink? Irving Janis, who coined the term, defines it as "a mode of thinking that people engage in when they are deeply involved in a cohesive

Table 7.5 Negative Roles

Roles	Description
Dominator	Refuses to allow others to express their opinions and dominates discussion
Blocker	Prolongs or stops decision making by foot-dragging and nitpicking
Self-Confessor	Distracts group by disclosing personal problems and by using group for personal therapy
Help Seeker	Constantly expresses own inadequacy and asks group for sympathy and compliments
Recognition Seeker	Spends time boasting about own accomplishments in order to be center of attention
Special-Interest Pleader	Manipulates group in interests of some other group; has hidden agenda
Playboy or Playgirl	Fails to take group seriously; spends time playing around and mocks serious behavior
Joker or Clown	Uses humor and horseplay to divert group from task

From Cragan/Wright. *Communication in Small Group Discussions,* 2nd ed. Copyright © 1986 Wadsworth, a part of Cengage Learning, Inc. Reproduced by permission. www.cengage.com/permissions.

in-group, when the members' strivings for unanimity override their motivation to realistically appraise alternative courses of action."[12] In groupthink, group members believe that they can do no wrong. This problem can occur when cohesion is too high, when group members are too similar (so that no new ideas challenge group consensus), or when the group is isolated from outside influences.

Groupthink has several symptoms. The first is an *illusion of invulnerability*. A group that is immersed in groupthink believes so strongly that it is the best that it loses all sense of reality. The second symptom is *belief in the group's own morality*. Members feel that their actions and beliefs are more valuable than those of people outside the group. This symptom is closely related to a third symptom, the tendency to hold *shared stereotypes*. Members take on an "us versus them" mentality, believing that anyone who opposes the group is stupid or wrong. Problems or failures are explained away by *collective rationalizations,* which allow members to stick to an ill-advised course of action even in the face of contrary information. Individual members who begin to doubt the group feel strong pressures toward *self-censorship.* They hesitate to speak up because they know they will encounter disapproval. In fact, an *illusion of unanimity* arises, whereby a doubting member believes that everyone else agrees with the group's chosen action. Should a dissenting member speak up, he or she is severely sanctioned as other members place *pressure on dissenters.* Finally, the leader and key members of the group are protected from outside information by self-appointed *mind-guards* who "protect" them from negative information.

As a result of the groupthink atmosphere, problem solving is disrupted. Members ignore alternatives, fail to test their ideas against reality, and refuse to make contingency plans. When people believe that they are superior and invincible, they feel no need to examine their ideas carefully. Janis analyzed several historical fiascoes and showed that symptoms of groupthink occurred in all of them, including America's failure to secure Pearl Harbor, its decision to invade the Bay of Pigs, the escalation of the Vietnam War, and the Watergate cover-up. And we can add the *Challenger* disaster to this list.

Groupthink does not occur only in famous historical cases; it also characterizes everyday groups. Any speech communication teacher who has taught a course in small-group communication can give examples of classroom groups that spent all their time telling themselves how great their project would be and almost no time working on the project. Talented people have a natural tendency to get lazy and overconfident unless they make special efforts to avoid groupthink.

> **Talented people have a natural tendency to get lazy and overconfident unless they make special efforts to avoid groupthink.**

How can groups guard against this kind of overconfidence? Groups can assign a member to take on the role of critic or devil's advocate. They can take criticisms and warnings seriously. When they hear themselves denigrating the competition or bragging about their own talents, they can become aware that they may be slipping into groupthink. And they can also make a rule that once a decision has been made, they will hold a second-chance meeting to review it and find its flaws. By carefully monitoring their behavior as they pass through the common stages of group development, groups can avoid serious errors in problem solving.

Improving Communication with Out-Groups

So far we have focused on communication within groups. But what about interaction between groups? How does being a part of one group affect how we think about and act toward members of another group? In this section we discuss how group membership offers us social identity, and how this identity may cause us to depersonalize and compete with people who belong to other groups.

But identity may be more complex than you think. Rather than having one identity, we have many. Each of us has a personal identity consisting of the characteristics that distinguish us from those around us. At the same time we have a social identity or, more accurately, a series of social identities that define us in terms of our similarities to others. When you describe yourself as cheerful or kind or brave, you are talking about your personal identity. When you describe yourself as a Republican or Democrat, a man or woman, a Christian or Muslim or Jew, you are referencing a **social identity**, an identity based on group membership. Scholars who take a *social identity approach* to studying groups go so far as to define them as collections of three or more people who "have the same definition of who they are, what attributes they have, and how they relate to and differ from specific out-groups."[13] Social identity theorists believe that groups create socially shared worldviews. They also believe that we favor in-group members (people in our own groups) and try to distinguish

Identity is arguably our most prized possession; it shapes the way we see ourselves, it affects our self-esteem, and it guides our actions.

ourselves from out-group members (people in other groups). So strong is this need to see ourselves as similar to some and different from others that even when our ties to others are tenuous and artificial, we still allow those ties to affect us.

A series of studies demonstrated this effect by using what is known as the *minimum group paradigm*. In a typical minimum group study, subjects are labeled as belonging to one of two groups and then asked to give money to each of the groups. Despite the fact that they get no money themselves, and despite the fact that they have no interaction with those who share their group label, subjects divide the money so that members of "their group" get more than members of the other group. Identification with a minimum group can be extremely tenuous. In one study, college students were asked to play a competitive game with someone they thought either had the same birthday as they did or had another birthday. Results showed that students tended to cooperate with those individuals with the same birthday but to compete against those with a different birthday.[14] If simply being categorized as similar to someone else leads to in-group bias, imagine how much influence real-life groups have over their members.

Social identity theorists believe that we hold *group prototypes* for every group we belong to. Group prototypes are mental images of the characteristics of group members, the values and norms they hold, and the differences between group members and outsiders. Within a given group, we will like members who match the group prototype and dislike members who fail to conform to the group prototype.[15] Furthermore, if we are strongly committed to a group, we ourselves internalize the group's norms and values, doing our best to fit the prototype by being like other group members. Research shows that members who act in accordance with the norms and values embedded in a group prototype gain the ability to influence others.[16]

We also use group prototypes to categorize and depersonalize members of out-groups, ignoring their unique characteristics. How can we explain this tendency to categorize others on the basis of their group identities? One reason is that depersonalizing allows us to reduce uncertainty. Assigning someone to a category suggests that he or she is like other people in that category; it allows us to say to ourselves, "I know who that person is because I know the group he belongs to." When people are uncertain or when the times in which they live are complex and confusing, they often join groups that have clearly defined or ideologically extreme prototypes.[17]

In addition to reducing uncertainty, holding strong positive in-group prototypes can increase self-esteem. By creating prototypes that favor in-group members, people can convince themselves, "My group is the best. Thank goodness I'm not one of *them*." Over time, this kind of thinking results in polarized perceptions such that out-group members are seen as more different than they actually are. Social identity theory, then, offers an explanation for prejudice and ethnocentrism and emphasizes the importance groups have in our lives. By being aware of our tendency to categorize and depersonalize others based on group membership, we may be able to, at least partially, make fairer and more reasoned evaluations of others.

> By being aware of our tendency to categorize and depersonalize others based on group membership, we may be able to, at least partially, make fairer and more reasoned evaluations of others.

GROUP DEVELOPMENT: PHASES IN PROBLEM-SOLVING GROUPS

Groups are not static. Over time groups develop and change. Norms develop, roles are embraced, and leaders emerge. As we saw in our discussion of interpersonal communication, couples go through recognizable stages as they create their relational cultures. So too do groups. In this section we begin by looking at phases in group development and then take up the topic of leader emergence in groups.

Phase Models: Mapping the Life of a Group

A number of scholars have tried to describe the phases that groups go through as they find ways to work effectively and productively. Despite slight differences in their models of group development, most scholars agree that groups go through approximately five phases.

In the initial phase, called by Bruce Tuckman the *forming* phase, members focus on getting to know one another and on deciding how to fit in to the group.[18] This stage is often characterized by tentative and awkward communication as members experience primary tension.[19] The best way to deal with primary tension is simply to *act in an open, friendly, and positive manner and to give members time to feel comfortable with one another*. It is not a good idea to force decisions during this period. In most cases, this tension will dissipate naturally; however, if it persists groups will be blocked from further development.

The second phase is generally described as a conflict phase, or, in Tuckman's term, a *storming* phase. Here a new form of tension, called secondary tension, arises as group members work out leadership and role distinctions. Susan Wheelan explains that "issues of power, authority, and competition are debated at this stage."[20] She believes that the conflict experienced in this stage, if properly resolved, can serve to define common values and can lead to increased cohesion. Members should *learn to expect periods of conflict and find ways to benefit from the energy and ideas that are generated during these periods*.

Once secondary tension has been resolved, the third phase, a *norming* phase, occurs as members openly work out group goals, norms, and roles, preparing themselves for the fourth, or *performing phase*. Groups are now ready to settle down to work. The goal here is to make good decisions, get the job done, and remain a cohesive unit. Members now feel comfortable in exchanging ideas.

In groups that have a formal end point, a fifth, *adjourning*, phase occurs. Depending on the success of the group in achieving its task, expression of positive feelings and congratulations may emerge, although occasionally anxiety about termination may occur.

Whereas most scholars see group development as passing through a series of orderly phases like these, others have argued that progress may not always be so clear-cut. Marshall Scott Poole, for example, offers a multiple-sequence model, in which he argues that groups often work on different problems simultaneously and may backtrack or even need to repeat earlier work.[21] Wheelan believes that the fact that groups do not always progress in an orderly fashion does not invalidate global phase models. She compares groups to individuals. While most people mature over time in fairly orderly ways, not all do. Some experience developmental delays or failures while others regress temporarily. "Some groups," she tells us, "like some people, will not mature. However, the majority of groups will develop cultures, structures, and processes that facilitate goal achievement."[22]

Leadership: How Groups Choose Leaders

What does it take to be a good leader? There is no easy answer to this question. Students of group behavior have answered this question in many ways. In this section we begin by looking at four different approaches to leadership. We then discuss some things to avoid if you want to be an effective leader.

Approaches to Leadership

Theorists who take a **trait approach** believe that the key to leadership lies in the personal characteristics of leaders. In his review of leadership research, Peter Northhouse found evidence that individuals who show intelligence, self-confidence, determination, integrity, and sociability are likely to emerge as leaders, although it is not yet clear if these same factors lead to successful group influence.[23] Other researchers argue that people who are charismatic, visionary, intellectually stimulating, and considerate of followers are likely to emerge as transformation leaders and may be in a position to influence others.[24] Still others take a different tack, identifying factors, or traits, that keep a person from becoming a leader, such as lack of participation, rigidity, authoritarian behavior, or negative communication.[25] Unfortunately, no one has been able to come up with a list of traits that, in all cases, distinguish leaders from nonleaders.

If traits can't always identify a leader, perhaps communication style can. Theorists who take a **styles approach** contend that what is important is not the personality of the leader but rather how he or she acts. A series of studies have argued, for example, that leaders who choose a democratic or participatory style are more effective than those who are either authoritarian or use a "hands-off" style.[26] Although a democratic style has been associated with positive outcomes, it too is not universally effective.

Perhaps, rather than looking for the one best style of leadership, it makes more sense to argue that different styles work in different situations. This is exactly what those who take a **situational approach** believe. But what aspects of the situation affect leadership? Kenneth Hershey and Paul Blanchard have argued that the maturity level of a group should dictate the leader's style, with a more directive style being suitable in the early stages of group development and a more delegating style being effective later in the life of the group.[27] Robert J. House and Gary Dessler, on the other hand, believe that the most important factors in determining leadership style are members' attitudes, in particular whether members believe they have the ability and opportunity to do their tasks effectively and whether they view completing the tasks as potentially rewarding.[28] Fred Fiedler offers another suggestion. He feels that variables such as the leader's relationship with group members, his or her power, and whether a task is structured or unstructured dictate the kind of leader who will succeed.[29] Finally, leader-member exchange theory contends that leaders should match their styles not to the situation, but to the characteristics of each member, substituting sensitivity to member needs for consistency.[30]

One of the factors that complicates research into leadership is the ambiguity of the term *leader*. Some people think of a leader as a single individual, someone who is appointed to manage a group. Others, however, believe that a leader is anyone who performs behavior that moves a group toward its goals. Under this latter view, called the **functional approach**, leadership can be shared, and what is important in understanding leadership is knowing the functions that have to be fulfilled in the group. Dennis Gouran offers an interesting way of thinking about leadership. He argues that leadership is the "art of counteractive influence."[31] By this he means that leadership is the art of getting a group back on track when it encounters obstacles such as arguments over authority, conformity pressures, disruptive behavior, lack of motivation, and the like.

Clearly, leadership is a complex process that cannot be summed up neatly. It is possible that there is a grain of truth in all of these theories. It is likely that leadership calls for personal traits that make the leader attractive to members. But it is also likely that leadership necessitates the flexibility to take on differing styles depending on the situation as well as the sensitivity to know how to keep the group moving in a positive direction. Gouran points out that leadership is more an art than a science:

> There does appear to be a kind of intuitive feel that some individuals have and others do not for the enactment of certain types of communicative behavior; it is very difficult to detect but it nonetheless can produce differences in leadership success. . . . Capitalizing on those subtleties that give one greater advantage definitely appears to be something of an art.[32]

How Not to Be Chosen Leader

Although the qualities that make people succeed as leaders appear complex, those associated with poor leadership are much easier to list. Fisher gives eight rules for how not to emerge as leader.[33] Although his intent is humorous, his list holds more than a little truth. If you don't want the responsibility of group leadership, try these suggestions. If, on the other hand, you want to help your group accomplish its tasks, these are behaviors to avoid.

RULE 1 Be absent as often as possible. And if you want to increase your chances of avoiding leadership still more, refuse to provide any excuse for your absence.

RULE 2 Contribute as little as possible. Here it helps to appear incompetent and uninterested as well as to be silent.

RULE 3 Volunteer to be secretary or record keeper. You run the risk of demonstrating your value to the group in this way, but because the secretary role is generally a secondary role, you can probably avoid major leadership responsibilities.

RULE 4 Be subservient and acquiescent, showing a total inability to come up with useful ideas of your own.

RULE 5 Be rude and verbally aggressive early in the discussion, and sulk and become apathetic later on when people are sharing ideas.

RULE 6 Become the group's joker. In this way, you get to be the center of attention, yet at the same time, you warn others not to take you seriously.

RULE 7 Come across as a know-it-all. The use of big words and a desire to talk about every topic under the sun should do the trick.

RULE 8 Show contempt for leadership, and attack and label others when they try to contribute.

STRENGTHENING GROUP DISCUSSION SKILLS

Communicating in groups is not always easy. In this section, we'll look at a few ways to become a more effective group member. We'll begin by discussing what makes groups intelligent and effective, including the importance of sharing information, creating positive group climates, and organizing problem-solving discussions. Finally, we'll review some of the standard formats for group discussion used in public settings.

Group Intelligence and Social Sensitivity

What makes a group intelligent? Why can some groups solve many different problems at a high level of accuracy while others can't? Until quite recently, most people would answer that what makes a group solve problems intelligently is a function of the individual IQs of group members. Groups with smart people solve problems in smart ways. Not so, suggest Anita Woolley and her colleagues at MIT who found, in a series of studies, that neither the average individual intelligence of group members nor the intelligence of the group's smartest member was as good a predictor of group success as were social sensitivity (as measured by members' ability to process non-verbal indicators of emotion) and the extent to which participation within the group is relatively evenly distributed.[34] In other words, Woolley found that the way that group members interact—how much attention and encouragement they give to one another—is at least as important as their individual intelligence and that groups have a general level of intelligence.

The Importance of Information Sharing: Uncovering Hidden Profiles

One of the reasons equal participation and social sensitivity create smart groups may be that they take advantage of collective knowledge. Groups thrive on information, yet too often group members fail to communicate what they know. The area of research that focuses on how and why members fail to share information has come to be called **hidden profile research**.[35] In a typical hidden profile study, group members are given information (the hidden profile) before discussing a problem. Some of the information is given to all members and some unique information is given only to individual members. Only when all the information is used can the group make a high-quality decision. What happens? Often the unique information is never discussed, and as a result optimal solutions are not reached.

One of the reasons that unique information is not offered is because information that everyone possesses is encouraged and repeated during deliberations and may overpower individual information. When members hear that others have the same information they do, they may take this as a validation that the shared information is important, and, as a consequence, unique information falls by the wayside. In addition, members may consciously decide to withhold unique information because they don't want to run the risk of losing credibility by contradicting the group.[36] They may also be motivated by a desire to avoid looking like a troublemaker, by a need to get their decision supported by the group, or by a desire to fit in to the group and make it more cohesive. Discussing something everyone agrees on can help members develop trust and interpersonal closeness and can establish common ground.[37]

Whatever the reasons, withheld information can lead to poor decision making. There are several ways to increase information sharing. Choosing group members who possess a range of information and encouraging them to discuss all possible alternatives before trying to solve the problem can lead to higher-quality solutions.[38] In addition, developing norms for critical evaluation can increase information exchange. Finally, studies have also shown that simply encouraging members to recall as much information as possible before deliberating will lead to better results.[39]

Creating a Positive Climate

Some years ago, Jack Gibb described the kinds of behaviors that can lead to competitive, defensive climates and those that can lead to cooperative, supportive climates.[40] Gibb believed that in a **defensive climate**, in which group members feel threatened, the group is unproductive. To the extent to which group members sense evaluation, control, strategy, neutrality, superiority, and certainty on the part of others, they close down and refuse to cooperate. By replacing these behaviors with description, problem orientation, spontaneity, empathy, equality, and provisionalism, a group can create a **supportive climate**.

Evaluation occurs when individuals are judgmental toward one another, when their comments imply that they are appraising and criticizing one another's behavior. *Description*, on the other hand, arouses little defensiveness, because it focuses on presenting feelings or opinions without assigning blame. It is better for a group member to express concern about a deadline by describing his or her feelings ("I'm concerned about getting the work done as soon as possible, because I have commitments at the end of the month") than by evaluating ("This group has got to stop wasting time and being lazy"). *Control* is another behavior that increases defensiveness. When members try to impose their will on others ("The only way to get this done is to …") rather than trying to collaborate ("Does anyone have ideas about how to get the job done?"), they are likely to meet resistance. The opposite of control is taking a *problem orientation*.

> By recognizing the need to be more supportive and open and by listening empathically, members can improve the social climate of their groups.

Strategy occurs when group members' behavior is prompted by hidden agendas. Feeling manipulated naturally leads to defensiveness. The corresponding supportive behavior is *spontaneity*, whereby the member communicates in an open and honest manner. *Neutrality*, although it sounds positive, can often signal indifference and a lack of commitment. On the other hand, *empathy* tells others that you understand their thoughts and feelings. As we saw in Chapter 6, the use of the paraphrasing response can indicate concern and empathy.

Superiority should be avoided as much as possible, for superior responses lead to jealousy and resentment. Instead, members should be careful to indicate *equality* by asking for others' opinions and weighing everyone's contributions equally. Finally, having too great a sense of *certainty* can lead to an unpleasant group climate. *Provisionalism*, by contrast, signals a willingness to listen openly to others' ideas. Group members should monitor themselves to make sure they are not inadvertently making others defensive. It is easy to come across as superior or certain even when you may not mean to. Without realizing it, we can easily hurt one another's feelings and make groups frustrating and unpleasant. By recognizing the need to be more supportive and open and by listening empathically, members can improve the social climate of their groups.

Enhancing Problem Solving

When left to their own devices, groups often jump from one idea to another. In fact, studies have shown that the average attention span of a group—the time it stays on a single topic—is approximately fifty-eight seconds.[41] One of the reasons group problem solving is so difficult is that groups have trouble staying on track.

To facilitate more orderly thinking, group members sometimes turn to the use of logical plans, or *agendas*, to guide their discussion. Agendas are often very useful when time is limited and task pressures are strong, because they focus on the task dimension. Their major disadvantage is that following a task agenda too closely or using agendas at every meeting may increase productivity at the cost of cohesiveness. Nevertheless, there are times when agendas can be extremely useful.

The Standard Agenda

In 1910, philosopher John Dewey described a rational process for solving problems that he called **reflective thinking**. Dewey believed that reflective thinking begins with a felt difficulty. We then examine that difficulty, think of possible solutions, evaluate them, choose the best one, and then implement it. The **standard agenda** is a six-step guide to solving problems that derives directly from Dewey's theories about reflective thinking.[42] Table 7.6 summarizes the six steps.

Table 7.6 Steps in the Standard Agenda

Step 1   Problem Identification
Group members clarify the problem, often by specifying the difference between a present state of affairs and a desired state of affairs. Problems should be concrete, clear, and solvable.

Step 2   Problem Analysis
Group members collect information about the problem, identifying factors that are causing the problem and factors that may help in solving the problem.

Step 3   Criteria Selection
Group members decide on the characteristics of a valid solution prior to discussing specific solutions.

Step 4   Solution Generation
Group members generate as many solution alternatives as possible.

Step 5   Solution Evaluation and Selection
Group members use previously selected criteria to evaluate each solution. The solution that best meets evaluation criteria is chosen.

Step 6   Solution Implementation
Group members follow through by putting the solution into effect.

The first step in the standard agenda is *problem identification*. Too often, groups jump into a discussion without a complete understanding of the problem they need to solve. A **problem** can be defined as a discrepancy between a present state of affairs and a desired state of affairs.[43] Defining the problem can often be the most difficult step in problem solving. Let's look at an example. Most of us feel that our campuses have a parking problem. But what does that really mean? Does it mean that there are currently not enough spaces? Or does it mean that there are plenty of spaces but that they are too far from classroom buildings? Or could it be that spaces are available at some times of the day but not at others? Each of these definitions calls for a different solution. Only when the definition of the problem is concrete and clear can the group move on to the next step.

> **Too often, groups jump into a discussion without a complete understanding of the problem they need to solve.**

Dan Rothwell gives two interesting examples of how the way a problem is framed affects the way it is ultimately solved.[44] In the first example, a service station manager learned that his soda machine was out of order when customers who lost their money complained. To solve the problem, he put an "Out of Order" sign on the machine. Customers ignored the sign, continued to lose money, and continued to complain. He finally solved the problem by changing the sign to read $2. No one bought the soda, and no one complained. In a second example, a convenience store had a problem with teenagers loitering outside. Instead of looking for ways to confront the students, the store owners simply piped Muzak into the parking lot. The kids found the bland music so objectionable that they soon found another hangout.

Rothwell explains that in both cases, the solution became achievable as soon as it was framed in the right way. In the first example, the service station manager stopped asking himself, "How can I let the customers know the machine is out of order?" and instead asked, "How can I stop customers from putting money in the machine?" In the second example, the proprietors were successful only after they stopped thinking in terms of force and started to ask, "What will motivate the teenagers to leave on their own?"

The second step in the standard agenda is *problem analysis*. David Johnson and Frank Johnson, drawing on the work of Kurt Lewin, suggest that one of the best ways to diagnose a problem is to view the current state of affairs as a balance between two opposing forces: restraining and helping forces.[45] Restraining forces are negative. If they prevail, the current state will get worse. Helping forces, on the other hand, are positive. If they are strengthened, the current state will move closer to the ideal. This kind of analysis is called **force-field analysis**. By listing restraining and helping forces, group members understand the problem better.

Assume that a school curriculum committee has decided that a new experimental course is needed to update current offerings. Through force-field analysis, the committee finds that one of the major restraining factors is parents' resistance to the course due to a misunderstanding of what the new course is all about. The committee also finds that the helping forces include current faculty members' ability to teach the new course and their willingness to support the idea. The group now knows that it can enlist the teachers' aid and that they should remove parents' fears.

The third step in the standard agenda is *criteria selection*. Before they begin to offer suggestions, group members should establish the criteria they will use in judging solutions. One group may decide, for example, that its solution must be rapid and reasonably cheap and that it must change the status quo as little as possible. Another group addressing another problem may decide that it wants a long-term solution and that money is no object. The time to decide on criteria is before members' egos get too involved in specific decision proposals.

The fourth step is *solution generation*. Here, group members attempt to generate as many alternative solutions as possible. To do this, they may use methods such as brainstorming, a method we will look at shortly when we examine ways to enhance group creativity. The important point is identifying a number of alternatives rather than being satisfied with the first one.

In step five of the standard agenda, *solution evaluation and selection*, alternative solutions are evaluated, and the best one is selected. Now it is a simple matter of looking at each solution and measuring it against each criterion. The solution that meets the most criteria (without causing additional problems) is the best solution. Finally, in step six, the group follows through with *solution implementation*.

Brainstorming: Increasing Creativity

Although a standard agenda can keep a group focused and can encourage members to think critically, it doesn't tell us much about how to generate new and creative ideas. One of the major blocks to idea generation is the tendency to reject potentially good ideas by evaluating them prematurely. **Brainstorming** is a technique in which members are encouraged to generate as many ideas as they can, as quickly as possible. They are instructed to say whatever pops into their heads, no matter how ridiculous it may sound. The idea is to collect a large pool of ideas and then go back and criticize them. Only after all ideas have been suggested is evaluation allowed.

David Johnson and Frank Johnson discuss several ways to encourage idea generation, methods that can be used by themselves or in conjunction with brainstorming.[46] One is called the *part-changing method*. Here, members think of new products or ideas by identifying old parts that might be altered. A group of furniture designers, for example, might decide to think of ways to change each part of a chair. They would then generate as many different colors, shapes, sizes, textures, styles, and so on as possible without worrying whether or not the ideas were feasible.

In the *checkerboard method*, the group draws up a matrix. One set of behaviors or characteristics is written in columns across the top of the matrix, and another set is written in rows along the left-hand side. Members then examine the spaces where rows and columns intersect to see whether they can generate any creative combinations. For example, a group with the task of inventing a new sport might list equipment or materials across the top of a matrix and actions or playing surfaces along the side. Although many of the resulting combinations might seem ridiculous, some just might work.

Finally, in the *find-something-similar method*, group members are encouraged to think of analogies. A group that wants to solve a parking problem might think of how bees, squirrels, shoe stores, dry cleaners, and so on store things. All of these methods encourage members to break away from standard ways of thinking and to become more open-minded and daring.

Nominal Group Technique

The standard agenda, brainstorming, and the Johnsons' methods for generating ideas are only some of the many techniques that have been devised to increase group problem-solving efficiency. An interesting variation combines parts of these procedures but cuts actual interaction to a minimum. This is **nominal group technique**.[47] In this technique, individuals generate solution ideas on their own and then meet to clarify these ideas. After all ideas have been listed and explained, members individually rank their favorite ideas. The rankings are then averaged, and the idea with the highest average is chosen. By asking members to work individually, the method avoids the problem of more aggressive members overpowering quieter members. By refusing to allow members to evaluate one another's ideas, the method eliminates potential conflict. This method is also less lengthy than full-blown discussion.

Brilhart and Galanes have modified this technique to involve more discussion.[48] After ideas are individually generated and rankings are computed and displayed, members begin to discuss the merits of the top ideas. The discussion continues until consensus is reached or until a vote is called.

Many additional methods exist to guide group problem solving, each with its own advantages and disadvantages. Being able to control a group and enhance its ability to work effectively are important skills for anyone who is interested in working with people. The more you learn about group dynamics, the more fascinating this subject will become.

Using Special Formats for Public Discussion

The techniques we have looked at so far were designed for groups to use in private deliberations. Occasionally, group discussion takes place in public, in front of an audience. In such a case, group discussion is used to increase audience understanding of a particular issue. **Public discussion formats** designed with this goal in mind include the symposium, the forum, the panel discussion, the buzz group, and the role-playing group.[49]

The Symposium

A *symposium* is a form of public discussion in which a number of experts give brief, prepared speeches on a topic. A typical symposium might concern a public issue such as child abuse. A sociologist might be invited to outline the extent and causes of the problem, a psychologist to discuss the symptoms and effects of abuse, a school administrator to speak on the role of teachers in discovering and reporting suspected cases, and so on. The role of the chairperson of a symposium is to introduce the problem, to present each speaker, and to sum up the discussion. The symposium is a fairly formal format that involves little interaction between participants and audience. To encourage more interaction, planners often combine the symposium with another format, the forum.

The Forum

A *forum* is a much more freewheeling form of discussion than is a symposium. In a forum, audience members share their comments and opinions with one another and are led by a moderator whose job is to announce the topic, to provide necessary background information, to set the ground rules for participation, and generally to control the discussion. When a forum follows a symposium, it allows audience members to express their feelings and to add their comments to those of the experts. Much of the success of the discussion lies with the moderator, who must keep the audience on track and make sure everyone is heard. When talk show hosts such as Oprah Winfrey or Dr. Phil go out into the audience to solicit comments, they are using a forum format.

The Panel Discussion

In the *panel discussion*, experts interact with one another in a small group while an audience listens. After the Los Angeles riots of 1992, for example, many communities organized panel discussions on the topic of police–community relations. These panels included police representatives as well as leaders from minority communities, educators, and local politicians. The goals were to allow interested parties to share their feelings and to discover ways to increase cooperation between law enforcement agencies and the public.

In a well-organized panel discussion, the moderator formulates the major topics to be discussed and informs the participants of these topics ahead of time. He or she introduces participants, organizes the discussion, and summarizes panelists' contributions. It is up to the moderator and participants to ensure that the discussion follows a logical plan, that participation is fair, and that enough time is allocated for each topic.

The key to moderating or participating in a panel is to be well informed, to listen carefully to others, and to make sure that the discussion is coherent. The panel format is particularly interesting because it combines small group and public communication. Panelists must share ideas and reach conclusions within the group while also communicating to an audience. This is no easy task.

The Buzz Group

Some discussion formats are expressly designed to be used as supplements to formal presentations. Their goal is to increase audience response to a speech or public discussion. One such format is the *buzz group*. Once the initial presentation is finished, audience members are divided into small discussion groups and are asked to respond to the speaker's topic. For example, a conference on the topic of wellness might begin with a speech on the importance of a healthy diet. To reinforce the speaker's points, audience members might be asked to divide into groups of seven or eight people, to make a list of factors that reinforce unhealthy eating habits, and then to think of ways to resist these negative influences. After members of each group have had time to discuss their ideas, a spokesperson reports the group's conclusions to the assembly as a whole.

The buzz session increases audience involvement by placing audience members in a small, friendly group. Members who might be intimidated by speaking up in a large forum often feel comfortable in the small-group context. In addition, discussion makes the speaker's points more personal and more memorable.

The Role-Playing Group

An even stronger way to involve audience members is through **role-playing**. In role-playing, people are placed in small groups, are given a scenario, and are asked to act out their responses. By experiencing a situation rather than passively discussing it, members can get in touch with their emotions and can practice new behaviors. After a role-play is over, the actors discuss what occurred and what they learned from the experience.

> By experiencing a situation rather than passively discussing it, members can get in touch with their emotions and can practice new behaviors.

Role-playing is often used to help people understand one another's point of view. In a workshop designed to increase child–parent interaction, for example, children and parents might be asked to switch roles, each playing the part of the other. This role reversal may help them understand one another's concerns and motivations. Role-playing is also often used to help people practice new or difficult behaviors. A campaign against drunk driving might ask high school students to practice taking the keys away from a friend who has had too much to drink. By rehearsing this response in a supportive group context, the students learn what to do if they are ever actually confronted with the problem.

Role-playing is not for everyone. If group members are too inhibited to play their roles or do not take them seriously, this technique will not work. If the scenarios revolve around highly sensitive issues, role-plays can become highly emotional and can get out of hand. In such cases, the presence of a moderator with training and experience is a must.

COMMUNICATING IN VIRTUAL GROUPS

In the past, most group communication occurred face-to-face (FtF). Increasingly, however, group communication is becoming mediated. Communication technologies now exist that can link group members at remote sites to one another, connect group members to information databases, allow members to communicate with individuals outside the group, and help to structure group tasks.[50]

Characteristics of Online Groups

Computer-mediated groups have unique features that distinguish them from face-to-face groups. As Robyn Parker has argued, virtual groups are not simply groups at a distance.[51] Not only are group members physically separated as they communicate, they may never even have met one another in person. In addition, their messages are often asynchronous, with members sending and responding to messages at various times of the day. Because virtual groups do not share a common location, the identification that comes from seeing each other daily or being familiar with on-site events does not occur.

These characteristics offer unique challenges to group members. Members may be slow to develop trust, and the reduction of social cues that is a result of computer mediation can lead to misunderstandings. In addition, incidental communication that might occur when members of FtF groups meet by chance at lunch or carry on a casual conversation in the parking lot is obviously restricted. Informal channels, which often support formal channels in on-site groups, are severely limited. Parker argues that virtual dynamics are more unpredictable than traditional group dynamics, and that virtual members have a more difficult time fulfilling the group maintenance functions that are necessary to build cohesion and trust. Finally, virtual groups depend on the ability of members to use technology effectively. When members lack access to or are unfamiliar with computer-supported technology, group communication can become impossible.

Are computer-mediated groups as successful and productive as face-to-face groups? In some cases, they are; in others, they are not. Certainly, strong commitments can and do emerge in Internet forums and problem-solving groups; nevertheless, effective group cooperation is not always the result. On tasks that involve idea generation, for example, computer-mediated groups appear to be more effective than face-to-face groups. On problem-solving and negotiation tasks, however, face-to-face groups have the advantage.[52] Members of mediated groups have also been found to be more negative and less polite than are individuals in face-to-face groups, although this depends on the group. Some groups allow uninhibited interaction, while others have strong politeness norms.[53]

A number of studies have also found a **participation equalization effect** in mediated groups. That is, at least in initial interactions, people communicating electronically participate more equally, presumably because the status cues that would normally make reticent members inhibited are not present. Over time, however, this effect dissipates as members establish status hierarchies.[54] Group members gain status online in many ways, including loquacity, skilled use of software, expertise and control of information, and clever performance.[55]

Working effectively in virtual groups is not always easy. Some people find it more challenging than others.[56] What does it take to be an effective virtual group member? One factor is the ability to work independently. Another is the ability to tolerate uncertainty and ambiguity. In addition, a willingness to trust others makes members valuable to a virtual group because trust fosters cohesiveness and satisfaction with group process. As Marshall Scott Poole points out, there is a cyclical relationship between trust and group effectiveness. When members trust one another, they are more likely to fulfill their obligations, which builds more trust and more commitment to the group.[57] Finally, the ability to accept and understand people who may be culturally different has been found to increase group effectiveness.

Whatever the challenges of computer-mediated group interaction, most organizations today find benefits in linking people who are geographically separated. Andrea Hollingshead and Noshir Contractor point out that organizations see real competitive advantages in having employees located in different time zones:

> Indeed, many group scholars now think of groups not just as collections of people but as knowledge networks made up of people and the media they use.

In some cases the members of these teams are "e-lancers" (electronic freelancers) who coalesce on a short-term project and then disperse. In other cases, the technologies have the potential to enable the organization to hire and retain the best people, regardless of location. . . . These changes have led scholars to call for a reconceptualization of groups as much more fluid, dynamic, multiplex and activity based.[58]

Cyber Vigilantes: Collective Knowledge in Virtual Groups

Many group scholars now think of groups not just as collections of people but as **knowledge networks** made up of people and the media they use.[59] These knowledge networks allow users to generate, share, edit, and construct collective knowledge that is beyond the scope of any single user.[60] And the ways virtual groups use their collective knowledge are creative and sometimes surprising. The technology associated with Web 2.0 makes it easier than ever for individuals who have never met to form groups and take collective action. In the past, virtual groups usually consisted of small work-related groups, but nowadays they can include hundreds of individuals working together for a common cause.

Pauline Hope Cheong and Jie Gong describe a case that raises interesting questions about the scope and ethics of pooling collective knowledge.[61] In 2008, at a restaurant in Shenzhen, a middle-aged man attempted to rape an eleven-year-old girl by violently pulling her into the men's room. After the girl escaped, her parents confronted the man, who laughed and announced that he was a senior government official immune from prosecution. The incident was reported online by several news portals, accompanied by clips from the restaurant's surveillance monitor, which recorded the man's verbal and physical threats. When the government attempted to downplay the incident, individual citizens banded together to uncover the identity of the perpetrator. Within two days the perpetrator's name, address, cell phone number, and license plate were posted online. The upshot of this act of cyber vigilantism was that the government was forced to act. According to Cheong and Gong, more than 1.8 million comments were eventually posted, and mashups consisting of satiric songs and videos were widely disseminated. What is your reaction to this story? At first glance, this use of collective knowledge appears beneficial: common citizens were able to hunt down a criminal and see that he was punished. Nevertheless, the Internet allowed them to act as vigilantes, and to some critics this is troubling. Like any form of communication, the many-to-many interactions enabled by new technologies can be used for good or can be misused.

BECOMING A MORE RESPONSIBLE COMMUNICATOR

Groups can bring out the best or the worst in us. At their best, they can produce the kind of synergy in which members outdo themselves. At their worst, they can be hotbeds of disagreement and personal ambition. It's easy for members to lose sight of group goals as they pursue individual agendas. This means that group members need to work hard to be responsible communicators for the sake of the group and shared goals. Following are issues to keep in mind as you interact with others in small groups:

- The behavior of each group member has consequences. As we saw in our discussion of groupthink, when policy-making groups go awry, there can be serious repercussions. Although the kinds of policy decisions we make in everyday life may not be earth-shaking, they still have an impact on the people who must live with them.

- In addition to showing concern for those outside the group who will be affected by group decisions, members should also show concern and respect for one another during group deliberations. This means giving each member's ideas a complete hearing. In some cases, it also means encouraging quiet members to speak up and listening patiently to those with whom you may disagree.

- Responsible group communication is unselfish. Of course, no one enters a group without a personal agenda; nevertheless, it's important to be as honest as possible about personal goals. It is irresponsible to manipulate others to gain selfish ends or to exercise personal power. Participants should not be coerced or manipulated into making decisions that have hidden outcomes and should make up their own minds on the basis of the best possible information available.

- To ensure high-quality decisions, it is important to enter deliberations with information that is as accurate as possible. You must also be willing to admit when you need further data; pretending to know more than you really do in order to save face or dismissing data that do not fit your personal biases is irresponsible. Because group members are under many pressures to solve problems rapidly, it's also important to avoid carelessness and premature consensus. Questions that arise during deliberations should be explored fully and thoughtfully.

- Group members have an obligation to express their views. Although it is often difficult to speak up, especially when groups are in the throes of groupthink, it is irresponsible to agree with a decision you do not support. Honest disagreement can only benefit group deliberations.

SUMMARY

We spend much of our social and work lives communicating in groups. This chapter looks at the special characteristics of group communication and offers advice for increasing group effectiveness.

A group is a collection of individuals who interact over time, becoming interdependent, developing unique patterns of behavior, and achieving a collective identity. Although it is difficult to say exactly how large a group can be before it ceases to be a group, it is safe to say that a small group must consist of at least three people. The ideal group size for effective communication is realized when the group is large enough to generate creative ideas yet small enough for equal participation.

People communicate in groups because the presence of others increases information, provides support, and helps members achieve individual goals. Successful groups create group synergy and are often more effective than their best members. Sometimes, however, groups take on tasks that are inappropriate, and social loafing or free-riding can occur. Like members of dyads, group members experience dialectical tensions. They must satisfy group and individual needs and must learn to balance task and maintenance roles. In groups, both the individual member and the group as a whole try to influence one another. If each meets the other's needs, commitment is high, and members pass through stages that deepen their involvement. If either party fails to meet its obligations, the group becomes unstable, and members drop out. To function effectively, members must also fulfill task and maintenance roles, working to get the job done and to ensure that the group atmosphere is pleasant, while avoiding negative individual roles and hidden agendas. When a group becomes too confident and fails to think realistically about its task, groupthink can occur. By assigning a member to act as critic, by taking criticisms seriously, and by holding second-chance meetings, groups can avoid groupthink.

Group membership is an important source of social identity. Members try to fit their groups' prototypes, and they often depersonalize those who don't fit. Categorizing others on the basis of group membership allows members to reduce uncertainty and bolster self-esteem.

Like dyads, groups go through phases. Often, the first is an orientation or forming phase and the second a conflict or storming phase. The third phase is usually characterized by norming, as members work out rules and roles. In the fourth, or performing, phase, groups settle down to work. Finally in the final or adjourning phase, members prepare to separate. Some groups pass through these phases in an orderly way, while others may simultaneously work on task, maintenance, and topic issues, returning to earlier stages if development is not smooth.

Groups must resolve issues of leadership as they develop. Scholars have used a variety of approaches to study leadership. The trait approach focuses on personal characteristics and the styles approach on the methods leaders use to influence members. The situational approach looks at the way external factors affect style choices, and the functional approach examines shared behaviors that help move the group forward. There are definite behaviors would-be leaders should avoid, including being absent, uncooperative, domineering, rude, or irresponsible.

Members can increase effectiveness by sharing hidden profiles, avoiding defensiveness, and using techniques such as the standard agenda, brainstorming, nominal group technique, and the like. Finally, they should be aware of the kinds of formats used in public discussions.

Groups today are often computer-mediated. Virtual groups are not just groups at a distance; they have unique characteristics that call for special skills. In addition to technological competence, members must be able to work independently, willing to trust others, and sensitive to cultural differences. On tasks involving idea generation, computer-mediated groups outdo face-to-face groups, but they fall behind when it comes to negotiation or problem solving. Online groups can also be uninhibited. In the early stages of group development, online members participate more frequently than do their offline counterparts, although over time, status hierarchies develop online too. Because more and more organizations find it advantageous to create computer-mediated groups, learning to take part in mediated group interaction is a necessary communication skill.

When individuals interact in groups, they bear an added ethical burden because their actions affect not only themselves but also the group as a whole. Honesty, concern for others, willingness to listen, and the ability to admit ignorance are necessary qualities of the ethical group member.

KEY TERMS

group   (164)

triads   (166)

group synergy   (167)

interpersonal needs   (167)

social loafing   (169)

additive tasks   (169)

free-riding   (169)

disjunctive tasks   (169)

group socialization   (170)

idiosyncrasy credit   (172)

task dimension   (173)

maintenance or social
    dimension   (173)

hidden agenda   (175)

groupthink   (176)

social identity   (178)

trait approach   (180)

styles approach   (181)

situational approach   (181)

functional approach   (181)

hidden profile research   (183)

defensive climate   (184)

supportive climate   (184)

reflective thinking   (185)

standard agenda   (185)

problem   (186)

force-field analysis   (186)

brainstorming   (187)

nominal group
    technique   (188)

public discussion
    formats   (188)

role-playing   (190)

participation equalization
    effect   (191)

knowledge networks   (192)

SUGGESTED READING

Beebe, Steven A., Masterson, John T., & Sherblom, John C. (2011). *Communicating in small groups: Principles and practices* (10th ed.). Boston: Allyn & Bacon.
> Provides a combination of theory, application, and skills, with expanded coverage of team building and critical thinking.

Hirokawa, Randy, & others. (2003). *Small group communication theory and practice: An anthology* (8th ed.). Los Angeles: Roxbury.
> A collection of readable essays from major scholars in the field; especially strong on small group theory.

Wheelan, Susan A. (2012). *Creating effective teams: A guide for members and leaders*. Thousand Oaks, CA: Sage.
> A sensible discussion of how to create and maintain effective teams that debunks some of the common but ineffective team-building strategies.

Organizational Communication

After reading this chapter,
you should be able to:

- Identify the four characteristics of organizations.
- Explain how organizational communication differs from other forms.
- Distinguish between formal and informal channels and between upward, downward, and horizontal information flow.
- Describe how structural diversity, transactive memory, and trust affect team effectiveness.
- Describe the steps in preparing for an employment interview.
- Explain how communication creates, maintains, and reinforces organizational culture.
- Use Trice and Beyer's taxonomy of organizational rites to identify aspects of the organizational culture on your campus.
- Discuss ways to build professional relationships in the workplace.
- Describe the effects of new technologies on organizational communication.
- Discuss ethical responsibilities in the organizational context.

E ach of us is affected by and, in turn, affects organizations.

O rganizations are everywhere. In the United States today, there is no way to escape their influence. Public school systems, organized religions, groups such as the Boy Scouts and Girl Scouts, hospitals, banks, charities and relief agencies, fast-food restaurant chains, and certainly the U.S. government, are all examples of organizations that have an impact, large or small, on our lives. Each of us is affected by and, in turn, affects organizations. As such, we are all "stakeholders" in the complex, goal-directed, social systems we call organizations.

This chapter is about communication in complex organizations. In looking at this communication context, we'll combine traditional and contemporary views of what organizational communication is. We'll begin by considering how information flows through organizations, examining informal pathways such as the organizational grapevine as well as more formal communication routes. We'll also consider the importance of building healthy workplace relationships. We'll then take a more interpretive view and discuss ways in which organizational cultures are created and maintained through communication. Finally, we'll focus on two specific skill areas, interviewing and use of organizational technology. Throughout, we'll concern ourselves with some of the ethical issues that confront organizations today.

WHAT IS AN ORGANIZATION?

An **organization** is a system consisting of a large number of people working together in a structured way to accomplish multiple goals. The college or university you attend, for example, is a complex organization that involves many people working together to achieve a common educational goal. Each person plays a different role depending on his or her position within the organization. Faculty, administrators, staff, and students have their own organizational identities and their own ways of behaving, and the success of the university depends in large part on each group's willingness and ability to fit into the university's structures. If, for example, faculty started to behave like students or students like administrators, the whole enterprise would likely fall apart (although the results might be quite interesting). So as you read this chapter, remember that you're already part of a complex organization. Consider how communication flows through your campus. Think about how power is distributed and used. And try to use what you learn about organizational communication to diagnose problems and understand the climate of the complex organization of which you are currently an integral member.

Characteristics of Organizations

Organizations have several characteristics that make them unique. Among these are interdependence, hierarchical structure, linkage to the environment, and a dependence on communication.

Perhaps the characteristic that best defines an organization is **interdependence**. Interdependence means that all the members within an organization are connected to one another. They share a common fate: what affects one part of the organization affects every other part. Interdependence is the reason people join organizations in the first place. People in organizations know that by working together, they can accomplish goals they could not achieve on their own.

In addition, organizations are hierarchical. A **hierarchy** is a system that is divided into orders and ranks. In a hierarchy, status and power are not distributed equally: some people are subordinate to others. The classic form of the hierarchical organization is the **bureaucracy**. In a bureaucracy, there is a clear chain of command. Jobs are usually specialized, and employees are rewarded on the basis of performance. When we use the term *bureaucracy* now, we generally equate it with red tape and inefficiency. However, when sociologist Max Weber first used the term, the bureaucracy was thought to be the ideal organization for Western industrial democracies because of its efficiency and impersonality.[1] Since Weber, the concept of strict hierarchical control has been criticized. Nevertheless, division of labor and recognition of status differences are still characteristic of most complex organizations.

It is important to keep in mind that, like other living systems, organizations are linked to their environments. Just like living creatures, organizations cannot survive without a healthy environment. And just like living creatures, organizations change (and sometimes destroy) their environments. An obvious example occurs when a manufacturing company depletes local resources. But there are other, less apparent, instances as well. When a large corporation moves its corporate headquarters its former community suffers. When a college or university expands, it creates pressures (for example, energy, transportation, and housing needs) as well as opportunities (both economic and cultural) for those who share its environment. Organizations must be aware of the damage they can sometimes cause. They must also be capable of adapting to changes in the environment that surrounds them.

It's common practice to talk about organizations as though they had an identity independent of the activities that define them. When the newspaper reports that "the Fed is lowering interest rates," the Fed seems to be a "thing." When we announce,

"I'll be working at MTV next year," MTV sounds like a place. But Tom D. Daniels and his colleagues point out that we should not think of organizations as "things," or as "places," but rather as elaborate and complicated forms of human behavior. In other words, "an organization is not merely a container for behavior. Rather, an organization literally is human behavior."[2] And one of the most important kinds of organizational behavior is communication. People in organizations argue, cooperate, make decisions, solve problems, and forge relationships.

One of the things that make organizational communication so important is that the very nature of the organization depends on the way members communicate. Marshall Scott Poole and Robert McPhee have pointed out the importance of communication in creating and maintaining organizational identity, or **climate**.[3] Taking what is called a **structurational approach**, they believe that there is a reciprocal relationship between organizational structures and organizational communication. How does this work? Well, as individuals settle into organizations, they begin to communicate in ways that they feel are appropriate to the organization. For example, they may learn that complaints and excuses are considered unprofessional. By following perceived rules—for example, by hanging tough when things get bad and taking criticism on the chin—they create an organizational climate that stresses personal accountability and individual responsibility. This climate, in turn, may generate new rules of behavior—such as the rule that employees should take tough stands and argue forcefully for their beliefs. Poole and his colleagues base their theories on the work of sociologist Anthony Giddens. Giddens believes that social structures (including organizational structures such as climate) are continually produced and reproduced by human interaction. Giddens once said that the structures in human societies are "buildings that are at every moment being reconstructed by the very bricks that compose them."[4] Organizations, too, are structures—structures built on a foundation of human communication.

© Underwood & Underwood/Corbis

Unless the organization works hard to build connections, workers can get lost in corporate bureaucracies.

Why Communicate in Organizations?

Good communication skills are absolutely essential to organizational life. It's through communication that people in organizations coordinate their efforts and achieve

their goals. When communication succeeds, the organization is likely to be effective and efficient and
workers satisfied and committed. When it fails, both
the organization and its individual members suffer.
Charles Redding, a scholar who studied organizations
for many years, lists just a few of the problems that
can occur when communication is faulty:

> **When communication succeeds, the organization is likely to be effective and efficient and workers satisfied and committed. When it fails, both the organization and its individual members suffer.**

> insensitive supervision, confusing instructions, fruitless meetings, deceptive announcements, vicious defense of "turf," biased (or entirely omitted) performance evaluations, misleading reports, empty promises, backstabbing tête-à-têtes with the boss, privacy-invading questions, sexist or racist harassment, scapegoating memorandum, clumsy explanations, paucity of information, conflicting orders, ambiguity (both intentional and unintentional), worship of inane regulations, refusal to listen to bad news, and rejection of innovative ideas—not to mention stubborn reliance upon autocratic, downward-directed messages in general.[5]

Only by learning to communicate effectively in organizations can we recognize and avoid problems such as these.

Being skilled in organizational communication can also enhance our careers. Organizations look for and reward employees "who understand how communication functions in an organization, who have developed a wide repertory of written and oral communication skills, and who have learned when and how to use those skills." Such employees have "more successful careers and contribute more fully to their organizations" than do people without these skills.[6]

Modes of Discourse in Organizations

Communication in the organizational context differs in some fundamental ways from everyday interpersonal or group communication. First, because organizations are hierarchical, members are expected to act not just as individuals but as incumbents of organizational positions. This latter identity puts some restrictions on communication. As Charles Conrad points out, even a strong personal relationship with a supervisor doesn't mean that we can communicate with that supervisor as we would with a friend. While at work, we have to maintain at least some degree of relational distance and detachment.[7] Because organizational communication is driven not only by our own personal goals but also by the need to work together to achieve common goals, it is more formal and deferential than communication in other contexts.

Second, there are unique types of communications, or communication *genres*, that occur only in organizations. Business letters, memoranda, meetings, interviews, and so on are widely recognized genres in American business.[8] Each genre is governed by rules of discourse that define not only what should and should not be conveyed but also how it should be conveyed. Letters of recommendation, for example, must speak to the qualifications of the candidate while avoiding irrelevant information. A recommendation letter (and this is a true example) that starts out, "Although

> **Part of fitting into an organization is knowing what you can and cannot say in certain situations and choosing the correct genre to convey your message.**

she is no beauty, you can count on her to get the job done," violates the rules of proper business etiquette, betrays a sexist bias, and gives irrelevant information. Part of fitting into an organization is knowing what you can and cannot say in certain situations and choosing the correct genre to convey your message.

Communication genres and the rules that define them are, of course, culture-specific. The American coffee break, for example, could be considered an informal communication genre. But what goes on there is not the same as what occurs when Japanese stop for tea. Bruce Feilor, who worked as a teacher in Japan, provides a perfect example when he describes the meaning of a uniquely Japanese organizational genre, the *aisatsu* tea-break. When Feilor first reported to his office, work ground to a halt as he and his principal were served cups of green tea and a plate of intricately wrapped sponge cakes. As he explains:

> *Aisatsu greeting ceremonies like this occurred in school and in my office no fewer than eight times in the course of a normal day. . . . That meant eight times a day everyone must rise and bow to the guest. Eight trays of tea that must be made, served, drunk, retrieved, and cleaned. Eight plates of sponge cakes stuffed with bean paste, fancy rice crackers, cookies, or plastic containers of jelly that must be eaten. It didn't seem to matter what was said in these meetings. Their purpose was to establish the unofficial paths along which tacit deals and arrangements are made. As I was . . . drinking tea and bowing to strangers, I was creating lines along which I could later walk, if need be.*[9]

Although the lines of communication may be different in the United States, they still serve the same ends: creating an atmosphere in which the work of the organization can be accomplished. To work effectively in organizations, one must know when to stick to well-worn paths and when to blaze new trails.

MANAGING ORGANIZATIONAL COMMUNICATION

Early scholars in the field of organizational communication were quick to realize that information is a precious organizational resource. They recognized that high-quality information is the fuel that powers organizational decision making and that the ability to create, analyze, store, and retrieve information is a source of power within any organization.

Understanding Formal and Informal Channels

It is common to distinguish between two kinds of channels: formal and informal. **Formal channels of communication** occur when information flows through a structured chain of command officially recognized by the organization. For example, if a worker hands in a report to his or her manager, who then sends it on to an immediate supervisor, information flows through formal channels. When information takes a more personal and less structured path, **informal channels of communication** come into play. When a sales representative meets the head of personnel's secretary in the lunchroom and discusses rumors about cutbacks, the worker is taking advantage of informal channels. Both forms of communication are essential to the life of the organization.

Formal Organizational Structure

Formal channels are often made explicit in an *organizational chart*, a visual representation of the organization's chain of command. Organizational charts, such as the Campus Safety Organizational Chart shown in Figure 8.1, specify formal relationships between organizational positions. They indicate where, in a hierarchy of responsibility and power, each job is located. They show who supervises whom, and they also illustrate preferred communication pathways.

Communication overload is a common problem in complex organizations.

As you can see in Figure 8.1, information can flow in several directions. **Downward flow** occurs when someone near the top of the organization sends a message to someone near the bottom (for example, when the associate director of campus safety sends a memo to the escort service supervisor). We find **upward flow** when a message travels from the bottom of the chart toward the top (for example, when a message from a records clerk ends up on the desk of the operations director). Finally, **horizontal flow** takes place when communication occurs between people at the same level (for example, when an investigator discusses an automobile break-in with a parking attendant and a patrol officer or when the heads of the community service, training, and administration departments meet to discuss budget needs).

Downward Communication. Instructions, appraisals, and announcements are examples of communications that typically flow downward. When a supervisor discusses the results of a yearly evaluation with a subordinate or explains travel policies to new employees, the supervisor is using downward communication. Unfortunately, employees in most organizations report dissatisfaction with downward communication. Daniels and his colleagues list some of the problems responsible for this dissatisfaction. Included are "inadequacy of information, inappropriate means of diffusing information, filtering of information, and a general pervasive climate of dominance and submission."[10]

Figure 8.1 Organizational Chart: Campus Safety Department at XYZ University

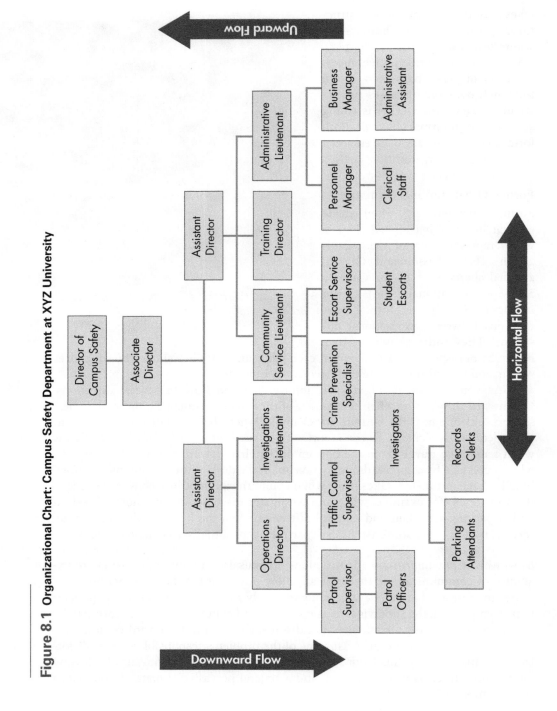

Dissatisfaction with the amount and type of information received is a serious problem in most organizations. Employees report, on the one hand, that they often don't receive enough information to do their jobs. On the other hand, they report receiving too much information. Often, they feel buried under an avalanche of forms, letters, memos, bulletins, reports, and emails. Given these seemingly contradictory responses, it is reasonable to conclude that organizational members receive a lot of information but that, unfortunately, it is not the information they want or need. This may occur because managers don't consider the needs of employees when they send out messages or because they don't choose the correct medium. Several scholars have found that organizational members receive too much mediated communication and not enough face-to-face communication from their superiors.[11]

> Dissatisfaction with the amount and type of information received is a serious problem in most organizations. Employees feel buried under an avalanche of forms, letters, memos, bulletins, reports, and emails.

Downward communication often contains information that is misleading or downright wrong. If you've ever played the game called "telephone," in which players pass on a message by whispering it to the person next in line, you know that messages change as they pass from person to person. This change is known as **message filtering**, and it is a serious problem in formal communication. As messages flow downward, the gist of the message may get lost in the process. The more links through which information must pass (the "taller" the organization), the more likely messages are to undergo distortion. Table 8.1 lists some of the kinds of distortion that occur during **serial transmission** (transmission of a message in a one-way direction from one person to the next).

A number of things can be done to improve accuracy during serial transmission. Managers can build redundancy into their messages and employees can ask for clarification when messages are ambiguous. Unfortunately, these simple solutions are rarely used because superiors are often too rushed to think carefully about their communications and subordinates are often reluctant to ask questions of their supervisors. Furthermore, both superiors and subordinates may not know that there is a problem. Managers in particular tend to overestimate the clarity and frequency of their communications.[12]

Table 8.1 Effects of Serial Transmission

Leveling	Details are left out as the amount of information in the message is reduced. The message grows shorter.
Sharpening	Certain high points are given special significance and elaboration.
Assimilation	Memory of the message is affected by the sender's frame of reference. Unfamiliar material is changed so that it makes sense to the sender.

From Johnson & Johnson, *Joining Together: Group Theory & Group Skills*, 4th Ed., © 1991, p. 159. Reprinted and electronically reproduced by permission of Pearson Education, Inc., Upper Saddle River, New Jersey.

Some message distortion is inevitable in any system that uses serial transmission, even when those involved do their best to communicate accurately.

Information may also be deliberately withheld. If managers anticipate that a piece of news will anger employees, decrease the organization's competitive edge, or be criticized by external stakeholders, they may decide to keep the information to themselves or even to lie about it. Unfortunately, this practice creates a climate of mistrust, damaging the credibility of future downward communication.

Upward Communication. Although most organizational messages flow downward, some flow from the bottom up. Typical of these are progress reports, warnings of job-related problems, and suggestions or feedback about organizational policies. When employees submit project reports, alert their superiors to changes in client needs, or express their objections to reorganization efforts, they are using upward communication.

Research shows that organizations often neglect upward communication, especially when it is negative or when it calls for organizational change. As a result, suggestion programs may be implemented in name only, with very little attention paid by either superiors or subordinates. Furthermore, upward communication is often distorted. Subordinates fear being seen as the bearers of bad tidings and tend to withhold information that will reflect badly on them. Research shows, for example, that subordinates who are insecure, who don't trust their superiors, or who are very ambitious tend to distort upward flow and withhold negative information.[13]

In addition, gatekeepers may affect upward flow. A **gatekeeper** is someone (such as an administrative assistant or receptionist) who is in a position to pass on or discard information. While gatekeepers can provide a valuable service by filtering out trivial messages, they can also suppress information that is badly needed. As we saw in Chapter 7, one of the characteristics of groupthink is the presence of self-appointed mind-guards who paint an unrealistic picture of events in order to protect the leader from negative information.

What can an organization do to improve upward flow? First, managers can seek out bad news and encourage subordinates to tell the truth, no matter how negative it may be.[14] In addition, unnecessary gatekeepers can be eliminated, or special channels can be provided to bypass cumbersome serial transmission. Some organizations have a special position called **ombudsman**. This person's job is to listen to workers at lower levels of the organization and pass their concerns directly to the top. Finally, the most important thing managers can do to increase upward flow is to establish a climate of trust and openness.

Taking Advantage of Informal Structures

In everyday life, people are connected to one another in complex and intriguing ways. It's not uncommon to meet a stranger and, after talking awhile, discover that you have friends in common, that you are in fact connected to one another through a network of acquaintances. It may be a small world after all. To find out exactly how interconnected the world is, psychologist Stanley Milgram set up an experiment in which he asked individuals from Nebraska and Kansas to try to contact strangers in

Massachusetts.[15] His subjects were each given a message and asked to send it to a personal acquaintance. The acquaintances were then asked to forward the message to someone they knew personally. This continued until the message reached its goal. Surprisingly, it took on average only five or six links. Milgram discovered that we are all part of a giant network, connected to others (including Kevin Bacon) by "six degrees of separation."

Acquaintance networks like those studied by Milgram also occur in organizations. People are linked to one another through personal relationships that often do not mirror the formal channels found in organizational charts. The problem with formal channels is that they are artificially constructed. Because they fail to take into account employees' social bonds and friendship choices, employees often bypass them by creating informal links to people they trust or like. Informal channels serve to counterbalance the inefficiency and distortion found in formal channels. When employees want to find out what's really going on, they may turn to informal channels. As Charles Conrad points out, "if organizational communication really was restricted to formal channels, most people, in most organizations, most of the time could honestly say that they do not know what is going on."[16]

> **We are all part of a giant network, connected to others by "six degrees of separation."**

The Grapevine. Informal channels are often referred to as the **grapevine**. When someone says, "I heard it through the grapevine," he or she means that the news came through an informal channel. Where did this usage arise? Evidently, during the Civil War, telegraph lines were threaded through trees in a complicated pattern resembling a grapevine. Later on, the term was adopted to describe any system of messages that does not follow a straight-line, predictable pattern.

Susan Hellwig and Keith Davis have both studied grapevine communication and have come to a number of conclusions. First, the grapevine arises because individuals have personal interests and needs that are not satisfied by formal channels. According to Keith Davis, "a lively grapevine reflects the deep psychological need

Fitting into an organization means understanding and accepting organizational culture. Usually, the rules are not expressed as clearly as they are in this photo.

Time & Life Pictures/Getty Images

of people to talk about their jobs and their company as a central life interest. Without it, the company would literally be sick."[17]

Second, although it's common to equate the grapevine with rumor, rumors make up only a small proportion of the information on the grapevine. The grapevine contains useful and valid information as well. Third, information on the grapevine may be incomplete, but it is quite accurate. In fact, it has been estimated to be anywhere from 75 percent to 95 percent accurate. Sometimes, it may even be more reliable than formally conveyed information. Conrad argues that it is also richer in content than formal communication, and because it usually operates on a face-to-face basis, it also allows for immediate feedback and clarification. Although managers may caution employees not to use the grapevine, their concern may be due to their own lack of control rather than to the grapevine's accuracy.

Network Analysis.   Informal communication can be very influential. Organizations should therefore understand and take advantage of informal networks. One tool for understanding networks is called **network analysis**, a method of mapping informal communication patterns. Network analysts can identify who is connected to whom in the organization. They can also specify the role each individual plays in an informal network. For example, some individuals, called **opinion leaders**, are at the center of things; they are the first people others go to for information. Other individuals, called **isolates**, have very few connections with coworkers; they are "out of the loop" when it comes to information. In times of institutional change, it makes sense for management to seek out and discuss the situation with opinion leaders rather than with isolates. If opinion leaders can be persuaded that a proposed change is good, they can influence others in their networks. It also makes sense to try to reintegrate isolates into the organization, especially if the isolates are keeping valuable ideas to themselves. Table 8.2 lists some other key network roles. As you look at the table,

Table 8.2 Network Roles

Boundary Spanner or Cosmopolite	An organizational member who has contact with individuals outside the organization's boundaries. Often, boundary spanners tend to occur at the top or bottom of organizations. They represent the organization and can bring valuable information into the organization.
Bridge	A member of a clique who has connections with another clique.
Clique	A group of people who communicate more with each other than they do with others in the organization. Members of cliques may have similar jobs or share a common status.
Isolate	Someone who is outside the informal network. An isolate has no links to any clique.
Liaison	Someone who connects two cliques without being a member of either one. A liaison may help spread information between people who might normally not speak to one another.
Opinion Leader	Someone within a clique who can influence the attitudes and actions of members.
Star	The member of a network connected to the most members.

ask yourself how you, as a manager, could use network analysis to enhance organizational communication.

Loose and Tight Coupling

Another distinction that describes organizational communication is the construct of coupling. Organizations may be either tightly or loosely coupled. Subunits within an organization that are closely connected and highly interdependent are characterized by **tight coupling**. In such an organization, anything that influences one part of the organization influences all parts. Information flow is rapid. Tightly coupled organizations are easy to control and standardize. But because subsystems are so closely connected, a problem that affects one part of the organization can affect all parts: in essence, subsystems are like dominoes—when the first goes down, the rest follow.[18] In fact, sociologist Charles Perrow suggests that one of the factors that led to the Three Mile Island nuclear accident was the fact that the system was so complex and so tightly coupled.[19]

> Sociologist Charles Perrow suggests that one of the factors that led to the Three Mile Island nuclear accident was the fact that the system was so complex and so tightly coupled.

When the relationship between subunits in an organization is relatively weak, the organization is characterized by **loose coupling**. Each unit acts in a relatively independent fashion, and an event that influences one unit may have only indirect effects on others. Here, information flow is more gradual. One of the apparent disadvantages of loose coupling, lack of standardization, may sometimes be an advantage. Because loosely coupled units are relatively independent, a given unit can respond rapidly and creatively to change. Of course, loose coupling does not always lead to positive results; units can also "preserve archaic, outmoded traditions."[20] Colleges and universities are prime examples of loosely coupled organizations. Individual departments are usually fairly autonomous and will defend to the death any attempt by an outsider to interfere with the academic decisions they make.

Building Effective Teams: Structural Diversity, Transactive Memory, and Trust

In the last section, we looked at downward and upward communication. In this section we focus on *horizontal communication*, the kind of communication that is used between people at the same level in the organization. Whenever we work with co-workers on team projects, we are engaged in horizontal communication. And more and more, organizations expect individuals to take part in teams. Unfortunately, not all teams are effective.

In the last chapter we saw that when group members pool resources they can be more productive than single individuals. We also saw, however, that group members do not always share unique information with one another, preferring instead to solve problems in familiar ways using commonly held information. Because information is the life-blood of organizations, and because single individuals can no longer know everything they need to in order to make optimal decisions, it is necessary for organizations to encourage information sharing. This section looks at several ways organizations can encourage knowledge-sharing including composing teams with diverse experts, keeping track of who knows what in the organization, and encouraging trust.

When people on a team come from the same organizational unit, share the same work methods, or have the same kind of training, there is often a danger that they will stay with the tried and true and be reluctant to accept creative ideas or try new approaches. To counter this danger, organizational experts now recommend the creation of work teams that exhibit **structural diversity**, that is, teams with members from different units within the organization and with different training and knowledge. For example, rather than composing a team entirely of employees from the research and development division at a single location, organizations who are creating new products may include employees from their marketing, sales, and human factors divisions as well. In this way the team can call on many areas of expertise. It has been shown that structurally diverse teams have a greater range of knowledge and see problems from more vantage points.[21]

But how does the organization determine who has expertise? And how does it make sure that information flows to the people who can best use it? The answer lies in keeping track of who knows what. When the organization has a systematic way to remember and identify who possesses expert knowledge, that is, when it possesses an effective **transactive memory system**, it is no longer necessary for everyone to know everything. Transactive memory systems "expand the total amount of knowledge available to members of work groups in organizations," because they allow the organization to make effective use of their employees' knowledge.[22]

Optimal transactive memory depends on an organization's ability to recognize expertise, to distribute new information to those who can make the best use of it, and to identify where to go when information is needed. How important is transactive memory? In some cases, it can be a matter of life and death. It has been argued, for example, that the *Columbia* space shuttle disaster of 2003 was at least partly due to the fact that the right information did not get to the right people.[23]

Despite the advantages that accrue when teams of experts work together, there can be communication challenges. It is sometimes difficult for individuals with different backgrounds to see things from one another's perspectives. Vocabulary can also be a problem when members use the technical jargon of their respective fields. The vocabulary of a senior chemist may be unintelligible to the people from advertising and vice versa. In addition, when organizational resources are limited, departments often compete for their share of the pie and may not communicate openly. For all of these reasons, the development of trust in teams is extremely important. **Trust** is an expectation that others will act in consistent and dependable ways. It is necessary for effective communication because it encourages employees to take risks and express themselves openly. Scholars have found that trust is associated with enhanced group and organizational performance, innovative behavior, effective crisis management, and overall satisfaction.[24] Trust has also been found to be an important predictor of success in virtual teams, a topic we will return to toward the end of this chapter.

INCREASING ORGANIZATIONAL SKILLS

To succeed in an organization you need to use all of the interpersonal and group skills we've talked about in previous chapters. In addition, you need to develop specific organizational skills. In this section, we look at the interviewing skills that gain you entry, the interpretive skills that allow you to fit into the organization's culture, and the relational skills that allow you to communicate professionally.

Interviewing Skills

An **interview** is a form of two-way communication having a predetermined and serious purpose in which participants ask and answer questions.[25] Interviews are used for many purposes: to orient and train employees, to survey their attitudes, to evaluate job performance, and to resolve complaints.[26] And of course interviews are used to select new employees. Since this latter form of interview is of immediate concern to most college students, we will look at it in some detail.[27]

Preparing for the Interview

Interviews are serious business. Talking off the cuff may be fine in everyday conversation, but it is not acceptable in a job interview. Preparation is a must. Interviewees should begin with a clear idea of their own strengths and weaknesses. They should also research the organization and prepare a cover letter and resume.

Before the interview, prospective employees need to review skills gained through coursework, personal experience, or previous employment. Facility in using computers, research ability, and graphic design skills are examples of *work-content skills*, skills that are directly related to a particular job. Skills that apply to a variety of situations and settings are called *transferable skills*. The abilities to define and solve problems, teach others, and manage time are examples. Finally, *self-management skills* include personal strengths such as flexibility, enthusiasm, and persistence. In addition to listing skills in these three areas, prospective employees should be prepared to discuss specific situations involving these skills. It is not enough for a candidate to tell an interviewer, "I can deal effectively with the public." The interviewer wants examples.

Before the interview, job candidates need to know as much as possible about the job they are seeking. By consulting standard reference books such as *Dun and Bradstreet's Career Guide* or *Hoover's Handbook of American Companies*, business magazines such as *Business Week* or *Fast Company*, company brochures and annual reports, and, of course, the Internet, candidates can walk in ready to answer two of the most frequently asked interview questions: "What do you know about our organization?" and "Why do you want to work here?"

Interviews are like exclusive parties: you can't crash the gate; you have to be invited. That means sending out resumes and cover letters that catch the eye of potential employers and make them want to

> Interviews are like exclusive parties: you can't crash the gate; you have to be invited. That means sending out resumes and cover letters that catch the eye of potential employers and make them want to meet with you.

meet with you. The cover letter highlights one's ability to do the job and motivates the employer to examine the resume. In the cover letter, prospective employees identify the position they are interested in, explain how they heard about it and why they are applying, emphasize how their qualifications meet job requirements, and make specific requests for an interview.

The resume is a profile of the candidate's background and qualifications. It communicates who the job seeker is. Because resumes are generally limited to a single page, every word counts. The resume should include contact information, a statement of career objectives, a summary of education and work experience, a list of special skills or interests, and the names, addresses, and phone numbers of references. It goes without saying that both letter and resume must be completely error free. A single misspelled word or grammatical error can be enough to eliminate the writer from further consideration. Employers have come to expect a certain format for resumes. An excellent source of information about current resume formats is the career services office at your school. Career counselors can offer more specific advice and show you models to follow. In the meantime, Table 8.3 gives you an example of what a resume should *not* look like. See if you can spot all the mistakes.

Answering and Asking Questions

Success in the actual interview is measured by how well candidates answer (and ask) questions. Although there is no way to anticipate all the questions the interviewer will ask, preparation and practice can help. Table 8.4 lists some frequently asked interview questions. By thinking about how to answer these questions and by practicing responses, you can increase the likelihood that you will present yourself effectively. As Table 8.4 also shows, not all the questions come from the interviewer. Interviewees are expected to ask questions. But watch what you ask. If your only concern is with salary, office size, and benefits rather than with the nature and challenges of the job itself, you will come across as self-absorbed. In most cases, it is best to avoid questions about salary in the first interview and to focus instead on learning about the organization and the position. Throughout the entire process, it's essential to demonstrate self-confidence, openness, and respect.

Like many things in life, the interview is not over until it's over. It is common nowadays for job candidates to follow up with a brief, professional letter thanking the interviewer for his or her time and restating your interest in the company. This gives a candidate one more chance to stand out from the crowd and make a positive impression.

Handling Inappropriate Questions

Although there are laws governing what can and cannot be asked in interviews, not all interviewers are sensitive about what they ask. Questions about marital status, plans for having a family, religious affiliation, politics, ethnic identification, and so forth are illegal. Yet it is possible that an interviewee may be asked such a question. What's the correct response? That's really up to each individual. There are a number of choices. The interviewee can

1. simply answer the question (although one should not feel pressured to do so).
2. politely refuse to answer and make the interviewer aware that the question was not appropriate.
3. discuss the underlying concern that may have prompted the question. For example, in asking a question about the candidate's family life, the interviewer's

Table 8.3 What's Wrong with This Resume?

PAT SUNDANCE

Local address:	Generic College, Generic, New York, 14850 **Permanent address:** 55 Main Street, Hometown, New Jersey.
Career Objective:	To use my people skills.
Education:	Generic College, Generic, New York Bachelor of Arts, May 2000 **Major:** speach communication **Minor:** Business **GPA:** 1.02 **Extracurricular Activities:** American Marketing Society, Skateboarding, Following Phish.
Experience:	Safety Patrol: John Paul Jones Elementary School. September 1990–June 1991. Asisted other students at crossings; gave out hall passes. Night clerk at Hollywood and Vine Video Store Anywhere, New York September 1999–June 1999. Rewound videotapes; learned names of all academy award nominated films since 1947; demonstrated people skills by talking with customers. Retail Salesperson at The Fissure Jeans Store Hometown, New Jersey June 2000–August 2000 Interacted courteously with customers; generated high volume of sales; solely responsible for handling customer complaints and returns; chosen salesperson of the month, July.
Special Skills:	Know how to use the computer, Lead singer in garage band.
References:	Robert Berlin High School Music Teacher George Patton High School Hometown, New York Illeana Cannes T.A., French 101 Anywhere College Anywhere, New York

Key to errors: No zip on permanent address. Phone number and email should be included. Career objective vague. Several misspelled words, including name of major. GPA should not be listed if below 3.00. Some extracurricular activities are better left unsaid. Experience should be noted in reverse chronological order, beginning with most recent employment. List only relevant experience. Describe work-related aspects of prior experience. Be specific about special skills and make sure they're job related. Why are there no references from Hollywood and Vine or the Fissure? Overall layout is poor. Incidentally, description of employment at Fissure is fine.

concern could be about the amount of overtime required by the job. An interviewee could respond by saying, "I understand that the job requires substantial investment of time. Let me assure you that there is nothing in my personal life that would keep me from performing any of the duties associated with this job."

Of course, if the questions are extremely offensive, the incident should be reported. In any case, it's important to remain calm and behave politely.

Understanding Organizational Cultures

The traditional approach to understanding organizations has been expanded, in recent years, by efforts to understand how organizational members make sense of organizations and share their understandings with others. In this section, we'll begin by

Table 8.4 Typical Interview Questions

Questions about Career Objectives and Goals
Some Typical Questions in This Category:

- What are your long-range career goals? How have you prepared yourself to reach these goals? What other personal goals do you hope to accomplish in the next ten years?
- Describe what you consider to be the ideal job.
- What characteristics do you believe are necessary for success in this field? Do you have those characteristics?

Interviewer wants to know: how your future plans relate to the organization, whether you have a realistic view of your career area, how goal directed and serious you are.

Use these questions to: demonstrate your knowledge of the field in which you hope to be employed, assure the organization that you have realistic goals, show a serious commitment to your career.

Questions about the Organization Itself
Some Typical Questions in This Category:

- Why are you interested in our organization?
- What do you know about us? What do you like best about our organization?
- What can you offer us?

Interviewer wants to know: whether you've done your homework, if you're a good match for the organization, if you intend to stay with the organization.

Use these questions to: show that you've taken the time to research the organization, demonstrate a positive interest in the organization, show that you understand the job that you're applying for.

Questions about Your Education
Some Typical Questions in This Category:

- How did you choose your college? Your major? If you had it to do over again, what would you change about your education?
- To what extent does your scholastic record reflect your abilities?
- What was your most rewarding college experience?

Interviewer wants to know: how thoughtful and goal directed you are, what your level of training and preparation is, whether you have the personal characteristics needed for the job.

Use these questions to: show your level of preparation; indicate characteristics, talents, and skills that are *job* related; indicate that you are serious and eager to learn.

Questions about Your Work Experience
Some Typical Questions in This Category:

- Tell me about the jobs you've held. What did you do exactly? Did you enjoy working there? Why did you leave?
- Did you encounter any problems at those jobs? How did you respond?

looking at what new employees do to understand new organizational cultures. We'll then expand the notion of culture by looking at how cultural understandings are conveyed through metaphors, stories, and rites.

Entering Organizational Cultures

Whenever a collection of people share common understandings, values, and perceptions, we can think of them as belonging to a common culture. Because people in organizations need to find a way to understand and manage what goes on around them, they create organizational cultures. In the words of Gary Kreps, **organizational culture** consists of collectively held "logics and legends about organizational life and the organization's identity."[28]

Table 8.4 Typical Interview Questions (*continued*)

- What is your greatest strength as an employee? Your greatest weakness?

Interviewer wants to know: what you will be like as an employee, what skills you possess, how your previous experience has prepared you for this position.

Use these questions to: demonstrate that you have what it takes to be an effective employee; show that you are responsible, willing to work, good with people, and so on.

Questions about You as a Person
Some Typical Questions in This Category:

- Tell me about yourself.
- What are your hobbies? How do you spend your free time? What kinds of books, magazines, or newspapers do you read?
- What personal accomplishment has given you the most satisfaction? Why?
- What is the most embarrassing thing that ever happened to you?
- What have you done that shows initiative?

Interviewer wants to know: how you relate to the profile of a successful employee, whether you have the necessary traits to fulfill job requirements, how articulate and focused you are.

Use these questions to: show concrete examples of job-related characteristics such as drive, ability to get along with others, and leadership; indicate

that you have a positive self-concept and are both confident and realistic about your abilities and experience.

Questions You Should Ask
Some Typical Questions the Interviewee Should Bring Up:

- How would you describe the organization's management style?
- Describe typical assignments for someone in this position during the first year. What are some typical problems that the person in this position may encounter?
- Tell me about your training programs.
- What industry trends do you feel will affect this company in the next five years?
- Earlier you mentioned . . . Could you elaborate?

Interviewer will be looking for questions that: show a sincere interest in the field and organization, indicate that you want to continue learning, demonstrate that you want realistic information on which to base your decision.

Use these questions to: show a sincere interest in the organization and its future, demonstrate a desire to advance, indicate that you want to grow professionally, show you were listening during the interview, let the interviewer know that you are interested in more than just salary.

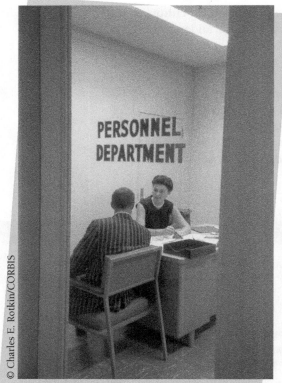

© Charles E. Rotkin/CORBIS

Maneuvering through employment interviews is a challenge for both interviewer and interviewee.

Newcomers should be helped to make sense of organizations. When newcomers enter an organization, they often have trouble understanding what is going on because their old scripts and schemata no longer work.

If you have ever lived or traveled abroad for an extended period of time, you may have experienced *culture shock*, a sense of disorientation that occurs when the rules you're used to playing by no longer work. That same sense may occur as individuals enter new organizational cultures. They need to know what's going on, and they need to find some way to adapt to their new surroundings.

Meryl Reis Louis argues that newcomers should be helped to make sense of organizations.[29] When newcomers enter an organization, they often have trouble understanding what is going on because their old scripts and schemata no longer work. As a result, they experience *surprise*, an emotional reaction to differences between life in the organization and life outside it. For Louis, surprise is the emotional state that occurs when one's expectations about the job or about oneself are disconfirmed. And surprise triggers the need for sense making.

When insiders in an organization encounter a surprising event, they can use their knowledge of the culture to help explain it or they can turn to friends and colleagues. But newcomers lack cultural knowledge and have no one to turn to. Their only way of understanding organizational events is to use models based on past experience. Unfortunately, these forms of sense making may not be useful. A newly employed recent college graduate who uses college experience to define what it means to "put in a hard day's work," for example, may be in for a rude awakening.

Louis believes that organizations must help newcomers learn the ropes. By linking newcomers with mentors and instituting early appraisal meetings in which superiors give newcomers feedback, organizations can eliminate many transition problems. "Secrecy norms, the sink-or-swim, learn-on-your-own philosophy, and sanctions against sharing information among office members," she argues, "are dysfunctional for newcomers and for their employing organizations as well."[30] Louis believes that newcomers should also be taught to understand the nature of entry experiences. They should learn to anticipate surprise and actively seek information from insiders. The newcomer who expects to experience organizational culture shock and who makes active efforts to learn the culture will be at a real advantage during his or her first year on the job.

Metaphors, Stories, and Rites

Newcomers can learn a lot about organizational culture by observing what goes on around them. But what, exactly, should they observe? In their classic article on communication cultures, Michael Pacanowsky and Nick O'Donnell-Trujillo suggested that organizational culture can be seen in communication practices, including metaphors, stories, and rituals.[31] By carefully observing these forms of communication, they argue, we can better understand an organization's underlying values, beliefs, and attitudes.

Metaphors and Stories. As we saw in Chapter 4, *metaphors* are linguistic expressions that allow us to experience one thing in terms of another. Metaphors both reflect and shape the way we see the world. This is as true in organizations as it is in our private lives. The metaphors that are used in corporate settings interest communication scholars because they embody basic aspects of organizational culture. For example, one organization may encourage the use of a family metaphor ("Here at Acme, you're part of a family who cares"), while another may see itself as an armed force ("We've got to go out there and blast the competition"). Cynthia Stohl explains how the family metaphor can affect employees:

> If we "see" our office group as a traditional family, then we expect people to take care of and protect one another. . . . [D]ominant behavior would be interpreted as fatherly or motherly[;] . . . weaker members would be treated as children, with fewer rights but much support. Our personal lives would be appropriate topics for discussion and rituals surrounding birthdays, the birth of a child, and other personal landmarks would be enacted.[32]

In an organization that uses a military metaphor, by contrast, life would be quite different. Charles Conrad describes a large West Coast toy manufacturer that takes a more military approach to organizational life. In this company, employees habitually talk about "fighting the battle" (working hard) and "taking no casualties" (being obsessed with quality). But, Conrad tells us, the most powerful expressions of the metaphor come directly from military slogans:

> "Be all that you can be" is used to justify voluntary overtime, and "lean, mean fighting machine" is used to explain reduction in the number of middle managers. Almost every normal work experience is explained in language reflecting the "army under siege" metaphor; almost every behavior desired of workers can be justified by referring to the metaphor.[33]

Clearly, the organizational cultures of these two companies are quite different.

Stories also help us make sense of organizational culture by reflecting company values. Conrad gives an example of how a story from the 3M Corporation embodies the key value "innovation should be encouraged."[34] According to the story, a junior employee discovered Scotch Tape by accident. His superiors didn't believe that there was a viable market for the product. So he slipped into the boardroom and taped members' materials to the conference table. The board members decided to give the new product a chance, and the rest, as they say, is history. Any new 3M employee hearing the story will quickly draw the conclusion that it is important to fight for one's ideas.

Another example of an organizational story concerns the actions of a young receptionist at IBM whose job it was to stop anyone from entering restricted areas without a badge. When Thomas Watson, Jr., then chairman of the board, walked up without a badge, she stopped him. According to a former IBM employee, this story was still circulating several years ago, and its interpretation was clear: at IBM, the boss gets no special treatment; everyone follows the rules. This interpretation is even clearer when it is compared to another story employees liked to tell. According to this companion story, the same situation occurred in a different organization, but instead of being understanding, the boss is reported to have said, "Don't you recognize my name? You should. It's on the checks you *used to* get. You're fired." Clearly, at least in these stories, IBM characterizes itself as a humane organization that "plays fair."

Rites and Ceremonials.   A more elaborate form of cultural life can be found in organizational rites and ceremonials. Harrison Trice and Janice Beyer define **rites** as publicly performed, "relatively elaborate, dramatic, planned sets of activities that consolidate various forms of cultural expressions into one event." A **ceremonial**, by contrast, is a "system of several rites connected with a single occasion or event."[35] Graduation, for example, is a ceremonial consisting of a number of different rites, including receptions, parties, award presentations, and the conferring of degrees. According to Trice and Beyer, rites have both manifest and latent consequences. The manifest (or public) consequence of graduation is recognition of the passage from student to graduate. The latent (or hidden) consequences, however, are more interesting. Graduations also celebrate the status of the college or university, reiterate the value of a college education, and remind participants that they are taking part in a practice that has a rich historical tradition. At the very least, they encourage both parents and students to believe that their sacrifices were worth it. Table 8.5 lists some of the kinds of rites that occur in organizations.

Trice and Beyer believe that rites play an important role in the creation and maintenance of strong organizational cultures and that strong cultures, in turn, help to produce effective organizations.[36] They advise managers to assess the hidden consequences of rites in their organizations in order to find out whether the rites are achieving desired effects. They also suggest that managers learn effective ceremonial skills. "Some flair for the dramatic and the ability to be expressive in speech, writing, and gestures," they tell us, "could be an asset in meeting the ceremonial requirements of managerial roles."[37] They go on to quote Karl Weick, "Managerial work can be viewed as managing myth, symbols, and labels. . . . [B]ecause managers traffic so often in images, the appropriate role for the manager may be the evangelist rather than the accountant."[38]

Rites play an important role in the creation and maintenance of strong organizational cultures.

Promoting Professionalism in Workplace Relationships

Getting along in an organization means more than simply passing on information efficiently or getting one's reports in on time. It also involves creating healthy relationships with one's coworkers. Too often, however, organizational relationships are marked by petty jealousies, resentments, stereotyping, and the like. In this section, we'll look briefly at why building good relationships is so important and so difficult in the organizational setting.

Workplace Relationships

Most of us treat strangers very differently than we treat those we know and trust. But where exactly do coworkers fit on the continuum between stranger and intimate? The answer is that they fit somewhere in

> Getting along in an organization means more than simply passing on information efficiently or getting one's reports in on time. It also involves creating healthy relationships with one's coworkers.

Table 8.5 Organizational Rites

Rites of Passage

Purpose: Rites of passage celebrate new role identities

Example: Army basic training, freshman orientation

Consequences: Facilitate transformation into new role while ensuring new member is as much as possible like previous members

Rites of Degradation

Purpose: Rites of degradation strip away power or remove incumbent from role

Example: Impeachment, student judicial hearing

Consequences: Strengthen organizational boundaries by defining who belongs and who doesn't; reaffirm value of role by punishing out-of-role behavior

Rites of Enhancement

Purpose: Rites of enhancement reward organizational achievement

Example: Academy Awards, student honor society induction

Consequences: Enhance status and value of organization, motivate individuals to strive, give organization credit for individual achievement

Rites of Renewal

Purpose: Rites of renewal improve functioning of organization

Example: Diversity awareness training, student government retreat

Consequences: Make members believe something is being done to solve problems; focus on some problems and avoid others; reinforce existing power structures

Rites of Conflict Reduction

Purpose: Reduce conflict and aggression

Example: Collective bargaining, grievance procedures

Consequences: Deflect attention away from problems; compartmentalize conflict

Rites of Integration

Purpose: Create common identity and commitment to organization

Example: Mardi Gras, end-of-semester party

Consequences: Permit catharsis; loosen norms temporarily in order to reaffirm their moral rightness; channel aggression

Adapted from Harrison Trice and Janice Beyer, "Studying Organizational Cultures Through Rites and Ceremonials," *Academy of Management Review, 9* (1984), pp. 653–669.

between. Because we spend so much time with them, it is natural to feel a personal connection and want to be friends. Yet we are in the organization to get a task accomplished; we certainly aren't paid to have fun and hang out. In the workplace, relationships must be professional, and part of fitting into an organization is figuring out just exactly what professional relationships are all about.

Professional relationships differ from personal relationships in at least two dimensions: choice and power. Choice is important. Although we choose our friends, we do not choose our coworkers; they are chosen for us by the organization. As professional consultant Bob Wall points out, "Companies do not bring people together to be friends. We are not there to develop some form of an extended family. Our primary purpose is to accomplish work, and the company is depending on us to be able to work together to make that happen."[39] Because employees are chosen for competence rather than personal compatibility, we may find ourselves working with people we would not otherwise choose as friends. Yet to work effectively together, we often have to put aside personal feelings of like or dislike.

Power is an added complication. Organizations are hierarchical; therefore, differences in power and status are natural and expected. This means that while organizational members should recognize that everyone in the organization, regardless of status, has a contribution to make, they should also understand and acknowledge role and status differences. It doesn't work to pretend that everyone is equal. The CEO and the guy or gal in the next cubicle don't do the same work, and the organization does not expect that they be treated exactly the same way.

Acknowledging status differences and putting aside personal feelings may not come naturally. Deferring to authority may make us feel uncomfortable. Because we are usually encouraged to be open and candid, being polite may appear phony. Therefore, when we enter the world of work, we may have to learn new sets of behaviors in order to act professionally. Table 8.6 lists some general guidelines for communicating on the job. As you read them, think about whether you agree or disagree with them and about how easy or difficult they might be to follow. Also ask yourself what other rules you would add. And keep in mind that different organizations will call for different kinds of communication, so general rules must always be modified in specific situations.

Of course, acting professionally doesn't mean keeping everyone at arm's length and never developing friendships. Professional relationships can and do turn into personal ones. But workplace relationships should be grounded in professional behavior. As Wall suggests, "It will be easier to build personal relationships when we know that we can work powerfully together and disagree without taking things personally. . . . It is simply easier to like people when we are able to work out the mechanics of working together."[40]

The Office Romance

People not only make friends at work but also occasionally fall in love. Handling workplace romance is particularly complicated. In the past, most organizations forbade office romances. If they were discovered, one partner (for heterosexual couples, it was usually the woman) would be asked to leave. Nowadays, attitudes are more relaxed. Several studies have surveyed both participants and observers and found the majority of respondents accepts office relationships and feels that they make little difference in terms of work performance.[41] Indeed, they have become so common that several modern etiquette books include advice for handling them. Grace Fox, for example, advises romantic partners to be discreet and tells them not to spend too much time together or send each other personal emails. She also advises them about what to do if the romance ends: "Don't tell your side of what happened around the office. Don't take it out on the person in meetings or in private. Treat each other as kindly as you can."[42]

Office romances are not without risks. They can disrupt work, cause perceptions that one of the partners is being given unfair advantages, isolate the lovers from the rest of the office, and affect the credibility of the organization in the eyes of

---

Table 8.6 Some Rules for Professional Behavior

- **_Understand and acknowledge that different people have different roles to play in the organization._**

  Acknowledge roles, but don't grovel or condescend. In addressing others, use formal titles until you're told to do otherwise. Let your superior initiate and set the tone and content of a conversation. In other words, don't corner the CEO in the hall and launch into a long conversation about your vacation.

- **_Remember that you're there to work._**

  Take care of personal business before or after work. It is inappropriate to make personal phone calls at the office if you are in an entry-level position. Similarly, you are not being paid to play computer games, download music, flirt, spend hours rehashing your personal problems, and the like. If others do so, disengage yourself politely.

- **_Manage time and responsibilities effectively._**

  Arrive on time and stay until closing. Take deadlines seriously. You may have managed to get extensions while you were in college, but the rules change after graduation. When you say you're going to do something, follow through.

- **_When it comes to relationships, balance inclusion and distance._**

  Greeting coworkers with a few friendly words, offering to help out in small ways, and inviting others to be part of group activities help build a positive climate. Refraining from asking nosy questions or looking through their desks shows that you respect coworkers' privacy. Find a way to be pleasant without being overly familiar.

- **_Remember that you share public space with others and must therefore take their comfort and concerns into account._**

  Your office is not your home, no matter how many hours you spend there. Don't assault others with heavy cologne, smelly sandwiches, or loud music. An office should look like an office, not a picnic area.

- **_Know when to put aside personal feelings._**

  Open expression of like and dislike (either to others' faces or behind their backs) can destroy a cooperative climate. Personal feelings are often irrelevant in a work environment, so learn to bite your tongue.

- **_Figure out how to handle disagreement and criticism._**

  Disagreement and criticism are normal parts of office life. Without criticism, how could we learn? When negative feedback is directed at you, don't take it personally. And when you're the one disagreeing, make sure that you focus on the issues, not the person.

Office romances are not without risks. They can disrupt work, cause perceptions that one of the partners is being given unfair advantages, isolate the lovers from the rest of the office, and affect the credibility of the organization in the eyes of clients.

clients. Because they play out in public, participants may lose control. Office romances are, in a sense, no longer dyadic relationships; they can affect the attitudes and behaviors of all coworkers. Indeed, Gary Alan Fine criticizes office romances and even goes so far as to suggest, "If the company is a family, an organizational romance is incest."[43]

Sexual Harassment

Although dating coworkers is becoming more accepted, there is a thin line between pursuing a personal relationship and assaulting coworkers with offensive displays of affection and intimacy. Pursuing a coworker who is not interested in a romantic relationship can be a form of sexual harassment and can destroy a working relationship. According to the Equal Employment Opportunity Commission (EEOC), *sexual harassment* consists of

> unwelcome sexual advances, request for sexual favors, and other verbal or physical conduct of a sexual nature . . . when submission to or rejection of this conduct explicitly or implicitly affects an individual's employment, unreasonably interferes with an individual's work performance or creates an intimidating, hostile or offensive work environment.[44]

It should be noted that the harasser may be a woman or a man and the victim does not have to be of the opposite sex. In fact, anyone affected by the offensive conduct—for example, a bystander who is forced to witness harassment—can be considered a victim. Sexual harassment is not a laughing matter. It violates Title VII of the Civil Rights Act of 1964 and can lead to serious legal repercussions.

According to Charles Conrad, harassment is more likely to occur in certain kinds of organizations than in others. When the organization defines the "normal" employee as male, when support systems for women and people of color are weak or nonexistent, when the organization is loosely coupled, and when power relationships between superiors and subordinates are unequal, there will be more incidents of harassment. Unfortunately, as Conrad points out, "each of these factors is present in most colleges and universities."[45]

Although some sexual harassment is intentional and egregious, some may be the result of stupidity or insensitivity rather than malice. While anyone would agree that unwanted touch, requests for sexual favors in return for job advancement, or sexual taunting clearly fall within the bounds of sexual harassment, is it sexual harassment if the victim overhears an off-color joke being told in the hall? Experts disagree. As Tom D. Daniels puts it, "It is very clear that you cannot do something such as put a pornographic photo with a sexual proposition couched in vulgar language on a coworker's office desk to taunt that person. Whether you can play songs with explicit lyrics on your portable CD for your own amusement during lunch break remains to be seen."[46] What constitutes a hostile work environment is currently being clarified in the courts. Regardless of the results, sexually suggestive behavior in any form has no place in the workplace. Restraint and respect should characterize all workplace relationships.

USING ORGANIZATIONAL TECHNOLOGY

Some of you may love technology; others of you may hate it. But whatever your attitude, you will be exposed during your working life to an array of new devices designed to make your work easier and more efficient. Whether these advances in technology live up to their promise or whether they complicate your life will depend on your ability to use them wisely. To be successful in today's workplace, it's essential to keep informed about new technologies. More important, it's necessary to recognize the ways in which technology changes the structure and operations of organizations.

Telecommuting

For many people, the virtual office is replacing the real office. Growing numbers of employees are *telecommuting*, working from their homes via electronic media. Champions of telecommuting have pointed out potential advantages. Organizations that encourage telecommuting save the money they normally spend on providing office and work sites, and workers do not have to relocate to get that perfect job. It has even been suggested that telecommuting can decrease traffic and pollution. In Los Angeles, for example, 60 percent of the city's notorious air pollution comes from automobile emissions.[47] Imagine how much more livable Los Angeles and other major cities could be if physical commuting were replaced by virtual commuting.

> As it becomes more feasible to work at home, the traditional separation between workplace and home may gradually disappear. When we can work anywhere, there is no way to escape the demands of the office, no time when parents are available exclusively to their children or husbands and wives to their spouses.

On the other hand, as it becomes more feasible to work at home, the traditional separation between workplace and home may gradually disappear. When we can work anywhere, there is no way to escape the demands of the office, no time when parents are available exclusively to their children or husbands and wives to their spouses. In *The Wired Community*, Stephen Doheny-Farina describes a typical telecommuter. Peg Fagen lives in Massachusetts and telecommutes to a New York office. She has equipped her home office with a "dedicated phone and fax line, computer and modem, e-mail and file-transfer connectivity, copier, and so on." She also hires a babysitter to supervise her preschool children. She is single-minded about her work time. "When she goes into her office, she is at work. When the sitter leaves or when the children awaken, she is at home. If the day's work is not completed when the sitter leaves, she returns to her office after the children have been put to bed."[48] She telecommutes successfully because she can manage her time wisely and because her boss knows and trusts her. Nevertheless, her decision has not been without costs:

"Co-workers with similar education, on-the-job experience, and time with the company have moved up the company's management ladder faster than Peg."[49]

Despite its convenience, telecommuting has drawbacks. Undisciplined workers may find it difficult to work without direct supervision, while workaholics may find themselves writing memos well past midnight. According to a report commissioned by *Mobile Office* magazine, home workers work more hours and experience more stress to meet deadlines than do office workers.[50] In addition, face-to-face informal networking and relationship building are not possible. Surveys show that telecommuters often fear a loss of "visibility and career momentum" when they don't have the opportunity to form direct, offline relationships with those who evaluate their job performance.[51] A final cost is to the development of a strong organizational culture. Corporate culture is created through the minutiae of everyday communications. As employees interact, they forge alliances and develop cohesion. Some of this interaction can be accomplished via corporate chat lines; however, text-based bulletin boards and video teleconferences don't allow the informality and frequency of face-to-face communication.

Virtual Teams

Although you may not end up working from home, it is quite possible that you will one day be part of a work group that communicates online. Because of advances in information and communication technologies (ICTs) and because of economic globalization, many organizations now ask their employees to join *virtual teams*, work groups whose members are separated geographically and whose communication is mediated by technologies such as email, telephone, groupware, videoconferencing, and the like.[52]

Virtual teamwork calls for heightened communication skills. Because communication is often asynchronous, members can experience frustrating time lags during communication. Although slow response time is often due to time zone differences or difficulty in accessing ICTs, it can lead members to believe their communication partners are lazy or nonproductive. Feelings of isolation can also occur in groups where members have never met face-to-face. Differences in cultural background can lead to misunderstandings. Finally, trust and group loyalty may be difficult to achieve. As Marshall Scott Poole and Huiyan Zhang point out:

> *Trust is the substrate of effective virtual teams. It substitutes for direct physical contact and the expectation that others will deliver, and it encourages members to meet their own commitments in order to maintain the trust that others have in them.*[53]

Although Sirkka Jarvenpaa and Dorothy Leidner have argued that swift, depersonalized, goal-directed trust can develop in virtual teams, this trust is quite fragile and temporal.[54]

To combat some of the problems encountered by virtual groups, organizations should use software that lets members know who is available online and what everyone has been doing. They should also create strong norms to coordinate and schedule work. To combat isolation, most communication experts suggest that virtual teams meet face-to-face at the beginning of every project and that leaders stay in telephone contact with every member. Organizations should also provide cross-cultural training for international teams. In addition, all members should also be trained to use a variety of ICTs, and access to up-to-date technology should be assured. Finally, organizations must choose the right people when composing teams.

What kinds of people should organizations look for? Research suggests people who are able to work independently, tolerate ambiguity, and motivate themselves are particularly effective in virtual teams.[55] In addition, individuals who are quick to trust others and are accepting of cultural differences seem to do well in this kind of setting. And, of course, facility in using ICTs is an important requirement. If you plan to work for a modern organization the ability to use and choose technologies wisely is a necessity you should prepare for now.

Finding the Right Medium for the Right Job

Computer-mediated communication (CMC) may be the latest thing, but that doesn't necessarily mean that it is the best thing. One of the drawbacks is that such communications use lean media rather than rich media. **Rich media** use a variety of channels to carry information whereas lean media use fewer channels. Face-to-face conversation, for example, is the richest medium because it contains the most verbal and nonverbal cues. Generally speaking, rich media are better than lean media when immediate feedback is important, when communicators need to know each other's emotional responses, or when the message contains very personal, highly charged news.[56] CMC may also discourage mutual problem solving, which is probably better done in a face-to-face context. On the other hand, CMC does provide a great deal of information very rapidly. Not only does it enhance distribution of simple announcements, it may actually improve information efficiency by bypassing formal channels. What is important is that communicators think carefully about what they want to accomplish with their messages and that they choose an appropriate medium.

Melinda Kramer offers a list of some of the factors that should affect choice of medium in a business context. Included are speed (How quickly does the message need to be there?), timing (Do you need an answer immediately or can you leave information to be dealt with later?), distance (How far does the message need to travel?), size of audience (How many people do you need to reach?), intimacy (How personal is the message?), talent (What media are both you and your receiver most comfortable with?), and cost (What is your budget?). Thus, if a message has to get out right away, if it doesn't need an immediate reply, if it is to go to many people at the same time, and if it is not personal, then email may be the way to go. On the other hand, if the material is sensitive, then a medium such as the telephone (where the receiver can hear your voice) or, better yet, a face-to-face meeting (with the full complement of verbal and nonverbal cues) is the right choice. Kramer reminds us, "Many business people choose the communication medium with which they are most familiar . . . without thinking about which medium will actually be the most effective. Instead of following old habits, you should evaluate the available media and select the one that best fits your communication goals."[57]

Alan Zaremba gives an example of what can happen when people react without thinking about the appropriateness of the medium. He reports that, in 1999, a counseling center in Boston received a phoned-in bomb threat. Taking the threat seriously, administrators knew that they had to notify the staff. How did they do it? By using a mass email asking everyone to vacate the building. The problem? Most of the employees were in a conference at the time, and even had they been in their offices, it's not likely that they all would have checked their email quickly enough. Luckily, the threat was a hoax. Had it not been, choosing the wrong medium could have led to disaster.[58]

In choosing the best way to send a message, it can be helpful to keep in mind the distinction made by Lee Sproull and Sara Kiesler between first-level and second-level effects of technology.[59] A **first-level effect** refers to what the technology is designed to do. For example, the first-level effect of email is that it allows us to communicate cheaply and immediately. A **second-level effect** is an unforeseen side effect of technology. Zaremba explains that second-level effects of email may be to make face-to-face encounters rarer, create a digital divide between those with access to computers and those without, and encourage flaming.[60] When choosing media, it is important to keep both kinds of effects in mind.

> If you've ever had to listen to someone else's cell phone conversation during a meal at your favorite restaurant or if you've been the recipient of an abrupt, dismissive email, you know how rude people can be in their use of electronic media.

Etiquette in the Wired Workplace

Just as there are rules of etiquette to help people develop workable relationships in the modern organization, so there are rules for the civil use of technology. If you've ever had to listen to someone else's cell phone conversation during a meal at your favorite restaurant or if you've been the recipient of an abrupt, dismissive email, you know how rude people can be in their use of electronic media. Table 8.7 lists some rules to follow as you employ electronic media.

Crowdsourcing and Organizational Problem Solving

As we saw in the last chapter, Web 2.0 has enabled new forms of information exchange and problem solving. Here we look at crowdsourcing, just one of the innovative ways organizations are using the Internet to harness collective knowledge. In **crowdsourcing**, organizations identify and articulate a need, then post an open call for proposals to meet that need. Threadless and iStockphoto are two examples. Threadless is a t-shirt company that crowdsources its designs through an online competition. Any individual can upload a design, which is then viewed and scored, with the highest scoring design being manufactured and sold online. iStockphoto sells royalty-free stock photography and animation submitted by amateur photographers.

Crowdsourcing is used to do more than sell products. The Doritos commercials shown on one of the Super Bowl broadcasts, for example, were produced through crowdsourcing, and large companies such as Boeing, DuPont, and Proctor and Gamble have awarded prizes, often ranging from $10,000 to $100,000, to promising solutions to research and development problems. Crowdsourcing is a way of taking advantage of "the wisdom of the crowd," and it can often produce solutions and products that are superior to those that could be developed in-house.

Media critics like Clay Shirky believe that practices like crowdsourcing capture what he calls "*cognitive surplus*," the resourcefulness and ingenuity that would normally be lost if Web 2.0 did not provide technology users with a creative outlet. It is his belief that when people blog or post to YouTube or answer a crowdsourcing proposal, they gain the personal satisfaction that comes from being actively creative, and society gains the end results of their inventiveness.[61] Not everyone agrees.

Table 8.7 Etiquette for an Information Age

Although etiquette may seem an antiquate idea, there are rules for using technology in an information age. Many etiquette experts now offer rules for polite interaction. Here are a few to consider.

Cell Phone Use in Public

Talking or texting in public places like restaurants or movies can be rude and disruptive. Moving to a more private place to take or place a call is considered polite.

Taking Calls During Other Interactions

Silence your cell phone in any conference or professional setting, including during class. During discussions the other parties deserve undivided attention. It is impolite and insulting to make or take calls while you are expected to listen.

Voice Mail

When recording your message to incoming callers avoid overly cute or offensive material that could offend a professional caller, and when you leave messages on others' voice mail, speak clearly and slowly. The person you call should not have to guess who called and what he or she wanted.

Conference Calls

Always remember to identify yourself when making a contribution and don't engage in whispered side comments or jokes.

Forwarding Messages from Others

Forwarding personal messages or photos meant only for you to other people who were not meant to receive the message is an invasion of privacy. Think how you would feel if everyone around you had access to your personal communications

Timing Phone Calls

Consider what the other person may be doing and time your calls appropriately. If you know someone is driving wait; speaking or reading texts while driving is dangerous and in many places illegal. And calling someone at two in the morning—unless you are sure they are awake—is just plain rude.

Screen Names and Ring Tones

Avoid choosing screen names that are risqué or silly, especially in a business setting. Although they may have seemed funny when you chose them, they can crease a bad impression. Also keep in mind that your ring tones create an impression of who you are. Consider what your boss or colleagues will think of you when your phone goes off.

Crowdsourcing has been criticized for its effect on the labor pool. The young film-makers whose ads were shown at the Super Bowl were certainly not paid at a professional level, nor were the artists whose designs won the Threadless competitions. And, when amateurs are willing to submit their photos for next to nothing, it is hard for professional photographers to make a living. In a critique of crowdsourcing, Daren Brabham likens the pay given to crowd members for their high quality work to a slave economy.[62] As with every other technical innovation, there is both an upside and a downside. Whether you consider crowdsourcing a clever business model or an exploitative practice depends on your perspective and professional goals.

BECOMING A MORE RESPONSIBLE COMMUNICATOR

In today's business environment, issues of responsibility are extraordinarily complex and critical. As the power of multinational organizations increases, so do troubling ethical issues. In an article on social responsibility in international business, Stanley Deetz lists just a few of the questionable business practices that occur in an organizational world where high-speed decision making hinders thoughtful ethical debate and internationalization and outsourcing make surveillance and control difficult. Values such as human rights, environmental protection, fair competition, and equal opportunity for all workers are abused in activities such as

> using prisoners as workers, moving operations to environmentally less restrictive communities, offering and taking bribes and payoffs, creating environmentally unsound or wasteful products, closing of economically viable plants in takeover and merger games, growing income disparity, declining social safety nets, malingering, harassment, maintaining unnecessary and unhealthy controls on employees, and advocating consumerism.[63]

In a world where practices like these can and do occur, organizations must work to create responsible and humane environments for those both inside and outside their boundaries. Listed below are a few guidelines that can help members of organizations act more responsibly.

- In most organizations, it's easy to pass the buck when it comes to ethical issues. As Charles Conrad points out, in bureaucratic structures, responsibility often falls between the cracks. Employees at lower levels who implement unethical procedures often excuse their behavior by pointing out that they were just following company policies and procedures. Employees at higher levels, who make the policies, do not feel any responsibility because they themselves don't actually have to make illegal or unethical decisions. As a result, in irresponsible organizations, unethical practices are always someone else's fault. Responsible organizations, on the other hand, encourage all employees to take an ethical stance.[64]

- Organizational cultures can be humane or inhumane. When they are humane, workers feel comfortable and supported and are able to work creatively. When they are inhumane, workers feel criticized and defensive and may be pressured to act in unethical ways to protect themselves. When organizations encourage mutual trust and support, employees are more satisfied with their jobs and display more commitment and loyalty to the organization. By refusing to play politics, engage in gossip, follow hidden agendas, or attack coworkers, employees can enhance the organizational climate and build a more humane culture. D. K. Banner and T. E. Gagne express it this way:

> [W]e create and maintain organizational forms consistent with our level of collective maturity and our shared identity. If we see ourselves as separate, fearful, shameridden people whose best hope for happiness is to manipulate our external circumstances so that they please us, we get the bureaucratic form. If we are willing to accept personal responsibility for expressing transcendent values, for living in true, spiritual identity, we will create flexible, nonhierarchical politics-free organizations. We create our own reality.[65]

- Responsible organizations encourage open communication. Since the 1960s, organizational communication experts have argued that effective organizations must establish an open communication climate in which subordinates have access to information on matters that affect their work lives and feel free to express their ideas and participate in decision making. Both scholars and practitioners have argued that when communication networks are open and participation is encouraged, organizations are likely to be productive and effective. To ensure open communication, organizations must provide forums for the voicing of opinions. But because many current forums are actually used to suppress conflict and to increase compliance rather than to foster a genuine exchange of ideas, companies must find new ways to encourage employees to express their own opinions, interests, and feelings.

- For too long, organizations have excluded large portions of the population. By opening up to employees who were formerly denied entry, organizations not only do the right thing, they also increase their ability to compete in a global economy. When organizations limit membership to people who think and act alike, they diminish creativity and problem-solving ability. When they expand their membership, they expand their perspectives. According to Deetz, "The presence of diverse goals, rather than creating costly conflict and impasse, creates the conditions whereby limited decisional frames are broken and the company learns."[66] But diversity must be more than an organizational policy. Members at every level in the organization must learn to value diversity and to overcome their discomfort with others who are different.

- It's a common belief that the only people affected by an organization are its employees and stockholders. In fact, the impact of organizational decisions is far ranging. Organizations affect the communities in which they are located, the customers who use their products or services, and even the physical environments that surround them. The groups that can affect or are affected by organizations—that have a "stake" in the organization—are called **stakeholders**. In a sense, they are as much a part of the organization as employees, and, as members of the organization, their values and needs must be taken into account. Responsible organizations recognize the legitimacy of their relationships with a wider community of stakeholders, acting as their stewards.

SUMMARY

An organization is a system made up of people working toward a common goal. Organizations have four characteristics: interdependence, hierarchical structure, linkage to their environments, and, most important from our point of view, dependence on communication. When communication fails, organizations experience problems in productivity and member satisfaction. Poor communication practices can also make the organization an unpleasant place to work by creating a negative organizational climate. By focusing on communication, managers and their employees can avoid problems and can increase their chances of organizational advancement.

To communicate competently in an organization, members must communicate with more formality than in other contexts. They must also master organizational genres, the unique forms of communication common to organizations. Of course, each organization will have its own rules for communication. What works in one organizational culture will not necessarily work in another.

Information is the lifeblood of organizations. As it circulates through the organization, it can follow a formal chain of command (the formal network) or a more unstructured pathway based on personal contacts and friendships (the informal network). Formal communication can move in an upward direction (from subordinate to superior), a downward direction (from superior to subordinate), or a horizontal direction (between employees with equal status). In U.S. organizations, most information flows downward. Unfortunately, employees are often dissatisfied with the amount and quality of downward flow. Sometimes, they receive too little information; sometimes, they receive too much; and sometimes, they receive deceptive or false information. Part of the problem is due to the fact that as messages pass between individuals, details are left out, elaborated, or changed to fit the communicator's own frame of reference. By building in redundancy and asking for clarification, communicators can overcome some of these difficulties in serial transmission.

Upward flow is less common in organizations, but it, too, can be distorted by employees who don't want to be the bearers of bad tidings or by gatekeepers who want to protect their superiors.

Informal structures, such as the grapevine, are also prevalent in organizations. Although we tend to think of the grapevine as a hotbed of gossip and false rumor, studies have shown it to be quite accurate, although often incomplete. One way to determine the informal structures in an organization is to do network analysis.

Horizontal communication can also be beset by problems. When people at the same level work together in teams, they may be reluctant to try new approaches, they may be unable to locate important information, or they may lack trust, especially in organizations in which departments are in competition. For this reason it is important for team leaders and managers to create teams that exhibit structural diversity, to maintain effective transactive memory systems, and to encourage trust.

Employees must know how to interview effectively, understand and fit into organizational culture, and act professionally. In order to gain admittance to an organization, individuals must prepare carefully for employment interviews by assessing their skills, preparing compelling resumes and cover letters, and researching the organization. During the interview itself they should use their answers to demonstrate competence and confidence as well as intelligence and respect. Once hired, individuals must find a way to fit into the organization's culture. By observing norms of conduct, metaphors, stories, and rites, the perceptive employee can uncover hidden values and assumptions and can begin to understand what is expected of him or her. Finally, organizational members must build professional relationships. By recognizing role differences and by remembering that personal desires and feelings must sometimes be subordinated to those of others, employees can create productive work relationships.

When sex and romance enter the workplace, interaction becomes complicated. Nowadays, more and more people are engaging in office romances. These interactions can be risky and must be handled with a great deal of discretion and skill. Sometimes, the presence of sexual attraction in the workplace can lead to serious problems, including sexual harassment. Any communication that creates an intimidating, hostile, or offensive work environment on the basis of verbal or physical conduct of a sexual nature counts as sexual harassment and is illegal under the Civil Rights Act of 1964.

In today's work culture, keeping up with technology is a must. At some time in their work lives, most members of organizations will be asked to join virtual teams composed of members who are separated geographically and whose communication is mediated. Virtual teamwork calls for heightened communication skills because working in cyberspace presents challenges such as frustrating time lags, unfair attributions about other members, feelings of isolation, and lack of trust. To combat these problems, organizations should work hard to connect members, provide cross-cultural training when necessary, and train members to use a variety of Internet communication technologies. Individuals who are independent and self-motivated, can tolerate ambiguity, are open to trusting others, and can choose the right medium for the right job do well on virtual teams.

Organizations should also encourage members to use the right medium for each job. Factors such as speed, timing, distance, audience size, intimacy, talent, and cost should be taken into consideration when choosing how to convey a message. It's also important to be aware of second-level effects associated with every medium.

As in other contexts, computer-mediated communication is changing organizational communication. Crowdsourcing is one way organizations take advantage of collective knowledge.

Every communication context raises ethical dilemmas. The organizational context is no different. By taking responsibility for one's actions, by trying to create a culture that respects the dignity of others, and by encouraging open discussion and respecting diversity, organizational communicators can create humane workplaces. In addition, organizational members should not develop an "us" versus "them" mentality; they should recognize that they are part of a wider community and take into account the needs and feelings of multiple stakeholders.

KEY TERMS

Listed below are the key terms used in this chapter, along with the number of the page where each is explained.

organization (196)	message filtering (203)	trust (208)
interdependence (197)	serial transmission (203)	interview (209)
hierarchy (197)	gatekeeper (204)	organizational culture (213)
bureaucracy (197)	ombudsman (204)	rites (216)
climate (198)	grapevine (205)	ceremonials (216)
structurational approach (198)	network analysis (206)	rich media (223)
formal channels of	opinion leaders (206)	crowdsourcing (224)
communication (200)	isolates (206)	first-level effect (224)
informal channels of	tight/loose coupling (207)	second-level effect (224)
communication (201)	structural diversity (208)	stakeholders (227)
downward/upward/horizontal	transactive memory	
flow (201)	system (208)	

SUGGESTED READING

Conrad, Charles, & Poole, Marshall Scott. (2004). *Strategic organizational communication in a global economy*. Belmont, CA: Wadsworth.

An intelligent survey of organizational communication with an excellent section on organizational culture.

Papa, Michael J., Daniels, Tom D., & Spiker, Barry K. (2007). *Organizational communication: Perspectives and trends*. Thousand Oaks, CA: Sage.

An overview of traditional, interpretive, and critical approaches to organizational communication combining case material and up-to-date research.

Shockley-Zalabak, Pamela. (2011). *Fundamentals of organizational communication* (8th ed.). Boston: Allyn & Bacon.

A good source for examples and cases of leadership, conflict, and globalization.

Public Communication

Public communication does not belong only to the famous—every day, all over the country, average people stand up and speak to audiences and, in doing so, make a difference.

After reading this chapter, you should be able to:

- Explain characteristics and purposes of communication in the public sphere.
- Know the social functions and personal consequences of public communication.
- Explain why it is important to understand audience beliefs, attitudes, and values.
- Understand how credibility, attractiveness, and power enhance speaker effectiveness.
- Use the Toulmin model to diagram and evaluate an argument.
- Give examples of authoritative, motivational, and substantive appeals.
- Distinguish arguments from cause, sign, generalization, and analogy, and identify the kinds of fallacies associated with each.

Consider the following situations in which public communication had a major impact on personal fortune and national consciousness.

- In one of the first of a long line of cases to be dubbed "the Crime of the Century," a celebrated lawyer took on the defense of two college students who had confessed to murder. In a summation that reportedly lasted for twelve hours, the lawyer presented one of the most eloquent attacks on capital punishment ever delivered.[1]

- During the Great Depression, when millions of Americans were struggling to survive, a president took office and rallied the nation, promising that there was "nothing to fear but fear itself."[2]

- A politician who had been accused of corruption resurrected his career with a single speech and was eventually elected president. Twelve years later, during his second term as president, he once again addressed the nation, this time as he resigned in disgrace.[3]

- Speaking the night before he was assassinated, Martin Luther King, Jr., the most famous civil rights leader in the United States celebrated the accomplishments of the movement and urged followers to continue their struggle, foreshadowing his own demise but holding out hope that his people would achieve equality.[4]

- The wife of a TV star, a young mother with AIDS whose seven-year-old daughter had already died, addressed a national political convention and described the kind of America she believed in.[5]

Clarence Darrow, Franklin Delano Roosevelt, Richard Nixon, Martin Luther King Jr., Elizabeth Glaser—none of these speakers is with us today, yet their words live on as compelling examples of how single individuals, communicating in the public sphere, can use the spoken word to influence audiences and sway public opinion. These speakers were all well known at the time they spoke. But public communication does not belong only to the famous; every day, all over the country, average people stand up and speak to audiences and, in doing so, make a difference.

In previous chapters, we looked at communication that involved relatively small numbers of people in face-to-face interaction. In this and the next chapter, we examine a different kind of communication: communication in which a single speaker addresses an audience to inform, persuade, or entertain. This chapter will provide a brief and very general introduction to the study of **rhetoric**, the art of designing public messages that can change the way in which audiences think and feel about public issues. Here, our concern will be in understanding the factors that make communicating in the public sphere unique and in discovering ways to evaluate public speeches. The next chapter is designed for those of you who want to gain practical speaking skills. It will examine some specific techniques that you, as a speaker, can use to construct and deliver effective public presentations.

WHAT IS PUBLIC COMMUNICATION?

Public communication is a one-to-many form of communication wherein a single speaker addresses a large audience. Although audience members may ask questions afterward, their major role during the speech is to listen to and evaluate what the speaker has to say. Clear organization, careful preplanning, and formal language style are the hallmarks of public speeches, which are the most traditional form of public discourse.

Characteristics of Public Communication

Public speaking differs from the forms of communication we have already studied. In the public context, the spontaneity and informality of interpersonal communication and the give-and-take of group discussion are replaced by relatively formal, preplanned messages and more rigidly defined communication roles. Public speakers and their audiences do not run into each other by chance, nor do they sit around and discuss whatever comes into their minds. Public speaking is usually prompted by an important event or issue. As a consequence, public messages are constructed with more care than are interpersonal messages.

> **Public speaking is usually prompted by an important event or issue.**

One factor motivating that care is audience size. Public speakers may address tens, hundreds, or even thousands of people. Their messages must therefore make sense to large, sometimes quite heterogeneous audiences. As we shall see, audience adaptation is one of the central challenges of communication in the public context. In addition, time is an important variable that affects public communication. Speakers do not have the luxury of slowly developing a relationship with receivers or of going back to reexplain poorly expressed ideas. Most public speeches are one-time-only occasions. The speaker must therefore make an immediate impact and must be completely clear from the outset. Public speeches are also relatively long. In conversations, turns are exchanged rapidly and rarely last longer than a minute or so. In public speeches, a single speaker may retain the floor for an hour or even longer. Audience members must therefore listen attentively for extended periods of time. Because this is hard work, the speakers must make the receivers' work as easy as possible. They must use simple structures that are easy to follow, employ transitions and repeated summaries, and do everything they can to capture attention.

The public speaker is also physically distanced from the audience. Conversational partners sit within a few feet of one another, but public speakers may be twenty or more feet from the audience. They must therefore speak loudly and clearly and use gestures and visual aids that can be seen at a distance.

A final characteristic of public communication is that it takes place in a different sphere from interpersonal or group communication. In interpersonal communication, talk focuses inward on personal matters. In public communication, the focus is wider. Issues and topics are focused outward, toward a community of individuals with shared interests. In other words, public communication occurs within the public sphere.

Communicating in the Public Sphere

When we communicate solely with our own interests in mind, we are acting in the **private sphere**. However, when we communicate as members of a larger community and our topic is of concern to many, then we are operating in the **public sphere**. Rhetorician Martha Cooper explains that

> the public sphere . . . is not a real place . . . in which you could sit down and have a conversation. Instead, it is an orientation that people take to parts of their lives. When something happens that seems to affect groups of people rather than single individuals, the public sphere is emerging. . . . [W]e can recognize that we have entered the public sphere when we find ourselves motivated by the needs of others as well as ourselves, by the needs of the community, rather than our own personal needs.[6]

> **When we communicate solely with our own interests in mind, we are acting in the private sphere. However, when we communicate as members of a larger community we are operating in the public sphere.**

What we say in the public sphere can affect the well-being of hundreds or even thousands of others. When sports celebrity Magic Johnson tested positive for HIV, he went public with the news. Had he kept his illness a secret, he could have retained some measure of personal privacy—at least for a while. By announcing the news immediately, however, he became a major figure in the battle against AIDS. His decision to make a public issue of his private circumstances had a dramatic impact on the attitudes of thousands of people.

Making a decision such as Johnson made would take a great deal of courage, for public communication involves risks and responsibilities. In fact, in contemporary

One reason for communicating in the public sphere is to create social change.

© Claudia Wiens/Alamy

society, many people shy away from public involvement. In discussing the reluctance of modern Americans to enter the public realm, Cooper argues that the mobility of modern society and the technical, specialized nature of the modern workplace weaken our ties with our communities. In addition, the diversity of contemporary society keeps many people from forming close bonds with those around them. As a result, our society emphasizes individualism more than community; we are constantly urged to make it on our own, to be our own person, and to look out for number one.[7]

Despite these difficulties, many people do take part in public debate. Environmental issues, in particular, have awakened people to the necessity of public involvement. And the success of grassroots groups such as MADD (Mothers Against Drunk Driving) has demonstrated that public communication is a powerful tool not only for dealing with public issues but for creating them as well. A generation ago, people bragged about how well they could drive while drunk, and driving with open containers was legal. Now our attitude is very different: drunk drivers are considered criminals. This change in attitude occurred in part because one woman, Candy Lightner, entered the public sphere. After a drunk driver caused the death of her daughter, Lightner formed MADD and began to take her message to the public. Today, she is a nationally recognized figure who delivers hundreds of speeches a year. She illustrates that one determined person can make a difference.[8]

WHY IS PUBLIC COMMUNICATION IMPORTANT?

Most people's attitudes toward public communication are mixed. On the one hand, we recognize how essential public discussion is to a democracy. Most of us believe that part of the responsibility of citizens in a free society is to take stands on public issues, and we know that public communication allows us to take that stand. Yet

Distrust of the art of rhetoric is not a modern phenomenon. Indeed, as early as the beginning of the fourth century B.C., Plato wrote about the fact that skilled public communicators could use rhetoric to dupe their audiences.

at the same time, we distrust much of what we hear in the public realm, dismissing the speeches of politicians or the arguments of lawyers as "empty rhetoric" or, worse, as manipulation or deception. This distrust of the art of rhetoric is not a modern phenomenon. Indeed, as early as the beginning of the fourth century B.C., Plato wrote about the fact that skilled public communicators could use rhetoric to dupe their audiences.[9] Plato recognized the power that knowledge of rhetoric can convey, a power that can be used to hide the truth as well as to reveal it.

Social Functions of Rhetoric

Rhetorician James Herrick admits that rhetoric can be used deceptively, but he also believes that it fulfills at least six positive social functions. By understanding and applying rhetorical principles, he argues, we discover facts about our world, test ideas, learn how to persuade others, shape knowledge, build community, and distribute power.[10] These six factors serve as an answer to the question: Why is public communication important?

Discovering Facts

An important aspect of rhetoric is the discovery of facts. Public speakers are expected to be well informed. This means that they must research their topics. Often, this process reveals new information. Engaging in the rhetorical enterprise means that both speaker and audience find out things about the world they had not previously known.

Testing Ideas

Rhetoric also provides us with "an important and peaceful means for testing ideas publicly."[11] In the process of putting together a public address, communicators test ideas, rejecting those that are illogical or unsupported and accepting others. Audience members too are part of the testing process. By listening with intelligence and by responding critically, audiences can demand that rhetoric be well reasoned and well supported.

Persuading Others

The art of rhetoric is one of the most important resources available to groups or individuals engaged in persuasive argumentation—"second only to the merits of their ideas." Knowledge of rhetoric helps lawyers prepare cases, candidates get elected, lobbyists make their cases, constituents persuade their representative, and committees debate the merits of proposals.[12]

Shaping Knowledge

Once facts have been discovered and presented and the ideas that derive from them have been tested, individuals within cultures come to accept these facts and ideas as true. Thus, public communication serves to create a body of knowledge. In this sense, truth is not something independent of communication; instead, it is a product of communication.

Building Community

If rhetoric is the tool that allows us to establish truth, it is also the tool that allows the establishment of community. After all, community consists of groups of people "who find common cause with one another, who see the world in a similar way, who identify

> If rhetoric is the tool that allows us to establish truth, it is also the tool that allows the establishment of community.

their concerns and aspirations with similar concerns and aspirations of other people."[13] And it is through public discourse that people come to share visions of the world.

Much of the time, the communities we build are local, but increasingly, communities can be electronically mediated. It is not uncommon to look for others who share our interests online. Anyone who has ever logged onto Facebook knows how easy it is to create and join groups with common interests.

Distributing Power

Finally, knowledge of rhetoric and the ability to speak publicly give us power. Herrick believes that rhetoric is connected to power in three ways. It gives us *personal power* by providing the skills needed for personal success and career advancement. It gives us *psychological power* by giving us the knowledge to shape the way other people think. And it grants us *political power* in that it gives us a voice. This latter point is important, for, as Herrick argues, "how influence gets distributed in a culture is often a matter of who gets to speak, where they are allowed to speak, and on what subjects."[14] The rise of social media has increased opportunities for average citizens to enter the public sphere. During Arab Spring, the democratic uprisings that occurred in the Middle East during 2010 and 2011, activists used social media like Facebook, Twitter, and YouTube to collect information, post videos, and organize protests. Although authoritarian regimes tried to silence them, the power of the Internet became the power of the people.

Personal and Professional Consequences

In addition to its social functions, skill in public communication has personal consequences. The ability to communicate in public is a necessary skill in most professional and managerial positions. As we saw in Chapter 8, modern businesses are held together by information. The ability to convey that information clearly and effectively is essential for professional advancement. As James van Oosting points out,

> speechmaking is integral to the business enterprise. Information must be conveyed; personnel must be motivated and directed; reports must be given; policies must be articulated and defended; meetings must be chaired; products and services must be sold. . . . Whether one gets up in front of a public gathering to introduce the company president or addresses a small sales staff the first thing each morning, one is engaged in public communication. . . . [P]ublic communication is [a] workday expectation and not some extraordinary assignment reserved for special occasions.[15]

EVALUATING PUBLIC COMMUNICATION

Whether or not you end up doing a great deal of public speaking, your life will be affected by those who do. Politicians will try to persuade you, religious leaders will try to inspire you, and lawyers may try to sway you. It is therefore important to think about ways to evaluate the strength and impact of the public speeches you are exposed to. In this section, we look at three factors that critics should use in evaluating public messages: the nature of the context in which public communication occurs, the relationship between speaker and audience, and appeals within the message itself.

Whether or not you end up doing a great deal of public speaking, your life will be affected by those who do.

Context and Rhetorical Situation

Like all acts of communication, public speeches are situated within contexts. When communication and context don't "fit," speakers stop being effective. To evaluate the impact of a public speech, it's necessary to begin with context. Factors such as the physical setting of the speech, the medium through which it is delivered, and the specific nature of the occasion are part of context. But so also are its wider historical and cultural setting and its argumentative history.

Physical Setting, Medium, and Occasion

As rhetorical critics James Andrews, Michael Leff, and Robert Terrill point out, "physical surroundings can have a real impact on the way a message is constructed and how it is delivered" because audience expectations are tied to settings.[16] For example, the style and delivery of a speech given in an open-air stadium to an audience of ten thousand are quite different from the style and delivery of a speech given in a college classroom, even when the purposes of the two speeches are similar. Vocal tone and language choices that are suitable for the first context will embarrass the audience in the second because the stadium demands a larger and more emotional style than does the classroom.

The medium of transmission is another aspect of context that affects public messages. A speech designed for TV will differ from one delivered in person because the conditions for reception are so different. Not only are television viewers distanced from the speaker, they are situated in a "noisier" environment, where they may be interrupted by the phone, by the dog asking to go out, or by a sudden urge to make a sandwich and grab a beer. Audiences in face-to-face contexts have less freedom to move around or multitask. On the other hand, they are freer to direct their attention to different aspects of the speech situation. The home viewer's perspective is entirely in the hands of the director who decides when to zoom in and when to get a shot of audience reaction. This is just one example of how media affect communication. In Chapter 11, we will deal with this topic in more detail, looking at how traditional and emerging media affect the way in which we process and send messages.

Another aspect of context is the nature of the occasion that has prompted the speech. An address that does not match its occasion cannot achieve its purpose. A speech delivered at a celebrity roast, for example, is stylistically very different from a State of the Union address. The form and substance of a funeral oration are not the same as those of a political keynote address or an opening argument in a murder trial. All the factors that make up the speech—its purpose, organization, language style, use of supporting materials, and the like—depend on the nature of the

> All the factors that make up the speech—its purpose, organization, language style, use of supporting materials, and the like—depend on the nature of the occasion.

occasion. Receivers have a sense of what fits into a particular context and will be unsettled if the speech does not meet expectations.

History as Context

There are broader aspects of context to consider as well. Every speech is given at a particular time in history and the events that surround the speech affect its reception. The attacks of September 11, 2001, for example, affected the way Americans thought about the world and their place in it. A speech criticizing America's posture in the Middle East would have been received very differently on September 12 than on September 10. Of course, events do not have to be of national significance to be part of a historical context. Campus or community events could well affect reactions to a speech. A recent hazing accident may well make an audience less receptive to a speech praising the fraternity and sorority system. Or a local case of police brutality may make it harder to argue for a stronger police presence on campus.

It is not just historical events that are of concern. Issues have a history as well. Unless an issue is completely new, it has been argued before, and these prior arguments may be known to an audience. Speakers who don't bother to find out what an audience has already heard are likely to spend valuable time "reinventing the wheel" by arguing points that have already been made or bringing up proposals that are likely to be rejected. Andrews and his colleagues refer to knowledge about how an issue has been treated in the past as **argumentational history**, and it is an essential aspect of context.[17]

Rhetorical Situation

The importance of context is probably best summed up by rhetorician Lloyd Bitzer.[18] In an article entitled "The Rhetorical Situation," Bitzer argues that of all the factors affecting public communication, situation is the most important because it both prompts a speaker to act and shapes the nature of his or her message.

For Bitzer, **rhetorical situations** consist of three parts: exigence, audience, and constraints. Bitzer believes that all acts of rhetoric are motivated by some *exigence*, or problem. Speakers decide to speak because they feel that something is wrong and hope, by speaking about it, to make it right. They therefore address an *audience* of people who can change the problem, either by altering their beliefs and attitudes or by taking direct action. Of course, the ways in which speakers respond to their audiences are affected by *constraints*, factors that control and shape the nature of the communication. The kinds of contextual features we've already discussed, such as medium of transmission or argumentative history, are constraints, as are things like the current beliefs and values of the audience and speaker characteristics such as credibility and argumentative skill.

Bitzer goes on to argue that every rhetorical situation demands a **fitting response**, a response that meets the demands of exigence, takes into account the audience, and is sensitive to constraints. For example, if a major natural disaster occurs, as it did in 2005 when Hurricane Katrina struck the Gulf Coast, and the government officials responsible for disaster relief fail to speak in a timely way, spend their time making excuses, or show a lack of understanding of the victims' plight, then we can rightly say that their rhetorical response failed. The rhetorical situation demanded a response, but the response that occurred did not fit the situation.

Bitzer's analysis is simple, yet it provides a powerful guide both for the speaker and for the rhetorical critic. Speakers must fully understand the rhetorical situation if they are to be effective; and audience members, if they are to respond thoughtfully and critically, must evaluate whether or not a given speech meets the demands of the situation. Bitzer's essay also offers a strong justification for the study of rhetoric. "In the best of all possible worlds," he tells us, "there would be communication perhaps, but no rhetoric—since exigencies would not arise. In our real world, however, rhetorical exigencies abound; the world really invites change—change conceived and effected by human agents who quite properly address a mediating audience."[19]

Great speakers create a community of listeners.

The Audience–Speaker Relationship

It is a truism in the field of rhetoric that speakers must understand and adapt their messages to audiences. Of course, the need to understand and set up a relationship with one's receivers is true of every kind of communication. We've seen its importance in interpersonal interactions as well as in group settings. In the public context, in which communicators often have no personal acquaintance with audience members, understanding where the audience is coming from is challenging. In this section, we look at some of the things that speakers must know about audiences and at how speakers create perceived relationships with their receivers.

> **It is a truism in the field of rhetoric that speakers must understand and adapt their messages to audiences.**

Audience Attitudes and Change

When audience members come to hear a speech, they bring prior beliefs, attitudes, values, and life experiences with them. In constructing messages, speakers must take

> When audience members come to hear a speech, they bring prior beliefs, attitudes, values, and life experiences with them.

into account what audience members may already be thinking. If speakers fail to do so, their messages will be misunderstood or rejected.

Psychologist Milton Rokeach believes that the human mind uses three kinds of cognitive structures: beliefs, attitudes, and values.[20] Because these structures organize perception and motivate action, it is essential that public speakers understand them. Table 9.1 summarizes these structures.

Beliefs.   **Beliefs** are the opinions that individuals hold about the world and about their place in it. "The world is round," "I am a worthwhile person," "Police can [or cannot] be trusted," "The capital of New York is Albany," and "Chocolate ice cream is delicious" are all examples. Obviously, beliefs differ in nature and importance. According to Rokeach, some beliefs are *peripheral beliefs*—that is, they are relatively inconsequential and easy to change. Matters of taste (such as one's belief about the relative merits of chocolate ice cream) and simple, unemotional facts (such as where the capital of New York is) are more peripheral than are beliefs about whether police can be trusted. Beliefs about whether the world is round or flat and about one's self-worth are more central, or core, beliefs. *Core beliefs* are basic long-term beliefs that cannot be changed without disrupting our entire belief structure. Core beliefs are more difficult to change than are peripheral beliefs. People defend core beliefs against attack. Yet when core beliefs are changed, other related beliefs change as well. Rokeach argues that beliefs are tied to one another in complicated ways. For this

---

Table 9.1 Structures in the Minds of Audience Members

Beliefs

Opinions about what is or is not the case. Beliefs differ in nature and importance.

- **Core Beliefs**

  Fundamental beliefs held for a long period of time. Some are shared with others ("The sun rises in the east"), and others are highly personal ("I believe that the world is an unfriendly place").

- **Peripheral Beliefs**

  Relatively inconsequential and less resistant beliefs about who is or is not an authority ("My dad will know what to do"), facts derived from authorities ("It's not good to bottle up your feelings"), or matters of personal taste ("Green is an ugly color").

Attitudes

Opinions that link an individual to a topic. Attitudes predispose a person to respond to a topic in a particular way. Attitudes have three dimensions.

- **Cognitive Dimension**

  What an individual knows about a topic ("There are X number of hungry children in America").

- **Affective Dimension**

  What an individual feels in regard to a topic ("I feel sad whenever I think about hungry children").

- **Behavioral Dimension**

  What an individual intends to do in regard to a topic ("I will donate money to feed hungry children").

Values

General and enduring opinions about what should or should not be the case.

reason, a speaker must understand not only what an audience believes but also how that belief is connected to other beliefs and how central it is to audience members.

Attitudes.   In addition to beliefs, people also hold attitudes. **Attitudes** are evaluative mental structures that predispose us to act in certain ways. "Studying is important and worthwhile" (or "Studying is a waste of time"), "Welfare programs help people" (or "Welfare only encourages idleness"), and "Candidate X's policies are nonsense" (or "X's policies are absolutely brilliant") are all attitudes. Attitudes are partially products of beliefs, but they are also products of emotions and desires.

Attitudes can manifest themselves in three ways. They can affect how we think, feel, and behave. Attitudes toward homelessness are an example. The *cognitive dimension* of our attitude toward homelessness consists of everything we know or choose to believe about it: its causes, its effects, and its solutions. An attitude's *affective dimension* consists of emotional reactions to the attitude object. Some people respond to the homeless with fear and distaste, others with pity and understanding, and still others with a mixture of emotions. How we feel about an issue is important because it can motivate us to take action. This leads us to the third way in which we exhibit attitudes: the *behavioral dimension*. An attitude's behavioral dimension consists of what we think should be done about the attitude object—for example, whether we intend to ignore homelessness or to take action.[21]

Most public speeches are designed either to reinforce or to change existing attitudes. Speeches may be designed to give people information about an attitude object and thus to affect the cognitive dimension, to stir our feelings and thus to change the affective dimension, or to get audience members to make a direct response and thus to act on the behavioral dimension. Often, a speaker's goal may be to affect all three dimensions at once.

Values.   Values are the strongest and most personal of the three cognitive structures. **Values** are convictions about what ought to occur or about what is or is not desirable and right. "World peace ought to be our highest goal," "Honesty is the best policy," and "Cleanliness is next to godliness" are examples. Values are stronger and more personal than attitudes, but they are less numerous. An individual may have thousands of beliefs and hundreds of attitudes but only ten or twenty values. Values are deeply held and are closely tied to audience members' identities. Making reference to a cherished value can be a powerful way to touch an audience. In the 1992 presidential election, for example, "family values" became an important catchphrase as each presidential and vice presidential candidate tried to show that his commitment to the family was greater than his opponent's.

Many authors have attempted to classify values. Rokeach, for example, lists eighteen values he believes people strive to achieve.[22] Table 9.2 defines these values. Which values do you think are important in your community? How committed are you to each value, and how would you respond to an appeal focused on that value?

Source Characteristics and Audience Response

From its inception, Western rhetoric has emphasized the importance of source characteristics in persuading an audience. As you may recall from Chapter 1, the Greek philosopher Aristotle believed that speakers have three tools with which to persuade an audience: **logos** refers to logical reasoning, **pathos** to emotional appeals, and **ethos** to the impression the audience forms of the speaker's character. Aristotle advises speakers to demonstrate intelligence, character, and goodwill in order to establish ethos. Although modern investigators take a slightly different approach to classifying the characteristics that indicate a speaker's character, they agree with Aristotle's basic premise that the success or failure of a speech depends on how the speaker is perceived by the audience.

It is quite natural for receivers to consider the source. Most of us would find a lecture on the dangers of avian flu more believable if its source was a noted research scientist than if it was delivered by someone with no medical credentials. In deciding on a vacation spot, most of us would respect the word of a friend we liked and trusted who had been there more than we would an advertising brochure. And most employees would comply with a directive from a boss more readily than they would an order from a summer intern. People who appear to us to be credible, attractive, and powerful have an advantage when it comes to communication and persuasion.

Herbert Kelman and William McGuire are two contemporary writers who have analyzed how source characteristics are related to audience response.[23] According to Kelman, audiences are influenced by sources in three ways: through internalization, identification, or compliance. **Internalization** occurs when audience members incorporate message content into their belief systems. When audience members think, "Yes, I agree; that argument makes sense to me and fits in with what I believe," they are experiencing internalization. What source quality leads audience members to internalize messages? According to McGuire, internalization occurs when the source possesses *credibility*; that is, when he or she is perceived to be believable and trustworthy.

Table 9.2 Rokeach's Terminal Values

A comfortable life (a prosperous life)	Inner harmony (freedom from inner conflict)
An exciting life (a stimulating, active life)	Mature love (sexual and spiritual intimacy)
A sense of accomplishment (making a lasting contribution)	National security (protection from attack)
	Pleasure (an enjoyable, leisurely life)
A world at peace (free of war and conflict)	Salvation (saved, eternal life)
A world of beauty (beauty of nature and the arts)	Self-respect (self-esteem)
Equality (brotherhood, equal opportunity for all)	Social recognition (respect, admiration)
Family security (taking care of loved ones)	True friendship (close companionship)
Freedom (independence, free choice)	Wisdom (a mature understanding of life)
Happiness (contentedness)	

In addition to internalizing a message, audience members may accept a message because they identify strongly with the source. **Identification** is based on the presence of a perceived relationship (either real or imaginary) between source and receiver. When audience members think, "By agreeing with the source, I will be more like him or her; we will have something in common," they are experiencing identification. Identification occurs when the source possesses *attractiveness*; that is, when he or she offers audience members an emotionally rewarding relationship.

Finally, audience members often respond favorably to sources who can meet audience needs or offer material incentives. This influence process is called **compliance**. Audience members experiencing compliance say to themselves, "It is in my own best interest to agree with the source." Compliance occurs whenever the source is perceived as possessing *power*, when he or she controls material resources desired by audience members. Table 9.3 summarizes these three influence processes and gives examples of ways in which speakers can increase ethos in each area.

Fox Photos/Getty Images

Without audience or exigence, the public speech has no purpose.

Credibility. Of the three kinds of source characteristics, credibility has captured the most attention in communication research. Although different authors identify different dimensions of credibility, most agree on two: expertness and trustworthiness. Speakers who show that they are knowledgeable about a topic establish *expertness*. Speakers who indicate a concern for audience interests demonstrate *trustworthiness*. Both characteristics increase credibility and consequently enable the speaker to influence and educate audience members.

Even before a speech begins, audience members have some feelings about the speaker's credibility; that is, they have preconceived notions of how expert and how trustworthy the speaker is. These notions may be the result of direct experience, advance publicity, or information given as the speaker is introduced. Once the speech begins, this initial credibility can rise or fall. A speaker without particularly impressive titles and credentials can increase credibility by delivering a carefully prepared and well-argued speech. Conversely, the credibility of a highly respected speaker can be undermined if the speech seems to have been thrown together at the last minute or if the speaker seems insincere.

Attractiveness.   All else being equal, the more attractive a speaker is, the more effective he or she will be. McGuire divides attractiveness into four dimensions: familiarity, similarity, physical attractiveness, and liking. Although new ideas are sometimes appealing, most of the time people are attracted by *familiarity*. Audiences often respond best to sources and ideas that seem "normal." Studies have also shown that the more often audiences hear an idea, the more attractive the idea becomes. Many years ago, Robert Zajonc demonstrated what he called the **mere-exposure hypothesis**, the idea that "simple repeated exposure to a stimulus" results in attraction.[24] These findings suggest that speakers will be perceived as more attractive if their ideas resonate

Table 9.3 Source Characteristics That Enhance Influence

The following table shows the kinds of characteristics that audiences value in public speakers. Note that the effectiveness of a given characteristic varies according to type of influence.

Influence Type	*Source Characteristic*	*Ways of Exhibiting Characteristic*
Internalization Influence based on convincing an audience to accept an argument as part of their belief system	**Credibility** Perception that the speaker can be believed	Speakers increase credibility by emphasizing expertness and trustworthiness.
Identification Influence based on creating a personal and positive relationship with audience members	**Attractiveness** Perception that the speaker is likeable and is someone with whom audience members would be comfortable	Speakers increase attractiveness by emphasizing familiarity, similarity, physical attractiveness, and liking.
Compliance Influence based on persuading audience members they have something to gain by agreeing or something to lose by disagreeing	**Power** Perception that the speaker controls a resource desired by the audience or has the ability to affect audience members' lives directly	Speakers increase power by emphasizing their legitimacy, control of rewards, and ability to act coercively as well as their access to scarce information and their willingness to associate with audience members.

Influence types are based on a taxonomy in "Processes of Opinion Change," by Herbert C. Kelman, 1961, *Public Opinion Quarterly, 25,* pp. 57–78. Classification of source characteristics follows that in "Attitudes and Attitude Change," by William McGuire, 1985, in Handbook of Social Psychology, Gardner Lindzey and Elliot Aronson, Eds. New York: Random House.

with ideas already accepted by audience members. The findings also suggest that it takes time for audience members to become comfortable with new ideas. The speaker who pushes new ideas too rapidly may be rejected.

> **All else being equal, the more attractive a speaker is, the more effective he or she will be.**

Closely related to familiarity is *similarity*. Typically, people are attracted to others who share their characteristics. Apparently, audience members identify more strongly with speakers who are like them than with speakers who are very different. This same effect occurs in modeling, wherein receivers are shown someone else being rewarded or punished for a given action. The more similar the model is to the receiver, the more likely the receiver is to act like the model.[25]

A source's *physical appearance* also affects an audience. A speaker whose physical appearance is average or above average has an advantage over one who is less physically attractive. Of course, physical attractiveness can sometimes backfire. Occasionally a speaker is too good-looking. Audiences who value credibility may be turned off by glamour. Nevertheless, if the audience is not overly concerned with expertise and if emotional identification is at stake, then a positive physical appearance is desirable.

Finally, a person who offers *liking*, who provides the social rewards of warmth, humor, and respect, will be perceived as attractive. Taken to an extreme and used as a tactic, presenting oneself as likeable is known as *ingratiation*.[26] Although ingratiation strategies such as flattery can be overdone and obviously insincere, audiences enjoy speakers who are genuinely warm, outgoing, and friendly.

Power.   The final way in which sources can influence others is through power. John French and Bertram Raven believe that **power** is exercised whenever an individual controls a valued resource.[27] According to their analysis, sources can achieve power in five ways: by occupying an important position in society, by offering material rewards in exchange for compliance, by threatening to punish disobedience, by gaining access to scarce information, and by exhibiting personal characteristics that others admire.

The last two of these power bases—the possession of information (which French and Raven call *expert power*) and the ability to offer social rewards through personal characteristics (which French and Raven label *referent power*)—are similar to expertness and liking, which have already been discussed. The first three power bases, however, are new to our discussion. The first of these, *legitimate power*, is evident when a source represents an important social institution. In such a case, the individual is powerful not because of personal characteristics but because of his or her position in the institution. The primary reason we obey police officers, judges, teachers, and the like is that we consider them legitimate authorities.

The second power base, *reward power*, is involved when an individual has a material possession that another person values. An employer who can give employees bonuses, raises, and promotions has reward power. The final power base, *coercive power*, exists when an individual can harm another or can take away valued possessions. A boss who can fire or demote a worker has coercive power. Employees usually comply with the requests and suggestions of their bosses because they realize both the harm and the good their bosses can do them.

Audiences differ in their attitudes toward power. Some people, called *high authoritarians*, are preoccupied with power and tend to identify with authority figures.[28] An audience made up of this kind of person is extremely impressed with symbols of power and will respect high-power sources. Other people are less likely to defer to the powerful. To assess their impact on an audience, sources should have a realistic view of their own power bases.

Relationships among Source Characteristics.   As we have seen, many characteristics affect responses to public communications. Generally, receivers look for characteristics that are relevant and appropriate to a given rhetorical situation. When the topic is serious and the goal is to inform or persuade, audiences want speakers to be expert and trustworthy. When the topic is less serious and the speaker's goal is to entertain, attractiveness may be more important. The relationships among source characteristics are complex. Indeed, factors that increase audience acceptance in one way may decrease it in another. Humor, for example, can increase attractiveness but may do little to enhance credibility or power. Perceived intelligence may increase credibility but may not make a speaker particularly well liked.

From the speaker's point of view, it is important to control audience perceptions. This does not mean, however, that speakers should try to be something they are not. Speakers are always better off sticking to their strengths. If they're not particularly funny, they should avoid telling jokes; if they're not well informed, they should not try to pass themselves off as experts; and if they don't have reward power, they would be foolish to make false promises.

From the audience's point of view, it is important to think carefully about how speakers affect us. If we let ourselves be swept away by warmth or charm when we should be considering whether or not the speaker actually knows anything about the topic, then we lower the standards for public discourse. Because audiences ultimately get the kind of speakers they deserve, it is important to consider the source.

> If we let ourselves be swept away by warmth or charm when we should be considering whether or not the speaker actually knows anything about the topic, then we lower the standards for public discourse.

Arguments and Appeals

Although perceived ethos can be an indication of the quality of public communication, it is a perception, and like other perceptions, it can be faulty. People who sound credible may have hidden agendas. Folks who seem attractive can be deceptive. And those with power do not necessarily have our best interests at heart. Therefore, it is important to pay close attention to the message itself and to the reasoning it employs.

The Structure of Argument: The Toulmin Model

Sometimes we accept a speaker's message without question; at other times, we need to be convinced. In the latter case, the speaker must provide an **argument**, an explanation of his or her reasoning. But not all arguments are equally valid. One method of testing arguments is to employ the Toulmin model.

Parts of an Argument. What constitutes a good argument? According to Stephen Toulmin, everyday arguments, the kind we use to convince one another, are made up of six parts: claim, qualifier, data, warrant, backing, and rebuttal or reservation.[29] Although a speaker may not refer explicitly to all six parts during a speech, preferring to keep some parts hidden, audience members who wish to test the validity of an argument should try to uncover the argument in its entirety. The Toulmin model, illustrated in Figure 9.1, is a great help in this regard.

Figure 9.1 The Toulmin Model

A General Diagram of an Argument

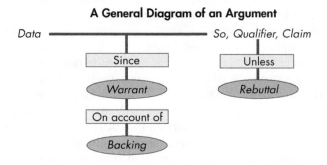

Example of an Argument Seeking to Justify the Claim "Harry Is a British Subject"

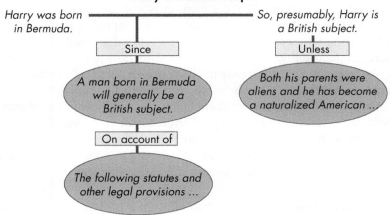

From *The Uses of Argument* by Stephen Edelston Toulmin, 2nd ed., Cambridge, UK: Cambridge University Press; p. 114. Reprinted with permission of Cambridge University Press.

The *claim* is what the speaker wishes the audience to accept. An argument succeeds if the audience accepts the claim, and it fails if the audience rejects the claim. Claims may be facts ("Smoking cigarettes is hazardous to one's health"), values ("Health is a positive value and should be safeguarded"), or policies ("Cigarette advertising should be banned").

Claims vary in strength. Some claims are absolute; others are less certain. The *qualifier* indicates the strength of the claim. Modifiers such as "always," "sometimes," "probably," "nine out of ten times," and the like are qualifiers that indicate the strength of a claim. Although some facts in this world are absolute, most knowledge is conditional. Unqualified claims often indicate that a speaker is overstating the case.

Intelligent audiences do not accept unsupported claims, even if the claims are qualified. Instead, audience members want evidence, or *data*, to support claims. In making public claims, speakers use statistics, illustrative examples, research results, expert testimony, eyewitness accounts, and the like as data.

Citing data does not guarantee that an argument will be accepted. Audience members must see a relationship between data and claim; that is, they must understand the reasoning that lets the speaker move from evidence to conclusion. The connecting link between data and claim is called the *warrant*. Ultimately, the argument lives or dies on the strength of the warrant. Warrants may or may not be spelled out explicitly during the speech, but they are always a hidden part of the argument.

Let's suppose that a speaker's claim is that the proportion of women faculty at a given school should be increased.[30] The data show that only 7 percent of the faculty are women and that, as a consequence, very few students have the opportunity to study with a woman teacher. What is the warrant that ties data to claim? In this case, the warrant is based on a value; the speaker is arguing that the presence of women faculty is worthwhile and desirable. Audiences who share the speaker's values will accept the warrant with little difficulty. Others will need additional evidence, called *backing*. Outlining the educational and social advantages provided by women faculty will provide this backing. When a warrant is well understood and acceptable, it needs no backing; when it is less acceptable, it may require detailed explanation.

The final part of the Toulmin argument is the *rebuttal*, or *reservation*. This consists of a statement of the conditions under which the claim does not hold true. What might constitute the reservation in the argument about employing female teachers? If women were less competent scholars or teachers than men or if their contributions were not particularly unique, then the warrant would not hold, and the argument would crumble. If a speaker believes that the audience has significant reservations in regard to a warrant, he or she may bring up the reservations and refute them. If the audience favors the warrant, the reservation may be omitted. In any case, it is a good idea for the creator of an argument to search for reservations to test the strength of the argument.

Using the Toulmin Model.   Speakers often offer their audiences only part of an argument. When should an argument be given in full, and when is the use of a partial argument justified? Most rhetoricians agree that when the warrant and its backing are known and accepted by an audience, the speaker need not go through a detailed explanation of the entire argument. If, for example, I live in a state where the speed limit is 65 mph, I will accept the state trooper's claim "You were speeding" on the basis of the data "I clocked you going 73 mph." The trooper does not need to spell out the warrant ("Anyone who exceeds 65 mph is guilty of speeding") or provide backing for it ("according to provisions of New York state traffic laws"). A visitor from a state where the maximum speed limit is more than 65 mph, however, might need to hear the entire argument.

Since the time of Aristotle, rhetoricians have argued that when a speaker is confident that audience members will correctly fill in missing parts of an argument, it is not only more efficient but also more effective to allow them to do so. That is, when people supply their own reasoning, they are more likely to be convinced than when the speaker presents the argument to them.

Of course, not every audience member fills in an argument as the speaker wishes. Reasoning that seems completely self-evident to a speaker may be flatly rejected by some audience members. In deciding how fully to frame an argument, the speaker must carefully consider the kinds of conclusions the audience will draw and the kinds of warrants it will accept.

When we make arguments, we are often vague about them. We know the conclusion we wish the audience to reach, and we usually have some data to support it, but at times we have trouble articulating the warrant, backing, qualifier, and rebuttal. By using the Toulmin

As audience members we can easily be swept away by emotional appeals, it is our responsibility to carefully evaluate a speaker's arguments.

© Bettmann/CORBIS

system to lay out our arguments, we can examine and clarify our thinking. And in evaluating a speaker's argument audience members should carefully examine the speaker's reasoning.

Types of Arguments

Adapting Aristotle's distinction between ethos, pathos, and logos, Wayne Brockreide and Douglas Ehninger argue that speakers have three kinds of warrants or ways of appealing to an audience.[31] Arguments can be based on authoritative, motivational, or substantive appeals.

Authoritative and Motivational Arguments.   An **authoritative argument** depends entirely on the authority of a source. Some sources are automatically trusted. In matters of health, the surgeon general is a good example. Let's assume the surgeon general has stated that a particular drug is dangerous and believes that it should not be sold. A speaker can use this statement as data to support the claim that the drug ought to be removed from the market immediately. We can outline the argument, including its implied authoritative warrant.

> **Data:** *According to the surgeon general, drug X is dangerous to public health.*
> **Claim:** *Drug X should be removed from the market immediately.*
> **Warrant:** *The surgeon general is an expert and trustworthy source whose recommendations should be followed.*
> **Reservation:** *Unless the surgeon general is politically motivated or her data are incorrect*

When parents tell their children to do something "because I said so," they too are using an authoritative warrant.

A **motivational argument** is based on the emotional needs of the audience. When a speaker uses a highly emotional appeal or urges audience members to accept a claim because doing so will satisfy a personal desire or need, he or she is using a motivational warrant. In the following example, the speaker relies on a visceral reaction of audience members. The argument is based on the speaker's belief that he and the audience share common feelings of pity and horror.

> **Data:** *Baby seals are being slaughtered.*
> **Claim:** *Laws should be enacted to protect the seals.*
> **Warrant:** *Brutality toward animals is emotionally repellent.*
> **Reservation:** *Unless animals do not have rights to humane treatment*

Whereas some motivational arguments are directed toward audience members' passions, others are directed toward members' needs. These kinds of motivational appeals assure audience members that a basic need will be fulfilled if the claim is accepted. To construct a need-focused argument, a speaker must understand the basic emotions and needs that drive an audience. Although needs are classified in several ways, the most familiar is **Maslow's needs hierarchy**. According to Abraham Maslow, humans have five basic needs.[32] The most urgent and basic of these needs are called *physiological needs*, the needs for food, water, air, warmth, and so on. Once these needs are satisfied, we concern ourselves with *safety needs*, our needs to be safe from external harm. Next come our needs for *love and belongingness*, and *self-esteem*. Finally, we experience the need for *self-actualization,* the need to reach our full potential. Later, Maslow came to believe that people may also be motivated by *curiosity needs*, the needs to explore and understand the environment, and by *aesthetic needs*, the needs for beauty, harmony, and balance.

Arguments can focus on any of these needs. Let's consider as an example a hypothetical advertisement for a new perfume.

Data: *(Visuals showing attractive male models being irresistibly drawn to a woman wearing Jungle Passion perfume.)*
Claim: *Buy Jungle Passion today.*
Warrant: *If you buy Jungle Passion, you too will be irresistible to men, and your needs for belongingness and love will be satisfied.*
Reservation: *Unless men find women attractive for reasons other than their scent*

Although this is not a particularly rational argument, it may be emotionally compelling if audience members' needs are strong enough and if members identify psychologically with the models in the advertisement.

Substantive Arguments.   A **substantive argument** connects data and claim through logic and reasoning. When a speaker shows audience members that the claim is the only rational conclusion, given the data, he or she is using a substantive warrant. As we shall see, certain standard patterns of argument are considered acceptable in our culture. These patterns include arguments from cause, sign, generalization, and analogy. Each takes a slightly different form and must stand up to different tests to be considered valid. Each also can be misused and can lead to faulty conclusions.[33]

Arguments from cause are common in the public context. Whenever a speaker tries to establish why something happened, he or she is using a causal argument. The following example shows how a causal argument might work.

Claim: *If my opponent is reelected, the economy will grow worse.*
Data: *Since my opponent took office, inflation has risen and unemployment has grown dramatically.*
Warrant: *These economic disasters were caused by my opponent's unwise fiscal policies.*
Reservation: *Unless these economic disasters were caused by factors beyond my opponent's control*

Establishing causal connections is not always easy. A valid argument from cause must establish four things: (1) that the presumed cause (Y) preceded the presumed effect (X) in time; (2) that Y can, in fact, lead to X; (3) that there is no other, more plausible cause that might explain X; and (4) that both X and Y were not due to a third, unexplained factor. Only when all four propositions are established can we be confident that a cause really does exist.

In attempting to prove cause, people often commit a **fallacy** (an error in reasoning) called the *post hoc fallacy* or doubtful cause fallacy. They assume that Y caused X simply because it preceded X. Superstitions are examples of post hoc fallacies. The driver who has an accident right after a black cat crosses the road and who assumes that the cat caused the accident is committing a post hoc fallacy.

Although the flaw in the black cat argument is fairly easy to see (unless you are unusually superstitious), some post hoc fallacies can be harder to spot. Assume, for example, that right after a new coach is hired, a team has a losing season. It is tempting to blame the loss on the coach, because bad coaching can sometimes cause a team to lose. But before we recommend firing the coach, we need to rule out other possible causes. We need to be sure that nothing about this year's team (say, the players' lack of experience) makes them uncoachable. We also must assure ourselves that no third factor (say, budget cuts) has kept both team and coach from doing an effective job. Assigning cause is a common activity, but it is more difficult to do correctly than it appears.

Arguments from sign are a second kind of substantive argument. An argument from sign seeks to predict one condition (X) by pointing to another condition (Y) associated with it. Arguments from sign should not be confused with causal arguments. Smoke, for example, is a sign of fire, but it is not the cause of fire. Most people would accept the claim "This building is on fire" on the strength of the data "The hall is full of smoke." Not all arguments from sign, however, are this straightforward. Let's look at a slightly more controversial example.

> **Claim:** *This year's freshman class will not do as well as previous classes.*
> **Data:** *The class SAT scores are substantially lower than previous class scores.*
> **Warrant:** *SAT scores are a good indicator of academic success.*
> **Reservation:** *Unless SAT scores are biased or other factors intervene that contradict their validity*

For an argument from sign to be valid, four things must be established: (1) that Y is a reliable sign of X, (2) that nothing has occurred to change the relationship between X and Y, (3) that a sufficient number of signs point to X, and (4) that there are no signs that contradict X. Let's look at the argument about test scores. People who oppose using standardized scores to predict success in school often argue that although test scores may indicate some students' achievement potential, other equally reliable and less biased predictors are overlooked. When people rely on only one sign and ignore others or when they imperfectly associate the sign in question with what they think it predicts, they are using fallacious reasoning.

Arguments from generalization seek to establish a general conclusion on the basis of data taken from a small sample of cases.

> **Claim:** *Jones will win the election.*
> **Data:** *Of 1,000 people surveyed, 57 percent said that they would vote for Jones.*
> **Warrant:** *The rest of the public will act as did the sample.*
> **Reservation:** *Unless the sample was unusual in some way*

Although professional pollsters following scientific procedures can generalize with amazing accuracy, the kinds of generalizations we make every day are often flawed. Four conditions must be met for a generalization to be valid: (1) the cases examined must be representative; (2) a sufficient number of cases must be examined; (3) the data must be up to date; and (4) any negative cases must be negligible.

In everyday life, we often generalize on the basis of one or two instances. Unfounded stereotypes and prejudices are examples of a kind of fallacy called *hasty generalization*. Hasty generalizations are based on too few cases or on unusual cases. If I were to draw conclusions about what students on your campus are like by surveying one student (say, the student who usually sits next to you in class), my generalization would probably be flawed. When I generalize on the basis of one case, I run the risk of choosing an atypical individual. The more cases I look at and the more careful I am to avoid selection biases, the more likely I am to reach valid conclusions.

Arguments from analogy seek to establish that two situations, X and Y, are alike.

Claim: *As president, I will be able to balance the budget.*
Data: *As governor, I balanced the budget.*
Warrant: *Being governor is similar enough to being president that success at the former level means success at the latter level.*
Reservation: *Unless I have not anticipated additional difficulties*

The validity of an argument from analogy depends on two conditions: (1) that the cases being compared are alike in all important respects and (2) that any differences between the cases are insignificant. Arguments such as "It worked for me, so it will work for you" are good examples. This argument obviously fails if the two people involved are very different from one another.

Some analogies are purely figurative. They are rhetorical devices a speaker uses to explain an idea to an audience, but they should not be taken literally. Such a **false analogy** was used by King James I. He argued that the monarch is the head of state and that just as the body dies when the head is cut off, so the nation dies without its king.[34] Although the analogy may be emotionally compelling, it is not substantive. Nations and bodies are not, in most important respects, governed by the same principles.

STRENGTHENING CRITICAL RECEPTION SKILLS

Much as we like to believe that people are rational and logical, it simply isn't true. Much of the time, we jump to conclusions, engage in wishful thinking, and believe what is easiest for us to believe. Psychologists who study the ways people reason find that most of us hold **cognitive biases** that distort our conclusions about the world. Evidence suggests, for example, that people exaggerate responsibility for their successes and minimize responsibility for their failures; give themselves more credit than they deserve for collective activities; exaggerate the extent to which others agree with them; and believe that they have a great deal more control over their destinies than they actually do.[35]

As audience members, we also often act as **lazy processors**.[36] We make up our minds about a speaker not by listening carefully to what he or she has to say but rather by looking at surface details. A less-than-confident listener, for example, may assume that a speech was good simply because everyone else liked it. An audience member with math anxiety may decide that any speaker who uses statistics must be intelligent. This kind of cognitive carelessness puts us at risk of being fooled by ignorant or unscrupulous speakers who feed us half-truths and fallacies. The only way we can guard ourselves against lazy processing is to learn to recognize some of the techniques used to fool audiences. Table 9.4 lists some ways speakers either deliberately or inadvertently create false arguments.[37]

BECOMING A MORE RESPONSIBLE COMMUNICATOR

It is common to think that the ethical responsibility for public communication lies only with the speaker. Certainly, anyone who takes on the role of public speaker bears the burden of being well informed and trustworthy. But audiences too have a responsibility for the outcomes of public communication. In the next chapter, we consider how speakers can become more responsible communicators. We would like to end this chapter by briefly turning our attention to the role of the listener.

As listeners, we act irresponsibly whenever we passively accept whatever we hear or when we allow personal needs and prejudices to blind us to facts. As au-

Table 9.4 Fallacies in Argument: Usages That Mislead Audiences

Ad Hominem

The speaker attacks someone's character in areas not necessarily relevant to the issue. By accusing a political opponent of infidelity, atheism, or a flamboyant lifestyle, the speaker diverts attention from the issue under discussion.

Slippery Slope

The speaker predicts that taking a given line of action will inevitably lead to undesirable effects. For example, it was once seriously argued that "If women are educated, they will be unable to bear children and the family will be destroyed." Slippery slope predictions often play on our fears.

False Dilemma

The speaker sets up an either–or situation, ignoring other possibilities. "America. Love it or leave it" and "You're either with me or against me" are two examples.

Straw Man

The speaker characterizes an opponent's view in simplistic terms and then easily demolishes it. Nixon's famous "Checkers speech" suggested that his only crime was in keeping a little cocker spaniel as a gift for his children. He had actually been accused of misappropriating campaign funds.

Non Sequitur

From the Latin, meaning "it does not follow." The speaker, using connectives such as *therefore, so,* or *hence,* makes two unrelated ideas seem logically connected. "It's been used for years; therefore, it must be good" is a non sequitur.

Glittering Generality

The speaker associates self or issue with a vague virtue word. "I believe in the American dream; my opponent will create the American nightmare" sounds good, but what does it mean?

Transfer

The speaker links own ideas with popular people or issues and links opponent's ideas with unpopular people or issues. Presidential candidates may portray themselves as following in the path of Washington or Lincoln, for example.

Plain Folks

The speaker attributes an idea to a member of the audience's own group rather than to self. Politicians often read letters from "average citizens" asking for help or thanking the politicians for enacting a given law.

Bandwagon

The speaker makes it appear that anyone who does not agree will be left out or will fall behind. "Fifty thousand people have already donated" legitimizes the act of donating and makes the nondonor feel abnormal.

Ad Populum

The speaker appeals to popular prejudices. "Unless we act now, the Japanese will soon own everything of value in this country" relies more on fear and ethnic prejudice than on a realistic threat.

dience members, we need to inform ourselves on important issues, follow arguments carefully, judge the adequacy of evidence, and critically evaluate the consequences of proposals. When unethical speakers persuade audiences to draw questionable conclusions, audience members are themselves partly to blame. Taking on the role of listener does not absolve a communicator from ethical responsibilities.

> **Anyone who takes on the role of public speaker bears the burden of being well informed and trustworthy. But audiences too have a responsibility for the outcomes of public communication.**

SUMMARY

This chapter examines the character of public communication and offers advice about factors audiences should consider in evaluating public messages. Public communication is a face-to-face, one-to-many form of communication wherein a single speaker addresses a large audience. It is more formal and less spontaneous than communication in other contexts and is affected by factors such as audience size, time, and space. Public communication also differs from interpersonal or group communication in that it takes place in the public sphere.

Rhetoric is the art of designing messages that can change the way audiences think and feel about public issues. Understanding rhetorical principles has both social and personal advantages. Socially, it allows us to discover facts, test ideas, advocate positions, shape knowledge, build community, and distribute power. Because the ability to communicate in public is a necessary skill in most careers, knowledge of rhetoric also leads to personal and professional success.

Three factors that audiences should consider in evaluating public messages are context, audience–speaker relationship, and message appeals. First, public messages must fit the context in which they are situated. Context includes factors such as physical setting, medium, and occasion as well as historical setting and argumentational history. That is, events that surround a speaking occasion have an effect on audience response, as does the way an issue has been argued in the past. One of the simplest yet most powerful discussions of the importance of context can be found in Bitzer's discussion of rhetorical situation. Bitzer believes that situation both motivates and shapes public discourse. Rhetorical situation consists of three parts, exigence (the problem addressed by a speaker), audience (receivers who have a stake in the outcome), and constraints (factors that affect the way messages are shaped). Rhetoric succeeds if it matches the demands of the rhetorical situation.

When speakers communicate in rhetorical situations, they seek to influence audiences. They can do this by targeting the beliefs, attitudes, or values of audiences. Audience members are also influenced by the personal characteristics they believe speakers possess. Three characteristics that affect audiences are a speaker's credibility, attractiveness, and power. Credibility refers to the extent to which a speaker is believable; it is affected by perceptions of expertness and trustworthiness. Attractiveness refers to the extent to which audience members want to maintain a relationship with the speaker and is affected by familiarity, similarity, physical appearance, and liking. Finally, power refers to the extent to which a source controls a valued resource. In addition to referent and expert power, legitimate power, reward power, and coercive power allow speakers to persuade audiences.

In evaluating public communication, audiences should not rely solely on their perception of source characteristics. It is also important to look at the appeals and arguments contained in a message. The Toulmin model provides one way of analyzing arguments and identifying gaps in logic. Audiences should also consider the nature of appeals. In authoritative appeals, arguments are based on expert opinions. In motivational appeals, arguments focus on audience needs such as the physiological, safety, love, esteem, self-actualization, curiosity, and aesthetic needs outlined by Maslow. In substantive appeals, logical argumentation based on cause, sign, generalization, and analogy is used.

KEY TERMS

Listed below are the key terms used in this chapter, along with the number of the page where each is explained.

rhetoric (232)	ethos (242)	substantive argument (251)
public communication (232)	internalization (242)	arguments from
private/public sphere (233)	identification (243)	cause (251)
argumentational	compliance (243)	fallacy (251)
history (238)	mere-exposure	arguments from sign (252)
rhetorical situation (238)	hypothesis (244)	arguments from
fitting response (238)	power (245)	generalization (252)
beliefs (240)	argument (247)	arguments from
attitudes (241)	authoritative argument (250)	analogy (253)
values (241)	motivational argument (250)	false analogy (253)
logos (242)	Maslow's needs	cognitive biases (253)
pathos (242)	hierarchy (250)	lazy processors (253)

SUGGESTED READING

Borchers, Timothy. (2011). *Rhetorical theory: An introduction*. Long Grove, IL: Waveland Press.

> In his excellent introduction to the history of rhetoric, Borchers takes on topics such as style and delivery, argumentation, theories of meaning, and rhetorical criticism as well as interesting discussions of gendered and non-Western rhetorical theories.

Herrick, James A. (2012). *The history and theory of rhetoric: An introduction* (5th ed.). New York: Prentice Hall.

> If you are interested in learning more about rhetorical approaches to the study of public communication, Herrick provides an excellent, readable summary of rhetorical theory from Sophists of ancient Greece to the works of contemporary writers.

Rybacki, Karyn Charles, & Rybacki, Donald Jay. (2011). *Advocacy and opposition: An introduction to argumentation*. Boston: Allyn & Bacon.

> If you want to hone your ability to create logical and effective arguments, turn to this well-written text that discusses arguing as a form of communication.

Preparing and Presenting Public Speeches

Public speaking offers the opportunity to speak up when it is important to do so, to develop ideas in one's own way, and to make a difference in the public sphere.

After reading this chapter, you should be able to:

- Understand how public speeches differ from other forms of discourse.

- Explain why it is important for speakers to understand audiences, and list some of the demographics that describe audience characteristics.

- List sources speakers can go to for information about audience motivations and attitudes.

- Explain the functions of the introduction and conclusion of a speech and describe techniques used in both.

- Identify the stock organizational patterns used to structure material in the body of a speech.

- Be able to write a formal speech outline.

- Know the difference between impromptu, extemporaneous, and manuscript delivery.

- Understand ways to manage speech anxiety.

- Identify effective and ineffective use of visual aids.

- Discuss the ethical responsibilities of the public speaker.

Consider the following situations in which you or someone you know might well be called upon to give a public speech.

- At your parents' twenty-fifth wedding anniversary celebration, you are asked to propose a toast and give a speech of congratulations.

- Your boss decides that you should explain the company benefit package to an assembly of new employees.

- Your child's teacher invites you to talk about your job during the school's career week.

- You are so outraged by a local politician's proposed law that you stand up and oppose it at a town council meeting.

Occasions like these are common. They are the kinds of everyday speaking situations that most of us encounter sometime in our lives, and it matters if we do them well. Some people respond to the challenge of public communication with fear and hesitation; others respond with grace and confidence. Luckily, a little knowledge and a lot of practice can transform the former into the latter. In this chapter, we look at ways to improve public speaking. In particular, we focus on audience analysis and adaptation, speech organization, delivery, and ways to use technology to enhance presentations. Reading this chapter cannot turn you into a Clarence Darrow or a Martin Luther King Jr. overnight, but it can give you some of the basic knowledge you need to prepare and organize presentations. And coupled with practice, it can give you the confidence to stand up and speak when you are called on to do so.

WHAT IS A PUBLIC SPEECH?

A **public speech** is a form of communication that is quite unlike most everyday interactions. It is an organized, purposeful, continuous presentation delivered in the presence of a relatively large group of receivers. In everyday interactions, receiver and sender roles switch back and forth; when giving a public speech, however, the speaker is the primary sender. In normal conversations, speaker and listener are usually personally acquainted. In the public speaking situation, by contrast, the speaker addresses a largely anonymous audience. In most informal settings, the communicators are situated within a few feet of one another. In public venues, they are commonly separated in space.

> In planning a public speech, speakers must find a way to establish a relationship with audience members, structure the speech so that it is both persuasive and easy to understand, and develop a compelling vocal and gestural style to keep the audiences' attention over an extended period of time.

PLANNING THE PUBLIC SPEECH

The conditions described above present the public speaker with a complex set of challenges. In planning a public speech, speakers must find a way to establish a relationship with audience members, structure the speech so that it is both persuasive and easy to understand, and develop a compelling vocal and gestural style to keep the audiences' attention over an extended period of time. In addition, speakers have to find ways to manage speech anxiety. This sounds like a tall order, but it is one that most of us can achieve with practice.

Creating a Relationship with the Audience

As we saw in Chapter 9, speakers need to create relationships with their receivers. To do so, they need to adapt their messages. We don't speak the same way to everyone, because every individual is different. For a kindergarten teacher to treat schoolchildren as though they were graduate students would be ridiculous. It would be equally ridiculous to confuse the life experiences of adolescents with those of senior citizens or to assume that people reared in remote rural communities have exactly the same experiences as do those from crowded urban centers. When we take into account the beliefs and life experiences of audience members and use that information in constructing a message, we are engaging in **audience adaptation**. Audience adaptation doesn't mean lying to please an audience; it means making a message relevant and understandable to the audience.

Audience Adaptation

A good communicator uses information about the audience in constructing at least three aspects of a speech: its central idea and structure, its supporting materials, and its style. A speaker must first decide on the purpose and central idea of the speech. If the speech is intended to inform, the speaker must present new and interesting information that is not too difficult or detailed. If the speech is intended to persuade, the speaker must avoid alienating audience members by advocating a proposal that is too extreme. In choosing the central idea of the speech, the speaker must know what the audience currently believes, what positions it might be willing to accept, and what positions it definitely rejects.

Assume for a moment that you are planning to argue that there is too much sex and violence on television. If members of your audience agree with you, you might advocate strong measures to combat the problem, including a boycott of products advertised on offensive programs. If your audience is less concerned about current programming, a better approach might be to show why current programming is objectionable. When an audience doesn't share your concern at all, you should identify the problem rather than offer a solution. In adjusting your proposal in this way, you are taking a realistic, incremental approach to persuasion.

The structure of the speech should also be adapted to the beliefs of audience members. With a hostile audience, for example, effective speakers begin by establishing common ground and then gradually move into their argument, presenting both sides of an issue rather than arguing for just one. With a favorable audience, however, a direct, one-sided appeal may be most effective.

Although politicians are adept at capturing and maintaining audience attention, every speaker must develop a compelling personal style.

Superstock/Glow Images

Speakers should also choose supporting materials with audience characteristics in mind. Assume that you support bringing a professional athletic team to your community and that meeting this goal involves raising money to build a new stadium. When speaking to a group of business leaders, you might stress the

People come to a speech with expectations. They want your speech to resemble their idea of the way a speech should sound.

economic advantages of your proposal; when speaking to the local PTA, however, you might mention that revenue from the use of the stadium may provide additional dollars for education and that the team will provide a new source of family entertainment. Good speakers choose appeals that are relevant to the audience.

Finally, the style of a speech should be adapted to the audience. Above all else, speeches must be understandable. It is not a good idea to try to clarify a concept

A successful communicator adapts to the audience. These children are clearly delighted with the performance.

by comparing it to a computer if the people in your audience are computer illiterate. If you are speaking to a group of engineers, however, this type of clarification might be a very good idea—provided that you know what you are talking about. It is also important to remember that people come to a speech with expectations. They want your speech to resemble their idea of the way a speech should sound. If you violate their expectations by using an unusual style, the speech will probably fail.

Audience Analysis

To make the adjustments just described, you must gather information about your audience. This can be done in a number of ways. **Demographic analysis** tells you about the groups to which audience members belong. Knowing the age, sex, educational level, religious affiliation, occupation, economic status, and cultural identification of audience members can help a speaker draw inferences about current beliefs and interests.

Age is an important audience variable. A story or example that appeals to a teenage audience may mean very little to listeners in their forties, whereas personalities and issues familiar to older listeners may be over younger listeners' heads. References to the 1960s, for example, can effectively build interest or illustrate a point if the audience is full of baby boomers, but these references can mystify an audience of teens.

Gender is another demographic factor that affects audience responses. Men and women are likely to have different views and concerns in some cases and identical responses in others. The trick is understanding which case is which. In earlier times, when women's place was thought to be in the private sphere and men's in the public sphere, audience adaptation was easy. Those days are, fortunately, long past, and men and women are now more equal. Nevertheless, even today's liberated men and women were raised in gender-specific environments and were encouraged to pursue sex-typed interests. This makes adaptation based on gender a difficult process. Stereotypic assumptions will only offend large segments of the audience, yet ignoring differences can be insensitive. As Stephen Lucas explains, "you must avoid false sex distinctions that do not exist and acknowledge true sex distinctions where they do exist."[1] To see just how difficult this is, try making your own lists of topics that are suitable for men and women without offending or stereotyping either group.

Lucas's rule should also be applied to other demographic categories, such as ethnicity, cultural identity, and geographic location. Speakers who address groups to which they themselves do not belong should be especially careful to check their assumptions by asking for feedback from people who belong to those groups. Speakers should also remember that collecting demographic data is not an end in itself. Data are useful only to the extent that they allow a speaker to answer specific questions: What motivates the people I am preparing to speak to? Why will they attend, and how do they feel about my topic? What approach will best help me inform or convince them?

A skilled speaker uses a number of sources to gather information about audiences.[2] One source is the local media. Bert Bradley suggests that speakers listen to local news broadcasts and subscribe to a local newspaper prior to a speaking engagement. News items show the kind of information that interests members of the community, editorials indicate opinions and concerns, and classified ads can provide useful information about economic conditions. Another source is personal interviews with individuals who are similar to audience members. Finally, if invited by an organization to speak, the speaker should spend some time with people in the organization and should read its official publications.

Structuring the Speech

Because public speeches are purposeful and because speakers communicate for extended periods of time, organization and structure are extremely important. Unless the speech is carefully constructed, audience members can lose interest or misinterpret the speaker's message. For this reason, public speeches are generally structured into three parts: introduction, body, and conclusion.

Introductions and Conclusions

Research shows that the beginnings and endings of arguments are remembered more than middle sections. Because introductions create initial impressions and conclusions sum up a speaker's points, they are extremely important to the structure of the presentation.

Functions of the Introduction.   The first function of the **introduction** is to create a desire in the audience to listen to the speech. As the speaker begins, audience members judge whether the speech will be lively or boring. If the speaker does not create interest at the outset, listeners are likely to tune out. Audience members also judge the speaker's qualifications. Therefore, the second function of the introduction is to increase audience confidence in the speaker. The speaker must introduce himself or herself to the audience and establish positive ethos. Finally, the third function of the introduction is to let the audience know what the speech is about. If audience members cannot figure out what the point is, they will stop listening. At some point in the introduction, the speaker must announce the **thesis**, or central purpose, of the speech. He or she may also use the introduction to foreshadow major points and themes (if the speech topic is complex) or to provide special information and definitions (if the topic is unfamiliar).

How does a speaker actually accomplish these goals? There are some standard ways in which speakers begin speeches: referring to the topic or occasion, offering a personal allusion or greeting, asking a rhetorical question, making a startling statement, using a quotation, telling a humorous anecdote, and offering an illustration. Table 10.1 lists and illustrates these techniques and explains how they are related to the functions of the introduction.

Functions of the Conclusion.   Just as the introduction is the speaker's first opportunity to make an impression on the audience, so the ending of the speech, or the **conclusion**, is the speaker's last chance to convince the audience. Both the introduction and the conclusion are extremely important, because audiences listen most closely and most critically at the beginning and at the end of a communication. Many novice speakers fail to take advantage of this phenomenon. They trail off or simply stop without warning the audience that the speech is ending. The conclusion must be as carefully crafted as the introduction and must generally do three things: signal that the speech is ending, reiterate the significance of the topic, and summarize the main ideas of the speech. If these functions are fulfilled, the audience leaves with a feeling of closure and an understanding of what the speaker expects them to know or to do.

> Just as the introduction is the speaker's first opportunity to make an impression on the audience, so the ending of the speech, or the conclusion, is the speaker's last chance to convince the audience.

As with the introduction, a speech may conclude in many stock ways. These ways, summarized in Table 10.2, include issuing a challenge or appeal, summarizing main ideas, using a relevant quotation, returning to an earlier illustration, offering an inducement for action or belief, and expressing one's own intention in relation to the speech topic.

Organizing the Body of the Speech

The part of the speech that lies between the introduction and the conclusion is called the **body** of the speech. Here, major ideas are developed and supported. It is important to organize these ideas so that audience members can follow the flow of the speech. Receivers who are exposed to written arguments can always reread a puzzling message. Receivers of spoken messages, however, must follow an argument as it is presented. To help them do this, speakers employ several devices. They **preview** the speech structure ("I'm going to give you three reasons why you should take action today"), use **transitions** to move the audience from one idea to the next ("Now let's look at the second reason"), and employ **internal summaries** ("So far, we've seen that there are financial and social reasons to act"). Even more important than these stylistic devices is the use of an overall organizational scheme that arranges

Table 10.1 Ways to Open a Public Speech

Type of Opening	*Example*
Reference to Topic A direct statement of subject; works well with motivated audience; less effective with skeptical or apathetic receivers	"I am here tonight to speak to you about a concern we all share, the problem of . . ."
Reference to Occasion A reference to the reason for the speech; allows speaker to acknowledge special occasions	"On the 100th anniversary of the founding of this great institution, it is fitting that we gather here to celebrate."
Personal Reference or Greeting An indication of one's relation to topic or audience; builds common ground; can backfire if greeting is too familiar or intrusive	"It's a pleasure to be here today. Ten years ago, I too was a new student. Like you, I wondered what the next four years would bring."
Rhetorical Question A question the speaker wants the audience to consider; involves audience; can offend if it makes assumptions about audience or asks members to make an uncomfortable choice	"What would you do if you had no place to live and no one to turn to for help? How long would you survive on the streets?"
Startling Statement A shocking statement of fact or opinion; increases attention and interest; can offend if silly or melodramatic	"Every six seconds another child becomes a victim of . . ."
Quotation A relevant quotation from a respected source; links speaker to source; can be trite or inapplicable	"As Shakespeare said, 'All the world's a stage. . . .'"
Humorous Anecdote A joke or story related to topic; shows speaker's warmth; can offend if poorly chosen	"This puts me in mind of a story. It seems there were three shipwrecked sailors . . ."
Illustration An extended example; makes topic vivid and concrete; can divert attention if point of illustration is not clear	"Let me tell you about what happened to one family whose lives were changed by our program. . . ."

Based on K. German, B. Gronbeck, D. Ehninger, and A. Monroe, *Principles of Public Speaking,* 18th ed. Copyright © 2013 by Pearson Education, Inc.

materials in ways that make sense to an audience. Over the years, researchers have identified several **stock organizational patterns**. These patterns include chronological, spatial, topical, causal, and problem–solution orders, as well as a special pattern known as the motivated sequence.

A **chronological order** arranges ideas according to a logical time sequence. If you were giving a speech on the history of the United States (putting aside for the moment the fact that this is too broad a topic for a single speech), you might decide to talk about North America before Columbus, the colonies prior to the Revolution, the Revolutionary period, the early Republic, and so on up to the present. It makes more sense to follow a past-to-present chronology. If you were given the job

---

Table 10.2 Ways to Close a Public Speech

Type of Closing	Example
Challenge or Appeal A direct request for action; lets audience know what to do next; not as appropriate if change desired is attitudinal rather than behavioral	"I encourage you to join with us now. . . ."
Summary A restatement of main ideas; increases audience comprehension	"There are, then, four ways we can protect ourselves. . . ."
Quotation A relevant quotation from a respected source; increases speaker credibility and inspires audience	"Let me close with the words Thomas Jefferson used when he stood in this hall exactly 200 years ago today. . . ."
Illustration An extended example; makes speech content concrete; can tie conclusion to earlier material	"So the next time you're ready to give up on yourself, remember what happened to the Jackson family. . . ."
Added Inducement A final reason for believing or acting; increases audience acceptance; can confuse if inducement is not clearly tied to proposal	"And if we work together now, not only will we be a happier and healthier community, but we will also. . ."
Personal Intention A statement of what the speaker is prepared to do; speaker leads by example and illustrates own trustworthiness	"I know I will be at the rally on Sunday, and I hope I will see you there too."

Based on K. German, B. Gronbeck, D. Ehninger, and A. Monroe, *Principles of Public Speaking*, 18th ed. Copyright © 2013 by Pearson Education, Inc.

of orienting new students to your campus, one way would be to take them through a typical day, from morning to evening. In both cases, use of a time sequence would help you to order your thoughts in a way that audience members could easily follow.

A **spatial order** arranges ideas according to physical location. The speech on U.S. history, for example, could be arranged geographically from east to west. In the orientation speech, you could employ a spatial order by taking your audience on an imaginary tour of the campus. As you would mentally pass each building or location, you could talk about a different aspect of campus life. For example, you might start at the theater and discuss the cultural life of the campus, move on to the gym and talk about athletics, proceed to the classrooms and discuss academic life, and so on. Of course, the success of this approach would depend on whether audience members were familiar with a map of the campus. For those unfamiliar with the campus, the use of slides or other visual aids could add interest and clarity.

A **topical order** divides the speech into familiar subtopics. Yet another way of organizing the orientation speech might be to divide the college experience into separate components: academic, social, cultural, and so forth. Or if you were explaining the kinds of majors available, you might discuss them in clusters: natural sciences, social sciences, humanities, and fine arts. Topical order works only when the subtopics seem to be sensible divisions of a field and when they are reasonably exhaustive. If a subtopic is unfamiliar to the audience, it should not be used. For example, if a student is not familiar with the term *social science*, this way of organizing the speech will be confusing.

The next two stock patterns are useful when a problem is the topic of the speech. When the speaker's goal is to discuss the causes and effects of the problem, a **causal order** may be used. Here, the speech is divided into two main parts. In the first, the factors that have led to the problem are discussed; in the second, the results of these factors are explained. Imagine a speech on the depletion of the ozone layer. The speech might first explain major causes of the problem and then talk about what will result if the problem continues. For speeches that offer a solution, **problem–solution order** is often used. As the name suggests, the two main divisions of this type of speech are the problem and the solution. Imagine a speech urging voluntary recycling. The speaker first establishes that a problem exists—that in many communities, landfills are completely full and alternative forms of waste disposal are unavailable. Having convinced the audience that a serious problem exists, the speaker then offers a solution (or a partial solution): voluntary recycling.

A final stock organizational pattern is called the **motivated sequence**. This five-part organizational plan focuses on making the topic and the claim relevant to audience needs. According to Alan Monroe, who developed this approach, the sequence follows a natural progression; that is, it mirrors the psychological reactions of receivers as they consider issues related to their needs.[3]

The five steps in the motivated sequence are attention, need, satisfaction, visualization, and action. In the **attention step**, which occurs in the introduction, the speaker's goal is to focus audience members on the message and to give them a reason for listening. Let's assume a speaker wants to convince audience members to begin to make financial investments for their old age. An audience of college-age people may not find this a very compelling topic. A startling statistic may serve here to gain attention. The speaker might say something such as, "In 2038, the year most of you will reach retirement, a dollar will be worth only X percent of its value today, a week's groceries will cost Y dollars, and rent on the most modest apartment will be Z dollars per month." If the numbers used are extreme, the audience will probably take note of them. Of course, the speaker's statistics should be taken from a reliable source so that they are believable as well as shocking.

The next step is the **need step**. Here, the speaker shows audience members that a present state of affairs is undesirable. In the investment speech example, the speaker uses the need step to establish that Social Security benefits alone will not be enough to allow audience members to live comfortably. The speaker's goal is to get the audience to think, "These things could happen to me if I don't take action."

Following the need step is the **satisfaction step**. Here, the speaker offers a plan to meet the need. In the example we have been discussing, the speaker has used the need step to induce fear of the future. Now he or she must show the audience that there is a simple and effective way to reduce the fear. Without this step, audience members may simply refuse to think about the issue. With a successful satisfaction step, however, they will see how their fear can be alleviated. At this point, then, our speaker shows how a reasonably modest amount of money can, over time, create a substantial retirement fund. The investment plan should be simple and easy to understand, and the use of complicated computations should be kept to a minimum, especially if the audience is not comfortable with numbers.

If the satisfaction step has worked, audience members are now thinking, "The plan seems simple and effective." To cement this idea and to motivate the audience to take action on the speaker's recommendations, the speaker next uses the **visualization step**. Here, the speaker describes concretely what will happen if the solution is adopted. In the investment speech, the speaker paints a picture of a retirement free from worry, a time when audience members can travel, pursue special interests and hobbies, and generally live comfortably.

Finally, in the **action step**, the speaker asks the audience to implement the proposal outlined in the satisfaction step. "So pick up one of our brochures, and open an IRA today" might constitute the action step and conclude the investment speech.

Outlining Main Points and Subpoints

Whichever organizational pattern you choose, be sure to develop your ideas fully and clearly in ways an audience will find sensible. One way to check your organization is to outline your speech. An **outline** is a kind of blueprint that shows the basic ideas in your speech. When you outline, you write out each of your main points and, below each main point, indicate the subpoints you wish to make. An outline allows you to see at a glance whether you are mixing up your ideas. Main points are usually indicated by Roman numerals and are written next to the left-hand margin; subpoints are indented. Table 10.3 illustrates an outline form and provides a summary of our discussion of speech structure.

MANAGING DELIVERY

In an everyday conversation, it's hardly necessary to worry about delivery. You talk in your natural tone, and if your partner wants you to speak more softly or more loudly or more clearly, he or she will ask you. In public, however, factors such as rate, volume, and articulation are important. Novice speakers often speak way too quickly, have trouble speaking loudly enough to be heard by everyone, and may not speak clearly. Type of delivery is also important.

Public speakers must match topic, occasion, and their own personal style in deciding whether to speak off the cuff, plan their speech ahead of time but deliver it conversationally, or read it from a manuscript.

> In an everyday conversation it's hardly necessary to worry about delivery. In public, however, factors such as rate, volume, and articulation are important.

Types of Deliveries

Traditionally, teachers of public speaking talk about three styles of speaking: impromptu, extemporaneous, and manuscript. **Impromptu speaking** occurs when the speaker is suddenly confronted with a rhetorical situation and is able, on the spur of the moment, to organize a message. Impromptu speaking does not mean

---

Table 10.3 An Example of Outline Form

How to Organize a Public Speech

I. A well-organized speech opens with an introduction.
   A. The introduction gets attention.
   B. The introduction establishes good will.
   C. The introduction orients listeners to the subject.

II. Every speech should have a thesis, or central purpose statement.
   A. The thesis explains the central idea of the speech.
   B. Ideas unrelated to the thesis should be eliminated.
   C. The audience must be able to identify the thesis.

III. Main ideas are included in the body of the speech.
   A. Organizing main ideas in outline form allows the speaker to check the organization.
      1. In outlines, subpoints are subordinated to main points.
      2. If an idea is subdivided, it should include at least two subpoints.
   B. Stock organizational patterns help the speaker arrange points in a sensible order.
      1. Chronological order arranges ideas according to time.
      2. Spatial order arranges ideas according to location.
      3. Topical order arranges ideas according to subject.
      4. Causal order arranges ideas into causes and effects.
      5. Problem–solution order arranges ideas into problems and solutions.
      6. Motivated sequence arranges ideas psychologically.

IV. Speeches end with a conclusion.
   A. A conclusion should provide a sense of closure.
   B. A conclusion should sum up the argument or present a proposal for action.
   C. The conclusion is the last thing an audience hears.

disorganized speaking. In fact, in impromptu situations, clear organization is a must. The more practiced a speaker is at public presentations and the more familiar he or she is with the topic, the more successful an impromptu speech will be.

Extemporaneous speaking is carefully preplanned but nonmemorized delivery. The extemporaneous speaker has researched and outlined the message but has not memorized its exact wording. Extemporaneous speeches are usually more immediate than memorized speeches; they allow the speaker to connect with the audience and choose the words that will have the greatest impact at the time. This is the method of delivery that is most favored in beginning public speaking classes.

Manuscript speaking, by contrast, involves very careful composition. In this form of delivery, the speaker reads from a printed page or teleprompter. Although beginning speakers often imagine that it would be easier to speak from a manuscript than to speak extemporaneously, it is actually very difficult to read with expression and quite easy to lose one's place. It takes a great deal of skill to avoid appearing wooden when reading. On the other hand, when precise wording is important, it is advisable to use a manuscript. No one form is better than the others. The nature of the rhetorical situation should dictate the type of delivery, and good public speakers become adept at all kinds of speaking.

Speech Anxiety

Most people who speak before large audiences experience some amount of **speech anxiety**. They may experience problems in speaking too fast or too slow, stammering, speech blocks, dry mouth, rapid heartbeat—the list goes on. This is entirely normal, and in most cases, the fear disappears over time. While you're waiting for it to subside, there are two measures you can take to reduce your apprehension. One is **cognitive restructuring**, in which you substitute adaptive thinking for negative thoughts. For example, instead of thinking, "I'll look like an idiot up there," you could think, "I know a lot more about this topic than anyone else in the class does, and besides they're just as scared as I am." The other is to use some form of **physical relaxation**, such as breathing deeply or consciously relaxing tense muscles. Both measures are based on the principle that it is impossible to experience two different mental or physical states at the same time. When you're thinking positively, it's hard to feel fear; when your body is relaxed, it's impossible to feel tense.

Speakers' use of gestures can be a powerful way of communicating.

© Bettmann/CORBIS

For most people, practice and a few simple actions will reduce tension. Raymond Ross lists six useful ways to become more confident. First, you should recognize and, if necessary, talk to someone about your fright; your instructor is a good source. By talking about it, you normalize your fear. Second, find a way to burn up excess tension by engaging in a simple, repetitive physical activity before you begin. Third, redirect your attention, for example, by concentrating on a given audience member or on objects on the back walls of the auditorium (but be sure you don't lose eye contact with your audience for long). Fourth, use a clear organizational pattern or a simple outline to keep from losing your place or forgetting a point. If you do blank out, try summarizing what you've said so far, as this will generally reawaken your memory. Fifth, unless you're giving your first Inaugural Address or accepting a Nobel Prize, your speech will not be recorded for posterity, so be realistic about its importance. Finally, concentrate on your message more than on yourself.[4]

If you are unusually apprehensive and find that your fear is debilitating or that it transfers to other communication situations, then you may want to take part in a program of **systematic desensitization**. In this process, you will learn to substitute deep relaxation for fear responses. You will be asked to list the situations that make you apprehensive, in order of severity; you will then be instructed on how to relax; finally, you will be asked to imagine each fear-producing situation while remaining relaxed. Over time, your fear reactions can be extinguished or at least reduced to the point at which they are manageable. Most college or university counseling centers offer some form of desensitization. Don't be afraid to use their services if you experience severe speech anxiety. Your reactions are something you learned along the way, and they can be unlearned with a little work.

INCREASING PUBLIC SPEAKING SKILLS

Many people avoid giving public speeches because they think that to speak in public, one must be a "born speaker." The truth is, of course, that no one is born able to speak in public. Even the greatest public speakers had to start somewhere. For many great speakers, that starting point was the realization that public speaking offers opportunities: an opportunity to speak up when it is important to do so, an opportunity to develop ideas in one's own way, and an opportunity to make a difference in the public sphere.

Some Guidelines for Speakers

Keep in mind that although each speech you give will be different, some general principles will help you to prepare to speak in public. Before speaking, you must *do serious research and preparation.* Researching your subject will increase your understanding of your subject area, build up your self-confidence, and, when incorporated into your speech, increase your ethos. It will also provide convincing data to back up your claims.

Once you have done sufficient research, you can start to develop your main points and arguments. First, make sure that your ideas make sense to you; then make sure they will make sense to your audience. This means that you must *make a special effort to be organized and clear.* Keep in mind that the audience has not researched and thought about the topic as you have and that conclusions that seem self-evident to you may not seem so to them.

Listening is a difficult, draining process, and audiences often become bored or distracted. *Incorporate vivid and interesting elements into your speech.* By using personal examples, concrete and immediate language, interesting anecdotes, and the like, you can keep your audience interested. Try also to make what you say relevant to audience members' life experiences.

Finally, you should *develop your own individual style.* What will make you worth listening to is the unique perspective you bring to a problem. If you can find a way to express original ideas in a personal style, you will have gone a long way toward becoming a good speaker.

Using Technology to Enhance Public Speeches

Although it is possible to give a compelling public speech without sophisticated audiovisual aids, most speakers realize that a well-placed chart, picture, or film clip can enhance a presentation. Nowadays, computer-generated multimedia presentations are a part of many traditional public speaking situations. They have been used effectively during final summations in trials and during nominating speeches at political conventions. Community groups employ them during year-end reports; teachers use them during lectures; and they are a large part of day-to-day business presentations. Certainly, slick visuals can never replace carefully organized and well-thought-out content; nevertheless, if visuals are well designed, they can add to the impact of a speech. Nowadays, none of us can afford to ignore a tool that is becoming an expected part of public communication.

> Nowadays, computer-generated multimedia presentations are a part of many traditional public speaking situations. Slick visuals can never replace carefully organized and well-thought-out content; nevertheless, if visuals are well designed, they can add to the impact of a speech.

Why Visual Aids Are Important

When used effectively, visual aids can increase audience attention, comprehension, and retention. First of all, visual images are often more compelling and emotionally powerful than words. As we saw in Chapter 3, receivers automatically attend to vivid images, especially if they are colorful or novel. Visual aids can also increase comprehension by making difficult concepts clear. A graph or diagram can help us to understand concepts that would be hard to put into words. In addition, visual images are often highly memorable, so they can stick with us long after we have forgotten the actual words a speaker used. Finally, use of well-designed visual aids can make a speaker appear credible to an audience. Of course, if visual aids are not carefully thought out, they can backfire. PowerPoint slides can bore an audience, graphs can be confusing, and video clips can act as distracters. And visuals that seem carelessly made or awkwardly presented can actually decrease credibility judgments.

How to Make Visual Aids More Effective

What are some things that make visual aids ineffective? Basically, visual aids don't work if:

- They draw attention away from the idea they are meant to illustrate
- They are difficult to see or understand
- They present too much information at once
- They are awkward or difficult to handle during the presentation
- Their relationship to the idea they are meant to illustrate is not clear

Visual aids should not distract. Because visual aids are so compelling, it is important that they not take attention away from the speaker. If you are going to display an object, for example, you should keep it hidden until it is needed. If you are using PowerPoint slides, show a blank slide until you reach the point in your speech at which you want to introduce the idea illustrated on your slide. In general, you should avoid using visual aids that need to be passed around the room. Stephen Lucas tells us that putting visual aids in the hands of the audience spells trouble. "At least three people will be paying more attention to the aid than to you—the person who has just had it, the person who has it now, and the person waiting to get it next."[5]

Visual aids must be easy to see. If a visual aid is too small or if it is messy and hard to decipher, it will work against you. On slides, you must consider font size, color, balance, and a variety of other design elements. Charts should be easy to understand and clearly labeled.

Visual aids can capture attention, but to be effective they should match the occasion and purpose.

© Bettmann/CORBIS

> **Because visual aids are so compelling, it is important that they not take attention away from the speaker.**

Visual aids should be simple. Generally, visual aids are used for illustrative or summarizing purposes. Don't try to get your entire presentation onto a poster or handout. A single slide with a picture, a chart, a quote, an animated cartoon, and five lines of text may show how clever you are at using PowerPoint, but it won't be effective. Remember, people come to hear a speech, not to read it.

Visual aids should be easy to handle. This rule is especially important with computerized or multimedia presentations. Electronic aids that need complex equipment to operate can invite disaster if the speaker isn't comfortable with the equipment or if something breaks. This means that you need to practice until you are completely confident. Asking the audience, "Hey, does anyone know how to turn on the projector?" doesn't create a positive impression. It is also necessary to have a backup plan. If you've misplaced your flash drive or the DVD player is not in the room, you should be prepared to give the speech the old-fashioned way.

Visual aids should be subordinate to the ideas they are meant to illustrate. The basic idea to remember is that visual aids are just that—aids. Their relationship to the points in a speech should be clear. Randomly chosen photos, no matter how beautiful, won't advance an argument or illustrate a thought. It is also important not to overuse slides; they should be used only when they will have maximum impact.

If these warnings are kept in mind, audiovisual aids can make a presentation polished and professional. Many software packages are available that can help you to design your presentation. Perhaps the most widely known is PowerPoint, which is, in fact, a very powerful tool. It can allow you to create and display text, photographs, clip art, charts, graphs, video clips, and audio clips with relative ease. It is definitely worth the time to become familiar with how this software works. But be careful. The more features you use, the more careful you need to be to make sure your style and tone are consistent and that every choice you make works to enhance your purpose.

BECOMING A MORE RESPONSIBLE COMMUNICATOR

From the very beginning of the study of rhetoric, ethics and communication have been linked. For the Greeks, ethical behavior was an important characteristic of the ideal communicator. Isocrates, for example, believed that dishonest communicators could do great harm; he therefore taught that "the argument which is made by a man's life is of more weight than that which is furnished by words."[6] Today, when technology has increased the ability of all communicators to reach mass audiences, the importance of ethical communication is at least as important as it was in classical times. Here are some simple guidelines to keep in mind as you engage in public communication, either in the community or in the classroom:

- A distinguishing characteristic of public communication is the power that is given over to the speaker. In the public context, the primary communication role is given to the speaker, and audience members expect facts that are true and proposals that are well considered. Whenever you speak publicly, even if only in the classroom, you are responsible for what you say. Delivering false information or half-formed ideas is a misuse of this power and a violation of trust.

- It is also a violation of trust for speakers to advocate positions that they themselves do not hold. As we've noted throughout this chapter, skillful public communicators adapt to their audiences. But adapting to an audience does not mean adopting their point of view. It means presenting your own ideas in a form that the audience can comprehend and appreciate. It is irresponsible to compromise personal ideals to tell an audience what it wants to hear in an attempt to gain acceptance or popularity.

- Skillful speakers can use their power either to inform or inflame. They can appeal to the best in people or to bigotry and hatred. They can use rational argument or resort to innuendo and simplistic slogans. In so doing, they demean their audiences. Assuming audiences are too stupid to understand or too weak-willed to make their own moral and ethical choices does great disservice and possible harm, for people who are lied to learn not to respect the truth and people who are treated as though they are irrational can become so. Responsible speakers treat their audiences with respect by rejecting these abuses of power.

- Speakers also show respect to audience members by encouraging independent decision making. They do so by presenting clearly and completely the best information available on a given topic at a given time. It is irresponsible to use methods that interfere with an audience's ability to make an informed choice, such as intentionally falsifying data, lying about one's own interest and intents, or misrepresenting the consequences of a proposed action. Paul Campbell expresses this idea when he instructs communicators on how to act more ethically:

  You avoid all hidden pressures and prejudices; you point out the consequences of given viewpoints whether they are favorable or unfavorable to your cause . . . and you always, always make it totally apparent that the audience must consciously and freely make its own choices.[7]

- Finally, as was pointed out in Chapter 9, audience members, too, have responsibilities. Listeners act irresponsibly when they passively accept whatever they hear or allow personal needs and prejudices to blind them to facts. Responsible listeners inform themselves on important issues, follow arguments carefully, judge the adequacy of evidence, and critically evaluate the consequences of proposals. When unethical speakers persuade audiences to draw questionable conclusions, audience members are themselves partly to blame. Taking on the role of listener does not absolve a communicator from ethical responsibilities.

SUMMARY

Most people, at some time in their lives, will be given the opportunity to speak in public. Those who have studied public speaking will be able to take best advantage of this opportunity. A public speech is quite different from the kind of communication we do every day: public speeches are organized, purposeful, continuous presentations in which a single sender talks to a large, anonymous audience for an extended period of time. This form of communication presents special challenges to speakers, who must create relationships with the audience, structure their speeches, and deliver them with confidence and force.

In planning their speeches, successful public speakers must adapt to the audience, keeping the audience in mind as they decide on the central idea they wish to convey, the structure of their speech, the supporting materials they will use, and the presentation style they will employ. This means that they must gather demographic information about the audience. Knowing things such as age, sex, educational level, religious affiliation, economic status, and cultural or ethnic identification can help speakers to understand audience motivations and attitudes. Demographic data can be obtained in a number of ways, including reading local newspapers, watching local news programming on TV, and interviewing individuals like those who will be in the audience.

Public speeches must be carefully organized. A typical speech is made up of an introduction, a body, and a conclusion. The introduction creates interest, establishes credibility, and orients the audience to the speaker's thesis. The conclusion signals the end of the speech, underscores the significance of the topic, and summarizes main ideas. The content in the body must be arranged in a logical order, often following a stock organizational pattern. By creating a formal outline, the speaker can check organization and subordination of ideas.

Delivery is an important aspect of public speaking. In planning the speech, speakers must decide whether to use impromptu, extemporaneous, or manuscript delivery. Speakers must also find a way to manage anxiety. Luckily, there are some simple actions that can ward off apprehension. In addition to cognitive restructuring and physical relaxation, speakers can talk about their fears, burn off tension before speaking, redirect their attention, and use clear organization. Being realistic about their

roles as speakers and focusing more on their message than on themselves can also help. In severe cases of stage fright, systematic desensitization can be used.

One cannot learn public speaking overnight; it takes practice and instruction. Nevertheless, some general principles can help a speaker to prepare. To ensure audience attention, comprehension, and retention, speakers should be organized and clear and should use vivid and interesting material. Finally, although they must adapt their speech to the audience members' needs and interests, speakers should never lose the unique perspective that makes a message their own.

Although there was a time when speakers used nothing but the spoken word to sway audiences, today's audiences expect speeches to be accompanied by sophisticated multimedia support. Well-designed visuals can compel attention, increase comprehension, make a speech memorable, and increase speaker credibility. Whether a speaker's audiovisual aids consist of posters and charts or computer-generated slides, they should be carefully planned. Efforts should be made to make sure they are not distracting, are easy to see, are simple, and are easy to handle. Most important, visual aids are just that—aids. They should always be subordinate to the ideas they are meant to illustrate.

A skilled public speaker can make a significant impact in the public sphere. With this power, however, goes responsibility. Speakers who deal in false information or half-truths violate audience trust. Speakers who use their power to inflame an audience rob its members of the ability to make independent informed choices. Responsible speakers treat their audiences with respect.

KEY TERMS

Listed below are the key terms used in this chapter, along with the number of the page where each is explained.

public speech (258)	stock organizational patterns (264)	visualization step (266)
audience adaptation (258)	chronological order (264)	action step (266)
demographic analysis (260)	spatial order (265)	outline (266)
introduction (261)	topical order (265)	impromptu speaking (267)
thesis (262)	causal order (265)	extemporaneous speaking (268)
conclusion (262)	problem–solution order (265)	manuscript speaking (268)
body (262)	motivated sequence (265)	speech anxiety (268)
preview (262)	attention step (265)	cognitive restructuring (268)
transitions (262)	need step (266)	physical relaxation (268)
internal summaries (262)	satisfaction step (266)	systematic desensitization (269)

SUGGESTED READING

Lucas, Stephen E. (2011). *The art of public speaking* (11th ed.). New York: McGraw Hill.

> Lucas provides a nice discussion of how to use PowerPoint effectively in public speaking situations.

McKerrow, Raymie E., Gronbeck, Bruce E., Ehninger, Douglas, & Monroe, Alan H. (2006). *Principles and types of public speaking* (16th ed.). Boston: Allyn & Bacon.

The fact that this basic public speaking text is in its sixteenth edition says it all. A solid introduction, this text presents everything you always wanted to know—and more—about how to speak in public.

11 Communication and the Media

I n a media culture, it is sometimes hard to distinguish fictional from factual reality.

After reading this chapter, you should be able to:

- Identify the characteristics of traditional media messages.

- List and explain the four classic functions of mass media.

- Give examples of ways in which the traditional media set agendas, create hegemonic messages, cultivate worldviews, and change expectations. Give examples of ways audiences resist media influence.

- Describe how consumers use newspapers, magazines, radio, and television and understand how the formats used by these media affect information processing.

- Identify the characteristics of new media.

- Be able to discuss the ways old and new media are converging and how convergence is making audiences more active.

- Understand how computer-mediated communication is used and how it enhances social interaction.

- Discuss how advances in cell phone technology are changing face-to-face communication.

- Be aware of ethical issues associated with computer-mediated communication.

I n the spring of 2009 researchers at Ball State University's Center for Media Design released a study demonstrating how important mediated communication is to the average American. At that time, we spent approximately eight hours a day in front of screens: TVs, cell phones, computers, and the like, and the time spent was almost identical for every age group. Television accounted for the largest amount of time, followed by computer usage, radio, and print media in that order. By 2013, as this edition went to press, TV programming was still the most popular way to spend one's time with media, although more and more young people were watching TV on their computers or hand-held devices and many were multitasking, checking social network sites, surfing the Web, or talking on cell phones while they watched their favorite shows. Both as consumers and as producers of messages, we are deeply involved with the media.[1]

Media fulfill many functions in our lives. Broadcast media, for example, provide us with access to information we could never gather on our own. They give us a front-row seat to events around the globe. When a devastating earthquake hit Haiti in 2010, TV camera crews from all the major networks were on the scene almost immediately. Not only did the media allow us to see the devastation, they gave us ways to become involved. In the first thirty-six hours after the disaster, more than seven million dollars was donated via text messaging.[2] The media, both traditional and new, allow us to reach out to help others.

We are no longer just passive consumers of media; we are creators as well. If we believe in something strongly we can broadcast our own message. In 2012, a twenty-two-year-old Christian named Jefferson Bethke posted a four-minute video called "Why I Hate Religion, But Love Jesus" to YouTube. It went viral. Overnight it garnered two million views and since then scores of millions have viewed it. Religion is no longer confined to churches, temples, or mosques, and everyone can have a say.[3] Similarly, during the freedom protests in the Middle East known as Arab Spring, photos taken by common citizens on their cell phones let the world know what was happening. The actions of average people are supplementing the work of professional reporters. We are contributing our own voices to collective knowledge.

Of course, not all media coverage is serious. We also value entertainment coverage. Fans at sporting events may spend only part of their time watching what is going on before them. Many listen to the play-by-play on portable radios and watch game highlights on giant TV screens. Without "six different camera angles, slow-motion instant replay, expert (color) analysis, and constant action," spectators feel that something important is missing from the game.[4] In a media age, real-life events may not be as complete or satisfying as mediated events.

When so much of our time is spent viewing TV, it is no wonder that many people dream about appearing on screen, perhaps as stars in the latest reality TV show. Reality TV is so big, in fact, that casting calls go out almost every week and text messages can alert potential contestants of the latest auditions. If the producers of reality programming have their way, everyone in the United States will get his or her "fifteen minutes of fame," as Andy Warhol predicted. In addition to talent shows, model searches, and survival ordeals, there are plenty of opportunities for "average people" to be on TV. As these words are being written, reality shows run the gamut from A (*Amazing Wedding Cakes, America's Next Top Model*, and *Are You Smarter Than a 5th Grader?*) to W (*Wife Swap, Worst Cooks in America*, and *Wipeout*).[5] Appearing on a quiz show can earn you money, and winning a modeling contest can (sometimes) launch a career, but why would people willingly expose themselves by appearing on *Hoarders* or *Intervention*? And when it comes to former shows like *Smile . . . You're Under Arrest!* in which criminals with outstanding arrest records are lured into elaborate comic stings before being arrested, or *America's Trashiest Weddings*, in which couples make wedding choices in questionable taste, why do people sign the release? For many people, it would appear, being seen on national TV is the ultimate legitimating experience.

And it's not just average people who want to become media stars. Politicians also have been quick to recognize the importance of making their presence known either by mounting their own Websites, by twittering about their day-to-day activities, or by becoming guests on talk radio or TV. Quick to criticize negative media coverage, they also are quick to seize the limelight. Shortly after his election, for example, President Barack Obama used a guest shot on *The Tonight Show* with Jay Leno to explain his economic stimulus package, and a few days later he held an online town-hall meeting to answer questions from the American public. Other politicians have appeared in commercials and have acted in skits on comedy shows like *Saturday Night Live*. In a media culture, it is sometimes hard to distinguish fictional from factual reality or politicians from performers.

These situations illustrate how important the mass media have become in our daily lives. Like it or not, we live in a media culture that affects how we experience the world and how we communicate with one another. In this chapter, we look at what it means to live in constant interaction with the traditional and emerging mass media.

THE TRADITIONAL MASS MEDIA

It has become common to distinguish between old and new media. The term **old media** refers to traditional one-to-many forms of mediated communication such as TV, radio, newspapers, and books. The label **new media** is used to describe digital information and telecommunication systems, including networked computing and mobile telecommunication.

Although this distinction is useful for organizational purposes, keep in mind that old and new media are rapidly converging, and that it won't take long for what we now consider new media to become old and for old media to take on new forms. In this chapter we'll start our discussion with the traditional media of mass communication and then turn our attention to some of the ways computer-mediated communication and mobile technologies are altering our lives and changing the nature of traditional media functions and formats. We'll then look at how old and new media are rapidly converging.

What Is Mass Communication?

Despite the attention that is currently being given to new media, traditional media are still an important and influential force in our lives. To understand how to interact with them more effectively, we have to begin by understanding what mass communication is and how it differs from other kinds of communication.

Defining Mass Communication

Mass communication is a form of communication through which institutional sources (often referred to as "the media") address large, diverse audiences whose members are physically separated from one another. Contact is indirect; devices for the transmission, storage, and reception of information are interposed between source and receiver. Mass communication is a powerful and pervasive mode of communication, and in modern societies, the media are important social institutions that reflect and affect the values and behaviors of large segments of the population.

Characteristics of Media Messages

Media messages are unique in at least three ways: (1) in major mass communication contexts, the source is a complex, profit-oriented organization rather than a single individual; (2) receivers are anonymous, dispersed in time and space, and heterogeneous in their interests and background; and (3) communication occurs through indirect channels that require specialized encoding and decoding technologies.

Institutional Sources.   In the communication contexts we have looked at in other chapters, the source has been a single individual who composes and delivers his or her own message. In mass communication contexts, messages are the products of complex organizations composed of individuals who perform specialized functions. To get a sense of how much internal specialization is involved in mediated communication, sit through the credits the next time you watch a film. You'll see that in addition to the director and actors, the film employs executive and associate producers, artistic directors, set dressers and costumers, lighting specialists, electricians, sound mixers, first- and second-unit camera operators, and a host of others. Making a movie costs millions of dollars, and production companies expect to make a profit. They must therefore appeal to the largest possible audience, a fact that is inevitably reflected in their products.

Invisible Receivers.   Another difference between interpersonal and mass communication lies in the relationship between source and receiver. Media sources have little, if any, direct contact with receivers. By the time audience members buy their popcorn and settle down in front of the screen, the cast and crew have long since packed up their equipment, struck the set, and moved on to other projects. In interpersonal contexts, sources and receivers are in direct contact; in mass contexts, feedback is indirect and delayed. Once a film or TV show is "in the can," the source's contribution is over. Media communicators must perform for invisible spectators.

Receivers are also invisible in another way: there are so many of them. Media audiences are huge. On a given night, 100 million viewers may watch a television special. These viewers represent a variety of ages and social classes; their backgrounds and interests may be extremely varied. Even with fairly specialized media, such as technical magazines, readers may number in the tens of thousands, and outside of the single shared interest that led them to purchase the magazine, they may have little in common. The problem of audience adaptation becomes particularly acute with such a heterogeneous public. Media messages cannot be individualized as can interpersonal messages. Being able to create messages that are widely acceptable is highly valued in the media industries.

> **Being able to create messages that are widely acceptable is highly valued in the media industries.**

A final characteristic of media receivers lies in the conditions under which reception takes place. With the exception of movie viewers, media receivers consume media messages alone or in small groups in fairly noisy environments. One source of noise is the competition of other mediated messages. It's important to remember that receivers' relationships with sources are voluntary and can be severed at any time. Audience members are free to turn off the radio if the DJ annoys them or to flip through TV channels until they find an image they like. When cable viewers have a choice of tuning in to any one of fifty different stations at a given time, the producers of a single program must work especially hard to capture an adequate share of the market.

Interposed Channels.   The use of interposed channels is a final characteristic of mass communication. Different media employ different technologies for the transmission and reception of messages, and these technologies make different demands on the resourcefulness of both source and receiver. Electronic media, for example, involve the use of special equipment to encode and decode messages. Not only does this equipment require a financial commitment, it may require technical expertise as well. Both producers and consumers must keep up with changing technologies.

Different media also require different cognitive skills. Books and magazines, for example, do not require costly equipment, but they do demand that the receiver be able to read the written word, an accomplishment that takes detailed instruction. The ability to "read" a message is actually demanded by every medium. To understand a TV drama, for example, viewers must be able to decode visual messages; they must accustom themselves to the language of camera angles, editing, scene composition, and so forth, just as directors must learn to tell a story in visual terms. Each medium has its own format, and successful media communicators understand their particular format.

How Audiences and Media Messages Interact

Mass communication is like every other form of communication in one way: sources and receivers form a relationship with one another. Since the beginning of the rise of the mass media in the United States, theorists have posed questions about this relationship, concerning themselves with the functions fulfilled by the media, the extent to which the media influence audiences, and the ways in which receivers process media messages. In this section, we look at some of the divergent viewpoints that have emerged as scholars have tried to understand the relationship between audiences and media messages.

Functions of the Media

Sociologist Charles Wright, expanding on a model first developed by political scientist Harold Lasswell, identifies four media functions: surveillance, correlation, cultural transmission, and entertainment.[6] Table 11.1 summarizes these functions.

The first media function is **surveillance**, the gathering and disseminating of information. Media sources affect receivers by providing them with news, by warning them of crises or dangers, and by giving them the instrumental information they need to get through a day. When we speak of the media as the "watchdogs of a free society," we are referring to the surveillance function. In general, this function is fulfilled by newspapers and by radio and television news programming.

The second function of the media is **correlation**, the analysis and evaluation of information. In addition to reporting facts, the media affect receivers by interpreting

Table 11.1 Media Functions

Surveillance	The gathering and disseminating of information
Correlation	The analysis and evaluation of information
Cultural Transmission	The education and socialization of receivers
Entertainment	The presentation of escapist material that provides enjoyment and gratification

news events and by analyzing social problems. The correlation function is most often found in the editorial pages of newspapers, on news analysis shows, and in magazine articles that analyze current issues.

The third function of the media is **cultural transmission**, or education and socialization. Not only do the media inform receivers about events, they also socialize receivers. By observing what characters do in television dramas, we internalize behavioral norms; by viewing films, we learn about our culture's history; and by reading magazines, newspapers, and books, we confront questions of values. Media personalities act as role models for us. Often, our learning is *prosocial learning*; that is, it reinforces social ideals and passes on cultural understandings from one generation to the next. Sometimes, however, our learning is essentially *antisocial learning*, reinforcing socially destructive behavior. The debate about the effects of televised violence on the behavior of children indicates a very real concern—that culturally transmitted messages may inadvertently undermine cultural values.

The debate about the effects of televised violence on the behavior of children indicates a very real concern—that culturally transmitted messages may inadvertently undermine cultural values.

The final function of the media is **entertainment**. The media offer receivers an escape from the problems of everyday life. Media provide enjoyment and gratification, help us to relax, allow us to experience vicarious adventure, and arouse our emotions. The entertainment function is fulfilled by almost every medium. Reading the newspaper, flipping through a magazine, and watching a TV show or a film are all ways that we give ourselves a break from the more serious aspects of our lives.

Of course, each of these functions can have negative side effects. Consider the surveillance function. News can as easily misinform as it can inform, and it can occasionally increase anxiety or cause panic. Too much information can even *narcotize*, or overwhelm and paralyze, an audience. When receivers are inundated with news reports, their knowledge of social problems may become superficial and their social concern may be replaced by apathy.[7]

The correlation, cultural transmission, and entertainment functions all have their negative sides as well. Simplistic commentary, for example, can increase passivity and can discourage social criticism. When anchors appear after every major broadcast to summarize what we have just heard, we may stop listening carefully or lose confidence in our own conclusions. Similarly, media socialization can reduce the ability of other institutions (such as

Media offerings must appeal to mass audiences.

Time & Life Pictures/Getty Images

families and schools) to set standards and can foster superficial, homogenized values. Finally, mindless entertainment can encourage escapism and can lower popular taste. The functions that the media fulfill appear to be mixed blessings.

Media Effects: An Overview

Do media messages brainwash a defenseless public, or are most people able to see through them? Do the media create desires, or do they simply give the public what it wants? Can the media instill values, or do they merely reflect values that already exist? The debate over these questions has resulted in two opposing schools of thought. According to the first, receivers are relatively passive; they accept media messages at face value and unconsciously allow media sources to tell them what to think. People who accept the first perspective believe in what has been called the **powerful effects model**.

According to the second point of view, far from accepting media messages as intended, audience members interpret messages according to their own preexisting beliefs and values and use these messages in unique ways. For people who hold this view, audiences are active processors who are quite capable of defending themselves against media influence. Those who accept this perspective employ a **limited effects model**.

During the last fifty years, the pendulum has swung back and forth between these extremes.[8] The earliest theories of mass communication tended to portray the media as extremely influential. Media influence was likened to a **magic bullet** or a **hypodermic needle** that could target unsuspecting audience members or inject them with a message. Receivers were seen as the passive victims of the all-powerful media.[9]

In the 1950s and 1960s, however, theorists began to take a closer look at the audience. They found that individuals were much more stubbornly resistant to media manipulation than had at first been assumed. According to the resulting **obstinate audience** theory, receivers were viewed as creative consumers who sought out media messages according to their own needs and interpreted messages in their own ways.[10] Media effects were thought to be mediated both by the receiver's personality and by his or her group allegiances.

Despite the popularity of this view, critics were left with a nagging feeling that audiences were not so resistant. Some theorists began to wonder just how much choice receivers really had. Therefore, beginning in the 1970s and continuing into the 1990s, theorists began to reconsider the power of the media to influence audiences. Of particular interest were the long-term effects of television viewing. Some theorists focused on uncovering hidden political agendas embedded in television programming; others looked at ways in which the media presented distorted views of society; and still others focused on specific effects like the correlation between media violence and aggressive behavior.

Adherents of each view still argue strongly for their own perspective. In the sections that follow, we'll take a brief look at some of the effects attributed to the media, as well as at characteristics that may make audiences at least somewhat resistant to media domination. After considering these arguments (which are summarized in Table 11.2), you be the judge.

What Media Messages Do to Receivers

Theories that argue for the power of the media generally argue one of four positions: that the media tell us what to think about, that the media tell us what not to think about, that the media present distorted views of the world, and that exposure to each new medium changes the way we process information and alters our expectations about how messages should be constructed.[11]

Media Agendas.   Very early on, critics identified the **agenda-setting function** of the media. According to this view, media **gatekeepers** select the issues they feel are most worthy of coverage and give those issues wide attention.[12] Receivers accept the gatekeepers' agendas without realizing that, somewhere along the line, an editor or producer is making choices about what to cover and what to ignore. As Norman Felsenthal remarks, "Neither an individual nor a society can give equal attention to everything. We are continually required to determine which problems get our immediate attention and which problems are simply endured or even ignored altogether."[13] The media often make decisions for us, alerting us today to a drug problem, tomorrow to a crisis in education, and the day after that to an erosion of family values. A movie-of-the-week about child abuse can trigger our interest in a normally overlooked problem, especially if it is followed up in other media. If, as a result of the movie, a weekly news magazine runs a feature about the problem and talk show hosts jump on the bandwagon, chances are that people will come to define child abuse as a serious issue. This is one way in which the media order our priorities.

Hegemonic Messages.   If media attention makes certain issues and information highly salient, it also makes some issues invisible. Critical theorists argue that the media reflect and reproduce only those ideas, meanings, and values that uphold the interests of the power elite and that they silence opposing views. According to these theorists, media messages are **hegemonic**; that is, media messages keep powerless

Table 11.2 Media Effects and Audience Resistance

How Media Affect Audiences	How Audiences Resist Media
Media influence receivers by:	**Receivers resist influence by:**
1. Agenda setting	1. Selective processing
2. Producing hegemonic messages	2. Conducting oppositional readings
3. Cultivating worldviews	3. Using media for individual gratification
4. Affecting cognitive practices and expectations	

groups from making their ideas known. Although the media may appear to present a variety of ideas and choices, this diversity is an illusion. Instead, the media reproduce and package a single message, or *dominant ideology*. Todd Gitlin, for example, argues that American TV encourages viewers to "experience themselves as antipolitical, privately accumulating individuals." Television supports the status quo and valorizes a consumer ethic while discouraging criticism of alternative economic or political arrangements.[14]

> **Critical theorists argue that the media reflect and reproduce only those ideas, meanings, and values that uphold the interests of the power elite and that they silence opposing views.**

The media also underrepresent and misrepresent certain social groups according to media watchdog site *Children Now*:

> *As America's primary storyteller and chief cultural exporter, television provides messages and images that contribute to the worldviews of millions. When certain groups are privileged, others subjugated, and still others altogether excluded, prime time sends skewed messages to viewers—especially young ones—that these groups are valued differently.*[15]

Does representation matter? Many would answer yes, arguing that media portrayals of gender, sexual orientation, race, ethnicity, age, disability, and so on affect how we see ourselves and others. If you're a person of color or member of another minority you know how frustrating it can be not to see yourself reflected realistically anywhere within the general culture. If you're not, it may not be too hard to imagine what it would feel like to be invisible.

Media content affects us in yet another way. Like other sources of stories and myths, the media convey not only what is normal and acceptable, but also what is irrelevant and wrong. As a result, people who disagree with the messages broadcast through the media often refuse to voice criticisms or objections for fear of being socially isolated or scapegoated. Elisabeth Noelle-Neumann's theory of the **spiral of silence** expresses this idea.[16] She believes that people who think their ideas are popular tend to express them; those who see themselves in the minority remain silent. As a result, only one side of any given issue receives notice. And groups outside the mainstream have almost no chance of making themselves heard, because the media refuse to legitimate their ideas. Not only do the media tell us what to think about, they also tell us what not to think about. It is a bit frightening to realize that, for the first time in history, the stories we hear and the values we are taught do not come from parents, schools, or churches, but from "a group of distant conglomerates that have something to sell."[17]

> **Like other sources of stories and myths, the media convey not only what is normal and acceptable, but also what is irrelevant and wrong.**

Cultivated Worldviews.   In addition to creating hegemonic messages, media can affect the extent to which we feel comfortable in our social worlds. **Cultivation theory**, originally developed by George Gerbner and his colleagues at the Annenberg School for Communication at the University of Pennsylvania, draws our attention to ways in which individuals come to accept the televised world as an accurate reflection of the real world. Unlike the hypodermic needle theories, which focused on ways in which specific messages or genres directly affect audiences, cultivation theory looks at how long-term television viewing affects viewers' beliefs about social reality.[18] Instead of an injection metaphor, cultivation theorists liken TV's influence to the kind of slow buildup that occurs as stalagmites form. They argue that, just as stalagmites grow over time from the steady dripping of limewater in underground caverns, so our views of what the world is like are built up from the images and representations we are exposed to over long periods of time.

One effect of cultivation is called **mainstreaming**: like critical theorists, cultivation scholars believe that television viewing creates widely shared, middle-of-the-road viewpoints that tend to support the status quo. Another effect of cultivation is a belief in what has come to be called the **mean world hypothesis**, the view that the world is a much more dangerous place than it actually is. For example, there is much more crime on TV than in the real world. As a result, viewers who spend a lot of time watching TV and don't have access to actual crime statistics come to view the world as violent and dangerous. According to cultivation theory, "heavy exposure to television violence cultivates insecurity, mistrust, and alienation, and a willingness to accept potentially repressive measures in the name of security."[19]

> There is much more crime on TV than in the real world. As a result, viewers who spend a lot of time watching TV and don't have access to actual crime statistics come to view the world as violent and dangerous.

Of course, not everyone is affected to the same degree. According to cultivation theory, it is *heavy viewers*, those who watch a lot of TV, who are most likely to experience cultivation. *Light viewers*, who presumably have alternative sources of information, are less affected. To date, research is somewhat mixed in its support for cultivation theory. However there is a general consensus that "television makes a small but significant contribution to the heavy viewers' beliefs about the world."[20]

Media Logics.   A final way in which the media may affect us has less to do with content and more to do with the form of media messages. According to this view, when new technologies emerge, they change the way we experience the world. They encourage certain kinds of messages and discourage others. Their very presence creates new social possibilities and changes existing power relations. For example, some critics argue that the electronic media have contributed to the emergence of an "imperial presidency." Elihu Katz sees the beginning of this trend in Franklin D. Roosevelt's "fireside chats." By broadcasting directly to the people, Roosevelt could bypass Congress.[21] Subsequent presidents adopted FDR's strategy, and modern presidents are now treated like media stars. Television focuses on "personalities," and it is easier to cast a single individual as a personality than it is to cast multiple characters, such as Congress or the judiciary.[22]

The creation of an imperial presidency is only one exemplification that media formats affect both the messages that are broadcast and the surrounding social structure. When Marshall McLuhan first stated that **"the medium is the message,"** he was expressing the beliefs that the channel through which a message is transmitted is as important as the message itself and that the channel, in fact, often determines which messages will be transmitted and which will be ignored.[23] According to McLuhan's theory, each medium has its own internal logic, and each affects how we experience the world. For example, print media have **linear logic**; that is, they transmit information in an orderly sequence, word after word, idea after idea. Print media encourage rationality and individuality. Television, by contrast, has **mosaic logic**, bombarding us with changing bits of information that we must cognitively reassemble. Television encourages sensory involvement.

Because television is what McLuhan refers to as a *cool medium*, it demands that viewers fill in detail. Performers who are too hard-edged and direct are not "cool" enough to succeed on TV, although they may be perfect for a "hotter" medium, such as radio. In fact, McLuhan explains John F. Kennedy's success in the 1960 presidential debates in terms of his relative "coolness" compared to the "hotter" Richard Nixon.

Although not everyone has embraced McLuhan's cool–hot distinction, many critics accept the idea that form is as important as content in affecting audience responses. As we accustom ourselves to different media forms, our cognitive practices and expectations change. Exposure to a constant barrage of highly arousing and rapidly changing images (such as those found on TV) changes the way we think. We become impatient with nonpictorial stimuli and with nondramatic messages. People raised on a steady diet of television may expect all information to be condensed, simple, short, and rapidly changing. Linear and detailed information may be rejected out of hand both by receivers and by media sources. Some media critics believe that our definition of information has been changed by the advent of television and that we all think in the language of TV, or, as we will see in the section on new media, in the language of the Internet.

> Exposure to a constant barrage of highly arousing and rapidly changing images (such as those found on TV) changes the way we think.

Robert P. Snow believes that our involvement with the language of television is so strong that it is changing the language of other media. Television viewers, used to the condensing and telescoping tendencies of TV, are demanding the same features in newspapers, books, and magazines, reading more tolerable for the TV generation.[24]

What Receivers Do with Media Messages

Our discussion so far has portrayed viewers as fairly passive recipients of media influence. But is this a fair portrayal? Many scholars argue that it is not. These scholars view receivers as selective, rational consumers of messages who are affected as much by their own needs and group memberships as by media goals and practices. To support this viewpoint, these scholars make three basic arguments: that audience members process messages selectively, that audiences are motivated to use media by private needs and desires, and that the meanings audience members assign to media messages are social constructions.

Selective Processing.   If everyone were to react to a given message in exactly the same way, the media would have very little trouble controlling receivers. Students of perception, however, know that this is not how perception works. People see the world in unique ways. As we saw in Chapter 3, we are capable of ignoring messages we don't like, of tuning out tedious or irrelevant details, of interpreting messages in original ways, and of forgetting inconvenient details. That is, we engage in selective exposure, attention, perception, and retention.

Selective exposure refers to people's tendency to avoid certain messages and to seek out others. Although we like to believe that we are open-minded and intellectually curious, many of us are not. Preexisting preferences guide us in the selection of media messages. Musical taste, for example, determines which radio station we listen to; a hard rock fan will not tune in to a station with an easy-listening format. Religious and political beliefs and values also affect media exposure; nonbelievers seldom watch televangelists, and political conservatives may refuse to read columns written by liberals. If we do expose ourselves to messages we usually avoid, we may do so to make fun of or criticize those messages, not to listen with an open mind. Most of the time, however, we don't go that far; we simply refuse to expose ourselves to messages we imagine we will not like. Media can hardly affect us if we don't tune in.

Even when we choose to process a message, we may engage in **selective attention**. That is, we may listen only to parts of the message. As we saw in Chapter 3, people's attention tends to wander, and messages must be vivid and novel if people are to process them. Advertisers, of course, are well aware of this fact and use music, color, sound effects, and other devices to make us pay attention.

Receivers are also not immune from **selective perception**, the process of assigning meaning to messages in selective ways. Ask two different people to explain what a book or a movie is about. Chances are, the explanations will be very different and will be affected as much by preconceived notions as by the intention of the media source.

Finally, receivers engage in **selective retention**, remembering only a small portion of any message. Studies have shown that "viewers of the network newscast can seldom remember more than three or four stories, or approximately 20 percent, just an hour after seeing the news." The average viewer is often ill-informed, even on issues that receive heavy coverage.[25]

Need Gratification.   Why do receivers turn to the media in the first place? Many theorists argue that they do so to fulfill preexisting needs. **Uses and gratifications research** focuses on the needs that motivate media consumers. This research argues that receivers are active and goal directed. Receivers know what they need, and they look for ways to get it. The media are only one of a number of competing sources of gratification. In Katz's terms, this approach "does not assume a direct relationship between messages and effects, but postulates instead that members of the audience put messages to use, and that such usages act as intervening variables in the process of effect."[26]

One of the earliest studies in this tradition was Herta Herzog's investigation of why women listened to radio soap operas.[27] Herzog determined that listeners used the soaps for emotional release, fantasy escape, and advice on how to deal with their own problems. Denis McQuail and his colleagues argue that the media, in general, are chosen to provide (1) diversion and emotional release, (2) substitute companionship and a shared social experience, (3) identity and value reinforcement, and (4) surveillance.[28] As we shall see in the section on new media, uses and gratification research is being employed to understand how consumers use the Internet and cell phones.

Reading Media Texts.   A number of theorists have focused their research efforts on describing how receivers make sense out of what they see and hear. These scholars argue that media reception does not take place in a vacuum and that receivers are not blank slates waiting to have a message inscribed on them. Instead, receivers are members of "interpretive communities" who actively construct meanings in accordance with their own social experiences. The theorists refer to the process of assigning meaning to media messages as "reading" and to the messages themselves as "texts." Scholars who take this approach argue that receivers are quite able to read media texts in ways that oppose the dominant ideology. Thus, it is possible for feminists to do an oppositional reading of the ways in which women are portrayed in romance novels or for members of ethnic minorities to recognize ethnic biases in news reporting.

> Receivers are members of "interpretive communities" who actively construct meanings in accordance with their own social experiences.

Rather than a given text having one hegemonic message, it may have multiple meanings, a condition known as **polysemy**. In this sense, media exposure is a process of negotiating between what lies in the text itself and what lies in the social and cultural context in which the text is experienced.

The debate over how much the media affect us continues to rage. Although little doubt remains that media messages are influential, the question of just how much power they wield remains open. As media consumers, we should be aware of the potential of the media to affect our lives. One way to increase this awareness is to understand media formats, our next topic.

Media Formats and Logics

Each medium is unique not only in the conditions under which it is received, but also in the way it is structured and in its internal logic. As a result, each has a distinctive capacity for influence.[29] In this section, we'll look briefly at the formats employed in some of the major media. We'll focus on newspapers, magazines, radio, and television; follow with a few words about film and books; and end with a discussion of media ethics. Table 11.3 summarizes major points.

Newspapers

Although tens of millions of newspapers are still sold each day, the format in which people prefer to receive news is changing. There is good news and bad news for

American newspapers. On one hand mobile devices are boosting access to and interest in news. Tablets, for example, let readers read and process long-form journalism. At the same time, print circulation continues to decline, and it is predicted that in five years many newspapers will offer print, home-delivered, versions only on Sunday.[30]

In addition to changes in format, changes in the profession of journalism are likely. Although no one knows yet what the newspapers of tomorrow will be like, everyone agrees they will change.

For example, Journalist Michael Kinsley has suggested that professional reporting in which trained journalists transmit facts laboriously collected from sources in the field may soon be supplanted by online forums and blogs in which communities of individuals share opinions full of emotion but with little regard to careful research. If his view is correct, how will our concepts of 'news' be changed? And how can standards of accuracy be maintained? Finally, will new forms of journalism have advantages over traditional forms? The outcome remains to be seen.

Newspapers aren't dead yet, however; *USA Today* and the *Wall Street Journal*, for example, are still thriving. While we wait to see what happens in the future, let's look at the traditional functions and formats that have made newspapers an important source of detailed information since the early 1800s.[32]

In addition to providing news in more depth than is possible through radio or television, newspapers provide other uses and gratifications. Reading is, in part, a routine way to pass time during transitional periods; because newspaper reading is seen as a useful activity, it allows us to take a break without appearing lazy. Newspaper reading is also a way to search out mundane information; people look to see what's on sale at the local department store or what's playing at the nearest movie

---

Table 11.3 Media Formats and Logics: Media Uses and Effects of Media Logics

Newspapers
- *Used to:* pass time, find mundane information, keep in touch with events, identify self as reader
- *Formats encourage:* focus on single events, avoidance of detail, interest in crises and dramatic events

Magazines
- *Used to:* pass time, find detailed information, gain access to valued subgroups
- *Formats encourage:* knowledge of detail, identity-related knowledge, unrealistic expectations, pressures to consume

Radio
- *Used to:* pass time, find mundane information, regulate moods, ease loneliness
- *Formats encourage:* conservatism, apathy, venting of emotion (through talk radio)

Television
- *Used to:* pass time, provide companionship, keep in touch with events, relax, find escapist entertainment
- *Formats encourage:* impatience with long or detailed material, interest in dramatic material, belief in ideal norms, dismissal of news that is not visually compelling

theater. As much as 60 percent of a newspaper may be devoted to ads. Readers don't complain, because the ads provide them with needed information.

Reading the paper is also a way of keeping informed on important news of the day, a way of taking advantage of the surveillance function that the press provides. People expect the press to act as watchdogs, and readership is especially strong when the community or nation is threatened by a crisis. Finally, reading a newspaper is an act of self-definition. When a reader opens the paper on the bus or in a local coffee shop, he or she sends the message "I am the kind of person who reads a newspaper."[33] So strong is this perception that one of the major goals of adults in literacy programs is to be able to read a paper in public.

Until recently, newspapers have taken the form of "hard copy." Information is laid out in two-dimensional space, and a variety of stories simultaneously compete for readers' attention. Readers skim the pages and select the items they find most useful or most appealing. News stories are typically written so that the most essential information appears in the first few paragraphs, leaving development to final paragraphs. This structure allows editors to cut a story from the end and readers to stop reading at any point without losing the most important information.

Newspaper format encourages certain kinds of communication: a focus on isolated events, a tendency to omit detailed analysis, and a temptation to focus on the unusual and the dramatic. The fact that the first paragraph of a news story must sum up the entire story leads to a focus on single events, and who, when, where, and what become more important than why. Coupled with the value placed on objective reporting, news stories tend to focus on concrete details that can be easily measured and counted: the size of a crowd, the number of days hostages have been held, the cost of a new bomber. News stories are less likely to explore why the crowd assembled, what sociopolitical factors led to the hostage taking, or whether the new bomber is needed.

In addition to providing a focus on events, newspaper stories search out the unusual and the dramatic. Although newspapers are designed to fulfill surveillance and correlation functions, they can't succeed unless they incorporate some level of entertainment as well. As any news reporter can tell you, "Dog Bites Man" is not news, but "Man Bites Dog" is. The more uncommon and sensational an event is, the more likely it will be reported. Reports of accidents and disasters are the most widely read of news stories, followed by reports of crime. As a result, "the world may seem more crime-ridden, conflict-filled, and/or absurd than it is."[34]

Kathleen Hall Jamieson and Karlyn Kohrs Campbell tell us that certain themes are considered especially newsworthy. These themes include (1) appearance versus reality (stories that uncover hypocrisy), (2) "little guys" versus "big guys" (accounts of conflict between the powerless and the powerful), (3) good versus evil (reports of crime and punishment), (4) efficiency versus inefficiency (exposures of waste and mismanagement), and (5) the unique versus the routine (the "Man Bites Dog" effect).[35]

In summary, the logic of newspaper discourse may result in events appearing isolated and separate, background information being overlooked and oversimplified, and crises and threats being exaggerated. The first two of these effects are partially offset by the analyses that appear in the editorial pages of a newspaper. It is here that the correlation function of the media is most evident. Given that TV news items are extremely short and concrete, receivers who want more thoughtful analysis of issues often turn to the print media for explanation and evaluation.

Magazines

The typical magazine is written to attract young, middle-class, reasonably well-educated readers, the people demographic analyses show are heavy purchasers. To make any further generalizations about readers is difficult, however, because magazines tend to specialize. More than do newspapers, magazines speak to and for particular segments of society. With the possible exception of magazines such as *TV Guide*, *Family Circle*, and *People*, which are sporadically read by large segments of the population, most modern magazines orient themselves to specific subgroups within the mass audience. The loyal readers who buy *Seventeen*, *Modern Photography*, *Field and Stream*, or *Heavy Metal*, for example, do so because these magazines understand their interests and identifications.

Magazines have always offered us glimpses into other worlds and images of who we could be.

© Bettmann/CORBIS

Readers may choose to read a magazine for a variety of reasons. Some readers simply use magazines as a means of killing time. Other readers are more involved, choosing a magazine that reflects the groups to which they wish to, or actually do, belong. *Vogue*, for example, appeals to a cosmopolitan, style-conscious, sophisticated female reader who wants to know the latest fashions in both clothing and pop culture. *Sports Illustrated*, on the other hand, is written primarily for male sports fans. In general, the reader of *Vogue* is not the reader of *Sports Illustrated*.

Magazines often provide instructions about how to become a member of a given group. The woman who wants to improve her social standing reads *Vogue* to pick up hints on how to look and act the part. A novice tennis player purchases a tennis magazine in order to improve his or her skills. Robert Snow tells us that specialized magazines show readers how to "act like insiders, how to gain the respect of others already firmly entrenched, how to avoid being gauche, . . . and the emotional sensations that should be felt when one is achieving success."[36] Magazines reflect the norms and values of their readers. Thus *Playboy* legitimates one set of values, and *Ms.* legitimates another.

Magazines can also serve as channels of communication to others. By publicly displaying a magazine, one can send a message about one's tastes and values. A copy of the *New York Review of Books* or the *Advocate* casually tossed on one's coffee table can let visitors know intellectual and personal interests that may become channels for conversation or identification.

Magazines in their paper form are one of the least ephemeral of the mass media. Electronic messages disappear immediately after broadcast (unless they are taped for future reference). Newspapers are quickly discarded. Magazines, however, are kept for several weeks and read intermittently. In layout, they fall halfway between a newspaper and a book. Articles are generally arranged sequentially and are meant to be read all the way through, although the latter part of an article is usually separated from the first part and placed at the end of the magazine. Titles and vivid illustrations are used to catch the reader's attention and to move him or her through the text. In fact, many magazines are as much for looking at as for reading.

The writing style in magazines is more narrative and personalized, often involving the use of first-person narrative. The use of a more direct form of address is in keeping with the identity function that magazines serve for readers. Magazine designers work hard to create a unique style for their magazines. Typestyle, photos, illustrations, and even ads reflect an overall image. The serious, functional, nonflashy format of *U.S. News & World Report* tells the conservative businessperson who reads it, "We are here not to entertain but to inform you." In contrast, *Vanity Fair* celebrates the ephemeral, using a style that is trendy and irreverent and filling its pages with glossy color photos of the rich and famous.

Increasingly, magazines offer readers online Websites that encourage more interactive involvement with content and that, at the same time, encourage readers to subscribe to the hard-copy version. Magazine Websites also often allow readers to shop online.

Magazines can offer us needed information and can provide serious analyses of important problems. They can also pander to voyeurism and can make us miserable by setting up unrealistic expectations. Some magazines are little more than gossip mills, invading the privacy of celebrities and "real people" alike to show us the sordid and the sensational. Images in magazines can also make us discontented with who and what we are. When the models in magazines set up expectations for an unrealistic level of youth or beauty or physical prowess, we may find ourselves pursuing impossible goals.

Radio

Over the years, radio use has changed. In the early days of radio, families gathered together in their living rooms to listen as their favorite serials and soaps unfolded. Radio was a "communal storyteller" as well as a source of information and musical entertainment.[37] Now, most listening occurs outside the home. Today, radio is a kind of "portable friend" that helps us through the day by giving us useful information, matching our moods, and keeping us company. Radio is a comforting presence that we rely on more than we imagine, as Altheide and Snow suggest:

> *Ask yourself if you can wash the car, clean house, study or read, or engage in a myriad of other activities without background radio noise. In these instances, radio is an integral part of the flow of the event. Indeed, without radio, some activity . . . would become awkward at best, and perhaps impossible.*[38]

Radio keeps people in touch with the world. In the words of a respondent interviewed in the early 1960s, "To me when the radio is off, the house is empty. There is no life without the radio being on."[39] Radio communication has a strong interpersonal dimension. Not only does the music and talk provide a quasi-social interaction for lonely people, but also "radio binds people together through common shared experiences and provides subjects to talk about with others."[40] It can link people within a given subculture, validating their group identity.

Not only is radio a companion, it is a companion who shares our identity, understands our moods, and makes few demands on our attention. Radio stations work hard to create a personal identity that audience members will accept and find attractive. Country, Adult Contemporary, Religious, Golden Oldies, Classic and Alternative Rock, Top 50, and Urban Contemporary—all are identities that stations form to establish a relationship with receivers. In addition, each station programs its selections to match audience needs and moods. Thus, wake-up music uses a lively rhythm and a tempo designed to get the audience going, whereas late-night broadcasts air more mellow and more romantic sounds. Even within a given time segment, programmers vary tempo from one selection to the next and, on a Top 40 station, rotate the top ten songs throughout a two- or three-hour period. Thus, the radio listener knows with a high degree of precision what he or she will be getting by tuning in.

Although a large part of radio content consists of musical selections, talk radio is also popular. Talk radio is an excellent example of the quasi-interpersonal nature of radio. Talk hosts interact with listeners, creating a forum for the exchange of ideas. Altheide and Snow predict that "as urban life becomes more privatized and socially fragmented, talk radio will function both as an opportunity for vicarious and overt participation and as a source of information on issues."[41]

In many ways, radio is the most local and "demassified" of the mass media. Like magazines, radio stations tend to be specialized, catering to particular subcultures within a community. Because of this, the accusations of undue sociopolitical influence that are often leveled at the more "mass" of the mass media have not been made against radio. Perhaps the most serious charge leveled at radio is that it is conservative and uncommitted. "By creating the impression of abundance and unlimited fun, listeners may be encouraged to stand pat and go on blithely ignoring issues and controversies that are critical in the long run."[42]

© Bettmann/CORBIS

When television first appeared, people were both fascinated and a bit fearful.

Television

In terms of audience penetration, "television is the *most mass* of all the mass media."[43] Despite earlier predictions that the Internet would rapidly surpass television in popularity, TV is still the medium of choice for most Americans.

Television fulfills many functions for its viewers. Like newspapers, it provides local and national news (although the amount and type of news provided are characteristics unique to the medium). Like magazines and films, it gives viewers a glimpse into alternative worlds, and, like radio, it provides companionship. Like many other media, television teaches and socializes, although critics sometimes bemoan its content. Finally, television serves as the most popular medium for relaxation and escapist entertainment. Watching TV has become such a habit that viewers often sit through programs they don't like rather than turning off the set. When television reception is knocked out, viewers feel anxious and at loose ends, so accustomed are they to TV as background noise. In a 1992 survey reported in the October 10–16 issue of *TV Guide*, viewers were asked, "Would you take a million dollars to stop watching TV forever?" The answer for large segments of those surveyed was a resounding "No!"

> Despite earlier predictions that the Internet would rapidly surpass television in popularity, TV is still the medium of choice for most Americans.

Because television is both auditory and visual, it (along with film) is the most perceptually compelling of all the media. Although sound is an important aspect of television, music and dialogue are often subordinated to visual information. Television is something we watch more than listen to. Television images are in constant motion, and a fundamental part of the logic of TV is a valuation of movement and change. Television has given us an appetite for highly arousing visual stimuli.

> Television images are in constant motion, and a fundamental part of the logic of TV is a valuation of movement and change. Television has given us an appetite for highly arousing visual stimuli.

Television has also accustomed us to time compression. Shows that move slowly (such as annual awards shows) are generally criticized. The more rapid the tempo, the better received a program is.[44] In both entertainment and news programming, we expect unnecessary details to be edited out, so that a story about a week in the life of a character happens in half an hour, and the gist of an hour-long speech is summarized in a ten-second "sound bite."

Another defining characteristic of television is that it is a very intimate medium. The most frequent shots are medium close-ups and close-ups that personalize the audience–actor relationship.[45] This means that television encourages psychological identification. When we turn on the set, we want to identify with the characters and personalities we see. The fact that we view television in our homes rather than in more public spaces further emphasizes how personal our relationship is to this medium.

Entertainment Programming.   In his discussion of the logic of television, Snow remarks on three features of television programming: speed and simplicity, a tendency to dramatize material, and a need to stay within the bounds of ideal norms. We'll look at how these work, first in entertainment programs and then in news programs.

It's important to remember that television is a business. Advertisers pay networks in an effort to gain substantial numbers of consumers. Every successful program must seize audience attention and hold it through the commercials. As viewers flip through the channels, a given show must be vivid enough to make them pause. The show must be simple enough that viewers can understand its premise immediately (even if they tune in halfway through the program), and it must be compelling enough to get viewers to stay tuned over commercial breaks. These factors affect the language of television.

Simplicity and brevity are important aspects of television discourse. Most programs have little time for detailed character or plot development. As a result, characters are stereotyped, and plots follow a simple beginning–middle–end structure. Situation comedies, for example, are organized around a simple problem or conflict that is inevitably resolved by the end of the show. Dialogue is written to ensure that viewers know exactly what is going on. Whereas in real life, a person might say, "Oh, there's Doug," a character on a TV soap says, "Look, there's Doug, Marcia's former husband who was falsely accused of the murder of old Doc Tyler and who's just been released from prison." Vocabulary must be simple and must convey plot intricacies instantly.

Extreme and dramatic situations are also a popular part of the logic of television entertainment. Characters are bigger than life, their lives more exciting or humorous or glamorous than ours. From the title to the final resolution, a show must maintain audience interest. In 1981, TV executive Ben Stein claimed that made-for-TV movie titles "must have sex, love, but especially human abuse. Human abuse works far better than sex. Sex can scare off people over 50. But roll it with abuse and you get everyone."[46] Other executives agreed that movies about love, sex, rape, or terror were surefire winners. Now, twenty years later, the principle remains the same. Just look through television listings during any sweeps week.

> Television producers can have it both ways: they can justify depiction of lurid and often ludicrous situations as long as these situations are placed in a moralistic frame. Television can titillate while remaining the most conservative of the major media.

The tendency to sensationalize material seems, at first glance, to contradict another important aspect of television content: reference to **ideal norms**. According to Snow, ideal norms are "the tradition of hard work, honesty, modesty, fidelity, and so on, which everyone upholds in principle."[47] A program such as the "Miss America Pageant" embodies the values of youth, feminine beauty, and love of God and country.

How do the sensational topics shown in TV movies fit in? The answer is that the resolution of sensational material always follows ideal norms: the rapist is punished, the drug user completes rehabilitation, the terrorist falls off a twenty-story building. The characters who commit crimes are evil, and the characters who solve crimes are noble. Television producers can have it both ways: they can justify depiction of lurid and often ludicrous situations as long as these situations are placed in a moralistic frame. Television can titillate while remaining the most conservative of the major media.

News Programming.   The values that inform entertainment programming can be found in nonentertainment shows as well. A perfect illustration is television news. A successful broadcast news item is brief, visually compelling, dramatic, and moralistic.

First, news reports are kept as short as possible—seldom longer than thirty seconds and usually about fifteen seconds long. In a fifteen-minute news broadcast, about twenty-five stories are told in about eighteen hundred words. Compare this figure to the one hundred thousand words found in an average daily newspaper, and you will see that television news skims the surface of events.[48] That this brevity leaves little time for detailed analysis or carefully explained background doesn't seem to bother news producers, whose concern is to keep viewers' attention throughout the newscast. Television executives assume that the average viewer is incapable of attending to a topic for long and that he or she will tune out if not kept constantly amused by slick production values—catchy theme music, colorful sets, reporters' happy talk, and the like.

Television news must also be highly visual, and a program usually leads off with the most visually interesting story. Thus, a fire may take precedence over a presidential press conference. Reporters and their subjects often go to unusual lengths to provide visuals. A reporter delivers news about the presidency while standing in the snow in front of the White House rather than sitting in the comfort of the studio, simply because location reporting is visually more interesting. A political candidate may announce a bid for a Senate seat while standing in front of Mount Rushmore, because doing so sends a visually symbolic message. During the war in Iraq, not only did reports from the field present dramatic visuals, but also specially designed graphics were used to lead into coverage, giving the war the look of a slickly produced action-adventure show.

> Although it is tempting to believe that all reporting is governed by the norm of objectivity and that events can be separated from values, this is usually not true.

Television reporters, like newspaper reporters, seek out the most dramatic stories they can find. The more unusual, conflict-filled, or violent a story, the more likely it is to be covered. Reuven Frank, former president of NBC News, has said, "Every news story should, without any sacrifice of probity or responsibility, display the attributes of fiction, of drama. It should have structure and conflict, problem and denouement, rising action and falling action, a beginning, middle, and an end."[49]

Although it is tempting to believe that all reporting is governed by the norm of objectivity and that events can be separated from values, this is usually not true. Media gatekeepers decide what is news and what is not and, in choosing what to report, tend to follow ideal norms. Driven by the need to create stories filled with conflict, reporters inevitably build their stories about "good guys" and "bad guys." International conflicts involving the United States are particularly open to oversimplified, "us-versus-them" reporting.

The Pervasiveness of TV Logic. In both entertainment and nonentertainment formats, television provides us with important services. It entertains, educates, and informs us. It can, however, be criticized on a number of levels. Perhaps the greatest criticism is that TV makes us want our everyday experience to come in short, vivid, entertaining form. According to an article in the *Los Angeles Times*, lawyers have had to change their style of presentation to more closely resemble a television courtroom scene. Some lawyers now call their strongest witnesses first and make their points in a rapid, dramatic way.[50] Members of the television generation are impatient with slow-moving events; with serious, detailed analyses of news events; and with narratives that deal with complex issues or personalities.

Television invites us into alternative realities. Unfortunately, these realities are seldom trustworthy. It oversimplifies, glamorizes, and sensationalizes everyday life. Some people buy into the glamorous lifestyles that they see, and they come to identify so strongly with favorite characters that they have difficulty separating fact from illusion. Soap opera actors frequently receive fan mail addressed to their on-screen personas.

Although most of us are not mesmerized by television to such a degree, we do regard media figures as role models. Children, especially, often take what they see quite literally. Joshua Meyerowitz has pointed out that one of the effects of television is to "obliterate childhood" by letting children see adult behavior that is otherwise kept from them and by showing children how to act like adults.[51] Children may also come to expect the adults in their world to act like those on TV. Today, when a young child can turn to her mother and ask, "Mommy, why can't you be like those ladies in the Pepsi commercial?" we have clear evidence that media images and values can affect everyday relationships.[52]

Another potential danger of television is the power of the visual image. When we see a picture of something, we assume that it is an objective representation of that thing. The fact that camera angle, shot composition, and the like might bias a perception seldom occurs to us. The possibility that people might be using the media to legitimate questionable causes is often ignored. One of the potential dangers of television is that we come to believe what we see on it.

NEW MEDIA: GOING GLOBAL AND MOBILE

Nowadays, we can communicate quickly and easily through networked computers and over cell phones. Most of us use these media in quite ordinary ways: to chat with friends, look up information, or make appointments. But some of the time, the new media are used in extraordinary ways. Consider the following examples.

In 2001, a young woman found herself stranded at sea off the coast of Bali. As her boat started to sink, she sent her boyfriend in England a text message asking for help, and he in turn contacted the U.K. coastguard, who made arrangements for an Indonesian gunboat to come to her aid.[53] The new media can, quite literally, be lifelines.

In the Muslim Middle East, one can order a phone with a compass that points toward Mecca and an alarm to signal prayer time. In some Christian countries, subscribers can sign up for daily text messages from the Pope and can even have the entire Bible downloaded to their cell phones, although the verses are written in text-message shorthand.[54] New media are being adapted to every aspect of our lives.

Of course, in addition to making life easier, new media can be used in tragically negative ways. A case in point occurred in 2010 when Tyler Clementi, a Rutgers freshman, committed suicide after discovering his roommate had used his Webcam to record Clementi's intimate encounter with another man, tweeted about it, and then shared the video with other students. In 2012, the roommate, Dharun Ravi, stood trial for invasion of privacy and bias intimidation, a hate crime. Cyberbullying is a real and significant problem.

Another use of new media is the habit, popular among some teens, of *sexting*, using their cell phones to send nude pictures of themselves to others.[55] A nationwide survey conducted in 2009 revealed that one in twenty teens have used their phones in this way without realizing that it is against the law. In some areas of the country, officials have begun to prosecute participants, arresting them on child pornography charges. Whether or not you believe these photos are actually pornographic, they can certainly cause embarrassment, because the photos are often widely circulated, sometimes out of spite. Whereas most people believe that what they text or email is private, a moment's thought should show that is not the case. The new media raise important questions of privacy.

Finally, to offer another example, a man in Dubai sent his wife, who was late to meet him, a text message that read: "Why are you late? You are divorced." A court later ruled that the divorce was valid.[56] These are just a few examples of the recent (and sometimes dismaying) ways in which individuals are adapting new media to meet their needs. As the new media become more accessible and powerful, people will undoubtedly think of even more unusual ways to integrate them into their lives.

In this section, we look at networked computing and mobile telecommunications, two of the most recent kinds of communication media. However, as we think about these communication technologies, we should keep in mind that they did not spring up overnight. New media are extensions of old media, and in the future, the personal computers and cell phones we use today will seem remarkably antiquated and will almost certainly have been revised, replaced, or reinvented.

Characteristics of New Media

Although cell phones and the Internet have been around for many years now, they are still considered

New media are extensions of old media, and in the future, the personal computers and cell phones we use today will seem remarkably antiquated and will almost certainly have been revised, replaced, or reinvented.

new media, in part because they have characteristics that distinguish them from more traditional forms of mediated communication.[57] Because new media employ digital technology, it is now relatively easy to combine words, images, and sound in a single format. Digitization gives media consumers more control and freedom than they had in the past. It allows new patterns of access and offers greater possibilities for interactivity and more access to information. Unfortunately, it can also lead to audience fragmentation and can erode privacy. Let's look at each of these characteristics in turn.

Digitization

As technology expert Nicholas Negroponte pointed out, new media are based on the "transmission of digital bits rather than physical atoms."[58] Think for a minute about the difference between snail-mail and email. Once upon a time, writing a letter to a friend overseas was a lengthy and laborious process. The message would have to be physically moved through space, and an overseas letter might take anywhere from a week to several months to get to the addressee. Now sending a message overseas is a much quicker process. When we type a greeting into our computer and hit the send key, the message is converted into digital bits that are processed almost instantaneously. Through the process of **digitization**, messages are converted into computer-readable electrical signals (or bits) that can be quickly processed, efficiently stored, and cheaply transmitted.

Multimedia Capability

One of the important benefits of digitization is the ability to easily combine different kinds of information—images, sounds, and words—in a single format. Of course, traditional media did some of this. Newspapers mixed written words and photos, and television merged images and sound. But digital technology allows us to combine diverse forms of information in very sophisticated ways. Any good Website will blend visuals and text, and most will provide access to video and audio content. To a generation raised with computers, it is hard to believe that people once lived in a world where combining media in sophisticated ways was difficult and, in some cases, impossible. Now our expectations about the use of multimedia are so great

One of the important benefits of digitization is the ability to easily combine different kinds of information—images, sounds, and words—in a single format.

that we often lose patience with messages that rely on only one kind of input. To be successful today, communicators must master computer technology and be able to create compelling multimedia presentations.

New Modes of Consumption

Digitization has not only transformed *what* information we experience but also *how* we experience that information. Once upon a time, in the not so distant past, if you wanted to make sure you didn't miss your favorite TV show, you stayed home the night it was broadcast. And before the advent of answering machines, cell phones, and text messaging, if you wanted to get in touch with a friend, you had to make sure he or she was near the (landline) phone to receive your call. Many new media messages are *asynchronous*, that is, receiver and sender do not have to be present at the same time in order to communicate. This means that you can contact friends at any time of day or night simply by texting or leaving a voice-mail or email message. It also means that

Time and space no longer act as barriers to communication and media receivers can set their own schedules.

you can consume traditional media messages when and where you want to. If you're busy when that TV show you want to see comes on, it's really not a problem. You can record it, view it whenever you want, rewind to see the parts you like again, bypass the boring bits, and even fast-forward through the commercials. Time and space no longer act as barriers to communication and media receivers can set their own schedules.

Interactivity

Recent computer applications have made it much easier for media users to become media producers. As a consequence, there is now a "more direct, interactive, and participative use" of computer-mediated communication than ever before.[59] On social networking sites like Facebook we can easily connect with others and share opinions; on Amazon.com we can rate and review products; on Wikipedia we can collaboratively edit information; and on community Websites like Second Life we can even construct virtual worlds. When we're not blogging or twittering, we can be remixing music, modding game content (using tools provided by game companies to design additional levels in game worlds), or creating short films for YouTube. This newfound ability to collaborate in the production of media content is often referred to as **Web 2.0**. This term refers more to the "explosion of creative and collaborative activity" that has occurred as a result of technical breakthroughs rather than to the breakthroughs themselves.[60] Admittedly, many of the traditional mass media have allowed some degree of audience involvement (think community TV stations and call-in radio shows), but nowadays the potential for audiences to become active has risen exponentially.

Whereas teenagers constitute the largest group of content creators and sharers, older users are also going online to blog, to publish photos or artwork, or even to create online profiles on social networking sites. When you log on to Facebook, don't assume everyone is your own age. Both MySpace and Facebook have several million users over the age of sixty-five. Says one eighty-eight-year-old grandfather, "I don't browse Facebook much, but I see that it is a way to get to the nitty-gritty of a person's character. Also [it's] a way to do something late at night when I can't sleep." So next time you post a photo or create a profile, be aware that your grandparents may be browsing your Facebook page.[61]

As we've seen in previous chapters, the new media allow interpersonal self-presentation, enable groups to work together online, and make it possible for organizations to harness the collective intelligence of globally dispersed members. The new media are also taking an increasingly important role in politics. During the 2008 election campaign, for example, 46 percent of Americans used the Internet to "get news about the campaigns, share their views, and mobilize others."[62] There were large increases in the viewing of online political videos and the use of social networking sites for political activity, with Americans not only going online to learn about the candidates, but also generating their own responses and promoting their own views. Campaigns have taken advantage of this activity by publishing talking points about their own and opposing candidates, "to give the public a tool kit they could use . . . in their conversations with friends and neighbors."[63]

Businesses and complex organizations are recognizing the advantages of connecting themselves with new media. Even the U.S. Army has gotten into the act. Recognizing that young Americans unfamiliar with the Army were unlikely to enlist, they developed an MMOG (massively multiplayer online game) called America's Army that allowed players to experience virtual military missions while exposing them to military values. Did it work? A 2004 marketing survey asked pro-military students the source of their favorable opinions. Nearly 30 percent cited their experiences playing America's Army.[64]

Interactivity is not without its perils. The online encyclopedia Wikipedia, for example, allows users to log on and add or edit existing entries. As the site explains, "Lots of people are constantly improving *Wikipedia*, making thousands of changes an hour, all of which are recorded on article histories and recent changes. Inappropriate changes are usually removed quickly, and repeat offenders can be blocked."[65]

Although the idea of a site that anyone can edit is appealing, it can also be open to abuse. In 2005, for example, a contributor anonymously posted false information in the biography of respected journalist John Seigenthaler Sr. The bogus information suggested that Seigenthaler had been involved in the assassinations of both John F. and Robert F. Kennedy and had lived in the Soviet Union for many years. The hoax began as a joke but soon got out of hand. For several months, the libelous entry stood until a friend of Seigenthaler discovered it.

Many, including Seigenthaler himself, were incensed. Clearly the new media have advantages. They expand our ability to share information and opinions in ways past generations could not have imagined. But equally clearly, they offer the prospect for abuse. The Seigenthaler case is but one example of the misuse and exploitation offered by sources like Wikipedia. When anyone can publish what they want to, it is likely that some of what is said will be distorted. Although it would be nice to believe that whatever we find out on the Internet is true, it obviously isn't. Internet sources, Wikipedia included, can be useful resources as well as forums for what is little more than informational graffiti. [66]

Access to Information

The new media have given us access to an unprecedented amount of information—good and bad. It's been many years since students with research assignments have had to trudge through the rain or snow to get to a library. Information is only as far away as their tablets or smartphones. Still, finding the right information is, at times, effortful. And search engines don't always get it right. If, for example, you're interested in finding out information about Ancient Greece and you input the keyword *Odyssey*, you're as likely to get Websites on the automobile or the program for gifted children as for the works of Homer. A solution to that problem is being developed right now: it's called **Web 3.0** and it promises to do away with time-consuming keyword searches. Instead, according to Web 3.0 developers, your browser will learn what you are interested in and do the work for you. Of course, whether we actually want our browsers to know that much about us and how we can stop them from sharing that information with others remains to be seen.

User Choice and Audience Fragmentation

New media offer users greater freedom of choice. In previous times, media gatekeepers chose what the public read, saw, and heard. Now audience members can actively search for the content they want, choosing to expose themselves only to ideas that match their values and interests. Although this situation gives receivers a great deal of freedom, it may have an unintended result: **audience fragmentation**. Audience fragmentation (or **demassification**, as it is sometimes called) refers to the fact that rather than being part of a single mass audience, people are now becoming members of separate, specialized audiences. As a consequence, they may no longer be exposed to information that could widen their knowledge, challenge their views, or create common ground with people who think differently. Some critics feel that as the people gain more control over what they see or hear, they will no longer be concerned with broad social issues.

> Some critics feel that as the people gain more control over what they see or hear, they will no longer be concerned with broad social issues.

Increased Surveillance

In earlier times, audiences were large and heterogeneous and, therefore, relatively anonymous. Media producers tried their best to gather information about audience members, but they often had to fall back on guesswork. And although skilled audience researchers could tell a lot about receivers, they had nowhere near the amount of knowledge that is available today. The technology that makes it easy for you to communicate by email or cell phone also makes it easy for large commercial or governmental organizations to monitor and predict your behavior. The use of intelligent software programs that gather consumer data and the presence of cookies (stored bits of data that allow Websites to authenticate user identity and track online choices) on computers mean that very little that goes on online is private. And the GPS devices that are so useful when you want to use your cell phone to get directions to the nearest restaurant also mean that your presence can be constantly tracked, even when your phone is off.

> **The technology that makes it easy for you to communicate by email or cell phone also makes it easy for large commercial or governmental organizations to monitor and predict your behavior.**

Computers can also automatically "compile dossiers about individuals by piecing together countless tiny, otherwise harmless shards of information about transactions, medical conditions, buying habits, and demographic characteristics."[67] What are the results of living in a world where it is becoming difficult, if not impossible, to remain anonymous? Many critics, following the lead of philosopher Michel Foucault, fear that the presence of constant surveillance may make people more passive, willing to accept "regulations and docility as part of the way every 'normal' person thinks and behaves."[68]

CMC: Computer-Mediated Communication

In the last decades of the twentieth century, the Internet became the newest mass medium, opening up a world of computer-mediated communication that has revolutionized the way we live our lives. Its movement from invention to popular phenomenon has been faster than that of any other medium to date. Ray Hiebert and Sheila Gibbons tell us that books took nearly 400 years to transform themselves from a curiosity for the elite to a mass medium. Newspapers took 200 years, while magazines required about 170 years. Sound recordings achieved mass popularity in about 60 years, movies in about 50, radio in about 40, and television in about 30 years. The Internet took even less time—about 15 years. In the early 1970s, the Internet, then called the ARPAnet, was a little-known network designed to link government computers so that scientists could exchange research data. By the mid-1990s, it was being used by millions of ordinary citizens around the world.[69] And Facebook, which launched in 2005, reported in 2012 having eight hundred million plus users.[70]

By now, we use it "for almost any human activity you can imagine, from shopping to sex, from research to rebellion."[71] We use it to talk with family and friends, colleagues, and even animals. Koko, the mountain gorilla who has learned to use American Sign Language, has actually participated in live Internet chats. On Earth Day 1998, as her trainer Penny Patterson translated and an assistant typed in Koko's thoughts, Koko expounded on such topics as "motherhood, pets, food preferences, friendship, love, and the future."[72]

How Do People Use the Internet?

Earlier, we looked at uses and gratifications research as it applied to media in general and television in particular. It's time now to look at the ways in which people use computer-mediated communication.

The popularity of Internet communication has increased dramatically over the years. A 2009 survey found that teens and members of Generation Y (those born between 1977 and 1990) use the Internet primarily for entertainment and social networking. They are much more likely than older users to look at online videos, play online games, visit virtual worlds, and download music. They are also more likely to keep in touch with others by writing and reading blogs and by logging on to social networking sites. Older generations use the Internet less for socializing and entertainment and more for seeking information, emailing, and shopping. Video downloads, online travel reservations, and work-related research, however, are pursued equally by both young and old.[73]

What general social functions does communication over the Internet fulfill? Hiebert and Gibbons discuss five in addition to *education*.[74] First, the Internet offers us *news and information*; most major newspapers now have online versions of their papers, including easily searched archives of articles in previous issues. Second, the Internet also serves as a site for *opinion, gossip, and rumor*; whether this function works to democratize information or to degrade is a debatable issue. Certainly, on the Internet, people are free to disseminate all kinds of ideas. In fact, if you want to see the variety available, log on to one of the alt.aliens newsgroups on Usenet. A third function of the Internet is to deliver *entertainment*. A fourth function is *advertising* products, a function that is abundantly clear to anyone who has been spammed (and I don't know anyone who hasn't). Finally, a fifth function is to affect public opinion by serving as a conduit for *public relations* messages. In general, these five functions seem similar to those of other media, although the depth of involvement and amount of interactivity seem to go well beyond those in traditional media.

The Social Impact of Social Network Sites

Whenever a new technology appears, it causes anxiety. As David Buckingham, an expert on the effects of media on children, points out, "new technology is often invested with our most intense fantasies and fears. It holds out the promise of a better future, while simultaneously provoking anxieties about a fundamental break with the past."[75] In the 1950s and 1960s, for example, when television was gaining hold, it was seen "both as a new way of bringing the family together, and as something which would undermine natural family interaction."[76] The same kind of fear has been attached to computer-mediated communication. Experts have worried about everything from physical damage (development of "Nintendo elbow" or epileptic seizures caused by computer games) and behavioral aberration (imitative violence, involvement with hate sites, or addiction to pornography). But the fear that has most captured the public's attention is the fear that individuals who use computers will become isolated, abandoning face-to-face interaction in favor of life lived in cyberspace and replacing the strong ties that exist between people in face-to-face relationships with the weak ties that connect people who have never actually met. The more time individuals spends on the Internet, it was argued, the less time they would be able or willing to devote to social interaction.

Although some early research did, indeed, find a negative relationship between sociability and Internet use, most of this work was done when using the Internet was an individual activity like watching TV. Once social network sites transformed Internet use into a form of social engagement, a different picture emerged. Although the inventors of networked computing had assumed that it would be used for file sharing rather than interpersonal interaction, Internet communication has played out as fundamentally social. Due, in large part, to the burgeoning of social network sites, Internet users, far from being social isolates, tend to use computer-mediated communication to support face-to-face relationships as well as to activate ties with casual acquaintances, and (less frequently) to initiate connections with strangers.[77]

Some theorists even suggest that online social participation can encourage a more open expression of one's feelings and thereby deepen friendships. An interesting offshoot of research on computer-mediated communication is that online connections such as email appear to have increased users' interest in letter-writing. Because letters slow communication down, "thus giving people more time to process their feelings, to put a greater effort into understanding others' expectations and to thinking in depth before they respond,"[78] Internet use may actually increase our ability to form rewarding relationships.

Recent studies have shown connections between Internet-mediated communication and a number of other positive social variables including social trust, civic engagement, and political participation. Today, the Internet is viewed as an important source of **social capital**,[79] a term that refers to the resources and advantages that occur from participating in social networks. Social capital accrues whenever members of social networks offer each other support, band together to get things done, or exchange information about their own areas of expertise. Many researchers now argue that the Internet, primarily through social network sites, creates social capital in two ways. It can strengthen the bonds between similar people who may then offer each other support and encouragement (*bonding capital*). It can also serve as a bridge to connect people who are different and who can offer each other new ideas and experiences (*bridging capital*). In both cases members of social networks benefit from their ties with others.

Some social critics have even argued that online virtual worlds like Second Life can actually serve as "third places," locations other than the home or workplace where people can congregate and interact socially as they do in offline brick-and-mortar neighborhood pubs or coffee shops. Although these cyberlocations do not provide deep emotional involvement, some argue that they "expose the individual to a diversity of worldviews." Role-playing and online gaming, some suggest, allow "individual and collaborative problem solving, identity construction, apprenticeship, and literacy practices."[80]

> **Although the inventors of networked computing assumed that it would be used for file sharing rather than interpersonal interaction, Internet communication has played out as fundamentally social.**

Cognition in a Hyperconnected World

As we've already seen, the Internet has widened our circle of friends and increased our store of information. Making connections of all kinds is easier and more convenient than ever. But are there other less obvious effects? Could the Internet be changing our minds? Many people think so. In this section we offer some speculations about the effects of Internet communication on our lives. First, we'll look at a survey conducted in 2011 by the Pew Research Center, a survey that asked experts to predict the effects on young people of growing up constantly connected to each other and the Web. Next, we'll review some research on how living in a wired world is affecting our thought processes. Finally, we'll offer some experts' views on the skills it will take to be successful in the future.

Speculating about the future effects of technology is, of course, a risky business. As we've seen, the uses of technology seldom match what their inventors envisioned, and the fears attached to new modes of communication are never completely realized. Nevertheless, thinking about the future is a worthwhile enterprise if it focuses us on the inevitability of change. Experts may not always be able to predict changes with complete accuracy, but there will definitely be changes.

Between the end of August and the end of October 2011, the Pew Research Center's Internet & American Life Project asked several thousand experts and stakeholders to look forward to the year 2020 and describe what young people's lives would be like. Responses were evenly divided between positive and negative predictions. On the positive side, a significant number of people believe that young people will be "nimble, quick-acting multitaskers," able to solve problems quickly by accessing collective intelligence via the Internet. On the negative side, respondents feared that young people would become accustomed "to a diet of quick-fix information nuggets" rather than deep and critical analysis of issues, and that they would be less patient and more dependent on instant gratification.[81]

One idea that emerged frequently in the Pew survey was the idea that the Internet is "rewiring" our minds. In *The Shallows: What the Internet Is Doing to Our Brains*, Nicholas Carr presents a convincing argument that the Internet is, indeed, changing the way we think. He cites research that shows the brain is extremely plastic and malleable. As the brain is given new tasks, it molds itself to accomplish those tasks, essentially reshaping itself. For example, a study of London cabdrivers found that the longer they had driven, the larger was the portion of their brains that handles spatial relationships and the smaller that portion that handles other memory tasks. Similarly as someone learns Braille, the part of the brain that is used to process visual stimuli begins to process information delivered through touch. And in people who experience profound loss of hearing and who can no longer overhear chance conversations, the part of the brain that governs peripheral vision grows stronger. In other words, the activities we habitually engage in can actually reform the architecture of our brains. And going online is one of those activities.[82]

How are our brains being changed? Carr answers that "Dozens of studies by psychologists, neurobiologists, educators, and Web designers point to the same conclusion: When we go online, we enter an environment that promotes cursory reading, hurried and distracted thinking, and superficial learning."[83] Although Internet use makes us better at skimming, scanning, and browsing and increases our hand-eye coordination, reflex response, and ability to process visual data, it also makes us less able to stay focused on a single source for very long. We can get to information more quickly, but we don't stay with it. Instead of reading, we "power browse."[84] Search engines encourage us to look at a small part of a document (the highlighted section) rather than read the whole.[85] In Carr's words, "We don't see the forest when we search the Web. We don't even see the trees. We see twigs and leaves."[86]

Websites as a Form of Communication

More and more of us are developing personal Websites. Whether the world needs any more Websites eating up bandwidth is debatable, but for now, they are an "inexpensive way to create an impression, polish your online persona, and tell the world something about yourself and your interests." By including photos, creative essays, poetry, and/or artwork, we can create an ideal self. By adding navigation links to our own favorite Websites, we can show off our interests and tastes.[87]

All of this assumes, of course, that our Websites are well designed and contain something interesting for others to view. This is not always the case for either personal or commercial sites. Jack Davis and Susan Merritt offer five design tips.[88] They believe that a well-designed Website is clear, visually and conceptually consistent, and uncluttered; uses contrast to make elements stand out; and employs cinematic techniques of storytelling such as personalization and emphasis on showing rather than describing. Other designers stress ease and simplicity.[89] Most designers warn against using graphics that take too long to load because people lose patience after ten or fifteen seconds. Jacob Nielsen and Marie Takir, for example, point out that the home page (especially the commercial home page) is like a lobby through which people pass on their way to somewhere else. People who enter the site want to get to the information they are seeking, not linger on the home page. Nielsen and Takir stress that "web design is interaction design" and urge designers to invest more time and effort in thinking about usability rather than decorative elements.[90]

If you decide to create a Web page, you should include certain elements. In addition to interesting and useful content, you will want to incorporate an attractive title at the top of the page that encourages visitors to scroll down, a clear site menu that tells visitors what you have to offer, useful navigation links that don't inadvertently strand your visitors in some remote outpost of cyberspace, and a way to contact you if they want to send a message. It is also a good idea to have some way to indicate new content, to give the date on which the site was last updated, and to provide copyright information where appropriate. The basic advice given by most designers is to keep it simple, organized, and clear—the same advice one might give about offline forms of communication.

> For many young people, being without a cell phone amounts to a kind of social death, a fate to be avoided at all costs. To members of "generation txt," having a cell phone is a necessity, not a luxury.

Mobile Telephony

One of the most popular of the new technologies in general use today is the mobile or cellular phone. For many young people, being without a cell phone amounts to a kind of social death, a fate to be avoided at all costs. To members of "generation txt," having a cell phone is a necessity, not a luxury. So pervasive is the cell phone today, that "many urban song birds have become adept at impersonating mobile tones and melodies."[91]

Uses and Gratifications

Mobile phones are an affordable, highly transportable way to stay in touch with friends and family. As Crispin Thurlow expresses it, "perhaps even more so than the telephone, the mobile phone and text-messaging are 'technologies of sociability.'"[92] In addition to their social functions, cell phones can be used to send and retrieve networked information. Many of today's cell phones have as much computing power as the largest and most expensive computers did only a generation ago.[93] Cell phones are not simply movable landlines. They have taken the networked computer and made it mobile. No longer is it necessary to be chained to one's desktop to retrieve information and send messages. Now access to the Internet is available anytime, anywhere.

Mobile technology, when coupled with short messaging service (SMS) technology, has yielded some highly inventive applications. For example, demonstrators in a number of countries, including the United States, have used their cell phones to organize and coordinate political protests. In Sweden, roving gamers, who have created and armed "bots," receive SMS messages about the geographic location of other players. When they get within range, they can shoot, and if their "weapons" are strong enough, they are credited with a "kill" that is posted online. In Japan, similar technology was used for matchmaking. "Lovegety" keychain devices signaled when another compatible Lovegety owner was within fifteen feet; in North America, a similar "Gaydar" device alerted members looking for same-sex matches. In Manhattan, a celebrity watch service makes it possible for fans to send one another sightings of favorite stars.[94] New technologies are also being integrated into traditional activities. During a 2009 performance of a Beethoven symphony at Wolf Trap, the National Symphony Orchestra sent out tweets explaining musical structure and references during the performance. Some symphonies even allow members to vote for encores by cell phone, and churches are encouraging inspirational tweets during services—electronic call and response.[95]

Although they are interesting, these ingenious uses do not constitute the bulk of cellular communication. Most people use their cell phones to communicate with family and friends. In a survey on text messaging done in the United Kingdom, Crispin Thurlow found most messages consisted of "friendship work," for example, apologies, words of support, and thanks. Short greetings were also frequently sent, as were plans for getting together and specific requests for information.[96] Although friendship work can be done face-to-face or through cell conversations, most of it is being done through texts. A survey done by the Pew Research Center in 2011 found that texting was the dominant form of daily communication for teens, with the median teen user sending sixty texts a day. For teens, texting was by far the most popular form of daily communication, followed by speaking on cell phones, face-to-face conversation, social network messaging, instant messaging, talking on landlines, and emailing.[97]

In her book *Alone Together: Why We Expect More from Technology and Less from Each Other*, Sherry Turkle discusses some of the reasons teens prefer texting over talking.[98] The young people she interviewed for her book felt much more anxious when speaking than when texting. They reported that texting allows them time to formulate their thoughts and produce the right impression. It is also less intrusive, as it can be read at a receiver's convenience. Phone calling, on the other hand, makes more demands on both sender and receiver. Callers must devote their full attention to the conversation and respond spontaneously. They must say just the right thing in just the right way and know how to end the call at just the right time.

Texting is a bit easier, although it, too, has its perils, for texts can be saved and passed around. To avoid saying something unfortunate that everyone can read, teens have been known to ask others to compose their messages for them, a modern-day version of *Cyrano de Bergerac*. Usually, however, texting doesn't require a carefully composed complex conversation. It is more often used to share feelings—one's immediate emotional state—than to transmit thought. Even if the entire "conversation," is "I'm so bummed," followed by a responding text of "I'm sorry," teens feel validated.[99]

Social Challenges of Cell Phone Use

Any technology presents social challenges. A cell phone may come with a user's manual that tells you how to operate the device, but social uses have to be figured out on the fly. One challenge of mobile technology is finding oneself in two different places at the same time. Talking to a distraught friend while walking along a busy sidewalk, for example, means negotiating two separate spaces: one physical and one psychological. Another problem comes in trying to allocate attention between the demands of one's copresent friends and one's ringing cell phone. Taking the call may signal to friends that they are unimportant, but not taking the call can lead to anxiety. The ability to handle these kinds of situations is becoming an important social skill.

An interesting effect of cell phone use is a general devaluing of time and a redefinition of what it means to be present. The term **approximeeting** has been used to describe a trend in which plans are made but then remain in flux. For activities that don't require specific time commitments, people often avoid making firm plans. Instead, they make loose arrangements that are forever changing. Thus, it is possible for nights out to be "characterized by endless deferrals and reshufflings of meetings and events which might never occur."[100] To make things worse, people seem to feel that as long as they make contact, they don't actually need to show up in person. Phoning or texting often counts as being there, allowing individuals to get out of dates they really don't want to keep.

If individuals can use cell phone calls to let people know where they are, they can also use such calls to lie about their whereabouts. It has been reported that individuals who are involved in illicit affairs find cell phones a boon, and suspicious spouses often check their partners' mobiles for signs of infidelity.[101] Other deceptive uses include *stage-phoning*, in which someone pretends to be making important calls to impress bystanders, or *phone-shielding*, in which someone pretends to take a call to avoid unwanted interactions.

> A cell phone may come with a user's manual that tells you how to operate the device, but social uses have to be figured out on the fly.

Despite the challenges, most people would not give up their cell phones. In her research on cell phone use, cybertheorist Sadie Plant sums up this feeling:

> *For all their reservations, the vast majority of the many contributors to this research found it impossible to imagine life without the mobile phone. . . . A young Afghan student in Peshawar said, "If I don't have my mobile with me, I feel as though I have lost something. I'm not OK. There's something missing. I turn off the ring tone when I take the bus, or when I'm in the mosque. But I never turn the mobile off."[102]*

As we've seen throughout this chapter, technologies are never used quite the way their inventors intend. Initially, SMS technology was designed for purely commercial purposes. It was soon taken over for social purposes, however, in much the same way that email came to dominate the Internet. The popularity of texting is "yet another example of how the human need for social intercourse—a kind of 'communication imperative'—bends and ultimately co-opts technology to suit its own ends."[103]

Today we are bombarded with media choices. Should we log on to MySpace, follow a celebrity Twitter, spend some time in Second Life, listen to our iPods, check out FriendFeed, surf through YouTube, or maybe just take a nap? It's no wonder some people are experiencing **e-fatigue**, a new term for media overload: "that mild, gnawing nausea that sets in once the marvels of a technology have worn off."[104]

One way to understand e-fatigue is to consider the life cycle of new technologies. According to Gartner, an information technology consulting firm that offers yearly predictions about the potential of new media, public response to a given media product goes through a series of five predictable **hype stages**. In what is called the *technology trigger* stage, people first hear about the new technology and become intrigued. Next, during the *peak of inflated expectations* stage, they are overwhelmed with excitement and unrealistic expectations. When the technology doesn't quite live up to its press, during the *trough of disillusionment* stage, it falls out of favor. At this point, the technology enters the *slope of enlightenment* stage, where people begin to redefine its nature and true worth. Finally, at the *plateau of productivity* state, the technology discovers what it was meant to do and finds its audience, which may be very different from what the developers imagined. As

Linton Weeks explains, "Eventually, people hold on to technologies that enrich their lives and jettison the rest."[105]

CONVERGENCE: THE INTERSECTION OF NEW MEDIA AND OLD

Media, whether new or old, are constantly converging with one another. Although we have looked at computer-mediated communication and mobile telephony separately, anyone with an iPhone or BlackBerry knows they are no longer separate. Media interact with and affect one another. Television, for example, has changed the design of newspapers. *USA Today* is print journalism's attempt to use the language of television, a language characterized by condensed information and visual contrast. Even textbooks are using "multicolored graphics, photos, boxed inserts, bold-faced types, and summaries" to make reading more tolerable for the TV generation, and soon versions for electronic readers may effect even more changes.[106]

When social robots become too real, they can seem uncanny. What is your reaction to this electronic companion?

YOSHIKAZU TSUNO/AFP/Getty Images/Newscom

As digitalization has taken hold in the new media, the traditional media have begun to realize its advantages and are busy converting from their traditional analog (nondigital) form. **Convergence** is the term used to describe this "coming together of computing, telecommunications, and media in a digital environment," as well as to describe the merging of Internet and traditional media companies.[107] Now, for example, TV news channels have their own Websites that can add more detail to a broadcast news item as well as hyperlinks to other sources of information. And entertainment programs can increase interactivity by inviting viewers to log onto connected Websites to chat with celebrities or to offer feedback through their cell phones.

In *Convergence Culture*, author Henry Jenkins provides countless examples of the synergy that exists between the old and new media. *The Matrix*, for example, is more than the three movies most mainstream viewers are aware of. The story continues in a series of comics, a massive multiplayer game set in the world of the Matrix, and a program of short animated films, all of which interconnect. Fans may follow the story across media, and "the consumer who has played the game or watched the shorts will get a different experience of the movies than one who has simply had the theatrical film experience."[108]

In the case of *The Matrix*, the producers actively planned the intersecting storytelling and encouraged collaborative authorship. In other cases, fans take over and produce sequels and related material based on a film or book. Fans of *Star Wars* have made their own movies with names like *George Lucas in Love*, *The Jedi Who Loved Me*, and *Boba Fett: Bounty Trail*.[109] Similarly, the Harry Potter series has encouraged young writers to insert themselves into the world of Hogwarts and write their own stories.

BECOMING A MORE RESPONSIBLE COMMUNICATOR

In this last section of the chapter, we'll look at some of the ethical dilemmas that creators of media messages face, as well as the ethical responsibilities of media consumers.

Ethical Issues for Media Practitioners

Because the media are in business to make money and because media communicators are human, the potential for unethical practices is great. Hiebert and his colleagues present an excellent discussion of the kinds of ethical problems media communicators face on a daily basis.[110] Although many of the examples they provide are related to news reporting, the ethical conflicts they discuss arise in all forms of media messages.

One problem media communicators face is *conflict of interest*, a situation that occurs when a media communicator's professional role conflicts with a personal interest. Does, for example, a reporter have the right to march in a public demonstration, as a *New York Times* reporter who attended a pro-choice rally did? Does this kind of activity damage a reporter's ability to report events objectively or decrease his or her credibility? And, to consider a more extreme case, does a reporter have the right to send out letters in support of an issue or a candidate? A Florida pro-choice reporter sent small wire coat hangers to 160 legislators in an attempt to dramatize the restricting of women's access to abortion. Did the reporter have the right to express her own views? What would you have done if you had been these reporters' editor? Would you feel the same way if they had taken a pro-life stand? In these cases, the reporters' right to act as private citizens clashed with their role as objective news sources. In the first case, the reporter continued to work; in the second, the reporter was fired.[111]

Media communicators also face problems concerning *truth, accuracy, and fairness issues*. The use of composite characters and reenactments are two examples of techniques that either mislead or utterly fabricate, depending on your point of view. In 1981, *Washington Post* reporter Janet Cooke was awarded a Pulitzer Prize for a compelling series about an eight-year-old heroin addict. When later it was revealed that the child she described did not exist but was a fictionalized composite, Cooke's career as a journalist was over. In another incident, ABC News came under fire for presenting a video segment showing a U.S. diplomat handing a briefcase to a Soviet agent. Ostensibly, the incident was taped during the actual transfer of secret information. In reality, however, the scene was a staged reenactment. What responsibility did ABC have to make clear to viewers that what was broadcast was not a real event?

Problems of accuracy are prevalent on the Internet where blogs operate without fact checking or editorial review, and false information can spread like wildfire. A case in point is the AptiQuant hoax of 2011 in which a (deliberately false) report that there was a strong scientific correlation between IQ and Web browser choice was posted online. AptiQuant reported this fake news as fact, and no one bothered to verify the item. No one appears to be watching the watchdogs.[112]

Methods of information gathering also present potential ethical problems. To gather information, most journalists promise confidentiality to their sources. But what happens if, off the record, a reporter finds out about a source's criminal activity? What if a reporter feels that he or she is being used by an informant? Is it ever right for a reporter to reveal confidential sources? And how should a reporter treat a source? Overzealous reporters have ambushed sources during interviews, have lied about their own identity, have bribed and threatened informants, and have even hacked into the personal phone messages of hundreds of ordinary citizens just to follow a news lead.[113]

Reporters have even set out to break the law to demonstrate problems in law enforcement. Should a reporter be encouraged to smuggle a fake bomb onto a plane to show lax security measures or make a drug buy to show how available drugs are? Are there limits to how far a reporter should go to get a story?

Privacy and propriety issues are also ethically gray areas. In an effort to get a compelling picture, is it right to invade a grief-stricken victim's privacy? Is every aspect of a public figure's life open for scrutiny? Is it defensible to pry into the private domestic arrangements of political candidates and to publish detailed exposés of their sex lives? What rights do crime victims have to keep their identities hidden?

Sometimes, reporters know that reporting a story can lead to *physical or emotional harm* or can encourage dangerous practices. What if a story gives people ideas about how to commit a crime or how to hurt themselves? In this regard, critics have voiced concern about articles on teen suicide encouraging more suicides and about exposés on cheating serving as lessons on how to beat the system. Covering terrorist activities is probably the prime example of this kind of ethical dilemma, because terrorist acts are primarily symbolic and depend on publicity for their effectiveness.

Although our focus has been on the news, ethical decisions arise in other areas of the media. Advertising certainly provides an arena for unethical communication, as does entertainment programming. The latter has been criticized for violence and sexually explicit material and for stereotypical portrayals of members of minority groups. And there are sins of omission as well as of commission. R-rated movies, for example, often show people involved in sexual situations yet seldom depict any discussion of condom use. Social psychologists argue that the behavioral scripts individuals internalize as a result of this modeling encourage potentially dangerous sexual practices. In the age of AIDS, do screenwriters have a responsibility in their scripts either to model safer sex or to stop modeling unsafe sex altogether?

The ethical questions that are raised in regard to media practices are complex and difficult. Each communicator must resolve them in his or her own way. Clearly, however, thoughtless, irresponsible actions cannot be tolerated, and media communicators must examine their own practices and must make decisions based not on expediency but on values.

Using Traditional Media More Responsibly

Given the huge amount of time Americans spend with the media and given the potential for media abuse, it's clear that we could all benefit from becoming more thoughtful and responsible media consumers. Some guidelines follow; consider others you would add.

- The media can convey hegemonic messages that reinforce role inequality between genders, among races and classes, and so on. Often, these messages go unnoticed or, when noticed, they are dismissed as insignificant. The first step in becoming more thoughtful about media is to recognize that we are affected by media messages. As media consumers, we need to judge carefully the truth and fairness of what we hear and see.

- Most of us don't deconstruct and question media texts and "facts" as carefully as we should because media representations often fit so nicely with what we want to believe. When we process only what we already find acceptable, we become lazy processors, passively soaking up information. Questioning media ideologies and becoming more informed about events make us more mindful about the information we are given. When we consume news, for example, we should make a commitment to check out facts and demand accurate information. If we don't, then the quality of the information we receive will continue to be low.

- When we encounter objectionable media messages, we need to think about our reactions. We may find certain kinds of media messages objectionable, but many of us consume them every day, thus reinforcing the production of even more extreme and offensive materials. Blaming media producers for poor quality and then eagerly consuming their products will do nothing to raise standards.

- Finally, in addition to tuning out objectionable material, we could all benefit from exploring new sources of information and entertainment. A steady diet of "junk" media isn't going to challenge us. We should be open to expanding our tastes by sampling new, more complex, and varied media menus.

Ethics for the New Media

We end this chapter with some ethical guidelines for you to consider as you interact electronically.

- The first and most important point to remember is that the people with whom you communicate online are real people with real feelings. They can be hurt and betrayed as easily as the people you meet offline. Don't let the anonymity of the Net lead you to dehumanize your conversational partners. Online you should observe the ethical principles that guide real-world relationships.

- The standards of decency that apply to interpersonal, group, and public interactions apply in cyberspace as well. Because we communicate with faceless others, we may be tempted to think that our actions are innocent. But as Michael Heim so eloquently puts it:

Without directly meeting others physically, our ethics languish. Face-to-face communication, the fleshly bond between people, supports a long-term warmth and loyalty, a sense of obligation for which the computer-mediated communities have not yet been tested. . . . The physical eyes are the windows that establish the neighborhood of trust. Without the direct experience of the human face, ethical awareness shrinks. . . . The machine interface may amplify an amoral indifference to human relationships.[114]

- Unethical practices can also occur in the workplace. More than one employee has been known to fire off foolish or insulting electronic memos without stopping to consider their effects. Not only is this bad form, it is dangerous. The "harmless joke" you sent to everyone about your boss may not seem so harmless when it's traced back to you. When email creates a hostile work environment, it is not only unethical, it is illegal. Think before you send messages that could annoy or insult coworkers.

- We know that gossip and misinformation thrive on the Net, perhaps because being "published" in cyberspace legitimizes information. Just remember that on a citizen's channel, anyone can say anything. We must therefore carefully evaluate the truth value of messages we receive and avoid posting information we have not checked for accuracy. When, simply by pressing a button, you can reach thousands of people who are primed to believe you, you take on additional ethical responsibilities.

- Finally, when it comes to cell phones, try to remember that they can be intrusive and disturbing. Strangers shouldn't be forced to hear your private disclosures. And people sitting next to you at the theater or the movies shouldn't have to put up with interruptions. It has gotten so bad that the New York City Council passed a law banning cell phone use during live performances and in museums. One Broadway actor, Robert Griffin, stopped a performance and threatened to walk off the stage if he heard one more cell phone ring. When in public, set your phone to vibrate or, better yet, turn it off.[115]

SUMMARY

This chapter looks at mediated communication. It begins by describing the language and logic of traditional mass media: newspapers, magazines, radio, and television. It then goes on to discuss the characteristics of new media with particular attention to computer-mediated communication (CMC) and mobile telephony.

In the traditional mass media, institutional sources address large, anonymous, heterogeneous audiences through interposed channels. Scholars usually talk about four functions of this form of mediated communication: surveillance, the gathering and disseminating of information; correlation, the analysis and evaluation of data; cultural transmission, the education and socialization of the audience; and entertainment. Although the impact of the mass media can be positive, it can also be negative by narcotizing audiences, increasing passivity, teaching antisocial behavior, and lowering popular taste.

There is lively debate about the extent to which mass media affect audiences. Early media theorists took a powerful effects view; they believed that audiences were largely powerless to resist media messages. Later theorists viewed audiences as more obstinate and resistant. Current theorists recognize that the media can set agendas, deliver hegemonic messages, cultivate erroneous worldviews, and change the way we think. But they also realize that audiences process media selectively, choose media according to their needs, and resist hegemonic messages with oppositional readings.

Consumers turn to different media for different reasons, some of which relate to the format of the medium. Newspapers are used to pass the time, gain practical information, keep in touch with public issues, and maintain a valued self-image. The newspaper format encourages focus on isolated events, a tendency to leave out detail, and a temptation to focus on the dramatic.

Magazines are more specialized and more personal than newspapers. They are read to pass the time, to gain information, and to learn how to live like "insiders." Radio has a strong interpersonal dimension, acting as a "portable friend" and binding people together through shared experience. Like magazines, radio is one of the most specialized of the media.

The medium of choice for most Americans is television. It provides news, gives us a glimpse of alternative worlds, and provides companionship. It also socializes us and provides entertainment. As a highly visual medium, it values movement, brevity, and intimate images. Entertainment programming favors speed and simplicity and tends to uphold ideal values. News programming tries to be brief, visuals oriented, dramatic, and moralistic.

It has become common to distinguish between traditional and new media. Six characteristics describe new media. First, they employ digital technology. Second, they make it easy to combine many different kinds of information in a single format. Third, time and space no longer act as barriers: media consumers can communicate anytime, anywhere. Fourth, new media allow new levels of interactivity; no longer are users passive receivers. Fifth, because media gatekeepers no longer have as much control over media content, consumers have more choice over what they see or hear. One result is audience fragmentation. Finally, new technologies make possible increased surveillance by commercial and governmental organizations.

Computer-mediated communication is the newest of the mass media, and its popularity has increased dramatically over time. Despite fears that CMC would isolate individuals from one another, it appears that it actually encourages interaction. Email is the most widely used form of CMC. Teens and Gen Ys use the Internet primarily for entertainment and social networking, whereas older users are more likely to seek information, email, and shop.

New technologies usually cause anxiety. With the advent of the personal computer came fears that computer use would lead to social isolation, but these fears were largely unfounded. Instead many argue that the social connections afforded by social network sites are a form of social capital. A more recent fear lies in the fact that the Internet may be changing the ways we think, making us more distractible and less patient with long-form text.

Both private individuals and businesses use the Internet to publish personal Websites. Because Websites create a first impression, they must be well designed. A well-designed Website is clear, visually and conceptually consistent, and uncluttered; uses contrast; and employs cinematic techniques. Most of all it is simple and easy to navigate, avoiding elaborate animation and art work. A personal Website should include interesting and useful content, an attractive title, and a clear site menu; useful navigation links; and a way to leave messages. Like all messages, computer-mediated messages should be simple, organized, and clear.

Mobile phones are another offshoot of new media technologies. They are an affordable, highly transportable way to stay in touch. Along with SMS (short messaging service) technology, mobile telephony offers new ways to stay in contact as well as new communication challenges. Cell phones have changed notions of time and space. People who are not present can be treated as though they were, and plans and schedules no longer have to be made in advance. So pervasive is the hype surrounding new media offerings that overload or e-fatigue often sets in.

Each new medium changes the media that have gone before. In response to new media technology, old media are converting to digital formats and are finding new ways to connect with audiences. Traditional and new media are converging as networked computing, telecommunication, and mass media are finding new points of connection.

Because of the effects of the media, media communicators must be concerned with such ethical issues as conflict of interest, fairness, appropriate ways of gathering information, privacy and propriety, and the risk of abetting physical and emotional harm. Media programmers must also take responsibility. We must be aware of the power of traditional media and refuse to reinforce questionable media programming. We must also be responsible users of computer-based channels, remembering that the standards of decency that apply in the "real world" apply in cyberspace as well.

KEY TERMS

Listed below are the key terms used in this chapter, along with the number of the page where each is explained.

old media (278)	hegemonic message (283)	uses and gratifications
new media (278)	spiral of silence (284)	research (287)
mass communication (278)	cultivation theory (284)	polysemy (288)
surveillance (280)	mainstreaming (285)	ideal norms (296)
correlation (280)	mean world hypothesis	digitization (299)
cultural transmission (281)	(285)	Web 2.0 (300)
entertainment (281)	"the medium is the	Web 3.0 (302)
powerful effects model	message" (286)	audience fragmentation (302)
(282)	linear logic (286)	demassification (302)
limited effects model (282)	mosaic logic (286)	social capital (305)
magic bullet (282)	selective exposure (287)	aproximeeting (309)
hypodermic needle (282)	selective attention (287)	e-fatigue (310)
obstinate audience (282)	selective perception (287)	hype stages (310)
agenda-setting function (283)	selective retention (287)	convergence (311)
gatekeepers (283)		

SUGGESTED READING

Campbell, Richard, & Martin, Christopher R. (2009). *Media and culture: An introduction to mass communication* (7th ed.). New York: Bedford/St. Martin's.

A popular, comprehensive, and current introduction to the field.

Carr, Nicholas G. (2010). *The shallows: What the Internet is doing to our brains*. New York: W. W. Norton.

A fascinating look at how living in a wired world is changing the way we think, based on solid research and personal experience.

Jenkins, Henry. (2008). *Convergence culture: Where old and new media collide*. New York: New York University Press.

A fascinating look at ways in which converging media are making it possible for all of us to become media producers.

Intercultural Communication

I n cross-cultural settings, even simple interactions can become complex.

F or communication to work, people must have something in common. If communicators know and respect one another, communication is relatively easy. They can predict one another's moods and meanings, they know what topics to avoid, and they can sometimes even complete one another's thoughts. Uncertainty and stress are at a minimum; communication is spontaneous, open, and comfortable.

Communicating with strangers is more difficult. If the strangers come from our own culture, we can at least base our messages on shared attitudes, beliefs, and life experiences; but if the strangers are from another culture, we may be at a loss. In such a case, uncertainty is maximized. The actual forms, and even the functions, of communication may be strange to us.

In cross-cultural settings, even simple interactions can become complex. Imagine for a moment that you're working in Morocco. A colleague has invited you to his family home for dinner but is a little vague about when dinner will be served, and you have to ask several times before fixing the time. That evening, when you enter your host's home, his wife is nowhere to be seen, and when you ask when she'll be joining you, the host looks flustered and says that she's busy in the kitchen. When his little boy enters, you remark on how cute and clever the child is, but rather than being pleased, your Moroccan colleague looks upset. Before dinner is served, you politely ask to go to the washroom to wash up. During the meal, you do your best to hold up your end of the conversation, but it's hard going. Finally, after tea and pastry, you thank the host and politely leave. You have a feeling the dinner party wasn't a success, but you don't really know what went wrong.

As it turns out, according to Craig Storti, almost everything you did in this social situation was inappropriate.[1] In Morocco, an invitation to dinner is actually an invitation to come and spend time. At some point, food will be served, but what's important is being together. Therefore, discussing the specific time you should come to dinner is like asking your host how long he wants you around; it also implies that your major concern is to be fed. Your questions about his wife and your compliments to his son were similarly inappropriate. It is not customary for a Moroccan wife to eat with guests or even to be introduced, and praising a child is considered unlucky because it may alert evil spirits to the child's presence. Washing up in the washroom was also impolite. If you had waited, your host would have arranged for water to be brought in to you in an expensive decorative basin that would have shown his good taste as well as his concern for your comfort. Finally, it was rude to carry on a conversation during dinner. Talking interferes with the enjoyment of the meal and can be interpreted as a slight against the food.

An isolated incident such as this is not terribly serious, but people who spend time in other cultures may encounter many such small misunderstandings, which over time can take their toll. If cultural differences can get in the way of a simple meal between friends, you can imagine how they might seriously affect complicated business or diplomatic relations. Because cross-cultural contexts add another layer of complexity to normal interactions, some grounding in intercultural communication is essential for anyone who travels abroad or interacts with strangers in this country.

Although cultural differences can sometimes cause misunderstandings, intercultural communication need not be doomed to failure. As Harry Hoijer has remarked, "No culture is wholly isolated, self-contained, and unique. There are important resemblances between all known cultures. . . . Intercultural communication, however wide the differences between cultures may be, is not impossible. It is simply more or less difficult."[2] Intercultural communication is possible because people are not "helplessly suspended in their cultures."[3] By developing an openness to new ideas and a willingness to listen and to observe, we can surmount the difficulties inherent in intercultural interaction. In Chapters 9 through 11, we have already seen examples of ways in which culture affects communication. This chapter extends that discussion by directly examining ways in which people from different cultures can learn to communicate more effectively.

> **By developing an openness to new ideas and a willingness to listen and to observe, we can surmount the difficulties inherent in intercultural interaction.**

WHAT IS CULTURE?

According to anthropologist Ruth Benedict, we spend our lives following the patterns and standards handed down to us by our cultures:

> *From the moment of birth the customs into which [an individual] is born shape his experience and behavior. By the time he can talk, he is a little creature of his culture, and by the time he is grown and able to take part in its activities, its habits are his habits, its beliefs his beliefs, its impossibilities his impossibilities.*[4]

As Benedict points out, we are, in an important sense, the products of our cultures.

Defining Culture

But what exactly is culture? Donald Klopf gives a simple definition. For him, **culture** is "that part of the environment made by humans."[5] According to this definition, culture includes all the material objects and possessions that a social group invents or acquires. Even more important, it includes the group's less tangible creations: the shared customs and values that bind its members together and give them a sense of commonality. Thus, culture includes a group's "collective answer to the fundamental questions . . . 'Who are we?' 'What is our place in the world?' and 'How are we to live our lives?'"[6]

> Culture includes a group's "collective answer to the fundamental questions . . . 'Who are we?' 'What is our place in the world?' and 'How are we to live our lives?'"

Characteristics of Cultures

Cultures are "templates for living" that have certain basic characteristics. Cultures are learned, shared, multifaceted, dynamic, and overlapping.

Cultures Are Learned

The first point about cultures is that they are learned. Americans act like other Americans not because we are innately predisposed to do so, but because we learn to do so. Much of our early training is an attempt to make us fit cultural patterns. If we do not learn the lessons of our cultures, we pay—"through a loss of comfort, status, peace of mind, safety, or some other value."[7] We may even be imprisoned or labeled insane for acting in ways that would be perfectly acceptable in other cultures.

To those familiar with them, cultural practices embody important values and traditions; to outsiders they may seem inexplicable or exotic.

© Alain Nogues/Sygma/Corbis

We are so well programmed that we seldom stop to think that culture is learned. Our cultural norms appear to be natural and right, and we can't imagine acting differently. Yet had we been brought up in Korea by Korean parents, an entirely different set of norms would appear natural. We would be culturally Korean. We would speak Korean, follow Korean norms and customs, and see the world in typically Asian ways. Although this point seems obvious, it is one we often forget. When we see someone from another culture act in ways we consider strange, our first impulse is to attribute the action to personality. For example, we label someone "pushy" who speaks more loudly and forcefully than we do; we seldom stop to realize that had we been brought up in that person's culture, we would probably express ourselves just as loudly and forcefully.

Cultures Are Shared

Another important characteristic of culture is that it is shared. Cultures are group understandings rather than individual ones, and belonging to a culture means acting according to group norms. For most people, fitting into a cultural group is very important. Being like others provides security, perhaps because we equate being alike with being right and being different with being wrong. Regardless of the reason, we learn very early to separate the world into "us" and "them," and we work very hard to make sure that others recognize which of the two we are. Little boys are mortified if they are mistaken for little girls; they will spend a good part of the rest of their lives living up to the masculine ideal. The wealthy do not wish to be thought poor; therefore, they act in ways that signal their status. Mistakes that mix "us" with "them" undermine our sense of self.

> We learn very early to separate the world into "us" and "them," and we work very hard to make sure that others recognize which of the two we are.

Because cultures are shared, we are not entirely free to act as we wish. Indeed, we spend a good deal of time proving who we are and living up to the expectations of others. This process of living out cultural rules is largely invisible and seldom difficult if we stay within a single culture. A white, middle-class, American male who associates only with others like himself seldom stops to think about the effects of national, racial, class, or gender rules on his beliefs and behaviors. Only when he steps outside his circle of friends, his neighborhood, or his country and experiences other cultures is he likely to see the extent to which culture affects him.[8]

People who frequently move between cultures are often more sensitive to the fact that culture is shared. Lawrence Wieder and Steven Pratt give an interesting example of the importance of shared cultural identity and the difficulties it presents for minority group members. In an article entitled "On Being a Recognizable Indian among Indians," Wieder and Pratt discuss ways in which Native Americans of the Osage people let one another know that they are "real Indians" rather than "White Indians." Wieder and Pratt's research not only illustrates the universal need to demonstrate cultural identity, but also shows how central communication style is to that demonstration.[9]

According to Wieder and Pratt, one of the primary differences between the communication styles of European Americans and Native Americans is the value the latter place on being silent. "When real Indians who are strangers to one another pass each other in a public place, wait in line, occupy adjoining seats, and so forth, they take it that it is proper to remain silent and to not initiate conversation."[10] Once Native Americans do engage in conversation with one another, they take on substantial obligations, among them the necessity of interacting whenever their paths cross. For students and businesspeople, this obligation may be burdensome, for it takes precedence over attending class or keeping appointments.

Talking like a "real Indian" also means being modest and not showing oneself to be more knowledgeable than other Native Americans. Being asked by a European American teacher to volunteer information in a group discussion in which other

Native Americans are present puts a well-informed Native American student in a difficult bind. To avoid appearing arrogant, he or she may simply refuse to participate.

The desire to avoid seeming immodest occurs in public speaking situations as well, where speaking is reserved for tribal elders. Only certain individuals are entitled to speak, and they often speak for someone else rather than for themselves. It is customary to begin a speech with a disclaimer such as "I really don't feel that I am qualified to express [the wishes of the people I am speaking for] but I'm going to do the best I can, so please bear with me."[11] Compare this custom to the rule taught by most European American communication teachers that a speaker should build his or her credibility at the beginning of a speech, and you will see how communication styles across cultures can conflict.

The need to use Native American styles of communication in front of other Native Americans often means the "real Indian" is misunderstood or misjudged by European Americans. Steven Pratt, who collected the primary data for this research and who is himself a participating member of the Osage people, reported instances in which his identity as a graduate student conflicted with his identity as a Native American. He and Wieder conclude thus:

> Being a real Indian is not a material thing that can be possessed and displayed. It consists of those patterns of appropriate conduct that are articulated in such a way that they are visible and recognizable to other Indians as specific Indian ways of conducting oneself. In the performance of these visible patterns, being a real Indian is realized.[12]

Although deciding how to display one's cultural identity may be more problematic for the Native American communicator living in a predominantly European American society, each member of a culture must prove himself or herself to other members by acting in ways that are culturally approved. Each of us acts out a cultural script.

Cultures Are Multifaceted

If we define culture as everything surrounding us that is not natural and biological in character, then culture clearly has many facets. At a minimum, culture affects language, religion, basic worldview, education, social organization, technology, politics, and law, and all of these factors affect one another.[13] As Edward Hall points out, if you touch a culture in one place, everything else is affected.[14]

> At a minimum, culture affects language, religion, basic worldview, education, social organization, technology, politics, and law, and all of these factors affect one another.

Table 12.1 gives an idea of the variety of interconnected activities that are found in virtually every culture. These activities are common to all people who live together in social groups and are thus examples of **cultural universals**, yet the enactment of these activities varies dramatically from culture to culture. In every culture, for example, people adorn their bodies, eat, educate their children, recognize family groupings, keep track of time, and so on. How people in a particular culture do these things, however, is unique. Although all people eat, what they consider edible and how they prepare food vary widely. The idea of eating dog, a food offered in many of the best hotels in South China, is considered revolting by most Americans. The idea of eating a ham and cheese sandwich, a perfectly acceptable meal for many Americans, is offensive to Arabs and Orthodox Jews. Thus, what is common practice in one culture may be taboo in another. To be functioning members of a culture, we must internalize rules governing a huge variety of activities; and to communicate with people from other cultures, we must recognize and learn to respect their customs.

Cultures Are Dynamic

Cultures are constantly changing. As economic conditions change, as new technologies are developed, and as cultural contact increases, old ways of doing things change and people must learn new behaviors. This important fact is one reason why memorizing lists of dos and don'ts is not the best way to prepare for intercultural contact. For just as soon as you've learned a rule about how to communicate with the "natives" of a culture, you'll find that the rule is obsolete. A better way to prepare for intercultural contact is to become sensitive to the kinds of differences that occur between cultures and to develop the ability to learn by observing.

Cultural Identities Are Overlapping

As our discussion of the communication patterns of some Native Americans showed, we belong to multiple overlapping cultures, some of which work together and some of which conflict. At a minimum, we all belong to national, regional, class, ethnic, religious, professional, age, and gender cultures. At various times, one or more of these identities may become crucial while the rest fade into the background.

> Memorizing lists of dos and don'ts is not the best way to prepare for intercultural contact. For just as soon as you've learned a rule about how to communicate with the "natives" of a culture, you'll find that the rule is obsolete.

Table 12.1 A Partial List of Cultural Universals

Anthropologists have studied common activities found in all cultures, included among them are the following:

Age grading and status assignments	Dancing	Folklore	Hairstyles	Marriage
	Education	Funeral rites	Hygiene	Puberty customs
Bodily adornment	Ethics	Gestures	Kinship	Rituals
Calendars	Etiquette	Giftgiving	Language	Sex restrictions
Childcare	Family	Gossip	Law	Taboo Foods
Cooking	Fear of Death	Greetings	Magic	Toolmaking
Courtship				

If we are lucky, our overlapping identities fit together into a coherent whole. If we are less fortunate, we experience conflicts. The woman who believes in equal rights yet belongs to a traditional culture in which women are subservient to men feels pressure from each identity. The immigrant who wishes to assimilate into his adopted country but does not wish to abandon tradition also experiences stress. The adolescent who is no longer a child and yet is not an adult has difficulty determining how to act.

Although multiple cultural memberships can cause stress, they can also be a source of strength, allowing us to be unique individuals rather than cultural clones. Seldom are any two people members of exactly the same cultures, and none of us manages to follow all of the rules of the cultures to which we belong. As Marshall Singer points out, "that is precisely what makes each of us humans unique. And while that makes for a more rich, varied, and interesting world, it also makes generalizing about people . . . that much more hazardous and difficult."[15] The task that confronts each of us is to find a unique sense of self in the face of our own conflicting cultural identities and to recognize when we speak to others that their cultural identities are also complex and overlapping.

Why Communicate Cross-Culturally?

Admittedly, communication becomes more difficult when people do not share the same attitudes and values. Why, then, should we bother to communicate cross-culturally? The answer is that we cannot afford to ignore people from other cultures. There may have been a time when people could spend their entire lives communicating only with others who shared their own cultural identities. In such a time, learning how to communicate across cultural boundaries was a luxury rather than a necessity. Nowadays, it is impossible to remain isolated from others, and **intercultural communication**, communication wherein sender and receiver come from different cultures, cannot be avoided.

Living in the Global Village

One reason for the rise in importance of intercultural communication is that the world is shrinking daily. We live in a global village where intercultural encounters are commonplace. Advances in telecommunication and transportation technology have changed our sense of distance and of place. We can board a plane in New York and be in Hong Kong or Singapore within a day. We can walk to the corner store and find products from every part of the globe. We can go to a local movie house and see the latest film from France or Hungary. We can switch on CNN and watch a military campaign in Somalia or a civil war in Bosnia from the comfort of our living rooms. It is no longer possible to remain isolated—from events, ideas, or cultural products.

Many of you will travel internationally, either on business or for pleasure, at least once in your life (if you have not already done so). Whether you travel as a business representative, diplomat or technical adviser, member of the military, student, teacher, or tourist, you will find yourself communicating with people whose beliefs, values, and ways of existing may be vastly different from yours. The greater your understanding of intercultural communication, the richer this experience will be.

Even if you don't travel outside the United States, you may still find yourself interacting with people from other cultures, for just as Americans travel abroad more and more frequently, so foreign nationals come to the United States. As individuals from Vietnam, Cambodia, Cuba, Haiti, the former Soviet Union, and a host of other countries come here to escape political upheaval or to flee war or famine, "contacts with cultures that previously appeared unfamiliar, alien, and at times mysterious are now a normal part of our day-to-day routine."[16]

Familiarity with the problems that arise when people communicate interculturally can ease the adaptation that both immigrants and host nationals must make. For adjusting to the global village is by no means easy. As Richard Porter and Larry Samovar express it, "The difficulty with being thrust into a global village is that we do not yet know how to live like villagers; there are too many of 'us' who do not want to live with 'them.'"[17]

Coming to Terms with Diversity

Of course, we don't have to look to newly arrived immigrants to experience intercultural communication. We are a country of many coexisting cultures. Americans from different ethnic or religious backgrounds may seem as alien as someone "just off the boat." It is becoming increasingly difficult to ignore the presence of **co-cultures** within our own country. Groups that were outside the mainstream several years ago are now demanding recognition and respect from majority cultures. Even when we speak the same language, we may find overcoming cultural differences difficult. Yet if we are to live in harmony with our neighbors, overcoming differences is a necessity.

Intercultural Communication and Personal Growth

Intercultural understandings serve not only to make contacts more comfortable, but also to enrich us on a personal level. Communicating with people from other cultures allows us access to the experiences of other human beings. Intercultural contact shows us that there are other ways to act in the world than those we have been taught; it widens our field of choices and stimulates our imagination.

> Intercultural contact shows us that there are other ways to act in the world than those we have been taught; it widens our field of choices and stimulates our imagination.

Students of intercultural communication often talk about the development of an **intercultural identity**, a sense of belonging to an original and a new culture at the same time. People who achieve this identity are more open to change and are willing to transcend their own cultural premises. Young Yun Kim expresses it this way:

Not all strangers may evolve this far in their adaptation process. Yet those who do will be able to enjoy a special kind of freedom, making deliberate choices for actions in specific situations rather than simply being bound by the culturally normative courses of action.[18]

BARRIERS TO INTERCULTURAL COMMUNICATION

Despite its importance, learning to communicate interculturally is extremely difficult. A variety of barriers keep people from different cultures from understanding one another. In this section, we'll look at some of the attitudes that impede our ability to communicate clearly with one another—attitudes such as prejudice, ethnocentrism, and a refusal to acknowledge differences. But before we look at these barriers, we need to understand how culture affects communication.

How Culture Affects Thought, Feelings, and Action

We have seen that culture is multifaceted, that it affects every aspect of our lives. That culture helps determine how we interpret reality, the emotions we feel, and the behaviors we enact should come as no surprise. In this section we look at how culture affects perception, role relations, goal-oriented behavior, worldview, and message making. In the process we will look at some of the ways cultures differ from one another.

Culture and Perception

As we saw in Chapter 3, perception is not simply a matter of receiving what already exists. Meaning is "not extracted from Nature but projected by people on it. People's behavior can be understood only in terms of their own constructs," and many of these constructs are products of culture.[19] When we perceive events and people, we attach values to them and make attributions about them. Our values and attributions are culture-specific, as the following example, reported by Donald Klopf, shows.[20]

Nancy, a native Californian, moved with her husband, an executive with an oil company, to Iran. Because the climate was very hot and humid, Nancy often wore shorts and casual tops when she went to the local market to shop. As she walked alone to the market one day, an Iranian man grabbed her and made lewd suggestions. Upset, she shook herself free and called the police.

Nancy, working from an American point of view, saw the Iranian as a degenerate and his behavior as an attack. The Iranian, however, was astonished by her reaction. When he looked at Nancy, he saw a prostitute, for in Iran, no other woman would ever appear in public in shorts or walk alone. From an Iranian

When we encounter a culture for the first time we may be puzzled about what is going on. Over time, what we see becomes commonplace.

© Aivar Mikko/Alamy

point of view, Nancy was giving clear signals that she was sexually available. Had Nancy known more about the culture in which she was a guest, the incident might have been avoided.

In *Beyond the Veil*, Fatima Mernissi describes the cultural codes that govern relations between the sexes in many Muslim countries. In these nations, she tells us, sexuality is territorial, and there are strict boundaries delineating the spaces belonging to each sex. Mernissi goes on to explain:

> *Women in males' spaces are considered provocative and offensive. If [a woman] enters [the male sphere], she is upsetting the male's order and his peace of mind. She is actually committing an act of aggression against him merely by being present where she should not be.*[21]

Of course, knowing the reasons behind the behavior of both parties does not necessarily lead to acceptance. The Iranian may still feel that behavior such as Nancy's is immodest, and Nancy may still find his behavior sexist. Nevertheless, cultural knowledge can place behavior in context and can reduce misunderstandings. Not knowing the values of another country can result in momentary embarrassment, as it did with Nancy, or can lead to the loss of millions of dollars and months of work, as the following story illustrates.[22]

An American engineering company spent months negotiating a huge contract with a Saudi Arabian firm. To signal the importance of the contract, the American executives bound their final proposal in costly leather. Unfortunately, they chose pigskin, unaware that Saudis consider the pig an unclean animal. Had the Americans wanted to insult their hosts, they could have found no better way. The proposal and binder were consequently burned, and the Saudi firm threw the American company out of the country. A cursory knowledge of religious custom could have averted this disaster. Unfortunately, however, no one had bothered to do basic research on Saudi beliefs.

Culture and Role Identities

Culture also tells us who to be and how to act. In every culture, people are classified according to factors such as age, status, occupation, gender, and so on. We do not expect the young and the old, princes and peasants, or men and women to act the same way; nor do we act the same way toward each of these groups. Being a good communicator means, in part, understanding role distinctions and adapting one's communication accordingly.

> We do not expect the young and the old, princes and peasants, or men and women to act the same way; nor do we act the same way toward each of these groups. Being a good communicator means, in part, understanding role distinctions and adapting one's communication accordingly.

An example of the way culture affects role identity can be found in varying attitudes toward age. The Ashanti of Ghana, for example, address all older men as "my grandfather," a title of respect.[23] The Maasai of East Africa also afford great honor to their elders. Lisa Skow and Larry Samovar explain that the Maasai equate age with wisdom and believe that those who are wise must be treated with special deference. Young people, no matter how clever, cannot reach the truth until they pass through all of life's stages.[24] The Chinese hold a similar view.

By comparison, Americans value youth more than age. Rather than welcoming old age, we see it as a time of diminished capacity. In fact, American beliefs about age may induce psychological states of "oldness." Carl Carmichael argues that "it is quite possible that many older people have aged prematurely by adopting the age-related characteristics they have come to believe must exist after a certain age."[25] If so, this is a dramatic example of the costs of false cultural beliefs.

Gender roles are also culturally derived. In parts of the Arab world, women do not work or drive cars, whereas in Israel and China, women do the same jobs as men. In parts of India, women must wait to eat until after men have finished, and in traditional Vietnamese households, women must eat smaller portions of food than men.[26] In modern America, these kinds of distinctions are seen as demeaning and offensive. Even the characteristics that we think are basic to the sexes may differ from culture to culture. According to Edward Hall, in Iran it is men who express their emotions freely, whereas women are considered to be coldly practical.[27]

Culture and Goals

Our cultures also tell us what goals we should pursue and how to pursue them. Americans have relatively high achievement motivation. We are generally characterized by **effort-optimism**, the belief that hard work will pay off. People in other countries may "expect to be rewarded on the basis of the social position of their family or clan" rather than on their own efforts, or in some cases they may not expect to be rewarded at all.[28] K. S. Sitaram and Roy T. Cogdell explain the difference between the attitude in some countries that individuals can do little to change their future and the attitude in other countries, such as the United States, that people are able to control their fate:

> If you ask a Hindu why he got only ten bags of corn from his land while nearby farmers got much more, he would say it was the wish of God. An American farmer's answer to the same question would be, "Hell, I didn't work hard enough."[29]

The goal-oriented nature of middle-class American culture is evident in popular slogans such as "No pain, no gain," and "Just do it." It is also evident in high stress levels and burnout. To people in many countries, Americans are overly ambitious. What we think of as a healthy work ethic, they see as needless effort or even arrogance.

Cultural Worldviews

In addition to affecting roles and goals, culture affects **worldviews**, basic notions of human nature, including the extent to which the individual self is valued. Larry Samovar, Richard Porter, and Nemi Jain argue that most Americans hold three basic beliefs about human nature: that humans are, at heart, rational; that humans are perfectible; and that human nature is highly susceptible to social and cultural influence.[30] The **rationality premise**—the belief that most people are capable of discovering the truth through logical analysis—underlies many American institutions, including democracy, trial by jury, and free enterprise, all of which are based on the idea that the average person can be trusted to make good decisions. The **perfectibility premise** is based on the old Puritan idea that humans are born in sin but are capable of achieving goodness through effort and control. Finally, the **mutability premise** assumes that human behavior is shaped by environmental factors and that the way to improve humans is to improve their physical and psychological circumstances. A belief in universal education follows from this assumption.

Dimensions of Cultural Difference

If culture affects the ways we think and act, it follows that people from different cultures think and act differently. But what are these differences? Is there any way to identify major dimensions of cultural difference? According to Geert Hofstede, there are five dimensions that describe cultural difference: power distance, uncertainty avoidance, masculinity/femininity, long-term/short-term orientation, and individualism/collectivism.[31]

Each dimension provides an answer to a fundamental question about the world and one's place in it. The first, **power distance,** addresses the question, "How should power and wealth be distributed?" In cultures with a high power distance orientation, both the powerful and the powerless endorse inequality as a fact of life, believing that it is natural and right that some people wield more power and have more resources than others (as well as bearing a greater responsibility for the welfare of the less fortunate). Power distance scores are generally higher in East European, Latin, Asian, and African countries and lower in Germanic and English-speaking countries.

The dimension of **uncertainty avoidance** focuses on the question, "How much risk and uncertainty is tolerable?" Cultures high in uncertainty avoidance dislike risk and change; they are essentially traditional, following strict codes and rules of conduct. Those low in uncertainty avoidance embrace change and are willing to take risks. According to Hofstede uncertainty avoidance is high in Eastern and Central Europe and German-speaking countries as well as in Japan and many Latin American countries. It is low in English-speaking and Nordic countries as well as in China.

The **masculinity/femininity** dimension centers on the question, "Are men and women essentially different from one another?" In masculine countries, differences are maximal; men are expected to be competitive and aggressive with women being meek, kind, and nurturing. In more feminine cultures, differences are less extreme, with men and women sharing similar characteristics. Hofstede reports that Japan, German-speaking countries, and some Latin countries like Italy and Mexico tend to be masculine, whereas the Nordic countries and the Netherlands are more feminine. Interestingly English-speaking countries like the United States tend to be moderately masculine.

A fairly recent addition to the list of cultural differences is that of **long-term/short-term orientation**. It addresses one's orientation to time, answering the question, "Is the present, past, or future more important?" Those who take a long-term orientation keep their eyes on the future; thrift and perseverance are highly valued. In short-term oriented cultures, a respect for the past and present are blended. Immediate need gratification, spending, and consumption are the norms, and preservation of face and traditional social status are valued. Most East Asian countries take a long-term orientation, with the United States, United Kingdom, Africa, and some Islamic countries taking a shorter-term view.[32]

Of all the dimensions identified by Hofstede the one that has gained the most attention is that of **individualism/collectivism**. The focus of this dimension is on the question, "What is the basic unit of society, the individual or the group?" Individualist countries believe that the most important social unit is the person, acting in his or her own interest. American individualism is evident from the fact that Americans are encouraged "to make their own decisions, develop their own opinions, solve their own problems, have their own things, and, in general, learn to view the world from the point of view of the self."[33] In fact, researcher Geert Hofstede found the United States to be the most individualistic of the forty nations he studied. The countries highest in individualism were Western or European countries, while those lowest in individualism were Asian or South American.[34]

The opposite of individualism is collectivism. In collectivist cultures, people believe it is right to subordinate personal goals for the good of others. For collectivists, shared identity is more important than personal identity. Harry Triandis and his colleagues argue that naming practices may reflect where a culture stands on the collectivist/individualist continuum. In Bali, they report, a person is referred to by his or her position in the family (for example, "the first son of X family" or "mother of Y"). Similarly, in China, one's family name (what we call the last name) comes first, followed by a personal name. In more individualist cultures, the personal name comes first.[35]

People in collectivist cultures are generally comfortable in **vertical relationships** (relationships in which some people are afforded more status than others), whereas individualists feel most comfortable in **horizontal relationships** (relationships with status equals). Members of collectivist cultures rarely compete on a personal basis, although they will fight fiercely for the good of their group. The converse is true in individualist cultures. In a collectivist culture such as Japan, for example, workers feel strong loyalties to their work groups, and the qualities sought in a leader are patience and the ability to listen.[36] Leaders in individualist cultures are more likely to be prized for quick thinking and an ability to take the initiative.

According to Triandis and colleagues, the most important collectivist values are harmony, face-saving, duty to parents, modesty, moderation, thrift, equality in reward distribution, and the fulfillment of others' needs. The top values for individualists are freedom, honesty, social recognition, comfort, hedonism, and reward distribution based on individual performance. Table 12.2 outlines some other differences between collectivist and individualist cultures.

Table 12.2 Rules to Increase Cooperation between Collectivists and Individualists

Some things individualists should keep in mind when interacting in collectivist cultures.

- Expect collectivists' loyalty to be to their own groups and expect them to match their values and personal styles to the group rather than to their own preferences.

- Collectivists value family and group relationships. Expect them to take time off from work to attend to family matters.

- Do not disclose personal information unless asked. Do share information on age, salary, and job position, information that will help the collectivist understand your social standing.

- Expect collectivists to be sensitive to loss of face. Avoid open criticism or refusal of requests.

- When trying to persuade collectivists, use arguments based on authority or the good of the group rather than on personal rewards.

- Do not jump into negotiations. Spend time getting to know others before getting down to business and expect delays.

- Negotiations may take a longer time than you are used to and decisions may change repeatedly.

- Gift giving is important. Make sure your gifts reflect the social standing of the collectivist.

- Do not expect to have as much privacy as you are used to.

Based on *The International Journal of Intercultural Relations,* 12, Harry C. Triandis, Richard Brislin, and C. Harry Hui, "Cross-Cultural Training Across the Individualism–Collectivism Divide," pp. 269–298.

Culture and Language Style

It almost goes without saying that people from different cultures often speak different languages and that difficulties in making oneself understood are an important barrier to cross-cultural interaction. But the problem is not just that people from different cultures use different words to express their thoughts. The thoughts they express may also be different.

One of the attitudes that most interferes with successful intercultural communication is the belief that everything that can be said in one language can be said in another, that meanings are directly translatable. This is simply not the case. A concept that is central to the language of one culture may be translated into another language only with difficulty. The Japanese concept of *amae* is an example. According to Edward Hall and Mildred Reed Hall, *amae* comes from the verb *amaeru*, "to look to others for support and affection." As Hall and Hall explain, *amae* has its roots in the psychological relationship between a child and his or her mother, but the child later transfers *amae* to teachers, bosses, and other authority figures. Although *amae* may be translated as "dependence," it is more than that: it is a willingly assumed, reciprocal relationship that blurs the distinction between the world of work and the interpersonal realm.[37] Because English speakers have no exactly comparable term, we may have difficulty grasping the subtleties of the concept. This does not mean that we can't learn to use the word when it is explained to us (after all, Hall and Hall give us a detailed description written in English), but it does mean the concept won't seem natural to us. One of the reasons that learning a foreign language is both frustrating and exhilarating is that it opens up new ways of viewing the world.

> One of the attitudes that most interferes with successful intercultural communication is the belief that everything that can be said in one language can be said in another, that meanings are directly translatable.

Culture affects not only semantic content but pragmatic rules as well. Our cultures tell us how to use language: how specific we should be, how openly we should convey our feelings, how much emotion we should reveal, and how formally we should speak.[38]

Context Dependence.   Some cultures value verbal precision; in such cultures, speakers must explicitly say everything they mean. The language is structured so that nothing is left to conjecture. Cultures that find meaning in the words rather than in the shared context in which communication occurs are called **low-context cultures**. In such cultures, the speaker assumes that the listener doesn't know very much about the situation and must be told everything explicitly. England, the United States, and other English-speaking nations are considered low-context cultures, as are many of the countries in Western Europe.

High-context cultures, on the other hand, don't consider it necessary to spell out messages as explicitly. Speakers don't bother to say what they believe listeners already know. They also believe that where and how something is said is as important as what is said. The Chinese language, for example, is highly contextual: many of the grammatical details we regard as important, such as verb tense or the distinction between the pronouns *he* and *she*, are not usually indicated. In Chinese, the same string of words can mean "he is going" or "she went." How do Chinese speakers know which is the intended meaning? From context. If the speaker has been discussing a past event and the subject of the conversation has been a woman, then everyone will know that the speaker means "she went." On the other hand, if the topic of conversation has been the current actions of a man, then everyone will understand the sentence to mean "he is going." In Chinese, it is often not necessary to say explicitly what can be inferred from context.

Not only is being explicit unnecessary in some cultures, it can be downright rude. In a high-context culture such as Japan, words are sometimes less important than tone of voice, eye contact, and other nonverbal cues. A "yes" may mean a number of things including "yes," "I don't know," "perhaps," or even "I hope I have said this unenthusiastically enough for you to understand that I mean no."[39] As you can imagine, these differences can cause problems. To the high-context speaker, low-context language can seem abrupt and insulting. And low-context speakers can become extremely frustrated and confused in high-context cultures.

Directness.   As we already saw in Chapter 4, the values associated with directness also vary from culture to culture. The following example, cited by Myron Lustig and Jolene Koester, is a perfect example of indirectness.[40] A Malaysian teacher is talking to a European American teacher. The Malaysian, who doesn't have a car, wants the American to drive him off campus for lunch but is too polite to ask directly. Instead, the Malaysian says, "Can I ask you a question?" "Yes, of course," the American answers. "Do you know what time it is?" "Yes, it's two o'clock," answers the American. The Malaysian then asks, "Might you have a little soup left in the pot?" Puzzled, the American asks for clarification, forcing the Malaysian to be more explicit. "I will be on campus teaching until nine o'clock tonight, a very long day for any person, let alone a hungry one!" Finally, the American catches on: "Would you like me to drive you to a restaurant off campus so you can have lunch?" The Malaysian teacher answers, "What a very good idea you have!" Although the authors do not reverse the dialogue, we can imagine that if it were the American who was hungry, the request would be much more direct: "I'm starving. Can you give me a lift off campus? I need to get lunch."

Members of indirect cultures often avoid overt statements, especially when being direct could cause embarrassment. Instead they use a variety of more subtle methods to get their meanings across. These include refraction (letting someone overhear what one wants him or her to know), covert revelation (letting personal views out in a disguised way), and mediation (waiting for someone else to relay the message).[41]

Expressiveness.   Expressive cultures are open when it comes to displaying emotions. Hugging, touching, laughing, and crying may not be out of place, even in the workplace. Eloquence is often valued. In other cultures, the opposite is true. In many cultures, emotional displays are seen as inappropriate and unprofessional. Iranians, for example, are very emotionally expressive. When angry, an Iranian's behaviors may consist of "turning red, invoking religious oaths, proclaiming his injustices for all to hear, and allowing himself to be held back."[42] Many southeast Asians, in contrast, value evenness and restraint and try to neutralize emotions. European Americans, in general, are somewhere in the middle.

Formality. A final dimension of intercultural language use is formality. Some cultures use language in a formal way. Protocol is very important, deference should be shown to superiors, and all messages should flow through proper channels. This kind of language use is found in cultures in which there is a distinct power hierarchy. Conversely, the goal of cultures favoring informal language is to reduce this hierarchy, get rid of red tape, and treat individuals as equals. The United States and Australia are well known for such informality.

Because culture affects so many aspects of our lives, it can be a barrier to effective communication. This is especially likely if we hold negative attitudes about cultural differences. In the following section, we will look at some destructive beliefs that can guarantee intercultural misunderstandings.

Attitudes That Diminish Understanding

Why are intercultural contacts so often frustrating rather than liberating? It is because we often enter them with preconceived attitudes that impede the possibility of understanding. Among these attitudes are stereotypes and prejudices, assumptions of similarity, a tendency to withdraw from novelty, and a deep belief in the superiority of one's own culture.

Stereotypes and Prejudices

The tendency to prejudge and stereotype members of other groups is one of the main barriers to intercultural understanding. Many people enter cross-cultural interactions with preconceived notions that make it impossible to find any common ground and that distort accurate perception. **Stereotypes**, which are "generalized second-hand beliefs that provide conceptual biases from which we 'make sense' out of what goes on around us, whether they are accurate or fit the circumstances," are one kind of preconception.[43] Although stereotypes fulfill certain

If cross-cultural interaction involves mutual respect, understanding is possible. If not, cultures clash and exposure to new ideas can result in culture shock.

Time & Life Pictures/Getty Images

functions (for example, reducing the anxiety that comes with uncertainty and making the world seem more predictable), they interfere with objective perception. Once we have decided that Germans are obsessed with order, that Japanese are workaholics, or that Central Americans lack ambition, we stop thinking about people objectively.

A **prejudice** is a special kind of stereotype, a "negative social attitude held by members of one group toward members of another group," an attitude that biases perception and provides a rationale for discrimination.[44] Prejudices are the products of in-group interaction; very rarely are they the result of direct contact with out-group members. People learn prejudices from secondary sources and seldom make any attempt to check their validity. Having decided that members of a target group are dangerous, unintelligent, or lazy, people who hold prejudices avoid contact.

> **Prejudices are the products of in-group interaction; very rarely are they the result of direct contact with out-group members.**

The purpose of prejudices is not to enable us to understand the world accurately but to "draw a line between in-group and out-group members, a line that divides those who are 'superior' from those who are 'inferior.' In drawing this line, people often use distorted data and unwarranted assumptions."[45] Table 12.3 shows some of the cognitive biases people use to keep their prejudices intact, biases that allow them to see differences where none exists or to distort differences that do exist.

Table 12.3 Cognitive Biases Used to Maintain Prejudices

Negative Interpretation	Interpreting everything the target group does as negative *Example:* If we see "them" relaxing, we interpret their behavior as shiftless and irresponsible; when we relax, we are simply unwinding after a hard day.
Discounting	Dismissing information that doesn't fit a negative stereotype *Example:* If one of "them" succeeds, it must be due to favoritism or luck; their success is simply the exception that proves the rule.
Fundamental Attribution Bias	Interpreting another's negative behavior as internal rather than external *Example:* If one of "them" is rude, it's because they're that way by nature; if one of "us" is rude, it's because we're under stress.
Exaggeration	Making negative aspects of out-group behavior seem more extreme *Example:* A simple argument is seen as a violent confrontation; a demonstration is reported as a riot.
Polarization	Looking for differences and ignoring similarities *Example:* An immigrant who has assimilated in almost every respect is still seen as one of "them" and as fundamentally different from "us."

Adapted from *Communicating Racism: Ethnic Prejudice in Thought and Talk* by Teun van Dijk, 1987. Newbury Park, CA: Sage.

Assumed Similarity

Almost as serious a stumbling block to intercultural understanding as prejudice is an unwarranted **assumption of similarity**, a refusal to see true differences where they exist. Assuming that everyone is "the same under the skin" may reduce uncomfortable feelings of strangeness, but it may also result in insensitivity. By assuming that members of a different culture see the world in the same way we do, we overlook real differences. When, for example, an American sees a foreign visitor smiling and nodding as the two interact, the American may assume the interaction is a success. It may be the case, however, "that the foreigner actually [understands] very little of the verbal and nonverbal content and [is] merely indicating polite interest or trying not to embarrass him or herself."[46]

Smiling is a good example of an assumption of similarity, for this "universal expression" takes on quite different meanings in different cultures. In some countries, it is considered extremely impolite to smile at a stranger; a smile may be interpreted as a sexual invitation or as a sign of derision. Foreign travelers in the United States may be insulted or taken aback by the Americans' friendly smile, as is evidenced by this Japanese student's comment:

> On my way to and from school I have received a smile by non-acquaintance American girls several times. I have finally learned they have no interest for me; it means only a kind of greeting to a foreigner. If someone smiles at a stranger in Japan, especially a girl, she can assume he is either a sexual maniac or an impolite person.[47]

Conversely, an American sojourner whose greetings are not returned may consider host nationals rude or standoffish. These misinterpretations are a direct result of failing to acknowledge that cultural differences in nonverbal behavior exist.

Let's look at one more example.[48] An American woman working in Tunisia stops by the local newsstand to get a copy of the *International Herald Tribune*. The vendor tells the American that he'll have the newspaper the next day, and instinctively adds the phrase *"N'sha'llah"* (God willing). The next day, when the American returns, there's no paper. The American is upset, because she interpreted the vendor's words as a promise. A Tunisian would have heard something quite different. To a Tunisian, the vendor's statement would have clearly meant: "I don't know if there'll be a paper tomorrow; in fact I doubt it, but it's not for me to say what may or may not happen in the future. That is in God's hands." In short, when the vendor said, "Yes, *N'sha'llah*," he meant "no." We can only assume that, over time, this sojourner will come to realize that in Tunisia, at least, "yes" does not always mean "yes."

Anxiety and Withdrawal

Other potential barriers to intercultural understanding are anxiety and tension. Novel situations almost always cause stress. A small amount of tension and excitement can be energizing, but a large amount is extremely debilitating. If you have ever lived in a foreign country, you know how exhausting it is to decipher an unfamiliar language or to find your way around. When the tension rises too high, individuals experience **culture shock**, "the anxiety that results from losing all of our familiar signs and symbols of social intercourse."[49]

When we're in our own cultures, we depend on familiar routines. We feel secure because we know what to expect from those around us. As Craig Storti puts it, "if we were not instinctively sure that people would be civil unless provoked, stay on their side of the road and stop on red, that shopkeepers would give us goods in return for money—if we could not routinely depend on these things happening—the resulting uncertainty would immobilize us."[50] In new surroundings, we may not be able to depend on any of these things; thus, we begin to feel isolated and adrift. It's ironic that the conditioning that makes it so easy for us to function at home is the very thing that makes it difficult for us to function abroad.

> When culture shock is severe, individuals develop feelings of helplessness and lowered self-esteem, a desire to return home, insomnia, depression, and even physical illness.

When culture shock is severe, individuals develop feelings of helplessness and lowered self-esteem, a desire to return home, insomnia, depression, and even physical illness. They become almost completely dysfunctional and may have to withdraw from contact with the native culture. During severe culture shock, people are likely to distort perceptions and feel hostility toward members of the host culture.

Although severe culture shock can be devastating, mild periods of stress followed by withdrawal can be productive. In her **draw-back-to-leap model**, Young Yun Kim argues that brief periods of culture shock may be "a necessary precondition for adaptive change, as individuals strive to regain their inner balance by adapting to the demands and opportunities of their new life circumstances."[51]

As sojourners experience stress, they often withdraw (the draw-back phase), engaging in tension-reducing behaviors that allow them an opportunity to reorganize their thoughts and feelings. Once they have processed cultural differences, they have the strength to continue to adapt (the leap-forward phase). According to Kim, some degree of stress is to be expected. By taking it easy when stress occurs, the individual avoids complete withdrawal.

Ethnocentrism

A final barrier to intercultural understanding is **ethnocentrism**, the belief that one's own culture is superior to all others and the tendency to judge all cultures by one's own criteria. Although it may be natural to believe that anything different is wrong, this is not a very productive attitude. Blaming people for not behaving the same way we do is irrational, especially when economic or physical factors may explain the difference. An ethnocentric American may be aghast to find out that people in another culture "waste" two hours of the middle of the day in resting. He or she may fail to consider that in that location, the temperature often rises well above ninety degrees and there is no air-conditioning. An ethnocentric individual may look down on the "natives" for using "primitive" farming methods without understanding that they have no money to buy modern machinery. In many cases, the way "they" do things makes sense, given their circumstances.

Samovar and his colleagues argue that it is naive to believe that our culture has all the answers. They ask us to consider the following questions:

> *The Jew covers his head to pray, the Protestant does not—is one more correct than the other? In Saudi Arabia women cover their faces, in America they cover very little—is one more correct than the other? The Occidental speaks to God, the Oriental has God speak to him—is one more correct than the other? The American Indian values and accepts nature, the average American seeks to alter nature—is one more correct than the other? A listing of these questions is never-ending. We must remember, however, that it is not the questions that are important, but rather the dogmatic way in which we answer them.*[52]

Unless we can admit that differences do not always mean deficiencies and that our culture is not necessarily superior in all things, we will never be able to establish the trust and respect that are necessary counterparts of successful intercultural interaction.

ADAPTING TO NEW CULTURES

Despite all the difficulties we have described, people do manage to adapt to one another. In this section, we explore how people from different cultures accomplish this feat.

All individuals who leave their home countries and immerse themselves in strange new lands experience stress. Some overcome this stress better than others, finding ways to feel at home with people who are quite different. Research has identified a number of factors associated with successful adaptation. These include the nature of the host culture, the personal attitudes and predispositions of the newcomer, and, most important, the kinds of communicative bonds the newcomer makes. For just as one maintains contact with one's own culture through communication, one's ability to enter a new culture successfully is also determined by communicative behavior.

> **Some cultures have more permeable boundaries than do others. Some make outsiders feel more at home than do others.**

Nature of the Host Culture

Some cultures have more permeable boundaries than do others. Some make outsiders feel more at home than do others. One factor associated with successful adaptation is the host country's attitude toward foreigners. If citizens of a country consider outsiders barbarians and infidels, then adaptation will be rough going.

Generally speaking, **cultural distance**, the extent to which two cultures differ, affects ease of communication. This point is illustrated in Table 12.4, which ranks cultural exchanges in terms of their relative difficulty. At the top of the table are cultural pairings with maximal difference. Japan and the United States, for example, are quite different in a number of important dimensions; as we have already seen, one of these cultures is collectivist, and the other is individualist. In addition, Americans have what Hall and Hall call a *monochronic* sense of time: Americans tend to segment and sequence time and to value speed. Although on the surface the Japanese may seem monochronic, below the surface they are *polychronic*, especially when it comes to interpersonal behavior. People in polychronic cultures change plans often and easily and consider schedules as objectives to be met, not as definite commitments. Thus, in polychronic cultures, it may take a lot longer to do things than in monochronic cultures.[53]

Another difference between Japan and the United States is that Japanese and English are very different languages. The distinction between them is much greater than, say, the distinction between English and French or German. Aspects of material culture (housing, transportation, and so on), as well as artistic and literary conventions, are also quite distinct. Although Japan and the United States are both quite advanced in technology, these two countries otherwise exhibit large differences.

Germany and the United States, in contrast, may differ in some ways, but these countries share more similarities. Although their languages, educational systems, managerial styles, and problem-solving approaches exhibit some differences, people in these countries share common beliefs and impulses as well as mutually familiar material cultures.

Toward the bottom of Table 12.4 are cultural pairings of people who speak the same language and live side by side in the same country. People from the same

Table 12.4 Cultural Distance

Cultural distance is the extent to which two cultures are culturally and physically different from one another. As distance increases, complete and accurate communication becomes more difficult. What do you think is the relative cultural distance between the United States and the following countries?

Australia, Canada, China, France, Germany, Italy, Japan, New Zealand, Saudi Arabia, South Korea, Spain, United Kingdom, Yemen

Answer:

English-speaking Countries such as Australia, New Zealand, Canada, and the United Kingdom are closest in cultural distance to the United States because they share a common language as well as a common history, and similar religious and social values. Adaptation for U.S. citizens will be relatively easy.

Western European Countries such as France, Germany, Spain, and Italy have moderate levels of cultural distance from the United States. Linguistic differences as well as some cultural patterns can make adaptation somewhat difficult; however, some many values and traditions are shared.

Asian and Middle Eastern countries such as South Korea, Japan, China, Yemen, and Saudi Arabia are more culturally distant from the United States. Adaptation is impeded by differences in written and spoken language, material culture, religious beliefs, and traditional values.

nation show the smallest amount of difference. Unfortunately, this does not preclude volatile interactions. Although Catholics and Protestants coexist quite peacefully in the United States, this obviously has not been the case in Northern Ireland. And although homosexuals and heterosexuals may share almost all aspects of national identity, the one difference that separates them may be highly salient to some—so much so that some heterosexuals may commit vandalism and acts of violence against members of homosexual cultures. In general, the more aspects of a culture that differ, the more difficult intercultural communication becomes.

Personal Predispositions

Having an open mind is clearly a prerequisite for adaptation. This brings us to a second factor related to intercultural interactions: the newcomer's personality. Included here are such factors as one's openness, resilience, and self-esteem. Some people have a low tolerance for ambiguity and find being an outsider distressing. Others lack confidence and may displace their feelings of anxiety onto those around them. Still others have great difficulty handling tension. Since adapting necessitates change and is always accompanied by stress, people with these predispositions will experience difficulty in adaptation.

In addition to personality variables, education and preentry training are important. The more a newcomer knows about a culture ahead of time, the more prepared he or she is for contact. The traveler who reads about the host culture and makes contacts with host nationals before entering that culture will be more comfortable in the new setting.

Communication Bonds

The third factor affecting successful adaptation is the way in which the newcomer interacts once he or she is in the host culture. Although openness and confidence can help, these internal predispositions must be implemented in actual communicative behaviors. In discussing the communicative aspects of adaptation, Young Yun Kim argues that a newcomer's exposure to communication networks in the host culture (what Kim refers to as *host social communica-*

Despite differences, people with open minds can learn from one another.

© Hugh Williamson/Alamy

tion) and his or her relationships with members of the home culture (*ethnic social communication*) are two important determinants of intercultural success.[54]

Kim believes that sojourners interested in *acculturation* (i.e., becoming part of a new culture) should expose themselves as much as possible to host social communication. They should make interpersonal contacts and familiarize themselves with mass communication within the host culture. They should also avoid depending too heavily on ethnic communication networks. The newcomer who interacts only with other foreigners, who refuses to make any attempt to learn the language, and who reads only books and newspapers from home needlessly isolates himself or herself. Although others who share the same ethnic identity can form a support group and can teach a newcomer the ropes, they often inhibit real cross-cultural contact.

Developing an open communication style is a key variable in successful adaptation. This means being willing to plunge in and explore new cultures with enthusiasm. It also means developing—often through trial and error—the behavioral competence to act in new ways that are more appropriate to one's new situation.

BECOMING A MORE OPEN COMMUNICATOR

As we have seen, misunderstandings occur not only between people from different countries, but also between people who live side by side. In fact, we may sometimes treat foreigners more respectfully and decently than we treat neighbors who, for one reason or another, we perceive as different. We end this chapter with some guidelines for becoming open- and fair-minded communicators, comfortable with both co-cultural and cross-cultural diversity.[55]

- Open yourself to new contacts. Although contact can reinforce negative perceptions, it can also disconfirm negative expectations. The best way to find out that "they" are not all alike is through contact. Unfortunately, we tend to associate and feel most comfortable with others who are similar. Think of your own circle of friends. How many of them are from a different racial, ethnic, or religious background? If your answer is none or few, you might consider widening your field of experience.

- Learn about the history and experiences of people from diverse cultures. One of the major complaints of minority cultures is that their history has been rendered invisible by dominant groups. Most people know very little about other co-cultural groups, and this ignorance is a barrier to understanding. By taking a course about, or by experiencing on your own, the cultural history of another group, you can gain a deeper understanding of its members' perspectives.

- Examine yourself for possible stereotypes. Prejudices and stereotypes are insidious; although these barriers are all too apparent in others, we may not recognize them in ourselves. The first step in becoming more fair-minded and open lies in admitting the possibility that some of one's judgments are unfair.

- Responsible and open communicators are willing and able to role-take. Role-taking means seeing the world from another's perspective—imaginatively taking on another's viewpoint. It means actively trying to understand how others make sense of their world and actively trying to experience what they feel. Although complete empathy is impossible, getting a better sense of what others think and feel is possible.

- Finally, each of us should work on becoming more self-confident. The better we feel about ourselves, the more likely we are to feel good about others and the more able we are to learn from them.

SUMMARY

Now more than ever, learning to communicate across cultures is important. This chapter discusses how culture affects us and how we can become more effective cross-cultural communicators.

Culture consists of all those parts of the environment constructed by humans, including the shared customs and values that create community, as well as material objects and possessions. Cultural understandings are learned, shared, multifaceted, dynamic, and overlapping. Cultural norms are learned from and shared with others, and we spend substantial amounts of time and energy proving to others that we are "real" members of our cultures and that we are different from outsiders. Cultures control many interrelated facets of our lives. In this sense, it is true that if you touch a culture in one place, everything else is affected. Moreover, cultures constantly grow and change, and people belong to multiple overlapping cultural groups. All of these factors make learning the rules of a new culture difficult.

Understanding culture is important in today's global village. As international business becomes more common and as cultural groups within our own country demand recognition and respect, it is less and less possible to avoid intercultural interaction. By improving cross-cultural communication, we can make contacts with members of other cultures more comfortable and can enrich our own intercultural identities.

Intercultural communication is difficult for several reasons. First, people from different cultures perceive the world differently, attaching their own culture-specific values to events. Second, people from different cultures have differ-ent attitudes toward roles. Third, cultures differ in the goals their members value. Americans, for example, are characterized by effort-optimism, whereas people in other cultures may be more fatalistic. Fourth, cultures affect worldviews, basic notions of self and humanity. Americans believe people are rational, perfectible, and mutable.

Cultures differ on a number of dimensions including power distance, uncertainty avoidance, masculinity/femininity, long-term/short-term orientation, and individualism/collectivism. Finally, language differences indicate that what can be said easily in one culture may be almost impossible to convey in another. Cultures differ in the values they assign to context, directness, expressiveness, and formality.

A number of attitudes diminish cross-cultural communication. When we stereotype, assume similarity while ignoring real differences, feel anxious about diversity, or take ethnocentric pride in the superiority of our own culture, we create blocks to understanding. Despite these barriers, intercultural communication can succeed. A number of factors are associated with successful adaptation to a foreign culture: the openness of the host culture and the degree to which it is culturally distant from one's own; the extent to which newcomers are open, resilient, and self-confident; and the willingness of newcomers to build bonds with members of host cultures.

Being comfortable with diversity is not easy. But by being as open as possible, by educating yourself on cultural issues, by challenging stereotypes, and by trying to see the world as others do, you will become a more confident and competent cultural communicator.

KEY TERMS

Listed below are the key terms used in this chapter, along with the number of the page where each is explained.

culture (321)	power distance (330)	low-context cultures (333)
cultural universals (323)	uncertainty avoidance (330)	high-context cultures (333)
intercultural communication (325)	masculinity/femininity (330)	stereotypes (335)
co-cultures (326)	long-term/short-term orientation (330)	prejudice (336)
intercultural identity (326)	individualism/collectivism (331)	assumption of similarity (337)
effort-optimism (329)	vertical relationship (331)	culture shock (338)
worldviews (329)	horizontal relationship (331)	draw-back-to-leap model (338)
rationality premise (330)		ethnocentrism (338)
perfectibility premise (330)		cultural distance (339)
mutability premise (330)		

SUGGESTED READING

Hofstede, Geert, Hofstede, Gert Jan, & Minkov, Michael. (2010). *Cultures and organizations: Software of the mind* (3rd ed.). New York: McGraw-Hill.

> A general discussion of ways to deal with the differences in how people from around the world think, feel, and act, by one of the foremost experts in cross-cultural communication and his colleagues.

Samovar, Larry A., Porter, Richard E., McDaniel, Edwin R., & Roy, Carolyn S. (2012). *Communication between cultures* (8th ed.). Belmont, CA: Wadsworth.

> A best-selling text that offers an overview of theory and research in intercultural communication.

Varner, Iris, & Beamer, Linda. (2010). *Intercultural communication in the global workplace* (5th ed.). New York: McGraw-Hill/Irwin.

> Illustrates how intercultural differences play out in organizational contexts, offering real-life examples and cases for analysis.

Methods of Discovery

When people know how to communicate skillfully, the quality of their lives and the lives of those around them is improved; when people lack this knowledge, their social and personal worlds can crumble.

After reading this chapter, you should be able to:

- Describe differences between commonsense ways of knowing and systematic ways of knowing.
- List the characteristics of scholarly research.
- Explain the five common tasks in communication inquiry.
- Define briefly the nine popular research methodologies from Table 13.3.
- Explain the purpose of rhetorical criticism and identify some contemporary critical approaches.
- Explain the purpose and methods used in ethnographic research.
- Describe the steps in conducting a survey.
- Describe the nature of and steps in experimental research.
- Understand the goals and methods of performance research.

There is a close link between communication theory and communication practice. When people know how to communicate skillfully, the quality of their lives and the lives of those around them is improved; when people lack this knowledge, their social and personal worlds can crumble. In short, discoveries about communication are important.

This chapter is about methods of discovery—methods scholars use to further their understanding of communication as well as methods you can use to widen your own knowledge. We begin by reviewing some of the basic research methodologies used by critics and communication scientists. Although you may not plan on becoming a professional scholar, professional methods can guide your own efforts to understand communication and can make you a more critical consumer of communication research.

We also look at some sources you can turn to for information about communication once this class is over. First, we will describe the kinds of courses offered in communication departments at large universities. Although not all of these courses may be offered at your school, each draws on a rich body of literature that is readily available. Second, we will discuss ways you can learn about communication both inside and outside of class. Once you have learned where to look, you will find sources of discovery all around you.

HOW IS COMMUNICATION RESEARCH DONE?

Forming hypotheses about the social world and looking for evidence to test those hypotheses are everyday activities. Our lives are guided, to a large extent, by commonsense theories of human action. When we try to explain the success or failure of a relationship or think up a strategy

> When we try to explain the success or failure of a relationship or think up a strategy for getting what we want, we are theorizing about communication.

for getting what we want, we are theorizing about communication. "We were so different; we never really had a chance" is a theory about relationships. "If I do a favor for her now, she'll have to repay me later" is a hypothesis about the way interpersonal influence works.

Problems with Commonsense Ways of Knowing

In everyday life, we often accept the first reasonable explanation we come across without asking whether there is another, better explanation for what is happening. Commonsense knowing is often biased. The first problem with commonsense knowledge is that we privilege our own experiences. Most people find it hard to accept generalizations that contradict what they have seen with their own eyes. Most project their own beliefs and motivations onto others. Thus, *our everyday models of human behavior are often models of our own behavior.*

We also let our own desires get in our way. We see what we want to see and turn a blind eye to information that makes us uncomfortable. Our prejudices make us dismiss anything that contradicts what we've decided is true. Our superstitions lead us to accept any message that gives us an illusion of control over unexplained events. Thus, *our everyday models of human behavior may also be models of what we wish were true rather than what is true.*

In everyday life, we also rely on simple **heuristics**, rules of thumb that allow us to avoid careful information processing.[1] When we encounter difficult information, we look for simple cues that tell us what to think. We may rely on authorities ("I didn't understand it, but my dad said it was true") or status cues ("The argument seemed odd, but after all, the author did go to Harvard"). We may look at formal aspects, rather than the content, of the message ("She used a lot of statistics and graphs, so she must know what she's talking about"). Too often, *our everyday models of human behavior are based on simplistic thinking.*

Systematic Ways of Knowing

Researchers try to avoid the errors that affect everyday thinking. In many ways, good researchers are like detectives or investigative reporters. They don't accept things at face value. They are suspicious.

> *To research is to search again, to take another, more careful look, to find out more. . . . What the research attitude presumes is that the first look—and every later look—may be prone to error, so that one must look again and again, differently and thoroughly each time.*[2]

Researchers often set out to overturn commonsense beliefs. In this sense, researchers "are professional troublemakers: they must challenge old beliefs, create new ones, and then turn the challenge upon those new ones."[3]

Lawrence Frey and his colleagues offer an excellent discussion of the characteristics of scholarly research. This discussion is summarized in Table 13.1. According to these authors, research has six basic characteristics: it is question oriented, methodological, replicable, self-critical, cumulative and self-correcting, and cyclical.[4]

The first characteristic of research is that it is *question oriented*. Research begins when the researcher encounters a state of affairs that needs explanation. Rather than simply accepting the status quo, the researcher formulates questions about it and then tries to answer these questions. At heart, research "requires the capacity to ask the right questions as well as a sense of what form the answer should take."[5]

Research is also *methodological*; that is, it is systematic and ordered, with built-in guarantees that the findings will be as accurate as possible. As we shall see, researchers are guided by systematic methods and procedures during their investigations.

That research is as careful and as accurate as possible does not mean that researchers lack imagination. Researchers must often make counterintuitive leaps and think their way past cultural biases. They also must devise imaginative ways of gathering information and testing hypotheses.

When Frey and his colleagues say that research must be *replicable*, they mean that it must be repeatable.

To research is to search again, to keep asking questions until we see what lies below the surface.

In many ways, good researchers are like detectives or investigative reporters. They don't accept things at face value. They are suspicious.

Table 13.1 Characteristics of Scholarly Research

• **Question Oriented**

"At the heart of all research is a question worth answering."

• **Methodological**

"Systematic procedures are used to ensure that researchers find and report what is accurate."

• **Replicable**

Other scholars must be able to "replicate, or reproduce, the entire inquiry process."

• **Self-Critical**

Scholarly researchers "openly evaluate the strengths and weaknesses of their own research studies."

• **Cumulative and Self-Correcting**

"The accumulation of information . . . allows for knowledge to evolve and grow."

• **Cyclical**

Research "ends up back where it started," with new questions emerging from previous answers.

From Frey, Lawrence R., Botan, Carl, H., Kreps, Gary L., *Investigating Communication: An Introduction to Research Methods*, 2nd ed., © 2000. Adapted and electronically reproduced by permission of Pearson Education, Inc., Upper Saddle River, New Jersey.

The methods employed must be so objective that if the research were conducted again, the same results would occur and the same conclusions would be drawn. A result that occurs only once in only one study may be due to some unusual aspect of the research (or the researcher) rather than to the underlying phenomenon the researcher is trying to explain. Scholars make an effort to test and retest their theories before they generalize about them.

> **Researchers belong to a community of scientists and critics, a community that works together to correct old mistakes and to discover new information.**

Scholarly research is also *self-critical*. This means that researchers make special efforts to disprove their own theories. A scholar should be his or her own most exacting critic. In addition, to make sure that research is replicated and criticized, researchers make their results public. They show their results to others for examination and questioning. To keep results secret violates the purpose of research, which is to further knowledge.

Another important characteristic of research is that it is *cumulative* and *self-correcting*. The first step in doing research is to review all of the previous studies on one's topic and to build on others' work. Researchers do not want to spend time and effort "reinventing the wheel." Researchers belong to a community of scientists and critics, a community that works together to correct old mistakes and to discover new information.

Scholarship is, then, ultimately *cyclical*. Just as good research begins with a question, it ends with another question. In the words of Frey and his colleagues,

> *a researcher begins with a sense of curiosity and a topic worth studying, asks questions and/or makes predictions, plans research carefully, carries out the planned research, analyzes the data to provide tentative answers, and starts all over again by posing new topics and questions worth asking.*[6]

Common Research Tasks

As we shall see shortly, researchers use a wide variety of methods in communication research. Some researchers rely on historical–critical methods, whereas others devise elaborate experiments. Nevertheless, all go through the basic activities shown in Table 13.2. The first task is to *find a subject of study and formulate a research question*. As Frey and his colleagues point out, inquiry is prompted by curiosity. The question a researcher attempts to answer in a given study is called a **research question**. The question should be specific and clear, for it will act as a guide throughout the research. Some researchers begin with a very specific question, whereas others start broadly and narrow the scope of their study as they proceed. For example, a researcher may be initially interested in political persuasion. The question "How do politicians persuade the public?" is so broad that a researcher could spend a lifetime on it and only scratch the surface. Researchers can narrow their focus by asking more specific questions. One interesting aspect of political communication is the use of surrogates, people who speak for a candidate. "What is the communicative role of surrogates in a political campaign?" narrows the focus, but the researcher must still decide which surrogates and which campaigns to study. An even more specific re-search question might be "What kinds of themes characterized the speeches of the vice presidential candidates in the last presidential campaign?"

An important part of framing a research question is defining key concepts and terms. The researcher who wishes to look at surrogates' roles must understand what a surrogate is and must be able to define the aspect of surrogates' communication behavior that he or she wants to investigate. The researcher who wants to study the effects of negative campaigning on a candidate's credibility and popularity must offer clear definitions of *negative campaigning, credibility*, and *popularity*.

Definitions are generally of two types: conceptual and operational. A **conceptual definition** explains the meaning of a term in a general, abstract way. *Credibility*, for example, might be conceptually defined as "the extent to which a candidate is seen by an audience as worthy of belief." An **operational definition** explains how a term will be measured in the study. An operational definition of *credibility* might be "the candidate's mean score on a ten-point rating scale of trustworthiness and expertness." An operational definition is necessary for measurement purposes. Although the researcher knows conceptually what negative campaigning means, he or she also has to know how to recognize specific examples of it. If a candidate refers to his opponent as "sleazy" and "dishonest," the characterizations are clearly negative. But what if the candidate refers to his opponent as a "liberal"? Is this a description or a slur? Before starting the study, the researcher must decide what to count as an instance of negative campaigning—an often quite difficult task.

In addition to formulating a research question and defining key terms, the re-searcher must *choose a particular research methodology*. Often, these tasks go hand in hand. The topic area may suggest a research methodology, or the methodology may guide formulation of the research question. Researchers use a variety of methodologies. Some researchers take a historical–critical approach. They might decide to investigate surrogate behavior by analyzing a given surrogate's public rhetoric. Other researchers might choose an ethnographic approach, actually joining a campaign to make behind-the-scenes observations. Still others might rely on survey methods, sending out questionnaires to track public opinion over the course of the campaign. Researchers with an experimental bent might even test whether certain kinds of information are more acceptable when attributed to a surrogate or when attributed to a candidate.

Table 13.2 Common Tasks in Communication Inquiry

Task 1	Formulate a research question
Task 2	Choose a research methodology
Task 3	Design a sampling strategy
Task 4	Gather and analyze data
Task 5	Interpret data and share results

Having chosen a research approach, the researcher must *design a sampling strategy* to decide who or what to study. The researcher who has decided to do a rhetorical analysis of surrogates' public speeches must determine which surrogates are of interest and which speeches to analyze. One researcher might decide to focus on a single individual (say, a presidential candidate's running mate), comparing speeches at the beginning, middle, and end of the campaign to see how themes and topics evolve. Another researcher might be interested in a single speech given at the nominating convention.

The researcher who opts to conduct a survey must decide what questions to ask and whom to ask. Because it is impossible to ask everyone in the country all the possible questions related to political persuasion, the researcher must choose a small subset of people and items. This process of sampling occurs in every case of research, no matter what the approach is.

Once the researcher has decided whom or what to study, he or she must *gather and analyze data*. For one study, the researcher might analyze data by poring over transcripts of public speeches, searching for themes and metaphors. For another study, data gathering might involve exposing subjects to an elaborate experimental manipulation and measuring their responses, and analysis might use statistical tests of significance. Regardless of the form of the data-gathering and -analyzing process, the final research activity is to *interpret the data and report the results*. The researcher must attempt to make sense of the data, draw conclusions about them, and share those conclusions with others.

FIVE CONTEMPORARY RESEARCH METHODS

There are many research methodologies. Table 13.3 lists only a sampling. In the next five sections, we will look at five methodologies in particular: rhetorical criticism, ethnographic research, survey research, experimental research, and performance as research. As we discuss each methodology, we will first describe the goals and procedures researchers follow when using that methodology, and we will then look at a representative sample of research so that you can see how these methods are applied.

Rhetorical Criticism

In everyday life, we frequently act as critics, analyzing and evaluating messages. Most of us enjoy expressing opinions; after attending a lecture or seeing a film, we like to discuss what we experienced. Our response may be a fairly simple description of what we liked or disliked about the communication, or it may be a more detailed analysis of the intended and unintended effects of the message on the audience. In either case, by discussing a message critically, we increase our understanding and appreciation of that message and of the communication process in general.

Rhetorical criticism is an extension and refinement of the everyday critical impulse; it is a systematic way of describing, analyzing, and evaluating a given act of communication. The kind of criticism we do in everyday life is often limited to a general description of how we personally react to a given message ("I really liked her speech. It was inspiring"). Although we may explain some of the things we liked about it ("The part where she described her childhood really hit home"), we seldom do so in much detail. Unless we are challenged, we do not spend a great deal of time making a strong case for our beliefs. We simply state our criticism and move on.

> Rhetorical criticism is an extension and refinement of the everyday critical impulse; it is a systematic way of describing, analyzing, and evaluating a given act of communication.

Rhetorical critics engage in a thorough examination of a given message and its effects, giving special attention to the situation that prompted the message as well as the social and personal constraints that affected the speaker. Rhetorical critics also examine the purpose, structure, and style of the message, evaluating the ways in which the speaker's rhetorical choices affected audience response.

Critics are careful to articulate the critical standards they use to judge a message. The same message may be evaluated in a number of different ways. One critic might look at arguments. Another might examine a speaker's metaphors. A third might look at the ideological values of a speech, and a fourth might analyze its social importance. Each evaluation can add to our understanding of how the message operates.

In their book *Communication Criticism*, Karyn Rybacki and Don Rybacki discuss the process of criticism. They argue that whatever the act being investigated is, the rhetorical critic has an obligation to do three things: to describe the significant qualities of a rhetorical act, to describe those aspects of the rhetorical situation that influenced the form of the rhetorical act, and to render a judgment about the quality and consequences of the rhetorical act.[7]

Steps in Rhetorical Criticism

Rhetorical criticism seeks to explain and evaluate a rhetorical act. A **rhetorical act** is any act of communication that influences the belief or behavior of an audience. Rhetorical acts can take many forms. An inaugural speech, a political cartoon, a propaganda film, a protest song, a satirical television show, an advertising campaign, an act of civil disobedience—all can influence an audience and may thus be classified as rhetorical acts.

In evaluating a given rhetorical act, the critic must take a critical approach. Each approach is based on a theory that defines rhetoric and the role of a critic, and each provides a slightly different set of criteria for judging rhetorical success. Table 13.4 gives a brief overview of some of the more popular contemporary critical approaches. Keep in mind, however, that critics may blend these approaches or develop new approaches in response to changing interests and ideologies.

Like all research, rhetorical criticism is designed to be shared. The rhetorical critic's goal is to increase understanding and appreciation of a rhetorical act. A rhetorical critic must make a strong case for his or her point of view by showing that he or she understands the context and the structure of the rhetorical act being judged and by providing support for critical claims. Rhetorical criticism is a rhetorical act in its own right, an act of argumentation that succeeds only when it enables us to understand and appreciate a message more fully.

Unity and Progress: An Example of Rhetorical Criticism

In March 2008, during Barack Obama's first run for the presidency, the pastor of Obama's church, Reverend Jeremiah Wright, made a series of inflammatory

---

Table 13.3 Popular Research Methodologies

Rhetorical Criticism

The rhetorical critic begins by choosing a rhetorical act to study. After describing its purpose, its audience, and its context, the critic examines the rhetorical strategies employed and evaluates their effectiveness.

Sample research questions:

- How did the president build audience identification in the last presidential campaign?
- How did the narrative structure that Spike Lee used in the film *Malcolm X* add to Malcolm's image?
- How did George W. Bush use metaphor to reach multiple audiences in his speech announcing the war in Iraq?

Content Analysis

Focusing on a text, the researcher systematically measures message content to determine how often a given unit of content occurs. The units studied may be general (themes, topics, viewpoints) or specific (kinds of words, grammatical forms). Results involve reporting the frequency of a given kind of content and relating frequencies to variables outside the text.

Sample research questions:

- What is the average number of violent acts on prime-time television shows on each of the major networks?
- Do Republican and Democratic senatorial candidates employ different kinds of symbols in campaign speeches?
- How do children's fairy tales portray family relationships?

Conversation Analysis

To describe the content, structure, and function of everyday spoken interaction, the researcher obtains a sample of talk, transcribes and examines it, and

draws inferences about it. Researchers frequently examine the sequential relationship, functions, and effects of the moves in a given conversation.

Sample research questions:

- What kinds of conversational moves do teachers use to encourage classroom participation?
- How are conversational openings and closings structured?
- What kinds of actions and utterances signal dominance in male–female interactions?

Ethnography

The researcher observes behavior in its natural setting. To describe the communication practices of a group of people, the researcher may actually "go undercover" as a participant. The researcher avoids imposing his or her own values and assumptions on the data. Instead of testing an existing hypothesis, he or she allows conclusions to emerge from observations.

Sample research questions:

- What are the primary functions of talk for male members of an urban, blue-collar neighborhood?
- How do middle-class mothers communicate to their children during play?
- How do established members of religious cults recruit and treat new members?

Unobtrusive Methods

Rather than openly observe people, researchers can opt to observe traces of their communicative behavior unobtrusively and draw conclusions from these observations. Researchers may focus on measures of erosion (how objects are worn down by use) or on measures of accretion (physical traces that build up over time).

statements suggesting that the 9/11 terror attacks were a just punishment for America's treatment of its African American citizens ("Not God Bless America, God damn America. . . . God damn America for treating her citizens as less than human"). Given Obama's connection to Wright, he had no choice but to respond, and, on March 18, candidate Obama delivered his "A More Perfect Union" speech,

Table 13.3 Popular Research Methodologies (*continued*)

Sample research questions:

- What museum exhibits are most popular (measured by wear and tear on carpets or amount of dirt on floors)?
- Is racial tension increasing at a certain high school (measured by kinds of graffiti in the school's public areas)?
- Which of a series of cover designs makes a brochure most appealing (measured by the number of each brochure removed from racks)?

Survey Research

To survey groups of people, researchers use either written questionnaires or face-to-face interviews to question subjects and record and code their responses. Researchers question a representative sample so that findings will be generalizable.

Sample research questions:

- What issues were most important in influencing young people to vote in the last presidential election?
- What kind of parental advice do young adults remember as being most influential?
- What do college students report as the most significant factors in choosing a romantic partner?

Experimental Research

Researchers systematically manipulate causal variables and measure the effects of their manipulation on subjects' responses. Extraneous influences are controlled or held constant in order to discern the relationship between specific variables. Responses are normally converted to numerical form and analyzed statistically.

Sample research questions:

- Does watching violent cartoons lead children to act aggressively toward one another?
- Is a one-sided or two-sided argument more effective for persuading a hostile audience?
- Are women more likely to turn to other women or to men when they need advice about career moves?

Performance Research

Researchers focus on analyzing the social and/or aesthetic meanings of performances. Sometimes they write about performances they have observed; at other times they uncover the meanings of texts by actually performing them. Through the process of re-creating a text for an audience, the researcher discovers and shares his or her understandings and findings.

Sample research questions:

- How did the play *Waiting for Lefty* work to attract workers to the labor movement in the 1930s?
- How can protesters use street performances to raise the consciousness of an audience?
- In re-creating a transcript of an oral history interview, what performance decisions did the performer make?

Mixed Methods

Researchers may combine several methodologies in a single study. For example, within the framework of an experiment, samples of talk may be collected under different conditions and then content analyzed. Ethnographic observations may be followed up with surveys. The term used to describe the process of approaching a research question from multiple perspectives is **triangulation**.

a significant statement on U.S. race relations. In "Race, Rhetoric, and Running for President: Unpacking the Significance of Barack Obama's 'A More Perfect Union' Speech," Susanna Dilliplane analyzes this speech, showing why it was a significant rhetorical moment in the campaign.[8] In her analysis, Dilliplane examines three aspects of the rhetorical situation: the specific challenges posed by the context in which Wright's comments and Obama's response occurred; the rhetorical strategy used to answer those challenges; and the place of this speech in the rhetoric of the campaign as a whole.

Dilliplane argues that Obama faced two challenges in responding to Wright. First, he had to reject Wright's extreme statements without rejecting the importance

---

Table 13.4 Contemporary Critical Approaches

Neo-Aristotelian Criticism

Using the concepts and principles set forth by Aristotle and other classical theorists, the rhetorical critic evaluates a speaker's rhetorical choices, examining modes of proof, structure and organization of arguments, and stylistic choices and delivery, as they affect audience response.

Genre Criticism

Critics discuss how a message fits into a genre, or specific type of communication. Traditional genres include the apologia (an apology, or defense of character), the eulogy, the political speech, the sermon, and so on. Rhetorical acts other than speeches also have their own genres—for example, the Western film or the romantic novel.

Burkean Dramatistic Analysis

Viewing symbolic acts as "drama," the critic analyzes how various aspects of a given "performance" (act, purpose, agent, agency, and scene) are symbolically represented and how they serve to evoke identification between speaker and audience.

Fantasy Theme Analysis

Working from the idea that we understand our world by telling stories about it, the critic examines the implicit narrative structure of rhetorical acts, describing the myths and fantasies that the acts convey. A fantasy theme analyst seeks to uncover fantasy themes (basic story lines and characters that dramatize a situation), fantasy types (recurring tales that embody the fears or values of a culture), and shared rhetorical visions (shared schemata for interpreting reality).

Social Movement Studies

The critic analyzes how a social cause gains adherents, how its members communicate to the public, and what their impact is on the culture at large. A social movement critic might study the rhetorical strategies of groups such as civil rights activists, the religious right, supporters of Jewish statehood, the right-to-life movement, and so on.

Cultural Ideological Criticism

The critic examines rhetorical acts for political messages and evaluates how these messages uphold or subvert existing power relations. Often, the critic evaluates what is left out of a message as well as what the message contains. Any political ideology, such as feminism or Marxism, may form the basis of criticism.

Social Values Criticism

Rhetorical critics look at the way cultural products (speeches, films, TV shows, etc.) represent a culture's basic values. Critics try to uncover ways in which rhetorical acts combine conflicting values. A social values critic might investigate how a rhetorical act synthesizes values such as individualism and community or morality and materialism.

of religious oratory in the history of African Americans' fight for equality. Second, he had to show constituents that that while he was a credible spokesman for the African American experience, he did not define himself solely as a black candidate. In other words, he needed to mobilize African American voters while retaining the support of white working-class Democrats and Independents as well as the national media. This meant that he had to strike a delicate balance between showing his understanding of Black voters' perspective while avoiding aligning himself with black stereotypes that could alienate white voters. In addition he needed to avoid the criticism of skeptical journalists who would be looking for consistency with past statements, "such as his repeated declaration that he self-identified as a black man."[9]

How did Obama overcome these challenges? Dilliplane argues he did so by using two interconnected themes: America as a nation moving toward fulfillment of its promise ("toward a more perfect union") and America as a country in which diversity gives birth to unity ("out of many, we are truly one"). Throughout the speech, he referred to these themes, first portraying the nation and himself as embodying these values, and then discussing Wright's behavior in light of them.

He began by quoting the Constitution, asserting that at its core it stood for the idea that America "could be and should be perfected over time," and implying that his campaign stood for this march toward progress. He then turned to the idea of unity through diversity by casting himself as a symbol of American diversity and therefore implying that he could speak "from and to diverse perspectives, particularly black and white perspectives."[10]

Having established the themes of progress and unity through diversity as basic American values, he then turned his attention to the topic of Reverend Wright and race. Dilliplane suggests that this section of the speech consisted of four rhetorical moves. First, Obama criticized Wright's view of American society by showing how his comments contradicted the twin themes of unity and progress. He stated that "Reverend Wright's comments were not only wrong but divisive, divisive at a time when we need unity" and that "he [Wright] spoke as if our society was static; as if no progress had been made."[11] Second, he attempted to validate and explain the important role of oratory in black churches. Third, he made an attempt to contextualize Wright's remarks, suggesting that although Wright was "imperfect," his views originated in an earlier struggle by the black church against segregation and inequality, from a time that America had left behind in its march toward progress. Fourth, he stated that just as he could not disown his own white grandmother's imperfect stereotypical views, he could not completely disown Wright's. "These people," he said, "are a part of me. And they are part of America, this country that I love." In brief, he was arguing that Wright, like the nation and himself, was made up of conflicting parts, but, as Dilliplane puts it, "these parts can unite into a larger whole that, although imperfect, is still greater as a result of its diversity."[12]

Although Dilliplane believes Obama's speech was largely successful, she suggests that there were a few potential risks in his rhetorical strategy. One risk occurred when he argued that, although there were some legitimate reasons for both African Americans and whites to feel anger (the former in reaction to slavery and discrimination, the latter in response to economic conditions), both black and white anger were counterproductive. In doing so, Dilliplane believes he could have offended black constituents by dismissing the use of righteous anger in traditional black oratory.

In addition, by portraying himself as a symbol of reconciliation, someone who could uniquely fulfill the task of bridging black and white perspectives, he set aside the opportunity to discuss specific policies to ameliorate racial problems with a strong call for action. Instead, in a final anecdote he portrayed two campaign workers, one an elderly black man and the other a young white woman, who found commonality in supporting his candidacy, implying, according to Dilliplane, that the proper response to racial tensions was "simply to join his campaign."

A third risk occurred when, at a press conference in April, Obama reversed himself by strongly denouncing further statements by Wright. This turnabout could have been criticized by the media as inconsistency; however, Obama avoided this criticism by again referring to his own history and his lifelong goal of reconciliation. "That's in my DNA, trying to promote mutual understanding to insist that we all share common hopes and common dreams as Americans and as human beings. That's who I am."[13]

Dilliplane ends her analysis by situating this speech in the context of Obama's campaign as a whole. She shows how the themes of progress and unity in the face of diversity can be found throughout his campaign rhetoric. In his 2004 convention speech, for example, he asserted that "there's no black America and white America and Latino America and Asian America; there's the United States of America."[14] In his 2008 announcement of his candidacy for the Democratic nomination, he declared, "beneath all the differences of race and region, faith and station, we are one people" and "I want us to take up the unfinished business of perfecting our union and building a better America."[15] Dilliplane feels that the simplest expression of these themes can be seen in his campaign slogan: "Yes, we can." She states, "Both themes were succinctly captured in this phrase: 'we' expressed unity; 'can' articulated a sense of purpose and motivation to act; and 'yes' conveyed resolve, as well as affirmation of the capacity to act and to succeed." Although she admits that by itself this slogan is open to other interpretations, she believes in the context of his speeches "its utility as a vehicle for conveying the two themes becomes important."[16]

In concluding her analysis, Dilliplane points out that Obama's use of the themes of progress and unity allowed him to connect his journey as a candidate with America's journey toward realizing its basic ideals, and thus it "constructed a powerful argument for supporting his election." She ends by quoting Obama's own words when he acknowledged that his campaign had been a success and that he had, in fact, become America's first black president: "If there is anyone out there who still doubts that America is a place where all things are possible, who still wonders if the dream of our founders is alive in our time, who still questions the power of our democracy, tonight is your answer."[17]

Ethnographic Research

If in everyday life we often act as critics, we also often act as ethnographers. Whenever curiosity about human behavior motivates us to observe others, we are engaging in our own private version of ethnography. Watching people and trying to figure out the rules that guide their actions are basic mechanisms for survival; without them, we wouldn't be able to fit into our own culture.

> **Whenever curiosity about human behavior motivates us to observe others, we are engaging in our own private version of ethnography.**

Like the rest of us, professional **ethnographers** learn from observation. Their reasons for observing behavior, however, are scientific, not personal. Ethnographers want to understand how members of other cultures interpret their world. To do so, ethnographers immerse themselves in a culture in an effort to see it through the eyes of its members. As Howard Schwartz and Jerry Jacobs point out, the ethnographer has two goals:

> First, he wants to learn the actor's "definition of the situation"—to see what the actor sees, know what he knows, and think as he thinks. Second, having accomplished this reconstruction of the other's reality, the researcher hopes to transcend this view, to see what the actor does not see—the formal features, processes, patterns, or common denominators that characterize the actor's view and situation.[18]

To achieve these goals, the researcher must make direct contact with the individuals he or she wishes to observe. As J. Kirk and M. L. Miller explain, ethnographic research depends on "watching people in their own territory and interacting with them in their own language, on their own terms."[19]

Steps in Ethnographic Research

If the ethnographer is to observe people in their own territory, he or she must assume a role. One approach is to observe people without their being aware of one's presence. The ethnographer who chooses to take this **covert role** goes "undercover" by becoming a member of the group being studied. To understand how cult members are socialized, for example, a researcher might join a cult in the guise of being a spiritual seeker. Or to understand the culture of a New York City cab driver, a researcher might drive a cab for several months. The problem with this approach is that it is deceptive. As the researcher forms relationships with group members, he or she may feel uncomfortable about lying to them. Another problem is in becoming so emotionally involved that one's ability to make objective observations is threatened.

Another approach is to take a more **overt role**. Here, the ethnographer enters the field as a scientist, and people know full well that they are being observed. The problem here is that when people know they are being watched, they may try to impress the observer. The ethnographer who takes an overt role must make special efforts to gain the trust of group members and to blend into the background as much as possible.

The key to ethnographic research is the ability to make accurate and insightful observations. Observations take the form of *field notes*, a record of critical events and behaviors accompanied by the ethnographer's self-observations, feelings, and interpretations. Field notes can run to thousands of pages in a lengthy study. Because it is hard to tell what details will be significant in the final analysis, good ethnographers note as much as possible as it occurs.

To gather data, the ethnographer may work with an *informant*, a member of the culture who is willing to show the researcher around, to answer questions, and to set up interviews with other people. Interviews are an important part of ethnographic research. By talking to as many people as possible about their communicative experiences, the researcher can check his or her own perceptions and can begin to understand how people within the culture view their own experiences.

Ethnographers must constantly be on the lookout for prejudices that may bias their ability to understand a culture. Although ethnographic research strives to be **presuppositionless research**, the researcher's own norms and values are hard to set aside.

The final step in ethnographic research is making sense of the data. Most researchers analyze their data inductively. This means that their conclusions flow directly from the data themselves rather than from a preexisting theory. Frey and his colleagues offer four criteria for good, inductively generated results. Conclusions should be

> believable, in that they should seem plausible to the reader. They should be comprehensive or account for all (or most) of the data. They should be grounded or tied clearly to the data. Finally, they should be applicable and lead to testable hypotheses and additional investigation.[20]

If You Can't Stand the Heat: An Example of Ethnography

Working as a chef in a restaurant is not an easy job. Dealing with heat, efficiently managing multiple orders, reacting to crowding, and being on one's feet for long periods of time can take a physical toll. Balancing managers' demands for efficiency and cost effectiveness with the need to express one's creativity and professionalism can be mentally trying. It's no wonder, then, that tempers often run high and stress is ever-present. Given these conditions, what can chefs do to manage their work lives and professional identities? In "Kitchen Antics: The Importance of Humor and Maintaining Professionalism at Work," Owen Hanley Lynch provides one answer. Chefs can use jokes, pranks, and humor. Drawing on years of kitchen experience including a one-year stint as a participant observer in a highly ranked restaurant as well as interviews with other chefs, Lynch provides an ethnographic study of ways humor can work to salve the inevitable strains of working in a high-stress profession.[21]

Lynch's research took place in a hotel kitchen with a large staff composed of one executive chef, twelve chefs (including the author), four cooks, and five trainee chefs. Lynch's role was that of a full-member participant observer, and his method included reflecting on his own experiences with kitchen humor as well as validating his observations by interviewing fellow chefs. As Lynch's goal was to understand how humor operated in the workplace, he paid particular attention to memorable messages, humorous situations that the kitchen staff remembered, retold, or, in the case of pranks, repeated many times. His goal was to uncover the meaning that motivated kitchen workers to repeat a joke and to consider ways in which the pranks he observed affected professional and organizational stability.

In addition to taking notes and personally analyzing humorous incidents, he conducted three rounds of interviews. In the first he interviewed twelve of his fellow workers, using an open-ended approach that allowed the interviewees to determine the content and scope of their comments. These interviews were then transcribed and used to refine the author's own observations. Three months later, a second set of interviews was undertaken, this time with two of the chefs who had already been interviewed. The purpose here was to make sure that the humor episodes Lynch had collected were accurately described. Finally a third round was conducted; this time, two additional chefs were asked to read Lynch's account of the episodes and his analysis and to confirm or disconfirm his interpretation. Thus, Lynch's analysis of the effects of kitchen humor combined his own year-long observations with critical feedback from coworkers.

Lynch found that humor was used in multiple ways: to maintain control and discipline in the kitchen, to preserve kitchen workers' professional identities, and to allow them to resist burdensome pressures. In his article, Lynch describes five types of humor used in the kitchen. In the first, which he calls *production control*, humor was used to control workers by ensuring that production standards were maintained. In one case, when salad preparation was slow, a banquet manager bet Mitchell, one of the cooks, that he (the manager) could make a salad order quicker. The result was a competition in which Mitchell, who knew that he would be teased mercilessly if he failed to win, was forced into competition. Although Mitchell did win, he also realized that he would be teased if, in the future, he didn't complete banquet requests on time. In another case, the executive chef saw that Ranger, one of the chefs, had failed to check the strawberries in a fruit display and that one of the strawberries had gone bad. The executive chef gave Ranger a choice: either eat the strawberry and forget about the incident, or be supervised and monitored for a month. Later on, when Ranger looked like he was about to do his job carelessly, the executive chef, egged on by other chefs, pelted him with blueberries. Although the executive chef's humor was aggressive, Ranger seemed to accept it. In commenting about the incident, Ranger said, "He gets his point across. I guarantee I check every strawberry thoroughly that I put out. I guarantee you." Here humor was used to cloak authority and make it more palatable to kitchen workers.

The second type of humor Lynch identified was *concertive control*. This is humor that group members themselves use to police their ranks and make sure that everyone complies with group standards and norms. The concertive control Lynch observed often involved pranks to test whether other chefs were on top of their game. One common trick was to place a pot handle over the flame and then return it to its original position. If the pot user was not alert, the resulting burn would quickly remind him or her to be more careful and more aware of what was going on. Other forms of abusive humor or teasing were used to point out work or attitude problems. Although Lynch admits that this kind of humor "broke legal and workplace safety laws" and was childish at times, he also argued that it ensured that chefs did their jobs according to professional norms.

Lynch labeled a third type of humor, *reification*. This is humor that strengthens in-group cohesion by excluding out-group members. In Lynch's restaurant this often took the form of speaking in one way to colleagues and another way to outsiders. For example, it was common for one of the chefs to make soups in the morning and for the other chefs to taste and comment on it, boasting about their creations, and sharing recipes and tricks of the trade. However, when a manager (considered to be an out-group member) would taste the soup and offer a compliment the chef would dismiss the compliment and tell him or her that the soup was simply made out of old scraps. This became a daily ritual whereby the chefs could maintain their belief in their superiority and distance themselves from management.

Lynch also observed a use of humor he called *safety valve resistance*. This is humor that allows workers a way of dealing with restrictive working conditions by reducing their sting, but not necessarily undermining them. In Lynch's restaurant, it was common for kitchen workers to use humorous nicknames for one another. Although these nicknames were used freely within the group, they were jealously guarded from outsiders, in particular from managers, who were not well liked because of their focus on industrial management. In one memorable case, one of the managers made the mistake of joking around and addressing a chef by his nickname of Tinker (a term that has negative connotations in some parts of Scotland and Ireland). This caused Tinker to "go off" on the manager, threatening to report him. The story of Tinker's confrontation with management was retold for weeks, with Tinker's reaction becoming more outrageous each time it was retold. Telling and retelling the story was a way to reduce the tension the kitchen staff felt toward management. When Lynch followed up by asking one of the interviewees what happens when someone who is not in the in-group jokes with people who are, he replied, "it's almost like they're invading our territory. Because they may make a joke to try and feel inclusive, when it's almost making them more exclusive because they don't understand why we do what we do."[22]

The final type of humor Lynch noted was *resistance humor*. This is humor that is used to express grievances and challenge practices deemed to be unfair. One example involved a new Food & Beverage director who decided to cut down on talking during work hours by separating the chefs and assigning each one to a single workstation. Because this hampered the chefs' ability to use ovens and tools located throughout the kitchen and because they enjoyed working together, they simply ignored the order. When the director persisted by posting a list that assigned each individual to a separate workstation, the chefs had nametags made with each other's names on them. When the director came into the kitchen he found five chefs working together, all sporting a name tag that said, "John." In this case the humor made it possible to resolve the impasse in a lighthearted manner.

Lynch's analysis shows that humor can be used in multiple ways by both superiors and subordinates. At times it can work as a control mechanism and at times it becomes an effective means of resisting control. In either case humor is a serious matter, and understanding how to use it effectively can be an important organizational skill.

Survey Research

Perhaps the most direct and straightforward way to learn about other people is to ask them questions. Survey research does just that. In **survey research**, an investigator chooses a sample of people to question, decides what to ask and how to ask it, and administers the questions in either written or oral form. He or she then codes responses and looks for meaningful patterns. Finally, the survey researcher draws conclusions from the data.

> Perhaps the most direct and straightforward way to learn about other people is to ask them questions. Survey research does just that.

Surveys may be used to describe a population or to test a hypothesis. They may be used to build theories of social behavior or to solve practical problems. Surveys are part of public opinion research, marketing studies, and program evaluations. Because surveys are used in so many contexts, you will likely be asked to design and conduct a survey someday.

Steps in Conducting a Survey

Survey researchers are often interested in describing the attitudes and communication behaviors of large groups of people. A pollster's ideal is to know how every American will vote. Practically, however, a pollster can question only a small fraction of the voting public. Luckily, it is not necessary to question every member of a **population** (the entire group a researcher wants to study) to get a good idea of what the population is like. By examining a **sample** (a small group of people representative of the population), the researcher can often draw very accurate conclusions about population characteristics.

There are good and bad ways to draw a sample; generalization is possible only if an unbiased sample has been chosen. To choose a representative sample, the researcher first chooses a **sampling plan**, a systematic method for choosing respondents for a study. Researchers use two general kinds of sampling plans: probability and nonprobability. **Probability sampling** allows generalizations because it assures the researcher that the sample is representative. In a probability sample, the researcher knows the exact probability that each member of a population will be included in a sample. For example, in **simple random sampling**, each member of the population has an equal chance of being in the sample. **Nonprobability sampling**

There are many ways to find out about others. Careful observation and systematic questioning are two "lenses" we can use to discover insights about human communication.

© H. Armstrong Roberts/CORBIS

does not give the researcher the same assurance. In nonprobability samples, some members of the population may have virtually no chance of being included whereas others may be overrepresented. A common form of nonprobability sampling is **accidental sampling**, whereby the researcher uses the most convenient people available.

Using nonprobability samples is risky. Imagine that you've been assigned to cover a presidential election for your college broadcasting station. Your task is to report the political views of students on your campus. With little time left before the election, you take the easy way out: you call all your friends and ask them how they intend to vote. The likelihood that this accidental sample will be accurate is very low because friends often share political views.

Simple random sampling, although costly in time and effort, significantly improves your chances of drawing a representative sample. If you were to use this method in our example, you would need a list of every student at your school as well as a computer-generated list of random ID numbers. You could then match the random numbers on your list to the student IDs, choosing for your survey only those students whose numbers came up. If you were to generate a sufficiently large sample (and if you could convince everyone in the sample to take part in the study), your results would closely approximate population figures.

Deciding whom to question is only the first step. A survey researcher must also frame questions and organize the survey. These steps are not as easy as they might seem. Like any other form of communication, questions can be misunderstood and misinterpreted. A researcher must take care that questions are answerable, unambiguous, and as nonthreatening as possible; that they focus on a single issue at a time; and that they do not lead the respondent to give a desired answer.

First, questions should be answerable; that is, they should avoid asking for information that the respondent does not know. "How many hours did you spend talking to friends last week?" is a difficult question; although some respondents might be able to give you a fairly accurate estimate, many would have no idea. Unfortunately, respondents often make up answers rather than admitting their ignorance, making data from this kind of question suspect.

Questions should also be unambiguous; that is, what the researcher is asking should be clear. "How many channels of communication do you use in your job?" is ambiguous. "I am going to read off a number of ways in which people communicate on the job. As I mention each one, tell me whether you have used it during the last week: memo, telephone, fax, . . ." is a much clearer way to ask the same question.

Questions should be as nonthreatening as possible; that is, they should avoid making the respondent feel guilty or incompetent. Questions about drug use, sexual behavior, or academic dishonesty are examples of topics that respondents may be unwilling to discuss. Explaining why these questions are necessary and assuring confidentiality may help respondents to overcome their reluctance. Sometimes, asking the question in an indirect form increases a respondent's willingness to respond. "Why do you think some students cheat?" may be more effective than "Why do you cheat?"

Double-barreled questions should be avoided. A *double-barreled question* asks several questions at once. "Do you believe that Governor Smith should be elected president because of her stand on the environment?" is really several questions rolled into one: "Do you believe that Smith should be elected?" is one question; "Do you approve of Smith's stand on the environment?" is another; and "Will Smith's environmental stand affect whether or not you vote for her?" is a third.

Another kind of question that should be avoided is the *leading question*. Leading questions are questions that indicate a preferred response. "Don't you think the depiction of women on MTV is shameful?" is a leading question. Generally, any question that starts with "Do you agree that . . ." is leading. A better phrasing would be "Consider the following statement. Do you agree or disagree with it?"

In addition to carefully considering the way in which a question is worded, the survey researcher is also concerned with the way questions are ordered. In general, easy-to-answer questions should be placed early in the questionnaire, and questions on sensitive topics should go toward the end. In addition, questions on a single topic should be grouped together.

Like other forms of communication, the survey interview should have a beginning, a middle, and an end. As Frey and colleagues point out, "how interviews are begun often determines whether, and then how fully, respondents cooperate."[23] In the beginning of a survey, the researcher must introduce himself or herself and state the purpose of the interview, the topic, how much time the survey will take, and whether the data will be confidential. At the end, he or she should thank the respondent for cooperating.

Researchers administer surveys in two general ways: through a face-to-face **interview** or through a self-administered **questionnaire**. Each method has advantages and disadvantages. Interviews allow the researcher to control what goes on during the survey and to clarify ambiguous questions. On the other hand, interviewers can inadvertently bias responses, and interviewers are relatively expensive to train and use. Mailed questionnaires are cheap and have the advantage of being anonymous, but there is no way to control for distractions. In addition, the response rate is often low, and the responses may not be statistically valid because those who choose to respond may differ in some important respect from those who do not respond.

Generally speaking, survey researchers convert responses into categories or numbers so that the responses can be statistically analyzed. Although this is relatively easy to do with responses to *closed-ended questions* (whereby respondents choose from a finite set of answers provided by the researcher) or *rating scales* (whereby the respondent rates an idea or an attitude on a numerical scale), it is more difficult to do with responses to *open-ended questions* (whereby the respondent is free to answer in his or her own words). With responses to open-ended questions, the researcher must find a way to categorize and compare responses. The researchers described in the next section used both responses to rating scales and content analysis to categorize responses to open-ended questions.

Coping with Separation: An Example of Survey Research

It takes skill and dedication to maintain relationships, even under the best of circumstances. When partners are physically separated, keeping relationships healthy can be particularly challenging. This is especially true during military deployment, when partners are separated for long periods of time by hundreds or thousands of miles, when anxiety is heightened due to the dangers of combat, and when opportunities to speak by phone or email may be sporadic and censored. In recent years over two million service members and reservists, about half of whom are married, have found themselves in this kind of situation. Although many military couples manage the challenges of long-distance relationships, others experience increased loneliness and anxiety, and decreased closeness and emotional support. What strategies allow some military couples to maintain satisfactory interpersonal ties while others fail to cope? In "Relational Maintenance during Military Deployment: Perspectives of Wives of Deployed U.S. Soldiers," Andy J. Merolla provides a preliminary answer to this question.[24]

Merolla's study is an example of exploratory survey research. To investigate day-to-day relational maintenance during military deployment, semi-structured interviews were conducted with thirty-three civilian wives married to deployed servicemen. Because for the majority of service couples it is the husband who is a member of the military and the wife who is a civilian, the sample consisted of female rather than male spouses. A convenience sampling plan was used; respondents were recruited from the social networks of graduate and undergraduate students at a Midwestern university.

A simple interview schedule focused questions on ways the respondents maintained feelings of connectedness with their husbands when they were away. Wives were encouraged to give examples of critical incidents—incidents during which they felt particularly connected and/or disconnected from their spouses. They were also asked about their use of communication media, their support networks, helpful advice they had received from others, and what they liked and disliked about separation.

Merolla's goal was to add to the literature on relational maintenance behaviors by answering two research questions: (1) "In what ways do partners maintain their relationships during deployment?" and (2) "What factors shape, facilitate, or complicate maintenance during deployment?"[25] As we saw in Chapter 6, relational maintenance behaviors are behaviors designed to "repair, sustain or enhance partners' relationship satisfaction, commitment, and stability."[26] Several typologies of maintenance strategies exist, listing anywhere from five to eleven strategies.[27] Although Merolla expected to find that some of these strategies would emerge in the present study, he also recognized that there are unique conditions that make relational maintenance in deployment challenging. Therefore, rather than asking respondents to respond to lists of previously identified behaviors, he used a more open-ended approach that allowed the wives he interviewed to come up with their own responses.

Merolla began data analysis by examining transcripts of the interviews for "thought units," statements that mentioned a single maintenance behavior. Reliability was ensured by comparing the units he identified with those identified by an independent researcher. The unitizing process yielded 505 units. Merolla then devised a category system to describe and classify the maintenance behaviors contained in these units, and then he coded each one into a category. To test coding reliability, a colleague separately classified the units. The final category system contained nine intrapersonal behaviors, ten behaviors involving mediated communication with one's partner, and five behaviors involving reliance on social network support.

Intrapersonal behaviors were maintenance strategies the wives themselves used, apart from interaction with their husbands or with others. By far the most commonly mentioned kind of intrapersonal behavior involved what Merolla called *sensory experience*: surrounding themselves with tangible reminders of the partner. Items such as photos, articles of clothing, favorite objects belonging to their spouses, or other relational symbols seemed to help wives feel connected. *Positive thinking and reminiscing* was the next most commonly cited behavior, followed by *focusing on self*, in which wives took up new hobbies or tried new experiences such as returning to school, to take their mind off worrying. Other intrapersonal behaviors (in descending order of importance) included *prayer, reflecting on perceived advantages, journaling, imagined interactions, future thinking*.

Mediated partner interaction was also an important maintenance strategy. Wives cited communicating by phone, letters, email, IM, video, and Webcam. The most important kind of mediated communication involved *debriefing talk*, in which spouses brought each other up to date on what has been happening in their lives. Although couples shared day-to-day information, *topic avoidance* was also a strategy; with so little time to communicate, couples avoided talking about anything negative. Instead their communication centered on *affection and intimacy*. Respondents also felt *creating and keeping communication routines*, for example, by using IM or email each day at a specific time, was important. *Future planning, openness, reassuring of safety, positivity*, and *faith talk* were also mentioned.

In addition to intrapersonal and partner communication, wives coped by making use of *social support networks*. Respondents mentioned finding comfort in chatting with others about their husbands (*family and peer updates*), keeping busy with friends in order to avoid worry (*preoccupation*), focusing on children (*support drawn from children*), and attending groups organized by the military (*military-facilitated support*).

Although these kinds of behaviors helped couples maintain a sense of connection, using them was not always easy. External factors like time limits, military monitoring, and the soldiers' lack of personal privacy made mediated communication difficult. Wives also differed in their preferences for certain modes of coping. Whereas most chose to draw on family support, others avoided it because of family stress or because too much talk of former times increased feelings of loneliness.

In his conclusion, Merolla points to what he thinks is one of the most interesting findings: the importance of "strategic creation of routine everyday talk." He believes that partners may have to perform behaviors strategically that, in non-deployment situations, are automatic and taken for granted. He also suggests that although routine small talk gives communicators a sense of normalcy, they should not rely on it totally. Instead routine interaction should be balanced by spontaneity, and small talk by deeper conversations.

Merolla is careful to point out that, whereas the behaviors his respondents cite may serve as a guide for individuals looking for ways to cope, they do not provide a universal recipe for happiness. Individuals need to learn what works best for them. In Merolla's words, "When confronted with long periods of non-contact with their spouse, partners can attend to their own education, health, or spirituality. When network members offer support that is unhelpful, partners can seek out the types of individual (and support forms) that better align with their needs."[28]

Experimental Research

In everyday life, we frequently have hunches about cause and effect. To test these hunches, we run naive experiments: we manipulate what we think might be the cause and wait to see the effect of this manipulation. A parent, for example, may decide that arguing with a child reinforces the child's negative behavior. To test this idea, the parent may stop arguing and see what happens. If the child's bad behavior ceases, the parent will probably conclude that it was caused by too much attention. Although not very scientific, this is an instance of everyday experimentation.

In **experimental research**, researchers are also interested in cause and effect.

> In everyday life, we frequently have hunches about cause and effect. To test these hunches, we run naive experiments: we manipulate what we think might be the cause and wait to see the effect of this manipulation.

The effect they want to explain is called the **dependent variable**, whereas the suspected cause is called the **independent variable**. If, for example, a researcher believes that giving an employee praise will cause that employee to feel more satisfied with his or her work, praise is the independent variable and satisfaction is the dependent variable.

All experiments involve manipulation, comparison, and control. To find out whether praise leads to satisfaction, for example, a researcher must *manipulate* the independent variable, praise. One way to do this is to choose two groups of workers, praise one group and not the other, and then *compare* the groups to find out which group was most satisfied. If the researcher carefully *controls* the experiment by making sure no other independent variables are at work, then any change in satisfaction is necessarily due to the effects of praise.

Steps in Doing an Experiment

Like survey researchers, experimental researchers want to generalize their findings. They want to discover general laws of cause and effect that apply in many different situations. To do this, they must choose the best possible sampling plan. A probability sampling plan is best, but if this is impossible to implement, the researchers must devise a sampling strategy that controls for as much bias as possible.

The way the researcher sets up a study is called the **research design**. In designing a study, the researcher must decide how the independent variable, or **treatment**, is to be administered and when the dependent variable is to be measured. The measurement of the dependent variable before the treatment is called a **pretest**; the measurement after the treatment is called a **posttest**. Some research designs are faulty and allow no conclusions to be drawn. Others are logically valid and can be used to demonstrate causal relationships.

To see what constitutes a faulty design, let's return to the praise–satisfaction experiment. Assume, for a moment, that the researcher did the experiment on a single group of workers. The researcher measured workers' satisfaction level, praised the workers at least once a day for two weeks, and then measured their satisfaction again. Assume also that satisfaction was greater after the two-week period than before. Would the researcher be justified in concluding that the change in satisfaction was due to the praise? The answer is no. The change might well have been due to other factors—perhaps the workload lightened during that period or rumors of a wage increase circulated. Because this design (called a *one-group pretest–posttest design*) used only one group, it is impossible to rule out alternative explanations.

The research design can be improved by adding a second, **control group**, which is equivalent to the first group in every way except that it does not receive the experimental treatment. If the satisfaction level of the control group stays the same over the two weeks while the satisfaction level of the treatment group rises, then the researcher can rule out alternative explanations. To ensure that the control and treatment groups are equivalent, the researcher should not use existing groups, for they may be different to begin with. Instead, he or she should randomly assign subjects to the experimental and control groups. The design used in this example is called a *pretest–posttest control group design* and is one of the strongest and most popular of the experimental designs.

In any experiment, the researcher must devise a way to measure the dependent variable. In the example we have been using, the researcher must measure satisfaction. To do so, he or she might use a simple yes-or-no question ("Are you satisfied with your job, yes or no?") and compare the percentages of workers in each group saying yes before and after the treatment. On the other hand, the researcher might use a more elaborate rating scale ("On a scale from one to ten, where ten indicates high satisfaction, how would you rate your feelings about your job?") and compare the average rating before and after the treatment. In any case, a measurement method must meet two criteria. It must demonstrate **reliability** (i.e., it must consistently yield the same results), and it must show **validity** (i.e., it must actually measure the dependent variable). If, for example, employees know that the boss will receive their answers to the satisfaction question, the results might not be valid; the results might reflect the employees' desire to please the boss and protect their jobs rather than the employees' actual degree of satisfaction.

Experimental researchers depend on statistical methods to help them analyze their data. They compute statistics that tell them whether their findings are due to random variation or to the presence of the independent variable. Although statistics provide an objective, numerical method for analyzing differences, it is still up to the researcher to interpret what these differences mean.

To Friend or Not to Friend? An Example of Experimental Research

Whenever we meet someone new we have decisions to make. At minimum, we need to determine whether the person is trustworthy, whether we should initiate a relationship or let well enough alone, and, if we want a relationship, the kind of relationship we want. Sometimes decisions like these are relatively easy to make. In face-to-face interactions, for example, when there is ample opportunity to observe and interact, the impressions we form have a good chance of being accurate. On social network sites, however, information is more limited and may not always be reliable. How then do visitors to online sites go about forming accurate impressions and deciding whether or not to form relationships with those they encounter? What information do they use and how does this information affect interpersonal decisions? These are the central questions addressed by Marjolijn L. Antheunis and Alexander P. Schouten in their study, "The Effects of Other-Generated and System-Generated Cues on Adolescents' Perceived Attractiveness on Social Network Sites."[29]

The authors begin their article by making a distinction between user-generated information that a site owner intentionally creates; other-generated information that is created by individuals other than the site owner, usually friends; and system-generated information that is created by the site itself. According to the authors, most visitors to social network sites realize that user-generated information is likely to be flawed. It is common knowledge that people don't always tell the whole truth about themselves and that online profiles are often carefully crafted to show their owners in the best possible light. A more reliable source of information would appear to be data generated by others (for example, comments and photos left on a site owner's wall) or by the system itself (for example, the sheer number of friends an owner has managed to collect). The purpose of this study was to investigate the extent to which other-generated and system-generated cues affect judgments of a site owner's popularity and attractiveness. The authors hypothesized that the more attractive an individual's friends are, the more positive the messages on the individual's wall, and the more friends a user has, the more attractive, popular, and extroverted he or she will be judged to be, and the more likely people will be to want to pursue a relationship.

The authors used a posttest-only experimental design. The study took place in the Netherlands. Four hundred ninety-five girls with accounts on Hyves, the most popular social network site in the Netherlands, made up the sample. They ranged in age from twelve to fifteen years. Each was asked to form an impression of a girl named Eline based on a (fictitious) online profile. The profile contained a photo of Eline, information about her (name, age, hobbies, and personal interests), photos of nine of her friends, two wall posts, and a system-generated count of her friends. Participants were assigned to one of twelve experimental conditions based on a combination of the physical attractiveness of Eline's friends (attractive or not attractive), the nature of the messages left on her wall (positive or negative), and the total number of friends she had collected (9, 269, or 665). After viewing their version of Eline's profile, each participant filled out scales measuring the amount of interpersonal attraction they felt for Eline, how physically attractive they found her, how extraverted they felt her to be, and whether or not they would be likely to accept her as a friend. These measures constituted the study's dependent variables.

Before running the actual study, the researchers had to create realistic levels of each independent variable. *Friend's physical attractiveness* was created by pretesting forty-six photos taken from actual Websites. Twenty-three adolescents rated the photos from (0) *very unattractive* to (10) *very attractive*. The nine photos that were judged to be most attractive and the nine photos rated most unattractive were used to reflect the two levels of friend attractiveness. *Number of friends* was determined by examining 280 random profiles of adolescents for number of friends. As 269 was the average, this number was chosen to represent a moderate number of friends. For the large number of friends condition, 665 was chosen as it was three times the standard deviation of the average. For the small number of friends condition, 9 was chosen, as the Hyves social network site is set up to show nine friends. Two sets of *friend messages* were used to illustrate positive and negative wall postings.[30] The two positive messages (translated from the Dutch) consisted of:

> "ELINE PARTYGIRL!! Was superfantasticamazing y'day! You're fun to go out with! Never ever had so much fun! Shall we go again soon?!?!??!"
>
> "Hey Girl. Thanks for your sweet reaction. Im really glad having a friend like U. you're right, it'll work out soon, I heard you tried to get everyone there. You're the best! LY4E."

The following messages were used for the negative condition:

> "Could you perhaps warn me when you pull a trick like that ... ?! It was def NOT funny. I thought we had a deal?"
>
> "ELINE. How was yesterday? You didn't go out with him again, did you? He is so pathetic."

To make sure that the independent variables were accurately represented, respondents rated the attractiveness of Eline's friends on a five-point scale from very unattractive to very attractive and the tone of the wall postings on a five-point scale from very negative to very positive. They were also asked if they thought Eline had few friends, an average number of friends, or a lot of friends, and they reported their own number of friends. The results indicated that the experimental conditions were perceived as the researchers intended and that the researcher's manipulation of number of friends closely matched the distribution of friends in the sample.

Data analysis showed that the physical attractiveness of Eline's friends affected perceptions of Eline's own attractiveness. Respondents who viewed attractive photos of Eline's friends rated her as more physically attractive than those who viewed unattractive photos of her friends, although friend attractiveness ratings did not affect Eline's popularity, extraversion, or the likelihood she would be chosen as a friend. Analysis also showed that the tone of the wall postings had an effect on ratings of Eline's social attractiveness and on the likelihood of accepting her as a friend. Respondents who viewed positive messages liked Eline more than those who viewed negative messages. In addition the nature of the messages also affected extraversion ratings, although not in the direction the authors had predicted. Respondents who read negative wall postings found Eline to be more extraverted than those who saw positive messages. Finally, number of online friends positively influenced perceived extraversion, but did not have an effect on either measure of attraction.

This study throws additional light on the way we form online impressions. Researchers often distinguish between two kinds of information: *identity claims* (controlled cues given off intentionally) and *behavioral residue* (unintentional information that contains cues about an individual's behavior). Both are used to form impressions, and both occur on social network sites. The photos and descriptions of likes and dislikes that profile owners intentionally publish are examples of identity claims. The wall postings and messages left by others as well as friend counts are examples of behavioral residue. Whereas the former are within a profile owner's control, the latter are often more difficult to manage. Many adolescent profile owners may not realize that they are being judged by the company they keep. And they may fail to appreciate the fact that messages intended just for them may have unintended consequences.

Performance as Research

In everyday life, we perform more than you might think. We tell stories, often imaginatively taking on the roles of the characters involved. We do impressions to amuse (or to mock). We take part in rituals, ceremonies, or religious rites. Often, these performances are liberating, allowing us to try on new identities and express unfamiliar emotions. They allow us to explore and work through feelings and ideas we may not even know we have. Our everyday performances are often acts of discovery.

> Our everyday performances allow us to explore and work through feelings and ideas we may not even know we have.

In the field of **performance studies**, communication scholars focus on a wide range of performances. Some researchers study the meanings in the performances of others, and others may perform themselves in order to gain insights into the meanings of texts and to share these insights with an audience. The performances researchers in this field study and enact are wide-ranging. They may study aesthetic products such as stage productions or performance art, but they may also choose to look for the meaning in everyday performances such as pageants, rites, and rituals. Those who choose to perform may create readings of plays, poems, or novels, but they may also perform folktales, enact natural conversations, or interpret oral histories.

Many researchers in this area use performance as a tool for research. They take a text, embody it with voice and movement, and share the product with an audience; as a result of actively engaging with the text, they come to understand the intricacies of its language and the power of its meanings. For these researchers, performing is a mode of inquiry as well as an aesthetic activity.

Steps in Performance Research

As in all of the methods we've looked at so far, the first step for performance researchers is one of *selecting*, of identifying a communication act or text for study. Performance researchers choose a text that has significance for them, whether that text is a literary work, a public speech, an autobiography, or the like. Ron Pelias calls the second step *playing*.[31] In this step, the researcher experiments with a variety of ways of interpreting the work. He or she tries on different voices and movements to see what these have to say about the meaning of the text. When the researcher feels that he or she has fully explored a number of possibilities, it is time to go on to the third step: *testing*. Here, the researcher tests interpretation against the evidence contained in the text. Says Pelias, "The researcher uses the other's text to guide his or her vocal and body work, and the researcher's vocal and body work help reveal textual dimensions."[32]

The fourth step involves *choosing*. Here the performer chooses a performance vision, a particular way of performing the text that will convey meaning to an audience. The performance may be very simple and direct, allowing the text's author to speak through the performer's voice and body. Alternatively, the performance may comment on the text so that distance is put between the author, the performer, and the audience. The fifth step is *repeating*. The performer repeats and rehearses the piece until it flows naturally, learning more in each iteration. Finally, step six is *presenting*. Here the researcher displays for others what he or she has come to understand. Following public presentation, the researcher often decides to write about what he or she has experienced. Pelias concludes:

> *Whether the researcher elects to report findings through public performance or written essay, the steps of selecting, playing, testing, choosing, repeating, and presenting are a method for examining the communication acts of others. They position the researcher to learn about others' discourse experientially, to come to know others by becoming them, to live in complete empathy, at least for a time, in the voice and body of others.*[33]

Performing Disaster, Understanding Personal Narratives of Loss, Identity, and Resistance: An Example of Performance Research

In the late winter/early spring of 2012, an unprecedented number of tornadoes swept across the United States, wiping out whole cities and leaving death and destruction in their wake. Stories of survival and loss filled news broadcasts and newspaper articles, as victims and viewers alike tried to make sense of the devastation. One way to think about the stories of survival that followed the tornadoes is to view them as performances, creative acts of communication during which survivors recreated their experiences for local and national audiences. The stories that so captivated the nation in 2012 are prime examples of an enduring form of communication known as disaster narratives, compelling personal stories that fulfill both individual and communal purposes.

In "Disaster Narrative Emergent/cies: Performing Loss, Identity and Resistance," Phyllis Scott Carlin and Linda M. Park-Fuller argue that disaster narratives constitute an identifiable genre of cultural performance. They identify key elements used to structure these narratives, analyze the functions fulfilled by disaster performances, and describe how the stories can be combined, rewritten, and staged to foster "dialogue, debate, and social action."[34]

The authors began by collecting as many examples of disaster narratives as possible. Examples were taken from natural and human-caused disasters occurring between 1880 and 2001, and were limited to historically recorded events experienced by multiple tellers. In all, five hundred stories were assembled, sixty of which were more closely reviewed. Common characteristics of the storytellers were identified, as well as five "keys," or aesthetic strategies, used to structure the stories.

The five key strategies used to structure the narratives consisted of:

- a recounting of whether or not there were premonitions that a disaster was about to occur; for example, tellers might describe strange sounds that preceded the event, or, conversely, they might note how surprisingly quiet, peaceful, and normal everything was.

- a description of the moment when the teller realizes something disastrous has occurred; for example, one individual, describing the moment an earthquake hit, referred to a "terribly frightening blackness," and the fact that he had "groped around on the sea of moving floors."[35]

- a dramatic report of damage, loss, and danger, including attempts to escape and accounts of miraculous rescues; a woman who escaped from one of the twin towers on September 11 described a cloud of smoke as a "monster chasing us. It was big, it was roiling, it was ugly, it was angry, and it wanted to kill me."[36]

- depictions of actions taken during the aftermath with special attention to the terror resulting from finding family members are missing.

- interpretation of the significance of the event in the teller's own life or in the life of his or her community, including identification of heroes and villains.

Although all five strategies were not always included in a single story, "whether the story was composed orally or in writing, and whether the story came from 1900 or 2001, several of the keys emerged in each of the narratives."[37]

After describing the five key elements used to structure the stories, the authors considered the functions fulfilled by the performative telling of disaster narratives.

They suggested that by telling their stories survivors were trying to make sense of what had happened to them. They were bearing witness to the event as a historical fact, to their own actions, and to the actions of others who tried to save or help those around them. Their stories also served as critical social commentary when, for example, they noted that the government had failed to provide aid to the poor or that evacuation plans were flawed. In summary, the authors tell us that disaster performances can heal individuals by restoring their sense of order and identity, preserving history, reinforcing an ethic of sacrifice, and calling for social change.

Although most disaster narratives consist of personal stories told by individuals to family members, close acquaintances or, in some cases, to reporters, they can form the basis of staged, artistic performances, theatrical pieces that are carefully constructed and presented to an audience by trained performers. When this occurs, individual stories take on significance the original tellers may not have recognized. Staged performance pieces based on field notes and other materials collected as part of an ethnography of a given cultural group and arranged for dramatic impact are called *ethnodramas*.

The appeal of ethnodrama, the authors note, is like the appeal of reality television—minus its formulaic, prepackaged nature. Ethnodrama is appealing because it is both authentic and theatrical. Scenic design, adaptation, and arrangement of materials can move audiences "beyond curiosity about disaster . . . toward action and change." To illustrate the power of ethnodramatic performances, the authors describe Playback Theatre, a theatrical group that performs improvised versions of audience members' personal experiences. A playback performance begins when a conductor, actors, and a musician introduce themselves with brief personal stories. Audience members are then invited to stand up and recount a story, prompted by questions from the conductor. The actors then improvise a performance piece based on the narrative they have just heard, often adding meaning by focusing on symbols or metaphors chosen by the teller. In one such performance, a young man from the audience told a story of a friend who could not return to his home after Hurricane Katrina because men with guns guarded a bridge he needed to cross. The actors picked up on the fact that the teller likened his friend to an illegal immigrant being excluded from the country by a broad river. They constructed a narrative involving boundaries, borders, and social inequality. The performance "opened" the original story to include a consideration of inequities in the way Katrina survivors were treated. In doing so, it offered new topics for consideration and discussion.

The authors note that U.S. culture has always been fascinated with tales of survival and triumph over adversity. "Beyond the inherent authenticity, dramatic action, and potential triumph that partially accounts for [their] popularity," these stories ask listeners "to become more reflexive, they build community among us, and they offer us hard-won hope."[38] The authors close by suggesting that it is time to address disaster stories using performance knowledge and skill. "To tell, and to participate in the telling through performing and bearing witness, is to further the struggle to resist annihilation; to enhance and to critique community memory; and, always, to honor those who suffered, those who cannot speak, and those who can never come home."[39]

LEARNING MORE ABOUT COMMUNICATION

The research studies we've looked at represent only a few of the ways scholars and critics gather new information and draw conclusions about communication. The five studies reviewed in the last section were taken from scholarly journals in the field of communication. Table 13.5 lists some additional journals that publish research in the field. One way to learn more about communication studies is to look through these journals for interesting articles. Doing so will give you a good sense of the kinds of topics that interest communication researchers today.

Subject Areas in Speech Communication

If you're not familiar with the field of communication—if this is your first exposure to the study of human message making—you may not be aware of the courses offered in departments of communication. Table 13.6 lists some of the major subject areas that make up this discipline, along with the kinds of courses that are offered at either the undergraduate or graduate level.

Table 13.5 Communication Journals

This list includes some of the scholarly journals that publish articles about communication, the association that publishes them, and the Web address of each association's home page.

National Communication Association
[http://www.natcom.org]
- *The Quarterly Journal of Speech*
- *Communication Monographs*
- *Communication Education*
- *Critical Studies in Media Communication*
- *Text and Performance Quarterly*
- *Journal of Applied Communication Research*
- *Communication and Critical/Cultural Studies*
- *Communication Teacher*
- *Review of Communication*
- *Journal of International and Intercultural Communication*

International Communication Association
[http://www.icahdq.org]
- *Human Communication Research*
- *Communication, Culture, & Critique*

- *Communication Theory*
- *Journal of Communication*
- *Journal of Computer-Mediated Communication*

Eastern Communication Association
[http://www.ecasite.org]
- *Communication Quarterly*
- *Qualitative Research Reports in Communication*
- *Communication Research Reports*

Central States Communication Association
[http://www.csca-net.org]
- *Communication Studies*

Southern States Communication Association
[http://www.ssca.net]
- *Southern Communication Journal*

Western States Communication Association
[http://www.westcomm.org]
- *Western Journal of Communication*
- *Communication Reports*

Table 13.6 Subject Areas in Speech Communication

Interpersonal Communication

The study of verbal and nonverbal exchanges in everyday interaction. Specialists in interpersonal communication study topics such as interpersonal influence, relational development and maintenance, impression formation, interpersonal attraction, gender and communication, and communication and the development of the self.

Courses include Interpersonal Communication, Gender and Communication, Family Communication, Conflict Management, and Therapeutic Communication.

Small-Group/Organizational Communication

The study of how communication helps people in groups accomplish goals and maintain group identity; the study of how communication operates in complex organizations. Specialists in small-group/organizational communication study topics such as group problem solving, conflict resolution, leadership, mediation and negotiation, superior/subordinate relationships, and organizational culture.

Courses include Small Group Decision Making, Business and Professional Communication, Leadership, and Employment Interviewing as well as courses in specialized professions, such as Health Communication or Legal Communication.

Public Communication

The study of communication in face-to-face, one-to-many communication settings. Specialists in the rhetoric of public communication study topics such as persuasion, propaganda, political communication, the history of public address, social movements, freedom of speech, and the ethics of speaking.

Courses include Public Speaking, Theories of Persuasion, Public Address, Rhetorical Theory, and Argumentation and Debate.

Performance Studies

The study of the ways people perform personal, cultural, or artistic scripts before audiences. Specialists in performance studies study topics such as

folklore and oral traditions; storytelling; performance art; the work of individual performers, such as stand-up comics or cultural icons; and the performance of literature.

Courses include Oral Interpretation, Readers' Theatre, Performance of Literature and Folklore, as well as courses specializing in a given author or genre, such as Performing Joyce or Performance and Analysis of Prose.

Mass Communication

The study of mediated messages created for a wide public audience. Specialists in mass communication study topics such as the history of the media, prosocial effects of the media, television and the family, media law, nonfiction film, and politics and the media.

Courses include Advertising, Public Relations, Broadcast Production, Introduction to the Mass Media, Journalism, and Media Criticism.

Intercultural Communication

The study of communication across cultural boundaries. Specialists in intercultural communication study topics such as interethnic and interracial conflict, verbal and nonverbal differences across cultures, forms of talk unique to a given culture, and ways to increase cross-cultural understanding.

Courses include Cross-Cultural Communication and a variety of specialized courses examining given cultures.

Language and Semiotic Systems

The study of code systems used to create messages in any of the contexts listed above. Topics include nonverbal message systems, semantic and pragmatic rules and their effects, dialect differences and social class, bilingualism, gender differences in language use, and conversational structures.

Courses include Language and Social Action, The Psychology of Language, Language Development, American Dialects, and Phonetics.

As you can see, the types of courses offered in departments of communication are both theoretical and applied. Some, such as public speaking, argumentation, and group discussion, help you improve your organizational and delivery skills. Others, such as interpersonal, family, and gender communication courses, focus on understanding and analyzing everyday interaction. You may choose courses that explore the history of our field (e.g., Classical Theories of Rhetoric), courses that develop your critical and analytic skills (e.g., Rhetorical Theory, Analysis, and Performance of Literature), or courses that prepare you for a specific communication-related career (e.g., Public Relations, Broadcast Production, Health Communication). The areas covered in departments of communication are far-reaching and varied.

Other Sources of Discovery

Although taking formal courses or reading books written by communication experts can increase your knowledge, you can learn more about communication in many other ways. One way is to explore other subject areas. There are connections between communication studies and all of the humanities and sciences. Psychology and sociology can offer insights into communication by illuminating human and group behavior, and anthropology can show us how communication practices differ from culture to culture. Literary criticism and linguistics can tell us more about how meanings are created and shared, whereas the study of music, art, and architectural design can help us see how different media transform expression. History and politics show us how events in the public sphere affect the subjects we communicate about as well as the ways we communicate about them. Indeed, it is difficult to think of any course in the humanities or social sciences that is not related to communication.

Curiosity about the world is the basic impulse behind all research. It is an impulse we are born with and one that guides us throughout our lives. Only when we no longer find the world interesting do we stop learning.

H. Armstrong Roberts/Corbis

Another way you can understand communication more fully is through reading novels and viewing plays and films. Not only are these forms of expression examples of rhetorical acts in their own right, they also illuminate our understanding of human behavior and therefore make us more sensitive to one another.

Finally, you can gain insight into communication by observing human interaction. This takes a willingness to stand aside and to watch and wonder. Curiosity is at the heart of all discovery—a curiosity that is initially attracted by anything odd or different and that proceeds to celebrate regularities in the "life that flows beneath the surface of things." If you develop that curiosity, you cannot help but learn about communication theory and practice.

SUMMARY

This chapter discusses methods of discovery: it describes the research process, examines five contemporary approaches to communication study, and outlines the structure of communication as an academic field.

Research is not exotic; it's something we do every day. Commonsense methods of discovery, however, are often biased. We privilege our own experiences, engage in wishful thinking, and rely too much on simple heuristics. Systematic research is more accurate and less biased; it is question oriented, methodological, replicable, self-critical, cumulative and self-correcting, and cyclical. Regardless of approach, researchers accomplish four tasks: they ask questions and define key concepts; they choose a method to guide their inquiry; they gather and analyze samples of communication acts; and they interpret these samples, sharing the results.

Five representative research methods are rhetorical criticism, ethnographic research, survey research, experimental research, and performance research. Rhetorical criticism is a systematic way of describing, analyzing, and evaluating rhetorical acts. In criticizing acts of influence, rhetorical critics use methods such as neo-Aristotelian criticism, genre criticism, Burkean analysis, fantasy theme analysis, social movement criticism, cultural ideological criticism, and social value criticism. Dilliplane's analysis of President Obama's "A More Perfect Union" speech is a good example of rhetorical criticism.

A second and very different kind of research is ethnography. Ethnographers try to understand how members of other cultures interpret their worlds. Ethnographers do this by observing behavior in natural surroundings to uncover rules that guide action. Ethnographers bracket their preconceptions and try to see the world without bias. Lynch's participant observation of kitchen antics is a good example of ethnographic research.

A third research method is survey research. Survey researchers describe populations by asking questions of systematically chosen samples. The questions must be answerable, unambiguous, and nonthreatening; researchers must avoid double-barreled and leading questions. The article on ways to cope with separation during military deployment by Merolla is a good example of exploratory survey research.

A fourth research method is experimental research. Experimental researchers manipulate independent variables to discover their effects on dependent variables. Experiments are controlled so that no unexpected factors invalidate conclusions about causal relationships. Measurement must be reliable and valid. The article by Antheunis and Schouten on impression formation in social network sites is a good example of an experiment.

A final research method involves either critically observing the performance of others or actively engaging in performance in order to understand the meanings of a text. By selecting, playing, testing, choosing, repeating, and presenting a text, the researcher learns more about the communication acts of others and shares this knowledge with an audience. The article by Carlin and Park-Fuller on disaster narratives is a good example of performance research.

The field of communication encompasses many interesting topics to study and many ways to study them. Whether your interest is in interpersonal, small-group/organizational, public, mass, or intercultural communication or in performance studies or language, you will find large bodies of research available and a variety of courses to take. But taking a course in speech communication is not the only way to learn more about communication. By reading and studying related topics or by simply observing life around you, you can continue to make discoveries about human communication.

KEY TERMS

Listed below are the key terms used in this chapter, along with the number of the page where each is explained.

heuristics (346)	survey research (361)	experimental research (366)
research question (348)	population (361)	dependent variable (366)
conceptual definition (349)	sample (361)	independent variable (366)
operational definition (349)	sampling plan (361)	research design (367)
rhetorical criticism (350)	probability sampling (361)	treatment (367)
rhetorical act (351)	simple random	pretest (367)
triangulation (353)	sampling (361)	posttest (367)
ethnographers (357)	nonprobability	control group (367)
covert role (357)	sampling (361)	reliability (367)
overt role (357)	accidental sampling (362)	validity (367)
presuppositionless	interview (363)	performance studies (370)
research (358)	questionnaire (363)	

SUGGESTED READING

Foss, Sonja K. (Ed.). (2008). *Rhetorical criticism: Exploration and practice* (4th ed.). Long Grove, IL: Waveland Press.

    Offers a clear explanation of a variety of critical methods, followed by sample essays by both undergraduate students and experts in the field.

Frey, Lawrence R., Botan, Carl H., & Kreps, Gary L. (2005). *Investigating communication: An introduction to research methods* (3rd ed.). Boston: Allyn & Bacon.

    An excellent, interesting, and comprehensive introduction to understanding and using research methods.

Notes

CHAPTER 1

1. Shands, Harley C. (1968). Crystallized conflict: Semiotic aspects of neurosis and science. In Carl E. Larson & Frank E. X. Dance (Eds.), *Perspectives on communication*. Milwaukee: The University of Wisconsin, Speech Communication Center, 128.

2. Lynch, John Patrick. (1972). *Aristotle's school: A study of a Greek educational institution*. Berkeley: University of California Press, 57, 93.

3. Bryant, Donald C. (Ed.). (1968). *Ancient Greek and Roman rhetoricians: A biographical dictionary*. Columbia, MO: Artcraft, 15–16.

4. Aristotle. (1954). *Rhetoric and poetics* (W. Rhys Roberts, Trans.). The Modern Library. New York: Random House, 1355b 26.

5. The material on the history of rhetoric is taken from two sources: Thonssen, Lester, Baird, A. Craig, & Braden, Waldo W. (1970). *Speech criticism* (2nd ed.). New York: The Ronald Press; and Harper, Nancy. (1979). *Human communication theory: The history of a paradigm*. Rochelle Park, NJ: Hayden Book Company.

6. Cicero. (1939). *Orator* (H. M. Hubell, Trans.). Cambridge, MA: Harvard University Press, 101. For a summary of Cicero's attitudes toward style, see Harper, 46–47.

7. Cicero, II. xliii, 182.

8. Plato. (1952). *Phaedrus, Gorgias* (Benjamin Jowett, Trans.). Oxford: Clarendon, 261.

9. Harper, 70.

10. Augustine. (1952). On Christian doctrine (J. F. Shaw, Trans.). In *Great Books of the Western World: Vol. 18*. Chicago: Encyclopaedia Britannica, IV.2.

11. *Ibid.*, II.1; Capes, W. W. (1877). *University life in ancient Athens*. London: Longmans, Green, and Co.

12. Augustine, II.2.

13. Arnold, Carroll C., & Frandsen, Kenneth D. (1984). Conceptions of rhetoric and communication. In Carroll C. Arnold & John Waite Bowers (Eds.), *Handbook of rhetorical and communication theory*. Boston: Allyn & Bacon, 27.

14. Golden, James L., Berquist, Goodwin F., & Coleman, William E. (1976). *The rhetoric of Western thought*. Dubuque, IA: Kendall/Hunt Publishing Company, 85.

15. Ehninger, Douglas. (1952, September). Dominant trends in English rhetorical thought, 1750–1800. *Southern Speech Journal*, 3–11.

16. For the original discussion see Hugh C. Dick (Ed.). (1955). *Selected writings of Francis Bacon*. New York: The Modern Library. For an excellent commentary, see Golden et al., 81–82. A new edition with a later publication date is also available. See Berquist, Goodwin, Coleman, William, Sproule, James M., & Golden, Ruth (2010). *The rhetoric of Western thought: From the Mediterranean world to the global setting, 10e*. Dubuque, IA: Kendall/Hunt Publishing Company.

17. Quotations from Bacon are taken from Golden et al., 82.

18. Leff, Michael C., & Procario, Margaret Orgen (1985). Rhetorical theory in speech communication. In Thomas W. Benson (Ed.), *Speech communication in the twentieth century*. Carbondale: Southern Illinois University Press, 4.

19. For a similar but more sophisticated example of source credibility research, see Bernstein, Arla G. (2000). The effects of message theme, policy explicitness, and candidate gender. *Communication Quarterly, 48*(2), 159–174.

20. Bormann, Ernest G. (1980). *Communication theory*. New York: Holt, Rinehart & Winston, 10.

21. From the reference list accompanying Gregg, Richard B. (1985). Criticism of symbolic inducement: A critical–theoretical connection. In Benson, 380–381.

22. From the table of contents of Arnold & Bowers, v–vi.

CHAPTER 2

1. Dance, Frank E. X. (1970). The "concept" of communication. *Journal of Communication, 20*, 201–210.

2. Dance, Frank E. X., & Larson, Carl E. (1972). *Speech communication: Concepts and behavior*. New York: Holt, Rinehart & Winston, 1–16.

3. For an interesting taxonomy of Internet forms, see Jensen, Klaus Bruhn, & Helles, Rasmus. (2011). The Internet as a cultural forum: Implications for research. *New Media Society, 13*, 517–533.

4. Book, Cassandra, et al. (1980). *Human communication: Principles, contexts, and skills*. New York: St. Martin's, 31–34.

5. For a general discussion of communication perspectives, see Fisher, B. Aubrey. (1978). *Perspectives on human communication*. New York: Macmillan.

6. Gergen, Kenneth J., & Davis, Keith E. (1985). *The social construction of the person*. New York: Springer-Verlag.

7. Fisher, B. Aubrey. (1982). A view from system theory. In Frank E. X. Dance (Ed.), *Human communication theory: Comparative essays*. New York: Harper & Row.

8. Watzlawick, Paul, Bavelas, Janet Beavin, & Jackson, Don D. (1967). *Pragmatics of human communication*. New York: Norton.

9. Aune, James Arnt. (1999). Catching the third wave: The dialectic of rhetoric and technology. In Thomas Rosteck (Ed.), *At the intersection: Critical studies and rhetorical studies*. New York: Guilford, 84–100, 85.

10. Condit, Celeste Michelle. (1999). The character of "history" in rhetoric and cultural studies: Recoding genetics. In Rosteck, 168–185, 169.

11. Sloop, John M., & Olson, Mark. (1999). Cultural struggle: A politics of meaning in rhetorical studies. In Rosteck, 248–265, 250.

12. Brummett, Barry, & Bowers, Detine L. (1999). Subject positions as a site of rhetorical struggle: Representing African Americans. In Rosteck, 117–136, 117.

13. Condit, 170; Nelson, Cary. (1999). The linguisticality of cultural studies: Rhetoric, close reading, and contextualization. In Rosteck, 211–225, 213.

14. Condit, 173.

15. The origins of cultural studies can be found in Williams Raymond. (1973). *The country and the city*. New York: Oxford University Press; and Thompson, E. P. (1966). *The making of the English working class*. New York: Vintage. For other influential sources, see Hall, Stuart, et al. (1978). *Policing the crisis: Mugging, the state, and law and order*. London: Macmillan; Grossberg, Lawrence, Nelson, Cary, & Treichler, Paula A. (Eds.). (1992). *Cultural studies*. New York: Routledge; Fiske, John. (1989). *Understanding the popular*. Boston: Unwin Hyman; and Fiske, John. (1994). *Television culture*. London: Routledge.

16. Hymes, Dell. (1974). *Foundations in sociolinguistics: An ethnographic approach*. Philadelphia: University of Pennsylvania Press.

CHAPTER 3

1. The original study is reported in O'Brien, Brian. (1959). How much can we see? In Robert S. Daniel (Ed.), *Contemporary readings in general psychology*. Boston: Houghton Mifflin, 270. It is retold and related to communication in Brooks, William D. (1974). *Speech communication* (2nd ed.). Dubuque, IA: William C. Brown, 23–24.

2. This definition is taken from the home page of the International Listening Association Website. See ILA (1996). International Listening Association. Retrieved from http://www.listen.org.

3. Nichols, Ralph G., & Stevens, Leonard. (1957). *Are you listening?* New York: McGraw-Hill, 12–13.

4. Wolff, Florence I., Marsnik, Nadine C., Tacey, William S., & Nichols, Ralph G. (1983). *Perceptive listening*. New York: Holt, Rinehart & Winston, 29.

5. Cooper, L. O. (1997). Listening competency in the workplace: A model for training. *Business Communication Quarterly, 60*(4), 75–84, cited in Brownell, Judi. (2006). *Listening: Attitudes, principles, and skills* (3rd ed.). Boston: Allyn & Bacon, 9.

6. Salopek, J. (1999). Is anyone listening? *Training & Development, 53*(9), 58–59, cited in Brownell, 9.

7. Brownell, 10. See also Bentley, S. C. (1998). Listening better. *Nursing Homes, 47*(2), 56–60; Anderson, D. A. (2000). Effective communicative and listening skills revisited. *Marine Crops Gazette, 84*(3), 60–61; Goby, J., & Lewis, H. (2000). The key role of listening in business: A study of the Singapore insurance industry. *Business Communication Quarterly, 63*(2), 41–51; Kemp, M. (2000). Listening skill saves time, increases effectiveness. *The American Salesman, 45*(9), 3–8; Feiertag, H. (2002). Listening skills, enthusiasm top list of salespeople's best traits. *Hotel & Motel Management, 217*(13), 20; Render, M. (2000). Better listening makes for a better marketing message. *Marketing News, 34*(19), 22; Steil, L. K., & Brommelje, R. K. (2004).

Listening leaders: The ten golden rules to listen, lead, and succeed. St. Paul, MN: Beaver's Pond Press.

8. James, William. (1890). *Principles of psychology*. New York: Holt; Neisser, Ulrich. (1961). *Cognitive psychology*. New York: Appleton-Century-Crofts.

9. Schneider, David L., Hastorf, Albert, & Ellsworth, Phoebe C. (1979). *Person perception* (2nd ed.). Reading, MA: Addison-Wesley.

10. For a brief description and comparison of social cognitive schemata, see Chapter 3 in Trenholm, Sarah, & Jensen, Arthur (2004). *Interpersonal communication* (5th ed.). New York: Oxford University Press. For a fuller discussion of some of the issues in schema theory as applied to media perception, see Wicks, Robert H. (1992). Schema theory and measurement in mass communication research: Theoretical and methodological issues in news information processing. *Communication Yearbook, 15*, 115–145. See also Garramone, Gina M. (1992). A broader and "warmer" approach to schema theory. *Communication Yearbook, 15*, 146–154.

11. Canter, Nancy, & Mischel, Walter. (1979). Prototypes in person perception. In Leonard Berkowitz (Ed.), *Advances in experimental social psychology: Vol. 12*. New York: Academic Press. See also Pavitt, Charles, & Haight, Larry. (1985). The "competent communicator" as a cognitive prototype. *Human Communication Research, 12*, 225–240.

12. For the original expression of construct theory, see Kelly, George A. (1955). *The psychology of personal constructs, Vol. I: A theory of personality*. New York: Norton.

13. Bargh, John A. (1988). Automatic information processing: Implications for communication and affect. In Lewis Donohew, Howard E. Sypher, & E. Tory Higgins (Eds.), *Communication, social cognition, and affect*. Hillsdale, NJ: Lawrence Erlbaum Associates, 18.

14. *Ibid.*

15. Crockett, Walter H. (1965). *Cognitive complexity and impression formation*. In Brendan A. Maher (Ed.), *Progress in experimental personality research, Vol. II*. New York: Academic; Delia, Jesse G., Clark, Ruth Anne, & Switzer, David E. (1974). Cognitive complexity and impression formation in informal social interaction. *Speech Monographs, 41*, 299–308; and Hale, Claudia, & Delia, Jesse. (1976). Cognitive complexity and social perspective-taking. *Communication Monographs, 43*, 195–203. For examples of studies on the impact of cognitive complexity in interpersonal relations, see Burleson, Brant R., & Samter, Wendy. (1990). Effects of cognitive complexity on the perceived importance of communication skills in friends. *Communication Research, 17*(2), 165–182; Samter, Wendy. (2002). How gender and cognitive complexity influence the provision of emotional support: A study of indirect effects. *Communication Reports, 15*(1), 5–16; Koesten, Joy, & Anderson, Karen. (2004). The influence of family communication patterns, cognitive complexity and interpersonal competence on adolescent risk behaviors. *Journal of Family Communication, 4*(2), 99–121.

16. Schank, R., & Abelson, Robert. (1977). *Scripts, plans, goals, and understanding: An inquiry into human knowledge structures*. Hillsdale, NJ: Lawrence Erlbaum Associates.

17. Sypher, Howard E., Donohew, Lewis, & Higgins, E. Tory. (1988). An overview of the roles of social cognition and affect in communication. In Donohew, Sypher, & Higgins, 35.

18. Bower, G. H., Black, J. B., & Turner, T. J. (1979). Scripts in memory for text. *Cognitive Psychology, 11*, 177–220; Loftus, E. F., & Zanni, G. (1975). Eyewitness testimony: The influence of the wording of a question. *Bulletin of the Psychonomic Society, 5*, 86–88; and Picek, J. S., Sherman, S. J., & Shiffrin, R. M. (1975). Cognitive organization and encoding of social structures. *Journal of Personality and Social Psychology, 31*, 758–768.

19. Petty, Richard E., Cacioppo, John T., & Kasmer, Jeff A. (1988). The role of affect in the elaboration likelihood model of persuasion. In Donohew, Sypher, & Higgins, 119. See also McGuire, William. (1985). Attitudes and attitude change. In G. Lindzey & E. Aronson (Eds.), *The handbook of social psychology* (3rd ed., Vol. 2). New York: Random House, 233–346; and Taylor, S. E. (1981). The interface of cognitive and "social" psychology. In J. H. Harvey (Ed.), *Cognition, social behavior, and the environment.* Hillsdale, NJ: Lawrence Erlbaum Associates.

20. Bargh, 28.

21. Langer, Ellen J. (1989). Minding matters: The consequences of mindlessness-mindfulness. In Leonard Berkowitz (Ed.), *Advances in experimental social psychology: Vol. 23.* New York: Academic, 137–173.

22. Baddeley, Alan. (1991). *Your memory: A user's guide.* New York: Macmillan, 82.

23. Weaver, Richard. (1953). *The ethics of rhetoric.* Chicago: Regnery.

24. Pratkanis, Anthony, & Aronson, Elliot. (2000). *The age of propaganda: The everyday use and abuse of persuasion.* New York: W. H. Freeman and Company, 75.

25. Henderson, John R. ICYouSee: T is for thinking— A Guide to Critical Thinking About What You See on the Web, Ithaca College Library, http://www.ithaca.edu/library/training/think.html.

26. Barnes, Susan. (2003). *Computer-mediated communication: Human to human communication across the Internet.* Boston: Allyn & Bacon, 125–126.

27. Henderson, op cit., www.ithaca.edu/library/training/think.html.

28. Gudykunst, William B., & Kim, Young Yun. (1997). *Communicating with strangers: An approach to intercultural communication* (3rd ed.). New York: McGraw-Hill, 265–266.

29. Chen, Guo-Ming, & Starosta, William J. (1998). *Foundations of intercultural communication.* Boston: Allyn & Bacon, 183.

30. Pratkanis & Aronson, 60–64.

31. Loftus, Elizabeth F. (1993). The reality of repressed memories. *American Psychologist, 48*, 518–537; Loftus, Elizabeth, & Loftus, G. R. (1980). On the permanence of stored memories. *American Psychologist, 35*, 409–420.

32. Brownell, 157–162.

33. Zuckerman, Marvin. (1988). Behavior and biology: Research on sensation seeking and reactions to the media. In Donohew, Sypher, & Higgins, 173.

34. *Ibid.*, 174.

35. Bargh, John A. (1984). Automatic and subconscious processing of social information. In Robert S. Wyler, Jr., & Thomas K. Srull (Eds.), *Handbook of social cognition: Vol. 3.* Hillsdale, NJ: Lawrence Erlbaum Associates.

36. Nisbett, R., & Ross, L. (1980). *Human inference: Strategies and shortcomings of social judgment.* Englewood Cliffs, NJ: Prentice-Hall.

37. An early statement of the cognitive response model can be found in Petty, Richard E., Ostrom, Thomas M., & Brock, Timothy C. (1981). *Cognitive responses in persuasion.* Hillsdale, NJ: Lawrence Erlbaum Associates.

CHAPTER 4

1. Orwell, George. (1949). *1984.* New York: Harcourt, Brace & World, 311. See also the appendix on Newspeak.

2. Lutz, William. (1989). *New double-speak.* New York: Harper & Row, 9.

3. Fromkin, Victoria, & Rodman, Robert. (1988). *An introduction to language* (4th ed.). New York: Holt, Rinehart and Winston, 4.

4. de Saussure, Ferdinand. (1966). *Course in general linguistics.* London: McGraw-Hill.

5. Chen, Guo-Ming, & Starosta, William J. (1998). *Foundations of intercultural communication.* Boston: Allyn & Bacon, 36.

6. Aristotle. (1963). *De interpretatione* (J. L. Ackrill, Trans.). Clarendon Aristotle Series. Oxford, UK: Oxford University Press, 43; Arnauld, A., & Lancelot, C. (1968). *Grammaire de Port-Royal* (R. Alston, Ed. and Trans.). Menston, UK: Scolar, 22; cited and discussed in Sperber, Dan, & Wilson, Deirdre. (1986). *Relevance: Communication and cognition.* Cambridge, MA: Harvard University Press, 5–6.

7. Carmichael, L., Hogan, H. P., & Walter, A. A. (1932). An experimental study of the effect of language on the reproduction of visually perceived forms. *Journal of Experimental Psychology, 15*, 73–86; Slobin, Dan. (1971). *Psycholinguistics.* Glenview, IL: Scott, Foresman, 103.

8. Mandelbaum, D. B. (Ed.). (1958). *Selected writings of Edward Sapir in language, culture and personality.* Berkeley: University of California Press, 162.

9. Slobin, 129.

10. Cohn, Carol. (1987). Sex and death in the rational world of defense intellectuals. *Signs: Journal of Women in Culture and Society, 12*(4), 690.

11. The latter example is taken from Lutz, 176. For additional examples, see 175–177.

12. Cohn, 713.

13. This list can be found online at http://www.ruf.rice.edu/~kemmer/Words04/neologisms/e.html#e. Other lists of neologisms can be found at http://www.neologia.org/html/neologism_sites.html, or simply google "neologisms."

14. James, Frank. (2012, March 29). Democrats embrace "Obamacare" to defang word's bite. *NPR.* Retrieved from http://www.npr.org/blogs/itsallpolitics/2012/03/29/149621814/democrats-seembrace-obamacare.

15. Galinsky, Adam D., Hugenberg, Kurt, Groom, Carla, & Bodenhausen, Galen (2003). Identity issues in groups. *Research on Managing Groups and Teams, 5*, 221–256. Retrieved from http://faculty.wcas.northwestern.edu/bodenhausen/reapp/.pdf.

16. *Ibid.*, 241; see also, Peters, W. (1987). *A class divided: Then and now.* New Haven, CT: Yale University Press.

17. *Ibid.*, 232.

18. The originators of CMM theory are Vernon Cronen and W. Barnett Pearce. One of the many sources on CMM is Cronen, Vernon, Pearce, W. Barnett, & Harris, Linda. (1982). The coordinated management of meaning. In Frank E. X. Dance (Ed.), *Comparative human communication theory.* New York: Harper & Row.

19. Lakoff, Robin Tolmach. (1992). *Talking power: The politics of language in our lives.* New York: Basic, 28.

20. McLaughlin, Margaret L. (1984). *Conversation: How talk is organized.* Beverly Hills, CA: Sage, 271.

21. My discussion of the differences between public and private forms of talk is based in part on Lakoff's discussion, but her ideas have been modified. For a discussion of this distinction as applied to relationships, see Trenholm, Sarah, & Jensen, Arthur. (1992). *Interpersonal communication* (2nd ed.). Belmont, CA: Wadsworth, chapter 2.

22. Grice, H. P. (1975). Logic and conversation. In P. Cole & J. Morgan (Eds.), *Syntax and semantics: Vol. 3.* New York: Academic, 41–58.

23. Lakoff, 45.

24. The four sets of questions were suggested by, but are not identical to, those used by Lakoff, 140.

25. Tannen, Deborah. (1990). *You just don't understand: Women and men in conversation.* New York: Ballantine.

26. Condry, John, & Condry, Sandra. (1976). Sex differences: A study of the eye of the beholder. *Child Development, 47,* 812–819; cited in Tannen, 1990, 228.

27. See, for example, Weatherall, Ann. (1998). Revisioning gender and language research. *Women and language, 21*(1), 1–9, and Kyratzis, Amy. (2000). Tactical uses of narratives in nursery school same-sex groups. *Discourse processes, 29*(3), 269–299.

28. Tannen, 1990, 44; Maltz, Daniel N., & Borker, Ruth A. (1982). A cultural approach to male-female miscommunication. In John J. Gumperz (Ed.), *Language and social identity.* Cambridge, UK: Cambridge University Press.

29. Tannen, 1990, 177–178.

30. Kramer, Cheris, Thorne, Barrie, & Henley, Nancy. (1978). Perspectives on language and communication. *Signs: Journal of Women in Culture and Society, 3*(3), 638–651, 638.

31. Crawford, M., & English, L. (1984). Generic versus specific inclusion of women in language: Effects on recall. *Journal of Psycholinguistic Research, 13,* 373–381.

32. Kitto, J. (1989). Gender reference terms: Separating the women from the girls. *British Journal of Social Psychology, 28,* 185–187.

33. Weatherall, 2.

34. Cameron, Deborah (1998). Gender, language, and discourse: A review essay. *Signs, 23*(4), 945. See also, Wareing, Shan. (1996). What do we know about language and gender? Paper presented to the Eleventh Sociolinguistic Symposium, Cardiff, September 5–7, cited in Cameron.

35. Aries, Elizabeth. (1996). *Men and women in interaction: Reconsidering the differences.* New York: Oxford, vii.

36. *Ibid.*, viii.

37. *Ibid.*, 205.

38. West, Candace, & Zimmerman, Don. (1987). Doing gender. *Gender and Society, 1*(2), 125–151, 140.

39. Tannen, Deborah. (1994). *Gender and discourse.* New York: Oxford University Press, 198.

40. Cameron, 6.

41. Aries, 204.

42. Miller, Ann Neville. (2012). When face-to-face won't work: Use of informal intermediaries to communicate interpersonally in sub-Saharan Africa. In Larry A. Samovar, Richard E. Porter, & Edwin R. McDaniel. *Intercultural communication: A reader.* Wadsworth/Cengage.

43. Eisenberg, Eric M. (1984, September). Ambiguity as strategy in organizational communication. *Communication Monographs, 51,* 227–241.

44. Bavelas, Janet Beavin, Black, Alex, Chovil, Nicole, & Mullett, Jennifer. (1990). *Equivocal communication.* Newbury Park, CA: Sage. Situations are modified from those used by Bavelas (68, 69); response alternatives are verbatim.

45. *Ibid.*, 260.

46. Mehrabian, Albert. (1967). Attitudes inferred from nonimmediacy of verbal communications. *Journal of Verbal Learning and Verbal Behavior, 6,* 294–295.

47. Reagan, Ronald. Address to the nation announcing the Reagan-Bush candidacies for reelection, January 29, 1984. Retrieved from http://www.reagan.utexas.edu/archives/speeches/1984/12984a.htm.

48. Berger, Charles R., & Bradac, James J. (1982). *Language and social knowledge: Uncertainty in interpersonal relations.* London: Edward Arnold, 203–204.

49. Tannen, Deborah. (1984). *Conversational style.* Norwood, NJ: Ablex.

50. Lakoff, 180.

51. Lakoff, George, & Johnson, Mark. (1980). *Metaphors we live by.* Chicago: University of Chicago Press, 4.

52. *Ibid.*, 5.

53. Huxley, Aldous. (1962). Words and their meanings. In Max Black (Ed.), *The importance of language.* Englewood Cliffs, NJ: Prentice-Hall, 4–5.

CHAPTER 5

1. Vanairsdale, S. T. (2011, November). Silent is golden: A chat with *The Artist's* leading man (and Oscar frontrunner) Jean Dujardin. *Movieline.com.* Retrieved from http://movieline.com/2011/11/21/silent-is-golden-a-chat-with-the-artists-leading-man-and-oscar-frontrunner-jean-dujardin/.

2. Ekman, Paul, & Friesen, Wallace. (1975). *Unmasking the face: A guide to recognizing emotions from facial expressions.* Englewood Cliffs, NJ: Prentice-Hall.

3. Mehrabian, Albert. (1970). A semantic space for nonverbal behavior. *Journal of Counseling and Clinical Psychology, 35,* 248–257.

4. Ekman, Paul. (1965). Communication through nonverbal behavior: A source of information about an interpersonal relationship. In S. S. Tompkins & C. E. Izard (Eds.), *Affect, cognition, and personality.* New York: Springer; Knapp, Mark. (1980). *Essentials of nonverbal communication.* New York: Holt, Rinehart & Winston, 11–15.

5. Knapp, 14.

6. Weimann, John M. (1977). Explication and test of a model of communication competence. *Human Communication Research, 3*, 195–213. See also Spitzberg, Brian H., & Cupach, W. R. (1988). *Handbook for interpersonal competence research*. New York: Springer-Verlag; and Spitzberg, Brian H. (1990). Perspectives on nonverbal communication skills. In Joseph A. DeVito & Michael L. Hecht (Eds.), *The nonverbal communication reader*. Prospect Heights, IL: Waveland Press.

7. Rubenstein, C. (1980). Body language that speaks to muggers. *Psychology Today, 20*.

8. Ekman, Paul, & Friesen, W. V. (1969). The repertoire of nonverbal behavior: Categories, origins, usage, and coding. *Semiotica, 1*, 49–98; Trager, G. L. (1958). Paralanguage: A first approximation. *Studies in Linguistics, 13*, 1–12.

9. Johnson, H. G., Ekman, P., & Friesen, W. V. (1975). Communicative body movements: American emblems. *Semiotica, 15*, 335–353.

10. Burgoon, Judee K., Buller, David B., & Woodall, W. Gill. (1995). *Nonverbal communication: The unspoken dialogue*. New York: McGraw-Hill, 28, 187–189.

11. Ekman, Paul, & Friesen, W. V. (1974). Detecting deception from the body or face. *Journal of Personality and Social Psychology, 29*, 288–298; Ekman & Friesen (1975); Zuckerman, Miron, DePaulo, Bella M., & Rosenthal, Robert. (1981). Verbal and nonverbal communication of deception. In Leonard Berkowitz (Ed.), *Advances in experimental social psychology: Vol. 14*. New York: Academic Press; Zuckerman, M., & Driver, R. E., (Eds.). (1985). Telling lies: Verbal and nonverbal correlates of deception. In A. W. Siegman & S. Feldstein (Eds.), *Multichannel integrations of nonverbal behavior*. Hillsdale, NJ: Lawrence Erlbaum Associates.

12. Burgoon, Buller, & Woodall, 281–287.

13. Charlesworth, W. R., & Kreutzer, M. A. (1973). Facial expressions of infants and children. In Paul Ekman (Ed.), *Darwin and facial expressions: A century of research in review*. New York: Academic Press; Eibl-Eibesfeldt, I. (1975). *Ethology: The biology of behavior*. New York: Holt, Rinehart & Winston.

14. Ekman & Friesen (1975).

15. Chen, Guo-Ming, & Starosta, William J. (1998). *Foundations of intercultural communication*. Boston: Allyn & Bacon, 90.

16. Buck, Ross. (1979). Individual differences in nonverbal sending accuracy and electrodermal responding: The externalizing-internalizing dimension. In R. Rosenthal (Ed.), *Skill in nonverbal communication: Individual differences*. Cambridge, MA: Oelgeschlager, Gunn & Hain.

17. Donaldson-Evans, L. (1980). Love's fatal glance: A study of eye imagery in the poets of the Ecole Lyonnaise [Monograph]. *Romance Monographs, 8*, 21; cited in Grumet, Gerald W. (1983). Eye contact: The core of interpersonal relatedness. *Psychiatry, 28*, 172–180, and reprinted in DeVito & Hecht, 126–137, 129.

18. Grumet, 129.

19. Hess, E. H. (1975). *The tell-tale eye*. New York: Van Nostrand; Andersen, P. A., Todd-Mancillas, W. R., & Clementa, L. D. (1980). The effects of pupil dilation on physical, social, and task attraction. *Australian SCAN of Nonverbal Communication*, 7–8, 89–96; Malandro, Loretta A., & Barker, Larry L. (1983). *Nonverbal communication*. Reading, MA: Addison-Wesley, 170–172.

20. For an interesting discussion of the function of the stare in initiating interpersonal relationships, see Wilmot, William. (1979). *Dyadic communication* (2nd ed.). Reading, MA: Addison-Wesley, 9–10.

21. Grumet, 133.

22. Miller, Patrick W. (1988). *Nonverbal communication* (3rd ed.). Washington, DC: National Education Society, 14.

23. Heinberg, P. (1964). *Voice training for speaking and reading aloud*. New York: Ronald; Burgoon, Buller, & Woodall, 68–70, also offer a good discussion of vocal qualities.

24. Malandro & Barker, 281–283; Burgoon, Buller, & Woodall, 68.

25. Bruneau, Thomas. (1973). Communicative silences: Forms and functions. *Journal of Communication, 23*, 17–46.

26. Basso, Keith H. (1992). "Speaking with names": Language and landscape among the Western Apache. In George E. Marcus (Ed.), *Rereading cultural anthropology*. Durham, NC: Duke University Press, 230; see also, Basso, Keith H. (1990). "To give up on words": Silence in Western Apache culture. In Donald L. Carbaugh (Ed.), *Cultural communication and intercultural contact*. Hillsdale, NJ: Erlbaum, 303–320.

27. Gonzalez, Alexander, & Zimbardo, Philip G. (1985, March). Time in perspective. *Psychology Today*, 21–26. For a copy of the instrument used to measure time perspective, see Zimbardo, Philip G., & Boyd, John N. (1999). Putting time in perspective: A valid, reliable individual-difference metric. *Journal of Personality and Social Psychology, 77*(6), 1271–1288.

28. Burgoon, Buller, & Woodall, 145. See also Hall, Edward T. (1959). *The silent language*. Garden City, NY: Doubleday.

29. Gonzalez & Zimbardo, 26.

30. Lyman, Stanford M., & Scott, Marvin B. (1967). Territoriality: A neglected sociological dimension. *Social Problems, 15*(2), 236–249. An abridged version is available in DeVito & Hecht.

31. Adams, R. S., & Biddle, B. (1970). *Realities of teaching: Exploration with video tape*. New York: Holt, Rinehart & Winston; Sommer, Richard. (1969). *Personal space: The behavioral basis of design*. Englewood Cliffs, NJ: Prentice-Hall; Malandro & Barker, 202–203.

32. Feilor, Bruce S. (1991). *Learning to bow: Inside the heart of Japan*. New York: Ticknor and Fields, 19; for another discussion of Japanese and American use of space, see Brake, Terrence, Walter, Danielle Medina, & Walker, Thomas (Tim). (1995). *Doing business internationally: The guide to cross-cultural success*. New York: Irwin Professional Publishing, 60–61.

33. Feilor, 20.

34. Burgoon, Buller, & Woodall, 77–79.

35. Burgoon, Judee, & Saine, Thomas (1978). *The unspoken dialogue: An introduction to nonverbal communication*. Boston: Houghton Mifflin, 70.

36. David, F. (1978, September 27). Skin hunger—An American disease. *Woman's Day,* 48–50, 154–156; cited in Malandro & Barker, 253.

37. Malandro & Barker, 253.

38. Knapp, 119.

39. See, for example, Wells, W., & Siegel, B. (1961). Stereotyped somatypes. *Psychological Reports, 8,* 77–78.

40. Knapp, 107.

41. Smith, Lawrence J., & Malandro, Loretta A. (Eds.). (1985). *Courtroom communication strategies.* New York: Kluwer.

42. Ruesch, Juergen, & Kees, W. (1956). *Nonverbal communication: Notes on the visual perception of human relations.* Berkeley: University of California Press.

43. Becker, Franklin D. (1977). *Housing messages.* Stroudsburg, PA: Dowden, Hutchinson & Ross, 4.

44. Becker, 5.

45. Burgoon & Saine, Chapter 4.

CHAPTER 6

1. Miller, Gerald R., & Steinberg, Mark. (1975). *Between people: A new analysis of interpersonal communication.* Chicago: Science Research Associates.

2. Miller & Steinberg. For a fuller discussion, see Trenholm, Sarah. (1991). *Human communication theory* (2nd ed.). Englewood Cliffs, NJ: Prentice-Hall, 161.

3. Allen, Woody. (1982). *Four films of Woody Allen.* New York: Random House, l05.

4. Gilbert, Paul. (2005). Social mentalities: A biopsychosocial and evolutionary approach to social relationships. In Mark W. Baldwin (Ed.), *Interpersonal cognition.* New York: Guilford Press, 299. See also, Cacioppo, J. T., Berston, G. G., Sheridan, J. F., & McClintock, M. K. (2000). Multilevel integrative analysis of human behavior: Social neuroscience and the complementing nature of social and biological approaches. *Psychological Bulletin, 126,* 829–843; Wearden, A. J., Tarrier, N., Barrowclough, C., Zastowny, T. R., & Rahil, A. A. (2000). A review of expressed emotion research in health care. *Clinical Psychology Review, 5,* 633–666; and Luecken, Linda J., Appelhans, Bradley M., Kraft, Amy, & Brown, Ana. (2006). Never far from home: A cognitive-affective model of the impact of early-life family relationships on psychological stress responses in adulthood. *Journal of Social and Personal Relationships, 23*(2), 189–203.

5. Cooley, Charles Horton. (1969). The social self: On the meaning of "I." In Chad Gordon & Kenneth J. Gergen (Eds.), *The self in social interactions, I: Classic and contemporary perspectives.* New York: Wiley, 87–91.

6. Rosenberg, Morris. (1967). Psychological selectivity in self-esteem formation. In Carolyn W. Sherif & Muzafer Sherif (Eds.), *Attitude, ego-involvement, and change.* New York: Wiley, 26–50; cited in Wilmot, William. (1987). *Dyadic communication* (3rd ed.). New York: Random House.

7. Rawlins, William. (1983). Openness as problematic in ongoing friendship: Two conversational dilemmas. *Communication Monographs, 50,* 1–13; Baxter, Leslie A. (1990). Dialectical contradictions in developing relationships. *Journal of Social and Personal Relationships, 7,* 69–88.

8. Wilmot, 169.

9. Cupach, William R., & Metts, Sandra. (1994). *Facework.* Thousand Oaks, CA: Sage, 3.

10. Brown, Penelope, & Levinson, Stephen C. (1987). *Politeness: Some universals in language usage.* Cambridge, UK: Cambridge University Press.

11. For some recent research on face needs and politeness, see Johnson, Danette I. (2007). Politeness theory and conversational refusals: Associations between various types of face threat and perceived competence. *Western Journal of Communication, 71*(3), 196–215; Johnson, Danette I., Roloff, Michael E., & Riffee, Melissa A. (2004). Politeness theory and refusals of requests: Face threat as a function of expressed obstacles. *Communication Studies, 55*(2), 227–238; Adrianne D. Kunkel, Wilson, Steven R., Olufowote, James O., & Robson, Scott J. (2003). Identity implications of influence goals: Initiating, intensifying, and ending romantic relationships. *Western Journal of Communication, 67*(4), 382–412.

12. Sieburg, Evelyn. (1975). *Interpersonal confirmation: A paradigm for conceptualization and measurement.* San Diego: United States International University. (ERIC Document Reproduction Service No. ED 098 634).

13. Wilmot, 148.

14. Knapp, Mark L., & Vangelisti, Anita L. (1992). *Interpersonal communication and human relationships* (2nd ed.). Boston: Allyn & Bacon; Wood, Julia T. (1982). Communication and relational culture: Bases for the study of human relationships. *Communication Quarterly, 30*(2), 75–83.

15. Knapp & Vangelisti, 39.

16. Baxter, Leslie A., & Wilmot, William. (1984). "Secret tests": Social strategies for acquiring information about the state of the relationship. *Human Communication Research, 11,* 171–202.

17. Altman, Irwin, & Taylor, Dalmas A. (1973). *Social penetration: The development of interpersonal relationships.* New York: Holt, Rinehart and Winston.

18. Duck, Steve. (1973). Interpersonal communication in developing acquaintance. In Gerald R. Miller (Ed.), *Explorations in interpersonal communication.* Beverly Hills, CA: Sage, 127–148.

19. Zhang, Shuangyue, & Stafford, Laura. (2007). A prototypical perspective on relational maintenance strategies. Paper presented at the annual meeting of the International Communication Association, San Francisco, California; available online from EBSCOhost. For a discussion of a range of relational maintenance strategies, see also Guerrero, Laura K., Andersen, Peter A., & Afifi, Walid A. (2001). *Close encounters: Communicating in relationships.* Mt. View, CA: Mayfield, 230–231. See also, Dainton, Marianne, & Gross, Jamie. (2008). The use of negative behaviors to maintain relationships. *Communication Research Reports, 25*(3), 179–191.

20. Canary, Daniel J., & Stafford, Laura. (1992). Relational maintenance strategies and equity in marriage. *Communication Monographs, 59,* 243–268.

21. Stafford, Laura, Dainton, Marianne, & Haas, Stephen. (2000). Measuring routine and strategic relational maintenance: Scale revision, sex versus gender roles, and

the prediction of relational characteristics. *Communication Monographs, 67*(3), 306–323. See also, Myers, Scott A., & Glover, Natica P. (2007). Emerging adults' use of relational maintenance behaviors with their parents. *Communication Research Reports, 24*(3), 257–264.

22. Weigel, Daniel J., & Ballard-Reisch, Deborah S. (2008). Relational maintenance, satisfaction, and commitment in marriages: An actor-partner analysis. *Journal of Family Communication, 8*(3), 212–229; Stafford, Laura, & Canary, Daniel J. (2006). Equity and interdependence as predictors of relational maintenance strategies. *The Journal of Family Communication, 6*(4), 227–254; Johnson, Amy Janan, Haigh, Michel M., Becker, Jennifer A., Craig, Elizabeth A., & Wigley, Shelley. (2008). College students' use of relational management strategies in email in long-distance and geographically close relationships. *Journal of Computer-Mediated Communication, 13*, 381–404; Buoy Kissick, Amana, & Yum, Young-Ok. (2007). Differences in relationship quality and maintenance behaviors between active parents and empty nesters. Conference paper presented at the annual meeting of the International Communication Association, San Francisco, California; available online from EBSCOhost. See also Canary & Stafford, 1992.

23. Guerrero, Laura K., & Chavez, Alana M. (2005). Relational maintenance in cross-sex friendships characterized by different types of romantic intent: An exploratory study. *Western Journal of Communication, 69*(4), 339–358; Canary, Daniel J., Stafford, Laura, Hause, Kimberley S., & Wallace, Lisa A. (1993). An inductive analysis of relational maintenance strategies: Comparisons among lovers, relatives, friends, and others. *Communication Research Reports, 10*(1), 5–14.

24. Myers, Scott A., Brann, Maria, & Rittenour, Christine E. (2008). Interpersonal communication motives as a predictor of early and middle adulthood siblings' use of relational maintenance behaviors. *Communication Research Reports, 25*(2), 155–167; Serewicz, Mary Claire Morr, Dickson, Fran C., Morrison, Jennifer, Huynh, Thi Anh, & Poole, L. Lori. (2007). Family privacy orientation, relational maintenance, and family satisfaction in young adults' family relationships. *The Journal of Family Communication, 7*(2), 123–142; Myers, Scott A., & Glover, Natica P. (2007). Emerging adults' use of relational maintenance behaviors with their parents. *Communication Research Reports, 24*(3), 257–264.

25. Goodboy, Alan K., & Myers, Scott A. (2008). Relational maintenance behaviors of friends with benefits: Investigating equity and relational characteristics. *Human Communication, 11*(1), 71–86.

26. Yum, Young-Ok, & Li, Han Z. (2007). Associations among attachment style, maintenance strategies, and relational quality across cultures. *Journal of Intercultural Communication Research, 36*(2), 71–89; Guerrero, Laura K., & Bachman, Guy F. (2006). Associations among relational maintenance behaviors, attachment-style categories, and attachment dimensions. *Communication Studies, 57*(3), 341–361.

27. Henson, Donna F., Dybvig-Pawelko, Kristin C., & Canary, Daniel C. (2004). The effects of loneliness on relational maintenance behaviors: An attributional perspective. *Communication Research Reports, 21*(4), 411–419.

28. Dainton & Gross.

29. Goodboy, Alan K., Myers, Scott A., & members of Investigating Communication. (2010). Relational quality indicators and love styles as predictors of negative relational maintenance behaviors in romantic relationships. *Communication Reports, 23*(2), 65–78, 67.

30. Dainton & Gross.

31. Goodboy, Alan K., & Bolkan, San. (2011). Attachment and the use of negative relational maintenance behaviors in romantic relationships. *Communication Research Reports, 28*(4), 327–336, 334.

32. Afifi, Tamara, Caughlin, John, & Afifi, Walid. (2007). The dark side (and light side) of avoidance and secrets. In Brian H. Spitzberg & William R. Cupach (Eds.), *The dark side of interpersonal communication.* Mahwah, NJ: Lawrence Erlbaum, 68. See also Smyth, Joshua M., & Pennebaker, James W. (2001). What are the health effects of disclosure? In Andrew S. Baum, Tracey A. Revenson, & Jerome E. Singer (Eds.), *Handbook of health psychology.* Mahwah, NJ: Lawrence Erlbaum.

33. Braithwaite, Dawn O., Olson, Loreen, Golish, Tamara, Soukup, Charles, & Turman, Paul. (2001). "Becoming a family": Developmental processes represented in blended family discourse. *Journal of Applied Communication Research, 29*, 221–247; Caughlin, John P., Golish, Tamara D., Olson, Loreen N., Sargent, Jack E., Cook, Jeff S., & Petronio, Sandra. (2000). Intrafamily secrets in various family configurations: A communication boundary management perspective. *Communication Studies, 51*, 116–134.

34. Johnson, David W. (1993). *Reaching out: Interpersonal effectiveness and self-actualization* (5th ed.). Boston: Allyn & Bacon, 179. Johnson gives excellent sample problems and responses, as well as good advice on how to respond helpfully.

35. *Ibid.*, 181.

36. *Ibid.*, 183–184.

37. *Ibid.*, Chapter 8, 205–265.

38. *Ibid.*, 222.

39. *Ibid.*, 231.

40. Chen, Guo-Ming, & Starosta, William J. (1998). *Foundations of intercultural communication.* Boston: Allyn & Bacon, 128. For a full discussion of the use of intermediaries, see Ma, R. (1992). The role of unofficial intermediaries in interpersonal conflicts in the Chinese culture. *Communication Quarterly, 40*, 269–278.

41. Reeves-Ellington, Richard H. (1993). Using cultural skills for cooperative advantage in Japan. *Human Organization, 52*, 203–215; quoted in Lustig, Myron W., & Koester Jolene. (1996). *Intercultural competence: Interpersonal communication across cultures* (2nd ed.). New York: HarperCollins.

42. Trenholm, Sarah & Jensen, Arthur. (2011). *Interpersonal Communication* (7th ed.). New York: Oxford University Press.

43. Walther, Joseph B. (1996). Computer-mediated communication: Impersonal, interpersonal, and hyperpersonal interaction. *Communication Research, 23*, 3–44.

44. Anderson, Traci L., & Emmers-Sommer, Tara M. (2006). Predictors of relationship satisfaction in online romantic relationships. *Communication Studies, 57*, 153–172.

45. Walther, Joseph B. (1996). Computer-mediated communication: Impersonal, interpersonal, and hyperpersonal interaction. *Communication Research* 23(1), 3–43; Walther, Joseph B. (1993). Impression development in computer-mediated interaction: A relational perspective. *Communication Research, 19*, 52–90.

46. Wallace, Patricia. (1999). *The psychology of the Internet*. New York: Cambridge University Press, 135. See also Parks, Malcolm, & Floyd, Kory. (1996). Making friends in cyberspace. *Journal of Communication, 46*(1), 80–97, and Anderson & Emmers-Sommer, 2006.

47. Haferkamp, Nina, & Kraemer, Nicole. (2009). When I was your age, Pluto was a planet: Impression management and need to belong as motives for joining groups on social networking sites. Paper presented at the annual convention of the International Communication Association, Chicago, IL.

48. Turkle, Sherry. (2011). *Alone together: Why we expect more from technology and less from each other*. New York: Basic Books, 182.

49. Toma, Cataline, Hancock, Jeff, & Ellison, Nicole. (2007). Separating face from fiction: An examination of deceptive self-presentation in online dating profiles. Paper presented at the annual meeting of the International Communication Association, San Francisco, California. Available online from EBSCOhost.

50. Smock, Andrew. (2010). Self-presentation on Facebook: Managing content created by the user and others. Paper presented at the annual meeting of the International Communication Association, Singapore; Van der Heide, Brandon, D'Angelo, Jonathan D., & Schumaker, Erin M. (2012). The effects of verbal versus photographic self-presentation on impression formation in Facebook. *Journal of Communication, 62*, 98–116.

51. Walther, Joseph, Van Der Heide, Brandon, Kim, Sang-Yeon, Tong, Stephanie, & Wesgterman, David. (2008). The role of friends' appearance and behavior on evaluations of individuals on Facebook: Are we known by the company we keep? *Human Communication Research, 34*, 28–49, 32. See also, Ellison, N., Heino, R., & Gibbs, J. (2006). Managing impressions online: Self-presentation process in the online dating environment. *Journal of Computer-Mediated Communication, 11*(2), Article 2. Retrieved rom http://jcmc .indiana.edu/vol11/issue2/ellison.html; Ellison, Nichole B., Steinfield, Charles, & Lampe, Cliff. (2007). The benefits of Facebook "friends": Social capital and college students' use of online social networks sites. *Journal of Computer-Mediated Communication, 12*(4). Retrieved from http://jcmc .indiana.edu/vol12/issue4/ellison.html.

52. Johnson, Amy Janan, Haigh, Michel M., Becker, Jennifer A. J., Craig, Elizabeth, & Wigley, Shelley. (2008). College students' use of relational management strategies in email in long-distance and geographically close relationships. *Journal of Computer-Mediated Communication, 13*, 381–404, 383.

53. Wang, Hua, & Andersen, Peter A. (2007). Computer-mediated communication in relationship maintenance: An examination of self-disclosure in long-distance friendships. Paper presented at the annual meeting of the International Communication Association, San Francisco, California. 22. Available online from EBSCOhost.

54. Johnson, A. J. (2008), 385.

55. Lyndon, Arny, Bonds-Raacke, Jennifer, & Cratty, Alyssa D. (2011). College students' Facebook stalking of ex-partners. *Cyberpsychology, Behavior and Social Networking, 14*(12), 711–715.

56. Meredith, Jessica P. (2010). Combating cyberbullying: Emphasizing education over criminalization. *Federal Communications Law Journal, 63*(1), 311+.

57. *Ibid.* quote is attributed to Patricia Agatston, coauthor of *Cyberbullying: Bullying in the Digital Age*.

58. Utz, Sonja, & Beukeboom, Camiel J. (2011). The role of social network sites in romantic relationships: Effects on jealousy and relationship happiness. *Journal of Computer-Mediated Communication, 16*, 511–527.

59. Hall, Jeffrey A., & Baym, Nancy. (2012). Calling and texting (too much): Mobile maintenance expectations, (over)dependence, entrapment and friendship satisfaction. *New Media and Society, 14*, 316–331.

60. For a discussion of the use of robots with elderly dementia patients, see Bemelmans, Roger, Gelderblom, Gert Jan, Jonker, Pieter, & deWitte, Luc. (2012). Socially assistive robots in elderly care: A systematic review into effects and effectiveness. *JAMDA, 13*, 114–120.

61. You can see a photo of the Hello Kitty robot at DreamKitty .com, http://www.dreamkitty.com/mm5/merchant.mvc.

62. For a good general discussion of companion robots and their social effects, see Turkle.

63. Sharkey, Noel, & Sharkey, Amanda. (2010). The crying shame of robot nannies: An ethical appraisal. *Interaction Studies, 1*(2), 160–190, 163. See also Sharkey, Noel, & Sharkey, Amanda. (2010) Living with robots: Ethical tradeoffs in eldercare. In Wilks, Yorick. *Artificial Companions in Society: Scientific, economic, psychological and philosophical perspectives*. (In press). Amsterdam: John Benjamins, 245–256; Turkle, Sherry, and others. (2006). Relational artifacts with children and elders: The complexities of cybercompanionship. *Connection Science, 18*, 4, 347–362.

64. Kramer, Melinda. (2001). *Business communication in context*. Upper Saddle River, NJ: Prentice Hall, 428. See also Harcourt, Jules. (1990). Developing ethical messages. *The Bulletin of the Association for Business Communication, 53*(3), 19.

CHAPTER 7

1. Jensen, Arthur D., & Chilberg, Joseph C. (1991). *Small group communication*. Belmont, CA: Wadsworth, 5.

2. Pittinger, R. E., Hockett, C. F., & Danehy, J. J. (1960). *The first five minutes: A sample of microscopic interview analysis*. Ithaca, NY: Martineau, 223.

3. Cited in Rothwell, J. Dan. (1992). *In mixed company: Small group communication*. New York: Harcourt Brace Jovanovich, 39.

4. For a good discussion of the problems of triads, see Wilmot, William W. (1987). *Dyadic communication* (3rd ed.). New York: Random House, 21–32.

5. Bormann, Ernest. (1990). *Small group communication: Theory and practice*. New York: Harper & Row, 2.

6. Rothwell, 41.

7. Schutz, William. (1958). *Firo: A three-dimensional theory of interpersonal behavior.* New York: Holt, Rinehart & Winston.

8. Johnson, David W., & Johnson, Frank P. (1994). *Joining together: Group theory and group skills.* Boston: Allyn & Bacon, 254.

9. Moreland, Richard, & Levine, John. (1982). Socialization in small groups: Temporal changes in individual-group relations. In Leonard Berkowitz (Ed.), *Advances in experimental social psychology: Vol. 15.* New York: Academic; and Moreland, Richard, & Levine, John. (1987). Group dynamics over time: Development and socialization in small groups. In J. McGrath (Ed.), *The social psychology of time.* Beverly Hills, CA: Sage.

10. Hollander, Edwin. (1958). Conformity, status and idiosyncrasy credit. *Psychological Review, 65,* 117–127.

11. There are many analyses of the *Challenger* case. See Jaksa, James, Pritchard, Michael, & Kramer, Ronald. (1988). Ethics in organizations: The *Challenger* explosion. In James Jaksa & Michael Pritchard (Eds.), *Communication ethics: Methods of analysis.* Belmont, CA: Wadsworth; Kruglanski, A. (1986, August). Freeze-think and the *Challenger. Psychology Today,* 48–49; Hirokawa, Randy Y., Gouran, Dennis S., & Martz, A. E. (1988). Understanding the sources of faulty group decision making: A lesson from the *Challenger* disaster. *Small Group Behavior, 19,* 411–433; Renz, M. A., & Greg, J. (1988). Flaws in the decision making process: Assessment of risk in the decision to launch flight 51-L. *Central States Speech Journal, 39,* 67–75.

12. Janis, Irving. (1972). *Victims of groupthink.* Boston: Houghton Mifflin.

13. Hogg, Michael A. (2005). The social identity perspective. In Susan A. Wheelan (Ed.), *The handbook of group research and practice.* Thousand Oaks, CA: Sage Publications, 136.

14. Miller, D. T., Downs, J. S., & Prentice, D. A. (1998). Minimum conditions for the creation of a unit relationship: The social bond between birthdaymates. *European Journal of Social Psychology, 28,* 475–481. See also Bourhis, R. Y., Sachdev, I., & Gagnon, A. (1994). Intergroup research with the Tajfel matrices: Methodological notes. In Mark Zanna & J. Olson (Eds.), *The psychology of prejudice: The Ontario symposium: Vol. 7.* Hillsdale, NJ: Lawrence Erlbaum.

15. Abrams, Dominic, Frings, Daniel, & deMoura, Georgina Randsley. (2005). Group identity and self-definition. In Wheelan, 343.

16. Hogg (2005), 141; Hogg, Michael A. (2004). Uncertainty and extremism: Identification with high entitativity groups under conditions of uncertainty. In V. Yzerbyt, C. M. Judd, & O. Corneille (Eds.), *The psychology of group perception: Perceived variability, entitativity, and essentialism.* New York: Psychology Press.

17. Abrams, Frings, & deMoura, 342; Marques, J. M., & Paez, D. (1994). The black sheep effect: Social categorization, rejection of ingroup deviates, and perception of group variability. In W. Stroebe & M. Hewstone (Eds.), *European review of social psychology: Vol. 5.* Chichester, UK: Wiley, 37–68; Marques, Jose M., Abrams, Dominic, Paez, Dario, &

Martinez-Taboada, Cristina. (1998). The role of categorization and in-group norms in judgments of groups and their members. *Journal of Personality and Social Psychology, 75,* 976–988.

18. Tuckman, Bruce W. (1965). Developmental sequence in small groups. *Psychological Bulletin, 63,* 384–399.

19. Fisher, B. Aubrey. (1970). Decision emergence: Phases in group decision making. *Speech Monographs, 37,* 53–66. See also Fisher, B. Aubrey. (1980). *Small group decision making* (2nd ed.). New York: McGraw-Hill.

20. Wheelan, Susan A. (2005). The developmental perspective. In Wheelan, 130.

21. Poole, Marshall Scott. (1981). Decision development in small groups I: A comparison of two models. *Communication Monographs, 48,* 1–24; Poole, Marshall Scott. (1983). Decision development in small groups II: A study of multiple sequences in decision making. *Communication Monographs, 50,* 206–232; Poole, Marshall Scott. (1983). Decision development in small groups III: A multiple sequence model of group decision development. *Communication Monographs, 50,* 321–341; Poole, Marshall Scott, & Roth, Jonelle. (1989). Decision development in small groups V: Test of a contingency model. *Human Communication Research, 15,* 549–589.

22. Wheelan, 123.

23. Northhouse, Peter G. (2001). Trait approach. In Peter G. Northhouse (Ed.), *Leadership: Theory and practice,* 2nd ed. Thousand Oaks, CA: Sage. For an overview of theories of leadership see Gouran, Dennis S. (2003). Leadership as the art of counteractive influence in decision-making and problem-solving groups. In Randy Y. Hirokawa, Robert S. Cathcart, Larry A. Samovar, & Linda D. Henman (Eds.), *Small group communication theory and practice: An anthology.* Los Angeles: Roxbury.

24. Gouran, 172. See also Aviolo, Bruce J. (1999). *Full leadership development: Building the vital forces in organizations.* Thousand Oaks, CA: Sage.

25. Hirokawa (2003), 170. For the original article see Geier, J. G. (1967). A trait approach to the study of leadership in small groups. *Journal of Communication, 17,* 316–323.

26. See Lewin, Kurt, Lippitt, Ronald, & White, R. K. (1939). Patterns of aggressive behavior in experimentally created "social climates." *Journal of Psychology, 10,* 271–299; Blake, R. R., & Mouton, Jane S. (1964). *The managerial grid.* Houston, TX: Gulf; and Blake, Robert Rogers, & McCanse, Ann Adams. (1991). *Leadership dilemmas—Grid solutions.* Houston, TX: Gulf.

27. Hershey, Kenneth, & Blanchard, Paul (1969). Life-cycle theory of leadership. *Training and Development Journal, 23,* 26–34.

28. House, Robert J., & Dessler, Gary (1974). The path-goal theory of leadership: Some post hoc and a priori tests. In James G. Hunt & Lars L. Larson (Eds.), *Contingency approaches to leadership.* Carbondale: Southern Illinois University Press.

29. Fiedler, Fred E. (1964). A contingency model of leadership effectiveness. In Leonard Berkowitz (Ed.), *Advances in experimental social psychology: Vol. 1.* New York: Academic Press, 149–190.

30. Graen, George B., & Ulh-Bien, Mary. (1991). Relationship-based approach to leadership. Development of leader-member exchange (LMX) theory over 25 years: Applying a multi-level multi-domain perspective. *Leadership Quarterly, 6*, 219–247.

31. Gouran, 172–182.

32. *Ibid.*, 181–182.

33. Fisher (1980), 223–225.

34. Woolley, Anita Williams, Chabris, Christopher, Pentland, Alex, Hashmi, Nada, & Malone, Thomas W. Evidence for a collective intelligence factor in the performance of human groups. *Science, 330*, 686–688. See http://singularityhub.com/2011/08/26/mit-unravels-the-secrets-behind-collective-intelligence-hint-iq-not-so-important/ for a discussion of this study and for links to a test that will allow you to find out your own social sensitivity scores.

35. For the original formulation of this research and review, see Stasser, Gerald, & Titus, William. (2003). Hidden profiles: A brief history. *Psychological Inquiry, 14*, 304–313.

36. Wittenbaum, Gwen M., & Bowman, Jonathan M. (2004). A social validation explanation for mutual enhancement. *Journal of Experimental Social Psychology, 40*, 40–169; Wittenbaum, Gwen M., & Park, Ernest S. (2001). The collective preference for shared information. *Journal of Personality and Social Psychology, 10*, 10–70.

37. Wittenbaum, Gwen M., Hollingshead, Andrea B., & Botero, Isabel C. (2004). From cooperative to motivated information sharing in groups: Moving beyond the hidden profile paradigm. *Communication Monographs, 71*(3), 298, 301. For a different model of information sharing see Bonito, Joseph A. (2007). A local model of information sharing in small groups. *Communication Theory, 17*, 252–280.

38. Brodbeck, Felix C., Kerschreiter, Rudolf, Mojzisch, Andreas, Frey, Dieter, & Schultz-Hardt, Stefan. (2002). The dissemination of critical, unshared information in decision-making groups: The effects of pre-discussion dissent. *European Journal of Social Psychology, 32*(1), 35–56.

39. Wittenbaum, Hollingshead, & Botero.

40. Gibb, Jack R. (1961). Defensive communication. *Journal of Communication, 11*, 141–148.

41. Bormann, 243.

42. Dewey, John. (1910). *How we think*. Lexington, MA: Heath. For a complete and detailed discussion of the standard agenda, see Wood, Julia T., Phillips, Gerald M., & Pedersen, Douglas J. (1986). *Group discussion: A practical guide to participation and leadership*. New York: Harper & Row.

43. Johnson & Johnson, 269.

44. Rothwell, 223–224.

45. Johnson & Johnson, 272–273; Lewin, Kurt. (1944). Dynamics of group action. *Educational Leadership, 1*, 195–200.

46. Johnson & Johnson, 320–321. The Johnsons draw their discussion from David, G., & Houtman, S. (1968). *Thinking creatively: A guide to training imagination*. Madison: Wisconsin Research and Development Center for Cognitive Learning.

47. Delbecq, A. (1975). *Group techniques for program planning*. Glenview, IL: Scott Foresman.

48. Brilhart, J. K., & Galanes, G. J. (1989). *Effective group discussion*. Dubuque, IA: Brown.

49. For a good discussion of different formats, see Barker, Larry L., Wahlers, Kathy J., Cegala, Donald J., & Kibler, Robert J. (1991). *Groups in process: An introduction to small group communication* (4th ed.). Englewood Cliffs, NJ: Prentice-Hall, especially Chapter 10.

50. Hollingshead, Andrea B., & Contractor, Noshir S. (2006). New media and small group organizing. In Leah Lievrouw & Sonia Livingstone (Eds.), *Handbook of new media: Social shaping and social consequences of ICTs* (Updated student ed.). Thousand Oaks, CA: Sage Publications, 116.

51. Parker, Robyn E. (2003). Distinguishing characteristics of virtual groups. In Randy Y. Hirokawa, Robert S. Cathcart, Larry A. Samovar, & Linda D. Henman. *Small group communication theory and practice: An anthology*. Los Angeles: Roxbury.

52. Hollingshead & Contractor, 127.

53. *Ibid.*, 121.

54. *Ibid.*, 1, 126–128.

55. Baym, Nancy K. (2006). Interpersonal life online. In Lievrouw & Livingstone, 46.

56. Poole, Marshall Scott, & Zhang, Huiyan. (2005). Virtual teams. In Wheelan, 365–366. Wheelan presents an excellent review of many of the factors affecting virtual teams, including personal characteristics.

57. *Ibid.*, 374.

58. Hollingshead & Contractor, 128.

59. See, for example Contractor, Noshir, & Monge, Peter R. (2002). Managing knowledge networks. *Management Communication Quarterly, 16*, 249–258; Katz, Nancy, et al. (2004). Network theory and small groups. *Small Group Research, 35*, 307–332; and Katz, Nancy, Lazer, David, Arrow, Holly, & Contractor, Noshir. (2005). The network perspective on small groups: Theory and research. In Marshall Scott Poole & Andrea B. Hollingshead (Eds.), *Theories of small groups: Interdisciplinary perspectives*. Newbury Park, CA: Sage, 2005.

60. Gunawardena, Charlotte N., and others. (2009). A theoretical framework for building online communities of practice with social networking tools. *Educational Media International, 46*(1), 3–16.

61. Cheong, Pauline Hope, & Gong, Jie. (2010). Cyber vigilantism, transmedia collective intelligence, and civic participation. *Chinese Journal of Communication, 3*(4), 471–487.

CHAPTER 8

1. Weber, Max. (1969). Bureaucracy (H. H. Gerth & C. W. Mills, Trans.). In J. A. Litterer (Ed.), *Organizations: Structure and behavior*. New York: John Wiley & Sons.

2. Daniels, Tom D., Spiker, Barry K., & Papa, Michael J. (1997). *Perspectives on organizational communication* (4th ed.). Boston: McGraw Hill, 3.

3. Poole, Marshall Scott, & McPhee, Robert D. (1983). A structurational analysis of organizational climate. In Linda L. Putnam & Michael E. Pacanowsky (Eds.), *Communication and organizations: An interpretive approach*. Beverly Hills: Sage.

4. Giddens, Anthony. (1993). *Sociology*. Cambridge: Polity Press, 18. For a detailed explanation of structuration theory, see Giddens, Anthony. (1984). *The constitution of society: Outline of the theory of structuration*. Berkeley and Los Angeles: University of California Press.

5. Redding, Charles, as quoted in DeWine, Sue. (1994). *The consultant's craft: Improving organizational communication*. New York: St. Martin's Press, xxiii.

6. Conrad, Charles. (1994). *Strategic organizational communication: Toward the twenty-first century* (3rd ed.). New York: Harcourt Brace, 3.

7. *Ibid.*, 5.

8. Yates, Joanne, & Orlikowski, Wanda J. (1992). Genres of organizational communication: A structurational approach to studying communication and media. *Academy of Management Review, 17*(2), 299–326.

9. Feilor, Bruce S. (1991). *Learning to bow: Inside the heart of Japan*. New York: Houghton Mifflin, 24–25.

10. Daniels, Spiker, & Papa, 115.

11. *Ibid.*, 116.

12. Callan, Victor J. (1993). Subordinate–manager communication in different sex dyads: Consequences of job satisfaction. *Journal of Occupational and Organizational Psychology, 66*, 13–27.

13. Krivonos, P. D. (1976). Distortion of subordinate-to-superior communication. Paper presented at the annual meeting of the International Communication Association, Portland, Oregon.

14. Downs, Cal, & Conrad, Charles. (1982). Effective subordinancy. *Journal of Business Communication, 19*, 27–37.

15. Milgram, Stanley. (1967). The small world problem. *Psychology Today, 1*(1), 60–67. Travers, Jeffrey, & Milgram, Stanley. (1969). An experimental study of the small world problem. *Sociometry, 32*(4), 425–443.

16. Conrad, 180.

17. Davis, Keith. (1980). Management communication and the grapevine. In Steward Ferguson & Sherry Devereaux Ferguson (Eds.), *Intercom: Readings in organizational communication*. Rochelle Park, NJ: Hayden Books, 55–66. Quoted in DeVito, Joseph A. (1997). *Human communication: The basic course*. New York: Longman, 348. See also Hellweg, Susan A. (1992). Organizational grapevines. In Kevin L. Hutchinson (Ed.), *Readings in organizational communication*. Dubuque, IA: Wm. C. Brown, 159–172.

18. Conrad, 310.

19. Perrow, Charles. (1984). *Normal accidents*. New York: Basic Books.

20. Daniels, 124.

21. For a discussion of the importance of structural diversity, see Cummings, Jonathon N. (2004). Work groups, structural diversity, and knowledge sharing in a global organization. *Management Science, 50*(3), 352–364. See also Cummings, Jonathon N., & Ancona, Deborah G. (2005). The functional perspective. In Wheelan, Susan A. (Ed.). (2005). *The handbook of group research and practice*. Thousand Oaks, CA: Sage Publications, 136.

22. Littlepage, Glenn E., Hollingshead, Andrea B., Drake, Laurie R., & Littlepage, Anna M. (2008). Transactive memory and performance in work groups: Specificity, communication, ability differences, and work allocation. *Group Dynamics: Theory, Research and Practice, 12*(3), 223–241, 223. For an early formulation of the theory, see Wegner, D. M. (1987). Transactive memory: A contemporary analysis of the group mind. In B. Mullen & G. R. Goethals (Eds.), *Theories of group behavior*. New York: Springer-Verlag.

23. Garner, Johny T. (2006). It's not what you know: A transactive memory analysis of knowledge networks at NASA. *Journal of Technical Writing and Communication, 36*(4), 329–351.

24. Ellis, Kathleen, & Shockley-Zalabek, Pamela. (2001). Trust in top management and immediate supervisor: The relationship to satisfaction, perceived organizational effectiveness, and information receiving. *Communication Quarterly, 49*(4), 382–398; and Lau, Dora C., & Liden, Robert C. (2008). Antecedents of coworker trust: Leaders' blessings. *Journal of Applied Psychology, 93*(5), 1130–1138.

25. Stewart, Charles J., & Cash, William B., Jr. (1991). *Interviewing: Principles and practices*. Dubuque, IA: William C. Brown, 3.

26. *Ibid.*, 5.

27. Much of the material about interview preparation is taken from "A Guide to Resume Writing," "Successful Interviewing," and "How to Write a Cover Letter," brochures prepared by Ithaca College Career Services. If your college does not provide similar guides, there are many popular books on the subject. See, for example, Medley, Anthony. (1992). *Sweaty palms: The neglected art of being interviewed*. Berkeley, CA: Ten Speed Press, or Krannich, Caryl. (1998). *Interview for success: A practical guide to increasing job interviews, offers, and salaries*. Manassas Park, VA: Impact Publications.

28. Kreps, Gary. (1984). Organizational culture and organizational development: Promoting flexibility in an urban hospital. Paper presented at the meeting of the International Communication Association, San Francisco; quoted in Goldhaber, Gerald M. (1993). *Organizational communication* (6th ed.). Dubuque, IA: Brown and Benchmark, 69.

29. Louis, Meryl Reis. (1980). Surprise and sense making: What newcomers experience in entering unfamiliar organizational settings. *Administrative Science Quarterly, 25*, 226–251.

30. Louis, 247.

31. Pacanowsky, Michael E., & O'Donnell-Trujillo, Nick. (1982). Communication and organizational cultures. *Western Journal of Speech Communication, 46*, 115–130.

32. Stohl, Cynthia. (1995). *Organizational communication: Connectedness in action*. Thousand Oaks, CA: Sage, 11.

33. Conrad, 86.

34. Conrad, 80–81.

35. Trice, Harrison M., & Beyer, Janice M. (1984). Studying organizational cultures through rites and ceremonials. *Academy of Management Review, 9*, 655.

36. *Ibid.*

37. *Ibid.*, 666.

38. Weick, Karl E. (1979). Cognitive processes in organizations. In Barry M. Staw (Ed.), *Research in organizations: Vol. 1*. Greenwich, CT: JAI Press, 42.

39. Wall, Bob. (1999). *Working relationships: The simple truth about getting along with friends and foes at work.* Palo Alto, CA: Davies-Black, 12.

40. Wall, 21.

41. Dillard, James. (1987). Close relationships at work: Perceptions of the motives and performance of relational participants. *Journal of Social and Personal Relationships, 4,* 179–193; Buzzanell, Patrice. (1990). Managing workplace romance. Paper presented at the annual convention of the Speech Communication Association, Chicago. See also DeWine.

42. Fox, Grace. (1998). *Everyday etiquette: A guide to modern manners.* New York: Berkeley Books, 78.

43. Fine, Gary Alan. (1986). Friendships in the workplace. Originally printed in Derlaga, Valerian J., & Winstead, Barbara A. (Eds.), *Friendship and social interaction.* New York: Springer-Verlag, 186–206. Quote is taken from version excerpted in Galvin, Kathleen M., & Cooper, Pamela (Eds.). (1996). *Making connections: Readings in relational communication.* Los Angeles: Roxbury, 274.

44. For a recent definition of sexual harassment, see www.eeoc.gov/laws/types/sexual_harassment.cfm.

45. Conrad, 400. See also Conrad, Charles, & Taylor, Bryan. (1994). The contexts of sexual harassment: Power, silences and academe. In Shereen Bingham (Ed.), *Conceptualizing sexual harassment as discursive practice.* Westport, CT: Greenwood Publishing.

46. Daniels, 232.

47. Doheny-Farina, Stephen. (1996). *The wired community.* New Haven, CT: Yale University Press, 93.

48. *Ibid.,* 89.

49. *Ibid.,* 90.

50. See Noble, Barbara Presley. (1994, June 15). Electronic liberation or entrapment? *New York Times,* D4; cited in Doheny-Farina, 95.

51. Shellenbarger, Sue. (1993, December 16). I'm still here! Home workers worry they're invisible. *Wall Street Journal,* B1; cited in Doheny-Farina, 95.

52. Poole, Marshall Scott, & Zhang, Huiyan. (2005). Virtual teams. In Wheelan.

53. *Ibid.,* 374.

54. Jarvenpaa, Sirkka L., & Leidner, Dorothy E. (1999). Communication and trust in global virtual teams. *Organization Science, 10,* 791–815; Jarvenpaa, Sirkka L., Shaw, Thomas R., & Staples, D. Sandy. (2004). Toward contextualized theories of trust: The role of trust in global virtual teams. *Information Systems Research, 15*(3), 250–267; also see Jarvenpaa, Sirkka L., & Tanriverdi, Huseyn. (2003). Leading virtual knowledge networks. *Organizational Dynamics, 31*(4), 403–412.

55. Poole & Zhang, 365. Kirkman, Bradley L., Rosen, Benson, Gibson, Christina B., Tesluk, Paul E., & McPherson, Simon O. (2002). Five challenges to virtual team success: Lessons from Sabre, Inc. *Academy of Management Executive, 16,* 67–79; Kirkman, Bradley L., Rosen, Benson, Tesluk, Paul E., & Gibson, C. B. (2004). The impact of team empowerment on virtual team performance: The moderating role of face-to-face interaction. *Academy of Management Journal, 47,* 175–192.

56. See O'Connell, S. E. (1988). Human communication in the high tech office. In Gerald M. Goldhaber & George A. Barnett (Eds.), *Handbook of organizational communication.* Norwood, NJ: Ablex, 473–482.

57. Kramer, Melinda G. (2001). *Business communication in context.* Upper Saddle River, NJ: Prentice Hall, 69.

58. Zaremba, Alan Jay. (2003). *Organizational communication: Foundations for business & management.* New York: Thomson/South-Western, 112.

59. Kiesler, Sara, & Sproull, Lee. (1991). *Connections: New ways of working in the networked organization.* Cambridge, MA: MIT Press.

60. Zaremba, 112; see also, Zaremba, Alan. (1996, January). Effects of e-mail availability on the informal network. *International Journal of Technology Management, 11,* 151–161.

61. Shirkey, Clay. *Cognitive surplus: How technology makes consumers into collaborators.* London: Penguin Books, 2010.

62. Brabham, Daren C. (2008). Crowdsourcing as a model for problem solving. *Convergence: The International Journal of Research into Media Technology, 14,* 75–90.

63. Deetz, Stanley. (1999). Multiple stakeholders and social responsibility in the international business context: A critical perspective. In Philip Salem (Ed.), *Organizational communication and change.* Cresskill, NJ: Hampton Press, 289.

64. Conrad, 330.

65. Banner, D. K., & Gagne, T. E. (1995). Designing effective organizations: Traditional and transformational views. Thousand Oaks, CA: Sage, 97; quoted in Salem, 25.

66. Deetz, 313.

CHAPTER 9

1. Darrow, Clarence. (1924, August 22). Closing argument: The State of Illinois v. Nathan Leopold and Richard Loeb. University of Missouri, Kansas City. Retrieved from www.law2.umkc.edu/faculty/projects/ftrials/darrow.htm. or do a Web search on "famous trials UMKC School of Law."

2. Roosevelt, Franklin Delano. (1933, March 4). First inaugural address. American Rhetoric. Retrieved from www.americanrhetoric.com/speeches/fdrfirstinaugural.html.

3. Nixon, Richard. (1952, September 23). Checkers. American Rhetoric. Retrieved from www.americanrhetoric.com/speeches/richardnixoncheckers.html; and Nixon, Richard. (1974, August 8). Resignation speech. American Rhetoric. Retrieved from www.americanrhetoric.com/speeches/richardnixonresignationspeech.html.

4. King, Martin Luther, Jr. (1968, March 3). I've seen to the mountaintop. American Rhetoric. Retrieved from www.americanrhetoric.com/speeches/mlkivebeentothemountaintop.htm.

5. Glaser, Elizabeth. (1992, July 14). American Rhetoric. Address to the 1992 Democratic National Convention. Retrieved from www.americanrhetoric.com/speeches.elizabethglaser1992dnc.htm.

6. Cooper, Martha. (1989). *Analyzing public discourse.* Prospect Heights, IL: Waveland Press, 5–6.

7. *Ibid.,* 5.

8. Lightner, Candy, & Hathaway, Nancy. (1990). *Giving sorrow words: How to cope with grief and get on with your life*. New York: Warner Books. Numerous Web pages give details of Ms. Lightner's work against drunk driving and her relationship to MADD.

9. Plato. (2004). *Gorgias* (Walter Hamilton and Chris Emlyn-Jones, Trans.). London: Penguin Books.

10. Herrick, James A. (2005). *The history and theory of rhetoric: An introduction*. Boston: Allyn & Bacon, 16.

11. *Ibid*. In making this point, Herrick also cites Perelman, Chaim, & Olbrechts-Tyteca, Lucy. (1969). *The new rhetoric: A treatise on argumentation* (John Wilkinson and Purcell Weaver, Trans.). Notre Dame, IN: University of Notre Dame Press.

12. Herrick, 18.

13. *Ibid.*, 23.

14. *Ibid.*, 20.

15. van Oosting, James. (1985). *The business speech: Speaker, audience, and text*. Englewood Cliffs, NJ: Prentice-Hall, 9.

16. Andrews, James R., Leff, Michael C., & Terrill, Robert. (1998). *Reading rhetorical texts: An introduction to criticism*. New York: Houghton Mifflin, 37.

17. *Ibid.*, 30–31.

18. Bitzer, Lloyd. (1968). The rhetorical situation. *Philosophy and Rhetoric, I*(1), 1–14.

19. *Ibid.*, 14.

20. Rokeach, Milton. (1968). *Beliefs, attitudes, and values*. San Francisco: Jossey-Bass.

21. For a discussion of current thinking about the three dimensions of attitudes, see Gass, Robert H., & Seiter, John S. (2003). *Persuasion, social influence, and compliance gaining*. Boston: Allyn & Bacon, 43–44, note 1, 70.

22. Rokeach.

23. Kelman, Herbert. (1961). Processes of opinion change. *Public Opinion Quarterly, 25*, 57–78; and McGuire, William J. (1985). Attitudes and attitude change. In Gardner Lindzey & Elliot Aronson (Eds.), *Handbook of social psychology* (3rd ed., Vol. 2). New York: Random House.

24. Zajonc, Robert B. (1968). The attitudinal effects of mere exposure. *Journal of Personality and Social Psychology, 9*(1), 1–27.

25. See Smith, Mary John. (1982). *Persuasion and human action*. Belmont, CA: Wadsworth, 202.

26. Jones, Edward E., & Wortman, Camille. (1973). *Ingratiation: An attributional approach*. Morristown, NJ: General Learning. For a discussion of ingratiation as a negotiation tactic, see Pruitt, Dean G., & Rubin, Jeffrey Z. (1986). *Social conflict: Escalation, stalemate, and settlement*. New York: Random House.

27. French, John, & Raven, Bertram. (1959). The basis of social power. In Dorwin Cartwright (Ed.), *Studies in social power*. Ann Arbor, MI: University of Michigan Press.

28. See Adorno, Theodor W., Frenkel-Brunswick, Else, Levinson, Daniel, Sanford Nevitt, .et al. (1950). *The authoritarian personality*. New York: Harper & Row.

29. Toulmin, Stephen Edelston. (1958). *The uses of argument*. Cambridge, UK: Cambridge University Press.

30. This argument is taken from Rottenberg, Annette T. (1985). *Elements of argument*. New York: St. Martin's, 118–126.

31. Brockreide, Wayne, & Ehninger, Douglas. (1960). Toulmin on argument: An interpretation and application. *Quarterly Journal of Speech, 46*, 44–53.

32. Maslow, Abraham H. (1970). *Motivation and personality* (2nd ed.). New York: Harper & Row, 35–58.

33. The distinctions between arguments from cause, sign, generalization, and analogy are standard, as are the tests of their validity. For further discussion see Ross, Raymond S. (1985). *Understanding persuasion: Foundations and practice* (2nd ed.). Englewood Cliffs, NJ: Prentice-Hall, 165–169.

34. Fearnside, W. Ward, & Holther, William B. (1959). *Fallacy: The counterfeit of argument*. Englewood Cliffs, NJ: Prentice-Hall, 25.

35. Sears, David O., & Funk, Carolyn L. (1991). The role of self-interest in social and political attitudes. In Mark P. Zanna (Ed.), *Advances in experimental social psychology* (Vol. 24). New York: Academic.

36. For research on lazy processors and heuristics, see Eagly, Alice H., & Chaiken, Shelly. (1984). Cognitive theories of persuasion. In Leonard Berkowitz (Ed.), *Advances in experimental social psychology* (Vol. 17). New York: Academic; Langer, Ellen J. (1978). Rethinking the role of thought in social interaction. In John H. Harvey, William J. Ickes, & Robert F. Kidd (Eds.), *New directions in attribution research: Vol. 2*. Hillside, NJ: Lawrence Erlbaum Associates; and Petty, Richard E., & Cacioppo, John T. (1986). The elaboration likelihood model of persuasion. In Leonard Berkowitz (Ed.), *Advances in experimental social psychology: Vol. 19*. New York: Academic.

37. For additional information on fallacies, see Fearnside & Holther; Rottenberg; Lee, Alfred M., & Lee, Elizabeth B. (1979). *The fine art of propaganda*. San Francisco: International Institute for General Semantics.

CHAPTER 10

1. Lucas, Stephen E. (2004). *The art of public speaking* (8th ed.). New York: Random House. Material cited is taken from the second edition, published in 1986, p. 72.

2. For an excellent discussion of sources to pursue in analyzing audiences see Bradley, Bert E. (1991). *Fundamentals of speech communication: The credibility of ideas* (6th ed.). Dubuque, IA: Brown, 93–95.

3. For a complete discussion of the motivated sequence, see any edition of *Principles and types of speech communication*. The latest edition (the 15th) is authored by Raymie E. McKerrow, Bruce E. Gronbeck, Douglas Ehninger, & Alan H. Monroe and was published by Allyn & Bacon in 2003.

4. Ross, Raymond S. (1983). *Speech communication: Fundamentals and practice*. Englewood Cliffs, NJ: Prentice-Hall, 193–199.

5. Lucas, 337.

6. Andersen, Kenneth E. (1991). A history of communication ethics. In Karen Joy Greenberg (Ed.), *Conversations on communication ethics*. Norwood, NJ: Ablex.

7. Campbell, Paul N. (1972). *Rhetoric-ritual*. Belmont, CA: Dickenson. For an overview of approaches to ethics, see also Johannesen, Richard L. (2002). *Ethics in human communication* (5th ed.). Prospect Heights, IL: Waveland Press.

CHAPTER 11

1. Stelter, Brian (2009). 8 hours a day spent on screens, study finds. *New York Times*. Retrieved from http://www.nytimes.com/2009/03/27/business/media/27adco.html?_r=1&adxnnl=1&adxnnlx=1323198878-Idzfe82ZySYP+zTXLxfohQ. If no longer at this address, available through New York Times online archive. A larger estimate of eleven hours a day is provided by a 2010 emarketer survey. The disparity is probably due to the double-counting of time spent using two different media in the latter study. See http://www.emarketer.com/blog/index.php/time-spent-watching-tv-tops-internet/. For descriptions of how TV was being viewed in 2011, see Consumer media usage across TV, online, mobile, and social. (2012). *Nielsonwire*. Retrieved from http://blog.nielsen.com/nielsenwire/online_mobile/report-consumer-media-usage-across-tv-online-mobile-and-social.

2. Mobile and Internet giving is a new way we can reach out to people in need. Palmer, Stacy. (2010, January 14). $7-million raised for Haiti via cell phones. *Chronicle of Philanthropy*. Retrieved from http://philanthropy.com/blogs/prospecting/7-million-raised-for-haiti-via-cell-phones/20648.

3. Hagerty, Barbara Bradley. (2012, February 7). A pulpit for the masses: YouTube, Christians click. *NPR*. Retrieved from http://www.npr.org/2012/02/07/146471341/wwjd-on-youtube-it-depends-who-you-ask.

4. Snow, Robert P. (1983). *Creating media culture*. Beverly Hills, CA: Sage, 29.

5. For a list of reality shows being broadcast during 2011, see http://realitytvmagazine.sheknows.com/2011/01/03/reality-tv-shows-for-winter-2011/.

6. Lasswell, Harold D. (1948). The structure and function of communication in society. In Lyman Bryson (Ed.), *The communication of ideas*. New York: Institute for Religious and Social Studies; Wright, Charles R. (1960). Functional analysis and mass communication. *Public Opinion Quarterly*, 24, 605–620; Wright, Charles R. (1975). *Mass communication: A sociological perspective* (2nd ed.). New York: Random House, 8–22.

7. Lazarfeld, Paul F., & Merton, Robert K. (1971). Mass communication, popular taste, and organized social action. In Wilbur Schramm & Donald F. Roberts (Eds.), *The process and effects of mass communication* (Rev. ed.). Urbana: University of Illinois Press, 565. For a good brief review, with examples, of the functions of the media, see Felsenthal, Norman. (1976). Orientations to mass communication. In Ronald L. Applbaum & Roderick P. Hart (Eds.), *Modules in speech communication*. Palo Alto, CA: SRA, 6–8.

8. For a summary of some of the major effects theories, see Littlejohn, Stephen W., & Foss, Karen A. (2010). *Theories of human communication* (10th ed.). Long Grove, Illinois: Waveland Press, Chapter 10.

9. Schramm, Wilbur. (1971). The nature of communications between humans. In Schramm & Roberts, 8.

10. Bauer, Raymond. (1971). The obstinate audience: The influence process from the point of view of social communication. In Schramm & Roberts. See also Klapper, Joseph. (1960). *The effects of mass communication*. Glencoe, IL: Free Press; and Weiss, Walter. (1969). Effects of the mass media of communication. In Gardner Lindzey & Elliot Aronson (Eds.), *Handbook of social psychology*. Reading, MA: Addison-Wesley.

11. Elihu Katz suggests this typology, although his examples differ. See Katz, Elihu. (1987). Communications research since Lazarfeld. *Public Opinion Quarterly*, 51(4), S25–S45.

12. See, for example, Shaw, Donald L., & McCombs, Maxwell E. (1977). *The emergence of American political issues*. St. Paul, MN: West Publishing.

13. Felsenthal, 31.

14. Gitlin, Todd. (1979). Prime time ideology: The hegemonic process in television entertainment. *Social Problems*, 26(3), 251–266; also reprinted in Horace Newcomb (Ed.), *Television: The critical view* (4th ed.). Oxford, UK: Oxford University Press, 510.

15. Children Now. (2000, May). *Highlights: Prime time diversity report, 2001–02*. Retrieved from http://www.childrennow.org/medoa/fc2002/fc-2002-highlights.htm, 2.

16. Noelle-Neumann, Elisabeth. (1984). *The spiral of silence: Public opinion—Our social skin*. Chicago: University of Chicago Press.

17. Gerbner, George. (1993). *Women and minorities on television: A study in casting and fate*. Philadelphia: University of Pennsylvania, Annenberg School of Communication, 1. The portions of this report pertaining to gender are summarized and analyzed in Michael R. Real. (1996). *Exploring media culture: A guide*. Thousand Oaks, CA: Sage, 181.

18. See, for example, Gerbner, George, Gross, Larry, Morgan, Michael, & Signorelli, Nancy. (2002). Growing up with television: The cultivation perspective. In Jennings Bryant & Dolf Zillmann (Eds.), *Media effects: Advances in theory and research*. Hillsdale, NJ: Lawrence Erlbaum Associates, 43–68.

19. The Museum of Broadcast Communications. Audience research: Cultivation analysis. *Museum of Broadcast Communication*. Retrieved from http://www.museum.tv/eotvsection.php?entrycode=audienceresec.

20. Ibid., 2.

21. Katz.

22. Felsenthal, 33.

23. McLuhan, Marshall. (1964). *Understanding media: The extensions of man*. New York: McGraw-Hill.

24. Snow, 162–163.

25. Book, Cassandra, et al. (1980). *Human communication: Principles, contexts, and skills*. New York: St. Martin's, 206; and Booth, Alan. (1970–1971). The recall of news items. *Public Opinion Quarterly*, 34, 604–610.

26. Katz, Elihu, Blumer, Jay, & Gurevitch, Michael. (1974). Uses of mass communication by the individual. In W. Phillips Davidson & Frederick Yu (Eds.), *Mass communication research: Major issues and future directions*. New York: Praeger, 12. For a brief summary and critique of uses and gratifications research, see Littlejohn.

27. Herzog, Herta. (1944). What do we really know about daytime serial listeners? In Paul Lazarfeld & Frank Stanton (Eds.), *Radio research, 1942–43*. New York: Dull, Sloan & Pearce.

28. McQuail, Denis, Blumer, Jay G., & Brown, J. R. (1972). The television audience: A revised perspective. In Denis McQuail (Ed.), *Sociology of mass communications.* Middlesex, UK: Penguin, 155–161.

29. Jamieson, Kathleen Hall, & Campbell, Karlyn Kohrs. (1992). *The interplay of influence: News, advertising, politics, and the mass media.* Belmont, CA: Wadsworth, 2.

30. Mitchell, Amy, & Rosenstiel, Tom. (2012). The state of the news media 2012. Major trends. Pew Research Center's Project for Excellence in Journalism. *Journalism .org.* Retrieved from http://stateofthemedia.org/2012/ overview-4/major-trends/.

31. Kinsley, Michael. (2006, September 25). Do newspapers have a future? *Time.* Retrieved from http://www.time .com/time/printout/0,8816,1538652,00.html.

32. Vivian, John. (2009). *The media of mass communication* (9th ed.). Boston: Pearson, 80.

33. Snow, 53.

34. *Ibid.,* 59.

35. Jamieson & Campbell, 24.

36. Snow, 91.

37. Hiebert, Ray Eldon, Ungurait, Donald F., & Bohn, Thomas W. (1991). *Mass media VI: An introduction to modern communication.* New York: Longman, 288.

38. Altheide & Snow, 21.

39. Mendelsohn, Harold. (1964). Listening to radio. In A. Lewis Dexter & David M. White (Eds.), *People, society, and mass communication.* London: Collier-Macmillan, 91.

40. Snow, 101.

41. Altheide & Snow, 26.

42. Snow, 121.

43. Felsenthal, 11.

44. Altheide & Snow, 31.

45. Jamieson & Campbell, 63.

46. Stein, Ben. (1981, July 25). Love, rape, highway, diary. *TV Guide,* 34–35; cited in Snow, 137.

47. Snow, 142.

48. Hiebert, Ungurait, & Bohn, 428.

49. Cited in Epstein, Edward J. (1974). *News from nowhere.* New York: Hastings, 4.

50. Ferguson, E. B. (1980, July 20). Media hype for fun and profit. *Los Angeles Times,* part VII, p. 5.

51. Meyerowitz, Joshua. (1983). Television and the obliteration of "childhood." In Sari Thomas (Ed.), *Studies in mass communication and technology.* Norwood, NJ: Ablex.

52. Snow, 157.

53. Tobin, Hugh. (2006). Fear of txt. *Institute of Public Affairs Review, 58*(1), 41. Full text also available online through *Academic Search Premier,* 20449474.

54. The almighty cell phone. (2006). *Wilson Quarterly, 30*(1). Full text also available online through *Academic Search Premier,* 03633275.

55. Teen "sexting" worries parents, schools. (2009, February 11). *CBSNEWS.* Retrieved from http://www .cbsnews.com/stories/2009/02/04/tech/main4776708.shtml; "Sexting" shockingly common among teens. (2009, January 15). *CBSNEWS.* Retrieved from http://www .cbsnews.com/stories/2009/01/15/national/main4723161

.shtml; and Associated Press. (2009, March 26). Girl, 14, faces porn charges for nude photos. *NPR.* Retrieved from http://www .npr.org/templates/story/story.php?storyId=102386952.

56. The almighty cell phone.

57. Discussion of the characteristics of the new media is taken from a number of sources. See, for example, Pavlik, John, & McIntosh, Shawn. (2004). *Converging media: An introduction to mass communication.* Boston: Allyn & Bacon, 15. See also McMillan, Sally J. (2006). Exploring models of interactivity from multiple research traditions: Users, documents and systems. In Leah A. Lievrouw & Sonia Livingstone (Eds.), *Handbook of new media: Social shaping and social consequences of ICTs* (Updated student ed.). Thousand Oaks, CA: Sage, 205–229.

58. McMillan, 206. For original discussion, see Negroponte, Nicholas. (1995). *Being digital.* New York: Knopf.

59. Harrison, Teresa M., & Barthel, Brea. (2009). Wielding new media in Web 2.0: Exploring the history of engagement with the collaborative construction of media products. *New Media & Society, 11,* 155–178, 157.

60. *Ibid.,* 157. See also, Madden, Mary, & Fox, Susannah. (2006, October 5). Riding the waves of "Web 2.0": More than a buzzword, but still not easily defined. Pew Internet & American Life Project. *PewInternet.* Retrieved from http://www.pewinternet.org/Reports/2006/Riding-the -waves-of-Web-20.aspx.

61. DeFalco, Beth. (2009, March 11). Grandpa is browsing your Facebook page. Associated Press. Retrieved from http://www.google.com/hostednews/ap/article.

62. Smith, Aaron, & Rainie, Lee. (2008, June 15). The Internet and the 2008 election. Pew Internet & American Life Project. *PewInternet.* Retrieved from http://www .pewinternet.org/Press-Releases/2008/The-internet-and -the-2008-election.aspx.

63. Jenkins, Henry. 2008. *Convergence culture: Where old and new media collide.* New York: New York University Press, 229.

64. *Ibid.,* 77. See also Au, Wagner James. (2004, April 13). John Kerry: The video game. *Salon.* Retrieved from http://www.salon.com/tech/feature/2004/04/13/battlefield _vietnam/. See also America's Army Website.

65. Retrieved 6/14/2006 from http://en.wikipedia.org/ wiki/Wikipedia:Introduction.

66. Retrieved 6/14/2006 from http://www.usatoday.com/ news/opinion/editorials/2005-11-29-wikipedia-edit_x.htm.

67. Rheingold, Howard. (2002). *Smart mobs: The next social revolution.* New York: Basic Books, 188.

68. *Ibid.,* 189. See also Foucault, Michel. (1977). *Discipline and punish: The birth of the prison.* London: Tavistock; and Foucault, Michel. (1980). In Colin Gordon (Ed.), *Power/knowledge: Selected interviews and other writings, 1972–1977.* New York: Pantheon.

69. Hiebert, Ray Eldon, & Gibbons, Sheila Jean. (2000). *Exploring mass media for a changing world.* Mahwah, NJ: Lawrence Erlbaum Associates, 306.

70. Protalinski, Emil (2012, February 1). Facebook has over 845 million users. *ZDNet.* Retrieved from http://www .zdnet.com/blog/facebook/facebook-has-over-845-million -users/8332.

71. Wallace, Patricia. (1999). *The psychology of the Internet*. New York: Cambridge University Press, 1.

72. *Ibid.*, 1.

73. Jones, Sydney, & Fox, Susannah. (2009, January 28). Pew Internet Project data memo: Generations online in 2009. Pew Internet & American Life Project. Retrieved from http://pewinternet.org/~/media//Files/Reports/2009/PIP_Generations_2009.pdf, 3.

74. Hiebert & Gibbons, 317–321.

75. Buckingham, David. (2006). Children and new media. In Lievrouw & Livingstone, 75.

76. *Ibid.*

77. Ellison, N. B., Steinfield C., & Lampe, C. (2011). Connection strategies: Social capital implications of Facebook-enabled communication practices. *New Media & Society, 13*(6), 873–892.

78. Antoci, A., Sabatini, F., & Sofini, M. (2011). Bowling alone but tweeting together: The evolution of human interaction in the social networking era. Retrieved from http://mpra.ub.uni-muenchen.de/34231/1/Tweeting_together .pdf, 5. See also Ellison, N. B., Steinfield, C., & Lampe, C. (2007). The benefits of Facebook friends: Social capital and college students' use of online social network sites. *Journal of Computer-Mediated Communication, 12*, 1143–1168; Park, N., Kee, K. F., Valenzuela, S. (2009). Is there social capital in a social network site? Facebook use and college students' life satisfaction, trust, and participation. *Journal of Computer-Mediated Communication, 14*(4), 875–901; Steinfield, C., Ellison, N. B., & Lampe, C. (2008). Social capital, self-esteem, and use of online social network sites: A longitudinal analysis. *Journal of Applied Developmental Psychology, 29*(6), 434–445; and Zhang, W., Johnson, T. J., Seltzer, T., & Bichard, S. L. (2010). The revolution will be networked: The influence of social networking sites on political attitudes and behavior. *Social Science Computer Review, 28*(1), 75–92.

79. Antoci, Sabatini, & Sofini, p. 2; Kobayashi, T., & Ikeda, K. (2008). The effect of PC e-mail usage on social tolerance: Focusing on the mediating effect of communication with heterogeneous others. *Research in Social Psychology, 24*(2), 120–130; and Miyata, K., & Kobayashi, T. (2008). Causal relationship between Internet use and social capital in Japan. *Asian Journal of Social Psychology, 11*, 42–52.

80. Steinkuehler, Constance A., & Williams, Dmitri. (2006). Where everybody knows your (screen) name: Online games as "third places." *Journal of Computer-Mediated Communication, 11*, 885–909, 888. For further discussion of gaming and online role playing, see Diehl, William C., & Prins, Esther. (2008). Unintended outcomes in Second Life: Intercultural literacy and cultural identity in a virtual world. *Language and Intercultural Communication, 8*(2), 101–118; Woods, Mathew. (2007). Login for love: Defining intimacy in the metaverse of Second Life. Convention paper presented at the National Communication Association annual meeting. Retrieved from EBSCOhost; Demetrious, Kristin. (2008). Secrecy and illusion: Second Life and the construction of unreality. *Australian Journal of Communication, 35*(1), 1–13; Shaw, Patrick, LaRose, Robert, & Wirth, Christina. (2006). Reaching a new level and other pleasures of massive multiplayer online games: A social cognitive theory of MMO usage. Paper presented at the International Communication Association annual meeting, Dresden, Germany. Retrieved from EBSCOhost.

81. Anderson, Janna Quitney, & Rainie, Lee (2012). Millennials will benefit and suffer due to their hyperconnected lives. Pew Internet & American Life Project. Retrieved from http://www.pewinternet.org/~/media//Files/Reports/2012/PIP_Future_of_Internet_2012_Young_brains_PDF.pdf.

82. Carr, Nicholas G. (2010). *The Shallows: What the Internet is doing to our brains*. New York: W. W. Norton, 2010, 29–30; the cab driver study can be found at Maguire, E. A., Gadian, D. C., & Johnsrude, I. S. (2000). Navigation-related structural change in the hippocampi of taxi drivers. *Proceedings of the National Academy of Sciences, 97*(8), 4398–4403; and Maguire, E. A., Spiers, H. J., & Good, D. C. (2003). Navigation expertise and the human hippocampus: A structural brain imaging analysis. *Hippocampus, 13*(2), 250–259

83. Carr, 115.

84. *Ibid.*, 129.

85. *Ibid.*, 89.

86. *Ibid.*, 89.

87. Wallace, 32.

88. Davis, Jack, & Merritt, Susan. (1998). *The Web design wow! book*. Berkeley, CA: Peachpit Press.

89. See, for example, VanderVeer, Emily, et al. (2002). *Creating Web pages: All-in-one desk reference for dummies*. New York: Wiley Publishers, 16–22.

90. Nielsen, Jakob, & Takir, Marie. (2002). *Homepage usability: 50 Websites deconstructed*. Indianapolis, IN: New Riders Publishing. A related Website can be found at http://www.useit.com/homepageusability.

91. Plant, Sadie. (2001). On the mobile: The effects of mobile telephones on social and individual life. Retrieved from www.motorola.com/mot/doc/0/234_MotDoc.pdf, 29. Original news report is from Gray, Chris. (2001, May 18). Now birds brag by mimicking mobiles. *The Independent*.

92. Thurlow, Crispin. (2003). Generation txt? The sociolinguistics of young people's text-messaging. Retrieved from http://www.shu.ac.uk/daol/articles/v1/n1/a3/thurlow 1001003-paper.html, 15.

93. Plant, 22.

94. Rheingold, 164–165.

95. Carr, 96.

96. Thurlow, 10.

97. Lenhart, Amanda. (2012, March). Teens, smartphones & texting. Pew Internet & American Life Project. Pew Research Center. Retrieved from http://www.pewinternet.org/~/media//Files/Reports/2012/PIP_Teens_Smartphones_and_Texting.pdf.

98. Turkle, Sherry. (2011). *Alone together: Why we expect more from technology and less from each other*. New York: Basic Books.

99. *Ibid.*, 198.

100. Plant, 65.

101. *Ibid.*, 55.

102. *Ibid.*, 65.

103. Thurlow, 2.

104. Weeks, Linton. (2009, March 31). It's not you, it's me: Breaking up with technology. *NPR*. Retrieved from http://www.npr.org/templates/story/story.php?storyID=101409144.
105. *Ibid.*
106. Snow, 19.
107. Pavlik, 19–20.
108. Jenkins, 104.
109. *Ibid.*, 147.
110. Hiebert, Ungurait, & Bohn.
111. Saul, Stephanie. (1989, July–August). Judgment call: Do reporters have a right to march? *Columbia Journalism Review*, 51; and Gersh, Debra. (1989, August 19). Question of conflict. *Editor and Publisher*, 11.
112. Whitehouse, Ginny. (2012). Pete/repeat tweet/retweet blog/reblog: A hoax reveal media mimicking. *Journal of Mass Media Ethics*, 57–59.
113. Marquand, Robert. (2012, March 13). Rebekah Brooks arrest: Phone-hacking scandal isn't going to fade. *Christian Science Monitor*. Retrieved from http://www.csmonitor.com/World/Europe/2012/0313/Rebekah-Brooks-arrest-phone-hacking-scandal-isn-t-going-to-fade.
114. Heim, Michael. (1993). *The metaphysics of virtual reality*. New York: Oxford University Press, 78–79.
115. Krotz, Joanna L. Cell phone etiquette: 10 dos and don'ts. *Microsoft*. Retrieved from http://www.microsoft.com/smallbusiness/resources/technology/communications/cell_phone_etiquette_10_dos_and_donts.mspx; and Stage actor Richard Griffith berates young man in audience for cell phone disturbance. (2006, June 2). *Textually.org*. Retrieved from http://www.textually.org/textually/archives/2006/06/012544.htm.

CHAPTER 12

1. Storti, Craig. (1990). *The art of crossing cultures*. Yarmouth, ME: Intercultural Press, 25.
2. Hoijer, Harry. (1954). The Sapir-Whorf hypothesis. In Harry Hoijer (Ed.), *Language in culture*. Chicago: University of Chicago Press, 94; cited in Singer, Marshall R. (1987). *Intercultural communication: A perceptual approach*. Englewood Cliffs, NJ: Prentice-Hall, 7.
3. The phrase comes from Diamond, C. T. Patrick. (1982). Understanding others: Kellyian theory, methodology and applications. *International Journal of Intercultural Relations, 6*, 403; cited in Singer, 8.
4. Benedict, Ruth. (1946). *Patterns of culture*. New York: Penguin, 2.
5. Klopf, Donald W. (1991). *Intercultural encounters: The fundamentals of intercultural communication* (2nd ed.). Englewood, CO: Morton, 31.
6. Trenholm, Sarah, & Jensen, Arthur. (1992). *Interpersonal communication*. Belmont, CA: Wadsworth, 368.
7. Klopf, 33.
8. For a discussion of cultural identity, see Singer, 46.
9. Wieder, D. Lawrence, & Pratt, Steven. (1990). On being a recognizable Indian among Indians. In Donal Carbaugh (Ed.), *Cultural communication and intercultural contact*. Hillsdale, NJ: Lawrence Erlbaum Associates, 45–64.
10. *Ibid.*, 51.
11. *Ibid.*, 61.
12. *Ibid.*, 63.
13. Samovar, Larry A., & Porter, Richard E. (1991). *Communication between cultures*. Belmont, CA: Wadsworth, 15.
14. *Ibid.*, 20.
15. Singer, 53.
16. Porter, Richard E., & Samovar, Larry A. (1991). Basic principles of intercultural communication. In Larry A. Samovar & Richard E. Porter (Eds.), *Intercultural communication: A reader* (6th ed.). Belmont, CA: Wadsworth, 6.
17. *Ibid.*, 6.
18. Kim, Young Yun. (1988). *Communication and cross-cultural adaptation: An integrative theory*. Philadelphia: Multilingual Matters, 145–146.
19. George Kelly, as cited in Diamond, 396–397.
20. Klopf, 57.
21. Mernissi, Fatima. (1975). *Beyond the veil: Male-female dynamics in modern Muslim society*. Cambridge, MA: Schenken, 81–86. For a discussion of a similar incident, see Storti, 66–67.
22. Klopf, 20.
23. Dodd, Carley H. (1987). *Dynamics of intercultural communication* (2nd ed.). Dubuque, IA: Brown, 44.
24. Skow, Lisa, & Samovar, Larry A. (1991). Cultural patterns of the Maasai. In Samovar & Porter, *Intercultural communication*, 90.
25. Carmichael, Carl W. (1991). Intercultural perspectives on aging. In Samovar & Porter, *Intercultural communication*, 130.
26. For examples of these kinds of differences, see Samovar, Larry A., Porter, Richard E., & Jain, Nemi C. (1981). *Understanding intercultural communication*. Belmont, CA: Wadsworth, 119; and Dodd, 45.
27. Hall, Edward T. (1959). *The silent language*. Garden City, NY: Doubleday, 67.
28. Argyle, Michael. (1991). Intercultural communication. In Samovar & Porter, *Intercultural communication*, 40; reprinted from Stephen Bochner (Ed.), *Cultures in contact: Studies in cross-cultural interaction*. Oxford, UK: Pergamon, 61–79.
29. Sitaram, K. S., & Cogdell, Roy T. (1976). *Foundations of intercultural communication*. Columbus, OH: Merrill, 51; cited in Samovar, Porter, & Jain, 94.
30. Samovar, Porter, & Jain, 73–74.
31. Hofstede, Geert. (2012). Dimensionalizing cultures: The Hofstede model in contest. In Larry A. Samovar, Richard E. Porter, & Edwin R. McDaniel (Eds.), *Intercultural communication: A reader*. Boston, MA: Wadsworth/Cengage Learning.
32. Hofstede, Geert. (2001). *Culture's consequences* (2nd ed.). Thousand Oaks, CA: Sage, 359.
33. Samovar, Porter, & Jain, 76.
34. Hofstede, Geert. (1982). *Culture's consequences*. Newbury Park, CA: Sage.
35. Triandis, Harry C., Briskin, Richard, & Hui, C. Harry. (1988). Cross-cultural training across the individualism-collectivism divide. *The International Journal of Intercultural Relations, 12*; reprinted in Samovar & Porter, *Intercultural communication*.

36. Hall, Edward T., & Hall, Mildred Reed. (1987). *Hidden differences: Doing business with the Japanese.* Garden City, NY: Doubleday, Anchor.

37. *Ibid.,* 54–56, 157.

38. Brake, Terence, Walter, Danielle Medina, & Walker, Thomas (Tim). (1995). *Doing business internationally: The guide to cross-cultural success.* New York: Irwin Professional Publishing, 54–59.

39. Brake, 54.

40. Lustig, Myron W., & Koester, Jolene. (1996). *Intercultural competence: Interpersonal communication across cultures* (2nd ed.). New York: HarperCollins, 125.

41. Brake, 57; see also, Stewart, Edward C., & Bennett, Milton J. (1991). *American cultural patterns: A cross-cultural perspective* (Rev. ed.). Yarmouth, ME: Intercultural Press, 97–98.

42. Quoted in Lustig, p. 253; the original source is Beeman, William O. (1986). *Language, status, and power in Iran.* Bloomington: Indiana University Press, 86.

43. Barna, Laray M. (1991). Stumbling blocks in intercultural communication. In Samovar & Porter, *Intercultural communication,* 348.

44. Trenholm & Jensen, 386.

45. *Ibid.,* 388.

46. Barna, 346.

47. *Ibid.,* 345.

48. Storti, 26, 64–65.

49. Oberg, Kalvero. (1985). Culture shock: Adjustment to new cultural environments. *Practicing Anthropology, 7,* 170–179.

50. Storti, 52.

51. Kim, 56–57.

52. Samovar, Porter, & Jain, 195.

53. Hall & Hall, 18–20, 115.

54. Kim.

55. Trenholm & Jensen, 404–405.

CHAPTER 13

1. Selltiz, Claire, Wrightsman, Lawrence S., & Cook, Stuart W. (1976). *Research methods in social relations* (3rd ed.). New York: Holt, Rinehart & Winston, 2.

2. For a good discussion of heuristic rules as they apply to persuasion, see Cialdini, Robert B. (1984). *Influence: How and why people agree to things.* New York: Morrow. For a more formal discussion, see Eagly, Alice H., & Chaiken, Shelly. (1986). Cognitive theories of persuasion. In Leonard Berkowitz (Ed.), *Advances in experimental social psychology: Vol. 19.* New York: Academic, 123–181.

3. Selltiz, Wrightsman, & Cook, 5.

4. Frey, Lawrence R., Botan, Carl H., & Krebs, Gary L. (2000). *Investigating communication: An introduction to research methods* (2nd ed.). Boston: Allyn & Bacon, 13–17.

5. Poole, Marshall Scott, & McPhee, R. D. (1985). Methodology in interpersonal communication research. In Mark L. Knapp & Gerald R. Miller (Eds.), *Handbook of interpersonal communication.* Newbury Park, CA: Sage, 100.

6. Frey, Botan, & Krebs, 17.

7. Rybacki, Karyn, & Rybacki, Don. (1991). *Communication criticism: Approaches and genres.* Belmont, CA: Wadsworth, 16.

8. Dilliplane, Susanna (2012). Race, rhetoric, and running for president: Unpacking the significance of Barack Obama's "A More Perfect Union" speech. *Rhetoric & Public Affairs, 15*(1), 127–152.

9. *Ibid.,* 134.

10. *Ibid.,* 135.

11. The text of President Obama's speech can be found online by searching "Obama's A More Perfect Union speech."

12. Dilliplane, 138.

13. These remarks were made at a press conference held on April 29, 2008, and can be accessed by searching "Obama's Remarks on Wright—New York Times." Wright's own subsequent comments can be found by searching "Transcript: Rev. Jeremiah Wright Speech to National Press Club."

14. A full transcript of this speech can be accessed online by searching "Obama's keynote address at Democratic National Convention."

15. A full transcript of this speech can be accessed online by searching "Barack Obama Announces Candidacy, 2007."

16. Dilliplane, 144.

17. A full transcript of this speech can be accessed online by searching "Obama's Victory Speech."

18. Schwartz, Howard, & Jacobs, Jerry. (1979). *Qualitative sociology: A method to the madness.* New York: Free Press, 48.

19. Kirk, J., & Miller, M. L. (1986). *Reliability and validity in qualitative research.* Newbury Park, CA: Sage, 9.

20. Frey, Lawrence R., et al. (1991). *Investigating communication: An introduction to research methods.* Englewood Cliffs, NJ: Prentice-Hall, 247.

21. Lynch, Owen Hanley (2009). Kitchen antics: The importance of humor and maintaining professionalism at work. *Journal of Applied Communication Research, 37*(4), 444–464.

22. *Ibid.,* 458.

23. Frey et al., 1991, 191.

24. Merolla, Andy J. (2010). Relational maintenance during military deployment: Perspectives of wives of deployed US soldiers. *Journal of Applied Communication Research, 38*(1), 4–26.

25. *Ibid,* 9.

26. *Ibid.,* 7; see also Canary, Daniel J., & Dainton, Marianne (2006). Maintaining relationships. In Anita L. Vangelisti & D. Perlman (Eds.). *The Cambridge handbook of personal relationships,* 727–743. New York: Cambridge University Press.

27. Stafford, Laura, & Canary, Daniel J. (1991). Maintenance strategies and romantic relationship type, gender, and relational characteristics. *Journal of Social and Personal Relationships, 8,* 217–242; Stafford, Laura, Dainton, Marianne, & Haas, Stephen M. (2000). Measuring routine and strategic relational maintenance: Scale revision, sex versus gender roles, and the prediction of relational characteristics. *Communication Monographs, 67,* 306–323; Canary, Daniel J., Stafford, Laura, Hause, Kimberly S., & Wallace, Linda (1993). An inductive analysis of relational maintenance strategies: Comparisons among lovers, relatives, friends, and others. *Communication Research Reports, 10,* 5–14; and Dindia, Kathryn, & Baxter, Leslie A. (1987). Strategies for

maintaining and repairing marital relationships. *Journal of Social and Personal Relationships, 4*, 1143–1158.

28. Merolla, 21.

29. Antheunis, Marjolijn, & Schouten, Alexander P. (2011). The effects of other-generated and system-generated cues on adolescents' perceived attractiveness on social network sites. *Journal of Computer-Mediated Communication, 16*, 391–406.

30. *Ibid.*, 398.

31. Pelias, Ronald J. (2000). Performance as method. In Frey, Botan, & Krebs, 253.

32. *Ibid.*, 234.

33. *Ibid.*, 255.

34. Carlin, Phyllis Scott, & Park-Fuller, Linda M. (2012). Disaster narrative emergent/cies: Performing loss, identity and resistance. *Text and Performance Quarterly, 32*(1), 20–37, 22.

35. Wick, Elizabeth, & Wick, Stanley. (1976). Unpublished letters to Wick family from the Guatemala Earthquake, 2. Quoted in Carlin & Park-Fuller, 23.

36. Fink, Mitchell, & Mathias, Lois. (2003). *Never forget: An oral history of September 11.* New York: HarperCollins, 68; quoted in Carlin & Park-Fuller, 23.

37. Carlin & Park-Fuller, 25.

38. *Ibid.*, 33.

39. *Ibid.*, 33.

Author Index

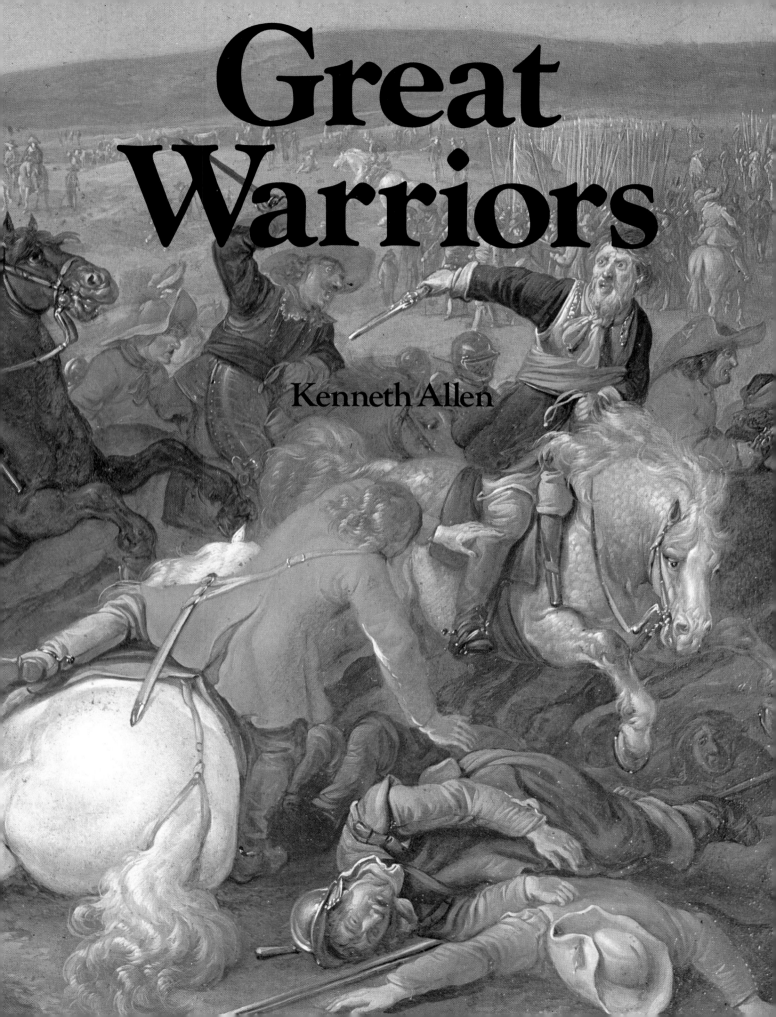

Great Warriors

Kenneth Allen

First published in 1979 by
Macdonald'Educational Ltd
Holywell House
Worship Street
London EC2A 2EN

ISBN 0 356 06786 6

Printed and bound by
Purnell & Sons Ltd
Paulton
Avon
England

Illustration credits
Key to the position of illustrations: (T) top; (C) centre; (B) bottom; and
combinations, for example: (TR) top right; (CL) centre left.

Artists
Peter Archer: 21, 28–29
Great Art Fraud (Gary Long): 10–11(B), 56
Hayward Art Group: 6–7, 20, 21 (BL), 31 (TL), 34–35
B. L. Kearley Ltd (Colin Andrew): 16–17
Linden Artists (Rob McCaig): 8–9, 18–19 (C)
John Martin & Artists (John Green): 25(BR), 40(R), 41(L), 50–51
The Parkway Group: 16(CL)
Tony Payne: 38, 39(TL)
Francis Phillips: 32–33
Trevor Ridley: 24–25(C)
Peter Sarson: 42(B), 43(BL), 58
Malcolm Smythe: 14–15, 18–19(T), 23(TL), 25(TR), 32–33(T),
40–41(C), 44(B), 46(BL)
Temple Art Agency (Jeff Burn): 22–23, 48–49
Temple Art Agency (Richard Hook): 12–13
Temple Art Agency (Alex Machin): 14(BL)
Lydia Thornley: 52–53

Photographs
Bibliothèque Nationale, Paris/Weidenfeld & Nicolson Archive: 35(CR)
(BL)(BR)
Bildarchiv Preussischer Kulturbesitz: 43(TL)
Courtesy of the Trustees of the British Museum: 26(T)(BL)
Courtesy of the Trustees of the British Museum/Weidenfeld & Nicolson
Archive: 33(BC), 40(CL), 41(CR)
Cooper Bridgeman Library: 36(T)
Werner Forman Archive: 30(TR), 33(BR)
Hirmer Fotoarchiv: 14(TR)
Michael Holford: 9(TR), 13(BR), 16(TR), 19(CR), 28(BR)
Imperial War Museum: 54(CL)(BL)(BC)(BR), 55(CR), 57(CL)
(BL)(BR)
A. F. Kersting: 29(BR), 37(C)
Keystone Press Agency: 46(TR), 56(TR), 58(TR)
Kungl. Husgeradskammeren: 4-5, 39(TR)
Mansell Collection: 18(CR), 26(BR), 28(BL), 39(BR)
Mas Barcelona: 27(L)(TR)
National Army Museum: 50(BR), 51(TR)
Novosti Press Agency: 45(CL)
Photoresources/Mike Dixon: 18(BR)
Courtesy of the Earl of Roseberry/Weidenfeld & Nicolson: 40-41(T)
Scala: 10(TR), 11(TL), 15(TR), 19(TC)(BR), 36(BR), 44(CL), 45(B),
47(TR)(BR)
Schloss Charlottenburg, Berlin/Robert Harding Associates: 42(TC)
Ronald Sheridan: 27(CR)
Snark International: 45(TR)
Swiss National Tourist Office: 17(BL)
Ullstein Bilderdienst: 43(BR)
Victoria and Albert Museum: (37(BR)(BL)
Western Americana: 46(BR), 49(T), 51(BL), 52(TR), 53(T), 58(BL)

The author and publishers would also like to thank Brigadier Peter Young
for his help in preparing this book.

Contents

Ramses II: Egyptian pharaoh

Ramses II was probably the greatest 'big-head' of ancient times. He was a very brave warrior, but he also always made sure that everyone knew of his victories and greatness.

He succeeded his father, Seti I, when still a young man. The first 15 of his 67 years' reign were spent in battle, leading his troops. We know he had a very high opinion of himself, because every detail of his battles was recorded on the walls of the great temples built throughout his kingdom. These details have been of great help to modern historians in tracing the history of his reign in the 13th century BC.

Soon after he came to the throne he learned that the powerful warrior nation of the Hittites was being joined by Nubians, Libyans and Syrians in order to make war on Egypt. This was a challenge he could not refuse. He gathered his own army of tough fighting men and marched to meet the invading force. The Egyptian army was triumphant everywhere it fought. No one, it seemed, could defeat it.

In the fifth year of his reign Ramses led a force to attack the Hittite capital of Kadesh. He took four divisions with him, each named after a god—Ra, Amon, Ptah and Sutekh. Ramses led the Amon division in his magnificent war chariot, the Ra division followed, with the other two divisions a day's march behind. None of the scouts saw any sign of the enemy so Ramses believed that they had left Kadesh and travelled northwards. He encamped with the Amon division to the north of the city while the Ra division made camp on the east side. No one realized that they had fallen into a clever trap until, at dawn, the whole Hittite army fell upon the Ra division. They cut it to pieces and drove the remnants back into the Amon camp.

To his dismay Ramses found that only a very small part of his two divisions remained. Many had been killed, others had taken flight. But he refused to be beaten. As the Hittites were busily plundering his camp, Ramses gathered together his remaining warriors. He drove them into the enemy's east wing, forcing it into the River Orontes nearby.

The Hittites closed in and a fierce battle followed. Fortunately at this vital moment the other two Egyptian divisions arrived and forced the Hittites back into Kadesh. But despite a bitter struggle, they were unable to capture the city. On returning to Egypt Ramses had every incident of these battles painted on the walls of his temples, a dramatic reminder of these earliest struggles for conquest and power.

Ramses eventually made peace with the Hittites which put both states on an equal power basis. During the next 50 years of peace Ramses managed to raise Egypt's level of economic prosperity. He also developed the arts, literature and building. His greatest achievements were the rock temple at Abu Simbel and the great hall at Karnak.

▶ A stone relief showing Egyptian soldiers carrying round topped shields, covered in cow-hide; bronze axes with wooden handles; spears and a large boomerang.

◀ Even in his own time Ramses' fame was greater than that of his father, Seti. He managed to make peace with the Hittites, after decades of fierce fighting. During the next 50 years of peace Ramses built many colossal monuments, often glorifying himself.

▼ Ramses II in his war chariot which enabled him to move around the battlefield with great mobility. The Egyptians adopted these chariots from the Hyksos who overran Egypt around 1700 BC.

▼ Each section of the Egyptian army was divided into five units named after a god, under whose sign it fought: Amon, supreme deity of Egypt; Ra, the sun god;

Ptah, the god who created the world; Phra, incarnation of Ra, and Set, god of violence. These corps of 10,000 foot soldiers went into battle surrounded by chariots.

Achilles: Trojan War hero

Every man in the Greek nation was furious. Helen, the most beautiful girl in the world, had been stolen away from her husband Menelaus, King of Sparta, by Paris, son of Priam, King of Troy. She had to be rescued—even though it meant war.

Soon a great armada of ships set out from Greece and the surrounding islands, heading for Troy. In overall command of the forces was Agamemnon, the brother of King Menelaus. With him went the greatest warrior of the Greek army, Achilles, son of Peleus and Thetis. Thetis had been warned that her son might die young, and when he was a baby had dipped him into the River Styx to make him invulnerable. Only his heel, by which she had held him, remained uncovered by the water.

The Trojan war was to last for ten years, and Achilles fought in many battles. From one city he raided, he captured a beautiful girl named Briseis, whom he loved dearly. Agamemnon, his commander, took Briseis from him. This angered Achilles so much that for a time he refused to fight. Patroclus, Achilles' friend, put on Achilles' armour and fought in his place. He was killed by the Trojan hero Hector, son of King Priam, who thought it was Achilles himself.

When he heard of this, Achilles immediately went out to avenge his friend, wearing armour newly made for him by Hephaestus, the god of metal-working. Achilles slew Hector in single combat and tied the body of the dead warrior to the tail of his chariot. He then drove it several times round the walls of Troy.

▲ Thetis carries Achilles' armour to him before he sets off for war. Zeus, King of the gods and men, had promised Peleus and Thetis that their son would be the most famous of all the Greek heroes to fight at Troy.

▶ Thetis, Achilles' mother, dips Achilles into the River Styx to make him immortal like her. The magic waters of the Styx did not cover his heel by which she held him. This was the only part of his body which could be wounded.

Hector's father, King Priam, was forced to enter the Greek camp to beg for his son's body so he could give it a ceremonial burial. The body was washed and then burned while the Trojan people mourned their hero.

But Hector was soon avenged. During a skirmish, Paris his brother, shot a poisoned arrow into Achilles' unprotected heel, killing him. From this incident comes the expression, 'Achilles' heel', meaning a vulnerable spot. Achilles' body was also burned and the ashes, together with those of his friend Patroclus, were buried in a golden urn on a headland high above the sea.

The fighting had now reached its tenth long year and still Troy remained untaken. The Greeks grew weary until the wise King Odysseus hit upon a brilliant idea which was sure to dupe the Trojans. The Greek fleet sailed away, leaving only the remains of their camp and a huge wooden horse standing on the shore. The unsuspecting Trojans were jubilant and hauled the trophy into the city, rejoicing that the war was over at last.

The rejoicing soon ended. At midnight, the Greek warriors who had hidden inside the horse crept out. They opened the gates of the city and let in the men from the Greek fleet which had returned to Troy under cover of darkness. Troy was destroyed and Menelaus was reunited again with his beautiful wife Helen, the cause of the long war and, indirectly, of the death of Achilles. The legend of this brave hero's deeds has inspired many other great men.

▲ A scene from the handle of a Greek vase showing Ajax, another Greek hero, carrying the body of Achilles. Ajax fought Odysseus for Achilles' armour but he lost and, as one legend tells us, eventually committed suicide.

▼ Achilles is shot in the heel by a poisoned arrow said to have been fired by Paris, Hector's brother. The heel was the only part of Achilles' body not to be protected and the great warrior died of the wound.

David: king of Israel

The men of the court of King Saul were very worried. Their king, Israel's first, had such a violent temper that everyone feared for his life. Someone suggested that a musician might be able to soothe the king's furious outbursts. So David, a shepherd's son, was brought from the country to become Saul's musician. He was a good harpist and his beautiful playing calmed the king and brought peace to life at court.

The peace was shortlived. Soon war broke out with the Philistines, the enemies of the Jews. David was dismissed from court as peacetime activities stopped while the Israelites busily prepared for war. Eventually the Israelite and Philistine armies faced each other. For some time there was no fighting.

▼ David about to behead Goliath who had been knocked out with a stone from a sling. Nobody from either side expected a mere shepherd boy to be victorious against the Philistines' giant champion warrior.

The Philistines demanded that the battle be decided by single combat between a warrior from each army. The Philistines' choice was Goliath, a giant of a warrior. He stood in the valley between the armies bellowing his jeers at the Israelites. No one dared face such an awesome opponent even though Saul had offered a rich reward to any man who would come forward.

To everyone's amazement David, the shepherd boy and musician, stepped forward. He volunteered to fight the giant. He was not a trained warrior but his faith in God gave him tremendous strength. Saul reluctantly gave permission for the boy to fight but ordered that he wear heavy armour for protection.

David refused all offers of armour and swords. He preferred to wear his simple shepherd's clothes and to use his familiar weapon—a sling. He ran down into the valley and picked some smooth, round pebbles from the bank of a brook. Then he returned to face his formidable enemy.

Goliath roared with laughter when he realized that the young boy before him was preparing to fight him. But David calmly slipped a stone into his sling and whirled it around his head letting it fly. The missile struck the unprotected forehead of Goliath who swayed and fell unconscious to the ground. David ran forward, drew the giant's sword from its sheath and cut off his victim's head.

The Philistines could not believe their eyes. They fled from their camp, chased by the Israelite soldiers who slew them as they ran. King Saul was so delighted with David's triumph that he made him his armour bearer. But as David's popularity grew with the people so did Saul's jealousy of the young hero.

David was forced to flee from Israel to save his life. He occupied himself with fighting wars for a foreign king until he heard of Saul's death in the Battle of Gilboa. He returned to Israel to become its king. Under David's leadership Jerusalem was made the capital of Israel, and he became the most powerful ruler in the area between the rivers Nile and Euphrates.

▼ A slingman from the palace of Kapara at Tell Halaf c.10th century BC. The sling is made up of a pad, usually of leather, attached to two thongs. After placing the sling-stone in the pad, the thongs are pulled taut, making the pad into a bag. The soldier holds the bag in his left hand and the ends of the taut thongs in his right hand above his head. He then whirls the sling with his right hand round and round to give it momentum, and releases the end of one thong. This opens the bag and frees the stone.

Alexander the Great

King Philip of Macedon looked at the tall youth who stood before him. 'My son,' he advised, 'look out for a kingdom worthy of yourself, for Macedonia is too small for you.' Little did he know then that his son Alexander was to become conqueror of most of the known world.

During his very brief reign of 13 years, from 336–323 BC, he conquered every great nation against whom he led his army, yet he was only 20 when his father died. His first battles were with various Greek states who rose against him; but by clever leadership, he managed to weld them all—Athens, Thebes, and Sparta—into a great army which fought alongside the men of Macedonia.

Alexander's next campaign was against Persia. Smashing through all opposition, he marched his men into Syria to defeat the Persian King Darius III at Issus in 333 BC. As a result, he was offered half of the Persian Empire but this was far from satisfactory. Alexander wanted to rule the whole of the Empire.

▲ Alexander riding into battle with one of his Macedonian foot soldiers.

Alexander's great march which built his Empire

▼ This map shows the eleven-year march that built a huge empire. Alexander first united Greece, then marched into Asia and on to Persia, where he defeated the Persians at Issus. He pushed south to Tyre and on to Egypt where he founded Alexandria. He returned to Persia to fight the Persians at Gaugamela, then on to Babylon. He marched on into India but eventually turned back and reached Babylon in 323 BC where he died aged 33.

◄ A coin showing the head of Alexander, one of the greatest generals in history. He was a brave leader who mastered the art of combining and manoeuvring his forces so well that he could adapt his methods of warfare to suit any situation.

► This stone and glass mosaic shows the fury of the Battle of Issus in 333 BC where Alexander's Macedonian forces smashed through the Persian archers and cavalry led by Darius. Darius fled in his chariot followed soon after by his demoralized men.

Alexander's Empire

0 |———| 1600 kilometres

His army quickly moved down the Syrian coast and invaded Egypt which was soon under Macedonian control. There he received the title Pharaoh of Egypt and gave his name to the city of Alexandria. He was worshipped as a god, but religious pomp and ceremony interested Alexander very little. War and conquest were his main interests. His wish to rule the entire Persian Empire came true when the Macedonian army completely defeated the Persian army at Gaugamela.

Alexander now ruled Egypt and Persia, which provided him with increased revenues as vast treasures poured in from the rich cities of the two nations. Gradually his army of tough Macedonian soldiers grew tired of warfaring. Many had not seen their families for ten years and wished to return home. But Alexander's great desire was to make all the peoples of the world into one huge family. Alexander spurred his men on to further achievements even though they probably grumbled about the icy mountains and waterless deserts they crossed before they reached northern India.

Here they met Porus, a great Indian Rajah, with his huge army of swift chariots, thousands of soldiers and hundreds of lumbering elephants. Despite the strength of the enemy, Alexander's men gained an overwhelming victory on the banks of the River Hydaspes. Finally, on reaching the mighty River Indus, he believed he had come to the shores of the ocean which encircled the world and agreed to march home.

It proved to be a most gruelling journey to Babylon and it was here that Alexander, now 33, fell ill. He died in the palace from which he had planned to rule the world. Not only did he leave behind an enormous empire but also a reputation which really deserves the title—great.

Hannibal: the Carthaginian

Hamilcar Barca, ruler of Carthage and a mighty warrior, was about to go to war. As he was making an offering to his gods he turned to Hannibal, his 9-year-old son, and asked him if he would like to go to war. When the boy nodded eagerly his father made him swear an oath of eternal hatred – to Rome.

Hannibal had always lived in an atmosphere of war. In time, his genius as a soldier became so respected that today he is regarded as one of the greatest warriors who ever lived. He learned the art of fighting beside his father who was killed in battle. He served under his brother-in-law Hasdrubal, who commanded the dreaded Carthaginian cavalry, and when he died Hannibal was appointed leader of the army.

◀ A coin showing the head of Hannibal who led the Carthaginian army against the Romans. He was regarded as a military genius by his friends and foes alike.

1 Felling trees for building rafts.
2 Half-finished raft.
3 When the elephants crossed one raft it was moved to the front of the line of rafts until the crossing was completed.

Aged 25 he headed a strong force of mercenaries and began the Second Punic War against the Romans which lasted for 17 years from 218–201 BC. The Romans expected to fight Hannibal in Spain but when they sent an army there they found he had moved on. Hannibal's army of 60,000 foot-soldiers, 18,000 cavalry and three dozen war-elephants had set off to cross the mountain passes into Italy.

His men were forced to struggle through the thick snow of the Alps. They crossed raging mountain torrents and through rocky passes where a sudden noise could start an avalanche. Would it really be possible to cross the Alps with elephants? Hannibal proved it was when he brought more than half his army onto Italian soil.

The Romans were astounded and hurriedly sent an army to meet Hannibal's forces. The Romans suffered heavy losses in two battles with the enemy by the River Trebbia and Lake Trasimene. Now the road to Rome itself was wide open but instead of taking the obvious route, Hannibal led his men southwards and fought against the largest Roman army that had ever gone into action.

Despite the size of the opposition, Hannibal's army almost annihilated the Roman army at the Battle of Cannae where over 70,000 Romans were killed or captured. It was Rome's worst defeat. Hannibal's outflanking tactics had overcome the superiority of the legionaries. Following this triumph, Hannibal's fortunes changed dramatically.

▼ Hannibal's elephants crossing the River Rhône on specially made rafts. The elephants were terrified of wading through the fast-flowing waters.

► A coin showing an elephant with a tower or castle strapped onto it in which soldiers travelled. Elephants were mainly used against cavalry because horses were frightened by their smell and size. Horses had to have special training before working beside elephants.

▼ The Alps which Hannibal's army was forced to cross in order to reach Italy.

His army was shrinking and his men were tired of endless campaigning. When Hannibal heard that a Roman army planned to attack his capital city Carthage, he left for home immediately. He lost the final battle against Rome at Zama in 202 BC. The Roman general Scipio used Hannibal's own tactics but had better troops at his disposal.

The Romans demanded that Hannibal be handed over to them as a prize captive but he fled for refuge to King Antiochus and later King Prusias in Asia Minor. He committed suicide by taking poison in 183 BC when Prusias was about to surrender him to the Romans. Hannibal, the military genius, inspired the Romans with awe, and 'Hannibal is at the gates' became a rallying call in later times.

Julius Caesar

Following the defeat and death of Hannibal, Rome became the capital of the greatest nation in the world. Its most famous citizen Julius Caesar first opened his eyes on 12 July in the year 100 BC.

He served with the army in the east, after which he became a prominent figure in Rome. He filled several public offices and was Consul in 59 BC. Then with Crassus, the richest Roman, and Pompey, then Rome's greatest general, he formed a partnership known as the First Triumvirate. He was made Proconsul (or Governor) of the province of Gaul, now France and Belgium, and for nine years fought against one Gallic tribe after another. In time, he had added all the lands west of the River Rhine to the expanding Roman Empire.

During the years 55 and 54 BC he took a Roman army across the Channel to invade the little-known island of Britain. He had no time to conquer the country as he would have wished, for he was forced to return to Rome where his enemies were plotting against him, with Pompey at the head of the conspirators. Caesar retained his own faithful soldiers even though the Senate demanded that they should be disbanded. He crossed the small River Rubicon, which marked the Italian frontier, with his army. He knew this action would lead to civil war.

He finally met Pompey at the Battle of Pharsalus in 48 BC and won an overwhelming victory. Pompey fled to Egypt where he was murdered as he stepped ashore from a small boat. Caesar moved on to Asia Minor where he fought Pharnaces, King of Pontus, at Zela. The Roman army was again victorious and it was here that Caesar wrote the famous words '*Veni, vidi, vici!*' – 'I came, I saw, I conquered!'

In 46 BC he returned to Rome to be made Dictator, (sole ruler) for ten years. He introduced many reforms at home, increased the number of Senators and gave parts of the provinces to those men who had served him loyally. He also introduced a new calendar, known as the Julian Calendar. It had 365 days and an extra day every Leap Year. The seventh month was renamed 'July' after Julius himself, who was born in that month. This is the calendar we still use today.

In 44 BC Caesar was made Dictator for life. He had statues of himself erected in temples and put his face on coins which made his fellow Romans very jealous. He became so arrogant and unbearable in his manner that Brutus, Cassius and other conspirators plotted to kill him to free the Republic.

Caesar did not have a personal guard. He went to a senate meeting and as he entered the hall several men, including Brutus, set upon him and stabbed him to death. Brutus recorded the event by issuing a coin with daggers and the fateful date '*Eid. Mar.*'—Ides of March (15 March), written on it. Thus Caesar's success brought him violent death.

▶ The Roman empire had expanded dramatically after almost 250 years of war. Rome now dominated the lands surrounding the Mediterranean, North Africa and Spain. Caesar added Gaul, Switzerland and some of Asia Minor.

▶ (below) Casear had been warned not to go to the Senate meeting. Death came suddenly from a group of conspirators who assassinated Caesar by stabbing him, on the fateful Ides of March, 15th March.

▼ A stone relief showing a powerful Roman war galley. The galleys were driven by two banks of oars. The crews of marines could board enemy ships as archers fired missiles from the towers.

▼ A detail from a Roman sarcophagus showing a battle between Roman soldiers and Germanic tribesmen. The soldier thrusts his sword into his enemy.

The Roman Empire in the time of Julius Caesar

Black Sea

Macedonia

Asia Minor

Greece

Mediterranean Sea

Egypt

▲ A bust of Julius Caesar as Chief Priest, an office he took at the age of 37. It was a position held for life and a great political honour for Caesar. He did not believe in religion but knew how to use ancient laws and traditions to gain greater power.

▼ Because of civil unrest in Rome, Roman politicians often arranged entertainments like this chariot race to gain popularity with the people. This terracotta relief from 1st century AD shows a charioteer wearing a cap and bands of leather round his chest for protection.

▼ Roman swords which were so important to legionaries for close-range fighting. They were used after the javelins or *pila* had been thrown.

Boudicca: Iceni queen

In AD 43 the Roman legions returned to Britain. This time, unlike the two brief raids of Julius Caesar, they intended to stay. At first, the Britons resisted strongly, so strongly in fact that the Emperor Claudius had to come from Rome with reinforcements. Eventually the British leader, Caractacus, was defeated and the Roman, Aulus Plautius, governed a very restless land.

Much of this unrest was due to the strange priests, the Druids, whose headquarters were in Anglesey in Wales. General Suetonius Paulinus, in command of the army, was determined to be rid of these troublesome Druids. In his absence in AD 61 Boudicca, Queen of the Iceni, led a great rising against the hated Romans. She had particular reasons for her hatred. On the death of her husband, King Prasutagus, she had been cruelly flogged by jeering Romans and her two daughters had been badly mistreated.

Soon other British tribes flocked to join her as she led an immense army south from the area which is now Norfolk. The first town they reached was Camulodunum, now Colchester, the Roman capital of Britain. This fell easily to Boudicca's troops, poorly trained and ill-equipped though they were. The whole town was burned to the ground and its inhabitants, men, women and children, killed. It was a ruthless slaughter.

▼ Some examples of Celtic weapons and armour made from bronze.

▼ Plans of Roman towns attacked by Boudicca.

Plan of Roman Camulodunum (Colchester)

Plan of Roman Londinium (London)

Plan of Roman Verulamium (St. Albans)

Excited by this easy victory, the Britons sped on to Londinium (London), where once again the ill-clad, badly armed natives poured into the town, killing everyone they saw. To complete the destruction they set fire to buildings as they passed.

Verulamium (St. Albans) was the next town to be attacked by Boudicca's forces. They were crazed with their recent victories, destroying all that stood in their way. People were killed without mercy and all traces of Roman influence destroyed. This was the third Roman town to be sacked by the rebellious Britons but no battle had yet taken place between the British and Roman forces. This would be a far greater test of Boudicca's strength.

▶ The Roman Legion was an offensive unit of about 5,500 men divided into ten cohorts of about 500 men each. The rigorous training consisted of marching, building camps, drill and use of weapons. The result was a well organized fighting force which was practically invincible.

▶ (above) 27 legionaries sometimes formed a *tortoise* or *testudo* with their shields.

► Boudicca riding her war chariot into her final battle against the Roman invaders. Although the Celtic forces outnumbered the Romans by 5 to 1, they were completely overwhelmed by the disciplined Roman legionaries.

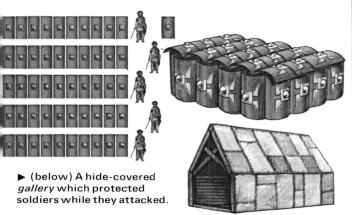

► (below) A hide-covered *gallery* which protected soldiers while they attacked.

Finally the Roman legions and the British warriors met somewhere in the Midlands. The Roman forces numbered 10,000 but they were outnumbered by 5 to 1 by the British. The battle was bloody and vicious and the British, though agile in their chariots, were no match at all for the well-trained, fit and highly organized Roman soldiers.

The wagons which carried the women and children blocked the line of retreat for the Britons, and mass hysteria broke out. The result was a terrible defeat for the British with an estimate of over 80,000 dead compared with 400 Romans killed. Boudicca fled from the battlefield and took poison, knowing her uprising had failed to crush the Romans.

Attila the Hun

In the 5th century AD a new and powerful threat appeared from the Steppes, an area now in Eastern Europe, beyond the shores of the River Danube. It was a fierce horde of warriors who seemed more like animals than men. They were short and hairy, clad in animal skins with flat faces and slanting, brown eyes. Their name was 'Ioung' or Hun.

There were more than 500,000 of these barbarians led by a terrifying warrior who was soon known to all Christendom as *Flagellum Dei* – the Scourge of God. His real name was Attila, and he became known as Attila the Hun.

He had been sent to Rome to be educated but learnt only to despise the ways of Roman society. His hatred of all things Roman caused him to swear that he would return to Rome but with an army behind him. In AD 450 his vow came true.

His huge army of Tartars ravaged Rome's Eastern Empire for several years until the Emperor Theodosius bought peace from him. Attila then headed west.

His army consisted mainly of horsemen on small, sturdy ponies who were the fastest fighting force ever known. Everywhere they went they sacked cities, towns and isolated villages. To Attila, might was right, and his famous boast was 'Where I have passed the grass will not grow again.'

Soon his men swept through deserted towns. News of his merciless treatment travelled ahead of his advancing army. He reached Orleans in present-day France, where he began a siege. But precious time had been lost. The Roman army with Aetius at its head had made an alliance with the Visigoths under Theodoric and the combined forces met Attila's Huns in Gaul.

Attila immediately abandoned the siege and chose what seemed a suitable position upon which to fight. It was a wide plain, the Campi Catalaunici, which is near Châlons, in France. At first it seemed as if the victory would go to Attila, for Aetius' army was giving way and Theodoric was killed.

▲ The barbaric Huns were constantly on the move and their homes were caravans on wheels, like the one pictured above. It was a simple construction of wood covered with skins sewed together to give protection from the elements.

▶ Whole tribes from Eastern Europe were on the run from Attila. His cruel horde of Huns destroyed everything and everyone they met. Villages were burnt, towns sacked and people killed unmercifully.

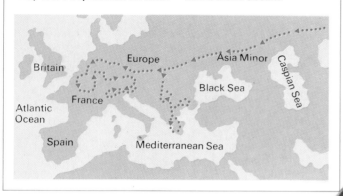
Certain victory for Attila suddenly turned to defeat. The Huns hastily retreated expecting to be followed, but, curiously, this did not happen. Attila gathered together his broken army with which he then attempted to invade northern Italy.

The Hun forces consisted of fewer men now, but this did not prevent towns from being destroyed or people from being killed or tortured. Rome was the next target, but Pope Leo I managed to persuade Attila to leave Italy in exchange for marriage to Princess Honoria accompanied by a vast dowry.

Attila was not able to enjoy this new life with its wealth, for he died suddenly on the following day. The decision to leave Italy without more fighting seems very strange indeed for the Hun who enjoyed having such a fierce reputation. The spring of AD 453 saw the end of the most famous warrior leader of all the Barbarian tribes.

▲ The Huns lived off their horses and did not carry bulky grain.

▲ Raw horse-meat, soaked in brine, was pressed under the saddle until it was soft enough to eat.

▲ Horse's milk, kept in leather bags, curdled into solid, cheesy balls.

23

Rollo: Duke of Normandy

'From the fury of the Northmen, O Lord, deliver us' must have been the prayer heard in churches all over Christendom from the year 800 and for two centuries afterwards. These Norsemen from Denmark, Sweden and Norway were men of the sea and of blood. In the dreaded, dragon-prowed longships they would appear from nowhere to attack coastal towns or sail up rivers to plunder, burn and kill.

The attacks were not confined to European waters. Some of these Vikings, acting both as pirates and traders, travelled along the rivers Volga and Dnieper while others tried to capture the fabulously rich city of Constantinople but found the walls too well guarded.

In the late 9th century the Vikings were only prevented from taking over Britain by the great efforts of King Alfred and the navy he created. France however was not so fortunate, and a number of weak kings allowed the Northmen to loot and kill almost as they wished. One of the greatest of the Viking warriors was Rollo, who was greatly feared by the French people.

However many troops the Frankish army put before Rollo and his men, it was always the Northmen who won. They fought with great bravery without fear of death. They believed that any warrior who died in battle would go straight to Valhalla, the Northmen's heaven, to feast with the other heroes.

In time, Rollo proved himself to be more than just a wild Viking, content to raid, kill and sail away. He captured Rouen in France and began to form a settled state around the city. The Christians watched with wonder as Rollo's leadership began to show a new way to peace and prosperity. Because of his ability Rollo was offered the lordship of the whole area (Normandy) between Epte and the borders of Brittany, provided he acknowledged the king as his overlord, lived in peace and became a Christian.

Rollo agreed to these demands and in 912, at St. Clair-sur-Epte, he was told to pay homage to the king, Charles the Simple, by kneeling and kissing his foot. Instead, Rollo summoned one of his men to do this for him. The man did not kneel but raised the royal foot to his mouth which sent the poor king toppling over backwards, to the delight of the Viking onlookers.

The new state was called Normandy (after Norman or Northman) and was ruled by Rollo who became known as Duke Robert. Rollo guarded his lands against attacks from other Vikings by strengthening the defences of the towns and improving law and order. His men married French women and the Vikings gradually adopted French customs, religion and language. Rollo's son, William Longsword, succeeded to the title. But it was another William, the Conqueror, who became the most famous descendant of Rollo, when he defeated King Harold at the Battle of Hastings and became William I, King of England, in 1066.

◄ A Viking longship c. AD 800. It was a canoe-like warship, long and narrow, and sat low in the water. It was made chiefly of oak, about 53 metres long and 5 metres wide. The huge mast carried a large, square sail, and the large steering paddle was attached to the stern on the starboard (right) side. There were usually sixteen pairs of oars for use in narrow waters or when the wind failed. The ships could operate anywhere, from deep seas to shallow rivers.

The Viking routes

▲ This map shows how far the Vikings travelled by sea and overland. Relics have been found proving they reached Iceland, Greenland, North America, Eastern Europe and Russia.

Viking relics

► (a) An intricately carved wooden ship's post c.9th century AD.

▼ (b) A Viking coin showing a Viking longship.

▼ (c) A Viking conical helmet with nose and cheek piece

▼ (d) A Viking 'byrny' or mail shirt made up of thousands of interlocking rings.

▼ A Viking in full battle dress. The iron sword was broad and two-edged. The wooden shield was bound by iron bars.

a

b

c

d

▼ Rollo (860-931 AD) became the first Viking Duke of Normandy. He spent 10 years attacking France before being offered land to settle there peacefully.

El Cid: Spanish hero

El Cid, the most famous of all Spanish warrior-heroes, is perhaps the most unusual hero in history. His real name was Rodrigo Diaz de Vivar but he is known as El Cid Campeador.

The first name comes from the Arabic *El Seid*, which means 'Lord'. The second name is Spanish meaning 'Champion'. The fact that his name is both Arabic and Spanish is revealing because he fought for both sides.

He first became famous during the wars against the Moors when his bravery in action earned him the name El Cid. He served under Ferdinand, King of Castile, who had spent much of his life fighting the Moors to regain land which is now Portugal. When Ferdinand died his son Sancho took over. It was while fighting for him that El Cid gained the title El Campeador.

Sancho was killed by his brother Alphonso who became King of Castile and Leon. He was pleased to keep the famous El Cid as one of his warriors. El Cid's first task was to fight Abdullah, the Moorish King of Granada. A great battle took place under the walls of Seville. El Cid routed the enemy, returning to King Alphonso with the treasures he had captured. But the friendship between the two men did not last long.

▲ The title page of the 1546 edition of *The Chronicle of the Cid*. The chronicle, a mixture of fact and fantasy, gives a clear idea of El Cid's heroic exploits.

After a quarrel with Alphonso El Cid went to seek his fortune elsewhere as a mercenary. He had a large number of soldiers who would fight for Moor or Spaniard provided the price was right.

El Cid had many exploits which were later included in the *Poema del Cid*, the oldest known Spanish epic poem. In this, his service with the Moors is hardly mentioned. He is shown as a fine example of knighthood, virtue and of Christian grace.

El Cid's greatest triumph came in 1094 when he led an army of 7,000 men against the city of Valencia. It was held by Moors. The garrison resisted and relief came with the arrival of the Almoravides tribe, the masters of Moorish Spain. But El Cid and his men captured Valencia, so gaining tremendous booty.

El Cid also took on royal powers and soon his kingdom comprised Valencia and all the surrounding country. In 1099 Valencia was again attacked by the Almoravides. The Moslem army had the superior position but El Cid encouraged his men to fight without fear. The result was a splendid victory for El Cid, one of the best yet achieved. But El Cid's happiness was not to last for long.

◀ A 15th-century Spanish woodcut showing medieval knights attacking a city, as they must have done in El Cid's time, working for the hero's Spanish or Moorish masters.

▲ Various scenes showing the Moorish soldiers in battle with the Christians from the colourful 13th century Chronicle of Alphonso X of Castile. You can see clearly the contrast between the heavy mail armour of the Spaniards and the traditional clothing of the Arabs.

◄ This woodcut shows the legendary Spanish warrior-adventurer, Rodrigo Diaz de Vivar-El Cid. He had most of the qualities expected of a medieval knight — a great and successful warrior who was brave in battle yet humane towards his enemies.

▲ The gateway of Santa Maria at Burgos through which El Cid rode on his way to exile. He was forbidden food or shelter by the King.

▲ The Golden Tower of Seville built around the 13th century. This shows the Moorish (or Arab-Islamic) influence in Spain which lasted for over 850 years, beginning in the 8th century.

Diego, El Cid's son was killed in battle at Toledo fighting for King Alphonso. El Cid was heartbroken. More battles took place against the Moors and El Cid was no longer so merciful with Moslem prisoners.

The loss of his son and the hardships and severe wounds received in battle had weakened the brave warrior. He died in July 1099. He was 56 and had spent almost all his life in battle. He is said never to have known defeat which is why his legend lives on in plays, poems and films. He represents the just and wise knight who was concerned for his friends without being barbaric towards his enemies.

Saladin: the great Saracen

The most memorable of the Moslem warriors was Saladin who proved on most occasions to have a more Christian-like nature than many of the Crusading Christian knights against whom he fought.

His full name was *Salah ed-Din* meaning 'Honour of the Faith', because he did his best to honour his faith as he saw it. He was born in 1138 at a time when the once great Moslem Empire was steadily falling apart. He came from a warlike race, the Kurds. His father was the governor of a large part of what is now known as Iraq.

Saladin was sent by the Sultan of Syria on an expedition against Egypt and when the Caliph of Cairo died he became ruler in his place. In 1174 the Sultan of Syria died. Saladin seemed to be the obvious choice as successor and he became the most powerful ruler in the Islamic world, with both Syria and Egypt under his command.

Saladin ruled wisely, and his main purpose was to win back for Islam the kingdom of Jerusalem. He led a great army of skilled horsemen into Palestine, proclaiming a Holy War. In 1187 Jerusalem was captured and the entire Christian lands, except for Tyre, became Moslem.

So began the Third Crusade led by two powerful kings, Richard the Lion-Heart of England and Philip Augustus of France. In time the struggle became a personal duel between Saladin and Richard.

▶ Saladin and Richard the Lion-Heart meet in a battle between Christians and Saracens. The cavalry from each side fight in a headlong clash after which the infantry moves in to slaughter the horsemen who have already fallen.

▼ (left) One of Saladin's Saracen warriors who was lightly armed with a short, sharp-edged scimitar, a dagger and bow and arrows. Being lightly armed enabled the Saracens to take advantage of speed and agility in battle.

▼ The Turks led by Saladin would have looked very much like these soldiers shown in this Arab painting. They would try to break the closed battle formation of the Crusaders by a series of hit-and-run attacks which started by firing volleys of arrows in quick succession.

Encouraged by an early victory, Richard led his army towards Jerusalem but it was the wrong season for such a march and he was forced to retire. There was soon unrest in the Christian army which made Richard approach Saladin with proposals for a truce. The 'Lion-Heart' demanded only the possession of Jerusalem and the wood of the true Cross. Saladin refused to surrender without a fight. The city was as dear to the Moslem as to the Christian.

A truce was finally reached in 1192 by which Saladin agreed to allow all pilgrims to visit the Holy City without hindrance. One pilgrimage was led by the Bishop of Salisbury who had a long talk with Saladin. He was interested to learn what the Christians said about both leaders. The Bishop answered fairly with the truth, 'My king stands unrivalled among all men for deeds of might; but your fame is also high and were you but converted to the true faith, there would not be two such princes as you and he in the whole world.'

Saladin praised Richard's valour in return, but added, 'For my part, I would rather be famed for skill and prudence than for mere audacity.' When he died in March 1193, Saladin was remembered for wisdom and kindness as well as for being the conqueror who stopped the conquest of the east by the west.

▼ The Krak des Chevaliers or Castle of Knights which was garrisoned by the Knights of St John. The Castle guarded Palestine's northern routes and stayed in Crusader hands for 161 years until 1271.

Yoritomo Minamoto: Samurai warrior

During the 12th century, Japan was torn apart by civil war. It was fought between two great ruling families, the Taira and the Minamoto. Their 30 years of struggle has since been compared with the English Wars of the Roses. The Taira, under their leader Kiyomori, proved more powerful and ruled the country for over 27 years. The men of the Minamoto clan and its followers were forced into hiding in remote places to avoid capture.

One young prince, Yoritomo Minamoto, narrowly escaped capture several times. On one occasion he hid in a hollow tree as a group of Taira men passed by. One soldier examined the tree but fortunately he was friendly and did not give away the prince's position to the other men.

When Kiyomori died the Minamoto followers joined forces under the leadership of Yoritomo. He proved himself to be one of Japan's greatest warriors and statesmen. War broke out again during which Yoritomo led his men from victory to victory. Both fighting families were led by military nobles who kept an army of personal retainers: tough, professional warriors.

▼ A Samurai dresses for battle. The ritual of arming could take a long time because he first bathed and perfumed himself so that if he died he would smell sweet.

▲ Samurai warriors in a fierce battle. Fighting was the Samurai's way of life and his commitment to the art of war was total. He had to endure hardship without complaint.

1. A cotton breech-clout which was the basic undergarment of a Samurai's costume.

3. Large pantaloons worn over the kimono, fitting loosely in the legs to allow freedom of movement.

5. Disposable thigh guards worn on horseback were often taken off for easy movement on foot.

2. A short-sleeved kimono or armour robe which was tied with a special knot.

4. Shinguards of cloth or leather were reinforced with strips of iron to give protection from the front.

6. Metal-cased sleeves made from a Japanese type of chain mail sewn on to a heavy cloth.

Samurai warrior in full armour

horns
crest
mask or mempo
iron collar or nodowa
shoulder guards or o-sode
body shirt or ho
armoured sleeve
short sword or wakizashi
thigh guard or haidate
sword or katana

▲ A Samurai warrior in full battle dress. The whole suit of armour weighed only 11½ kilos and the wearer could move about with ease. The Samurai code demanded that he should live and die with a sword in his hand. Rigorous training kept the Samurai keen and alert at all times.

These men were called Samurai, an honourable class, who in time became nobles in their own right. They galloped into battle wearing iron masks, elaborate armour and wielding deadly, razor-sharp swords. The sword meant much more to a Samurai warrior than just a weapon. It was a sacred object placed beside him at birth and after death.

It was strange that during this time of civil war, an emperor had appeared to rule Japan. He was nothing more than a puppet ruler, his court was just a symbol. The real power in Japan was in the hands of the most powerful ruling family. Yoritomo, the real leader, asked the emperor to grant him a new title, that of Shogun or, more correctly, *Seii-taishogun*, meaning, 'Barbarian-suppressing commander-in-chief'. His wish was granted and, as Japan's first Shogun he appeared to follow the emperor's commands while actually keeping the real power. The emperor led the government but Yoritomo led the warriors.

After his death in 1199 his two sons were soon disposed of but Yoritomo's wife, the lady Masako, took over control of his forces. She used the members of her family, the Hogo, to help her rule. This family controlled Japan for well over a century. Her position may well be compared to that of Elizabeth I of England.

7. A sheath for the body, made from rows of lacquered iron scales, included armoured skirt panels for the hips.

9. An iron collar, with a metal bib for extra protection, helped to guard against decapitation.

11. A glowering mask of lacquered iron which was strong enough to blunt a spear point, covered the face.

8. Broad shoulder guards of threaded iron scales (lamellae) hung from the shoulders.

10. A cotton skull cap, which helped to cushion the weight of the helmet, is tied over the warrior's head.

12. A visored helmet with an armoured fringe that guarded the back of the neck, completed the costume.

31

Genghis Khan: Mongol leader

The Mongol Khan gave a cry of surprise as he reached forward and prised open his newly-born son's hand. It contained a clot of hard blood like a small, red stone. The chieftain saw this as a sign referring to his recent victory over his rival chieftain Temujin, so he gave his own son the same name.

Thirteen years later, in 1175, the Khan died and the young Temujin became the new leader of his tribe. Nobody would accept leadership by such a young and inexperienced boy. His mother persuaded some of the tribes to follow him. Others were engaged in constant battles until Temujin was old enough to take command.

As the first to rule all the Mongol tribes Temujin changed his name at their request, to Genghis Khan or Cheng-sze, meaning 'Perfect Warrior'. The tribes met under his nine-tailed white banner to form a truly fantastic fighting force. It was not long before they were on the move, in search of new grazing grounds for their cattle combined with the less peaceful wish for plunder and the usual spoils of 12th-century war.

Britain

Europe

Atlantic Ocean

Africa

Extent of the Mongol Empire

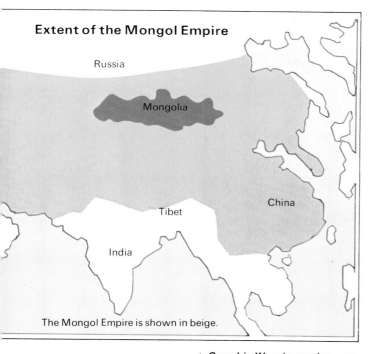

Russia

Mongolia

China

Tibet

India

The Mongol Empire is shown in beige.

▲ Genghis Khan's empire was the biggest the world had known. It stretched from the Sea of Japan in the east to the mouth of the Danube in the west. Marco Polo, the explorer, said of him, 'Genghis Khan was a man of courage, wisdom and prudence . . . he used his power with insight and sound judgement.'

◄ Genghis Khan leads his terrifying Mongol hordes into battle. The Mongols were highly skilled horsemen who shot their arrows from the saddle while riding at full speed.

► (right) A Persian painting showing Genghis and his troops during his conquest of China. Genghis's fame spread far and wide. Early references to his life are found in Persia, China and India.

► (far right) The Mongol armies prepare to attack a Chinese fortress. This miniature is taken from the Indian 'History of the Mongols'. Akbar, who had the scene painted, was descended from Genghis Khan.

It was not long before Genghis' army of Mongols and Tartars swept across Central Asia, killing two-thirds of Persia's population and destroying cities they found en route. It was not a wild horde of untrained horsemen like those led by Attila. The Mongol army, known as the 'Golden Horde', moved at high speed. The horsemen shot their arrows from the saddle as they galloped into action. The army was organized into three toumans or groups of cavalry, each consisting of 10,000 horsemen.

None of the enemies could stand up to the strength of the Mongol army, and Genghis Khan was able to achieve a series of incredible conquests. In 1213 he began his conquest of China, storming and then crossing the Great Wall. It was a great campaign that lasted for two years.

The Mongol Army then turned westwards, going on to conquer Armenia, western Turkestan and India down to Lahore. By 1222 his captains had reached as far as the shores of the Black Sea. Twenty years later Genghis' warriors had captured almost the whole of Russia and lands as far west as Silesia and Hungary.

By the time the formidable Genghis Khan died in 1227, he ruled the biggest empire the world had ever known. It stretched from the Pacific Ocean to the mouth of the River Danube. The building of such a vast and rich empire did not happen by luck. It was Genghis Khan's ability to think and act quickly when dealing with the movement of his troops which made him successful. No warrior before or since has achieved so much with so many uneducated and unorganized people.

The Black Prince

There was no settled peace between England and France in the years 1337 to 1453, and the period is now known as the Hundred Years' War. In August 1346 the army of King Edward III of England had been forced to retreat by the much larger army of King Philip VI of France. When the English reached the village of Crécy, Edward decided to turn and fight his enemy even though the English troops were outnumbered by 4 to 1.

The English took a position on a slight hill with the army arrayed in divisions, one of which was commanded by Edward, the Prince of Wales, King Edward's son. He was 16 years old and this was to be his first battle. He always wore black armour which soon earned him the name 'The Black Prince'.

King Edward had barricades erected behind which he placed his special weapon. This was hundreds of archers armed with long bows. The French army had no idea what was in store for them when they began their attack on the morning of 26 August 1346. They used heavily armoured knights who were totally confident of victory. Suddenly the air became white with a hail of feathered shafts as the English archers fired their arrows at a rate of 20 a minute. The French cavalry had no chance as horses crashed to the ground. Wounded men fell, unable to rise again because of the weight of their armour.

A messenger came from the Black Prince to ask for reinforcements but the king refused to help so long as his son was not injured or dead. Edward wanted his son to win his knight's spurs by fighting to the end without help from other knights.

Crécy was a crushing defeat for the French but an excellent training ground for the Black Prince. Ten years later in 1356 he led an army of 10,000 men through France to meet the huge French army which numbered 60,000. On 19 September 1356 a battle between the two armies was fought at Poitiers. The result was similar to the Battle of Crécy.

The English archers let fly their deadly volleys. Once again the heavy armour of the French knights was little protection against the arrows which struck them with such incredible speed and precision.

The French king was forced to surrender and the battle ended in a complete victory for the Black Prince. The French lost around 10,000 men and the English perhaps 1,000. After further battles in Spain the Black Prince died in June 1376. He never wore the crown of England but his son became Richard II.

▼ The most deadly weapon ever used in battle was the longbow and arrows. The staff, usually made from yew, was 1·8 metres long.

► Two maps showing the position of Crécy in France (left) and the positions of the English and French divisions in the battle (right).

◄ The bowman strung his bow just before firing. The string was made from hemp or silk which the archer waxed regularly.

▲ In battle the archer stuck several arrows in the ground in front of him so that they could be fired at great speed.

▲ The longbow needed strength, skill and practice for effective use. The pull was about 35-45 kg which made it impossible to hold the aim for very long.

► The archer wore a guard or bracer to protect his arm against the slap of the string.

England

Canterbury

Dover

Calais

Agincourt 1415

Crécy 1346

St Vaast

France

Poitiers 1356

Crécy Grange Wood

English baggage

Wadicourt

EDWARD

Battle of Crécy

PRINCE EDWARD

ALENÇON

Crécy

LORRAINE

BRITISH
Men at arms and dismounted knights
Longbows
Welsh spears
FRENCH
Mounted men at arms
Genoese crossbows
Infantry

▲ Spanning a bow with a windlass. The biggest drawback to the crossbow was its slowness because it took time to span, load and fire. The crossbow's effective range was about 90 metres and the rate of fire was 1 to 2 arrows a minute.

▲ The Battle of Poitiers in 1356, a great victory for the English, was won by the large numbers of long-bowmen. They could fire up to 12 arrows per minute, twice as many as the French crossbowmen.

◄ A pavilion which was put up near the battlefield so that knights could rest and eat in comfort when not engaged in battle.

► A foot soldier fights with a knight who has lost his horse. The ordinary soldier's armour was simple.

Akbar: Moghul emperor

The grandson of Genghis Khan, Kublai followed in his footsteps and became the ruler of more people than any monarch before him. After his death his great empire fell apart but many of his descendants also became famous. One was the Mongol chieftain of Turkestan, Timur, known as 'Tamburlaine the Great'.

A century later, another of Genghis Khan's descendants, called Babur, became the military conqueror of northern India and the founder of the great Moghul Empire of India. By the time Akbar came to the throne in 1556 India was a divided land because of the weakness of Humayun, Akbar's father.

Akbar was only 13 when he became emperor, but he was helped by his guardian Bairam Khan who had been one of his father's most trusted generals. He was ruler of Delhi, Agra and Sambhal but powerful enemies surrounded him. Soon a huge army under the leadership of Hemu attacked Delhi. It consisted of 100,000 foot soldiers and cavalry and 1,500 elephants. When they met in battle in November 1556 Akbar's forces totalled only 20,000, and the Moghuls were only saved by a lucky accident. An arrow struck Hemu in the eye and he fell unconscious. His army, now without a leader, turned and ran.

Akbar commanded one of the divisions in the battle but his heart was not really in warfare. He much preferred to hunt and play polo. He left most of the control to his adviser Bairam who eventually tried to gain too much power and was captured by Akbar's men as a rebel.

Akbar spared Bairam's life but he was killed shortly afterwards by an Afghan enemy who bore him a grudge. Akbar left the problems of war and government to his family until his foster brother Adham Khan killed Akbar's chief minister. Akbar was so furious that he killed his foster brother. At 19 years of age he became master of his empire. He improved its organization both in military and civil matters and kept close watch on his nobles, who ran the army and his provinces and districts.

He became noted for his religious tolerance and married a Hindu princess from the Rajput tribes of northern India. The Rajputs were the greatest warriors in India and were to fight with the Moghuls for the next century.

Akbar continued the policy of expanding his empire at every opportunity, usually 'under the guise of engaging in hunting'. He used an assortment of arms in addition to heavily armoured war elephants which were kept in the rear. At the Battle of Chitor in 1567, Akbar used mining and the 'sabat' or covered way to attack the fort. Eventually, a year later, the fort was captured and a brutal massacre followed.

When Akbar died in 1605 the Moghul Empire was secure because he had turned his enemies into strong allies by being firm, kind and just to all subjects.

◀ A bridge of boats broken by Akbar on his elephant while crossing the River Jumna in 1561.

▼ (below left) The poor receive food while the Emperor talks to his advisers, in this scene in the Moghul Palace in Bombay.

▼ Akbar enjoyed the action of tiger hunting which was excellent practice for real battles against India's enemies.

◀ Burbal's house at Fatehpur-Sihkri, Agra. This magnificent palace, made from red sandstone, was built by Akbar in 1569 in honour of his son's birth.

▼ Bullocks hauling the large, heavy cannons Akbar used in his many battles and sieges. This picture, painted at the time of the great Moghul Emperor, shows the frenzied activity of war.

Gustavus Adolphus: Swedish king

Almost from the day of his birth, Prince Gustavus Adolphus was trained for the time when he would become King of Sweden. Even at the early age of 9 he began to share in his father's government and impressed those who came into contact with him with his kingly manner and wide knowledge.

On the death of his father in 1611, he came to the throne, aged only 17. He was soon a popular leader with nobles and ordinary people alike. His self-confidence soon spread to his subjects, especially when they fought with him in war.

For many years Sweden had been dominated by Denmark which had taken much of its land. Gustavus was determined to win it all back, but first he had to train his army. He increased the discipline and rigid battle training of all the men. He cleverly linked pikemen and musketeers and increased the numbers of musketeers used in battle. He also used the *salvo*, a method by which the Swedes could fire a simultaneous three-rank volley when the enemy was almost upon them.

The Swedish army was now almost invincible and before he was 20 years old Gustavus had forced Denmark to return territory taken from Sweden. By 1630 he had enlarged his kingdom around the whole eastern shore of the Baltic Sea, having successfully fought against Russian and Polish forces.

Gustavus wanted to help the Protestant cause in Germany. With the aid of France he entered the Thirty Years' War which lasted from 1618–1648. The Swedish army was now the best equipped, best trained, best disciplined fighting force since the Roman legions. The men had proper uniforms which protected them from the weather, and flintlock muskets which meant faster and more accurate firing.

The soldiers were supplied from fixed depots instead of foraging and living off the land. They were forbidden to attack hospitals, churches and schools, and they obeyed Gustavus completely. When he wished to punish the enemy he ordered his men to loot and kill, but they only did this at his command – not to satisfy their own wishes.

► Gustavus Adolphus leads a victorious charge at the head of the cavalry. His military tactics became the model for other leaders.

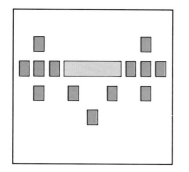

Pikemen

Musketeers

▲ A typical formation of pikemen and musketeers as used by Gustavus Adolphus.

The Swedish army was fanatically loyal to its leader and this enabled Gustavus to score two great victories in Germany. The first was at Breitenfeld in September 1631 when the Swedish forces met the Austrian Imperial army led by Count Tilly. The Swedish army won the battle with only 2,000 losses compared to the enemy losses of almost 20,000.

The next major conflict was at Lützen in November 1632 when Gustavus' forces met the Imperial army under its new commander Wallenstein.

Gustavus personally led his men into action and it was while riding to take control that he lost his life. The army did not give up but fought all the harder and eventually won the battle but with severe losses. Gustavus did not manage to create a united Protestant Europe, but he is remembered for his military genius in combining the use of infantry, cavalry and artillery, so that his army became the most professional of the day. He changed forever the way in which wars were to be fought in Europe.

► Gustavus before the Battle of Lützen which was to be his last military action. He was killed in November 1632, aged 38.

◄ Pikemen and musketeers in the Swedish army of Gustavus Adolphus. After the well trained musketeers had fired their volleys two ranks at a time, the pikemen, armed with pikes about 4 metres long, would charge in upon the enemy. The pikemen then fell back and allowed the musketeers to fire their second volley.

Cromwell: Roundhead leader

In front of Britain's Houses of Parliament stands a statue of one of its most famous members. In one hand he holds a sword, in the other a Bible. Both sum up what the man is remembered for. He was a soldier ready to fight for what he believed in. He was also a devout Puritan who cared for the right of every man to worship God in his own way. The statue is that of Oliver Cromwell.

Born in 1599, he was educated at his local grammar school, then at Cambridge. After graduating he returned home to become a gentleman farmer, but that soon bored him. In 1628 he was elected to Parliament as member for his home town of Huntingdon. For a time he was hardly noticed except for his rather uncouth manner and his fervent Puritanism.

▼ (left) A plan of the Battle of Naseby, 14 June 1645, showing the positions of the Royalists and Parliamentarians.

▼ A Royalist cavalry officer. He wore long hair, plumed hat and fine clothes, ornamentation which was despised by the Puritan followers of Cromwell. The light red sash distinguished the royalist supporters.

Main battles and sieges during the Civil War

Preston

Ch

Wo

Pembroke

Glouc

Br
Lans

Taunto

✠ Stratton

Exeter

Lostwithiel

✠
Plymouth

When Cromwell entered Parliament, King Charles I had been on the throne for three years and was already at odds with his Parliament. Matters came to a head in 1642. Cromwell was determined that Parliament should defend its rights so he went home to raise and drill a troop of horse. Each man was hand-picked. Each had to be sincere, determined and God-fearing. These men later became known as Cromwell's 'Ironsides', a nickname he was given at the Battle of Marston Moor.

Supporters rallied throughout England. Some were on the side of the king, some on the side of Parliament. Civil war began in August 1642. Families were split and brother was to fight against brother. The first battle was fought at Edgehill on 23 October 1642.

The beheading of Charles I in January 1649 by a Flemish painter. Charles I is shown in the top left corner, with the executioner at top right. He was 48 years old and had reigned for almost 23 years. Below left the king is led to his execution; below right, people dip their handkerchiefs in the blood of the 'martyred' king.

✠ Battles
◙ Sieges

Newcastle

York
◙

◙ Hull

Marston Moor
✠
Adwalton Moor

Naseby
✠

Edgehill
✠ Cropredy
Bridge
◙
◙xford   Brentford
✠ Newbury   ✠
oundway   Maidstone
own

The Royalist troops won, but at Marston Moor on 2 July 1644 the Parliamentarians were victorious. This was largely owing to the thorough training Cromwell had given his men.

In 1645 he was promoted to be second-in-command of the Parliamentary New Model Army. The men in this army were strictly disciplined and were allowed no swearing, no bad behaviour. They had to promise complete obedience to God and to their commander, Cromwell.

This New Model Army defeated the king's forces at Naseby in June 1645. Charles surrendered to the Scots who handed him over to Parliament. There was a long and bitter trial after which Charles was beheaded in Whitehall on 30 January 1649.

◄ A Parliamentarian cavalryman wearing a metal corselet, buff coat, blue sash and large, stiff leather boots. The 'lobstertail' helmet has a three-bar facial protection.

► A broadsheet produced in 1685 recalling 'the sad events of the late unparalleld rebellion', shows some disturbing events which had occurred during the English Civil War.

Cromwell now became the most powerful man in England, bringing in a Republic, to be controlled by Parliament. Ireland and Scotland resisted him and he had to lead his men again, storming Drogheda and winning the Battles of Dunbar (3 September 1650) and Worcester (3 September 1651). He was then declared 'Lord Protector' and governed all three countries – England, Scotland and Ireland.

He died peacefully on 3 September 1658, on the anniversary of his victories at Dunbar and Worcester. He was buried in Westminster Abbey. When Charles II came to the throne, however, Cromwell's body was dug up and, on the anniversary of Charles I's execution 12 years earlier, it was hung on the gallows at Tyburn.

Frederick the Great

The rough and tough old Frederick, the first King of Prussia, was a very disappointed man. He intended that his son, also named Frederick, should become an even greater warrior than himself. He had great plans both for his small country and for his son. To his disgust, however, the young prince was not interested in military matters. He preferred music, literature and art. As the prince grew older these interests increased and the king grew more and more displeased with him, often showing his anger in public.

Then quite suddenly the prince's attitude changed and his father's stern discipline began to take effect. In 1740 he came to the throne as Frederick II. He was now 28 years of age and most of the first 23 years of his 46 years' reign was to be spent in war. He ruled as absolute monarch of Prussia until his death in 1786.

At that time the two most powerful nations in Europe were France and Austria. Frederick resolved that Prussia would be the third. To help him in this attempt he took over the disciplined army created by his father. This included a special guards regiment in which every man was well over 2 metres tall.

Almost as soon as he was crowned, Frederick demanded that

▲ Frederick the Great by Glume.

Queen Maria Theresa of Austria return four duchies to their rightful owner, Prussia. She scornfully refused, so Frederick invaded Silesia and won the Battle of Mollwitz in April 1741. Soon the Prussian king's courage and brilliant tactics had secured the whole of Silesia for his country. Peace was signed at Dresden in December 1745 but it was not to last long. The Seven Years' War began in 1756 during which almost all the continental powers took up arms against Prussia.

Prussia and Britain formed an alliance against their opponents France and Austria. Prussia was soon facing three invading armies from France, Austria and Russia. Frederick was defeated at Kolin in June 1757 but his military genius brought about victory over the French and Austrians at Rossbach in November. The Austrians were again defeated at Leuthen in December 1757.

The Prussian army combined the qualities of speed, endurance, steadiness and precision which enabled Frederick to keep his enemies at bay. The Prussians were fighting against impossible odds and victories were mixed with defeats. The strain of the war began to tell on all the countries involved as money and manpower ran low.

▼ A Prussian flintlock musket used by Frederick's well drilled troops. The use of a double-edged iron ramrod, stronger than the usual wooden one, increased the rate of infantry fire to four rounds per minute.

1. Loading a flintlock was not difficult. Powder and ball in a cartridge were put down the barrel and rammed home. The cock was pulled back to the half-cock position.

2. Powder was put into the priming pan next to the touch hole. The sparks fell into this powder to fire the charge so it had to be kept dry.

3. The next step was to close the pan cover. This protected the priming powder and kept it dry. The weapon was now loaded and ready.

4. The cock was pulled back. As the trigger was pressed it flew forward and pushed the cover clear. This struck sparks into the priming and so fired the gun.

France and Britain made peace in Paris in 1763. Russian troops withdrew and Frederick was forced to make a separate peace with Austria at Hubertusburg in February 1763. Silesia was held by the Prussians but no other frontiers in Europe changed.

The war did establish Prussia as a great military power in Europe and chief rival to Austria. Frederick's main task after the war was to enable the country to recover its losses. He acted generously to the people but insisted on maximum efficiency and economy.

The devastation of war was quite soon put right and the army was kept at full strength. In 1764 Frederick made an alliance with Catherine the Great of Russia. With the help of Russia and Austria he acquired West Prussia after the partition of Poland in 1772.

Frederick worked hard in the service of his subjects. He was a 'benevolent despot', which meant that he ruled as a dictator but with the good of his people in mind. He had made Prussia a truly great power. He had doubled its territory and trebled its population.

Frederick really earned his title 'Great' because of his military genius and flexibility. His well drilled troops could move more quickly than those of his enemies. Most of the battles in which Prussian troops fought were against greater numbers of men, but Frederick's army usually won. Frederick had laid down the beginnings of the German Empire. Soon the other German states rallied round Prussia, the strongest country. It was in Frederick's time that the feeling of German Nationalism first began.

▼ Frederick's army often used the Austrian 12-pounder cannon which was drawn by a team of ten or twelve horses. Ammunition was carried on two three-horse carts. It consisted of 70 roundshot (solid iron cannon balls), and 30 rounds of canister (cylinders of sheet metal or wood which enclosed scores of walnut-sized shot).

▲ Some of the uniforms worn by the Prussian army under Frederick. He believed in discipline which applied to smartness in dress, as well as to battle formation.

► The Prussian Army at Breslau in 1742. The rigid columns of musketeers with fixed bayonets must have terrified the enemy.

Napoleon

Ask almost anyone who was the most famous Frenchman that ever lived and the chances are that they will answer – Napoleon. Yet he was not a Frenchman. He was born on the island of Corsica. This had been acquired from Genoa by France in 1769, the year before his birth.

When he was only 10 years old his father sent him to a military academy in France. Here the other students made fun of the thin, quiet boy who was shorter than most of the others. They laughed when he spoke French with a Corsican accent. How could they know that he was to become one of the world's greatest conquerors? In 1789 a revolution broke out in France putting the country in turmoil. Four years later Napoleon, now an artillery officer, had become the idol of his men.

At that time France was governed by five 'Directors' who had no military experience. Napoleon. felt that someone stronger should lead the country. He had the army behind him and in 1799 he dismissed the government and became First Consul of France.

Most of his time, however, was spent in wars abroad. He defeated the Austrians at Marengo and Austerlitz, the Prussians at Jena and the Russians at Eylau and Friedland. He was virtually the master of Europe. He made his brothers Kings of Spain, Holland and Westphalia. His brother-in-law became King of Naples. He had himself crowned as Emperor of France in December 1804 when he was 34.

Only England with her strong navy stood out against France. In 1812 Napoleon decided to invade Russia. This proved to be a terrible mistake as most of his army died in the harsh Russian winter.

In October 1813 the French suffered another defeat at the Battle of Leipzig. Soon after this the Austrians, Prussians and Russians invaded France and Napoleon was forced to abdicate. He went into exile on the island of Elba but he stayed there for less than a year.

He plotted to escape, landed in France, and gathered around him a large army. On 15 June 1815, at Waterloo, one of the most famous and most important battles in history was fought. The battle raged all day but the British soldiers stood firm against the charges of the French cavalry. When the German Marshal Blücher arrived in the evening with his army of Prussians, the battle was already over. France was completely defeated and Napoleon was forced to abdicate. He was exiled again, this time to St. Helena, where he died in 1821. Yet even before then the 'Little Corporal', as his devoted soldiers called him, had become a legend.

◄ Napoleon Bonaparte rose from a very poor family in Corsica to become Emperor of France in 1804, aged 34 years. Many portraits were painted showing him in rich clothes and a regal pose.

◄ At the height of his power Napoleon controlled, or was allied to, most of Europe except for England, France's traditional enemy. Continual warfare brought hardship to the French troops. They were exhausted after fighting an average of seven battles per month during the height of the Napoleonic wars.

✕ Battles of Napoleonic War
▉ Napoleon's Empire
▤ Controlled by Napoleon
▨ Allied with Napoleon

▼ Napoleon marched his troops into Russia in June 1812 and reached Moscow in September after a gruelling 804 km march. The Russians refused to surrender, preferring to set fire to Moscow.

► An illustration from 'The Game of Heroes of the French Empire', showing a French Hussar and a Sapper in the uniform of Napoleon's day. Bearskins, swords, pistols, rifle and cannon are shown in the border around the players.

LE JEU DES HÉROS DE L'EMPIRE FRANÇAIS.

▼ The Battle of Eylau in North Prussia in February 1807. It was a bloody and inconclusive battle and one of the most difficult in Napoleon's career. The Russians were forced to retreat and signed the Treaty of Tilsit in July 1807.

Garibaldi: Italian patriot

There had been a time when Italy was one of the most powerful countries in Europe. From Rome, her legions had marched to conquer much of the world. From Rome, the Pope controlled the Christian Church throughout the whole of Western Europe. But a series of invasions by other nations from the 5th century on had torn apart the once proud country.

In 1807, the year when a future liberator named Giuseppe Garibaldi was born, the Italians were crushed beneath the iron heel of the Austrians. It seemed impossible that Italy would ever break free. But a series of revolutions – especially the French Revolution of 1789 – set Italians hoping and planning. The Congress of Vienna that met in 1814–15 divided Italy into eight separate kingdoms, with the Austrians more firmly in control than ever. Things seemed hopeless.

But a number of Italian patriots still met secretly to scheme and work for the day of liberation. They were led by a young Genoese idealist named Giuseppe Mazzini. The movement was called 'Young Italy'. One who was very moved by Mazzini's talk of an Italy freed from Austrian rule was the young sailor Giuseppe Garibaldi.

▼ In Garibaldi's time Italy was divided into many states. It was not until 1870 that the whole of Italy was united as one Kingdom under the rule of Victor Emmanuel II.

▲ Giuseppe Garibaldi was born in 1807 in Nice, which was then part of Italy. He dreamed of a united state of Italy just as it had been in Roman times over a thousand years ago. As a young sailor he joined a group called 'Young Italy' to fight for unity.

Twice he raised the standard of revolt; twice he failed. In 1834 Garibaldi had to escape to South America with a death sentence hanging over him. While there, he formed the 'Italian Legion', led an army in a local revolution and became known as the 'Hero of Montevideo'. After 14 years' exile he returned to Italy to take part in the revolution of 1848.

This, too, ended in utter failure and Garibaldi had to flee once more. This time he reached New York where he became a successful businessman, amassing a considerable fortune.

In 1859 Austria went to war with France. This was Garibaldi's chance! He sailed at once for Italy and raised a small army. But France made peace with Austria so his now famous army of a 'Thousand Red-Shirts' landed in Sicily and crushed the army of the king of Naples (to whom Sicily belonged).

With 25,000 men he crossed to the mainland of Italy. He had only to appear before a town for it to open its gates to him. French troops were still in the Papal State of Rome but in 1870 they were withdrawn and Italy was free at last. Garibaldi died in 1882 but his name as a freedom fighter lives on.

▲ Some of Garibaldi's Red Shirts struggle with Bourbon troops at the Battle of Sessa, in the Sicilian campaign of 1860. The Red Shirts were international volunteers from all over the world fighting for the freedom of Italy.

► Garibaldi and his troops land at Marsala in May 1860 to help the peasants of Sicily in their revolt against the French Bourbon government. This paved the way for Garibaldi to capture Naples, another step towards Italian unity.

◄ Garibaldi meets Victor Emmanuel, King of Sardinia, who became King of Italy in March 1861. This was possible because of Garibaldi's successful campaign in southern Italy during the summer of 1860.

General Robert E. Lee

'John Brown's body lies a-mouldering in the grave', sang the people of the northern states of America. They were singing about an American soldier who had been hanged by the men of the South after being captured during a raid on the arsenal at Harper's Ferry. The song, telling of a man they regarded as a martyr, became the marching song of the Union.

John Brown had died for being opposed to slavery, like his fellow Northerners. His death began a struggle which, in time, became full scale war after Abraham Lincoln was elected President of the United States in 1860. Seven Southern states decided to leave the Union, and joined together to call themselves the Confederate States of America.

The first shots, in what was to be the American Civil War, were fired at Fort Sumter, held by Federal (Northern) troops. Like all such wars it was to be a terrible struggle, brother fighting brother and father fighting son. During its four years (1861–65) four million men took part in the fighting.

Before the war began, President Lincoln called upon the country's outstanding soldier, Robert E. Lee, to take command of the United States' forces. But Lee was a Southerner from Virginia and he chose to fight with the Confederates. He soon proved to be a very brave man and an outstanding general. This was shown when, in 1862, he won a number of victories in the 'Seven Days' Battle' which for a time made the South supreme.

In May of the following year he won a great victory at Chancellorsville. But in July 1863 came defeat. A battle was fought at Gettysburg, only a small market town but the junction of several roads. Lee, leading the bulk of his army into Union territory, was marching east. At the same time, General George Meade, with a strong Federal army, was moving north. They clashed at Gettysburg in a battle that lasted for three horror-filled days. At first it seemed as if Lee would win but on the third day he was forced to retreat. This one battle cost the lives of 7,058 men.

▶ General Robert E. Lee inspired tremendous hope and loyalty in his men during their hard fight for the Southern Confederate cause. Whenever he rode before them on his horse 'Traveller' the soldiers were greatly cheered and showed their affection for their leader.

Lee was later defeated at Chattanooga (in November 1863) by General Ulysses Grant who then sent his generals Philip Sheridan and William Sherman to encircle Lee's dwindling forces. By the spring of 1865 the Confederate troops were completely cut off and on 9 April, Lee was forced to surrender at Appomattox Court House.

It has been said that there are few instances of greater nobility than the way in which he accepted defeat. His surrender ended the war.

Soon afterwards he was pardoned and became President of Washington College, Lexington, for five years until his death in October, 1870. He was mourned by North and South alike.

▲ The Battle of Gettysburg, July 1863, from a painting by Paul Philippoteaux. The battle ended in terrible defeat for the Confederate troops under General Lee's command.

▼ Field hospitals during the American Civil War were simple makeshift places for basic treatment. Casualties on both sides were very high. The total of dead and wounded reached 800,000 by the end of the war.

Cetewayo: Zulu warrior

'The *impis* are coming! The *impis* are coming!'

That was the warning that caused terror among the scattered farms and isolated villages on the Transvaal border towards the end of the 19th century. The *impis* were the regiments of Zulu warriors. They were tall, muscular men armed with deadly spears or clubs, and protected by oval, skin-covered shields.

They lived in Zululand, a region of south-east Africa – between Natal and the Transvaal in South Africa. At the beginning of the 19th century most of Natal had been occupied by the Boers (or Dutch farmers) until in 1843 the British took over. An uneasy period followed in which there were several raids across the border by Zulu warriors from small tribes.

Then a great Zulu chieftain united them and became their ruler. He was Cetewayo, chief of the Zulu nation. The British High Commissioner, sensing trouble, ordered Cetewayo to disband his army. He received no answer, and in January 1879 a British force under Major-General Lord Chelmsford moved in to deal with the troublesome natives. Chelmsford had a force of 5,000 Europeans and some 8,000 natives. His plan was threefold: to crush the Zulu in battle, to destroy their capital of Ulundi, and to capture Cetewayo.

Chelmsford split his army into three groups, sending each into Zululand by different routes. This type of campaign was new to him. He was advised by Boers to protect his camps at night with a *laager* or circle of wagons, and to send out scouts in all directions, but he ignored their advice. He was also unaware that Cetewayo led an army of 40,000 warriors who had sworn to wash their spears in blood . . . British blood!

On the morning of 22 January 1879, Chelmsford moved out of his camp at Isandhlwana to reconnoitre, leaving some 1,200 men to protect it. He had hardly gone when Cetewayo appeared with at least 20,000 men. When Chelmsford returned he was shattered to find that almost half the men he had left at the camp had been killed.

An officer of the 1st King's Dragoon Guards

▼ Some typical uniforms of the British Army in South Africa around 1879.

An officer of the 58th Foot Regiment

A sergeant of the 24th South Wales Borderers

▲ Frederick Augustus Thesiger, 2nd Baron Chelmsford, General Officer commanding British troops in South Africa.

At the same time Cetewayo sent another *impi* to attack a nearby post at Rorke's Drift. The garrison here was far smaller than at Isandhlwana – just over 100 officers and men – yet it managed to drive the Zulus back with musketry and then at bayonet point.

Reinforcements were soon arriving from England and in July 1879 the British army reached Ulundi where Cetewayo and his warriors awaited attack. It proved a great victory for Chelmsford. Cetewayo was captured and his country divided up and given to minor chiefs. These soon began to fight amongst themselves, however, and Cetewayo was recalled. In 1884, after a year's rule, he died, and three years later Zululand ceased to exist. It had become a British colony.

► The 24th (2nd Warwickshire) Regiment at Isandhlwana, 22nd January 1879. They lost 21 officers and 581 men. The Zulus inflicted the worst defeat a modern army has suffered from men without firearms.

► Zulu warriors in battle dress wearing armbands made from furs and feathers. They carried oval shields made from oxhide, spears or assegais, and clubs or knobkerries.

knobkerry

assegai or spear

shield

▲ Cetewayo, leader of the Zulus, 'a man of considerable ability, much force of character and . . . a dignified manner'.

Sitting Bull: Indian chief

When the first settlers arrived in America they were well received by the people whom Columbus, in error, had named 'Indians'. They were eager to trade and treated the newcomers with kindness and courtesy. It was only when the early pioneers began to cross the Appalachian Mountains that the trouble began.

For a time the fighting was of no great consequence – young braves attacking wagon trains or the encampments of the 'pale faces'. The real trouble began in 1849 when gold was discovered in California and when thousands of prospectors – the 'Forty-Niners' – began to pour into the territory. And it was Indian Territory!

This was too much for the great tribes – the Cheyenne, Arapaho, Cherokee, Comanche and the Sioux. The braves put on their war-paint, mounted their fast little ponies and went on the warpath.

But what chance did they have with their spears and bows and arrows, especially when the government sent in soldiers – the Bluecoats – armed with rifles and often with artillery? Yet the tribes fought bravely. They were fighting for their lands and to preserve their way of life. One by one, however, they were forced to submit, leaving their free life on the great open plains, to go into reservations provided for them by the government. Finally only the Sioux and a few others stood out, inspired by the great Sioux chief, Sitting Bull.

▲ Sitting Bull was one of the ablest leaders of the Sioux nation. His name means 'A Buffalo Bull resides permanently among us'. This shows how respected he was: the buffalo was highly honoured by all Plains Indians.

► Scenes from Sitting Bull's pictographic diary which shows him:
1 Storming a Crow camp, taking 30 scalps.
2 Killing a frontiersman.
3 Bagging a bearer of dispatches.
4 Killing a Crow warrior.
5 Duelling.
6 Scalping a teamster.
7 Striking an Irishman.
8 Stealing a drove of horses.

1

2

3

4

5

▲ Custer's last fight on 25 June 1876, at the Battle of the Little Big Horn. Despite warnings from his Indian scouts and his friends, Custer with only 250 men attacked an Indian camp containing between 1,500 and 3,000 warriors. The result was a complete victory for the Sioux, Cheyenne and Arapaho. Custer's forces had been wiped out in less than an hour.

Two small armies under generals Terry and Cook were ordered to deal with the chief and his troublesome Sioux. In April 1876, Sitting Bull called a great council of his own chiefs – Crazy Horse, Spotted Eagle, Black Moon and others, together with chiefs of the Cheyenne and Arapaho. They took part in the terribly painful Sun Dance and then, exhausted from loss of blood from self-made cuts, Sitting Bull had a vision. He saw white soldiers upside down – a sure sign of victory.

Soon scouts came in to tell him that horse-soldiers were riding towards their camp. It was the crack 7th Cavalry commanded by Colonel George Custer. Although told by his own scouts that a strong Indian camp lay ahead, Custer did not stop. He was looking for personal glory. Instead, on June 25, 1876, he found death. Something like 3,000 Sioux surrounded his detachment of 250 men and when General Terry arrived he found only the corpses of soldiers. It had been Custer's Last Stand.

But even the proud Sioux finally had to yield to the might of the Bluecoats. Sitting Bull and a few braves fled to Canada, but returned reluctantly in 1881 to live on a reservation. Nine years later he was about to lead one last uprising but his cabin was surrounded and a brief skirmish followed. When the cavalry arrived they found the bodies of white men and braves. Amongst them was the greatest of all the Indian warriors – Chief Sitting Bull.

6

7

8

Richthofen: air ace

Captain Oswald Boelcke looked at the eager young faces of his pilots and smiled. With such men, and the new Albatros single-seater aircraft, he would sweep the sky clear of enemy planes.

Boelcke was Germany's leading 'ace' and had been ordered to train and fly with these pilots, two of whom he had especially asked for – Erwin Bohme and Baron Manfred von Richthofen. To these young pilots Boelcke was like a god as, day after day, he took them into the air until he felt that his *Jagdstaffel* (fighter squadron) was ready.

On 17 September 1916, with him leading and the rest in 'V' formation behind, they soared skywards, looking for the enemy. Soon a squadron of bomber planes escorted by two-seater fighters was sighted.

▶ A German Albatros D5A which was superior in speed, armament and rate of climb to the planes of the Royal Flying Corps.

◀ Captain Roy Brown of 208 Squadron, a Canadian who shot down Richthofen on 21 April 1918, so ending the career of the legendary 'Red Baron'.

▶ An artist's impression of a Sopwith Camel, as flown by Roy Brown, in a dog-fight with Richthofen.

▼ Von Richthofen with members of his fighter Squadron, Jasta II, in 1917. His dog Moritz, standing to his left, was the only living thing for which he seems to have had any affection.

▼ The Red Baron dressing before take-off. He wears sheepskin boots, fur hat, scarf and fur trimmed goggles to give him protection.

The Jagdstaffel swept down on them out of the sun. Later, back at their airfield, Boelcke congratulated them all, especially young Richthofen who had shot down his first plane.

Boelcke was to score 40 victories. Disaster struck during a 'dog-fight' (a battle of several planes) when his wing tips touched those of Bohme's plane. It was only for a moment – but his machine went spinning earthwards and crashed.

Inspired by his leader's death, Richthofen resolved to beat his master's total. He had already shot down six enemy machines. He was destined to equal and then double the other's record. He was to be credited with 80 confirmed 'killings' – the largest number by anyone in any war.

Richthofen was put in command of the squadron, now known as 'Jagdstaffel Boelcke' and led it to continual victory. The bullets spitting from the black-crossed fighters proved too much for the slower and more cumbersome bombers and fighters then flown by the British and French. He scored his eleventh victory during this time. It was especially notable for his victim was Major Hawker V.C., one of Britain's own aces.

Richthofen's great day came on 13 April 1917, when he downed his 41st plane. This exceeded the total of his master. By then he was famous throughout Germany and the British called him the 'Red Baron', for his Fokker triplane was painted completely red.

The 'Red Baron' met his end on 21 April 1918. As he closed in on a British fighter he did not notice that a Sopwith 'Camel', piloted by Captain Roy Brown, was on his tail. There was a short burst of fire and the Fokker crashed behind British lines. The pilot was dead. He was buried with full military honours and later a British pilot flew over Richthofen's aerodrome to drop a message of high regard from R.A.F. pilots.

▼ Planes of Richthofen's Jasta II (Albatros D III's) at Douai in France in March 1917. Richthofen's aircraft is second from the front, without an Iron Cross on the tail.

◄ Von Richthofen's room decorated with war trophies, the serial numbers of enemy aircraft he had shot down. He claimed to have shot down 80 enemy aircraft.

► The Fokker Triplane entered service with the German forces in August 1917. It was used very successfully because of its manoeuvrability and good firepower. It was only used by the best German pilots including Manfred von Richthofen.

Orde Wingate: British officer

Two spruce-looking British officers were seated in a club in Burma when a bearded, bare-footed and foul-smelling man passed them. One lieutenant, newly arrived from England disdainfully asked, 'Who let such a person in here?' The other hissed urgently, 'Shut up you fool – he's a brigadier – he's Wingate!' Both officers then shot to their feet giving a smart salute to a man who had already become a legend.

Wingate had just returned from a foray into the jungle where as usual, he had shared the hardships of his men. Apart from their human enemy, the Japanese, they had to struggle across rivers or through prickly undergrowth where scorpions hid under stones and huge king cobras reared up in their path. Above all there was always the pitiless sun and the wet, steaming heat of the jungle. But these men carried on because they had absolute faith in their leader – the strange, and often rebellious Orde Wingate.

▲ Brigadier Charles Orde Wingate talking to his men at the transit camp of an outpost on the Burma-Assam border.

▲ The Chindits became a serious threat to Japanese forces. Their presence behind enemy lines proved that the Japanese were not indestructible and this gave other troops in India and Burma renewed confidence.

▶ Some Chindits preparing to demolish a railway bridge. The Japanese depended heavily on the railways to transport troops, supplies and ammunition.

He had been called by Lord Wavell to help stem the advance of the Japanese in Burma. After inspecting the territory, Wingate suggested that he should form and train long range penetration columns to become fast-moving guerilla columns. These would slip past the Japanese and attack them from the rear. Their name – 'Chindit' – came from the strange beast which stands before Burmese pagodas. The half lion, half griffin kept out devils and is called a *Chinthe*.

After intense training by Wingate, the Chindits crossed the River Chindwin into Burma in February 1943. They included soldiers from Britain, Gurkhas from Nepal and Burmese warriors who were fighting to free their homeland. Each man carried a week's rations. Other supplies were transported by R.A.F. 'planes. Sometimes, despite radio contact, the Chindits were hidden by the thick jungle foliage. Without supplies the men lived on coconuts, eggs and chickens.

The Chindits infiltrated as planned and it became obvious that 'Wingate's Circus', as the men called themselves, were more than a match for the Japanese. At the end of the same year, Lord Mountbatten, Supreme Allied Commander in south-east Asia, arrived to give Wingate fresh orders. The Japanese were preparing to invade India but he was determined that they should not. Wingate was the right man to stop the enemy's advance.

In February 1944 Wingate and his Chindits returned to the fighting they knew so well. They held back a major Japanese offensive mounted during the following month. On 15 April, when they made contact with Indian soldiers, their task was done. But Wingate was not there to see it. Although only 41 years old he had died in a 'plane crash on 24 March 1944. It was less than three weeks before the victory had been won – a victory for which he had been mainly responsible.

▼ Typical jungle hats and simple wooden crosses mark the graves of two fallen Chindits. Death was often caused by tropical diseases, such as malaria and typhus, and by the terrible jungle conditions.

▼ One of the last photographs of Wingate before his death in an air crash in March 1944. Wingate proved that guerilla warfare could be highly successful in the jungle behind enemy lines.

Patton: American general

In so many ways Patton, the American, was similar to Wingate, the Englishman. Like him, he had no time for officers who fought the war from behind a desk. He liked to be where the action was. Like Wingate he was tough, and a hero to his men. He frequently ignored direct orders if it suited him.

His task was plain – to defeat the enemy. As he himself said, 'War is very simple, direct and ruthless. It takes a simple, direct and ruthless man to wage war.' And ruthless he certainly was!

In November 1942 U.S. troops had invaded North Africa but had been defeated in battle. Their morale was very low. Then Eisenhower, the U.S. Supreme Commander, sent in Patton to take command. He burst like a whirlwind into the headquarters of the American II Corps and proceeded to shake up everybody. A 'tough guy' had arrived! His men became used to his grim, set face, and the pair of pearl-handled revolvers that swung at his waist.

They also realized that Patton preferred to lead his men into action himself, something most unusual for a general. His courage and toughness gave him the nickname – old 'blood and guts'. His leadership paid off for he led an action on 12 July 1943 at Gela (El Guettar) in Tunisia. Twice he was thrown back but, using his tanks with great skill, he turned possible defeat into victory.

▲ Patton, known as 'blood and guts', studied military history in great detail. He realized men were fearless in battle only if inspired by their leaders. He was strict with his men in order that they would react coolly in war, spurred on by their will to win at all costs.

◄ General Montgomery takes note of General Patton's ivory handled Colt Peacemaker revolver which he often carried. Montgomery and Patton had much in common as popular leaders of the British and American troops.

► Patton's 3rd Army used Sherman M4/A3 tanks in their push across Europe into Germany. These tanks had a crew of 5 men, 500 horse power and a maximum speed of 41 kph on roads. Their range was 160 km.

On 10 July 1943, Sicily was invaded. Patton commanded the U.S. 7th Army and when the whole island was in Allied hands (17 August 1943) he was ordered back to England. His aggressive attitude had already made him unpopular with many generals both British and American. But Eisenhower knew Patton's worth. He knew what he could do and how well he inspired his men.

Soon after the allies had invaded France (D-Day, 6 June 1944), Patton flew in to take command of the U.S. 3rd Army. His men responded well to his leadership and soon American tanks had smashed a way out of the Normandy bridgehead and were racing across France.

Patton had previous battle experience with tanks in World War I. He moved his squadrons so fast that he was ordered to slow down because he was leaving the rest behind.

War in Europe ended on 8 May 1945, and Patton was made military governor of Bavaria. He soon lost this position for he was a soldier not a diplomat. On 9 December he was in a motoring accident and died soon afterwards. He was buried in the U.S. military cemetery at Hamm, in Luxembourg, on Christmas Eve 1945. He was a genius on the battlefield who seized his opportunities and exploited them to the full. His aim was to win at all costs in the shortest time.

▲ (a) The Tiger, Panzerkampf-wagen VI used by German troops. This had a crew of 5, a battleweight of 56 tons, 700 bhp, a fuel capacity of 125 gallons, a maximum speed of 37 kph and a range of 118 km.

▲ (b) The Mark 4 Churchill III tank used by British troops in World War II. This had a crew of 5, a battleweight of 39 tons, 350 bhp, a fuel capacity of 182 gallons, a maximum speed of 25 kph and a range of 193 km.

How to find out more

Ramses II Books: *From the beginning to Alexander the Great* by Colin and Sarah McEvedy (Rupert Hart-Davis), *Ancient Egypt* by Lionel Casson (Time-Life International), *Ancient Empires* ed. by S. G. F. Brandon (Reader's Digest Assoc.). Films: *The Egyptian, Cleopatra*.

Achilles Books: *Golden Tales of Greece* by Sir Compton Mackenzie (Aldus), *Myths of Greece and Rome* by H. A. Gurber (Harrap), *The Greek Armies* by Peter Connolly (Macdonald Educational). Film: *Helen of Troy*.

David Books: *The Bible as History* by Werner Keller (Hodder & Stoughton), *David* by Duff Cooper (Jonathan Cape), *Warrior and King* by Frank Slaughter (Hutchinson), *David the Shepherd Boy* by Helen Wheaton (Scripture Union). Films: *David and Bathsheba, Solomon and Sheba*.

Alexander Books: *The Campaigns of Alexander* translated from Arrian (Penguin), *The Age of Alexander* translated from Plutarch (Penguin), *Alexander the Great* by L. Du Garde Peach (Ladybird), *Alexander the Great* (Macdonald Educational Starters).

Hannibal Books: *Hannibal's Place in History* by Sir Denis Proctor (Oxford University Press), *Hannibal* (Macdonald Educational Starters), *Hannibal* by L. Du Garde Peach (Ladybird), *Hannibal and the Enemies of Rome* by Peter Connolly (Macdonald Educational).

Julius Caesar Books: *Julius Caesar* by Alfred Duggan (Faber), *The Assassination of Julius Caesar* by J. C. and A. B. Davis (Franklin Watts), *One Day in Ancient Rome* by Kenneth Allen (Tyndale), *The World of Ancient Rome* by Giulio Giannelli (Macdonald). Films: *Julius Caesar, Ben Hur, Spartacus*.

Boudicca Books: *The Great Invasion* by Leonard Cottrell (Evans), *Boadicea* by Betty King (Robert Hale), *Crimson Harvest* by K. Allen (Robert Hale), *The Rebellion of Boadicea* by R. Dudley and G. Webster (Routledge).

Attila Books: *The History of Attila and the Huns* by E. A. Thompson (P. Greenwood). Film: *Attila*.

Rollo Books: *Rollo, Duke of Normandy* ed. Jump (Liverpool University Press), *The Normans in Europe* by Linda Yeatman (Chambers), *William the Conqueror* by L. Du Garde Peach (Ladybird).

El Cid Books: *El Cid and his Spain* by Ramon Menendez translated by L. Pidal (F. Cass), *The Poem of El Cid* edited by Ian Michael (R. Hamilton and J. Perry), *In Search of the Cid* by Stephen Clissold (Hodder and Stoughton). Film: *El Cid*.

Saladin Books: *Saladin* by Geoffrey Hindle (Constable), *Saladin* by Andrew Osmond (Hutchinson), *Sultan of the Holy Swords* by Kathrine S. Walker (Dobson), *Early Islam* by Desmond Stewart (Time-Life International). Films: *Richard and the Crusaders, Richard the Lionheart, Ivanhoe, The Black Knight of Walworth*.

Yoritomo Minamoto Books: *Tales of Old Japan* by A. B. Mitford (K. Paul), *Japan* by Martin Hurlimann and Francis King (Thames and Hudson), *The Samurai of Japan* by Michael Gibson (Wayland). Films: *The Seven Samurai, Rashomon*.

Genghis Khan Books: *The Life and Times of Genghis Khan* (Hamlyn), *Genghis Khan and the Mongol Empire* by Malcolm Yapp (Harrap), *The Story of Genghis Khan* by Charles King (Dent). Film: *Genghis Khan*.

The Black Prince Books: *History of Edward III* by Mackinnon (Boydell Press), *Edward the Warrior* by Brenda Honeyman (Robert Hale), *Age of Chivalry* by Arthur Bryant (Reprint Society). Film: *Henry V* (which shows armour similar to that used at Crécy).

Akbar Books: *Akbar and the Moghul Empire* by John A. Harrison (Harrap), *The Great Moghuls* by Bamber Gascoigne (Jonathan Cape).

Gustavus Adolphus Book: *Gustavus Adolphus and the Rise of Sweden* by Michael Roberts (English University Press). Film: *Queen Christiana* (his daughter who died in 1689).

Cromwell Books: *Cromwell* by David Storey (Jonathan Cape), *Cromwell and his Roundheads* by John Wroughton (Macmillan), *Oliver Cromwell* by John Buchan (Sphere), *Cavaliers and Roundheads* by Michael Gibson (Wayland). Film: *Cromwell*.

Frederick the Great Books: *Frederick the Great* by G. Walter Hubatsch (Thames and Hudson), *Frederick the Great* by Nancy Mitford (Penguin), *The Army of Frederick the Great* by Christopher Duffy (David and Charles).

Napoleon Books: *Napoleon* by John Bowle (Weidenfeld and Nicolson), by Vincent Cronin (Penguin), by Stephen Pratt (Wayland), *Napoleon, Man and Myth* by Richard Jones (Hodder and Stoughton), *The Story of Napoleon* by L. Du Garde Peach (Ladybird). Films: *Napoleon and Desiré, War and Peace, Maria Walewska*.

Garibaldi Books: *Garibaldi* by Denis Mack Smith (Prentice-Hall), *Garibaldi of the Red Shirts* (Macdonald Educational).

General Robert E. Lee Books: *Lee of Virginia* by William E. Brooks (Greenwood Publications), *Robert E. Lee* by Peter Earle (Weidenfeld and Nicolson). Film: *The Red Badge of Courage*.

Cetewayo Books: *The Zulu War* by David Clammer (David and Charles), *The Washing of the Spears* by Donald R. Morris (Jonathan Cape), *Uniforms and Weapons of the Zulu War* by C. Wilkinson-Latham (Batsford). Film: *Zulu*.

Sitting Bull Books: *Photographs from the Smithsonian Institution* by Joanna C. Scherer (Octopus), *The Trailblazers* (Time-Life International), *Bluecoats and Redskins* by Robert Utley (Cassell), *Sitting Bull* by Alexander B. Adams (New English Library). Films: *Stagecoach, Broken Arrow, How the West Was Won, A Man Called Horse*.

Manfred Von Richthofen Books: *The Red Baron* by P. Kilduff (Bailey Bros.), *The Red Baron* by Nicholas Wright (Sidgwick and Jackson), *Aces High* by A. Clark (Fontana), *Richthofen* by William E. Burrows (Hart-Davis), *The Great Air War* by Aaron Normal (Macmillan). Films: *The Blue Max, Sky Devils, Dawn Patrol, The Red Baron*.

Orde Wingate Books: *The Chindits* by Mike Calvert (Pan/Ballantine), *Campaign in Burma* by Frank Owen (Arrow), *Wingate in Peace and War* by Derek Tulloch (Macdonald).

Patton Books: *Through Mud and Blood* by Bryan Perrett (Robert Hale), *Patton, The Commander* by H. Essame (Batsford), *Decisive Battles of the Second World War* ed. Peter Young (Arthur Barker). Films: *Patton, Lust for Glory, Battleground, Battle of the Bulge*.

PLACES TO VISIT

British Museum; Victoria and Albert Museum; Tower of London; National Army Museum; Imperial War Museum; Artillery Museum, Woolwich; RAC Tank Museum, Bovington, Dorset; RAF Museum, Hendon; Shuttleworth Collection, Biggleswade; The American Museum, Claverton, Nr Bath.

Index